Architecture in Global Socialism

Architecture in Global Socialism

Eastern Europe, West Africa, and the Middle East in the Cold War

Łukasz Stanek

Princeton University Press

Princeton and Oxford

Contents

VI   Abbreviations

1   Chapter 1
Introduction
Worldmaking of Architecture

35   Chapter 2
A Global Development Path
Accra, 1957–66

97   Chapter 3
Worlding Eastern Europe
Lagos, 1966–79

169   Chapter 4
The World Socialist System
Baghdad, 1958–90

239   Chapter 5
Socialism within Globalization
Abu Dhabi and Kuwait City, 1979–90

303   Epilogue and Outlook

308   A Note on Sources
315   Acknowledgments
319   Notes
336   Bibliography
347   Index
356   Image Credits

Abbreviations

ARCHIVES AND REPOSITORIES

AAN	Archiwum Akt Nowych, Warsaw, Poland
AESL	Architecture and Engineering Services Limited, Accra, Ghana
AKDC	Aga Khan Documentation Center, Massachusetts Institute of Technology, Cambridge, MA, US
ANR	Arhivele Naționale ale României, Bucharest, Romania
BA	Bundesarchiv, Berlin, Germany
BSC	Sir Basil Spence Collection, Historic Environment Scotland, Edinburgh, UK
CAA	Commonwealth Association of Architects, London, UK
CAC	Canadian Architecture Collection, McGill University, Montreal, Canada
CCF	Library of Congress, Confidential US State Department Central Files, Washington, DC, US
CDA	Constantinos A. Doxiadis Archives, Athens, Greece
DAA	Durzhavna agentsiia "Arkhivi," Sofia, Bulgaria
FN	Filmoteka Narodowa, Warsaw, Poland
GSD	Graduate School of Design, Special Collections, Harvard University, Cambridge, MA, US
GTA	Archiv, Geschichte und Theorie der Architektur, Eidgenössische Technische Hochschule Zürich, Zurich, Switzerland
IFA	Institut français d'architecture, Paris, France
IRS	Leibniz-Institut für Raumbezogene Sozialforschung, Erkner, Germany
KAB	Kamarata na arkhitektite v Bulgariia, Sofia, Bulgaria
LC	Library of Congress, Washington, DC, US
MARKhI	Moskovskii arkhitekturnyi institut, Moscow, Russian Federation
PRAAD	Public Records and Archives Administration Department, Accra, Ghana
RGAE	Rossiiskii gosudarstvennyi arkhiv ekonomiki, Moscow and Samara, Russian Federation
RGANTD	Rossiiskii gosudarstvennyi arkhiv nauchno-tekhnicheskoi dokumentatsii, Moscow, Russian Federation
RIBA	Royal Institute of British Architects, London, UK
SARP	Stowarzyszenie Architektów Polskich, Warsaw, Poland
ZDA	Zbigniew Dmochowski–Archiwum, Gdańsk University of Technology, Gdańsk, Poland

NEWSPAPERS, JOURNALS, AND OTHER PERIODICALS

BN	*Baghdad News*, Baghdad
BO	*Baghdad Observer*, Baghdad
DG	*Daily Graphic*, Accra
DT	*Daily Times*, Lagos
EN	*Evening News*, Accra
EP	*Energoprojekt*, Belgrade
GT	*Ghanaian Times*, Accra
IT	*Iraq Times*, Baghdad
KT	*Kuwait Times*, Kuwait
MEC	*Middle East Construction*, Sutton, UK
NC	*Nigerian Chronicle*, Calabar
NN	*New Nigerian,* Kaduna
RZ	*Rynki zagraniczne,* Warsaw
WA	*West Africa,* London
WABA	*West African Builder and Architect*, Accra
WAP	*West African Pilot*, Lagos

Architecture in Global Socialism

1.1. Africa Hall (Women's Hall 6), Kumasi (Ghana), design 1964–65. Architects Office UST, John Owusu-Addo/ Miro Marasović (chief university architect), Nikša Ciko (architect in charge).

Chapter 1
Introduction
Worldmaking of Architecture

"I remember very well these Eastern European architects, because it was the first and the last time that a white man had an African boss in Ghana"—this is how a Ghanaian architect recalled his encounters with architects from socialist countries in 1960s Accra.[1] For him, and for many other Ghanaian professionals, the encounters with Eastern Europeans were part of the extraordinary moment of independence that entailed a disruption and fundamental reorganization of places assigned to Africans and Europeans during the colonial period, including places of work.[2] When writing this book, I listened to many recollections of such encounters. A Ghanaian architect told me about his education in the Soviet Union, and gave me a brief lecture on what Soviet architecture was all about.[3] Another recalled Hungarian professors and Czech professionals in Ghana's first school of architecture (figure 1.1).[4] The staff of the monumental National Arts Theater in Lagos, Nigeria, pronounced with a sense of pride the long name of Technoexportstroy, the Bulgarian firm that designed and built the structure in 1977. The pronunciation of the name of Polish architectural scholar Zbigniew Dmochowski is more of a contentious matter in Nigeria, but all architects whom I met in Lagos knew his drawings of Nigerian vernacular architecture, which continue to be used as teaching aids in architectural schools in the country. A Nigerian administrator recounted his collaboration with Romanian and Yugoslav contractors on the expansion of Lagos in the 1970s.[5] Planners and academics from Baghdad told me about the "Polservice master plan" of the city, delivered in 1973 by Polish planners, which still waits to be replaced by a new one.[6] An Iraqi architect showed me drawings of the Amiri Diwan complex in Kuwait City, designed in collaboration with a large group of Czech and Slovak architects, while a Sudanese architect in Al Ain recalled the winning entry of the design for the Municipality Building, by a Bulgarian enterprise.[7]

These conversations were complemented by studies of buildings and documents from Accra, Lagos, Baghdad, Abu Dhabi, and Kuwait City—the five cities focused on in this book. During field trips to West Africa and the Middle East, I visited housing estates, schools and hospitals, theaters, sports facilities and community centers, along with military infrastructure and industrial facilities designed by architects and engineers from socialist countries during the Cold War, and often built by contractors from Eastern Europe. Varying in technical condition and in ways of use, they continue to provide frameworks for everyday lives, to create points of concentration, and to set extension vectors for urbanization processes, and they are sometimes celebrated as monuments to decolonization and national independence. Construction industries in these cities often rely on materials produced by factories set up by state-socialist enterprises, and local architectural and planning schools use curricula that evolved from initial iterations cowritten by professionals from socialist countries (figure 1.2). In turn, decision makers often work on the basis of master plans, survey maps, building norms, and other regulatory frameworks that resulted from those exchanges.

The Cold War brought about new geographies of collaboration that fundamentally impacted a myriad of locations, including West Africa and the Middle East.[8] Yet while Eastern European architects, planners, and construction companies are vividly remembered by professionals, inhabitants, and the general public in Ghana, Nigeria, Iraq, the United Arab Emirates (UAE), and Kuwait, their engagements in the Global South have been almost completely written out of Western-based historiography of architecture.[9] This blind spot, in turn, has reinforced a reductive conceptual framework by means of which architecture and, more generally, urbanization in the Global South have been understood.

This book advances these debates by taking as its starting point the recent scholarship about worldwide mobilities of architecture. During the last two decades, research about "nomadic expertise" and "global experts" has greatly expanded the historiography of twentieth-century architecture.[10] Scholars have studied late-colonial networks and their prolongation into the postcolonial period, networks of Western-based development-aid and financial institutions, professional organizations of architects, and the emergence of the global market of design and construction services dominated by Western Europe and the United States.[11] While the studies of the mobility of modern architecture often began by following such figures as Le Corbusier or Louis Kahn, the best among them extended their focus beyond Western architects toward their local collaborators, partners, students, and followers.[12] In this way, these studies entered into dialogue with architectural scholarship in countries that emerged from the colonial rule, such as India or Egypt, and those that were never part of European empires, such as Iran or Japan.[13] Historians demonstrated modern architecture's capacity to respond and adapt to a variety of climatic, environmental, technological, and social conditions, and showed how its international forms were appropriated to convey programs of nation building in, for instance, kemalist Turkey or mandate Palestine.[14] Studies of foreign encounters expanded the radar of historians toward until-then little-known figures, such as Constantinos Doxiadis or Maxwell Fry and Jane Drew, and organizations

1.2. Advertisement of Foreign Trade Organization for Complete Industrial Plants (Cekop, Poland), 1958.

such as the International Union of Architects, UNESCO, and corporate architectural offices.[15] In turn, commissions abroad became opportunities for learning and experimentation that impacted metropolitan practices including, for example, infrastructural projects, type designs, and planning regulations as implemented in French North Africa.[16] The discovery of colonial implications of modern architecture facilitated the reassessment of its biopolitics through categories of race and gender.[17] These studies were developed in conversation with broader accounts of global urbanization processes as shaped by Western European colonialism and imperialism, and analyses of the accelerated "urbanization of the world" as the driving force of global capitalism.[18]

Yet if the merits of this scholarship are magnified by its impact on general architectural historiography, so are its omissions. In contrast to a surge of interest of Cold War historians in the political, economic, institutional, and cultural interconnections between Eastern Europe and the decolonizing world, scholarship about architecture's mobility after World War II has maintained an almost exclusively Western focus.[19] As a consequence of the reliance on Western archives, publications that discuss the work of foreign architects in Cold War Baghdad, for example, are limited to several years in the 1950s and later in the 1980s, while omitting the two decades in between, during which Iraq was allied with socialist countries.

By contrast, this book shows that urban histories of twentieth-century Baghdad and numerous other cities in the Global South cannot be understood without accounting for the exchanges with Eastern Europe and socialist countries elsewhere.[20] Recording these exchanges requires a broad survey of architectural mobilities between these regions, including the flows of blueprints of buildings and master plans of cities, construction

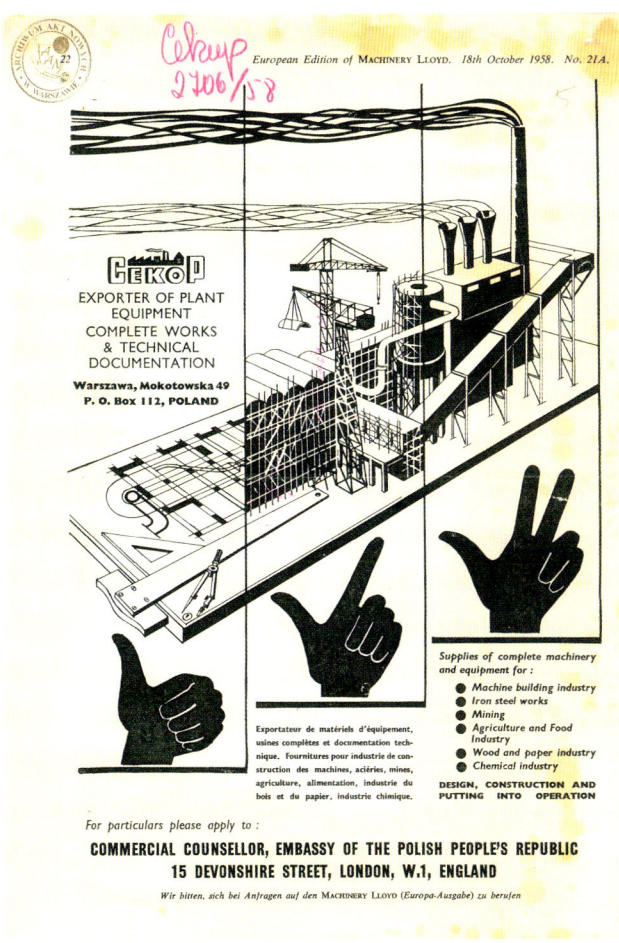

INTRODUCTION

materials and machinery, design details and images, norms and regulations, teaching curricula and research methodologies, as well as labor, both intellectual and manual. By studying these flows, this book expands architectural history toward the history of urbanization, understood as a production and transformation of the built environment, with housing, social services, industrial plants, and infrastructure, but also involving the processes of territorial regulation and representation, and socialization, learning, and routines embedded in everyday lives.[21]

The following chapters reconstruct these engagements on the basis of new archival material from Eastern Europe, West Africa, and the Middle East. But besides complementing urban histories of these regions, this material necessitates a revision of the ways in which urbanization processes in the Global South have been theorized. In particular, this book challenges the dominant conceptual reduction of these processes to the path-dependences of the colonial encounter with Western Europe and results of the globalization of capitalism, and shows how urbanization in the Global South was differentiated by the collaboration of local professionals and institutions with those from socialist countries.[22] Capturing this differentiation requires a comparative study of architectural mobilities from across Cold War divides and their impact on urbanization processes on the ground. Accordingly, in the following chapters I study five locations that received architects, planners, and contractors from multiple networks: Ghana under Kwame Nkrumah (1957–66), Nigeria between the First and the Second Republic (1966–79), Iraq from the coup of Qasim to the first Gulf War (1958–90), and Kuwait and the UAE during the last decade of the Cold War.

During the periods described by this book, Ghana, Nigeria, Iraq, the UAE, and Kuwait engaged with socialist countries to varying degrees, while being neither Soviet satellites nor Marxist-Leninist regimes. Rather than belonging to a socialist world, the elites of these countries cultivated several other regional and global alliances. Accordingly, while constituting some of the main destinations for Eastern European architects, planners, and contractors from the 1950s to the 1980s, these countries received also professionals from Western Europe, North America, the nonaligned countries, and experts of international institutions. As sites of competition and, sometimes, collaboration of professionals across and within geopolitical boundaries, Accra, Lagos, Baghdad, Abu Dhabi, and Kuwait City offer privileged vantage points for a study of the bifurcations of networks of architectural and construction expertise during the Cold War, and their changing dynamics. These bifurcations also included those among the socialist countries themselves in the wake of the split between the Soviet Union and Yugoslavia (1948), followed by the creation of the Non-Aligned Movement (NAM, 1961), and the split between the USSR and Mao Zedong's China in the course of the 1960s. In turn, when seen from the South rather than from the West, countries in Eastern Europe did not appear as a homogenous "Soviet bloc" but revealed distinct political ambitions and constraints, economic interests, technological profiles, industrial capacities, and architectural traditions.

The protagonists of this book worked within and across these multiple and often antagonistic networks that intersected in Accra, Lagos, Baghdad, Abu Dhabi, and Kuwait City. Architects, planners, and contractors from socialist countries and their local counterparts strived to avoid obstacles stemming from differences between these networks and to exploit advantages resulting from them. By focusing on their work, this book shows how Cold War engagements in West Africa and the Middle East differentiated urbanization processes on the ground, and shaped their conditions for the years to come. In so doing, it contributes to a more heterogeneous and antagonistic historiography of global urbanization and its architecture.

ARCHITECTURAL MOBILITIES SEEN FROM THE SOUTH

The comparative perspective offered by this book is more than an analytical tool: it was the basic experience of decolonization.[23] A case in point is a set of articles celebrating the 48th anniversary of the October Revolution published in 1965 in Ghana, the first country to gain independence in sub-Saharan Africa (in 1957), which embarked on the path of socialist modernization under its first leader, Kwame Nkrumah. Articles published in the Ghanaian newspaper *Daily Graphic* drew comparison between Ghana and Soviet Central Asia. The contributors stressed the Soviet support for decolonization worldwide, and presented Central Asia as a colonial territory of tsarist Russia that had been liberated by the Soviet Union.[24] Soviet industrialization, modern agriculture, mass education, and welfare distribution in Central Asia were extensively discussed, and particular attention was given to housing. Based on Soviet statistics, the articles argued that "the Soviet Union has surpassed the United States of America, for instance, not only for the total number of apartments it builds, but for per capital dwelling construction, as well."[25] Such comparisons were frequently published in the Ghanaian press in the 1960s, and besides housing, they included military equipment and household appliances, agricultural production and standards of living, sports achievements and fine art. The *Daily Graphic* and other newspapers reported almost every day about delegations coming to Accra from all over the world, they cheered the accelerated pace of arrivals of foreign technicians and advisors, and they commented upon machines and consumer objects put on display in Accra by trade representatives of both socialist and capitalist countries. Comparison was an empowering experience, because it challenged hierarchies of power and prestige inherited from the colonial period—but it was also a frustrating one, as it was based on often exaggerated and incommensurable statistics fed by the propaganda machineries of Cold War rivals.

If independence came with a discovery of the world beyond the colonial metropolis, the former colonial centers remained points of reference for the newly established states. In Accra and in the other four cities discussed in this book, the predominant point of reference was Britain. The state apparatuses and economies, militaries and mass media, cultural and educational institutions in Ghana, Nigeria, Iraq, and the Gulf countries had been shaped by Britain or were modeled according to British precedents. This included architecture and planning, as well as the construction and construction-materials industries, and legislation, education, and research in these areas.[26]

In Ghana and elsewhere, independence rarely meant the severance of financial, professional, educational, and technoscientific exchanges between former dependent territories and the metropolis.[27] Those exchanges were perpetuated by institutions charged with technical assistance and development aid for the British Commonwealth and, after the UK joined the European Community in 1973, trans-European aid agencies such as the European Development Fund.[28] British architectural schools established during the Empire, such as Liverpool and Manchester, continued to attract students from former colonies, and some among them adapted their curricula to the needs of architectural and planning practices outside Europe, as was the case in London with the Department of Tropical Architecture at the Architectural Association and with the Development Planning Unit at University College.[29] Building research stations in Britain continued to provide services for architects and contractors across the Commonwealth, and British-based publications continued to circulate among professionals, in particular those educated in the UK. Professional organizations such as the Royal Institute of British Architects, its Overseas Relations Committee, and the newly formed Commonwealth Association of

Architects (1965) strived to defend the interests of British architects in the Commonwealth, sometimes clashing with the newly established Institutes of Architects in Ghana, Nigeria, and elsewhere.[30]

Dominance of British architects, engineers, and construction firms was a concern for governments in the newly independent countries, which aimed to offset this influence by accepting and sometimes inviting professionals and organizations from elsewhere. These included development-aid agencies and commercial firms from other Western European countries, among them France, Italy, West Germany, the Netherlands, and Belgium, as well as new actors from Scandinavia and Israel.[31] Representatives of the latter argued that they offered a more equitable mode of collaboration with independent nations because Israel was "free of the taint of the colonial exploiters"—an argument that the socialist countries made, too.[32] By the 1970s, contractors and, sometimes, architects from South and East Asia, including Pakistan, India, South Korea, and Japan, entered what was by then a booming construction market in North Africa, the Middle East, and elsewhere.[33] In Iraq and the Gulf during the period this book covers, a crucial role was played by architects, planners, and contractors from other Arab countries, including Egyptian, Lebanese, and Palestinian professionals, deeply intertwined with pan-Arabism and supported by transnational professional organizations, journals, and conferences.[34] Regional exchanges in construction began to emerge in West Africa, too, within the Economic Community of West African States (ECOWAS), founded in 1975. This book offers an insight into this gradual differentiation of architectural and construction services, which increasingly challenged the dominance of Britain in the former British colonies and dependencies in West Africa and the Middle East.

A major opportunity to offset that dominance came from the United States. Based on the experience of the Marshall Plan for Europe and aid programs for Japan, President Truman's Point Four Program of 1949 established the institutional framework for US technical assistance and development aid.[35] In the first decade following implementation, the allocation, volume, and composition of this and other US aid programs depended on decision makers influenced by the modernization theory formulated by Walt Whitman Rostow, who argued that the United States should support developing countries in the "take off" phase leading to industrial growth, in this way "inoculating" them from communism.[36] Typically, US aid grants required recipients to purchase construction materials and services from American firms, themselves supported by cheap loans provided by the government. These commissions opened the path of commercial expansion for American architects, planners, and construction companies in Africa and Asia from the 1960s onward.[37] Such expansion was one of the aims of US aid summarized in 1955 by the journal *Architectural Forum*, together with "building up the basic welfare of other nations, creating climates unfavorable to communism, readying countries for industrialization and democratic independence, making them prosperous enough to buy more of our products."[38]

The dynamics of these activities were evolving and relied on military spending for US interventions abroad and shifts in US aid policies, from their consolidation under President Kennedy to imposing neoliberal policies on aid recipient countries under the Reagan administration some two decades later.[39] By the 1970s, organizations created by the Bretton Woods agreements (1944), including the International Monetary Fund and the World Bank, became major instruments in the US-led campaign for the liberalization of the international economy, including the reduction of barriers on trade and capital.[40] That objective was translated into specific financial instruments used in the construction of development projects. For instance, credit agreements for the construction of schools, signed between the World Bank and governments of developing countries, required the latter to obtain goods and services on a competitive international basis, in order to secure the most economical solution but also to expose local contractors to external competition and "socialize" their countries into the globalizing capitalist economy.[41]

Another path toward diversifying the economic actors on the ground, including actors engaged in urbanization processes, was offered by the Non-Aligned Movement (NAM). Building on earlier experiences of forging international ties between anticolonial movements, in particular the conference of African and Asian states in Bandung (Indonesia, 1955), NAM was formalized in 1961 on the initiative of President Tito of Yugoslavia, Prime Minister Nehru of India, President Nasser of Egypt, President Nkrumah of Ghana, and President Sukarno of Indonesia. The NAM countries postulated decolonization, disarmament, and the restructuring of the world economy in order to assist developing countries, along with their emancipation from the cultural dominance of European empires.[42] All countries focused on in this book, including Ghana, Nigeria, Iraq, the UAE, and Kuwait, were NAM members, if sometimes reluctant ones, and encouraged economic collaboration within NAM. Yet with the exception of Yugoslavia, such collaboration in architecture and construction proved difficult for the member states, as their economies were similar rather than complementary. The same was the case with other transnational organizations in the Global South, such as the Organization of the Petroleum Exporting Countries (OPEC, since 1960), the Tricontinental Conference (since 1966), and the pan-Islamic World Muslim League (since 1962), even if their members occasionally mobilized architecture as part of technical assistance or charity work.

In contrast to disappointing economic collaboration within NAM, the bloc was more effective in formulating demands for global economic reform and for development-aid distribution. A crucial platform for formulating and implementing those demands was the United Nations, whose organizations such as UNESCO, the Expanded Programme of Technical Assistance, and the Human Settlements Programme (since 1978) became major funding bodies for investment in developing countries.[43] Following independence, African, Asian, and Latin American countries were in the majority at the UN, where their representatives voiced alternative visions of the international economy to those of the United States, based on a redistribution of power between developed and underdeveloped parts of the world.[44] This vision culminated in the UN Conference on Trade and Development (UNCTAD, since 1964), which aimed at the internationalization of protectionism for less developed countries. UNCTAD called for favorable conditions on trade for primary products, transfer of financial resources and technology to developing countries, and their full sovereignty over their national resources, including the right to nationalization, regulation, and supervision of international corporations—among the latter, Western contractors and engineering firms operating in Africa and Asia.[45] By the 1970s, NAM argued that the fundamental division of the world was that between the underdeveloped "Global South" and the industrialized "Global North," which held on to its structural advantages in the world economy.[46]

Such a redemarcation clashed with the Eastern bloc discourse of "the world...divided into two camps: the camp of peace, democracy, and socialism, and the camp of imperialism," as a resolution of East Germany's communist party put it in 1952.[47] In this vision, socialist countries belonged to the same anti-imperialist "camp" as the countries on the path of decolonization, the latter term rarely used in Eastern Europe, as it suggested that independence was a gift of the imperial powers rather than a result of a struggle.[48] After the death of Stalin (1953), solidarity between socialist and the newly independent countries was the main expression of socialist internationalism that defined much of the foreign policy of the USSR and its Eastern European satellites.[49] Nikita Khrushchev, the first secretary of the Communist Party of the USSR (1953–64), pronounced that African and Asian countries "need not go begging to their former oppressors for modern equipment. They can get it in the socialist countries."[50] Under Khrushchev, this support was part of the principle of "peaceful coexistence," or competition with capitalist countries on an economic basis. This competition took the form of worldwide promotion of the socialist model, or "path," of development, which aimed to unleash productive powers in developing countries based on science, technology, and education, thus allowing a high level of social welfare. The similarities, reflections, and mutual borrowings between this path and American modernization theory did not preclude differences between them, however. While during the first postwar decades both Western and Soviet advisors stressed the importance of state interventions and elements of central planning, instead of a Western emphasis on the "free" market economy, the Soviets supported the development of a command economy and a justice-oriented welfare distribution.[51]

The reference for promoting socialist development in the newly independent countries was the Soviet modernization of the Central Asian and Caucasian Republics and the grafting of this development path in satellite states in Eurasia.[52] In particular, the Soviets pointed to what until the early 1960s appeared as the successful extension of this path to China, which resulted in industrial investments, residential neighborhoods, social infrastructure, urban and regional planning delivered by Soviet experts, as well as several highly visible, Soviet-designed buildings in Shanghai and Beijing (figures 1.3 and 1.4).[53] The Soviet Union also assisted North Korea and recruited its Eastern European satellites for this task (redirecting parts of East German war reparations to North Korea).[54] As a consequence of long-term Soviet technical assistance, the construction industry, building regulations, and architectural education in several Eurasian countries, above all in Mongolia, were predominantly shaped by the Soviet Union. Some of this technical assistance was coordinated by the Council of Mutual Economic Assistance (Comecon), the economic organization founded in 1949 and consisting of the Soviet Union and its European satellites, later joined by Mongolia, Cuba, and Vietnam (figure 1.5).

In contrast to those experiences, upon their arrival in West Africa and the Middle East in the late 1950s, Soviet administrators, architects, planners, and technicians needed to win over local decision makers in competition with other actors on the ground. Newly gained prestige stemming from the launch of Sputnik (1957), the earth's first artificial satellite, and the virgin lands campaign, which initially boosted agricultural production in Soviet Central Asia, gave credibility to the socialist modernization path, in particular as the Soviets insisted that this path needed not to be emulated but rather adapted to conditions on the ground. Soviet anticolonial rhetoric gained the sympathy of the first generation of independent leaders wary of the United States as an ally of former colonial powers that had assigned the Global South an unfavorable position in world markets.[55] Those leaders often presented Soviet-inspired modernization programs in terms of socialist modernization, sometimes qualified as "African" socialism in Ghana under Nkrumah or as "Arab" socialism in Iraq under the Baath Party. By following such appropriations, this book contributes to recent scholarship in Cold War history that has challenged the discourse on African and Asian leaders as "proxies" of the "superpowers." This research has shown that governments of developing countries often had the upper hand in allocating resources granted within the framework of Soviet technical assistance. For example, despite sending Indonesia over one-fifth of its total aid budget for "nonsocialist developing countries," Soviet advisors found themselves with little leverage in their dealings with the Sukarno

1.3. Exhibition Center in Beijing
(People's Republic of China), 1952–54.
Viktor Andreev, K. D. Kislova, Tai Nianshi.

1.4. Exhibition Center in Beijing
(People's Republic of China), 1952–54,
detail. Viktor Andreev, K. D. Kislova,
Tai Nianshi.

INTRODUCTION

1.5. Friendship Monument, Ulaanbaatar (Mongolia), 1971. A. Khishigt and others.

1.6. Nikita Khrushchev and President Sukarno inspect the model of the National Stadium in Jakarta (Indonesia), 1960. R. I. Semergiev, K. P. Pchel'nikov, U. V. Raninskii, E. G. Shiriaevskaia, A. B. Saukke, N. N. Geidenreikh, I. Y. Yadrov, L. U. Gonchar, I. V. Kosnikova.

regime, and the hundred-thousand-seat National Stadium in Jakarta was constructed without regard to Soviet recommendations (figure 1.6).[56]

Collaboration with the USSR and other socialist countries was also attractive to those West African and Middle Eastern governments that, unlike Nkrumah in Ghana, did not follow a socialist development path. Besides military and geopolitical concerns shared with the USSR, governments of many developing countries appreciated the favorable terms on which socialist countries offered their technology, goods, and services. The tender submissions from Comecon countries, in particular for industrial facilities, were not always the cheapest, but the authorities from the Global South valued the training opportunities for local staff, the use of local resources, and the favorable terms of payment offered by the socialist countries. In particular, the form of barter—the exchange of goods for goods without direct intervention of money—allowed the bypassing of constraints of international markets and avoided the use of exchangeable ("hard") currency, in short supply in both socialist and most developing countries. Barter agreements on favorable terms offered by the Soviets and their satellites resulted in the exchange of Cuban sugar, Egyptian cotton, Indonesian rubber, and Ghanaian cocoa for arms, machinery, consumer goods, and fully equipped facilities from socialist countries. These agreements also involved specialized services, such as those of architects, planners, technicians, and construction companies, as well as contributions to architectural and engineering education.[57]

By the 1970s, socialist countries were increasingly abandoning trade policies based on anti-imperialist solidarity, and they began to see the Global South as a reservoir of raw materials and mobile labor. Yet governments of many Asian and African countries continued to welcome Eastern Europeans as a means of stimulating economic competition between foreign enterprises.[58] These governments used the socialist countries as a source of technology and know-how, as a palliative against the rigors of hard-currency constraints, and as a way to realize projects the West was not willing to fund, in particular in the oil and steel sectors.[59] In addition, assistance from socialist countries allowed leaders of developing countries to achieve a better negotiating position toward the West and other donors, including China. In the wake of the Sino-Soviet split, Mao Zedong contrasted the Soviet Union and the United States ("the two largest international oppressors and exploiters") with the majority of developing countries and China as their champion.[60] Architecture and construction were a central part of Chinese technical assistance projects in Mongolia in the late 1950s and early 1960s, and later in Sri Lanka, Guinea, Ghana, Mauritania, Somalia, and Tanzania, where China stepped in to construct the Tanzania-Zambia Railway (1970–75).[61]

Another incentive to work with Eastern Europe was notorious shortages in the professional workforce in West Africa and the Middle East. Professionals from Comecon countries were employed by administrative and planning institutions at municipal, regional, and state levels. For example, planners from socialist countries worked for the planning offices of Aleppo (Syria), Addis-Ababa (Ethiopia), Algiers (Algeria), and many other cities (figures 1.7 and 1.8).[62] In the course of the 1970s, when Czech, Slovak, and Polish planners and sociologists were hired to work on the master planning of Algiers, a group of Romanian architects was employed by Algeria's University of Constantine, where they shaped its architectural program according to the curriculum of the Ion Mincu University of Architecture in Bucharest.[63] Educational, research, and advisory roles held by Eastern Europeans in schools of architecture in Kumasi (Ghana), Zaria (Nigeria), and Baghdad were particularly important and are discussed in this book. Architects from socialist countries also worked in private architectural offices, including those at the forefront of

1.7. Design of the Governmental Center in Addis Ababa (Ethiopia), 1979. Ministry of Urban Development and Housing in Addis Ababa, Charles Polónyi and others.

1.8. Planning of the historical center of Aleppo (Syria), early 1970s. Urban Planning Office of the Municipality of Aleppo, Henryk Roller and others.

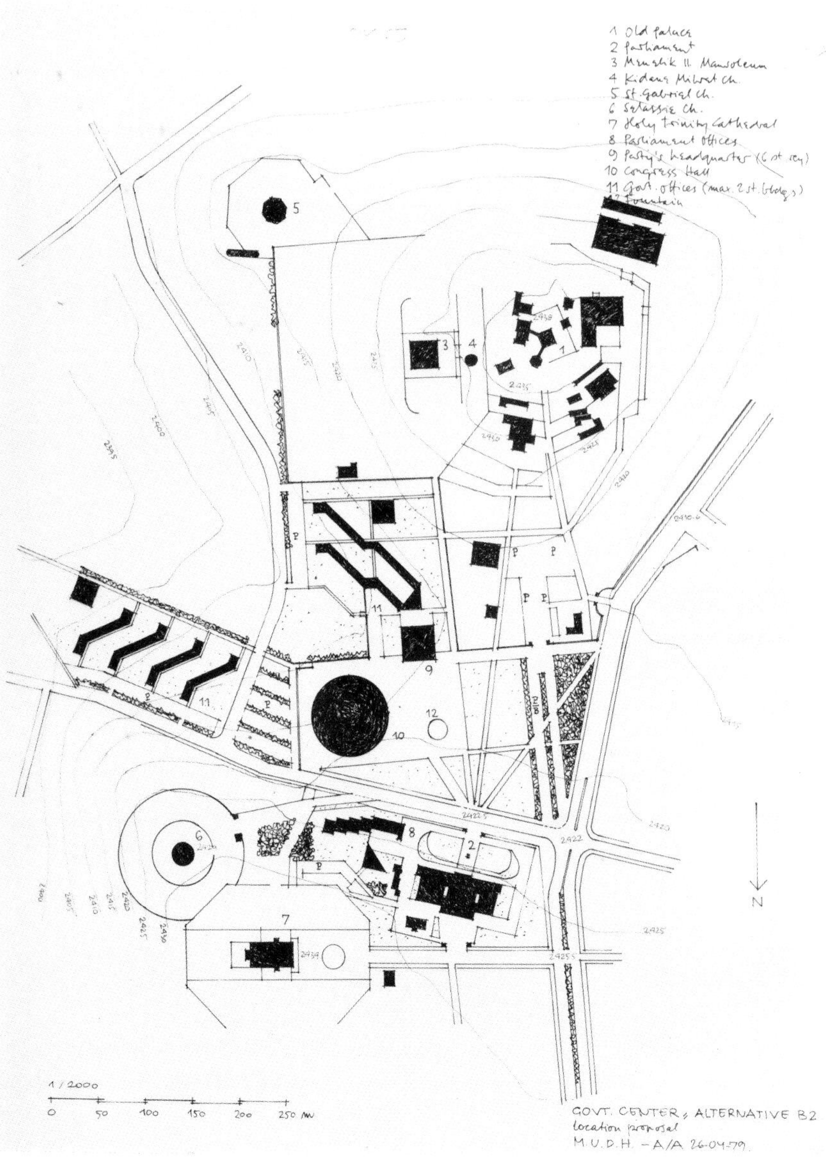

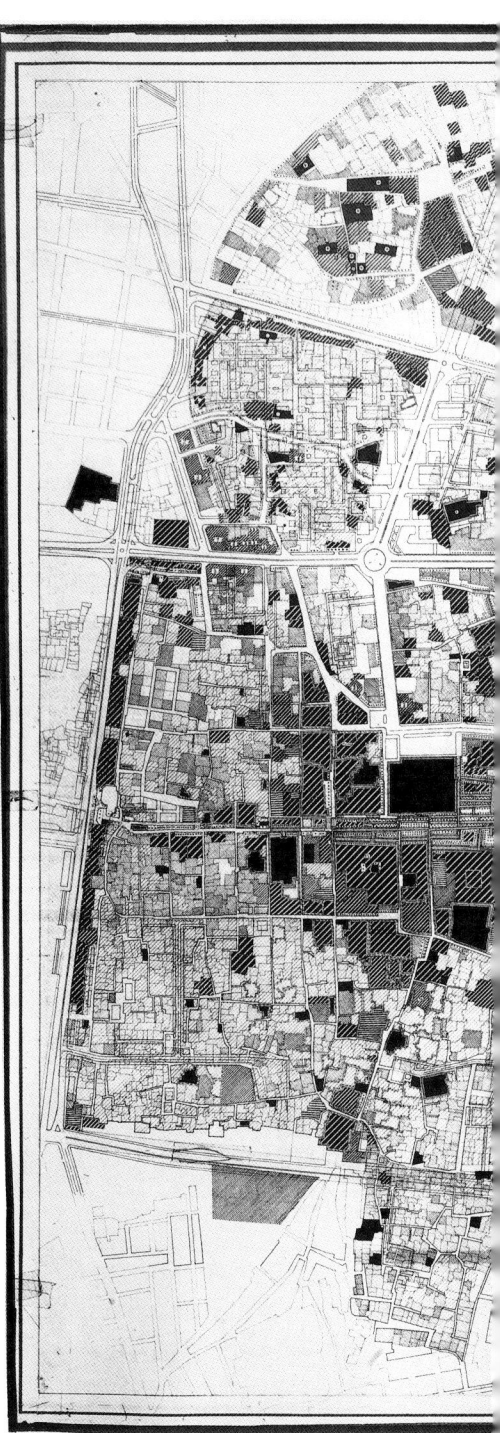

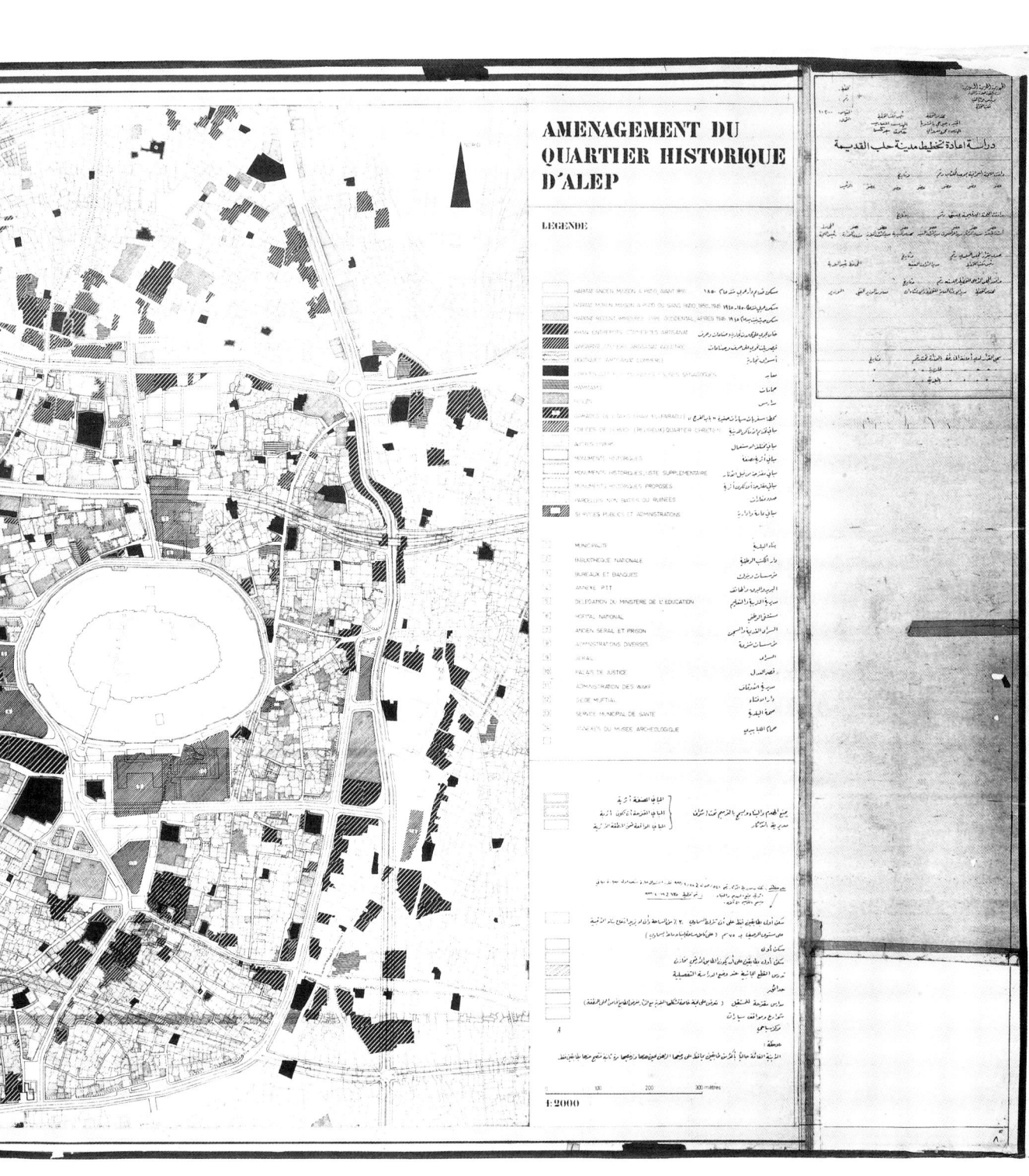

14 CHAPTER 1

< 1.9. Institute of Oceanography, Conakry (Guinea), 1970s. A. Shchusev, E. Sokolov, A. Novozhilova, A. Legostaev. "Sovetskaia arkhitektura za rubezhom," *Arkhitektura SSSR* 6 (1984): 109.

< 1.10. Monument of Agostinho Neto in Luanda (Angola), design 1979, model. E. Rozanov, V. Shestopalov, E. Shumov. "Sovetskaia arkhitektura za rubezhom," *Arkhitektura SSSR* 6 (1984): 112.

architectural discourse and practice in Lagos (Augustine Egbor), Baghdad (Kahtan Awni, Mohamed Makiya), and Kuwait City (Gulf Engineering Office, Kuwait Engineering Group).

Politicians, administrators, managers, and experts in the Global South did not necessarily share the same incentives to collaborate with Eastern Europe, and even more often these incentives differed from the ideological aims, geopolitical objectives, and economic and industrial policy interests of the USSR and its satellites.[64] The following chapters show how shifts in those goals from the 1950s to the 1980s were mediated through architectural transfers, starting with few highly visible buildings donated within the framework of Khrushchev's "gift diplomacy" to economic agreements that directly benefited the USSR under First Secretary Leonid Brezhnev (1964–82), often with countries that produced raw materials. By the 1960s, the new Soviet leadership criticized Khrushchev-era policies for their lack of economic analysis. However, despite this critique, the Soviet Union continued to send substantial sums to developing countries, in particular those considered on a "noncapitalist" development path, while not being able to match aid given by the West, in particular by the United States.[65] Much Soviet assistance was delivered by means of military support given to Soviet allies and resistance movements, which dominated Soviet involvement in Africa and Asia over the course of the 1970s, and this assistance sometimes included architectural programs, too (figures 1.9 and 1.10). Despite Soviet disenchantment with revolutions in Africa and Asia by the 1980s, and cuts to technical assistance programs, Soviet architectural projects abroad continued to perpetuate the ambiguous relationship between "aid" and "trade" that characterized Khrushchev's gifts. For Soviet economists, this ambiguity was conveyed by the principle of "mutual advantage" that they used to characterize the specificity of foreign trade with socialist countries. In the final decade of the Cold War, however, Soviet design institutes began to pursue commercial commissions, often tapping into old contacts initiated under Khrushchev, for instance housing commissions in Guinea.[66]

Whereas Eastern European satellite countries broadly followed the objectives of foreign policy set by the USSR, they had the capacity to bypass, stall, and at times obstruct and divert those objectives. Their activities abroad were also dependent on their economic exchanges with the Soviet Union, which were characterized by complex, evolving relations of exploitation and subsidy, the latter mainly by means of Soviet oil and gas sold to the satellites below international prices.[67] The chapters that follow show how changes in the political economy under Bulgarian leader Todor Zhivkov, Poland's Edward Gierek, and Romania's Nicolae Ceaușescu modified trajectories, volumes, and composition of architectural export from these countries. So, too, did the reorganization of economies toward "market socialism" in Yugoslavia and Hungary in the last decades of the Cold War. Geopolitical concerns specific to particular countries also played a role, with the West German policy of détente (*Ostpolitik*) resulting in a shift toward commercial aims of architectural export from East Germany (German Democratic Republic, or GDR). Until the 1970s, the latter had been dominated by attempts to subvert the Hallstein Doctrine (1955–69), under which West German governments had declined to recognize any nation that recognized their eastern counterpart (figure 1.11).[68] The Ostpolitik also opened a path for Polish architectural exports toward a more commercial approach, having been used until West Germany's recognition of Poland's western border (1970) to stabilize the international standing of the country, notably in the UN. For Tito and Ceaușescu, architectural export was instrumental in their ambitions for leadership of the developing world, as both countries aimed at straddling multiple worlds. In particular, Yugoslavia's foreign trade benefited from the country's increasing integration into the capitalist market, its associated membership in Comecon, and its leadership in NAM.

In the 1960s, solidarity with the postcolonial world was central to the legitimization of communist regimes, and the engagements of Eastern European architects abroad were presented as part of the international struggle against imperialism. However, in the following decade such presentations were less prominently featured in mass media and the professional press. With the promise of consumption becoming pivotal to the social contract between the communist parties and the Eastern European societies, accounts of exported architectures provoked unfavorable comparisons with architectural production at home, both in quantity and in quality.[69]

This shift in the climate of opinion reflected the redefinition of the objectives of foreign trade by the socialist countries. In the aftermath of the oil embargo of 1973, architectural, engineering, and construction firms from many Comecon countries flocked to oil-producing countries in North Africa and the Middle East, just as their Western European and American competitors did. The latter targeted those markets in search of commissions that shrank in the West as a result of the oil crisis. In contrast, increased export activities from socialist countries resulted from the "kiss of debt," or pressure to repay credit that these countries obtained from Western financial institutions. However, the economic modernization of socialist countries and the industrial leap that was planned to follow and that was supposed to finance their model of consumer societies and repay their debts never materialized. In order to finance those debts, Bulgaria, Hungary, Poland, Romania, and Yugoslavia responded by raising exports to countries able to pay in convertible currencies, or in products resalable to the West, such as crude oil.[70] This included the export of construction services that was particularly beneficial to the national economy, as a Polish study argued in the 1970s. Such export required low capital intensity, did not deprive the domestic market of goods and services, allowed for a "secondary hard-currency output" (as Polish employees deposited foreign earnings in Polish banks), and facilitated knowledge and technology transfers to Poland.[71]

While few of these claims would remain unchallenged in the years to come, the emphasis on export meant increased pressure on architects,

1.11. Apartment blocks in Kilimani (Zanzibar), 1969. Heinz Willumat (project architect), and others. Ludger Wimmelbücker, "Architecture and City Planning Projects of the German Democratic Republic in Zanzibar," *Journal of Architecture* 17, no. 3 (2012): 417.

planners, and managers of construction companies. However, yielding to compulsory "hard-currency plans" was not the only reason for architects and state companies from socialist countries to seek and accept contracts abroad. Such contracts ensured high levels of employment, for which there had been little justification after the conclusion of postwar reconstruction in Eastern Europe. Since the 1960s, this was a major motivation for such offices as Poland's Miastoprojekt-Kraków or the Hungarian Design Institute for Public Buildings (Közti) to actively seek commissions abroad, for example through participating in international competitions and tenders.

To see architectural circulation from socialist countries as part of a larger circuit of oil, money, goods, and services connecting oil-producing states in North Africa and the Middle East with Western and Eastern Europe may explain the shift in the patterns and volume of architectural engagements by the mid-1970s. The export of architectural and construction services from non-Soviet Eastern Europe to several countries around the Mediterranean accelerated during the final two decades of the Cold War, but not from the USSR, which was able to gain convertible currency by expanding its exports of fossil fuels to Western Europe (since the 1960s). At the same time, and in contrast to the USSR's dominant presence with the Marxist-Leninist regimes in Angola, Mozambique, or South Yemen, several nominally socialist governments in the Global South grew wary of Soviet influence and thus favored non-Soviet socialist countries. For one example, in a meeting in 1972, a Libyan envoy told Ceaușescu that in spite of Libya's friendly relations with the USSR, Libya felt uneasy about collaborating with such a large country and would prefer Romania to step in.[72] Such accounts, and the perspective from the Global South more generally, challenges the received vision of the socialist world as consisting of satellites revolving around the Soviet Union at the center. Instead, this book shows that the capacity of that center to concentrate, aggregate, attract, and integrate went hand in hand with its propensity to repel, disperse, fragment, and stir up competition. This combination of centrifugal and centripetal forces further differentiated architectural mobilities from Comecon countries.

VESSELS OF ARCHITECTURAL RESOURCES

Rather than aspiring to a complete account of architectural travels from socialist countries during the Cold War, this book focuses on several points on the triangular trajectory between Eastern Europe, West Africa, and the Middle East. In so doing, the following chapters offer more concentrated glimpses into the changing motivations, priorities, and geographies of the actors involved. Some individuals were able to cover the entire triangle. They included Zoran Bojović from Yugoslavia (Serbia), who designed buildings in Nigeria and in Iraq, all supervised by engineer Aleksandar Slijepčević; the architects Kuno and Stanka Dundakova, a Bulgarian couple who worked in Nigeria, Kuwait, and the UAE (figure 1.12), as did Tibor Hübner from Hungary; and another couple, Polish architects Grażyna Jonkajtys-Luba and Jerzy Luba, who worked in Ghana and Nigeria before traveling to Libya. While the Lubas were directly employed by local institutions, whether state-owned or private, Hübner worked for Közti, a design institute from Hungary, and Bojović and the Dundakovs traveled on contract with contractors from their countries: Energoprojekt and Technoexportstroy (TES).

These are the main actors in architectural mobilities discussed in this book: individual architects and planners as well as aggregate actors, including design institutes and state contractors offering services in both design and construction. Their work abroad, whether in other socialist countries or in "nonsocialist" ones (as Ghana, Nigeria, Iraq, the UAE, and Kuwait were classified in Eastern Europe), was carried out within a broad network of national institutions. They included ministries in charge of foreign trade, foreign affairs, construction, and others; central planning institutions; communist parties and their dependent bureaucracies; technical assistance organizations; state-socialist banks; and foreign trade organizations. Other institutions included research, training, and scientific centers; the army and its engineering divisions; trade unions; mass organizations including those for youth and women; producers of construction materials, machinery, and equipment; international solidarity committees, and cultural and sports organizations. While enlisted into centralized chains of command, the activities of these institutions at various levels were not always coordinated, and neither were their aims and motivations unanimous. They were complemented by bilateral organizations, including intergovernmental committees established between socialist and African and Asian countries, and multilateral ones, including permanent commissions of the Comecon, in particular its Commission for Construction and Commission for Technical Assistance.

Design institutes from socialist countries were often the first to be approached with requests concerning projects abroad. These were typically large organizations employing hundreds of professionals, sometimes connected to particular ministries. Among them were Soviet town planning institutes, such as the State Institute for the Planning of Cities (Giprogor), Institute for Town Construction Projects (Gorstroiproekt), and Central Scientific Research and Design Institute for Town Planning (TsNIIEP gradostroitel'stva). They were responsible for master plans of cities in Cuba (Havana, 1960s), Mongolia (Ulaanbaatar, 1954, 1963, 1971), Afghanistan (Kabul, 1964), and Iran (Ariashahr, today Fuladshahr, 1968), often in collaboration with local planners (figures 1.13 and 1.14).[73] Planning offices from Yugoslavia, Poland, and Czechoslovakia delivered master plans for

1.12. Cover of a catalogue of Bulgarproject with the design of the sports grounds in Ilorin (Nigeria), 1970s. Bulgarproject (Bulgaria), Kuno Dundakov, Stanka Dundakova, and others.

1.13. The center of Ulaanbaatar (Mongolia). Master plan by Giprogor (USSR), 1954.

1.14. Ariashahr, today Fuladshaht (Iran), 1960s. I. Badanov, S. Volkov, D. Grishin, G. Zosimov, I. Konovalov, B. Lun'kov, A. Repetii, V. Serzhantov. "Sovetskaia arkhitektura za rubezhom," *Arkhitektura SSSR* 6 (1984): 103.

INTRODUCTION

1.15. Master plan of Conakry (Guinea), 1963. Zagreb Urban Planning Institute (Socialist Republic of Croatia, Yugoslavia).

1.16. Master plan of Tripoli (Libya), 1979–83. Warsaw Development Consortium (WADECO, Poland).

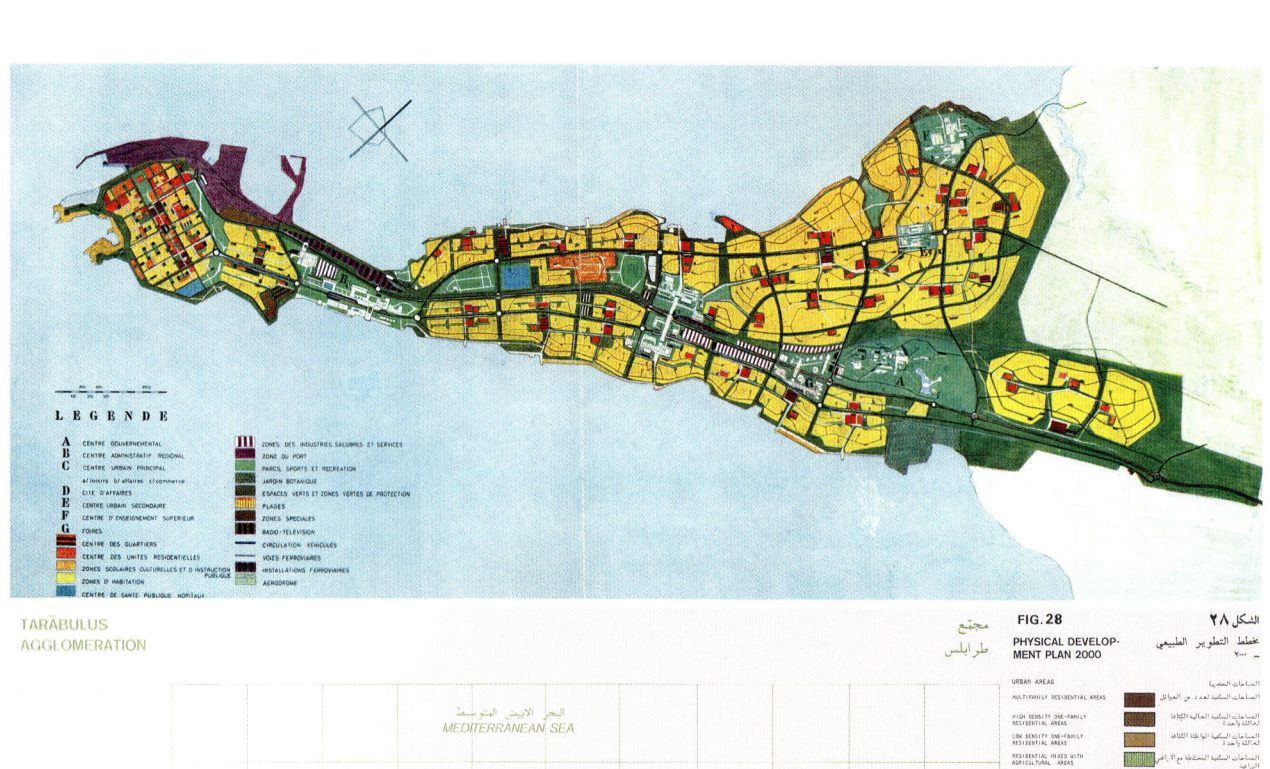

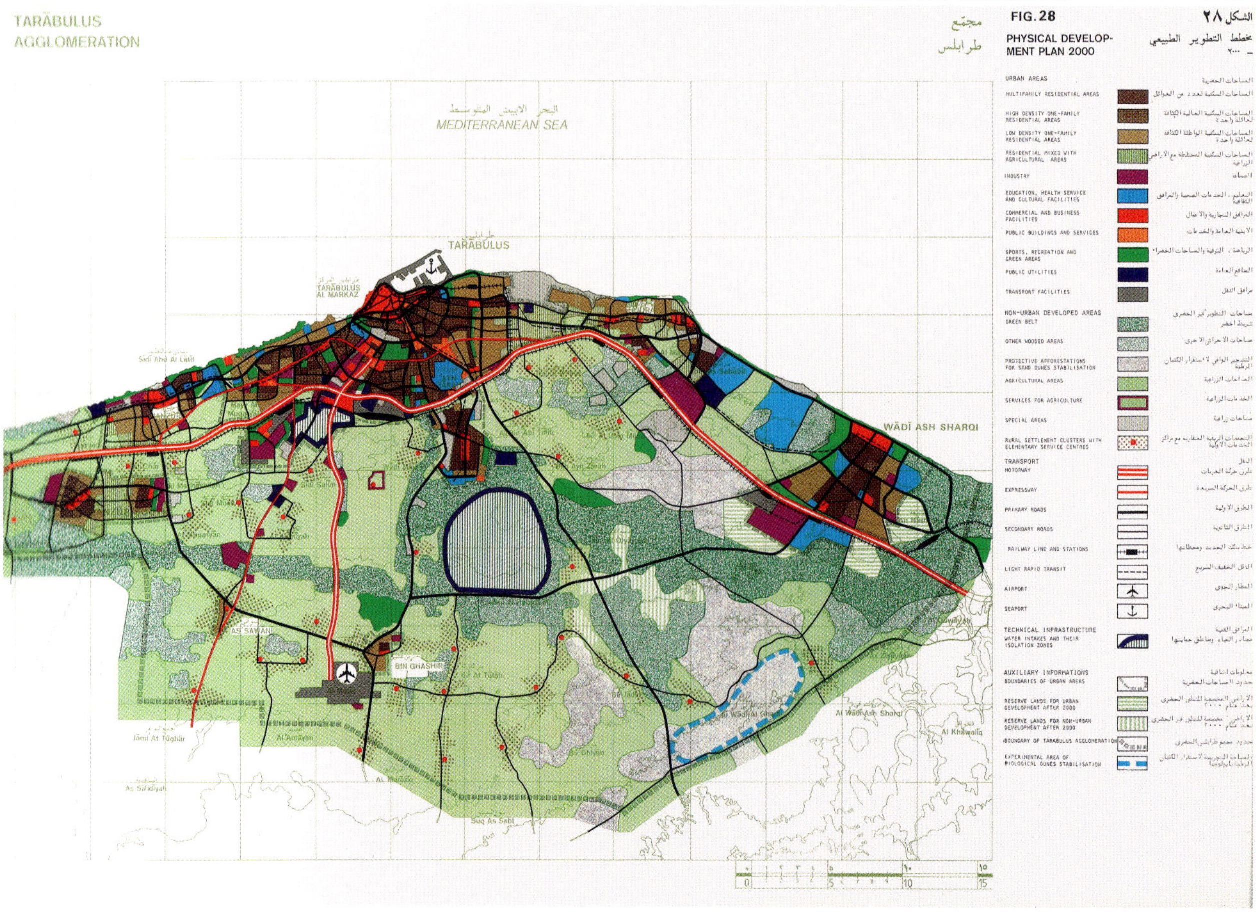

1.17. House of Culture and Youth Theater Complex in Darkhan (Mongolia), 1978. L. Kataev, E. Antipova, V. Shifrin.

Conakry (Guinea, 1963), the Tripolitania region and its particular cities (Libya, 1983), and Tunisia's tourist development (1966), among many others (figures 1.15 and 1.16).[74]

In general, plans delivered by design institutes abroad reflected their specializations, with distinct Soviet design institutes responsible for schools, hospitals, housing, industrial facilities, and theaters built in African and Asian cities (figure 1.17). Design work in other socialist countries was often equally differentiated, including industrial design institutes that specialized according to particular industrial branches. Several producers of high-end equipment and machinery also offered comprehensive designs of building envelopes for their products. For example, the architectural section of Carl Zeiss, the optical instruments manufacturer from the East German city of Jena, designed planetariums for the instruments produced by Zeiss.[75]

While Zeiss built upon the prewar history of the firm, most design institutes from Eastern Europe were founded after World War II. In their work abroad, they drew upon their experience of postwar, state-led reconstruction and development, and their representatives were eager to claim the specificity of their experience and the competence stemming from it. Accordingly, Bulgarians promoted their tourist architecture at the Black Sea coast, while Czechs and Slovaks advertised renovations of historic Bohemian and Moravian towns, Poles showcased the reconstruction of Warsaw, and East Germans promoted their country's system of "complex" (that is to say, comprehensive) industrialized construction, then extended the country's achievements in sports toward a claim to competence in sports architecture.[76] Authorities from the South were often decisive in shaping these profiles—for example, by soliciting the import of plants in one rather than another industrial sector, or by requesting that scholarships offered to their students by a particular socialist country were assigned in a specific discipline. The local authorities typically decided about the distribution of design and construction commissions among particular Comecon countries, as was the case, for example, when a Polish-Syrian team took over from the Soviets the planning of the new town at the Soviet-designed Tabqa Dam over the Euphrates River in Syria (figure 1.18).[77]

The claims to a specific expertise were hardly exclusive among Eastern European countries, and they rarely coincided with attempts at specialization as advocated by Comecon, which aimed at a "socialist international division of labor" as the basis of intersocialist economic integration.[78] Comecon's Permanent Commission for Construction coordinated

INTRODUCTION 21

technical assistance in architecture and construction to its least developed members. In contrast, there is little evidence of coordination among Comecon countries in commercial commissions in the Middle East and North Africa. Design institutes often extended their remit when working abroad—for example, the commissions of Közti in Arab countries included not only health, school, and sports facilities, but also residential districts (figures 1.19 and 1.20).[79] Some aggregate actors discussed in this book, such as Energoprojekt and TES, constantly adapted their structures, workflow, and recruitment procedures to fit the requirements of African and Asian markets in order to be more competitive. By the 1970s, they also competed against organizations from other socialist countries in open tenders organized by African and Middle Eastern governments.

Energoprojekt and TES represent the second dominant type of architectural actors mobilized in socialist countries: state contractors that offered both design and construction services. As was the case with the design institutes, these companies were typically established during the postwar reconstruction period and put in charge of large-scale industrial works and civil-engineering infrastructure; such tasks also dominated their subsequent export activities. This genealogy was often reflected in their names, such as Energoprojekt, created in 1951 in Belgrade (Yugoslavia) to provide design and consultancy services within hydro- and thermal-power generation and water management. Other companies included Yugoslavia's Ivan Milutinović (PIM) and Rad from Serbia, as well as Ingra from Croatia and Beton from Macedonia, Arcom and Romproiect from Romania, and Budimex from Poland. Most of them worked on commissions both in their home countries and abroad, but some, including TES, worked exclusively abroad.[80]

The "design-and-build" procedure these contractors offered was favored by West and North African and Middle Eastern governments, and resulted in such highly visible projects as the National Arts Theater (Stefan Kolchev for TES, 1977) and the International Trade Fair (Zoran Bojović for Energoprojekt, 1977), both in Lagos, as well as the Sudanese Parliament building in Khartoum (Cezar Lăzărescu and the Design Institute Carpați, 1972–78), and many others (figure 1.21).[81] Commissions abroad given to these enterprises were sometimes restricted either to design

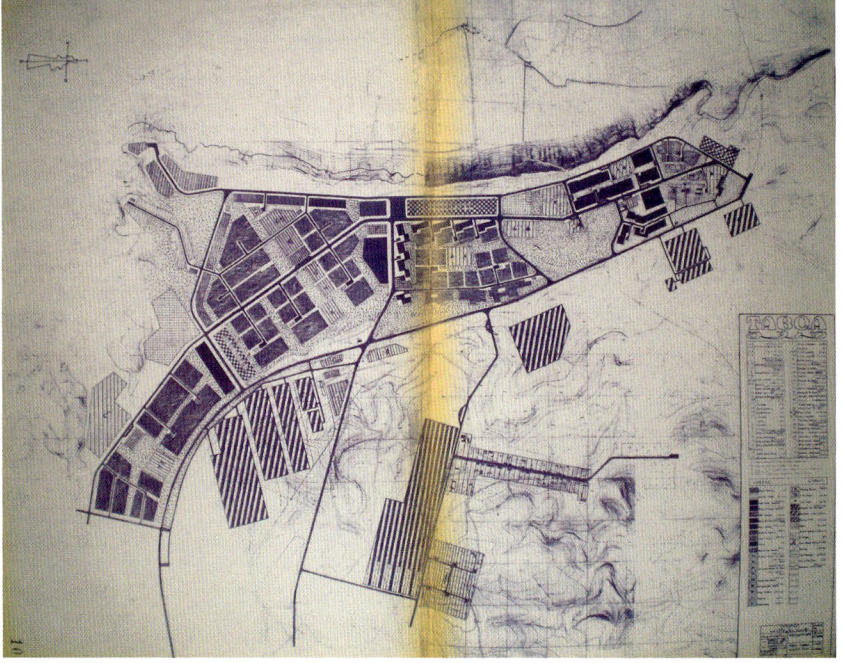

1.18. Master plan of al-Tabqa (Syria), 1968. Claude Dagher, Krystian Seibert, and others. Syrian Arab Republic, General Organization of the Euphrates Project, "Tabqua Town: Final Report on the Plan of the Town," Damascus, 1968.

1.19. 5 July 1962 Stadium, Algiers (Algeria), 1965–72. Közti (Hungary), András Egyházi, Sándor Ázbej.

1.20. Housing estate in Jijel (Algeria), 1971. Közti (Hungary), Ildikó Halmágyi.

INTRODUCTION

Ready for any project
Anytime
Anywhere in the Republic of Zambia

ZECCO
A Zambian company for the people of Zambia

- building branch
- airconditioning department
- concrete factory
- electrical department
- plumbing department
- ZECCO furniture factory
- ZECCO steel factory

THE FINDECO BUILDING, LUSAKA.
Designed by UNICO

ZAMBIA ENGINEERING & CONTRACTING CO. LTD.
Head Office: P.O. Box 306, LUSAKA.   Telephone: 73770/74652
Mukwa Road, Heavy Industrial Area.   Telex: ZA4225

July 1978 In Situ page 29

< 1.21. Parliament Building, Khartoum (Sudan), 1972–78. Arcom (Romania), Design Institute Carpați (Romania), Cezar Lăzărescu and others. "Palatul Adunării Poporului din Khartoum. Republica Democratică Sudan," *Arhitectura* 6 (1979): 13.

< 1.22. Findeco House in Lusaka (Zambia), 1972–76, advertisement. Energoprojekt (Socialist Republic of Serbia, Yugoslavia), Zambia Engineering & Contracting Company (ZECCO, Zambia), Dušan Milenković, Branimir Ganović. *In Situ* (July 1978): 29.

tasks (Administration Center Hamma in Algiers by TES's Dimitar Bogdanov, 1987) or to construction (the Ministries Complex built in Kuwait City by Energoprojekt, 1981).

Many of these organizations combined various in-house specialists, from landscape and urban designers to interior architects, but also engineers and construction managers, quantity surveyors, graphic designers, IT specialists, and translators. Experts from the industry and research institutes were recruited, too. This capacity to tap into a countrywide pool of experts was presented to potential partners as a major advantage of a socialist centralized and planned economy.[82] Moreover, research centers that supported work abroad included the Institute of Tropical Architecture in Gdańsk (Poland), the Architecture and Civil Engineering University in Weimar (GDR), and the International Postgraduate Course of Urban and Regional Planning for Developing Countries in Szczecin (Poland). Researchers at the Patrice Lumumba University in Moscow, including Anatolii Nikolaevich Rimsha, authored guidelines and manuals that were used by Soviet architects abroad, and were distributed within the socialist bloc.[83] These research centers, supported by a growing number of institutes specializing in African and Asian studies, and by architectural and planning departments and other higher-educational institutions, examined urbanization processes in Africa and Asia, studied architectural and engineering solutions appropriate for the Global South, and sometimes compiled market surveys for state-socialist enterprises that operated abroad. Graduates of Eastern European universities coming from Africa and Asia were hired at times by state-socialist contractors operating outside Europe.

The authorities from most socialist countries put pressure on contractors to use construction materials from their countries of origin to maximize income, resulting in some cases in custom-made series of construction materials earmarked for export. Another way to avoid purchases from third parties was to produce components in factories set up alongside construction sites in West and North Africa and the Middle East. Besides managers, designers, and engineers, contractors from Eastern Europe typically brought qualified foremen on site, who supervised and trained the local workforce. Employment of local workers was sometimes required by the governments of the receiving countries, as was collaboration with local partners. In Zambia, Guinea, Nigeria, Kuwait, and the UAE, for instance, Eastern European companies were required to establish joint ventures with local firms and individuals (figure 1.22). This book discusses several instances of such collaboration, including the Lagos-based joint venture Nigerian Engineering and Construction Company Ltd. (NECCO), established in 1974 by Energoprojekt and the Nigerian government.

By the 1970s, however, few contractors from socialist countries could avoid purchases of third-party construction materials and equipment because of their shortages in Eastern Europe and their low quality. In turn, Western companies employed Eastern European firms as subcontractors in projects commissioned by North African and Middle Eastern governments. In this sense, during the two final decades of the Cold War, individuals and companies from socialist countries working in foreign markets collaborated as much as competed with those from the West. Precedents can be found earlier for such collaborations across Cold War divides—in 1960s Afghanistan, for instance.[84] However, during détente such commercial "tripartite" contracts between local enterprises and those from socialist and capitalist countries burgeoned in North Africa, the Middle East, and elsewhere (figure 1.23).[85] The Eko Hotel in Lagos, designed by Nigerian architect Oluwole Olumuyiwa in collaboration with a New York–based firm and constructed by Bulgaria's TES under the supervision of an American contractor (1977), is one example among many (figure 1.24).[86] These entanglements between Southern, Western, and Eastern actors resulted in new patterns of division of labor, which often persisted after the end of the Cold War.

Work on foreign commissions by design institutes and contractors was often the path for architects, planners, and engineers to individual contracts with institutions abroad, including planning institutes, research centers and universities, municipal or national authorities, and sometimes private offices. Individual architects were eager to sign such contracts, motivated by professional ambition and determined to practice architecture outside the constraints exerted by party bureaucrats and construction companies under state socialism. By the end of the Cold War, work abroad had become a genuine learning experience, in particular in the booming oil economies of North Africa and the Middle East, where newest construction technologies and design innovations coming from the West were tested and explored. Know-how from abroad was at times brought back to socialist Eastern Europe, including, for example, the Chinese experience of planning the special economic zones, which Polish urban planner Piotr Zaremba attempted to import to Poland in the 1980s.[87] The opportunity to travel and see the world, rare in most socialist countries where citizens did not own their passports, was an important incentive, too. Financial perks were another motivation, as professionals on export contracts were paid, at

1.23. Ministry of Defense, Kabul (Afghanistan), 1964. Mieczysław Wróbel and others.

1.24. Eko Hotel, Lagos (Nigeria), 1977. Oluwole Olumuyiwa, Lagos (Nigeria), in collaboration with Warner, Burns, Toan & Lunde, New York (US); constructed by Technoexportstroy (Bulgaria) under the supervision of the Bechtel International Corporation (US).

least partially, in convertible currencies. In this way, they benefited from hugely favorable exchange rates between those currencies and Eastern European currencies, notwithstanding obligatory fees and taxes paid to state-socialist institutions.

However, opportunities to work abroad often entailed considerable personal costs for the professionals involved, including separation from families and frustrations about the limited control over life and work conditions, in particular when compared to their local counterparts and Westerners. The case of a Bulgarian foreman who spent months in the Libyan desert without much to do besides work, a Romanian couple in Algeria unable to see their small children for two years, a Polish architect handing over a third of her salary every month (in cash) to a Polish trade representative in a Kuwaiti cafe, and an East German engineer instructed to remain in Baghdad during its bombardment by the Iranian army are reminders that there is nothing inevitably emancipatory in mobility.[88]

All contracts abroad, whether a design or design-and-build commission or an employment contract, were mediated by foreign trade organizations (FTOs), another key actor in the architectural engagements of socialist countries abroad. Created after World War II with the aim of importing machinery and licenses for postwar reconstruction and industrialization, FTOs were soon charged with the export of goods, services, and technical know-how in order to gain foreign currency necessary for import purchases. Besides buying and selling on behalf of state-socialist enterprises, FTOs organized technical support for equipment and machinery sold abroad, and studied foreign markets.[89] A brochure of the Czechoslovak FTO Polytechna also counted to its remit the cooperation with the UN and the management of Czechoslovak technical assistance to developing countries.[90] Furthermore, Polytechna was in charge of marketing Czechoslovak enterprises, among them architectural offices.[91]

FTOs typically specialized according to industrial branches, with some responsible for export of construction services (Czechoslovakia's Strojexport, East Germany's Limex), and others in charge of the export of labor, such as Polytechna, Intercoop in East Germany, Tesco in Hungary, Polservice in Poland, and Romconsult in Romania (figure 1.25). With the decentralization of the economy in Yugoslavia over the course of the 1960s, the introduction of "market socialism" in Hungary, and attempts at stimulating competition elsewhere in Eastern Europe, selected contractors in those countries were given the prerogatives of FTOs so that they could export directly and were financially incentivized to do so. In general, aggregate actors commissioned to work abroad were required to sign contracts with a responsible FTO and the foreign commissioner. In turn, individual architects leaving for abroad signed agreements with their home employer, their prospective employer abroad, and the FTO in charge of export of labor (figure 1.26).

In the following chapters, individual architects, design institutes, and contractors mediated by FTOs are studied as vessels of architectural mobilities, that is to say, conveyors of architectural resources from socialist Europe. These resources included architectural designs and master plans, construction materials and technologies, technical details and functional typologies, building norms and urban standards, academic curricula and research methodologies, images and discourses. In this book, I pay particular attention to the one resource that was both mobilized in these networks and was mobilizing others: the labor of architects, planners, contractors, administrators, managers, educators, foremen, and workers. In particular, I study modalities of labor; its specialization, division, remuneration, and taxation; its trajectories, speed, and rhythms. I also focus on places of work as sites where new collective subjectivities emerged and where global projects of solidarity were tested and challenged, confirmed or refuted.[92]

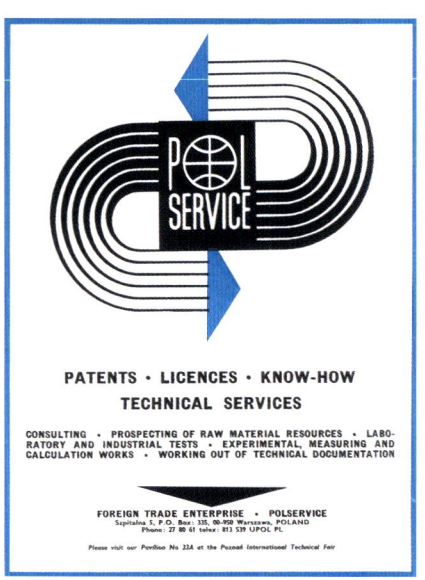

1.25. Advertisement of Polservice (Poland). *Polish Fair Magazine* 3 (1973): 39.

1.26. National Library in Damascus (Syria), 1974–84. Jan Jacek Meissner, Małgorzata Mazurkiewicz, Marek Dunikowski, Wojciech Miecznikowski.

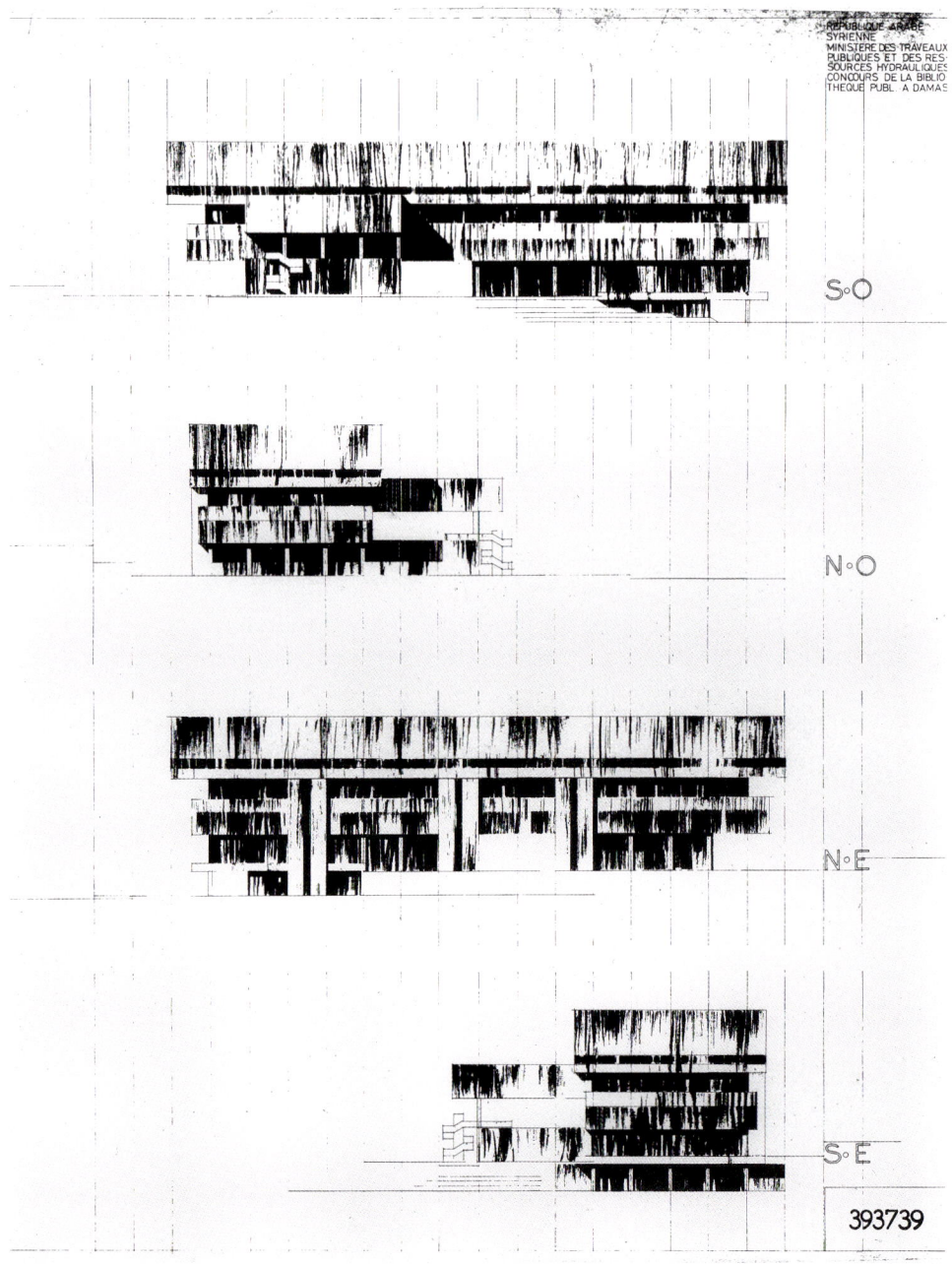

When mobilized abroad, this labor could be many things, and its modalities appear differently depending on the archive interrogated. In documents of FTOs and journals specializing in foreign trade such as Poland's *Rynki zagraniczne* (Foreign Markets), labor was discussed as a fungible resource, whose mobility from Eastern Europe was part of larger packages stipulated by export contracts. However, such a view has been contested by some protagonists of this book, and Karlheinz Schlesier, an East German designer of a housing complex in North Vietnam, affirmed in a recent interview that "[East German] architectural export never has existed."[93] For Schlesier and his colleagues, work abroad was, above all, a professional experience. Along such lines, in architectural magazines and individual portfolios of architects, their labor appeared as an outlet of creative capacity and cultural competence to adapt the principles of modern architecture to local technological, cultural, material, and social conditions. In turn, in engineering journals architectural labor was primarily represented as a carrier of a technological expertise, whose translations to conditions on the ground were informed by concerns of stabilization and reproduction of the expected performance that would create path-dependencies and "collateral dividends" for the countries concerned. Each of these three modalities—export, adaptation, and translation—applied to many instances of architectural labor, but not necessarily to all, and, for example, what could not have been exported might have been adapted.

SOCIALIST WORLDMAKING

When introducing their technical assistance to the developing countries, representatives of the Soviet Union and the Comecon countries often insisted on its specificity, from the socialist path of development and its spatial frameworks, to the technologies and techniques of its implementation. In retrospect, economic historians and historians of technology, architecture, and urban planning questioned such statements and pointed to the intense exchanges of know-how and technology across the Cold War divides.[94] They included, for example, the borrowing of Anglo-American layouts in Soviet urban typologies, and the appropriation of Western European technology in Soviet prefabricated housing systems, two of USSR's main export products. Read in this way, the Cold War discourse of distinction and confrontation may appear as a mere smokescreen that covers the fundamental entanglement of postwar architectural culture.

However, entanglement does not preclude antagonism. In order to study the ways in which architectural mobilities from socialist countries introduced antagonism and difference into urbanization in the Global South, in this book I focus on the deployment of architectural resources in Cold War Accra, Lagos, Baghdad, Abu Dhabi, and Kuwait City. I will account for the dynamics of these processes by developing the concept of worldmaking, building upon the work of several writers.

These writers include French urban theorist Henri Lefebvre, who in the course of the 1970s coined the concept of world-forming (*mondialisation*) in order to point to the world as an emerging dimension of practice. The world in this understanding does not imply a bounded space carved out from the surface of the planet. It is not divided into the "First," "Second," and "Third" worlds, identified in 1952 by French demographer Alfred Sauvy with capitalist, socialist, and developing countries.[95] Neither does it map into the three "pillars" of the postwar world-system, as distinguished by Samir Amin, including the socialist-democratic compromise, "Sovietism," and the nationalist project of Bandung.[96] Rather, the world is a contested and plural category; it is an abstraction, but a "social" or "concrete" abstraction that becomes "true in practice."[97] The experience of a world thus understood is that of diversity, connection, and multiplication of points of attachment, which Martinican writer, poet, and theorist Édouard Glissant called worldness (*mondialité*). Contrary to earlier experiences of the world, Glissant wrote by the end of the Cold War that "the thrust of the world and its desire no longer embolden you onward in a fever of discovery: they multiply you all around."[98] Following both writers' theorizing of the world as a historically specific dimension of practice, imagination, and experience, I understand worldmaking as the production of the world from within its many, often antagonistic, possibilities.

For Glissant, *mondialité* is opposed to what since the 1970s has been studied in Anglo-American scholarship under the term "globalization." This overarching process was conditioned upon the deregulation of financial systems after the end of the Bretton Woods agreement (1971); the industrialization outside the West, beginning with Southeast Asia; the increasing economic integration of global trade that undermined the bipolarity of the Cold War; the global development-aid system promoted by institutions of the UN and the organization's global standards concerning health, the environment, and human rights; as well as new information and communication technologies, including digital ones, and the acceleration of speed and scale of mass transportation.[99] In this book, I develop the concept of worldmaking by insisting on the difference between worldmaking and globalization. I am not, however, opposing one to the other in the manner in which globalization was contrasted with *mondialité* by Glissant, and with *mondialisation* by the French philosopher Jean-Luc Nancy.[100] Rather, in what follows I understand globalization as just one among many possibilities of worldmaking.

Socialist countries offered alternative possibilities. While the global dimension of socialism was explicitly present in the movement since its beginning in the nineteenth century, after the October Revolution the Soviet Union became the center of socialist worldmaking, both as the heart of the global network of revolutionary movements, and as the kernel of an expanding system of socialist states.[101] The term "global socialism," used in this book's title, refers to these and other projects of global cooperation that were practiced by institutions and individuals from socialist countries, including architects, planners, and construction companies working abroad. Even if the "socialist commonwealth" declared by Khrushchev never materialized, and socialist worldmaking remained between the descriptive and the normative, it produced frameworks of interaction and of exchange of very real things, among them architectural resources.[102]

Initiated within the Soviet state and then extended after World War II to its satellites across Eurasia, under Khrushchev these exchanges were opened toward decolonizing countries that were encouraged to follow the socialist path of development. Chapter 2 argues that the claim to that path's global applicability was predicated on its adaptation to conditions outside the USSR, and that architecture, planning, and construction technology played a key role in this adaptation. By focusing on two Soviet blueprints of residential districts in Nkrumah's Ghana, this chapter demonstrates how Soviet architecture, planning, and construction technologies were adapted to the climatic, social, and economic conditions of West Africa. Soviet housing in Ghana, while never built, became a precedent for the mobility of Soviet prefabricated technologies and urban typologies to tropical regions in Africa, Asia, and Latin America.

Chapter 2, however, makes it clear that architectural production in Nkrumah's Ghana was far from dominated by the Soviet Union. In charge of this production, instead, was the Ghana National Construction Corporation (GNCC), a state agency responsible for building and infrastructure programs after Ghana's independence in 1957. Along with being the local partner for Soviet organizations, GNCC employed architects from other socialist countries, including Bulgaria, Hungary, Poland, and Yugoslavia.

Despite circulating within state-socialist networks, few among those architects identified with Cold War confrontations. Rather than exporters of the socialist path of development, they saw themselves as members of one world of the international culture of modern architecture. Accordingly, the juxtaposition of the Soviet blueprints for Ghana with GNCC's architectural production, including the International Trade Fair in Accra, shows that modern architecture under Nkrumah was not imported from the Soviet Union or elsewhere. Rather, it was coproduced by Ghanaians and foreigners who tapped into resources circulating in competing networks of global cooperation that intersected in the country.

The argument that transfers of the socialist development path did not exhaust international engagements of architects, planners, and contractors from socialist countries is reinforced in chapter 3. This chapter focuses on Nigeria in the 1970s, a country whose elite was generally hostile toward socialism and not attracted by socialist modernization. The presence of Eastern Europeans in Nigeria came about owing to attempts by the federal government to diversify the set of foreign enterprises working in the country. Socialist regimes were happy to oblige, and to benefit from Nigeria's oil boom.

Accordingly, rather than referring to the socialist path of development, Eastern European architects and planners who found themselves in Nigerian cities such as Lagos, Calabar, Zaria, and Jos sought other references in order to make sense of the tasks at hand. Borrowing from recent discussions on the "worlding" of African and Asian cities, I study ways in which these architects and planners imagined worlds they shared with West Africans. In particular, they pointed to the shared experience of foreign domination over Eastern Europe and West Africa during the long nineteenth century, which resulted in both regions in economic backwardness and cultural dependency. Socialist propaganda argued that the experience of overcoming of such predicaments in postwar Eastern Europe was the basis of the region's solidarity with decolonizing countries, and offered an example to follow. But rather than accepting this rhetoric, most protagonists of that chapter referred to longer traditions of Eastern European architectural culture to identify tools and procedures they might employ in Nigeria.

In that sense, chapter 3 shows the work of architects, planners, and contractors from socialist countries as a "worlding" of Eastern Europe, or the appropriation of its experience of economic modernization and cultural emancipation to the tasks at hand in Nigeria. The study of the master plan of the city of Calabar (1969), designed by a Hungarian team, shows how its head, architect Charles (Károly) Polónyi mobilized his earlier experience of architecture and planning in rural areas of postwar Hungary, which he saw as "not very far from…a developing country."[103] Rural territories were also in the focus of the research on vernacular building cultures in Nigeria by Polish architect and scholar Zbigniew Dmochowski and his team. In this research, Dmochowski implemented drawing and surveying techniques from prewar Poland in order to open the way toward a "modern school of Nigerian architecture."[104] Last, Yugoslav designers and Yugoslav and Nigerian contractors of the International Trade Fair in Lagos (1977) embraced the peripheral position shared by Eastern Europe and West Africa as an opportunity to work across multiple worlds and mobilize resources from various centers. Yet while showing how this chapter's protagonists employed historical analogies between Eastern Europe and West Africa, their work also reveals limits to these analogies and ambiguities of Eastern Europe's own colonial history.

While chapter 3 shows worldmaking as a precarious affair, practiced by people "'cast out' into the world," chapter 4 discusses worldmaking as an overarching practice of international trade.[105] This practice was conveyed by the concept of the world socialist system, coined by Soviet economists, which promised an alternative international division of labor that would end the economic exploitation of the Global South by the Global North. The core of the world socialist system was the Comecon, but the system also included affiliated countries, among them Iraq (from 1973). Chapter 4 shows how Comecon and Iraqi architects, planners, and contractors contributed to the urbanization of Baghdad by instrumentalizing differences between the emerging global market of design and construction services and the political economy of the world socialist system.

That political economy defined conditions of labor of architects, planners, and technicians from socialist countries and the terms of their collaboration with Iraqi partners. These conditions, in turn, facilitated specific design methodologies and the technopolitics of construction in Iraq. I make this argument by revisiting the master plans of Baghdad delivered by Miastoprojekt-Kraków and its General Housing Programme for Iraq (1976–80), as well as residential districts by Romania's Arcom and Romproiect; infrastructure in Iraqi cities by Bulgarian, East German, and Soviet design institutes; public buildings by Yugoslav firms; and teaching curricula at the Department of Architecture in Baghdad to which architects from Czechoslovakia and Poland contributed. By focusing on collaboration between East German and Romanian firms on the Baghdad slaughterhouse project (1974–81), the chapter argues that specific profiles of state-socialist actors resulted from path-dependencies forged by economic instruments and political bargaining within the world socialist system.

Chapter 5 opens with one of the most prominent buildings in Abu Dhabi: the Municipality and Town Planning Department. Designed in Bulgaria, it was constructed in 1985 by an Abu Dhabi–based contractor and a number of subcontractors from the region and elsewhere. This building, as well as others delivered by Eastern Europeans in the UAE and Kuwait

1.27. Joint Factory 718, Beijing (People's Republic of China). Constructed in 1957 according to the design of Ipro Dresden (GDR), the factory is today the seat of the Goethe Institut in Beijing.

during the final decade of the Cold War, differs from those discussed in the preceding chapters. It did not result from intergovernmental agreements, but rather from increasingly aggressive attempts by state-socialist companies to enter foreign markets. In so doing, their managers left out references to socialist internationalism and introduced themselves to prospective clients as carriers of technological expertise on par with their Western competitors. Furthermore, the Abu Dhabi building broke with the tradition of modern architecture, however modified or adapted, which had characterized the foreign work of architects from socialist countries in previous decades. Instead, it reflected the requirement of "Arab-Islamic culture," increasingly formalized in the UAE and Kuwait by the late 1970s in response to disenchantment with post-oil urbanization in the Gulf.

That combination of technical and cultural expertise was the condition for integrating Eastern European architects and contractors into the Western-dominated and increasingly globalized market of design and construction services in the Gulf. Chapter 5 argues that Bulgarian and other Eastern European actors had acquired that double expertise during their previous engagements in North Africa and the Middle East in the 1960s and 1970s. Over the course of their work abroad, these actors learned to comply with Western building norms, specification standards, financial regimes, technological systems, and construction-management procedures. They also became acquainted with aesthetic and cultural proclivities of governmental clients in Arab countries. In so doing, they became agents of an integration of state-socialist design and construction economies into the Western-dominated, global economic order. With the Gulf becoming one of the paradigmatic places of architecture's globalization at the turn of the twenty-first century, chapter 5 rewrites the genealogy of those processes by situating them within a longer history of socialist projects of worldwide cooperation.

Read together, these chapters show how Eastern European architects, planners, and construction companies and their counterparts in West Africa and the Middle East practiced worldmaking. They did so either by working within frameworks and networks of socialist projects of global solidarity and advancing them against their competitors, or by working across such competing frameworks and networks. In this way, the concept of worldmaking offers a different image to that of a curtain, either iron or nylon, that has informed most studies of Cold War architectural transfers to date. In this book, the Cold War appears as a clockwork mechanism in which cogs of antagonistic worldmaking projects sometimes gnashed and ground, and sometimes complemented each other to mutually productive effect.[106]

What was produced was urbanization. Individual and aggregate actors circulating in networks set up and sustained by socialist countries contributed to all dimensions of urbanization distinguished by urban theorists Neil Brenner and Christian Schmid, including the production and reproduction of territories and structures, their regulation, representation, and appropriation in everyday life.[107] In West Africa, the Middle East, and elsewhere, urbanization processes continue to be conditioned by structures, forms, landscapes, technologies, norms, standards, and institutions coproduced by Eastern Europeans, West Africans, and Middle Easterners during the Cold War (figure 1.27). In turn, professionals who returned to Eastern Europe from export contracts contributed, and sometimes continue to contribute, to the urbanization of the region after the end of socialism. By revisiting these engagements, this book is not an excavation of failed projects of globalization but offers instead a heterogeneous and antagonistic genealogy of a world that is more urban and more global than ever before.

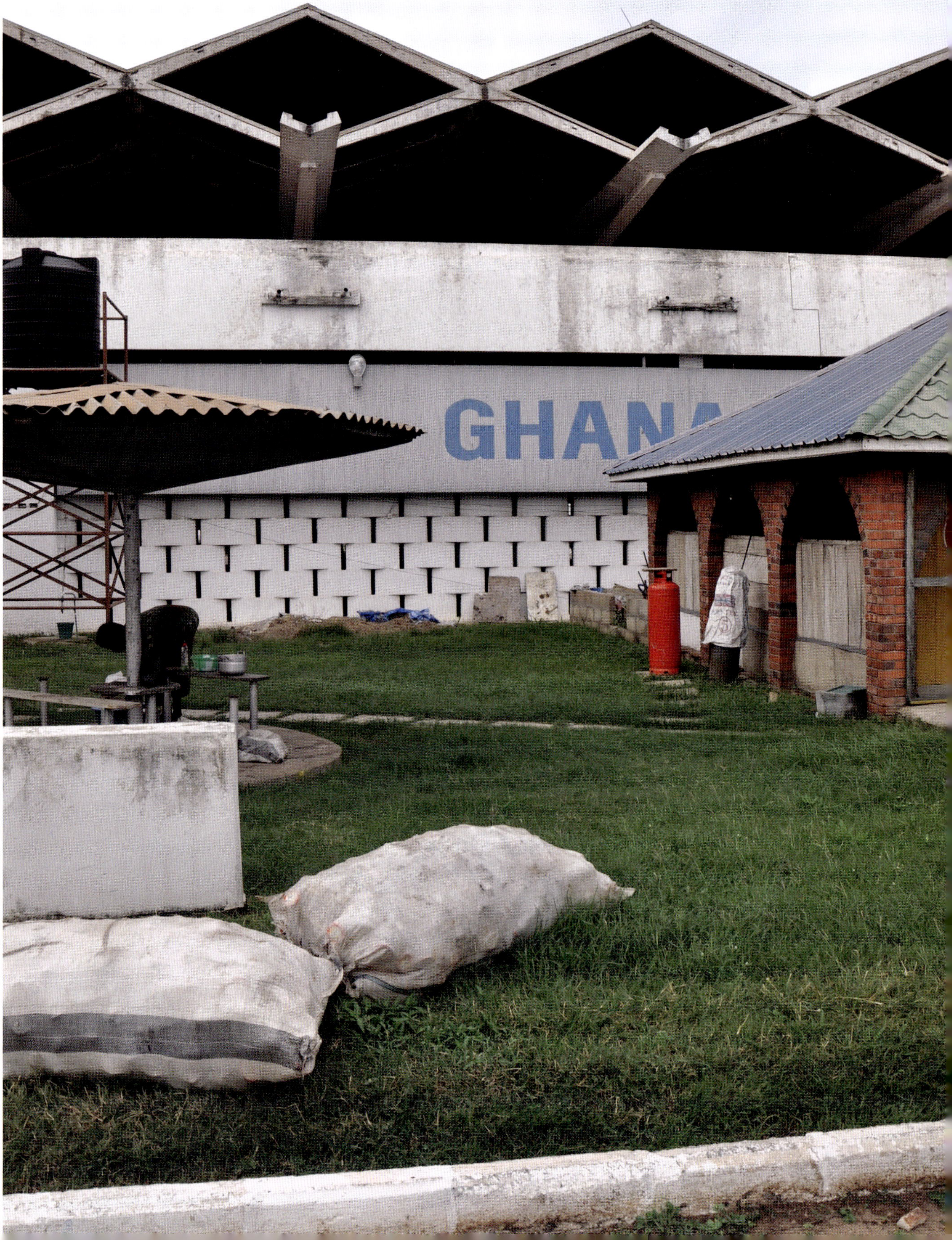
GHAN

Chapter 2
A Global Development Path
Accra, 1957–66

2.1. Pavilion A ("Made in Ghana" pavilion), International Trade Fair, Accra, 1962–67. GNCC, Vic Adegbite (chief architect), Jacek Chyrosz, Stanisław Rymaszewski (project architects).

When seen from Labadi Road, the buildings of Accra's International Trade Fair (ITF) appear among abandoned billboards, scarce trees that offer shade to resting taxi drivers, and tables next to the road where coconuts, bottled water, sweets, and telephone cards are sold (figure 2.1). ITF's buildings border the settlement called La, where streets meander between houses, shops, bars, schools, and shrines, while at the seashore on the other side of Labadi Road, a luxurious housing estate is under construction next to upscale hotels overlooking Labadi Beach.

    The government of Kwame Nkrumah, Ghana's leader after the country achieved independence from Britain (1957), initiated ITF in 1962, but it was opened on February 1, 1967 by Joseph Arthur Ankrah, who had led the putsch that toppled Nkrumah (1966) (figure 2.2).[1] Once conveying a sense of radical modernity, many of the trade fair buildings appeared to have suffered from underinvestment when visited in 2012. The aluminum roof of the round entrance pavilion had collapsed, and the pavilion stood empty, left unoccupied just as the concrete structure of what had been planned a decade ago as the first air-conditioned ITF exhibition building. Yet most other structures—those built as permanent, those intended to be temporary, and those added in an unplanned manner—were in use, rented out during exhibitions taking place every few months, political rallies, and religious services. By 2012, ITF had around two hundred tenants, the majority of them Ghanaian firms, but also West African ones.[2] Around the compound, melancholy was mixed with grand ambitions for a new beginning, and in the manager's office one could admire bird's-eye renderings delivered by Dublin-based architects, which showed a spectacular vision for replacing most of the original buildings.

The ITF was designed and constructed between 1962 and 1967 by the Ghana National Construction Corporation (GNCC), the state organization charged with design, construction, and maintenance of governmental buildings and infrastructure in Ghana. The designers of the trade fair were two young architects from socialist Poland, Jacek Chyrosz and Stanisław Rymaszewski, employed at GNCC, with the Ghanaian Victor (Vic) Adegbite as the chief architect. Chyrosz and Rymaszewski traveled to Ghana on a contract with Polservice, the foreign trade organization (FTO) mediating the export of labor from Poland. At GNCC, they worked together with Ghanaian architects and foreign professionals, many of the latter coming from socialist Bulgaria, Hungary, and Yugoslavia.

This collaboration reflected the alliances with socialist countries forged by Nkrumah's government and the Convention People's Party (CPP), which he headed. Since his tenure as prime minister during the shared Ghanaian-British rule (since 1952), Nkrumah and the CPP envisaged Ghana as a modern nation that was leading Africa's decolonization, anti-imperialist struggle, and the unification of the continent. Nkrumah's beliefs had been shaped by Marxist and pan-Africanist debates that pointed to the interdependence between imperialism and capitalism.[3] Nkrumah argued that a socialist planned economy within a one-party state was the means to do away with "poverty, hunger, illiteracy, disease, ignorance, squalor, and low productivity," which he laid out on the eve of independence as the goal of the government.[4] By the early 1960s, this program of a fundamental political, social, economic, and infrastructural modernization was supported by the Soviet Union and its satellites. Along with Guinea (independent since 1958) and Mali (independent since 1960), with which Ghana formed a confederation, Nkrumah's government was approached by the socialist countries within Khrushchev's policy of "peaceful coexistence." For the

2.2. International Trade Fair, Accra, 1962–67. GNCC, Vic Adegbite (chief architect), Jacek Chyrosz, Stanisław Rymaszewski (project architects).

Soviets, West Africa became a testing ground for the global transferability of the socialist path of social and economic development, and for its superiority over capitalism. The Soviets argued that this path (or "model"), when adapted to the conditions of West Africa, would allow Ghana to match the fast-track economic development of the USSR, an argument that was well received by Nkrumah.

Yet contrary to previous Soviet experiences of transferring the socialist path of development to Eurasia, upon their arrival in Accra, they found themselves in direct competition with actors already present on the ground. These were coming from Britain, Ghana's former colonial metropolis and largest trade partner, and the United States. US-based institutions, among them the World Bank, granted Ghana loans for its infrastructural investments, in particular the Volta River Project, a development scheme conceived by the colonial administration and relaunched after independence.[5] International organizations, including the UN and its Technical Assistance Programme, were present in Ghana, too. Furthermore, by the 1960s, the networks of socialist countries were bifurcating, and Chinese envoys arriving in Accra presented Nkrumah with a socialist alternative to the Soviet model. Such alternatives were also offered by Yugoslavia and other members of the Non-Aligned Movement, of which Ghana was a founding member. Accra became also a center for the Pan-African Movement, which Nkrumah had the ambition to lead.

The GNCC operated across these competing and often antagonistic networks that intersected in Ghana. The corporation tapped into these networks and negotiated antagonisms between then, and in this sense its architectural production is best understood as a practice of worldmaking. These networks provided the corporation with a range of resources, including labor, building materials, construction technologies, technical details, images and discourses, and building norms and standards. The admission of these resources to Ghana and their transfers between particular networks were regulated by specific entrance protocols and gatekeeping procedures, such as contracts underwritten by foreign governments, technical assistance programs, and trade agreements.

Yet while this mode of operation seemed to bypass Cold War antagonisms, those became unavoidable when, by the early 1960s, GNCC was enlisted in the program of implementing the socialist path of development embarked on by the CPP. In order to address the ways in which Cold War antagonisms informed the architectural production of the corporation, I will discuss its two major projects: Soviet plans for residential districts in Ghana (left unrealized), and the International Trade Fair in Accra. The residential-district plans adapted Soviet construction technologies and urban typologies to climatic conditions in West Africa. Had they been built by GNCC as intended, those districts would have resulted in a radical change in the everyday lives of their inhabitants, but also in a transformation of the Ghanaian construction industry in accordance with the socialist path of development.

In contrast, that path was not on the minds of the designers of ITF, who saw themselves as part of an international culture of modern architecture being practiced in Ghana since the late-colonial period. However, this aspiration was challenged by British architects in Accra, who mobilized Cold War categories to claim an irreducible difference between "nonfree" architectural labor under socialism and architectural labor in the "free" Western world. Though that categorization is untenable, I will show that conditions of labor under socialism did distinguish architectural mobilities from Eastern Europe from those of Western actors. In this sense, the reading of the design and construction of ITF will capture both sides of the worldmaking dynamics in GNCC production: the appropriation of resources from competing global networks operating in Ghana, and the articulation of antagonisms between those networks.

ARCHITECTURE FOR INDEPENDENT GHANA

During the first decade after independence, Accra changed dramatically. This change comes to the fore in the juxtaposition of two maps of the capital: one published in 1958 by the Kingsway Department Store in Accra, and the other published seven years later by the Survey of Ghana.[6] The former map shows the city as inherited from the colonial period, when Accra grew around the port starting from three European strongholds at Jamestown, Ussher Town, and Osu (figure 2.3). After the city became the seat of the British colonial administration in 1877, its growth accelerated, leading to the emergence of a business and an administrative area, and new housing districts for Africans and Europeans that complied with the colonial policy of residential segregation (since 1885). The Kingsway map depicted a collection of respectable buildings accumulated during the final decades of the British rule, such as the art deco Roman Catholic Cathedral and the historicist Arch of Independence, the Supreme Court, the Parliament House, and the University College in Legon. Depictions of the Kingsway Department Store, the Bank of Ghana, the Ambassador Hotel, and the modest terminal building of the Accra Airport exemplified modern architecture as it had been adapted to tropical conditions during the postwar period in the colony.

2.3. "The Kingsway Street Map of Accra," 1958.

None of those buildings, with the exception of the university, were depicted on the 1965 map, which showed Accra as fundamentally modern and looking toward the future (figure 2.4). The landmarks represented were either recent buildings in the modern idiom or technical structures: the parabolic Presidential Tribune at Black Star Square, the Flagstaff House, the Police Headquarters at the Ring Road, the State House Complex, the Kwame Nkrumah Circle fountain, new buildings of the Korle Bu Hospital, and telecommunication towers. Other recent buildings, such as the Ministerial Area, are shown in figure-ground, and the site of the future ITF is marked and annotated. All these are linked by an overarching traffic network covering a much larger territory than the one shown on the Kingsway plan, thus demonstrating Accra's rapid expansion in all directions from its original nuclei.

Architectural Resources for Ghana

The transformation of the city conveyed by the contrast between these two maps resulted largely from GNCC's work and that of its predecessor, the Ghana National Construction Company. The latter had been created in 1958 as a joint venture between the government-owned Industrial Development Corporation (60 percent) and the Israel Construction Company—Solel Boneh (40 percent).[7] The collaboration between the Ghanaian government and the Israeli firm reflected Nkrumah's fascination with the Jewish state and was supported by Golda Meir, then Israel's foreign minister. Meir specifically singled out Solel Boneh, with its construction and civil engineering experience in the Middle East since the 1930s, as a diplomatic tool rather just an economic agent.[8] The joint Ghanaian-Israeli venture was put in charge of the construction of major infrastructure works in Ghana, residential buildings, and several iconic projects, including the Black Star Square tribune and the Cabinet Offices at Osu Castle (figure 2.5). The joint venture was also committed to the training of Ghanaians, both within the company and by funding scholarships for Ghanaians to study in Israel and in Ghana, at the newly opened (1958) School of Architecture, Town Planning and Building at the University of Science and Technology (UST) in Kumasi, the first school of architecture in sub-Saharan Africa.[9]

By 1962, Nkrumah's rapprochement with North African Arab countries resulted in a cooling of relations with Israel. Within the shift toward a state-led socialist economy, the Ghana National Construction Company was nationalized and merged with the former colonial Public Works Department (PWD) to create GNCC. During colonial rule, PWD had been in charge of design, construction, renovation, and maintenance of governmental buildings, then after independence it was subsumed under the Ministry of Works and Housing (as the Division of Public Construction), before being included into GNCC.[10] This genealogy resulted in the persistence of colonial technoscience at GNCC, including the continuous use of specifications, technical papers, and handbooks published since the early twentieth century by PWD branches in West Africa, guidelines published by various Ghanaian ministries, and manuals by British architects and planners with experience in British West Africa.[11] These provided recommendations about architectural typologies and urban layouts, type projects for housing and social facilities, information about vernacular construction, pragmatic solutions for sanitation facilities, suggestions for ways of handling local and imported materials in the climatic and social conditions in West Africa, and typical details. These publications were available to and used by architects working in the post-independence PWD and later in GNCC.[12]

Continuity between colonial and post-independence planning institutions in Ghana included personnel, and that continuity was targeted by the policy of Africanization enforced by Nkrumah's government.[13] In the

INDEX
N
E
S
W
ACCRA
UNIVERSITY OF GHANA
ACHIMOTA
ANUNMLE
ABOFU
ABLENKPE
APENKWA
TESANO
POLICE TRAINING DEPOT
KOTOBABI
MAMOBI
ALAJO
KPEHE
ACCRA NEW TOWN
NIMA
KANDA
KOKOMLEMLE
ACCRA INTERNATIONAL AIRPORT
AIRPORT RESIDENTIAL AREA
BURMA CAMP
CANTONMENTS
LABADI
BUBIASHI
KANESHIE
ASYLUM DOWN
ADABRAKA
RINGWAY ESTATE
MATAHEKO
ABOSE OKAI
WEST RIDGE
EAST RIDGE
CHRISTIANSBORG
SABON ZONGO
AGBOGBLOSHI
VICTORIABORG
LARTE BIOKORSHI
KORLE DUDOR
USSHER TOWN
JAMES TOWN
MAMPROBI
KORLE GONNO
GULF OF GUINEA
Edition of 1963
Reference No. X2520

< 2.4. "Accra. Compiled, Drawn, and Photo-lithographed by the Survey of Ghana," 1965.

2.5. Presidential Tribune at the Black Star Square in Accra, early 1960s. Ghana National Construction Company.

years leading to independence, supervisory positions had been increasingly assumed by Ghanaians, including Kojo Gyinaye Kyei, A. K. Amartey, O. T. Agyeman, and Vic Adegbite. Adegbite's biography reveals the internationalization of Ghanaian architecture. A graduate of the architectural school at Howard University in Washington, DC, Adegbite received a UN fellowship to specialize in housing design at the Inter-American Housing Center in Bogotá, Colombia, and traveled to study housing programs in Jamaica and Puerto Rico. He returned to Ghana in 1956, where he became the head of the Ghana Housing Corporation, and was responsible for such prominent designs as the Ghana Farmers' Office and the headquarters of the CPP (both 1960).[14] While most Ghanaian architects taking up leadership positions in the early 1960s were educated in the UK and the United States, by the end of the decade they were joined by those trained in the Soviet Union. These included Ghanaians who received scholarships to study at the Moscow Architectural Institute (MARKhI), among them E.G.A. Don Arthur, who studied at MARKhI between 1962 and 1968, as well as Moses Tulasi (1962–68) and Edwin Kankam (1963–69).[15] Over the course of the 1960s, a growing number of Ghanaian architects, educated abroad or in Kumasi, entered the labor market and, by the end of the decade, began to create the first Ghanaian private offices, such as Architectural Design Partnership, Associated Consultants, and Architectural Associates.

That process was a gradual one, however, and in the first years after independence PWD and GNCC depended heavily on a foreign workforce. Until the early 1960s, smaller type buildings were designed and constructed by PWD/GNCC, while more prestigious, singular buildings were designed by British architects based in Accra or abroad and then executed by PWD/GNCC. Several of those architects subscribed to principles of "tropical architecture," a name self-assigned by a group of architects and urban planners operating within the British late-colonial and Commonwealth contexts, who adapted principles of modern architecture according to local conditions outside Europe.[16] In former British West Africa, which had

A GLOBAL DEVELOPMENT PATH

included Gambia, the Gold Coast (the colonial name of Ghana), Nigeria, and Sierra Leone, tropical architecture was represented by buildings by Maxwell Fry and Jane Drew, the authors of *Tropical Architecture in the Humid Zone* (1956), and by Architects Co-Partnership, James Cubitt, John Godwin and Gillian Hopwood, and Kenneth Scott.[17] Based on longer traditions of construction in the British colonies and protectorates in Africa and Asia, in the wake of decolonization tropical architecture came to be presented by its protagonists as an international community of professionals offering their services to newly independent states.

After independence in Ghana, several proponents of tropical architecture continued to receive commissions there, including Kenneth Scott, who designed the Kumasi Stadium (1958), the Korle Bu Hospital and its extensions in the 1960s, and the Volta River Authority building in Tema (1964).[18] The National Archives Building (1959) in Accra, designed by Nickson, Borys & Partners, joined the National Museum (1957), designed by Fry, Drew, Drake & Lasdun, among such projects (figures 2.6 and 2.7).[19] Fry, Drew, and their associated partners also designed a number of housing projects in Ghana, as did Architects Co-Partnership, and Miles Danby.[20] Several new structures were built in Kumasi, where the UST campus became a major construction site, including those designed by Gerlach & Gillies-Reyburn as well as by Barnes, Hubbard & Arundel.[21] A. Gilmour designed several carefully detailed private bungalows whose wooden frames offered an alternative to the concrete structures of Scott's Accra villas.[22] Several "tropical" architects were guest teachers at the School of Architecture, Town Planning, and Building at UST in Kumasi, and continued to participate in discussions about the future of Ghanaian cities.

British contractors continued to play important roles in Ghanaian architecture after independence, including Taylor Woodrow, which provided commissions to British architectural and engineering firms. Others included Ove Arup & Partners, which opened offices in West Africa during the 1950s, and George Paton, in charge of the landmark Ambassador Hotel in Accra and its subsequent extensions.[23] Yet while Jane Drew argued in 1960 that a country like Ghana "does not worry whether the architect is a local or a foreigner," in the following years this was no longer the case.[24] Over the course of the 1960s, GNCC increasingly kept design commissions, such as the International Trade Fair, for itself. Nevertheless, British professionals did play an important role in the ITF design, for which the functional program was drafted by R.H.C. Hammond, a British expert in exhibition design who worked on ITF since 1963, hired in the framework of British Technical Assistance Programme.[25] Most ITF construction materials—from louver windows and the aluminum sheets for the entrance pavilion's round roof to the fountain on the exhibition grounds and fittings for particular pavilions—were shipped from Britain (figures 2.8 and 2.9).[26]

From the early 1960s, construction activities in Ghana were supported by a number of bilateral agreements between Ghana and the countries of the British Commonwealth, including Canada, which provided construction materials, blueprints, equipment, and training staff for Accra's Technical Training College.[27] They were joined by architects from Western European countries that granted credit to Ghana, including a group of Italian architects who delivered a design for the waterfront of Central Accra (unrealized).[28] The new Accra Airport terminal was credited by the French government and designed and constructed in the mid-1960s by French companies.[29] Dutch engineers were working at the Korle Bu estate projects as well as at ITF.[30] In 1964, a West German housing corporation was commissioned by the Ghana Housing Corporation to design a neighborhood of single-family houses in Teshie Nungua, Greater Accra, constructed after the end of Nkrumah's regime.[31]

2.6. National Archives Building, Accra, 1959–62. Nickson, Borys & Partners.

2.7. National Museum, Accra, 1957. Fry, Drew, Drake & Lasdun.

A GLOBAL DEVELOPMENT PATH

43

Several foreign architects arriving in Ghana were hired by GNCC. They included the African American architect J. Max Bond Jr., who designed the celebrated Bolgatanga Library (1965), and several other buildings, such as the Studio and Practice Hall for the National Orchestra in Accra (1964) (figure 2.10).[32] The United States was an increasingly important political and economic partner, and several US foundations sponsored buildings in Ghana, including the construction of the drama studio of the Art Council.[33] US-based foundations also supported the Greek office of Constantinos Doxiadis, which delivered a master plan for Tema (the contract was signed in 1961), and designed various housing typologies for the new seaport town, from blocks of flats to an "experimental" typology of row-housing for lower income groups. Other commissions for Doxiadis included the master plan for the Accra-Tema-Akosombo metropolitan area (since 1961), and the plan for Accra's central area (figure 2.11).[34] Furthermore, town planning in Ghana was consulted by experts sent by the UN.[35]

British, Commonwealth, Western European, and US architects were joined by professionals from socialist countries. Following the opening of the Soviet embassy in Accra (1959) and the Ghanaian embassy in Moscow (1960), Ghana formalized diplomatic relations with other socialist countries from Eastern Europe.[36] The staff of the US embassy in Accra was astonished by the appearance of unfamiliar cars on the streets, such as Skodas, Volgas, and Moskvichs, and alarmed by the increasing presence of Soviet technicians, among them flight and ground crews for the six Ilyushin Il-18 airliners bought by the government in 1960. A memorandum sent by the US embassy to the State Department in 1960 listed twenty-eight projects by the Soviet Union planned for Ghana, as well as nineteen projects by Yugoslavia,

2.8. International Trade Fair, Accra, 1962–67, Africa Pavilion under construction. GNCC, Vic Adegbite (chief architect), Jacek Chyrosz, Stanisław Rymaszewski (project architects).

2.9. International Trade Fair, Accra, 1962–67, one of the temporary pavilions under construction. GNCC, Vic Adegbite (chief architect), Jacek Chyrosz, Stanisław Rymaszewski (project architects).

2.10. Library in Bolgatanga, mid-1960s. GNCC, Vic Adegbite (chief architect), Max Bond (project architect). Max Bond, "A Library for Bolgatanga," *Architectural Forum* (March 1968): 67.

2.11. Master plan for the Metropolitan Area of Accra and Tema. Doxiadis Associates. "Accra–Tema–Akosombo Regional Programme and Plan Interim Report," *Ekistics* 11, no. 65 (March 1961): 269.

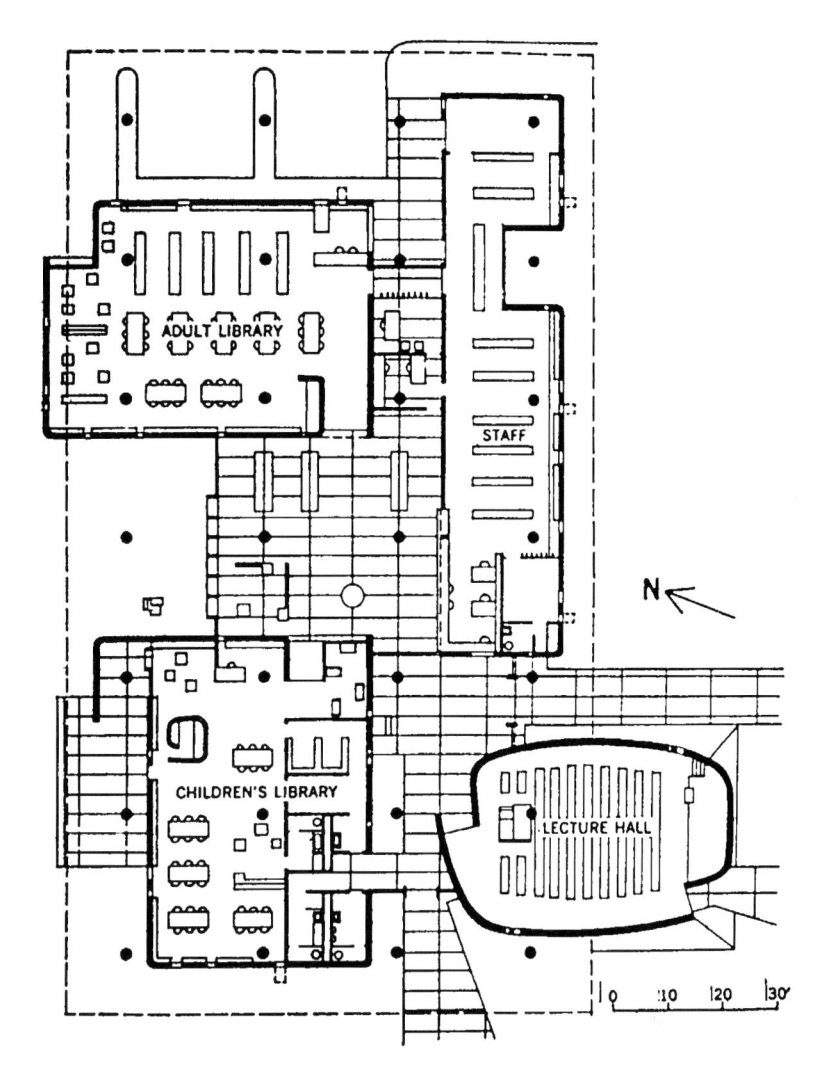

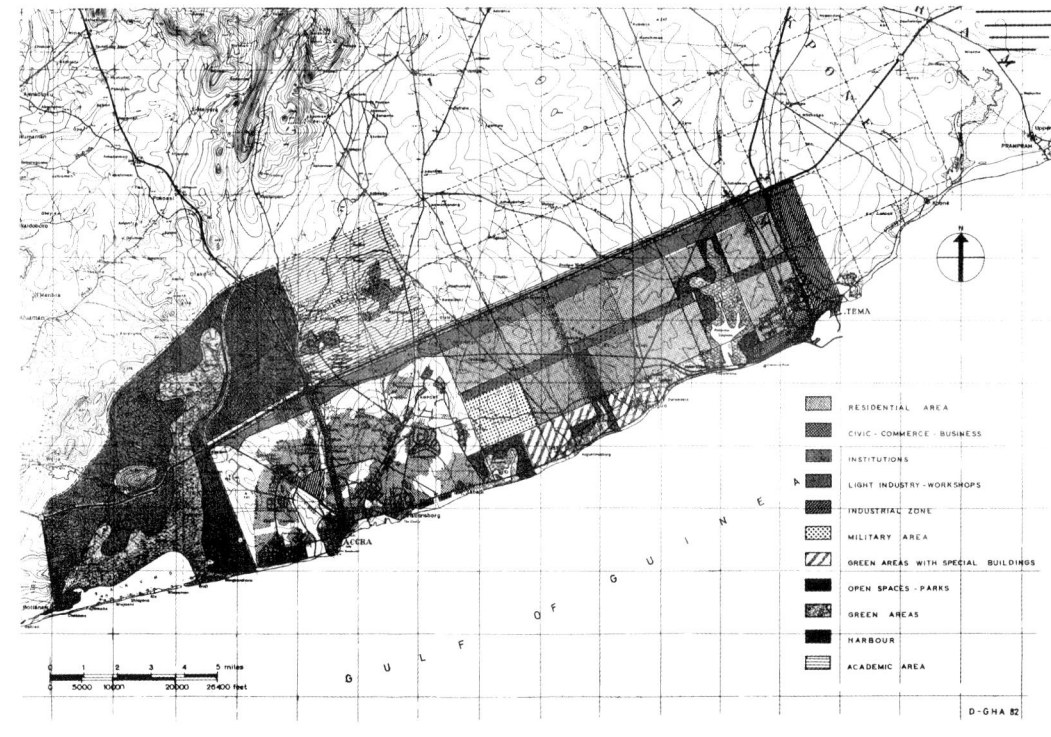

A GLOBAL DEVELOPMENT PATH 45

eighteen by Poland, ten by Czechoslovakia, nine each by Hungary and China, eight by Bulgaria, seven by Romania, five by East Germany, and four by Albania.[37] By the early 1960s, most of those countries would already have organized trade exhibitions in Accra, and local press in 1962 reported that more than fifty technicians from socialist countries were working in the capital.[38] In his memoirs, the US ambassador in Guinea (1961–63) chose to deride Soviet involvement in West Africa as incompetent, yet original wires from the US embassy in Accra during the period struck a rather different tone.[39] The embassy's rapporteur described the Eastern bloc's activities as "conducted quietly and correctly" and acknowledged that "within a relatively short time the Communist World has gained an appreciable measure of acceptance and respectability on the local scene."[40]

This presence of Soviet and Eastern European personnel reflected Khrushchev's opening toward West Africa. Since the late 1950s, "cultural and economic achievements of the Soviet Union" were popularized by Soviet propaganda material distributed in Ghana, Guinea, and Mali. Radio Moscow launched broadcasts targeting African listeners in French, English, and Hausa, while the Soviets circulated printed materials, established field bureaus for the chief Soviet information agencies and newspapers, granted fellowships for Africans to study in the Soviet Union, and trained specialists on Africa.[41] African studies in the USSR grew rapidly from the late 1950s, including the Institute of Africa, created in 1959 at the Soviet Academy of Sciences, which was expected to provide expertise to support Soviet policy toward African countries.[42] In 1960, the Peoples' Friendship University was opened in Moscow as part of Khrushchev's "fraternal assistance" to developing countries, with training offered in medicine, agriculture, economy, and engineering to a growing number of students (over four thousand in 1972).[43] Renamed for Patrice Lumumba after the Congolese leader was killed in 1961, the university became a hub of knowledge production on Africa, as were other specialized institutes established in Czechoslovakia, East Germany, Hungary, Poland, and Yugoslavia over the course of the 1960s.[44]

Soviet propaganda in Guinea, Mali, and Ghana was focused on the promotion of the socialist path of economic and social development.[45] Economic competition with capitalist countries was at the core of Khrushchev's policy of "peaceful coexistence," which aimed at "verify[ing] in practice whose system is better," as he had declared in 1955.[46] Khrushchev's confidence in the Soviet path was based on rates of economic growth, which since the end of World War II were higher in the USSR than in Western economies, while Soviet advances in science and technology culminated in the launch of the Sputnik satellite, and the virgin lands campaign resulted in record harvests by newly established state farms in western Siberia and the Kazakh Soviet Socialist Republic (SSR).[47] These attainments were discussed at length in the Ghanaian press, and the newspaper *Ghanaian Times* published a first-hand account in 1961 of Nkrumah's visit to Czechoslovakia, Hungary, Poland, Romania, Bulgaria, the Soviet Union, and East Germany. The journalist wrote that socialist countries have achieved "full scale employment, all-level free education, free medical attention, cheap good houses for workers, and many other facilities."[48] This assertion was illustrated by architectural examples from socialist countries, which in Ghana in the early 1960s were more visible to the general public than architecture from the West. The daily press reproduced images of newly constructed public buildings and housing districts in Beijing, Shanghai, Moscow, Leningrad, Rostov-on-Don, Budapest, Warsaw, Constanța, and East Berlin, as well as the new "socialist" towns Dunaújváros in Hungary and Nowa Huta in Poland, which Nkrumah visited in 1961.[49]

Soviet leadership was clear about what the socialist path of development meant. In the late 1950s, the State Committee on Economic

Cooperation, the agency charged with coordinating Soviet technical assistance programs, explicitly included references to learning from the experience of the Soviet Central Asian and Caucasian Republics.[50] In particular, lessons for less developed countries were to be found in the mechanization of agriculture based on collective and state farms and the industrialization and creation of large-scale infrastructure. The latter were to be protected by strict limits set for the presence of foreign capital, and by the nationalization of existing enterprises. This development path, with the state as the main engine of growth, differed from what Western advisers in Ghana were suggesting, including the British economist William Arthur Lewis, Nkrumah's chief economic advisor until 1959. Lewis's industrial plan for Ghana advocated unrestricted access to foreign investors for a period of five to ten years, in order to foster an industry directed at exports.[51]

The Central Asian Republics, where the Soviet modernization path was implemented in a non-European setting, became privileged sites for visits by delegations from Africa, Asia, and Latin America, including Cuba. They were widely represented, for example, during the 1965 international economic seminar in Tashkent, which discussed "the experience in socialist construction of union republics of Central Asia and Kazakhstan, the experience of forming and developing industrial complexes, territorial-production and sectoral complexes."[52] These delegations included Ghanaians, and after a visit to the Kirghiz SSR, a *Ghanaian Times* journalist compared the republic to Africa and reported on its progress in terms of agriculture, industrialization, and higher education.[53]

Such analogies were made also in architecture and urban planning, resulting in new candidates for comparison of architectural solutions that, until independence, had been largely restricted to Britain as the colonial center. In other words, decolonization allowed for what urban theorist Jennifer Robinson recently called "experimental" comparison, or "thinking cities through elsewhere," beyond established candidates for comparison.[54] In the conditions of the Cold War, new geographic connections and new claims about affinities, however inchoate and speculative, became opportunities for juxtaposing cities that had never been juxtaposed before. Such experimental comparison sometimes brought about innovations in the ways these cities were conceptualized and practiced, including the reflexive and self-reflexive practice of architects and planners.

The book *Town Planning in Hot Climates* (1972) by Soviet planner Anatolii Rimsha can be read as an instance of such experimental comparison.[55] Rimsha was the head of the Department of Civil Construction Engineering at Patrice Lumumba University with an extensive experience abroad.[56] By using Atkinson's classification of tropical climate, Rimsha argued that the southern republics of the USSR shared conditions of hot-dry climate with a number of locations, including such countries (or parts of them) as Algeria, Libya, Egypt, Sudan, Mali, Ethiopia, Yemen, Iraq, Iran, Afghanistan, Mongolia, and Chile.[57] By the time Rimsha's book was published, Soviet architects and planners worked in all those countries by "thinking" African and Asian cities "through" Tashkent and Samarkand (Uzbek SSR), Dushanbe (Tajik SSR), Yerevan (Armenian SSR), Ashgabat (Turkmen SSR), Bishkek (Kirgiz SSR), and Tbilisi (Georgian SSR). New residential buildings, schools, housing districts, transportation planning, landscaping, and overall master plans from those cities were extensively reproduced and commented on in Rimsha's book, as were specific guidelines and recommendations, such as optimum walking distances to various service facilities in a residential community normed by planners in Uzbekistan.[58] Furthermore, work in Central Asia exposed Soviet architects to Islam, which was described as a component of "national heritage." (By the 1950s, this was the only socially and politically acceptable discourse on

Islam in the Soviet Union, even if large parts of the population unofficially continued to practice their religion.)[59] Besides restoring mosques and madrassas understood as part of national heritage, Soviet architects referred in their practice to spatial dispositions and, in particular, ornamental forms of Islamic architecture in Central Asia.[60] These forms have been applied to cultural buildings designed in the idiom of socialist realism and, since the 1960s, to prefabricated shading devices and mosaics on mass-constructed residential buildings. For some scholars, including the architectural historian Veronika Voronina, studies of Islamic architecture in Central Asia in the 1950s provided for a bridge to surveys of vernacular buildings in the Middle East and West Africa, including Ghana, and to broader overviews of architecture and urban design in Africa (figure 2.12).[61]

Along with arguing for the applicability of the specific experience of architecture and planning in the southern republics of the USSR to countries in hot-dry zones across all continents, Rimsha's book made a broader point. By showing how planners in the USSR adapted principles of Soviet urbanism to climatic conditions and "national traditions" in Central Asia, he demonstrated the adaptability of those principles to extra-European contexts and posited them as a global model. The concept of the *mikroraion* (plural: *mikroraiony*), or micro-district, was a case in point. First introduced in the USSR in the 1930s as a translation of the American "neighborhood unit," then reappraised by Soviet planners after 1945, the mikroraion returned over the course of the 1950s, when it became the fundamental unit of Soviet planning. Each micro-district consisted of housing for five thousand to fifteen thousand inhabitants, isolated from main roads and equipped with social facilities in a park-like landscape.[62] Rimsha argued that elements of a mikroraion "may have different compositional plan structures depending on local natural and climatic conditions and the social and economic way of life and traditions of the people."[63] For example, planners in the Uzbek SSR claimed to have based their designs of the micro-district on *mahallas*, the traditional sociospatial units of Uzbek communal life that were recognized and incorporated into the local governance of the republic.[64] The adaptability of micro-district typology to hot-humid, hot-dry, and temperate climates was shown in Rimsha's book by means of examples, among them Soviet layouts for Kabul (within the master plan co-designed by Rimsha, 1962–64), and for Accra (figure 2.13).[65]

By the early 1960s, the Nkrumah government embarked on the implementation of the socialist path of development. After the experience of international isolation during the Congo crisis (1960) and after Western funding for the Akosombo Dam was secured (1961), Nkrumah decided to intensify contacts with Moscow, and then to abandon the Second Development Plan (1961) and to adapt the Seven-Year Development Plan (1963), aiming at a socialist transformation that included the nationalization of major companies such as GNCC.[66] Ghana's president wrote to Moscow that his objective was "the rapid industrialisation and electrification [of Ghana], but also accelerated development and mechanisation of the agriculture."[67] Such fast-track, state-led development allowed for the creation of employment and redistribution of welfare. Furthermore, the Soviet Union provided models for mass organizations, including the Young Pioneers for school-age children; the Builders' Brigade (later: Workers' Brigade), or nationwide network of work camps for young people who were trained in agricultural practice, construction, and craftwork; as well as the Trades Union Congress, the National Council of Ghana Women, the Young Farmers' League, and others.[68] The government in Accra emphasized that "modern scientific socialism" was adequate for Ghana because it allowed preservation of principles and ideals of a traditional communalistic society.[69]

2.12. Measured drawing of the house of Abdullah-Bey in Bukhara (Uzbek Soviet Socialist Republic, USSR). Veronika Leonidovna Voronina, *Narodnye traditsii arkhitektury Uzbekistana* (Moscow: Gosudarstvennoe izdatel'stvo arkhitektury i gradostroitel'stva, 1951), 20.

2.13. Arrangement of residential groups according to local climatic conditions. Anatolii Nikolaevich Rimsha, *Gorod i zharkii klimat* (Moscow: Stroiizdat, 1975), 193.

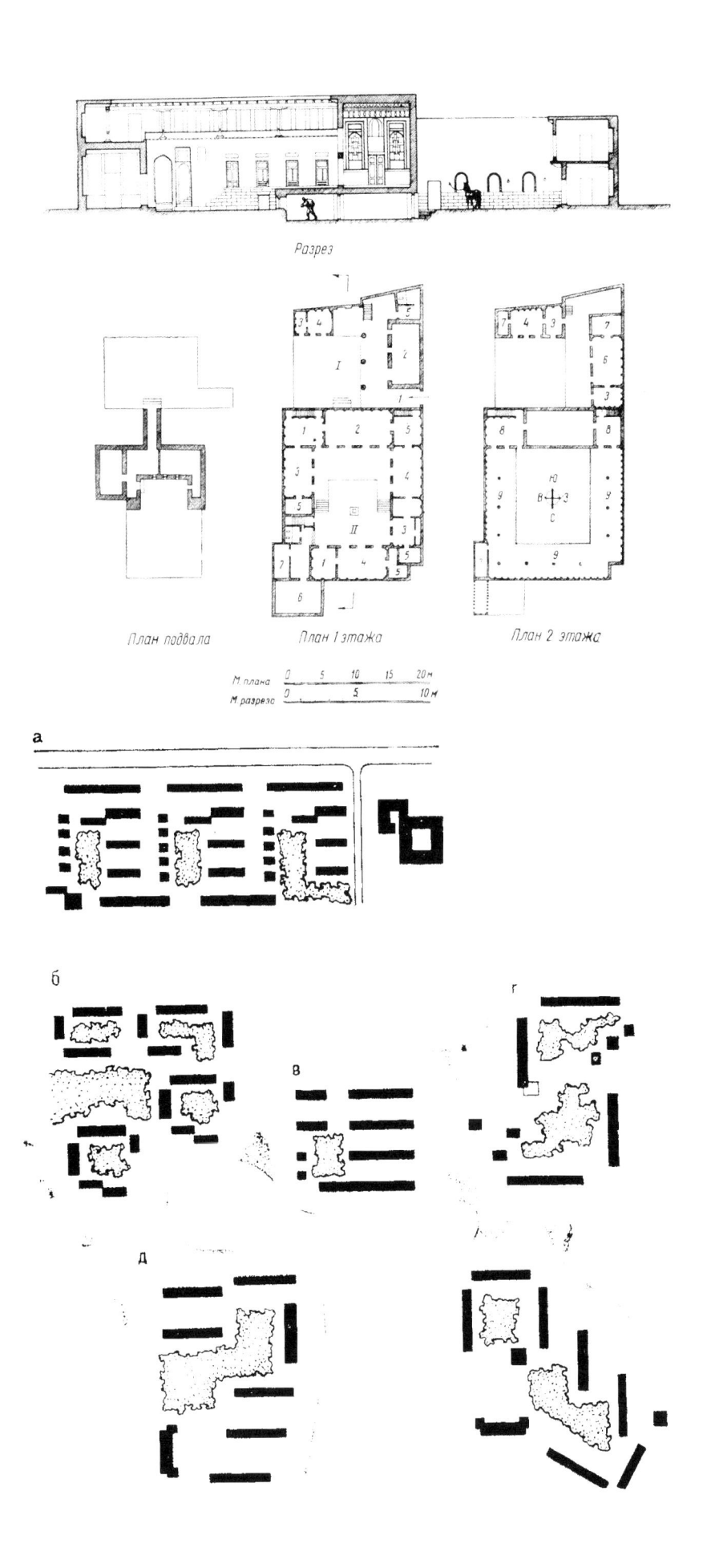

A GLOBAL DEVELOPMENT PATH

The first treaty of economic and technical assistance and cooperation by Nkrumah's government and the Soviet Union was signed in 1960.[70] State companies from the USSR and socialist countries were contracted to design and construct industrial facilities, including cement factories and steel-rolling mills that furnished the basis for Ghana's construction industry.[71] The Ghanaian government contracted designs for shoe factories and plywood plants from Czechoslovakia, a bus-assembly plant from Hungary, print works from East Germany, and a sugar refinery from Poland, among others.[72] Several of these ensembles included supporting social amenities and housing, including staff bungalows, workers' hostels, and social facilities at Asutsuare as part of the Polish-designed and equipped sugar-mill complex, and bungalows at the Bui Dam on the Black Volta River and the textile factory in Tamale, both Soviet projects.[73] Since 1961, the coordination of agreements with Eastern European countries was the remit of Ghana's Committee for Economic Cooperation with Eastern Countries.[74] Agreements with Eastern bloc countries were followed by those with Yugoslav companies, contracted to deliver slaughterhouses and a naval base at Sekondi, among other projects, and with the People's Republic of China.[75] It was in Accra in 1964 that Zhou Enlai, China's prime minister, announced the "Eight Principles" that would define China's aid to Africa in the decades to come.[76] Zhou's visit was followed by Chinese investment in the textile factory in Juapong, northeast of Accra (1965).[77]

Contracts for nonindustrial projects were signed as well, in particular for housing. In June 1961, Ghana and the Soviet Union agreed for nine Soviet architects and engineers to be sent to Ghana to prepare studies for the design of residential districts in Accra and Tema.[78] These districts were to be constructed by GNCC from large-scale prefabrication elements produced by a factory delivered by the Soviets. Initially, the Accra district seemed to have been envisaged as part of the Korle Lagoon development project in the capital, which included a culture and leisure center, a sports center, public beaches, and a spectacular African Unity Tower.[79] The Soviets were to construct a hotel with two hundred beds in Accra, as well. Neither design was realized, as was the case with a design of large-scale seashore development in Central Accra, delivered by Bulgarian architects who suggested a landscape of cultural facilities, including a cinema, a casino, and two large stadiums (Dimitar Katsarov and the Glavproekt team) (figure 2.14).[80]

Polish architects Chyrosz and Rymaszewski recalled that upon receipt of the Bulgarian design, architects at GNCC rejected it as unsuitable to Ghana's economic capacities.[81] Signals about similar miscalculations came from Guinea, from where the Ghanaian press reported on the "uneven quality" of Eastern technical aid, "administered without proper regard for the country's needs."[82] In response, governmental officials in Accra assured the public that "whatever happened elsewhere, we in Ghana are in full and absolute control of every single project."[83] Where architectural labor was concerned, the most effective way of maintaining such control was for Ghanaian institutions to hire Eastern Europeans, and this was how PWD and later GNCC operated. The architects from socialist countries in service of those organizations turned out to have much more impact on the urbanization of Ghana than any large-scale project shipped from Moscow or Sofia.

While the work of Soviet organizations in Ghana was an instance of socialist multilateralism (with the nation-state and its organizations being the primary entity of architectural engagements), GNCC can be seen as a venue of socialist cosmopolitanism: an experience of transnational collaboration of Ghanaian actors with architects from various socialist countries.[84] These included Hungarian Charles (Károly) Polónyi, who worked at the corporation in 1963 and 1964 on a contract with the International Organization for Technical-Scientific Cooperation (Tesco),

2.14. Cinema-Theater in Accra, early 1960s. Glavproekt (Bulgaria), Encho Balukchiev. "Kompleks 'kraibrezhna zona' v Akra–Gana," *Arkhitektura* 7 (1964): 34.

2.15. Osu Castle, extension to the offices of the prime minister, Accra, 1960s, postcard. Ghana National Construction Company and GNCC.

an FTO that managed the export of intellectual labor from Hungary.[85] Polónyi designed the Flagstaff House housing project (1964) and others in Accra, industrial facilities in Accra and Tema, and numerous proposals for Osu Castle, or Christiansborg, the seat of the government (figure 2.15).[86] In 1964, he left Accra to join the international group of teachers at the School of Architecture at UST in Kumasi, which included Czech architect Jan Skokánek as well as Yugoslav (Croatian) architects Miro Marasović, Berislav Kalogjera, and Nebojša Weiner, and engineer Zvonimir Žagar. The Croatian professionals were contracted by the Zagreb-based combine Ingra, which specialized in export of construction, and by Yugoslav institutions in charge of technical assistance. These architects and engineers made significant contributions to modern architecture in Ghana, both through their teaching and through buildings they designed as employees of the Development Office (later the Architects Office) at UST (figure 2.16).[87] Another teacher and practitioner at UST was Croatian architect and sculptor Niksa Ciko (1962–68), who had come to Accra in 1960. For two years, Ciko was employed by PWD as architect at the Police Section, where he designed police stations and staff quarters, among other projects, including the presidential zoo in Accra.[88] During the 1960s, PWD/GNCC also employed at least four Bulgarian architects. They were responsible for governmental buildings in Accra and other cities; among them was Ivan Naidenovich, superintendent architect for schools.[89]

The largest group of foreign architects at GNCC during the 1960s, at least twenty-six architects, came from Poland. Engineers and technicians in a separate group were responsible for execution drawings and supervision of construction sites: seven Polish engineers worked on the ITF project alone, and Polish foremen were employed to train Ghanaian workers.[90] On top of this, at least five Polish architects and planners were working at the Town and Country Planning Division (TCPD), headed by Ghanaian planner Peter Turkson.[91] These significant numbers reflected the more general pattern of distribution of Polish experts on Polservice contracts, for whom Ghana was the main destination in the mid-1960s (with 102 people).[92]

Besides Chyrosz and Rymaszewski, the group of Polish architects at PWD/GNCC included Jan Laube, who designed numerous educational facilities in Accra; Jarosław Nowosadski, who was responsible for a number of health-care facilities; Jakub Kotliński, who was the superintendent architect responsible for hospitals; and Kazimierz Sierakowski, who was the superintendent architect for police stations.[93] In Rymaszewski's role as superintendent architect of the exhibition section, he collaborated with Chyrosz not only on ITF but also on Ghanaian pavilions at international trade fairs in Lagos (1962), Poznań (Poland, 1963, 1965), Niamey (Niger, 1965), and on the Ghanaian exhibition for the Expo '67 in Montreal.[94]

2.16. Students participating in the course "Structures and Structural Design" taught by Zvonimir Žagar, School of Architecture, Town Planning and Building, UST, Kumasi, Ghana, 1965.

> 2.17. State House Complex (Job 600), Accra, 1965. GNCC, Vic Adegbite (chief architect), Witold Wojczyński, Jan Drużyński (project architects).

> 2.18. State House Complex, Accra, 1965. GNCC, Vic Adegbite (chief architect), Witold Wojczyński, Jan Drużyński (project architects).

> 2.19. State House Complex, Accra, under construction, 1965. GNCC, Vic Adegbite (chief architect), Witold Wojczyński, Jan Drużyński (project architects).

A GLOBAL DEVELOPMENT PATH 53

Witold Wojczyński and Jan Drużyński, together with Adegbite, designed Job 600, comprising the Banqueting Hall, the Conference Hall, and the renovation of the colonial State House with a high-rise hotel constructed behind it (1965) (figures 2.17, 2.18, and 2.19).[95] The complex was built for the summit of the Organization of African Unity (OAU) and testified to the importance given by Nkrumah to ideas of pan-Africanism, but it also became one of his most notorious projects. It was carried out when Ghanaians were suffering from economic decline, including wage freezes, severe inflation, and unemployment in an increasingly oppressive, one-party state.[96]

Among the thirty-one Polish architects and planners working in the 1960s for PWD, GNCC, and TCPD, eight were women. This significant share reflects the high status of women architects in Poland since the interwar period, and career opportunities open to professional expatriate women in 1960s Ghana, in line with the official discourse of the CPP.[97] Polish sculptor Alina Ślesińska was invited to Ghana, and her design for the monument to Kwame Nkrumah was realized on the grounds of the Ideological Institute in Winneba, constructed by GNCC (figure 2.20).[98] Hannah Schreckenbach, an

2.20. Monument of Kwame Nkrumah, Winneba, 1965. Sculpture by Alina Ślesińska.

54 CHAPTER 2

émigré from East Germany who had studied in Karlsruhe (West Germany) and London, became superintendent architect at GNCC and was responsible for a large number of prominent projects, including extensions of the Parliament House in the 1970s, before moving to a teaching position at UST in Kumasi.[99]

With architects from Ghana, Bulgaria, Hungary, Poland, Yugoslavia, and Germany at GNCC, joined by professionals from the United States, the Philippines, and India, the corporation contributed to the internationalization of architecture in Ghana.[100] There were several places where these architects could meet professionals circulating in other networks. Among such places was UST in Kumasi, which became a site of exchange between Ghanaian, American, British, and West German architects and their fellow professionals from Hungary, Poland, and Yugoslavia. Several architects crossed Cold War divisions, including Charles Polónyi, invited to join UST by Dean John Lloyd (1964), who was aware of Polónyi's activities as a member of the international architectural group Team 10.[101] Also belonging to both worlds were émigrés from Poland who had settled in the UK during or after World War II, who had come to the Gold Coast as colonial officials and then stayed in Accra after 1957. These included Eligiusz Daszkiewicz, a graduate of the Polish School of Architecture that had opened in Liverpool during the war, and Olgierd Wojciechowski, who worked at PWD and later GNCC as chief architect, under his assumed name, Ludlam.[102] A small number of expatriate architects at GNCC cooperated with private firms in Accra; this was the case with Hannah Schreckenbach.[103]

Ghanaian Architecture on Its Own Terms

During the 1960s, GNCC and its predecessors were in charge of construction and, increasingly, of design of roads and airport runways in Ghana, industrial facilities, as well as housing, educational and research institutions, culture facilities, commercial buildings, administrative, military, and police structures, buildings for tourism and leisure, and urban layouts. When seen from the point of view of private archives of Hungarian, Bulgarian, Polish, and Yugoslav architects who designed many of those buildings, they appear as points on personal creative trajectories, carrying along discussions in architectural culture in Budapest, Sofia, Warsaw, and Zagreb. Addressed along such lines, the Flagstaff House apartment block in Accra by Charles Polónyi would be seen in continuity with his hotels designed in the Lake Balaton region in Hungary, while the modernist reinterpretation of a historic palace by Bogdan Wnętrzewski in the buildings of the Ideological Institute in Winneba would appear as carrying on the monumental modernism of Warsaw, and the (unrealized) design for the colonnaded Parliament building in Accra by Z. Doychev would be a belated example of socialist realism from Sofia.[104] When seen from Eastern European capitals, GNCC production foregrounds the heterogeneity of architecture in socialist countries during the late 1950 and early 1960s.

However, GNCC architecture looked very different from Accra. From that vantage point, the work of the corporation hardly appeared as a sum of European "modernisms." GNCC responded to the technopolitical road map of reshaping Ghana's economy, culture, and society that was formulated by Nkrumah, officials of the CPP, intellectuals, and journalists. Headed by Ghanaians with international education and experience, the GNCC production was accompanied by self-aware discourse in the Ghanaian daily press. It is to the latter that I will turn to account on Ghanaian terms for the contribution of GNCC to the modernization of the country. Since professional criticism on architecture in early 1960s Ghana hardly developed beyond a small circle of British architects, grouped mainly around the Accra-based journal *West African Builder and Architect*, and since it was only slowly complemented by voices from UST in Kumasi, a focus on the daily press offers a broader view of discussions accompanying the work of GNCC.

In what follows, I will focus on three major daily newspapers in Ghana: the *Evening News* (founded in 1948 by Nkrumah as the *Accra Evening News*), the official CPP newspaper and always at the forefront of the ideological battle; the *Daily Graphic* (established in 1950); and the *Ghanaian Times* (founded in 1958).[105] This press was tightly controlled by the CPP, which took over or shut down most newspapers that deviated from the party line. Most of the articles were unsigned, and their authors seem to have been a heterogeneous group consisting of journalists but also practicing architects, state officials, and academics. These texts and the accompanying photographs of GNCC buildings, often shot by the journals' own photographers, suggested to their readers how to speak about the buildings under consideration, how to look at them, how to use them on an everyday basis, and how to feel at home in these new structures. The newspapers almost always omitted the names of European architects at GNCC, and presented the architecture of the corporation as a result of collective work of Ghanaian organizations. In this sense, this discourse needs to be seen as part of the overarching process of appropriation of resources brought to Ghana by Cold War networks.

As presented in the press, Ghanaian architectural production was far from homogeneous. In the wording of a *Daily Graphic* headline (1961): "Modern Buildings Are Simple in Form—But Old Designs Are Still in Use."[106] The "old designs" included vernacular forms, such as the mosque in Wa, and buildings that followed colonial typologies, including primary schools and health centers.[107] These had typically been constructed by local communities by means of self-help programs, often with some financial support from the government. Many had been built with local materials in resettlement villages in the framework of the Volta River Project and the creation of the Lake Volta reservoir.[108] In standard school designs produced by GNCC, pitched roofs and verandas were sometimes combined with expressive elements in reinforced concrete, such as staircases in the Accra Academy extension (Anna Gadomska and Jan Laube for GNCC, 1967). These elements undermined the sharp opposition between "old designs" and "modern buildings."[109]

However, it was the latter, those "modern and novel designs," that gave Accra and other Ghanaian cities "a new look."[110] Until the early 1960s, "modern designs" were generally delivered by private architectural practices in Accra and Kumasi and constructed by PWD or GNCC; later, they were designed directly by GNCC. As an index of the "changing face of Ghana," these straddled various visual idioms, from tropical architecture through expressive compositions such as the Tamale Cathedral (1963), to sophisticated appropriation of vernacular forms, such as the Regal Cinema in Accra (Jan Laube for GNCC, 1970).[111] Some of these buildings were called "modern" or "modernistic" by Ghanaian commentators in order to describe the specific experience of the structures.[112]

"Modern buildings" did not constitute a discrete category, delineated by sharp borders, but rather a broad field, defined by a number of points of radiation. Among them were higher buildings that appeared on the skyline of Accra, such as Job 600, the Korle Bu Hospital, and the new Police Headquarters (1962), which in the terminology of a Ghanaian commentator was a "modernistic" composition of large surfaces of shutters placed in an overarching structural frame.[113] That building was featured in the press when it was opened by Kwame Nkrumah, "the Architect of the new Ghana," and included into photographic accounts of "the new Ghana Kwame Nkrumah is building" (figure 2.21).[114]

Portraits of the leader often appeared on patterned backgrounds of such structures as the CPP headquarters and the Trades Union Congress

2.21. Kwame Nkrumah visits the construction site of the State House, mid-1960s.

2.22. "The Great Architect of Ghana Comrade Kwame Nkrumah Seen Admiring the New National Headquarters of the Convention People's Party." *Evening News*, March 7, 1960, 1.

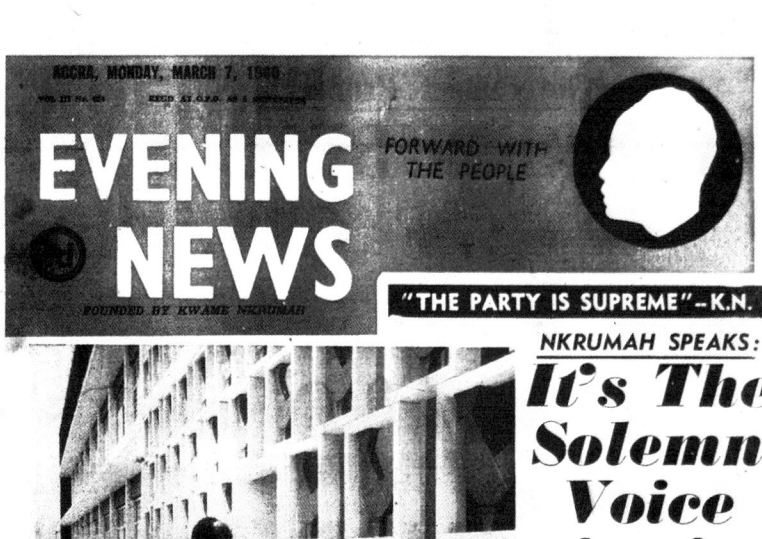

A GLOBAL DEVELOPMENT PATH

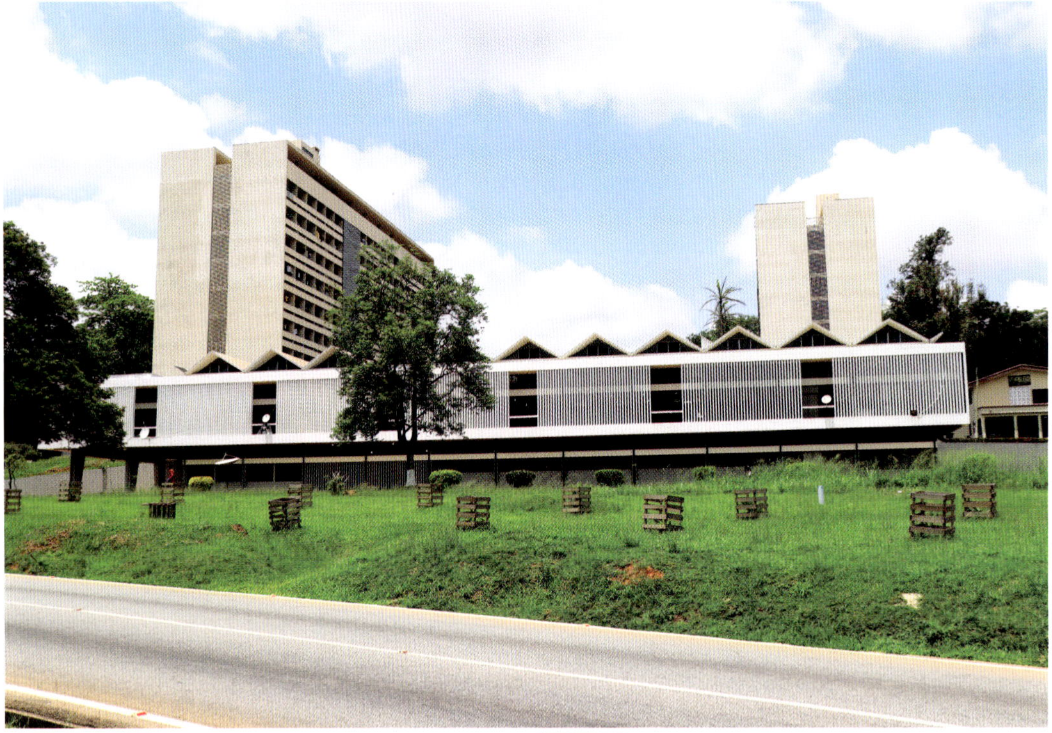

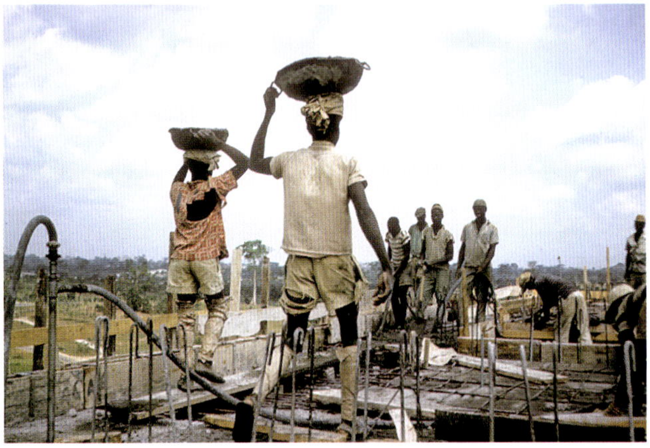

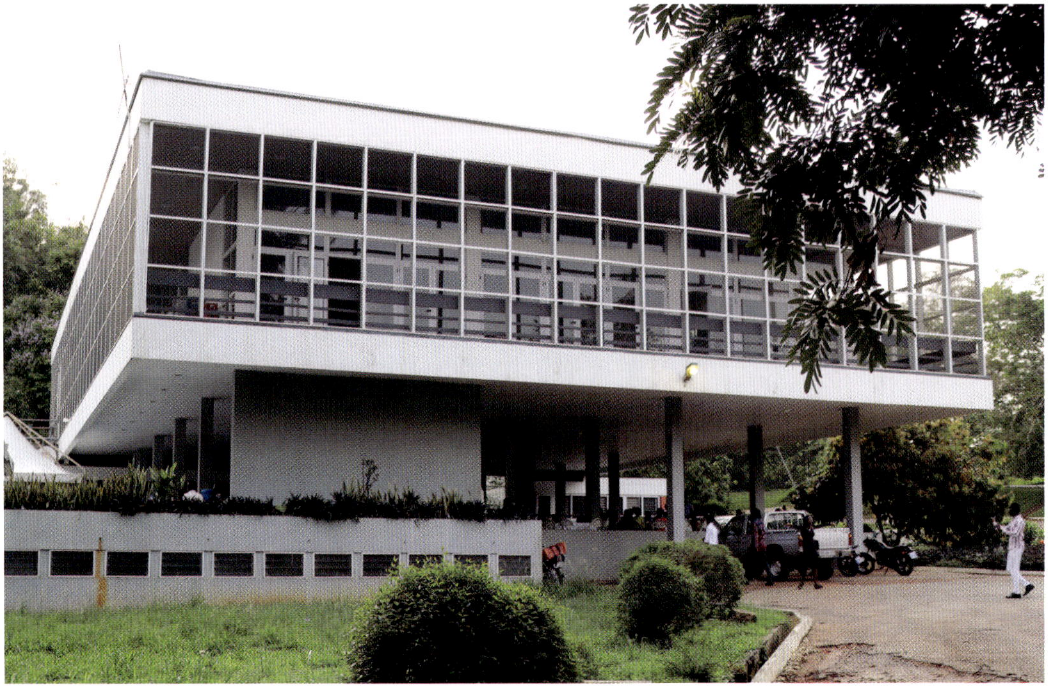

< 2.23. Unity Hall (Hall of Residence 5), Kumasi, 1963–68. Architects Office UST, John Owusu-Addo (architect in charge), Miro Marasović (senior architect).

< 2.24. Unity Hall, Kumasi, 1963–68, construction site, March 1966. Architects Office UST, John Owusu-Addo (architect in charge), Miro Marasović (senior architect).

< 2.25. Senior Staff Club, Kumasi, 1964. Architects Office UST, Niksa Ciko (architect in charge), Miro Marasović/John Owusu-Addo (chief university architect).

2.26. Africa Hall (Women's Hall 6), Kumasi, design 1964–65. Architects Office UST, John Owusu-Addo/Miro Marasović (chief university architect), Niksa Ciko (architect in charge).

2.27. Peduase Lodge near Aburi, Ghana, 1959. GNCC, Vic Adegbite.

building (Arthur Lindsay and Associates, 1961), discussed as part of "Nkrumaistic architecture and planning" and as a "revolutionary display of architectural maturity in Nkrumaist Ghana" (figure 2.22).[115] The university campus in Kumasi was among the most commented-upon examples, with the Unity Hall, the Faculty of Architecture, the Senior Staff Club, the Vice-Chancellor's Lodge, the Africa Hall, the Faculty of Pharmacy, and several administrative and social buildings. They were designed in the course of the 1960s by Yugoslav (Croatian), Czech, British, and Ghanaian architects in the service of the university (figures 2.23, 2.24, 2.25, and 2.26).[116] While the designs of many of these structures drew upon the experience of British architects during colonialism, some Ghanaian commentators pointed to them as proof of the radical break with the colonial period.[117] The press contrasted photographs of dilapidated sheds from before independence ("what Britain thought fit for the African") with the new housing projects, including those in Tema.[118] The association of modern architecture with Nkrumah's rule came to the fore most dramatically in a list of buildings singled out as targets for bomb attacks by, presumably, conspirators planning to overthrow Nkrumah in 1961. That list, made public by the police, included the CCP headquarters and the Trades Union Congress, as well as the extension of Osu Castle, the Tribune at the Black Star Square, and other modern buildings.[119] This association continued after the end of the regime, when accusations that Nkrumah had squandered state resources and appropriated them illegally often included mentions of Job 600 and the Peduase Lodge, the presidential holiday resort and retreat near Aburi designed by Vic Adegbite (1959) (figure 2.27).[120]

Nkrumah's portraits on the background of modern public buildings introduced a more general visual syntax that was conveyed by hundreds of black-and-white photographs of buildings that were published in the Ghanaian press during the 1960s. At its most abstract level, this syntax

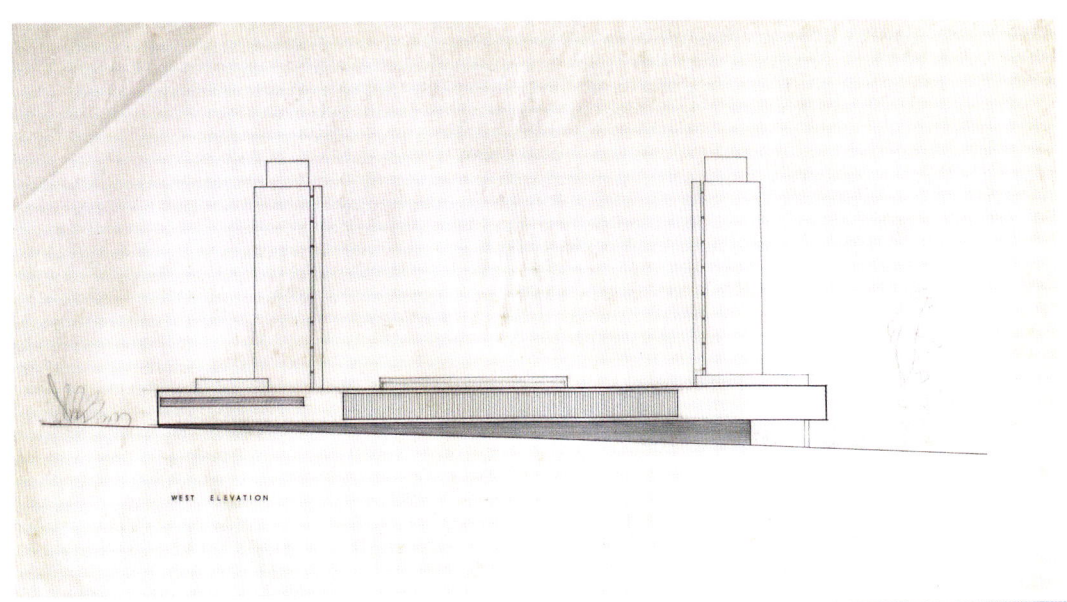

A GLOBAL DEVELOPMENT PATH

was that of line and surface: a balcony railing on the background of a wall; delicate profiles framing glass and openwork screens; a slab of ceiling visually detached from the wall by a sharp shadow; a structural frame capturing the entire volume of the building; a patterned surface of cement bricks. Infrastructure projects conveyed this syntax, too, including the perfect geometry of the landscape divided by roads and pedestrian passages, conveyed by aerial photographs of Black Star Square and Kwame Nkrumah Circle. The latter, presented together with an account of state agricultural farms, was considered part of Nkrumah's "Socialist reconstruction plan."[121] This fascination with straight lines and smooth surfaces was shared by numerous authors who described suave movements of the eye or of cars. One among them was particularly impressed by the new road from Adomi to Tema, which "like a Roman Road…goes on for miles in a straight line" and allows for the car to move "so smoothly over its very good surface that one could relax and enjoy the very pleasant scenery of the surrounding countryside."[122] Improvements in infrastructure allowed people to see the country with new eyes, and those returning to Ghana after a stay abroad would recognize that the country "has progressed in all fields…particularly in the field of architecture."[123]

The capacity of modern architecture to provide frameworks for the social body to be both united and differentiated conveys the spatiotemporal dynamics of modernization in Ghana. In photographs published in the daily press, newly constructed buildings appear as points of attraction for Ghanaians to gather. At the same time, against the backgrounds of these buildings, their users become identifiable as members of specific social and professional groups, distinguished by attributes such as uniforms of the Young Pioneers and the Workers' Brigade, or nursing aprons (figure 2.28).[124] In the press, modernization appeared as spatiotemporal redistribution, with graduates of the Women's College in Aburi—an extension to a college designed by Fry and Drew in 1955—expected to challenge men for "top jobs."[125] GNCC architecture facilitated and stabilized in time and space the emerging socioeconomic order, the social division of labor, and the distinction between private and professional life. For example, the press reported that the state-owned People's Shop in Accra (1962) was open until late and hence "prevented many workers from running away from their jobs to shop during business hours" (figure 2.29).[126] A similar emphasis on the differentiation between private and professional places and moments was conveyed by the apartment houses for nurses at the Korle Bu Hospital, which, as a governmental minister explained, were developed out of consideration for the women's private life.[127]

In the Ghanaian press of the 1960s, architecture appeared as unifying places and moments that had been separated under colonial rule according to ethnic or "tribal" categories, and as redividing them according to principles of a new societal organization. This redistribution pertained to all key aspects of Ghanaian life, including work, family and gender relations, and relationships between ethnic groups. It straddled all scales, starting with the inherited spatiotemporal divisions in the family house, a neighborhood, or a village, which were undermined by the participation of young people in the activities of the Young Pioneers and the Workers' Brigades, and ending with the whole urban territory. With independence, the racial segregation of cities was undone, and all urban spaces were supposed to be returned to the collective body of Ghanaians, or the "masses" in the discourse of the CPP. "Houses for the people, factories and public buildings meant to serve the interest of the masses are springing up daily in all corners of the country," wrote an author shortly before the coup.[128] Housing was presented as a basic right for all Ghanaians, with housing estates for low-income groups particularly emphasized in CPP's program. These included blocks of flats built by GNCC on Switchback Road between 1964 and 1967, designed

2.28. The seventh Independence Anniversary celebrations at the Black Star Square in Accra, 1964. *Evening News*, March 7, 1964, 1.

2.29. People's Shop, Accra, 1962. Ghana National Construction Company.

A GLOBAL DEVELOPMENT PATH

by Rymaszewski, who delivered twenty type designs of housing during his work at the corporation.[129] Low-income housing estates were also constructed in Accra's Kaneshie and Lartebiokorshie neighborhoods. Each of the buildings in the latter neighborhood, finished in 1962, consisted of six apartments equipped with a kitchen, bathroom, and toilet.[130] Another example was "magnificent" workers' residences in Tema, "cheap houses for the people," as the title declared.[131] Repetition of buildings on the allotments was by no means seen as monotonous—rather, it was a sign of plenty. This visual effect was also conveyed by the repetition of the same photographs, which returned over and over again in the press, not always with the same captions.

However, Ghanaian housing production was not limited to low-cost housing, and it reflected the social differentiation within Ghanaian society after independence. Press descriptions of new housing estates read as lessons in such differentiation, including articles on housing policies that showed images of housing for low-, middle-, and high-income groups, with subtle differences in architectural expression.[132] This differentiation continued in articles on students' hostels and on temporary accommodation available to visitors according to their income—from economic motels in Accra, consisting of modest bungalows, to the expressive composition of volumes and large-scale surfaces of openwork screens and wide windows in the spectacular first-class hotel in Takoradi (figure 2.30).[133] Readers learned to recognize luxury in modernist designs conveyed by variations in volumes, materials, details, and patterns—and journalists never failed to mention the costs of each construction. This included, in particular, the "luxurious" Ambassador Hotel, and the "elegant" VIP apartments near the Korle Bu Hospital.[134] Such luxury was condemned as ostentatious when it pertained to villas owned by a minister or a chief justice, typically built in the former European areas of Accra (a condemnation often preceding a purge). It was praised, however, when it was seen as a benefit for all, such as the "luxury Tema Community Centre."[135]

The spatiotemporal redistribution performed by newly constructed buildings helped Ghanaians "eradicate the colonial mentality," which had

2.30. Students' housing at the University of Ghana, Legon, design 1966. GNCC, Vic Adegbite (chief architect), E. Lartey (engineer in charge), E. Daszkiewicz (project architect).

been "induced" by their "contact with Europe," as the foreign minister, Kojo Botsio, put it during the opening of the Workers' College in Accra.[136] An image of this new architecture in itself could perform a disciplining function, as one Joe Joseph argued in the *Daily Graphic*. Joseph exhorted his fellow citizens to prepare for the 1965 OAU summit, urging taxi drivers to be polite and creditable to visitors coming to Accra, and bus conductors, managers of hotels, and shop assistants to be helpful and appear neat, and he asked the general public not to use the gutters and street walks as dumping grounds. This long list of urbane virtues was triggered by the view of the "affectionate 'Job 600' towering high" on the horizon. Its photograph was reproduced next to Joseph's article so that his readers could appreciate the didactic effect of this building—many of whom had probably questioned the funding priorities of the government.[137] Perhaps it was the "insulting white" and the "concentrated gleam" of this building that Ayi Kwei Armah had in mind when, in his novel *The Beautyful Ones Are Not Yet Born* (1969), he described the "disturbing ambiguity" of architecture of Nkrumah's Accra. Armah wrote that this architecture both attracted "the massive anger of a people in pain" but also drew onto itself "the love of a people hungry for just something such as this."[138]

Built around the colonial-era State House, Job 600 demonstrated the ambition of GNCC architects to integrate the past into new spaces of representation of the Ghanaian state. During the decade preceding independence, conflicts around history were a crucial way for expressing economic and political tensions in Ghana, in particular the rivalry between the Ashanti-led National Liberation Movement and the CPP. The latter claimed to speak for all those disenfranchised by the traditional order epitomized by the Ashanti Empire and its involvement into the slave trade.[139] However, after the CPP gained hegemony in the country, the regime moved to incorporate the precolonial and colonial past into the project of Ghana's modernization. In particular, the preservation of architectural heritage was included into the remit of the National Museum and Monuments Board, including adobe mosques in Central Ghana, European forts around Cape Coast, and British colonial bungalows in Kumasi.[140] Several colonial and vernacular buildings were surveyed by Jan Laube and Rymaszewski by means of measured drawings, and such surveys were also produced by the international staff and students of UST in Kumasi.[141] Appropriating the colonial past into the new visual coherence of the Ghanaian state could mean a careful placing of volumes in a historical context. This was the case with the extensions of Osu Castle: while the project of the cabinet wing adjusted volumes and open galleries to the proportions of the historical structures, the extension of the chapel wing of the castle included a vertical white cube furnished with bay windows of reinforced concrete, and gargoyles that evoked military architecture.[142]

Yet the true challenge was to turn precolonial heritage into a resource for the independent society. "We have a culture which we are proud of and determined to preserve," claimed one author, and a letter to the *Daily Graphic* editor urged the preservation of Ashanti temples as a part of the "world history of religious architecture."[143] "[B]lending Ghanaian, traditional life with modern ways of living" was presented as a pressing task for architects and urban planners, who were called upon to design buildings according to "traditional and cultural patterns."[144] A favorably discussed example was the Junior Staff Housing at Osu Castle (1961), designed by architects at PWD. One enthusiastic reviewer asserted that this ensemble "expresses the fusion of African and European cultures needed in Ghana today," in contrast to "foreign types dumped down here regardless, as is unfortunately so often the case."[145]

The search for continuity with vernacular typologies also characterized some of the work of GNCC architects. The negotiation between vernacular and modern forms was at the center of the design of a chief's residence in Bolgatanga by Vic Adegbite and Jacek Chyrosz (1962): an orthogonal house under a flying roof, surrounded by a set of semicircular screens evoking vernacular buildings of the Bolgatanga region and at the same time regulating sun exposure and airflow.[146] This building was planned to be constructed of sandcrete and stabilized earth bricks, in line with those voices demanding imported materials be abandoned in order to end Ghana's economic dependence on industrialized countries, and to "project African personality in our buildings."[147] The expectation to convey Ghana's cultural specificity was also addressed in the ITF design. However, rather than quoting specific building traditions of particular ethnic groups, when designing the round entrance pavilion of the Fair Chyrosz and Rymaszewski chose the form of an umbrella, the symbol of power and prestige in West Africa, which they saw as a more general cultural reference.[148]

COLD WAR ANTAGONISMS IN GHANAIAN ARCHITECTURE

The architectural production of GNCC was occasionally presented in the Ghanaian press as instrumental in the "transition from colonial status to socialist Ghana."[149] Since the early 1960s, GNCC was an agent of this transition, in charge of the construction of industrial facilities, housing, and social services, which fundamentally redistributed the times and spaces of everyday life for large groups of Ghanaians. Furthermore, the implementation of the socialist path of development required the reorganization of the construction industry, with GNCC taking over state design and construction commissions, and with the development of the state-owned construction-materials industry.

The most advanced translation of the socialist development path into an architectural and urban design in Ghana was the blueprint of two housing districts, in Accra and Tema, planned by Soviet architects for GNCC to construct. However, neither design was realized. Rather than supporting the vision of a socialist modernity, most architects from socialist countries working at GNCC perceived themselves as belonging to an international culture of modern architecture. The following reading of the Soviet designs together with GNCC's International Trade Fair will both evidence this ambition to bypass Cold War antagonisms and show how it was challenged in a way that brought back those antagonisms to the fore.

Soviet Housing for the Developing World

In 1964, the Soviet architectural journal *Arkhitektura SSSR* published two articles: "Notes on the Architecture of Ghana" by Veronika Voronina, and "Modern Housing in Ghana" by Irina Filippovich.[150] The articles gave an informative account of architecture in Ghana, starting with vernacular building traditions in the country, covering European military architecture in Ghana from the seventeenth and eighteenth centuries, and then paying particular attention to recent buildings and urban layouts in Accra and Tema. Based on their visits to Ghana, Voronina and Filippovich focused on ways in which architects and planners responded to climatic conditions in the humid tropical zone and spelled out design solutions for sun protection and ventilation in terms of urban layout, landscaping, design of buildings' volumes, their internal dispositions, wall sections, and technologies and materials required. The articles gave an overview of recently constructed housing projects and health and educational buildings in Ghana, and commented on locally available building materials, both traditional and modern, the use of color in Ghanaian architecture, and the integration of local art into buildings. In this way, they would have been instructive for Soviet architects practicing in West Africa. For that purpose, the journal

2.31. Master plan of Accra, 1958. TCPD. B.A.W. Trevallion, Alan G. Hood under the direction of W. H. Barrett, "Accra: A Plan for the Town: The Report for the Minister of Housing" (Accra: Town Country Planning Division, 1958).

reproduced drawings of building layouts, mostly designed by British architects in the late-colonial period.[151] The authors paid particular attention to collective housing typologies such as hotels, student hostels, and blocks of flats, among the latter one in Tema designed by Soviet architects.[152]

Housing was an urgent task, wrote Filippovich, in a country where the majority of the population lived in slums.[153] The scale of the housing crisis in Accra had been conveyed by the city's master plan delivered in 1958 by the Town and Country Planning Division of the Ministry of Housing (figure 2.31).[154] Since World War II, the city experienced a population explosion that only accelerated after independence, and between 1957 and 1960 the number of inhabitants grew from just below 290,000 to 340,000.[155] Most new inhabitants were coming from rural areas, attracted by employment possibilities in Ghana's main commercial and administrative center. According to the planners in charge of the 1958 plan, the housing crisis was exacerbated by the diminishing ability of the population to build houses by their own means, uncertain land tenure, and rising costs of building materials. A large proportion of inhabitants were accommodated in inadequate housing made worse by the lack of stormwater drains, piped water, sewage and garbage disposal, tree planting, and community services in general.[156]

However, governmental intervention was impeded by the complex land ownership structure, with land owned either by the government, individuals, chiefs in the name of the community (over which the government had some statutory management power), or families (with individuals

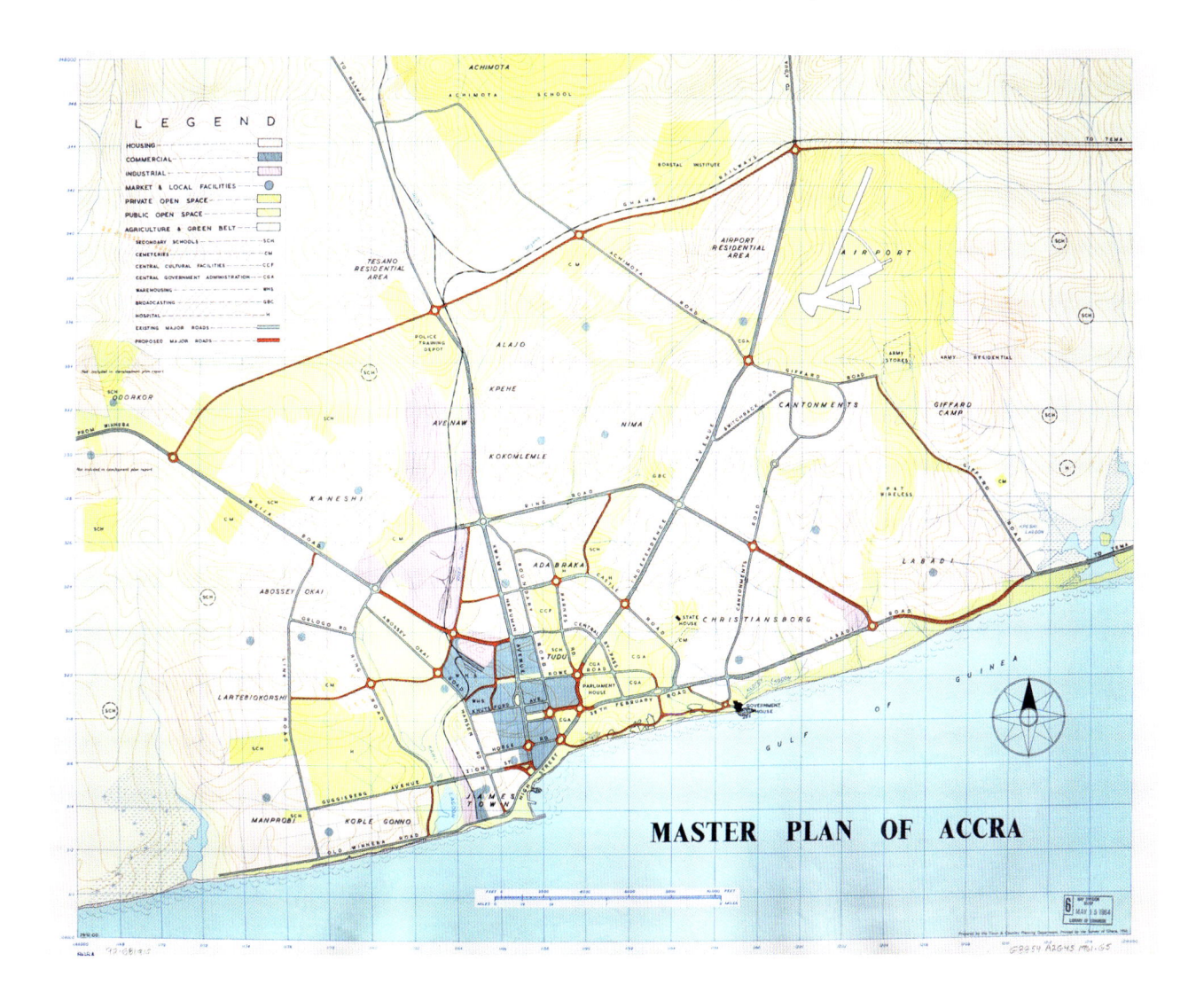

A GLOBAL DEVELOPMENT PATH

holding limited rights to dispose of land).[157] Further inflating the costs of housing were restrictive, British-based building standards that gave preference to imported construction materials and banned small plot sizes.[158] In an earlier response to the housing crisis, the (colonial) 1951 Development Plan had proposed a series of measures, from subsidized housing (distributed mainly among governmental officials) to loan schemes for housing.[159] The authors of the 1958 master plan of Accra argued that, given the scale of the problem (60 percent of the population had no means of access to the housing market), emphasis should be placed on the distribution of serviced land within self-help construction schemes.[160]

After independence, the government allocated significant funds for the provision of housing. Nkrumah argued that "full employment, good housing, [and] equal opportunity for education" were part of the "socialist path to progress."[161] Financed by state housing agencies, including the State Housing and the Tema Development Corporations, housing was promoted for political and social reasons, but also as a means to stimulate economic development. In particular, the emphasis on housing in national-development plans and annual budgets under Nkrumah was part of the general support for the building and construction-materials industries. Those industries were considered instrumental for economic development, as they created employment, reduced dependence on imported materials, and thus conserved foreign currency.[162]

Soviet propaganda material in Ghana and accounts by Ghanaian journalists from the USSR pointed to the Soviet Union as a country where such integration of housing policy and national economic and spatial planning was most advanced.[163] Soviet housing programs were studied by Ghanaians visiting the Soviet Union. Among them was GNCC's Vic Adegbite, who participated in a 1963 tour to the USSR organized for professionals from Latin America, Africa, Asia, and the Middle East by the UN Technical Assistance Programme. That study tour focused on housing policy as well as administration, legislation, and financing of housing projects, their design, construction, and research. During their visits to Soviet design and research institutions, building sites, housing estates, and industrial plants in Moscow, Leningrad, Kiev, and Sochi, participants became acquainted with development and utilization of traditional and modern building materials and structural components, industrialized construction methods, design procedures, and application of cooperative methods to residential constructions in rural areas.[164]

According to Nikolai Baranov, deputy chairman of Gosgrazhdanstroi (State Committee for Civil Construction and Architecture), who greeted the tour participants, the Soviet housing program reflected and benefited from the principles of the socialist economy, including the integration of state construction and construction-materials industries with centralized research and planning activities based on state ownership of land and means of production.[165] The Soviet Union had been chosen for the study tour because Soviet rates of housing construction were the highest in the world, and because of the unprecedented level of mechanization of construction in the USSR. Since the late 1950s, Soviet housing systems based on large-scale prefabricated components and type plans had been adapted to various climates of Soviet republics, from permanently frozen soil in subarctic regions to hot-dry Central Asia, thus providing a range of examples that were potentially useful for study-tour participants coming from various climatic zones.[166]

The housing programs studied during the tour reflected the shift in Soviet architecture and urban planning toward mass-produced, industrialized housing. That shift had been announced to the wide public in the speech by Khrushchev at the All Union Conference of Builders, Architects and Building Industry Workers (1954), then was codified by the Soviet

Construction Norms and Rules for mass housing in the second half of the 1950s. These redefined the main tasks for housing programs as the supply of compact, economical apartments to Soviet citizens, and directed design and construction efforts toward optimizing apartments minimal in size, based on efficient, economical structural schemes and methods of construction. Those requirements were reflected in the nationwide competition for mass-produced prefabricated residential buildings throughout the USSR (1957), which resulted in the design of the first "series," or construction systems made up of a certain range of prefabricated elements, and standard designs assembled from those elements.[167]

By the end of the 1950s, large prefabricated panels became the basis for mass-housing districts in Soviet cities across a vast territory between the Baltic Sea and Siberia. The buildings were typically five stories high (to avoid the construction of an elevator, required under Soviet norms for buildings above five stories), and were arranged into mikroraiony. Adegbite and other study-tour participants visited the paradigmatic among these, Block 9 of Moscow's Novye Cheremushki district, completed in 1958. This mikroraion consisted of residential buildings connected by footpaths with a kindergarten, a school, a movie theater, a cafeteria, and two stores. In Soviet cities, mikroraiony were combined into residential districts, themselves assembled into urban districts forming larger units of a given city.[168] This nested-settlement system was the basis for the programming of social facilities according to urban norms applied across the USSR.

Gift Diplomacy

The Soviet plans for the two districts in Ghana were the most comprehensive attempt at transferring principles of the Soviet housing program to West Africa. Both projects benefited from other Soviet experiences in the region: in Guinea under President Ahmed Sékou Touré, and in Mali under President Modibo Keita. Those experiences included the adaptation of Soviet designs and technology to local conditions, and the testing of specific financial and legal frameworks underpinning Soviet architectural mobilities.

Guinea was the first West African country to sign a treaty of economic and technical cooperation with the Soviet Union (1959). When France severed all relations with its former colony after Guinea had refused to join the French Community (1958), the USSR offered assistance, as did other socialist countries, including Bulgaria, Czechoslovakia, East Germany, and China, which constructed several buildings in Conakry, the capital, including the monumental National Assembly Building (Chen Deng'ao and Wang Rongshou at the Beijing Design Institute, 1967) (figure 2.32).[169] Based on credit granted by the USSR, the Soviets constructed industrial, health, educational, and sports facilities in Conakry and elsewhere in the country. Among these was the Polytechnic Institute in Conakry, for fifteen hundred students, designed by Giprovuz, the State Design Institute for Higher Educational Institutions, which had significant experience abroad, including in Vietnam, Burma, Afghanistan, and Cameroon (figure 2.33).[170] The complex was completed in 1964 and handed over as a self-contained, fully operational environment furnished with Soviet equipment and staffed, in the years to come, largely with Soviet personnel. Its auditoriums, libraries, accommodations for students and staff, and the adjoining sports complex with a swimming pool and a stadium with twenty-five thousand seats acquainted Soviet architects with challenges and solutions concerning the protection of buildings against tropical rain and sun. That these challenges were considerable is shown by recurring problems with water protection of the façade of the Camayenne Hotel in Conakry, designed by the Moscow design institute Mosproekt 1

68　　　CHAPTER 2

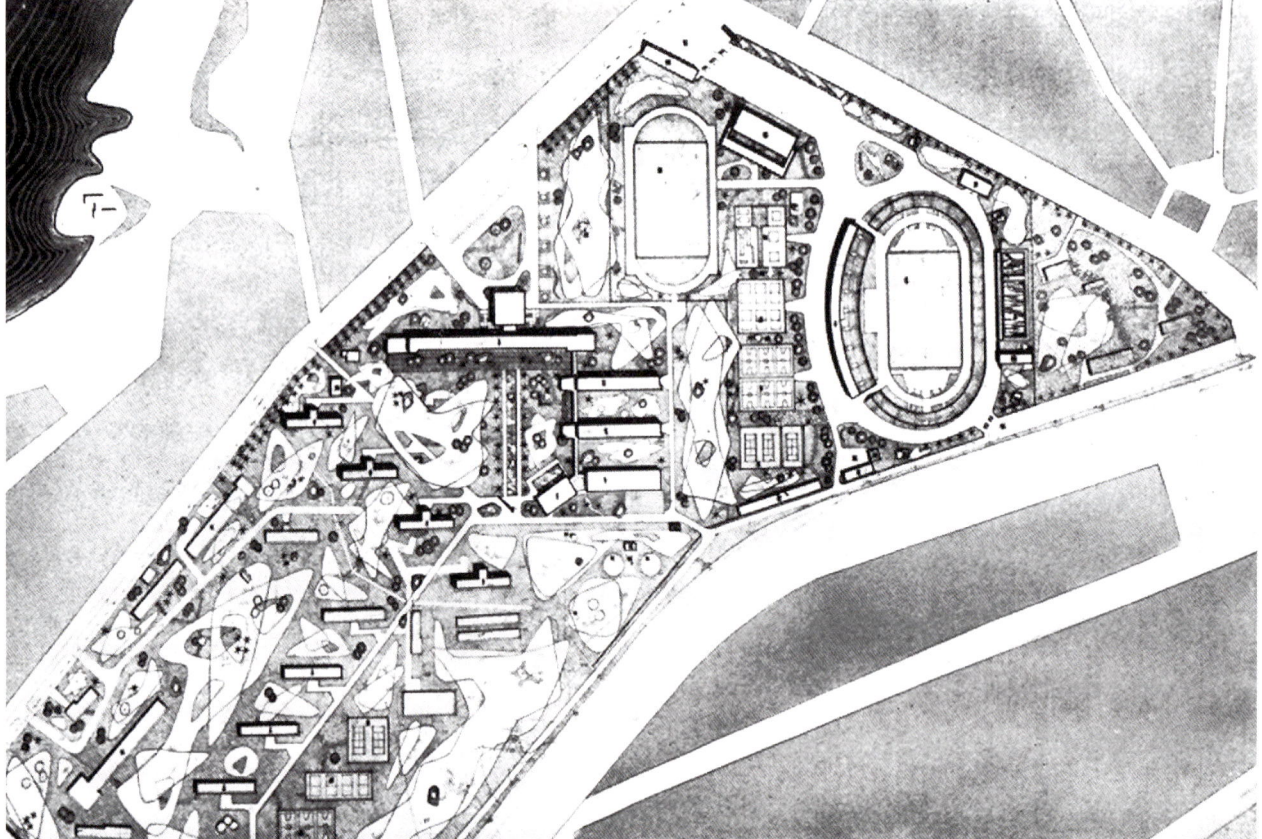

< 2.32. National Assembly Building, Conakry, Guinea, 1960s. Beijing Design Institute (People's Republic of China), Chen Deng'ao, Wang Rongshou. Chen Deng'ao, *Redai Jianzhu* (Beijing: Zhongguo jianzhu gongye chubanshe, 1989).

< 2.33. Polytechnic Institute in Conakry, Guinea, 1964. Giprovuz (USSR), L. Afanas'ev and others. "Raboty Giprovuza za rubezhom," *Arkhitektura SSSR* 9 (1976): 52.

< 2.34. Hotel Camayenne, Conakry, Guinea, 1964, postcard. Mosproekt 1 (USSR).

(1964) (figure 2.34).[171] Soviet planners also considered constructing a factory for prefabricated concrete elements for residential buildings in Guinea, for which they extended a Soviet prefabrication system with new elements adapted to the requirements of the tropical climate, tested by means of an "experimental" mock-up built in the USSR.[172]

With these projects, the Soviet Union demonstratively stepped into the role of the provider of technological expertise for West Africa, a role reserved until then for Britain and France. In this sense, they illustrated Khrushchev's dictum that newly independent nations could obtain modern equipment and technology from socialist countries rather than being dependent on their former colonial metropolises.[173] At times, Soviet functionaries, architects, and engineers working abroad acknowledged in internal reports the limitations of Soviet prefabrication technology and compared it unfavorably with prefabrication systems offered by Western firms to developing countries.[174] But they described Western technical assistance as driven by interest in raw material extraction and achievement of monopolistic positions, and contrasted it with the Soviet self-professed goal to ensure the economic independence of West African countries. In this rendering, Soviet assistance aimed at the creation of modern national industry, the utilization of the available natural resources, and the rising of agricultural production, in this way contributing to the improvement of the living standards of the population.[175]

Nothing exemplified this attempt at differentiation from the West better than Soviet "building-gifts." Gifted buildings conveyed a vision of a socialism of abundance resulting from the Soviet Union's fast-track modernization and prepared the ground for political and economic collaboration with African governments. Socialist gift-giving suggested a temporary negation of the commodity form and aimed at establishing a bond stronger than a mercantile relationship, symbolizing in this way the difference between socialist and capitalist systems.[176] Soviet gifts encouraged the imagining of an international order that broke radically with patterns of colonial exploitation. While such gifts manifested socialist solidarity with "oppressed people" around the world, they also were an intrinsic part of socialism, with the "voluntary work" of the population reciprocated by paternalistic "gifts" by the party leadership, such as "democratic luxuries" of clothing brands in East Germany and tobacco in Bulgaria.[177] A similar discourse was adopted in Nkrumah's Ghana, when the country's Trades Union Congress was given a new building as a "gift" by the government in recognition of the workers' contribution in the "struggle for Independence."[178]

Just as gift-giving in socialist countries conveyed an entire spectrum of political relations, from loyalty through distance to confrontation and violence, so did socialist gift diplomacy.[179] In particular, its requirement for nonimmediate reciprocity brought about intrinsic risks for both sides of the transaction: as argued by Marcel Mauss, every gift requires a counter-gift, but as pointed out by Pierre Bourdieu, the counter-gift needs to be given neither too early nor too late, in order not to appear as trade.[180] Consequently, the temporal delay meant that reciprocity, which the Soviets expected from African leaders, sometimes did not materialize; while the upkeep of some of the donated buildings turned out to be prohibitively expensive. The delineation between gifted buildings and those financed by credits granted to African governments was not always sharp, and some projects that had initially been underwritten by the Soviets were subsequently transformed into gifts, as was the case with a hospital in Kisumu (Kenya, 1968).[181] Such delineations were further blurred by the fact that projects financed by means of Soviet credit were often called "gifts" by commentators in the USSR.

A GLOBAL DEVELOPMENT PATH

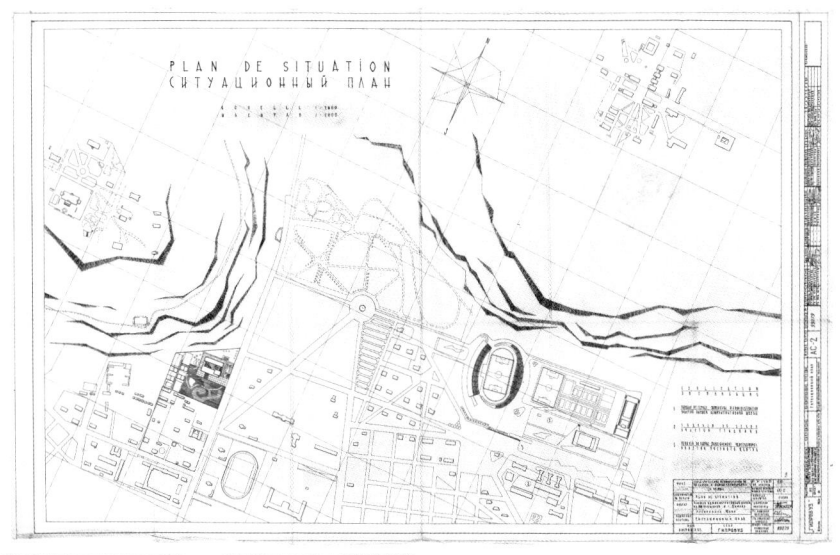

2.35. Higher Administration School, Bamako (Mali), design 1962, situation plan. Giprovuz (USSR), L. Afanas'ev and others.

2.36. Higher Administration School, Bamako (Mali), design 1962. Giprovuz (USSR), L. Afanas'ev and others.

2.37. Professional Training Center, Housing for 300 students, Bamako (Mali), design 1962. Giprovuz (USSR), L. Afanas'ev and others.

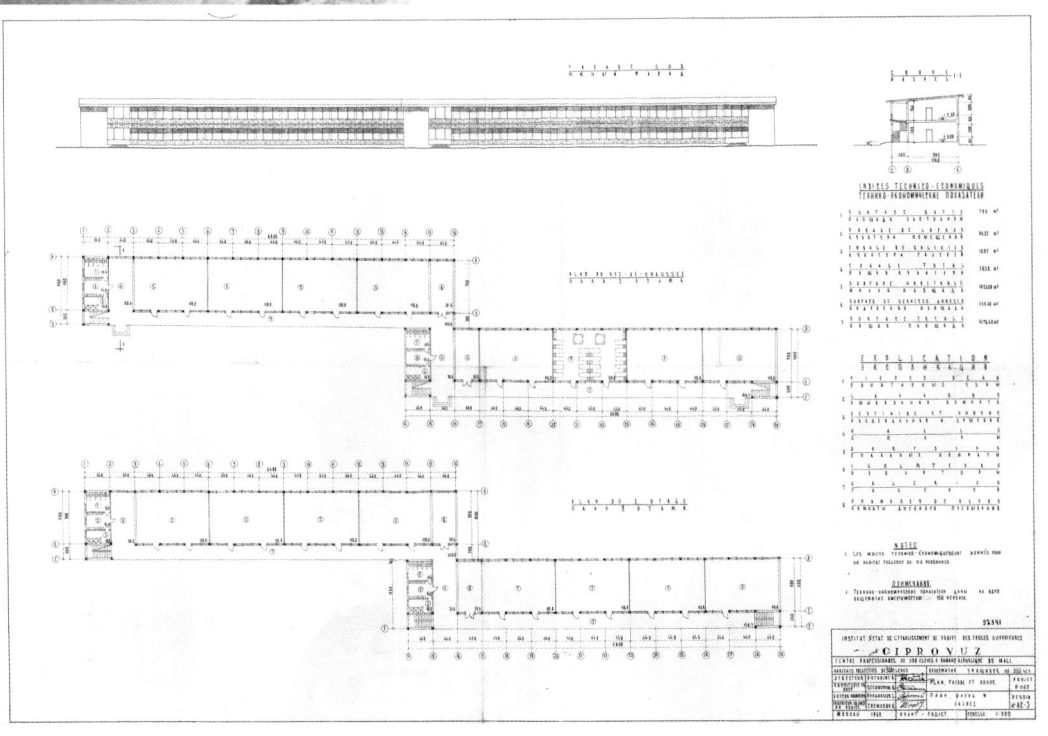

Among the most visible Soviet gifts for West Africa were three buildings in Bamako, the capital of Mali, a former French colony that gained its independence in 1960. As part of the extensive Soviet aid program to Mali, which included the construction of a stadium in Bamako paid from Soviet credits, the USSR donated the center for agriculture education in the city of Katibougou, and two educational buildings in Bamako: the Medical College and the School of Higher Administration, all designed by Giprovuz in the early 1960s.[182] The School of Higher Administration was gifted by the Communist Party of the Soviet Union to the Sudanese Union Party of Keita in order to "permit the party cadres...to acquire the theoretical base of scientific socialism, indispensable for the construction of a socialist society" (figures 2.35, 2.36, and 2.37).[183]

The agreement concerning the school in Bamako offers a glimpse into the legal framework of a Soviet building-gift, which resulted in specific decisions concerning materiality, design procedure, and construction that reverberated in other Soviet engagements in the region, including those in Ghana.[184] The agreement was signed in August 1963 in Bamako between two Soviet organizations, the FTO Tekhnoexport and the Soviet Ministry of Installation and Special Construction Work, and the Bamako-based, state-owned National Contracting Company Sonetra. In the agreement, the Soviet organizations were called "customers" and their Malian counterpart was called the "contractor." The Soviet customers agreed to pay the Malian contractor (in local currency) for its work, and to provide it with design documentation free of charge, as well as materials and equipment that were not produced in Mali. The two Soviet organizations also agreed to send specialists to train Malian workers on the construction site and to supervise them. In addition to constructing the buildings, Sonetra agreed to deliver workers and equipment, and materials produced in Mali. They also pledged to provide housing for Soviet specialists, paid by the Soviet side.[185]

This agreement shows that, far from being a mere mode of distribution of architecture, the status of a gift had several consequences for the design and construction process. First, the agreement limited materials, technology, and labor used in the construction to two countries, the Soviet Union and the recipient country, here Mali. Almost all materials and machinery were Soviet, including cement. While the agreement reserved the possibility for the Soviet side to purchase third-party materials and equipment, such purchases were unlikely, given the tendency by the USSR to save on foreign currencies. This insistence on Soviet materials in West African projects sometimes proved counterproductive, when the Soviet side was required to replace faulty components, as was the case with the Camayenne Hotel.[186]

Second, the budgets of gift projects were often inflexible. The agreement stipulated that after the beginning of construction work, any budget changes would need to be approved by Soviet authorities, who were not only averse to such changes but also took a great deal of time to review them, leading to delays. To maximize savings, Soviet reviewers were eager to get rid of all "excesses" and decorative elements initially proposed by the architects in the Bamako designs, including canopies, cantilevers, and reflective pools.[187] The framework of a building-gift allowed for much tighter budgetary control than was the case with investments funded by Soviet loans, which, to the frustration of the creditors, sometimes included "prestige projects" with little impact on the recipient countries' economic development.[188]

Budgetary concerns might have been a major reason for limiting the involvement of the gift-takers in the design process once the initial agreement had been signed.[189] In the case of the Bamako school, the review process in Moscow led to significant revisions of the design. For example, Soviet reviewers rejected the application of asbestos-cement proposed by the designers and pointed out the poor performance of that material in earlier

Soviet projects in Guinea—a conclusion showing the accelerated accumulation of Soviet technoscientific knowledge about sub-Saharan Africa.[190]

By the mid-1960s, Soviet architects could already rely on guidelines compiled by Soviet organizations for several African countries, and in the years to come, on broader overviews, often produced by scholars at the Lumumba University in Moscow (figure 2.38). These guidelines facilitated the extension to foreign locations of the Soviet practice of modifying standardized designs to meet specific site conditions (the *priviazka* system, literally meaning "tightening" or "binding").[191] For instance, technical guidelines for the design of facilities constructed with the technical assistance of the USSR in Guinea and in Ghana were published in 1961 and 1962, respectively.[192] These guidelines were obligatory for Soviet design institutes and organizations that worked in these countries. In the case of Ghana, they included information on climatic and seismic conditions and the local construction industry, they recommended construction materials and their way of use, they specified the dimensions of the structural modules and lighting standards, and they suggested solutions for engineering, ventilation, and sewage designs. The document was accompanied by a note written by Ghanaian architect E.Y.S. Engmann, employed at that time at the Ministry of Public Works, who corrected some of the Soviet recommendations and qualified others.[193] During the review process in Moscow, designs for West African countries were checked against these country-specific guidelines.

2.38. Shading devices. Vladimir M. Firsanov, *Arkhitektura grazhdanskikh zdanii v ulsoviiakh zharkogo klimata* (Moscow: Vysshaia shkola: 1971), 259.

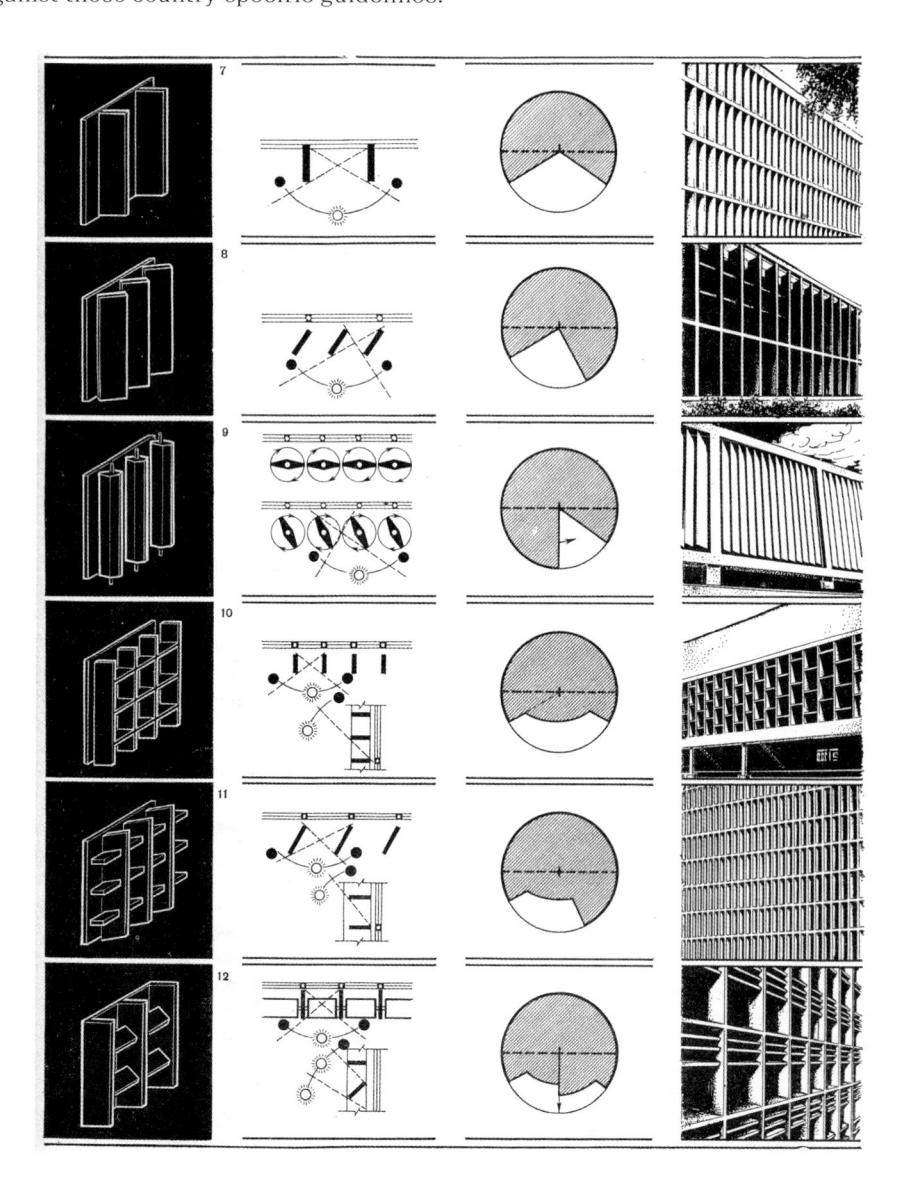

A rigorous review process was a general feature of Soviet architectural culture. But such a process was particularly important in the case of building-gifts, since the gift giver never fully cedes responsibility for the gift. That obligation was confirmed by the afterlife of Soviet gift projects, including continuous Soviet support for the schools in Mali, and for the hospital in Kisumu.[194] Other socialist countries took responsibility for their gift projects, too, including gifts to West African countries donated by China in the 1960s, which were renovated in the 1980s and 1990s at the expense of the Chinese government in order to make their initial benefits sustainable.[195]

Socialist Modernity for Ghana

While gifts comprised but a small part of the total number of Soviet-constructed buildings in West Africa during the Cold War, the concerns that characterized gift giving informed design decisions for a much larger group of Soviet projects in 1960s Ghana, Guinea, and Mali. The majority of those projects were not donated but were funded by credits granted by the Soviet Union. West African countries used those credits to pay for Soviet services and goods, including the work of architects and engineers, equipment, machinery, and industrial products. The credits would be repaid by means of local goods, typically agricultural products and raw materials, such as bauxite from the Soviet planned and constructed plant in Kinda (Guinea), then later by industrial products. In other words, these were barter transactions based on exchanges of goods and services, cleared on a periodic basis. Soviet readiness to accept payments in goods was acknowledged by Western commentators as a distinctive feature of Soviet foreign trade with West African countries, and as an incentive from the African point of view.

Those principles were the basis for the first agreement on economic and technical assistance and cooperation signed by Nkrumah's government and the Soviet Union in 1960. The terms of the agreement were highly favorable for Ghana and conveyed the blurred boundary between socialist aid and commercial transactions. The USSR agreed to assist Ghana in the construction of a number of industrial plants and in the establishment of vocational education to train specialists in industry, construction, and agriculture.[196] Soviet organizations that were to carry out this work were to be paid by Ghana from a credit line granted by the USSR at the favorable interest rate of 2.5 percent (compared with 6 percent, the typical rate requested by UK institutions).[197] As was the case in the agreement with Guinea and Mali, Soviet technological products and machinery were to be exchanged for agricultural goods (cocoa beans, in particular) with an estimated value set above the price on the international market.[198]

A share of the credit granted by the treaty was allocated by the Ghanaian government to the design and construction of two residential districts, one in Accra and one in Tema. The district in the harbor town Tema, where the Soviets had already planned a fish-processing plant, was designed for eleven thousand people (figure 2.39). The plan followed the master plan of Tema by Doxiadis Associates, which consisted of twelve housing communities, an industrial zone, the town center, and recreation areas.[199] Soviet planners were put in charge of the area between the Sakumono lagoon and the seashore, called Community 3 in the master plan. The district in Accra, twice as large and intended for twenty-two thousand people, was located in the northwest of the city, along the road to Takoradi (figure 2.40). This location opened a new direction for Accra's urbanization, as residential land use had not been foreseen there by the 1958 master plan or by the master plan of the Accra-Tema metropolitan region by Doxiadis Associates.[200]

CHAPTER 2

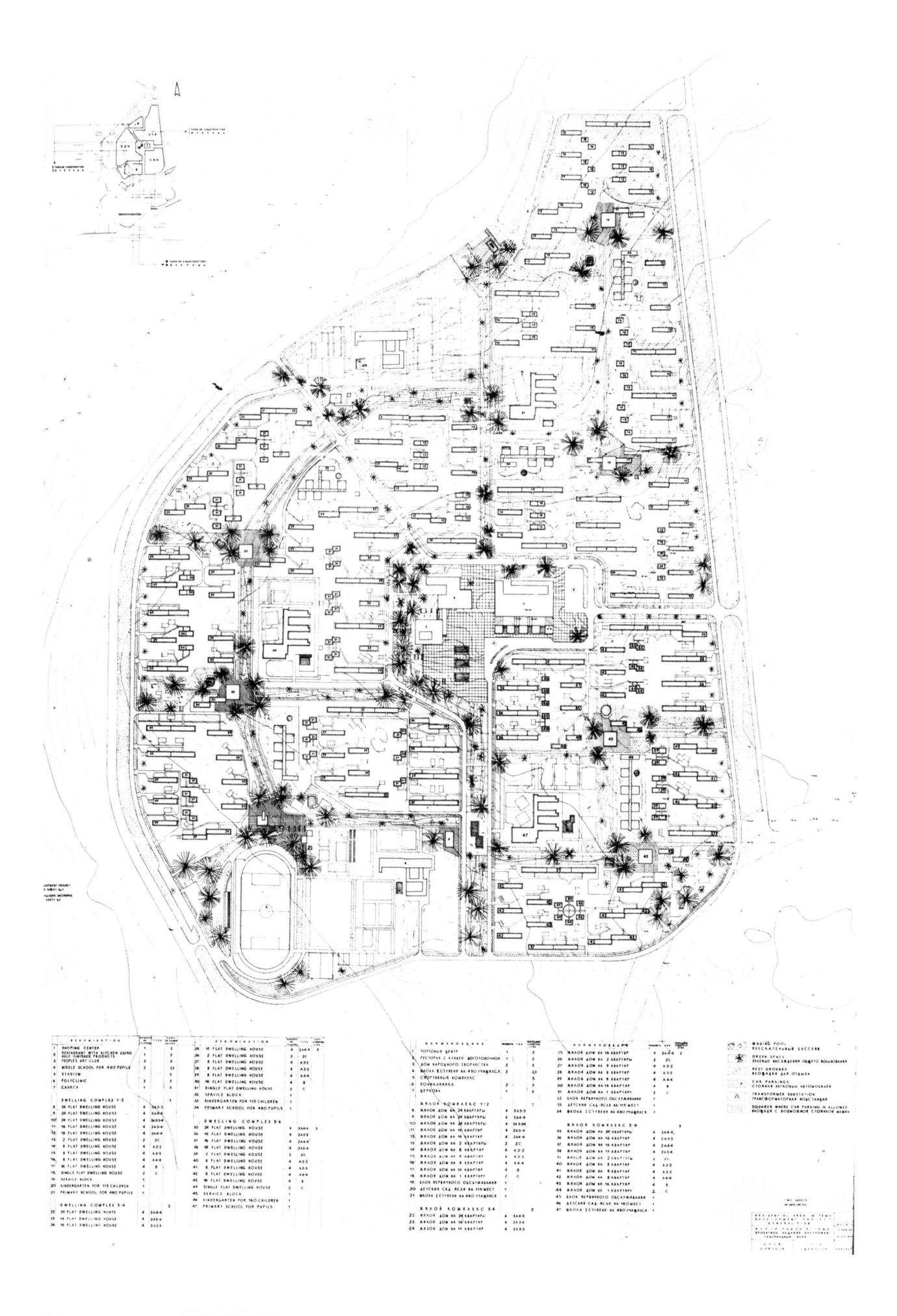

< 2.39. "Residential Area in Tema Development Project, General Plan." Giprogor (USSR), S. Raitman, I. Bukreev, and others.

On the Ghanaian side, both projects were approved by the Ministry of Works. They were to be executed by GNCC under Soviet supervision by means of large-scale prefabricated elements produced in Ghana in a factory imported from the USSR. GNCC's staff was to be put in charge of assembling and operating the factory, after being trained by Soviet specialists. Ghanaian organizations provided Soviet planners with site-specific information, including topographical maps and geological surveys, as well as data required for quantity surveying and standards for sewage networks and vegetation.[201] Further information was collected by Soviet planners during their site visits to Ghana.[202]

From the Soviet side, the design institute Giprogor (State Institute for the Planning of Cities) was in charge of the architectural and urban design. Giprogor was created between 1929 and 1932 from the merger of several Soviet planning institutions. With fifteen hundred employees, its remit straddled preparatory research for urban planning, design of new towns and neighborhoods, and design of housing and social facilities. Giprogor shaped the principles of Soviet urban planning centered on the industry, with the supply of labor force used to calculate other factors, such as the number of inhabitants and social infrastructure.[203] In turn, Giprostroiindustriia (State Design Institute for the Construction of Industrial Buildings) was in charge of the design of the prefabrication system and the factory that would produce the elements.[204] The Soviets agreed to ship all necessary mechanical equipment to Ghana, including transportation vehicles for the prefabricated elements and cranes. The design was consulted with a number of other organizations at the level of the Russian Republic, and on the All-Union level, including design institutes specializing in educational and commercial buildings, and the Academy of Construction and Architecture. The work was monitored by Gosstroi (State Committee for Construction), the Ministry of Foreign Affairs, and the Ministry of Foreign Trade, with the latter in charge of the contract and negotiations with Ghanaians.[205] The negotiations were coordinated by the Soviet consulate in Accra.

The preliminary project was accepted by the Ghanaian side in 1962, execution drawings were completed in 1964, and the construction of the district in Tema was planned for the following year. As was the case with the gift projects for Mali, Soviet planners limited the use of third-party materials needed for the construction of the residential buildings and, with the exception of louver windows to be bought in Britain, all materials, technology, machinery, and labor were of Soviet or Ghanaian origin. As with the Bamako projects, the Tema layout had undergone a series of thorough reviews in the Soviet Union before its complete documentation was sent to Ghana.[206] However, in summer 1964, after the documentation and the formwork for the prefabricated elements had been shipped to Accra, the Ghanaian counterparts demanded that the dimensions of rooms be enlarged, including their height (to 9.6 feet, or 2.93 meters).[207] A group of Soviet specialists, including architect S. Raitman and engineer S. Maroko from Giprogor, as well as representatives of other design institutes involved in the project and of the supervising ministries, were sent to Accra in early 1965 to address the demands of the Ghanaian side. Raitman and his colleagues were alarmed, and pointed to added costs and further delays, in particular since the construction of the prefabrication factory in Accra was already advanced. They also pointed to the fact that the height foreseen in the original project was consistent with other buildings designed in Ghana at that time, including those planned by Doxiadis. The Soviet specialists reported that it was Adegbite who insisted on the extension of the height, and this decision was confirmed by the Planning Committee of Accra and Tema with the explanation that higher quality houses were desired by the population and would serve longer.[208] The Soviets yielded to this demand, and went back to their drawing

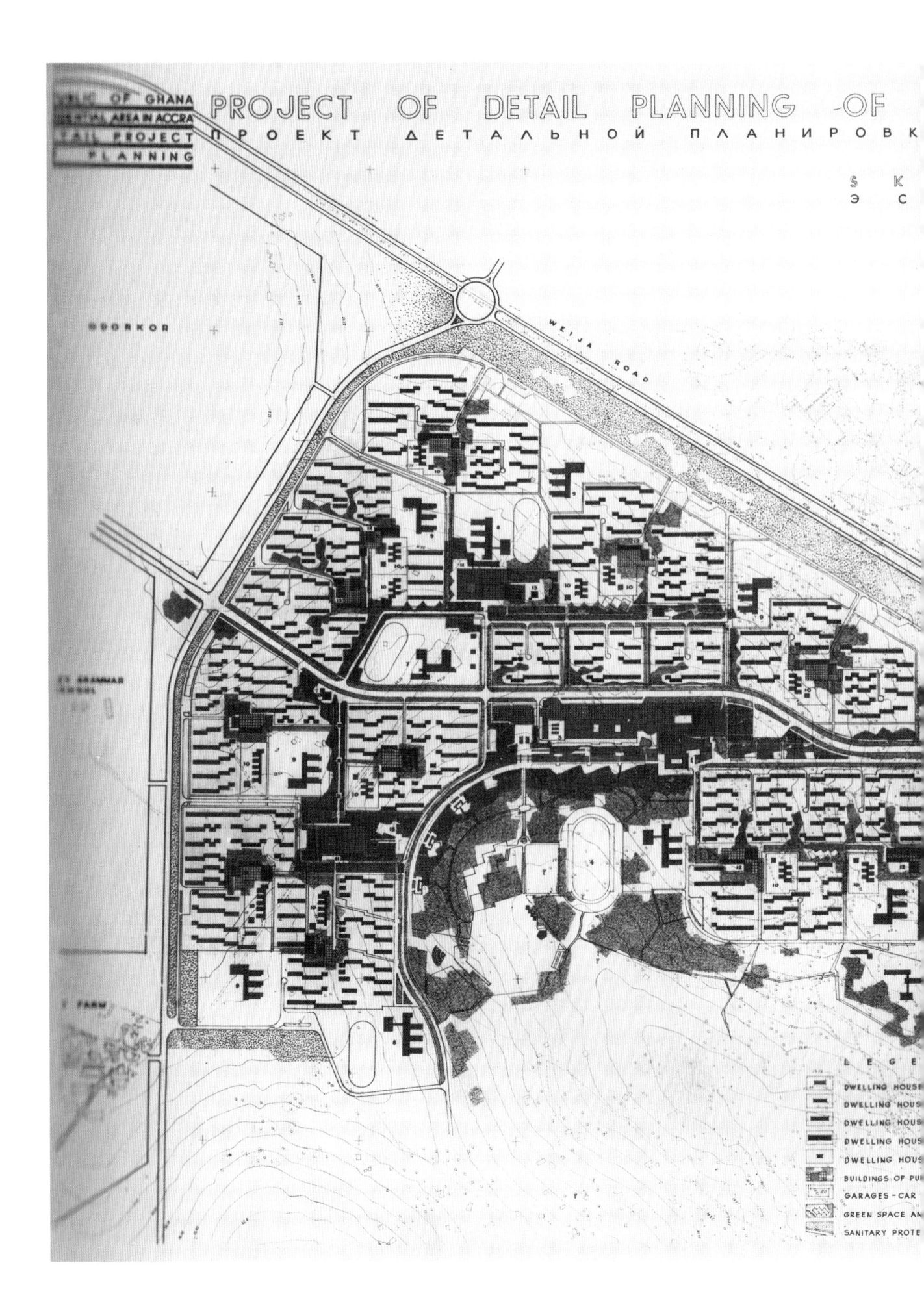

PROJECT OF DETAIL PLANNING OF
ПРОЕКТ ДЕТАЛЬНОЙ ПЛАНИРОВК

STATE OF GHANA
DWELLING AREA IN ACCRA
DETAIL PROJECT
PLANNING

ODORKOR

WEIJA ROAD

LEGE
- DWELLING HOUS
- DWELLING HOUS
- DWELLING HOUS
- DWELLING HOUS
- DWELLING HOUS
- BUILDINGS OF PU
- GARAGES - CAR
- GREEN SPACE AN
- SANITARY PROTE

2.40. "Residential Area in Accra. Project of Detail Planning," design 1962. Giprogor (USSR), S. Raitman and others.

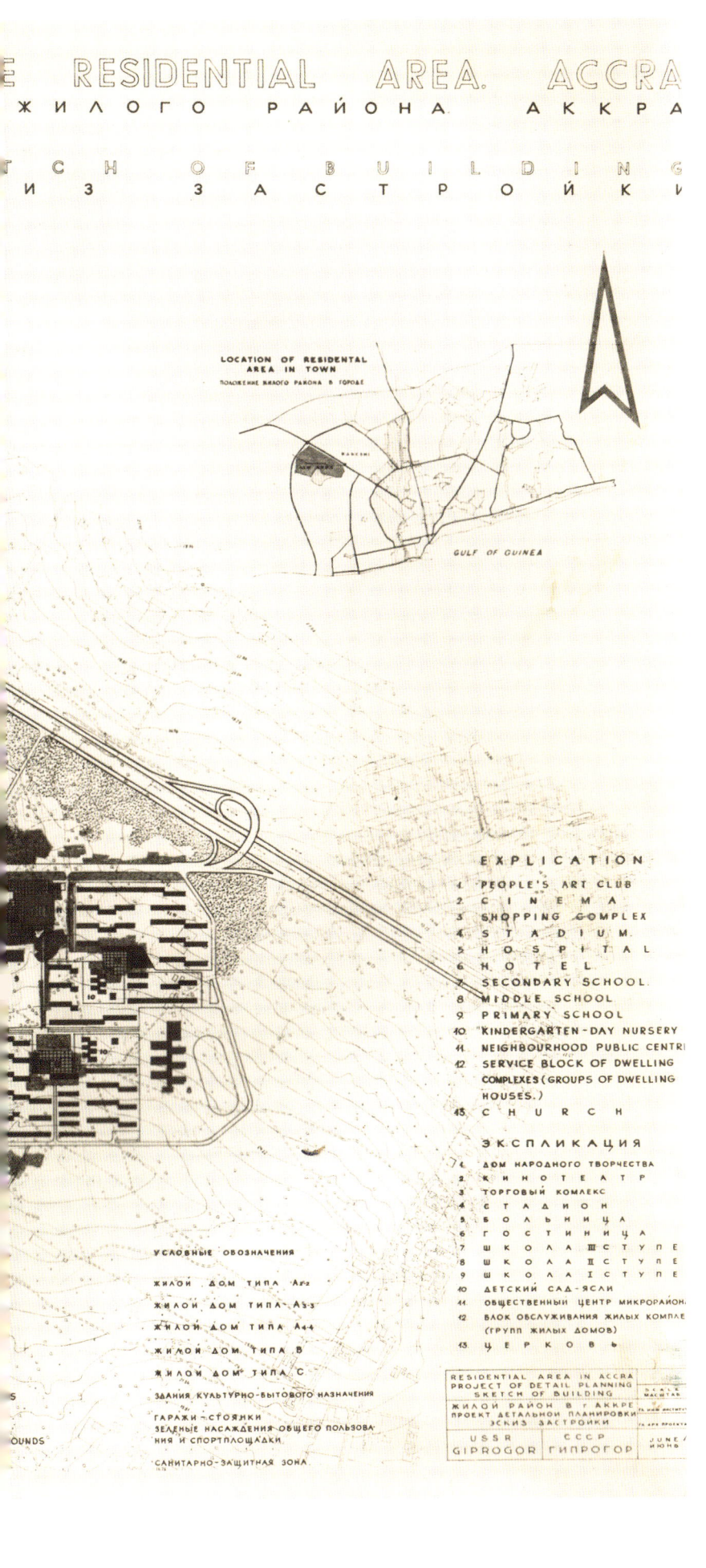

boards, although the final agreement with the Ghanaian side did not seem to have been reached.[209] By summer 1965, the Soviet factory near Accra was reported to be operational. However, its production was suspended a few months later in the wake of the coup, and neither residential district would be built.[210]

Both residential-district plans were unmistakably products of Soviet architectural culture. They were designed by S. Raitman and his team as nested systems of settlement units. The Accra district consisted of fourteen residential complexes (up to two thousand residents each), complemented by blocks with primary services. The residential complexes were, in turn, grouped into three mikroraiony (up to ten thousand residents), each of them with their own centers; functions serving all three mikroraiony were located in the district center. The Tema district was organized into six residential complexes, with each of their centers including a shop, a canteen, a social club, service rooms, and a park with sport facilities (figure 2.41).

2.41. "People's Art Club of Residential Area, Accra," design 1962. Giprogor (USSR), A. Panfil', A. Ustinov (project architects), and others.

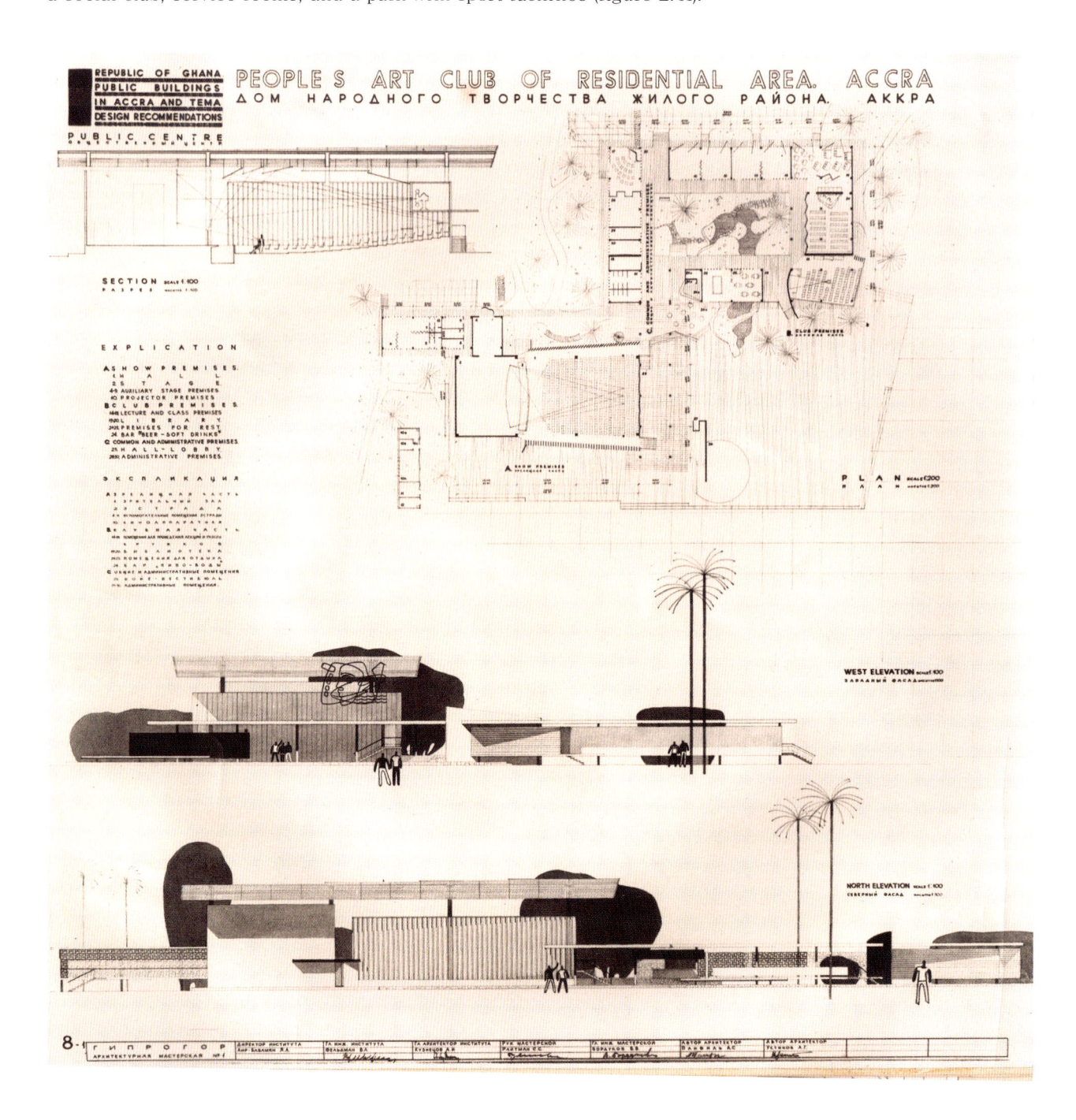

2.42. "Service Block for House Groups with 1600–1800 Inhabitants," design 1962. Giprogor (USSR), A. Panfil', A. Makarycheva (project architects), and others.

The program of the district's center included a "people's art club" with a lecture room, a library with a reading room, and a cinema hall, among other facilities, a canteen, a shopping center and market, and a service block including ateliers, postal services, and others. Nurseries, kindergartens, schools at various levels, and sports facilities were distributed according to Soviet norms. Pedestrian pathways among green spaces connected facilities with residential buildings. Streets with segregated traffic were designed in compliance with Soviet standards.[211]

Plans for the social, educational, commercial, health, and cultural facilities were typically delivered in pavilion layouts, to be constructed either from prefabricated elements or cast on site in monolithic frames. Their flexible spaces allowed for a variety of arrangements, and so the service block could accommodate celebrations, lectures, dance parties, and training courses, as demonstrated by drawings showing various possible arrangements of the block's public areas (figure 2.42).[212] The program of these facilities conveyed a sense of a socialist everyday, with community clubs providing venues for collective enjoyment, and kindergartens and day-care centers allowing mothers to take up professional jobs.[213] Domestic work was to be reduced by canteens selling precooked food for inhabitants.[214] In drawings sent from Moscow to Accra, those facilities were presented as an airy architecture with light roofs, glass walls, openwork grids, crisp neon signs, and atmospheric vegetation.[215]

The choice of apartment blocks as a housing typology, while not unprecedented in Ghana, was also a direct reflection of Soviet practice. In line with housing programs in the USSR, the main advantage of multifamily housing was economical, but Soviet authors pointed out that multistory buildings also came with advantages in terms of climate control. Their height could be used to catch the breeze and thus improve

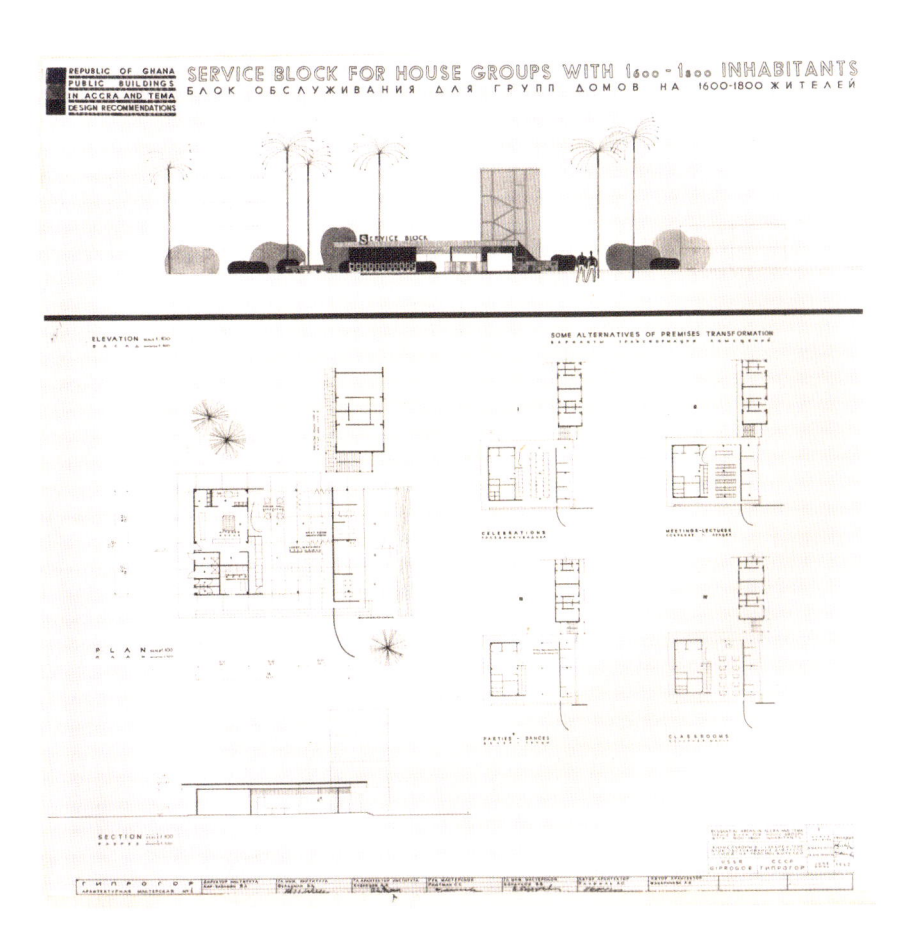

A GLOBAL DEVELOPMENT PATH

cross-ventilation, and galleries and loggias could serve for access, as protection against the sun, and as an extension of living spaces (figure 2.43).[216]

The prefabrication system that the engineers at Giprostroiindustriia designed for Ghana was a modification of the Soviet system I-464.[217] This system consisted of external walls assembled from room-size panels, and floor panels supported at the perimeters by transverse and longitudinal walls.[218] Introduced in 1958, the I-464 system became the most widespread in the USSR and it was produced in two hundred plants across the country. I-464 translated the demand for low-cost, high-speed construction of housing that characterized Khrushchev's outlines of housing policy into the operational possibilities of Soviet industry in the 1950s. It was economical in terms of the use of material, simplicity of prefabricated elements, and their limited number; it had a high level of "factory readiness," as the walls and ceilings required no further treatment; and the equal weight of elements optimized the load on construction cranes. In the Soviet Union, the I-464 system was adapted to various climatic conditions in the republics, and to specific soil conditions (such as permafrost) and seismic risks (a central concern of Soviet architects over the course of the 1950s). Regional design institutes in Tbilisi and Tashkent adapted the I-464 system for application in the Caucasus and Central Asia, including the introduction of shading devices, loggias, and verandas.[219]

Some of those elements, including adjustable shades for windows and doors, were used in the Tema project, as were technical solutions concerning foundations, walls, and joints used to alleviate seismic risks in the area, classified according to Soviet norms (figure 2.44).[220] An openwork panel was designed especially for projects in Ghana then added to the system. In order to adapt to climatic conditions in Ghana, the architects added a supplementary protective layer of concrete to vertical elements and additional waterproofing to roof elements. However, such decisions resulted in prefabricated elements that were heavier than initially foreseen and could not be lifted by standard cranes (figure 2.45).[221] In order to test the structural performance of newly designed components, the Soviets constructed an "experimental" mock-up of a whole "section" of the building,

2.43. "Dwelling Houses in Accra and Tema. House A4–4. Elevations," 1964. Giprogor (USSR), A. Panfil' (project architect), and others.

> 2.44. Prefabricated elements for housing projects for Accra and Tema, 1962. Giprogor (USSR).

> 2.45. Standard details for housing projects for Accra and Tema, 1964. Giprogor (USSR), S. Raitman (project architect), and others.

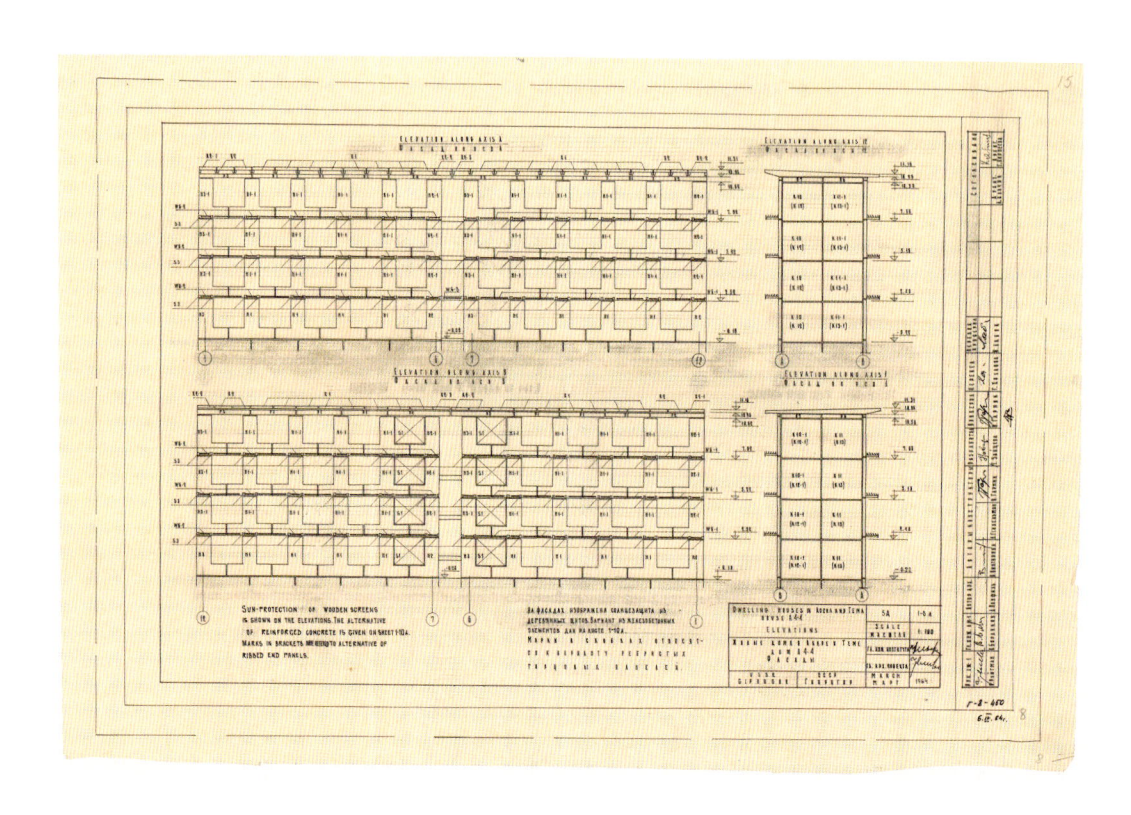

A GLOBAL DEVELOPMENT PATH

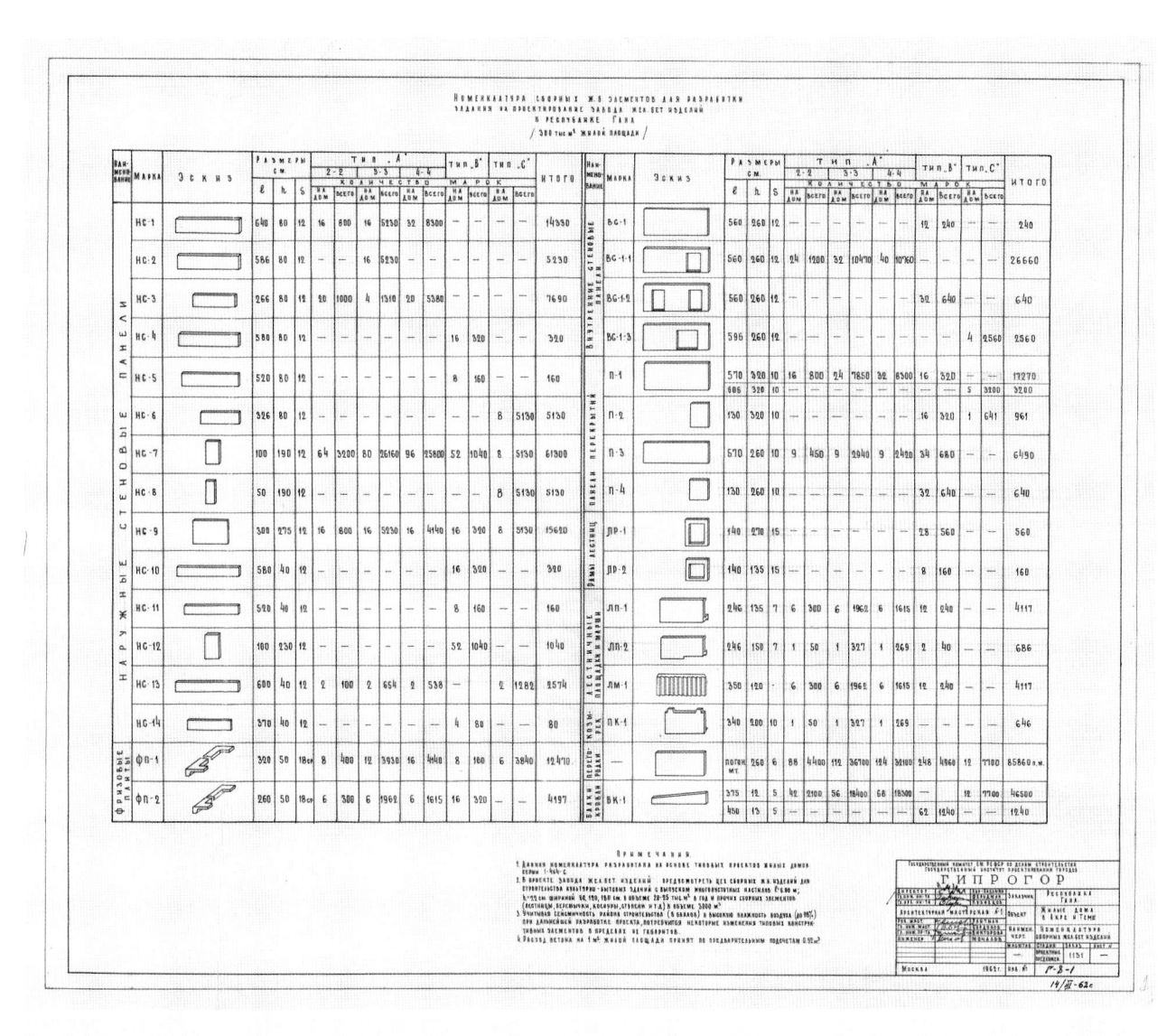

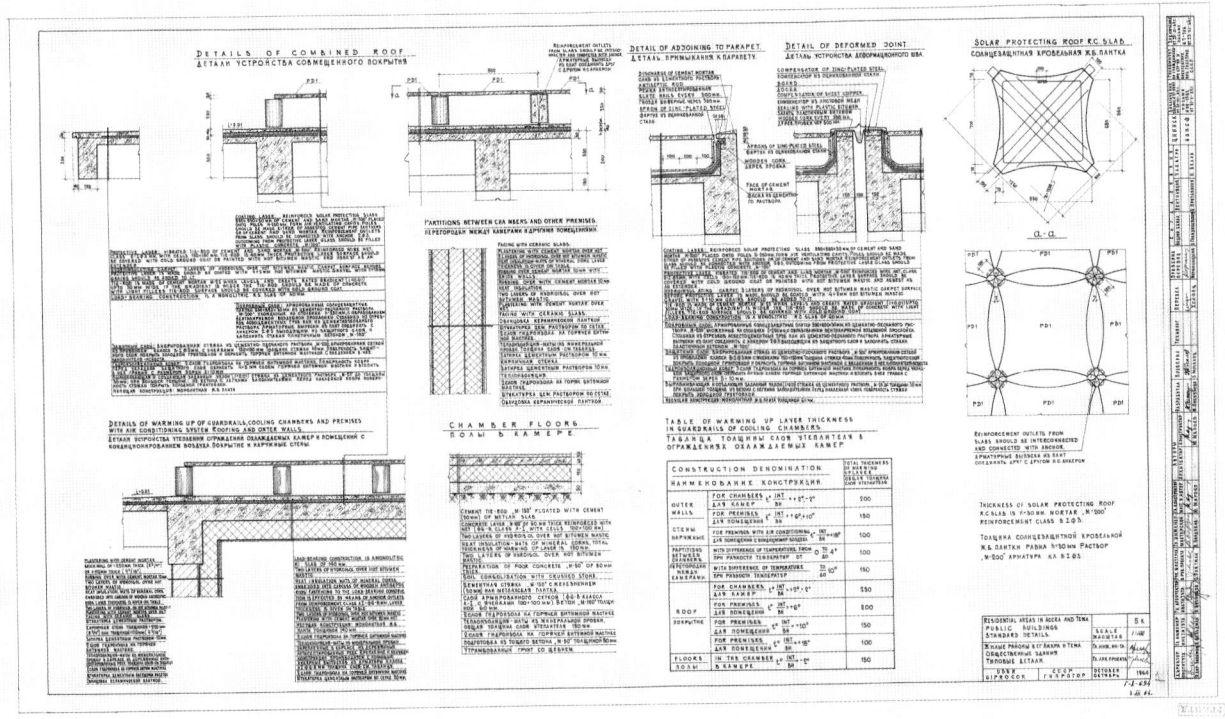

or its part accessible from one staircase. First planned on the Black Sea coast to approximate Ghana's climate, it was eventually built in a factory near Moscow, where it was used to test the prefabricated elements, the processes of their assembling, and the appropriateness of the equipment, resulting in several revisions of the design (figure 2.46).[222] Further revisions were made in the wake of the visit of the Soviet specialists to Ghana. In addition to reducing costs, enhancing technical performance, and simplifying the construction process, these modifications responded to the demands of the GNCC, such as the inclusion of external spaces for each flat.[223]

Building layout was adapted to Ghana's climate. The original I-464 system apartment layouts were four- and five-story buildings consisting of three or four sections.[224] The designs for Ghana were more varied, and included a four-story building with apartments of one to four rooms, and a two-story building with five- to six-room apartments (figure 2.47).[225] While sections in the original I-464 building designs in the USSR were inseparable, sections in the designs for Ghana were structurally independent. Accordingly, A. Panfil', L. Il'chik, G. Korneeva, and other architects in charge of the housing designs could propose stepped layouts to accommodate site topography and enhance the architectural variety of the ensemble. Single-family two-story buildings were designed as well, and applied in the master plan either as detached houses or combined in a row layout. All buildings were east-west orientated to protect them from the sun, and distances between apartment blocks were enlarged over the course of the design process to allow for better airflow within the district.[226]

Ventilation concerns also impacted the design of individual buildings. In particular, architects did not employ Gosstroi's recommended layouts of four apartments accessible from a single staircase landing, which would result in buildings two rooms in breadth.[227] Rather, all buildings for Ghana were designed with single-room breadths with two (external) longitudinal load-bearing walls (figure 2.48). Single-room breadth plans followed housing layouts constructed in West Africa since the late-colonial period and were recommended by "tropical" architects as optimal for cross-ventilation.[228] In Giprogor's Ghanaian apartments, this layout allowed for the cross-ventilation of each room, including the living room (with windows on both sides) and bedrooms, accessible through a "loggia-corridor." However, in comparison to apartments constructed in the Soviet Union, a single-room breadth plan reduced to two the number of apartments accessible from a staircase landing, a decision that increased the usable square meterage cost.

Giprogor planners ignored the decision of the Doxiadis Associates master plan to differentiate Tema housing typologies according to income

2.46. Housing project for Tema, mock-up, Ochakovo (USSR, today Russian Federation), winter 1964/65. TsNIIEP zhilishcha, Giprogor (USSR).

2.47. Housing project for Tema, plan of the ground floor, 1964. Giprogor (USSR), A. Panfil' (project architect), and others.

2.48. "Dwelling Houses in Accra and Tema. List of Series Houses," 1964, schematic plans, sections, and elevations. Giprogor (USSR), L. Il'chik, G. Korneeva, A. Panfil' (project architects), and others.

groups, and differentiated the apartments instead according to family size, in line with Soviet practice.[229] Typical I-464 system housing layouts designed in the Soviet Union followed the so-called Vesnin layout, which maximized living spaces by using the living room as the link between entrance hall and bedrooms, and by situating the kitchen and the sanitary facilities near the entrance.[230] The first principle was followed by layouts in Ghana, in which the living room connected the entrance area and the loggia-corridor providing access to bedrooms. As in Vesnin layouts, the kitchen was located next to the entrance and was provided with a "cooking porch" separated by a grate: a design acknowledging the importance of external spaces for domestic work in Ghana. However, the cooking porch left no space for sanitary facilities near the entrance, and they were located at the end of the loggia-corridor. As in the USSR, all apartments were planned with access to water, plumbing, and electricity.[231]

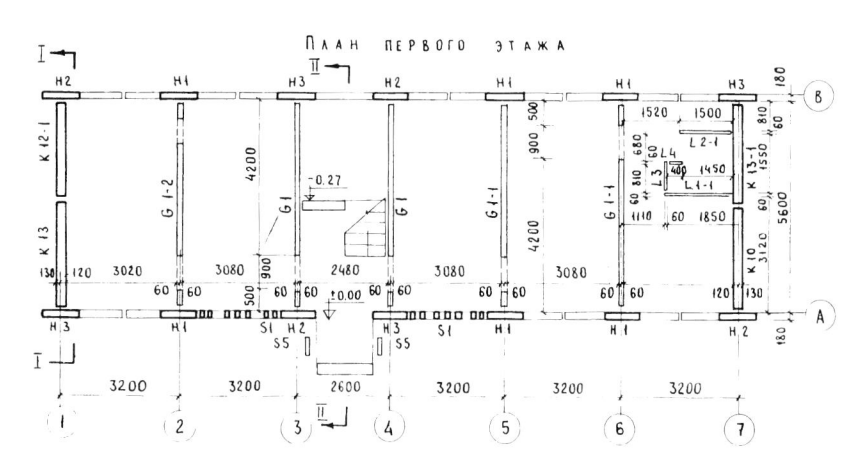

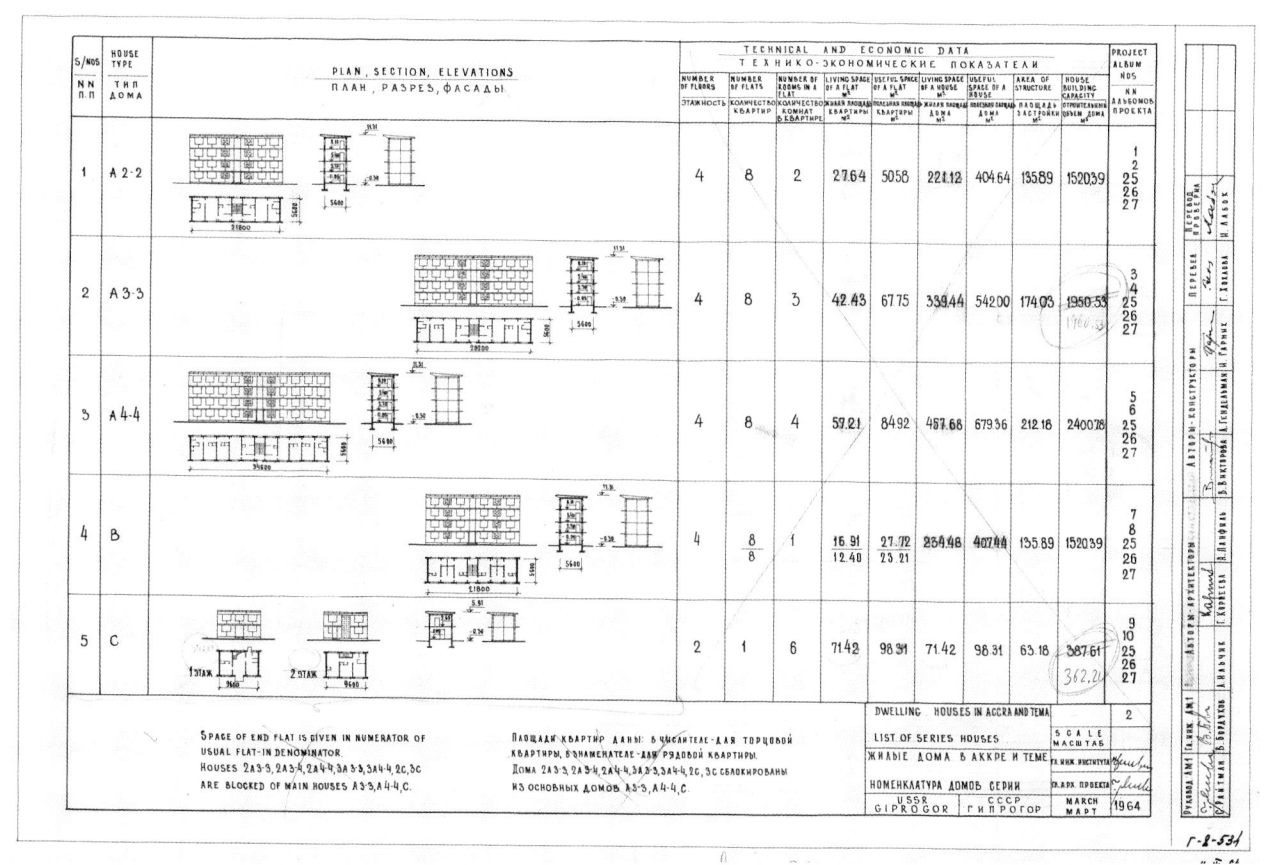

A GLOBAL DEVELOPMENT PATH

This close reading of the projects in Accra and Tema shows that Giprogor planners went to great lengths in adapting principles of the Soviet housing program to conditions on the ground. What underpinned this adaptive work was a distinction between conditions that required the Soviet model to be modified and those requiring no such modification. The criteria of this distinction come to the fore in the comparison between the Giprogor housing layout and others designed for Ghana around independence—in particular, in the contrast between the Soviet "experimental" mock-up and the real-life "experimental" housing that Doxiadis Associates had designed for Tema.

For Soviet planners, the main concern of their "experimental" mock-up was the structural feasibility, seismic resistance of the building, and the process of the assembling of the elements; further experiments were planned in Ghana to test the performance of the concrete used by the factory.[232] In contrast, the focus of Doxiadis Associates' row-house typology was its ability to facilitate the transition of Tema's inhabitants from a rural to an urban way of life. Such a transition was the purpose of the garden, which allowed for urban agriculture and an incremental growth of the house to accommodate the extended family; the garden also helped ensure the requirement of privacy attributed to rural communities.[233] Layouts accounting for distinct ways of life of specific professional or ethnic groups had been in the focus of several architects in Ghana since the late-colonial period, and included housing plans for workers in aluminum-smelting townships (Mayer & Whittlesey, 1955–56), rehousing schemes for the population of Tema (Fry, Drew, Drake & Lasdun, 1951–58), and the resettlement project in Accra for fishermen in Ussher Town who belonged to the Ga ethnic group (Alcock and Richards, 1952). The latter was, as with the Soviet layouts, a multistory apartment block. In line with the gender-based occupancy of the traditional Ga compound, this design separated men and women with children on each floor, and accommodated the functional differences between the women's part with a cooking balcony and movable partitions, and the men's part with an area for mending nets.[234]

If the Soviet planners decided not to differentiate apartments according to ethnic, vocational, or income categories, their decision did not stem from ignorance about heterogeneity in Ghanaian society or from lack of awareness about earlier housing layouts in Ghana. Architects at Giprogor

2.49. "Labadi Slum Clearance. Basic Map—Master Plan Proposals," mid-1960s. TCPD, Peter Turkson (chief planner), Grażyna Jonkajtys-Luba, Jerzy Luba.

2.50. International Trade Fair, Accra, with leisure area at the shore and the development of La, mid-1960s. GNCC, Vic Adegbite (chief architect), Jacek Chyrosz, Stanisław Rymaszewski (project architects).

knew the latter well, and they closely studied the schemes of Doxiadis Associates, which they used in the review process in Moscow to assess the costs of the Soviet housing layouts for Tema.[235] Their designs subscribed, rather, to the Khrushchev-era imperative of providing an egalitarian living space in uniform standard, at the lowest possible costs and in the shortest possible time. Such vision resulted in the adaptive work performed by the Soviet planners, including climatic comfort and functional adaptation (cooking porch), while the economic imperative resulted in a uniform design that would allow the maximizing of the economies of scale allowed by the mass prefabrication system. But in order to benefit from such economies, the construction of the Soviet factory for prefabricated elements would need to be supported not only by a fundamental reorganization of the GNCC planning process but also by an integration of the Ghanaian construction and construction-materials industries within a centralized, state-led planning framework. The Soviets argued that such a decisive shift was necessary for putting an end to Africa's economic dependence on the West, and after the Sino-Soviet split, they contrasted this strategy with Chinese aid based on incremental change.[236] In this sense, rather than being limited to two neighborhoods, the Soviet layouts need to be read as catalysts that were to trigger a fundamental transformation of the Ghanaian economy toward the socialist development path.

Architectural Labor in the Cold War

In the wake of the 1966 coup and of the revision of the Nkrumah-era planning that followed, the construction of both Soviet neighborhoods was abandoned. This revision also concerned other investments, including the scaling back of the design of Accra's International Trade Fair. Because of ITF's strategic location between Accra and Tema, the trade fair was conceived as part of the large territorial restructuring of the envisaged Accra-Tema metropolitan region.[237] That restructuring had included the introduction of a new traffic system, for which ITF was to constitute a node.[238] A central component of this development was the "slum clearance"

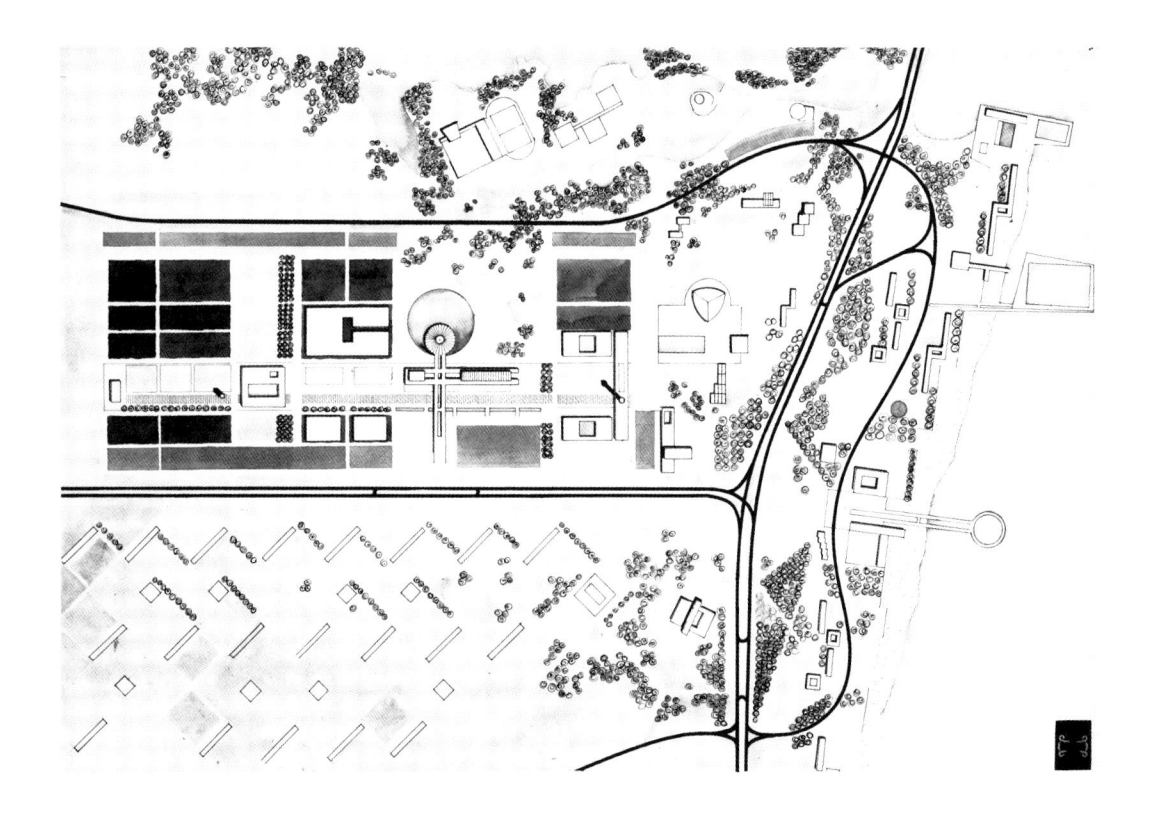

A GLOBAL DEVELOPMENT PATH

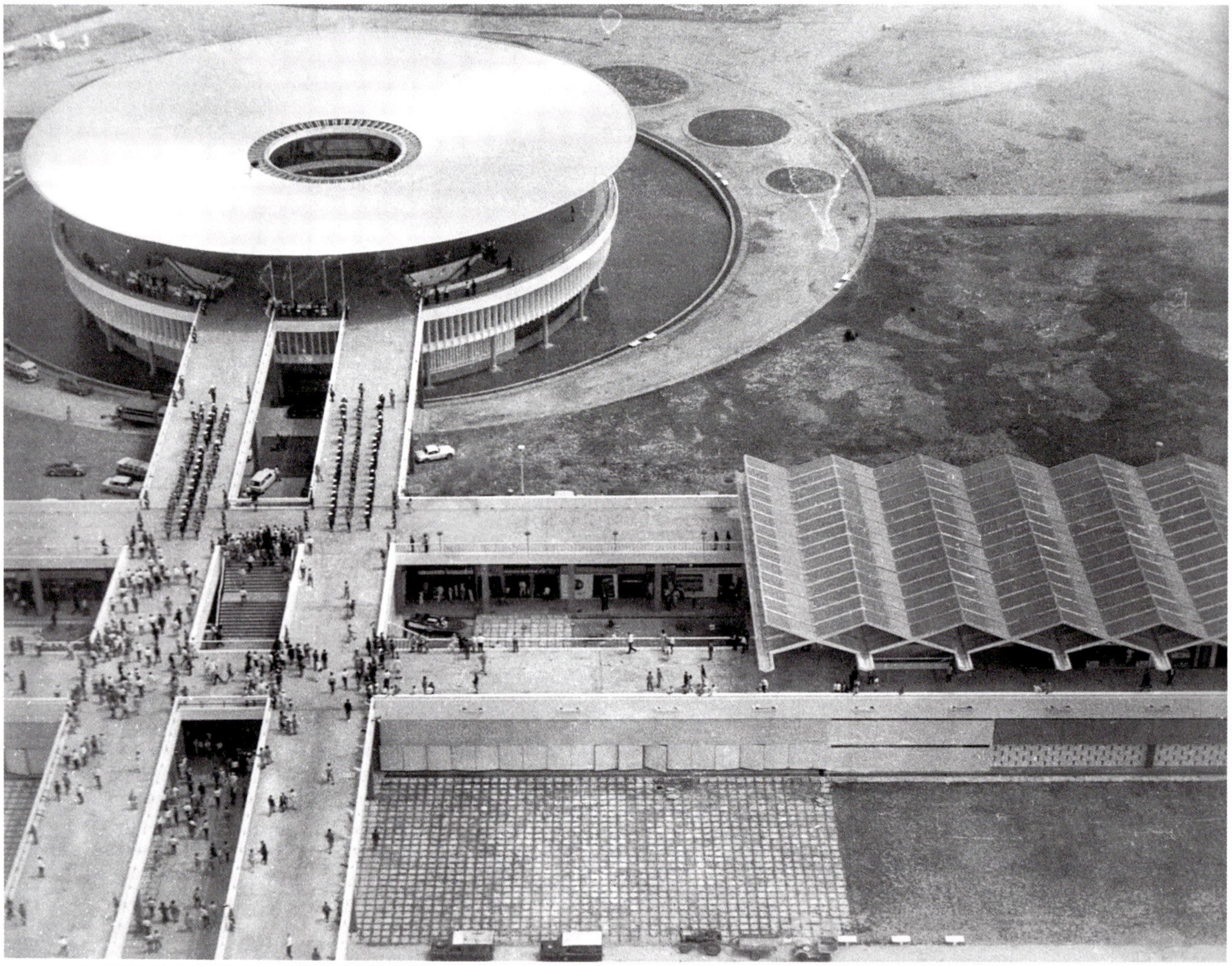

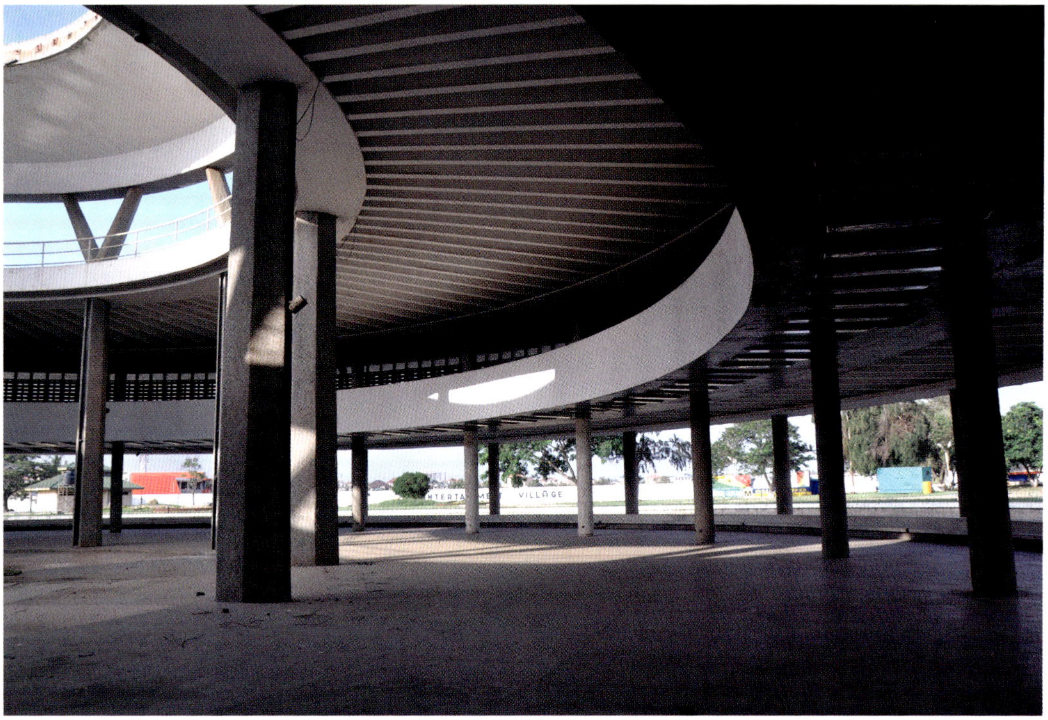

< 2.51. International Trade Fair, Accra, 1962–67, Africa Pavilion and Pavilion A, aerial view. GNCC, Vic Adegbite (chief architect), Jacek Chyrosz, Stanisław Rymaszewski (project architects).

< 2.52. International Trade Fair, Accra, 1962–67, Africa Pavilion. GNCC, Vic Adegbite (chief architect), Jacek Chyrosz, Stanisław Rymaszewski (project architects).

2.53. International Trade Fair, Accra, 1962–67, temporary pavilions. GNCC, Vic Adegbite (chief architect), Jacek Chyrosz, Stanisław Rymaszewski (project architects).

of ITF's immediate neighbor, the district of La, for which TCPD delivered a master plan with new social facilities, public spaces, and infrastructure integrated into the ITF's utility networks (figure 2.49).[239] The investment around the ITF site also included a layout for Labadi Beach, with a program of leisure, tourist, cultural, and sports facilities, free-floating between roads and vegetation, sometimes accompanied by proposals to rebuild Labadi completely (figure 2.50).[240]

Upon the opening of ITF in February 1967, only parts of the traffic network in La had been built, and the seaside leisure area was scaled back to a small pavilion. Other elements of the trade fair deemed "extravagant and unnecessary" were left out, including a hundred-meter tower planned for the southern end of the area.[241] The composition for ITF exhibitors was also reshuffled. Under the overarching topic of "Developing Africa," and with the explicit aim of creating an "atmosphere of confidence and trust" for foreign investors, the trade fair was instrumental in Ghana's reopening toward the West.[242] Consequently, the pavilions of Great Britain and the United States were among the most prominent ones. India was represented as a member of the Commonwealth, rather than as a member of the Non-Aligned Movement, since Nkrumah's attempt to position Ghana as one of the leading nations of that movement, along with Egypt, India, and Yugoslavia, had been abandoned after the regime change. Collaboration among African countries was favored, not as a way of carrying on with Nkrumah's vision of a pan-African union, but with the more modest aim of stimulating trade within Africa. Accordingly, displays representing African countries were gathered prominently in the round entrance pavilion, located at the end of the ramp through which visitors accessed the compound. From there, they dispersed to Pavilion A (the "Made in Ghana" pavilion) and permanent and temporary pavilions rented to Ghanaian state firms, foreign firms, and foreign governments (figures 2.51 and 2.52).[243] The latter included Czechoslovakia, East Germany, Hungary, Poland, and Yugoslavia, while the Soviet Union and the People's Republic of China were absent (figure 2.53).[244]

This rearrangement reflected the differentiated position of the new Ankrah regime toward socialist countries: while Soviet, Chinese, and East German advisers were expelled from Ghana in the wake of the coup,

A GLOBAL DEVELOPMENT PATH

professionals from other socialist countries were invited to stay and contribute to the development of the country along with specialists from the West.[245] The new regime embraced a vision of a "mixed economy" that would "marry the best in the capitalist and socialist patterns of development."[246] Photographs from the ITF construction site published in the Ghanaian press seemed to prove this point, as they showed Polish designers working for GNCC in friendly conversation with British advisers and US experts.[247] ITF's architecture, with its abstract geometry of volumes, levitating roofs, and rhythmic patterning, appeared to be part of such an international professional culture as well. The trade fair had nothing to do with the socialist-realist style that the educated Ghanaian public could have associated with buildings in socialist countries, as those had been reproduced in the press under Nkrumah and were occasionally seen in Ghana, for instance in historicist forms of the pavilion of the Chinese Trade exhibition in Accra (1961).[248] If anything, ITF resembled buildings constructed in Accra since the late-colonial period by British architects within the tradition of tropical architecture. However, in spite of the shared design culture of the architects involved, a closer look at ITF will show how its production articulated Cold War antagonisms.

The comparison of design principles of ITF with those of tropical architecture offers an entry point into this discussion. According to Drew and Fry, the "main considerations influencing architectural design in the tropics" were climate, local materials and technologies, and people's needs and aspirations.[249] Climate was also the first concern for the architects of ITF, and both its layout and its particular buildings were designed with

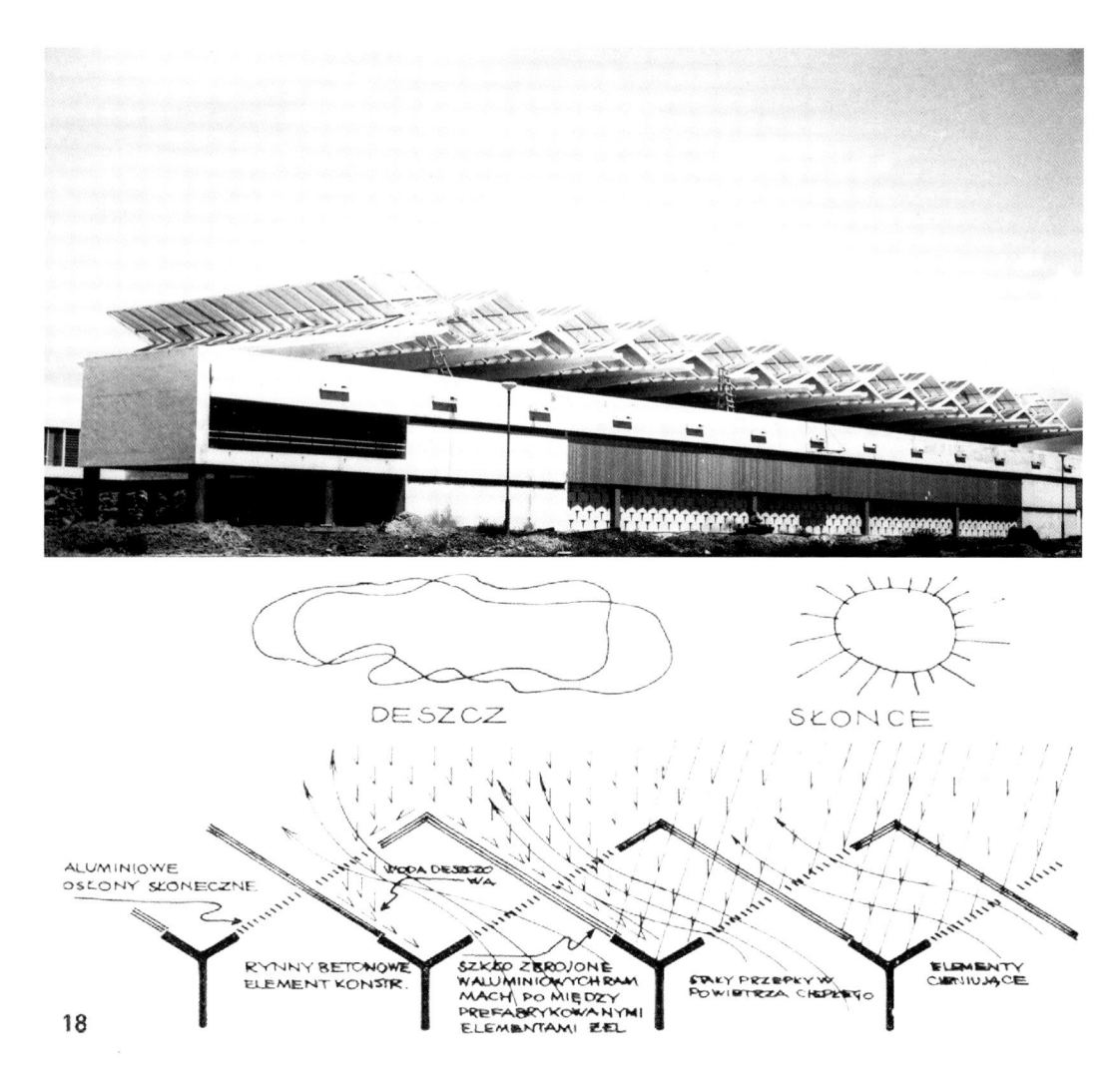

2.54. International Trade Fair, Accra, 1962–67, Pavilion A under construction. GNCC, Vic Adegbite (chief architect), Jacek Chyrosz, Stanisław Rymaszewski (project architects).

2.55. International Trade Fair, Accra, 1962–67, diagram of Pavilion A. GNCC, Vic Adegbite (chief architect), Jacek Chyrosz, Stanisław Rymaszewski (project architects). Jacek Chyrosz and Stanisław Rymaszewski, "Międzynarodowe Targi w Akrze, 1.2.1967–19.2.1967," *Architektura* 4 (1969): 146.

2.56. International Trade Fair, Accra, 1962–67, Pavilion A, details. GNCC, Vic Adegbite (chief architect), Jacek Chyrosz, Stanisław Rymaszewski (project architects).

2.57. International Trade Fair, Accra, 1962–67, Timber Industry Pavilion. GNCC, Vic Adegbite (chief architect), Jacek Chyrosz, Stanisław Rymaszewski (project architects).

natural ventilation, open to breezes from the ocean, with pronounced eaves providing shade and protection from rain, open brickwork of the walls offering shade and ventilation, and roofs raised above the buildings and volumes raised above the ground to secure airflow.

In the design process, climate was abstracted into an operative model by means of a section that isolated particular factors (daylight, glare, rain, ventilation) and reassembled them into a single drawing. This was consistent not only with the approach advocated in *Tropical Architecture* but also, more generally, with the privileging of the section in the management of the climatic conditions in postwar architectural culture.[250] The section was the main design tool for all buildings of ITF. The designers of the round entrance pavilion conceived it by rotating the section around its central symmetry axis, and in Pavilion A, the section was projected on the façade, which, in this way, was turned into a pedagogical diagram demonstrating the principles of rainwater disposal, ventilation of the building, control of glare, and access of sunlight (figures 2.54 and 2.55).[251] It was this very same approach of designing a building by means of a section that had won one

A GLOBAL DEVELOPMENT PATH

of the second prizes for the team of Polish architects (to which Chyrosz belonged) in a competition for the culture center in Leopoldville, today Kinshasa in the Democratic Republic of Congo (1959). This success opened doors to Ghana for the first group of Polish architects, allowing them to demonstrate a previous engagement in sub-Saharan Africa.[252]

Drew and Fry's second postulate, of using local materials and technologies, was a challenge with which they and other "tropical" architects working in West Africa struggled. As had been the case with such prominent buildings in Accra as the National Museum and the National Archives, the main materials of ITF were reinforced concrete and cement blocks, steel construction for roofs, and aluminum covering (figure 2.56). All those materials, including louver windows, another emblematic detail of tropical architecture, were imported in early 1960s Ghana, since the Ghanaian building-materials industry was only slowly taking off. However, several temporary ITF buildings were constructed by GNCC from local materials, including the Cocoa Industry Pavilion, designed by Jan Laube, and the Timber Industry Pavilion by Chyrosz and Rymaszewski, which in their words was "truly African architecture" (figure 2.57).[253] The Timber Industry Pavilion was a hanging structure of plywood shades supported by mahogany pillars. The plywood was produced in Ghana from local hardwood and tested for resilience to the West African climate and insects.[254] More generally, during the construction of ITF, GNCC (which had been restructured after the coup) was assisted by local contractors, including other state firms and private ones comprising both international firms with representatives in Accra and local contractors operated by expatriates or Ghanaians.[255] Last, Drew and Fry's third recommendation, that of accounting for people's needs and aspirations, when applied to ITF, displayed the challenge addressed by *Tropical Architecture*: the imperative to respond to needs of a rapidly modernizing population from within this modernization process, which included the modernization of those very needs.[256]

2.58. International Trade Fair, Accra, 1962–67, Pavilion A. GNCC, Vic Adegbite (chief architect), Jacek Chyrosz, Stanisław Rymaszewski (project architects).

In other words, ITF subscribed to principles of tropical architecture to no less of an extent than its own most visible examples in Accra and encountered the same challenges that "tropical" architects faced in their work. ITF's affiliation with tropical architecture was emphasized in retrospect by its designers and was conveyed by photographs taken by Chyrosz shortly before the trade fair's opening. These showed the rhythmic patterning of varying surfaces, slender pillars on contrasting backgrounds, and deep shadows emphasizing the volumes. In another photo taken by Chyrosz, a low viewpoint makes a railing appear as a colonnade, almost as monumental as schools by Fry and Drew shown in black-and-white photographs in a 1955 issue of *Architectural Design* (figure 2.58).[257]

This aspiration of Polish architects to participate in an international community adapting the principles of modern architecture to tropical conditions was supported by publications that began to appear in Poland in the early 1960s. For example, papers published by Maciej Ziółek, a scholar from Warsaw's Institute of Building Technology, gathered basic information about climatic factors a designer needed to take into account, and their influence on detailing and materials.[258] Ziółek, writing in 1968 about demand for this knowledge "in view of the recent rise" of interest in the export of construction materials, design, and construction services from Poland, referred to the work of countries and institutions that "had a long experience and major achievements in construction in tropical climates."[259] Among such institutions, he listed the Tropical Building Section of the Building Research Station in Watford (UK) and the Department of Tropical Architecture at the Architectural Association in London, as well as the Centre Scientifique et Technique du Bâtiment in Paris, the School of Research and Training in Earthquake Engineering in Roorkee (India), and other institutions in the United States, the USSR, Japan, the Netherlands, Belgium, Australia, Israel, and South Africa, along with Ghana and Nigeria.[260]

Guidelines issued by these institutions were included in the bibliography of Polish, Soviet, and other Eastern European authors writing about construction in tropical climates. In these publications, examples of architectural and urban layouts, as well as materials and details (such as shading devices and roof sections), were based on solutions published by Western authors circulating in the networks of tropical architecture, including George A. Atkinson, Jeffrey Aronin, Drew and Fry, Danby, and the Olgyay brothers.[261] In contrast to accounts in the Polish daily press about the foreign work of Polish architects, professional publications in Poland rarely elaborated on ideological or geopolitical questions. Such topics were listed in the curriculum of a one-year course offered to experts recruited by Polservice and organized by the Center for African Studies at the University of Warsaw (established in 1962). However, they did not play a major role in the curriculum either, which focused instead on surveys of African countries, language courses (English, French, and basic Arabic, Hausa, Swahili), and practical advice (medical and legal).[262]

While Western literature on building in hot climates was well known and referred to by Eastern European authors, there was hardly any reverse flow of knowledge. In particular, the International Trade Fair was absent from publications that sustained the discourse of tropical architecture, despite the fact that the ITF architecture subscribed to principles spelled out by Drew and Fry, and shared with tropical architects in Accra materials, contractors, modes of representation, and architectural precedence. Particularly striking is the absence of any presentation of ITF's architecture in the journal *West African Builder and Architect*, which featured prominent buildings in Ghana and Nigeria associated with tropical architecture during the 1960s, and which became a major vehicle for the promotion of the designers of those buildings. This absence cannot be explained by a lack of awareness about ITF on the part of the editors of the journal, given that images of the trade fair's entrance pavilion appear in an advertisement for Naco louver-window systems that ran in two issues.[263] Furthermore, short notes about ITF were included in the "Developments in Ghana" section, which registered economic, technological, and industrial news relevant for architects practicing in the country.[264] Nor was it likely that the journal's editors deemed the trade fair in Accra not significant enough to feature on their pages, as ITF was among the most visible projects of the decade in West Africa, appearing on the covers of magazines in Ghana.[265]

The main reason for the omission was the fact that *West African Builder and Architect* was invested in the interests of British architects in West Africa. Edited by Anthony Halliday, who worked for Drew and Fry, the journal featured architects who were members of the Royal Institute of British Architects (RIBA).[266] This was the very group whose economic interests had been undermined by GNCC, which was increasingly taking over control of the entire building process, from design to construction. With GNCC's withdrawal from commissioning architectural designs to individual architects, those architects had to rely on commercial investors, who were under threat by Nkrumah's nationalization policy.[267] The competition between GNCC and other architects in Accra sometimes took direct forms—for example, Nkrumah invited both Kenneth Scott and Witold Wojczyński of GNCC to submit designs for his private theater.[268] At an institutional level, the competition between these two groups was reflected in the existence of two professional organizations of architects in the first half of the 1960s: the Gold Coast Society of Architects, founded during the colonial period (1954), and the Ghana Institute of Architects, founded in 1962. Most architects from socialist countries working for GNCC were members of the latter, including Chyrosz and Rymaszewski.[269]

Yet on the pages of *West African Builder and Architect*, this economic rivalry between RIBA architects and those of GNCC was translated into what Carl Pletsch called the "Cold War division of social-scientific labor." In Western discourse, the Cold War appeared as a mode of production of knowledge in which cultural works were assumed to be produced only by the "First," "democratic," and "free" world; in contrast, the "Second" socialist world could, at best, produce industrial and engineering works.[270] Within Western Cold War discourse, labor under socialism appeared as "nonfree," forced labor; hence, it could not produce cultural objects, which require, according to this discourse, the work of free, creative, and spontaneous subjects.[271]

In other words, architects from socialist countries in 1960s Ghana perceived themselves as members of one world of international architectural culture, along with professionals from Britain and the West. But in fact, the worlds these professionals belonged to were not exactly the same, and transfers between these worlds were subject to gatekeeping procedures. In reports in the Ghanaian press about socialist countries, their technical prowess and their cultural achievements were presented in tandem. In contrast, the condition of visibility within Western discourse of a cultural object from a socialist country—and its condition of entry into the market of intellectual labor controlled by Western institutions—was its translation into a technical object, deprived of cultural capital. This devalorization procedure was conveyed by Drew and Fry, who in *Tropical Architecture* compared the massive change under way in the "tropical zone" to changes in the USSR, but noted that the latter were operating under "coercion" and for that reason were of lesser value.[272] That such a devalorization procedure stemming from the Cold War division of social-scientific labor permeated *West African Builder and Architect* was manifested in the ways in which ITF was accounted for in the "Developments in Ghana" section. In those notes, ITF was discussed as an infrastructural undertaking and as an engineering project, with text suggesting that GNCC was the contractor rather than the planning office. The designers of the buildings were not mentioned, and neither drawings nor photographs were published.[273]

Bulgarian, Hungarian, Polish, and Yugoslav architects at GNCC would have strongly objected to the description of their work for the corporation as "nonfree." While many of them were dissatisfied with constraints imposed on their work under socialism, they perceived their employment at GNCC as an alternative to their work back home, not as its extension. This perception came to the fore in the conflicts between Polish architects and Polservice, which had difficulties in disciplining the architects to pay the obligatory monthly fee to the FTO. Polish architects also seemed to have shared with some of their Ghanaian colleagues the skepticism about the requirements of discipline and sacrifice that characterized the discourse on socialist labor both by the CPP and by Poland's communist party.[274] In response, representatives of Polservice in Warsaw reminded Polish specialists that they were not dispatched to Ghana as "economic migrants" and appealed to their sense of duty as well as to the legal obligations stipulated in their contracts with the FTO.[275] However, when in Accra, many functionaries of the regime presented themselves as pragmatic: Rymaszewski recalled that the Polish trade counselor "told us on our arrival in Accra that they didn't need people for slogans but people who could get things done."[276] This was a prevailing approach: although Polservice did take political views into account in recruiting for contracts abroad, professional experience and knowledge of English were more important criteria and could trump political disloyalties toward the regime—in particular since Ghanaians participated in the last round of recruiting interviews in Warsaw. Few architects from Poland and Hungary working in Ghana were card-carrying members of the communist party in their respective countries; neither Chyrosz, Rymaszewski, nor Polónyi were party members.

In their recollections, Hungarian, Polish, and Yugoslav architects described their motivation to leave for West Africa as multifaceted, but rarely stemming from political convictions. Architects who applied for positions in Ghana were driven by professional ambition, including the possibility of realizing design work and of leading large projects, such as the International Trade Fair. A rare opportunity to travel and to leave behind the austerity of war-damaged socialist Europe was another reason to go. Grażyna Jonkajtys-Luba recalled that she arrived from Warsaw to Accra with her husband, architect Jerzy Luba, leaving behind multiple jobs at various planning offices, hours of commuting, and an apartment shared with other families. Upon their arrival in Ghana, the Lubas discovered a spacious villa, lavish beaches, car trips across the country, and parties with colleagues at GNCC ("My Ghanaian boss, Vic Adegbite, taught me how to dance the twist," recalled Rymaszewski).[277] By contrast, Hungarians, Poles, and Yugoslavs often perceived Soviet technicians as isolated from Ghanaians, not least because of their limited knowledge of English.[278]

In general, Eastern European architects hired by GNCC engaged in a delicate balancing act between the necessity of maintaining links with state institutions at home and the strategic loosening of those links. While FTOs responsible for the export of labor to Ghana, including Polservice and Tesco, encouraged contracted architects to facilitate new commissions for Polish and Hungarian companies, those architects did not always follow these instructions and sometimes advised against the purchase of Eastern European machinery.[279] More often than not, they were skeptical about their professional prospects on returning to Europe and were invested, rather, into networking in Ghana. For Rymaszewski, that strategy paid off: after returning to Poland in 1967, he traveled two years later to Ghana to work on the second edition of ITF (1971). That contract was signed against the recommendation of Polservice, but at the explicit wish of Ghanaian authorities.[280] In this way, Rymaszewski was able to bypass restrictions of Polservice contracts, which typically limited stays abroad of experts to three years. After that period, they were obliged to work in Poland for the same amount of time before being eligible to apply for another contract abroad.[281] The maximum span of such contracts and other regulations (including restrictions on traveling with family members) differed from country to country, with Yugoslavia being the most liberal, followed by Hungary and Poland, and with East Germany and the USSR being most restrictive.

The work of GNCC architects from socialist countries was hardly "non-free" in any meaningful sense. Nevertheless, their conditions of labor were distinct from those of other foreign architects in Ghana. The recruiting, remuneration, taxation, division, and specialization of architectural labor in contracts abroad were conditioned according to the organization of such labor in the socialist country concerned, and by principles of socialist foreign trade, starting with the state monopoly on this trade, that was exercised by FTOs. This conditioning applied to both types of architectural labor discussed in this chapter: the work of architects employed by a socialist design institute charged with projects abroad, such as the Soviet Union's Giprogor, and the work of architects directly hired by a foreign institution, such as GNCC. As I will show in the following chapters, the political economy of state socialism continued in the years to come to define the work abroad of architects from socialist countries. It distinguished their work from that of other actors until the final decade of the Cold War, thus long after the vision of the socialist path of development ceased to be the driving force for the mobility of architecture from Eastern Europe.

CONCLUSION: SOCIALIST WORLDMAKING AND ITS ARCHITECTURE

Contemporaneous Western authors commenting on "Soviet bloc" engagement in West Africa in the 1960s pointed out that the region's geopolitical significance hardly warranted the scale of investment by socialist countries in Ghana, Guinea, and Mali.[282] However, the work of Eastern European architects in West Africa showed that the relevance of this region in Soviet policy stemmed from its role as a site where the applicability of the socialist path of social and economic development was tested as a global project. Blueprints of districts in Accra and Tema testified that this adaptation aimed both at a new type of daily life and at a radical transformation of the construction industry in Ghana. While those projects remained unrealized, the work of their designers was not lost, as it informed future Soviet engagements in Africa, Asia, and Latin America.[283] Like earlier in Ghana, these engagements were defined by the concerns to implement Soviet typologies and technologies in a way that facilitated the general economic development of the countries in question, adapted them to the local climatic, social, and technological conditions, and involved local decision makers and professionals in the planning and the construction process. While the organization of design labor in Ghanaian, Guinean, and Malian projects was advanced in subsequent Soviet engagements abroad, the dynamics specific for gift economies never ceased to reverberate in these engagements, as I will argue in chapter 4. That continuity persisted despite the shift in Brezhnev's African policy, which was geared either toward economic agreements that directly benefited the USSR or toward military aid provided to Soviet allies and resistance movements.

Countries allied to the Soviet Union, however, were neither the sole nor the dominant destinations for architects, planners, and construction companies from socialist countries in Africa and Asia. Most prominent among those destinations were countries whose governments negotiated their positions across Cold War rivalries, rather than siding with one hegemonic bloc or the other, even when they were often nominally socialist or ruled by socialist parties. These included Syria under Hafez al-Assad (after 1971); Iraq after the Abd al-Karim Qasim coup d'état in 1958, then under the Baath Party and Saddam Hussein; Afghanistan between 1953 and 1973, when the Afghan government accepted assistance from both sides of the Iron Curtain; Algeria under the Boumédienne regime (1965–78); and Libya under Muammar Gaddafi (after 1969). By the 1970s, this list was extended by several states with elites openly hostile to socialism, such as Nigeria, the United Arab Emirates, and Kuwait. Employed by state offices and private firms in those countries, architects from socialist Europe worked in competition and at times in cooperation with architects from the West and those in service with international organizations, along with architects from regional networks and local professionals and administrators.

In this sense, their work continued to contribute to the worldmaking of architecture discussed in this chapter: an architectural production that drew on competing practices of global cooperation. These dynamics characterized the production of GNCC in Ghana, which resulted in material structures, industrial assembly lines, and infrastructural networks, but also—as reviews in the Ghanaian press showed—in images and narratives that conveyed a sense of anticipation, elation, and direction during the country's first years after independence. The fact that this production was based on resources appropriated from antagonistic networks did not make those antagonisms disappear but, rather, rendered them subject to negotiations the outcomes of which were unpredictable, as the contrasting fates of Soviet districts and ITF in Accra have shown.

What did not disappear, in particular, were differences in political economy, which informed the mobility of architects circulating in these competing networks and facilitated their conditions of labor. As this chapter indicated, and as the following chapters will show, these differences could translate into constraints, which professionals from socialist countries and their local counterparts strived to avoid, or into opportunities, which they exploited. Whether a hindrance or a competitive advantage, such differences were at the core of the worldmaking of architecture this book describes.

3.1. National Arts Theater, Lagos, 1972–77. Technoexportstroy (Bulgaria); Stefan Kolchev and the Regional Planning Office of the City of Varna (Bulgaria); Building Research Institute (Bulgaria).

Chapter 3
Worlding Eastern Europe
Lagos, 1966–79

In Lagos, architecture is likely to be overlooked. Buildings hardly differentiate a landscape defined by topography and infrastructure—unless topography and infrastructure make them stand out. That is the case with the National Arts Theater: those arriving onto Lagos Island by the Third Mainland Bridge cannot miss the oval building emerging above the lagoon as a vortex for people, vehicles, and everything else that circulates in Nigeria's economic center and Africa's largest metropolis (figure 3.1). This prominent location was the starting point for the theater's design, delivered by Bulgarian architect Stefan Kolchev and his team from the Regional Planning Office of the city of Varna and the Building Research Institute from Sofia.[1] Based on Kolchev's earlier blueprint for the Palace of Culture and Sports in Varna, which the Nigerian delegation visited in 1972 and accepted as the "prototype" for the new National Theater, the team designed a sequential experience of the building: from a concrete volume recognizable from afar, through the round base open to gardens around the complex, to its opulent interiors in marble, aluminum, colored class, ceramic, and wood, decorated with artworks by Nigerian artist Erhabor Emokpae (figures 3.2, 3.3, and 3.4).[2]

The National Arts Theater was constructed in 1977 by Bulgarian state firm Technoexportstroy (TES) as the main venue for FESTAC '77, the Second

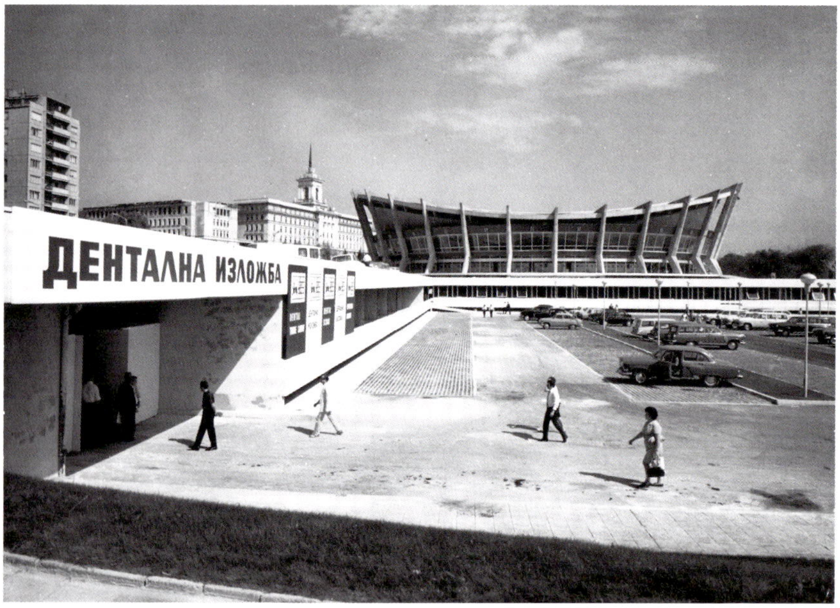
ДЕНТАЛНА ИЗЛОЖБА

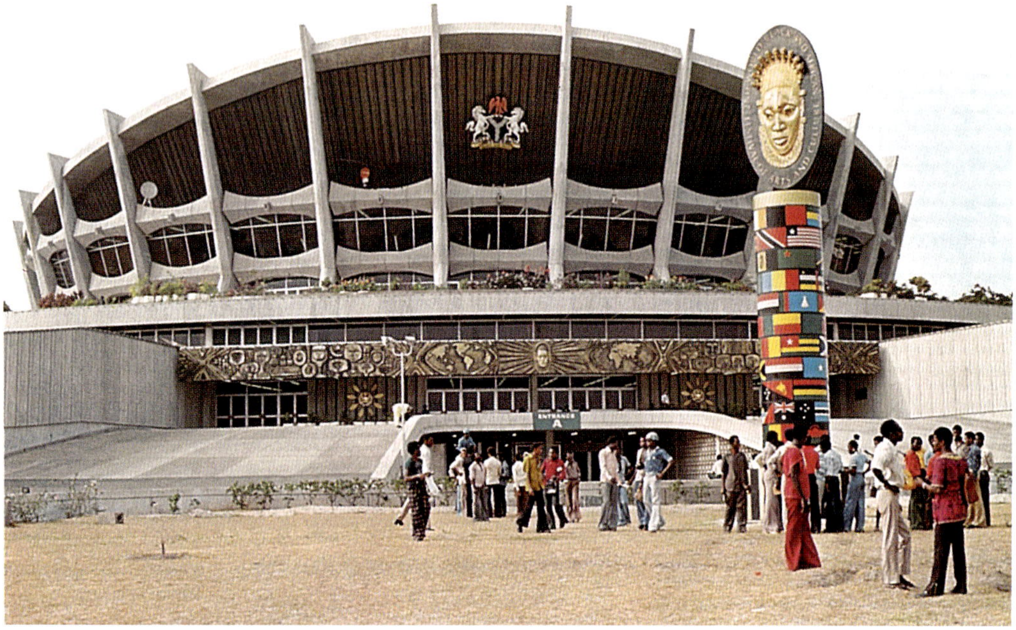

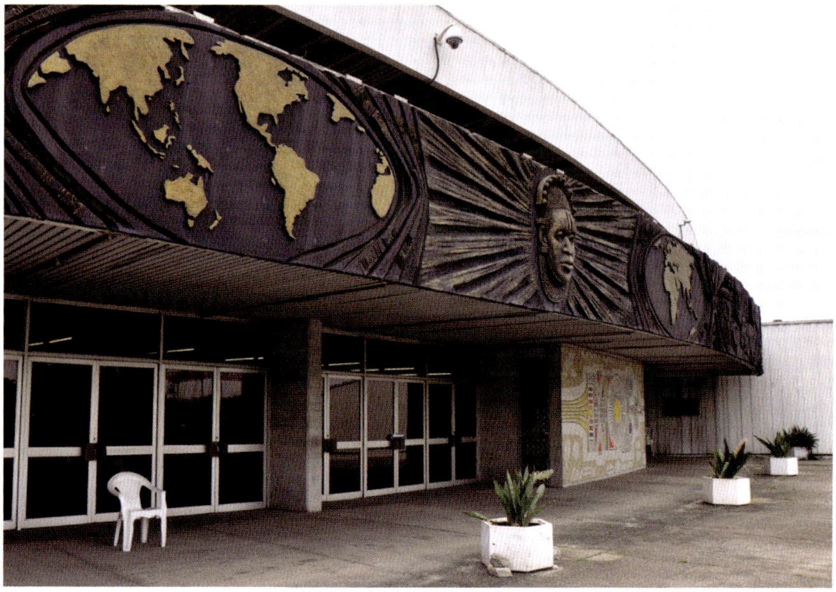

< 3.2. Palace of Culture and Sports, Varna (Bulgaria), 1968. Stefan Kolchev.

< 3.3. National Arts Theater in Lagos during FESTAC, 1977. Technoexportstroy (Bulgaria); Stefan Kolchev and the Regional Planning Office of the City of Varna (Bulgaria); Building Research Institute (Bulgaria); artworks by Erhabor Emokpae. "Festac '77," *New Directions* (April 1977): 8.

< 3.4. National Arts Theater, Lagos, 1972–77, entrance area. Technoexportstroy (Bulgaria); Stefan Kolchev and the Regional Planning Office of the City of Varna (Bulgaria); Building Research Institute (Bulgaria); artworks by Erhabor Emokpae.

World Festival of Black and African Culture. It was the center of an entire set of buildings designed and built for FESTAC, numerous of them by companies from socialist Europe. Along with the theater, TES was responsible for the construction of the Eko Hotel on Victoria Island, and for the design and construction of a hotel and race course in Kaduna in northern Nigeria, followed by the sports grounds in Ilorin (1979).[3] Energoprojekt of Yugoslavia was in charge of the International Trade Fair (ITF) in Lagos, and Romania's Romconsult and Design Institute for Housing and Urban Technical and Social Infrastructure designed housing and social facilities in Festac Town, the accommodations site for artists and visitors master-planned by Doxiadis Associates.[4]

For companies from socialist countries, Lagos in the 1970s was a very different environment from that of Ghana during the Nkrumah era a decade before, where many of their architects had gained first experiences in West Africa. Instead of encountering post-independence enthusiasm, their arrivals in Nigeria coincided with the end of a violent civil war between the central government and the eastern region, the secessionist state of Biafra (1967–70). The end of that war was followed by the oil boom. The fourfold leap in the world-market price of crude oil in 1973 permitted the funding of the ambitious Third National Development Plan (1975–80). The plan included modernization of the rural sector, the overhaul of education and healthcare, construction of new traffic and telecommunication infrastructure, and investments into parastatal industrial production. FESTAC was the high point of this effort, testifying as much to Nigeria's preponderance in Africa as to the extravagance of a rentier state ruled by bureaucrats and politicians living off the licenses and royalties from foreign corporations.[5]

Unlike Nkrumah and his collaborators in Ghana, Nigeria's political class felt no affinity with socialism. After the country's independence in 1960, Nigeria's governments neither sought nor accepted aid offered by the Eastern bloc within Khrushchev's opening toward West Africa, and the socialist countries' diplomatic presence was restricted. Though Nigeria joined the Non-Aligned Movement (NAM), it became one of the least active members. This attitude continued when the First Republic was ended by a military coup and General Yakubu Gowon became the head of state (1966–75). Diplomatic relations with socialist countries improved during the civil war, when the Soviets and several of their allies sent aircraft and advisers to assist the federal government, in contrast to the West's reluctance to do so. However, Soviet materiel was paid for in hard currency and, occasionally, by barter; hence the Gowon government insisted on the economic character of these exchanges, an approach that continued under the regimes of Murtala Muhammed (1975–76) and Olusegun Obasanjo (1976–79).[6] In the aftermath of the civil war, socialist countries continued to support Nigeria's demand for Africa's political independence and for more favorable trade terms for non-industrialized countries, as demanded by the UN Conference on Trade and Development (UNCTAD).[7] In turn, Nigeria's government encouraged state firms from Eastern Europe to operate on its market and to benefit from the oil boom, and thus to offset the dominance of Western firms.[8]

The presence in Nigeria of TES and other companies from socialist countries came about due to this set of political and economic considerations. However, this chapter is less concerned with intergovernmental agreements and focuses more on individual encounters between Eastern European architects and planners and their Nigerian counterparts. These encounters did not always observe diplomatic protocols, as Charles (Károly) Polónyi remembered from the eastern Nigerian city of Calabar. In his memoirs, the Hungarian architect recalled that after his presentation of the master plan of Calabar (1969), he was confronted by a Nigerian journalist: "You are communists, we are not. Will you propose the nationalization of private property?"[9] (figure 3.5). In contrast to the developmentalist fantasy of free-floating, perfectly mobile technological expertise, the audience in Calabar was aware that besides machinery and materials, Eastern European companies brought with them institutional frameworks and convictions about how things should be done. Anxious that Hungarian planners would impose solutions foreign to West Africa, some in Calabar wondered how people belonging to a different world entirely, a socialist world, would know what to do in Nigeria, and how to do it.

To the Calabar audience, community and competence appeared connected. That link resurfaced in another question at the conference, as Polónyi recalled: "'You are Hungarians. You never had colonies. You don't have any tropical experience. Do you consider yourselves competent to prepare a master plan for a city in West Africa?'"[10] This question conveyed the double bind of a postcolonial condition, where the condemnation of British colonial exploitation, held responsible for many of Nigeria's predicaments, went hand in hand with the recognition that tapping into the expertise of the former colonial metropolis might be necessary to overcome those very predicaments. The arrival of Eastern Europeans added a new variable to these postcolonial dynamics, for until the end of World War II and decolonization, few Eastern Europeans who were not scholars or missionaries had visited West Africa.[11] Yet while the Ghanaian press under Nkrumah looked at this absence from Africa with a sympathy toward nations not implicated in colonial exploitation, to many in Nigeria during the following decade, that absence testified to a lack of expertise about the region.

Questions about Eastern European competence to work in West Africa, such as those posed to Polónyi in Calabar, were posed many times to other architects and planners from socialist countries. This chapter is an extended response to these questions. In what follows, I will argue that the protagonists of this chapter embraced the connection between community and competence, and claimed that Eastern Europeans and West Africans indeed inhabited the same world. This world was not, evidently, one that followed the socialist development path, but it was a larger one. It was the world of those striving to overcome the triple predicament of underdevelopment, colonization, and peripherality.

Eastern European architects and planners, on their arrival in newly independent countries in Africa and Asia, realized that these countries shared many economic, social, and cultural predicaments specific to Eastern Europe since the nineteenth century. Polónyi and others sensed that those commonalities stemmed from shared historical experiences, and speculated that colonial occupations in Ghana and Nigeria had similar consequences to occupations of Eastern European territories by neighboring empires during the long nineteenth century: Prussian and Habsburg

3.5. Charles Polónyi and Udoakaha Jacob Esuene, the Military Governor of the South-Eastern State of Nigeria, Calabar, 1969.

from the west, and tsarist and Ottoman from the east. Eastern Europeans emancipated themselves at the end of World War I and, like African societies would half a century later, they then faced the challenges of transforming economies, largely underdeveloped and mainly rural, and cultures, systematically devalorized by Western European epistemologies that divided the world into modern and traditional, civilized and barbaric, central and peripheral. The response offered by postwar socialist modernization to those predicaments was just the most recent addition in a longer effort to address them, an effort to which the region's architects and planners had contributed since the mid-nineteenth century.

In other words, while Polónyi and others from Eastern Europe traveled to West Africa within state-socialist networks, once on site they practiced worldmaking based on a recognition of commonalities that transgressed the official boundaries of socialist internationalism and exceeded the dichotomies of the Cold War. Eastern European architects recognized these commonalities as opportunities to put into practice their disciplinary and professional culture in order to formulate situated responses to West African challenges of modernization. This extension of the historical Eastern European experience beyond the region, however riddled with blind spots, is what I will call in this chapter the "worlding of Eastern Europe," in reference to studies on the "worlding" of African and Asian cities.[12] In recent years, this concept has been given multiple meanings in the analysis of urban transformations in the Global South since the end of the twentieth century. For example, in her analysis of Asian cities Aihwa Ong understood worlding as practices that instantiate visions of the world in formation that are irreducible to a singular logics of urban change, and that destabilize established criteria and standards of global urban modernity.[13] In turn, AbdouMaliq Simone described a "worlding from below" in Southern cities as practices of people "'cast out' into the world," and studied the ways in which Africans at the outset of the twenty-first century deployed the city as a resource for operating at the world level.[14] Building upon the latter study, in what follows I understand the worlding of Eastern Europe as a practice of small groups and individuals from the region who found themselves in Lagos, Calabar, Jos, Zaria, and other Nigerian cities and tried to make sense of these unfamiliar locations by forging alliances and developing sensibilities that connected these places and people with where they came from. In so doing, they extrapolated the validity of Eastern European architectural culture toward the entire ("Third") world, often in a speculative and experimental manner.

In their work in Nigeria, Polónyi and his colleagues drew on specific concepts and tools that Eastern European architecture and planning had formulated in response to conditions of underdevelopment, colonization, and peripherality. Such concepts and tools had been accumulated since the nineteenth century, had been advanced in the interwar period, often in the framework of international organizations such as the International Congresses of Modern Architecture (CIAM), and were incorporated into programs of state-led modernization after World War II. The planning instruments, institutional frameworks, survey techniques, and ideas about an architect's social and political responsibilities, developed within this long tradition, were employed, adapted, and sometimes challenged in 1970s Nigeria. At the same time, this chapter will emphasize limits to analogies between Eastern Europe and West Africa, and point out that during their travels to Africa, some of the protagonists were confronted with ambiguities in the historical past that they claimed to share with Africans. In this sense, the worlding of Eastern Europe did not simply mean an extension of Eastern European experience toward Africa; at times, it also meant an African perspective on Eastern Europe.

I will begin with Polónyi's responses to the questions posed to him in Calabar. In particular, I will show how his work on the city's master plan had been prepared by his earlier projects. They included contributions to regional planning of rural, underdeveloped areas of postwar Hungary, then advanced by Polónyi's work in Ghana. Second, I will focus on the survey of vernacular architecture in Nigeria by Polish architect and scholar Zbigniew Dmochowski, who launched this survey as an explicit attempt to undo the devalorization of indigenous Nigerian cultures as a result of colonial rule. In so doing, he and other Eastern Europeans were instrumental in the decolonization of institutions of architecture in Nigeria. In the third part of this chapter, I will return to the landscape of FESTAC and show how the peripheral position vis-à-vis dominant centers of knowledge production, which Polónyi, Dmochowski, and others saw as a predicament common to Eastern Europe and West Africa, was turned into a technique of assessing, comparing, and combining resources from various centers. This procedure will be studied by focusing on the legal entity of a joint venture established by Yugoslav company Energoprojekt and the Nigerian government, which was instrumental in the construction of the International Trade Fair and other buildings in Lagos.

CHARLES POLÓNYI AND THE WORLDING OF THE HUNGARIAN VILLAGE

"I had not made a big mistake when I compared a Hungarian village or an agrarian town with those of the Gold Coast," Charles Polónyi stated in his memoir *An Architect-Planner on the Peripheries* (1992).[15] While his supervisors in Budapest sometimes ridiculed such comparison, he maintained that his work in the late 1950s rural Hungary, parts of which were "still not very far from…a developing country," had prepared him for West Africa.[16] This included his work as architect and planner in Accra and as educator at the School of Architecture, Town Planning, and Building at the University of Science and Technology (UST) in Kumasi.

During the Calabar conference, it was to that earlier work in Nkrumah's Ghana that Polónyi referred in order to refute the suggestion that he lacked "tropical experience." At the same time, he carefully avoided any reference to the socialist modernization pursued by Nkrumah, or to Cold War geopolitics from which the Hungarian presence in Ghana stemmed. Following his long-held view that "technological and economic necessities are stronger than ideology," Polónyi rejected the association between planning approaches and political positions.[17] Representatives of the Nigerian government concurred, and their presentation of the Calabar plan omitted any references to socialism. Instead, they described members of Polónyi's team as "heirs to a long tradition of town planning in Austria & Hungary," with Hungary being "one of the first countries in Europe to develop Town Planning about a century ago."[18]

Polónyi responded along similar lines at the Calabar conference when queried about his "communist" proclivities toward the nationalization of private property. Never a member of the Hungarian communist party, he was motivated to leave for West Africa in part because of his unease with politics and policies in early 1960s Hungary. Accordingly, during the press conference he pointed out that public ownership of land was not restricted to socialism, and did not necessarily involve large-scale nationalization of land property. Rather, it had been promoted within the European planning tradition from Ebenezer Howard at the turn of the century to CIAM in the prewar period.[19] It was within this tradition that Polónyi situated Eastern European architectural culture, and he considered that its specific contributions were strategies of tackling rural underdevelopment. He argued that such responses, or "the lessons of the village" in the expression of architectural historian Ákos Moravánszky, lend themselves to be extended toward West Africa, and presented his work as a case in point.[20]

Global Backwardness

Polónyi's argument echoed the work of Eastern European economic historians, economists, and planners who, since the late-nineteenth century, had conceived of the region as a testing ground for the study of backwardness, and constructed strategies for overcoming it. That work accelerated during the interwar period and, in particular, during World War II in preparation for postwar reconstruction, first in Europe and then on the global scale. In the words of Ignacy Sachs, Polish economist and advisor to Nkrumah: since "Eastern and southern Europe were part of the capitalist periphery…the challenges they encountered in the 1930s were very similar to those faced by the developing countries after the war: land reforms that were too timid, excess of rural population, unfavorable terms of trade between agricultural and industrial goods, mass urban unemployment as a consequence of the 1929 crisis, need for a more active state support for the incipient industrialization, and difficult relations with foreign capital."[21]

During World War II, plans for postwar reorganization of Eastern Europe were drafted by émigrés from the region working in British institutions, including Paul Rosenstein-Rodan (born in Kraków and educated in Vienna) at the Royal Institute of International Affairs in London, and Michał Kalecki (born in Łódź and educated in Warsaw and Gdańsk) at the Oxford Statistical Institute.[22] In their work, "the countries between Russia, Germany, and Italy," dominated by extensive rural economies with poor, underemployed, or unemployed populations, were constructed as a scientific model of global backwardness, characterized by specific economies, specific responses to crises, and specific positions in the international division of labor. The construction of such a model was made possible by statistical data about economy and population gathered and published before World War I. Scholars had continued to collect that data in newly independent countries in the region during the interwar period, when such statistics were made available to international organizations for comparison.[23]

Based on this data, economists from Eastern Europe began to envisage scenarios of tackling backwardness, including the proposal by Rosenstein-Rodan of a "big push" in favor of reconstruction based on planned, large-scale, state-directed industrialization with stress put on the development of infrastructure and education.[24] During and after World War II, this proposal was translated into development plans for postcolonial and underdeveloped countries, including Ghana, mediated by the first generation of UN officials and consultants of the World Bank, among them Kalecki and Rosenstein-Rodan.[25] Upon their returns to Warsaw in the mid-1950s, Kalecki, Sachs, and other like-minded, left-leaning, but not always communist economists contributed to research programs and institutions specifically focused on "less developed" countries. Among these was Kalecki's graduate seminar on the topic (established in 1958), where participants and invited speakers, many from developing countries, discussed reports from the field, analyzed actual plans, and played Kalecki's "planning games," such as a draft plan for "Cocoaland" that built on experience gained in Ghana by Polish planners. Other Warsaw institutions included the Research Center of the Economy of Less-Developed Countries established in 1961, and the UN-funded Higher Course in National Economic Planning for Economists from Less-Developed Countries. Scholars attached to those institutions often became economic advisors to the governments of Ghana, India, Cuba, Mongolia, and elsewhere.[26]

The same data that became the basis for economic models of backwardness in interwar Eastern Europe was used by architects from the region to address backwardness by means of architecture and spatial planning. A key platform for these debates was CIAM, the organization that pioneered the use of statistical data and its visualization in comparative urban analysis. CIAM members from Czechoslovakia, Hungary, and Poland were among the first to extend the organization's debates to underdeveloped rural areas in their respective countries, and to rethink architects' tasks with regard to the countryside in view of technological, political, and economic changes of the modern world. The Functional Warsaw plan (1934) by Szymon Syrkus and Jan Chmielewski is a case in point. Based on data provided by Warsaw's Office for the Regional Plan, their plan encompassed rural areas, extending urban planning toward regional planning.[27] It was presented in Zurich and in London during the meeting of the CIAM executive committee (1934), and impacted CIAM's stance on regional planning in the following years. It led to the emphasis on the interaction between town, region, and country during the organization's fifth conference (1937), where Syrkus presented a paper on rural areas and discussed questions of "rural urbanization" with representatives from Hungary, France, and Italy.[28]

Recognition of the specificity of architectural and planning practice in Eastern Europe led to the creation of the short-lived regional group CIAM-East by architects from Austria, Czechoslovakia, Hungary, Poland, and Yugoslavia. The development of backward rural areas was a central theme during the group's meetings in Budapest and in Brno and Zlín in Czechoslovakia (1937), and on the Greek island Mykonos (1938). Within CIAM-East, rural areas in Eastern Europe were analyzed both in their regional specificity and in relation to world economy, as proposed by Hungarian architect Farkas Molnár, who in 1936 envisaged a study "on a global scale" of countries bordering the Danube River.[29]

Both aspects of the Eastern European countryside came to the fore in the work of Hungarian architect and architectural historian Virgil Bierbauer: a protagonist of modern architecture in Hungary and editor of the Budapest-based modernist journal *Tér és Forma* (Space and Form). Bierbauer offered a new take on the debate about the village in Hungarian architectural culture, which had since the late nineteenth century revolved around questions of ornament, material, and national style.[30] In his report to CIAM (1937), Bierbauer urged rethinking the development of backward rural areas of Hungary, where the majority of the country's population lived, within the context of the global division of labor, hence in direct competition with mechanized agriculture in the Americas, as well as in the view of changing patterns of food consumption in Europe.[31] Ways out of this condition were hampered by unequal distribution of land in interwar Hungary, where a third of arable lands were controlled by large estates, the owners of which had a disproportionately large influence over governmental affairs. In contrast, a third of all peasants were either landless agricultural workers or smallholders who could not provide a decent living for their families solely from their meager landholdings. The lack of a paved road system and of storage facilities for perishable goods further prevented the modernization of agriculture and the improvement of living standards among the rural population.[32] The situation in neighboring countries was similar, and earlier statistical data showed that backward areas of the Habsburg Empire had been comparable in terms of productivity per capita and living standards to southern Italy, China, colonial India, and other parts of what after World War II was termed the "Third World."[33]

In the search for solutions, Bierbauer turned to historical patterns of Hungarian settlements, and in particular "agrarian towns": large, extended settlements that had emerged in Hungary after Turkish rule, such as the town of Kecskemét with an area of 93,000 hectares (double

3.6. Plan of the agricultural town of Hajdúböszörmény (Hungary), 1782.

the size of the Department of the Seine, as Bierbauer informed his francophone CIAM audience) (figure 3.6).[34] Agricultural towns consisted of a nucleus with industrial, commercial, and religious functions surrounded by belts devoted to residences and agricultural production.[35] Bierbauer saw such rural-urban settlements as the model to follow, including their socioeconomic organization into cooperatives that pooled resources and comanaged agricultural production and administration. As was the case with other members of the CIAM-East group, he turned to regional planning to plan the Hungarian village on multiple scales, starting with the settlement network in the region, through the design of service centers, complemented by housing, both individual and collective. These would be designed and built with the participation of the local cooperatives, their layouts adapting traditional means of construction to modern technology and the possibilities of mass prefabrication.[36] The interest in vernacular architecture as a resource of modernization was conveyed by two issues of *Tér és Forma* that Bierbauer devoted to vernacular architecture, and by his *History of Hungarian Architecture* (1937).[37]

The position of Bierbauer and the CIAM-East group was strongly opposed in interwar Hungary by a traditionalist group that drew entirely different lessons from the Hungarian village. They warned about the destruction of local identities by Western-style modernization and promoted the idea of a "Garden Hungary" as a middle land between an organic community and an industrial city.[38] While Polónyi had personal ties to architects in both groups, the extension of his work from postwar Hungary to independent Ghana and Nigeria was based on the worlding of the Hungarian village as proposed by Bierbauer's survey. In that survey, this village appeared as global, being both part of the global division of labor (closely dependent on technological shifts and food consumption patterns around the world), and part of the global geography of underdevelopment. The generalization toward the postcolonial world of this condition opened the way to the generalization of specific architectural and planning responses to it.

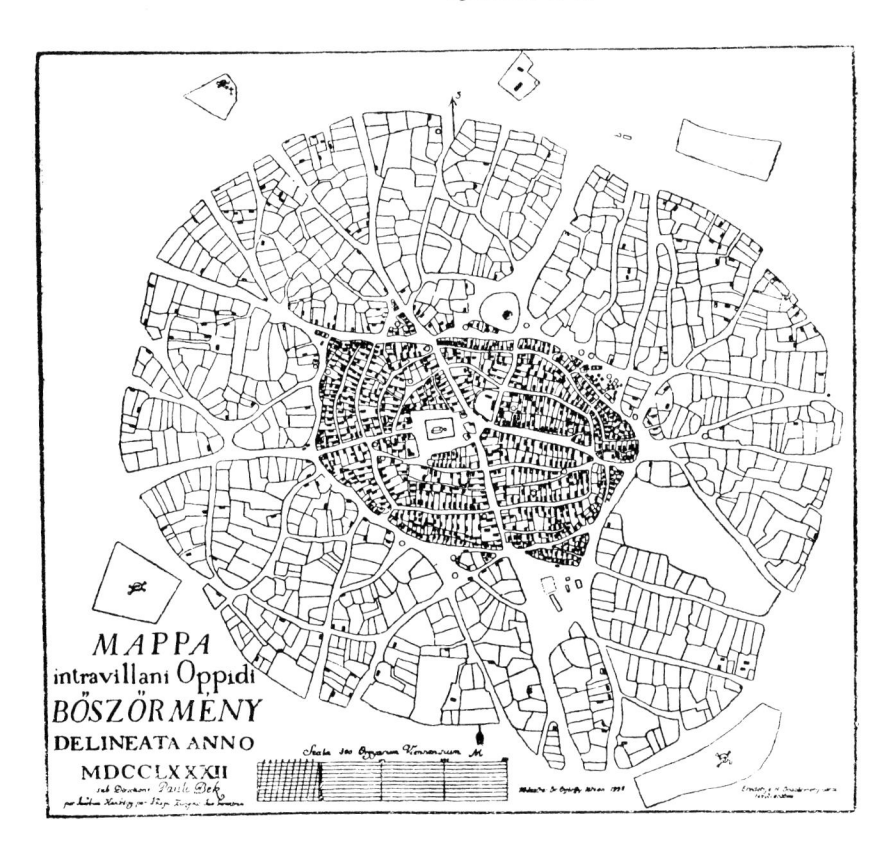

From Architecture to Regional Planning and Back

Based on prewar experiences and debates, including those within CIAM, regional planning became a central tool in postwar reconstruction and state-led development in socialist Eastern Europe, and was high on the list for technical know-how offered to developing countries since the 1950s. Within a broader argument that the Eastern European experience of overcoming backwardness was useful for developing countries, planners from the region spelled out advantages of Eastern European regional planning.[39]

In West Africa, that argument was made by Polish planner Wiktor Richert, who taught the Postgraduate Course in Regional Planning at UST in Kumasi together with Ghanaian sociologist and urban planner Austin Tetteh. Richert argued that "development experiences of countries which took this arduous road already"—such as Poland—were more relevant for Ghana than "ready-made patterns of developed countries, however modern and scientifically founded."[40] Major differences notwithstanding, parallels between Poland and Ghana straddled the creation of new statehood and the modernization of agriculture, industry, services, and infrastructure, Richert argued in his book *Regional Spatial Planning in Ghana* (1973).[41]

His argument was supported by Piotr Zaremba, planner and head of the International Postgraduate Course in Urban and Regional Planning for Developing Countries at the University of Technology in Szczecin, Poland (established in 1965). After visiting West African countries in the early 1960s, Zaremba wrote that newly independent countries have "no time to wait" and need to make investment decisions on multiple scales in a short period of time. Thus, instead of "old classical Town and Country Planning methods," such as elaborate surveys or master plans for selected cities, developing countries should make use of simplified town, regional, and national physical planning applied in the reconstruction of Poland after World War II.[42] Application of those procedures would allow, according to Zaremba, for a rapid conversion of rough surveys into strategic investment decisions, along with an integration of physical and economic planning, and simultaneous elaboration of local and regional plans.[43]

Several planning instruments advocated by Richert and Zaremba were grafted into Ghana's National Physical Development Plan (1965). This document translated into spatial terms the decisions of the Seven-Year Development Plan (1964), which had served as the blueprint for Ghana's economic and social reconstruction and development after independence (figure 3.7).[44] Prepared by the Town and Country Planning Division (TCPD) in Accra, headed by Ghanaian planner Peter Turkson, the declared objectives of the Physical Development Plan resembled those of postwar reconstruction in Eastern Europe, including increasing living standards, and diversifying the economy, its specialization, and integration into regional (West African) economic exchange.[45]

To achieve those goals, both plans turned to Polish postwar planning, which advocated the use of "perspective plans"—that is to say long-term economic plans, usually drafted for fifteen to twenty years to be in sync with urban planning.[46] This planning instrument was most likely introduced in Ghana by the Polish members of the physical-planning team at TCPD (economist B. S. Kwiatkowski and architects Zbigniew Filipow and Jerzy Luba), along with members of the National Planning Commission (economist Jan Drewnowski) and its advisors (economist Czesław Bobrowski, one of the conveyors of the Graduate Seminar on Less-Developed Countries in Warsaw).[47] Besides providing an outline for perspective planning in spatial terms, the most explicit impact of socialist planning ideas on the Physical Development Plan was its proposal to abandon the regional division of Ghana stemming from the colonial period and to redemarcate the country into "economically viable" regions, capable of specialization

3.7. "National Physical Development Plan for 1963–70. Infrastructure—Growth Areas to Be Created by Infrastructure." Ghana Town and Country Planning Division. *National Physical Development Plan, 1963–70* (Accra: State Publishing Corporation, 1965), fig. 7e.

and of a balanced distribution of infrastructure and social services. The inspiration for such redrawing of administrative regions was coming from socialist countries, where it "has become a common practice," argued the plan's authors.[48]

While the plan was suspended after the toppling of Nkrumah, controversies about regional planning continued in Ghana, and Richert criticized the country's return to short-term planning. Those plans, advocated by experts of the World Bank, were seen by Richert as conveying the interests of international capital.[49] He continued arguing for a radical transformation of Ghana's spatial structure beyond patterns inherited from the colonial period. Such radical change, he argued, was constitutive of the "planning imagination," and it defined the socialist project, including the objective of undoing the difference in living conditions in rural and urban areas.[50] Richert saw regional planning as a tool for this task because it allowed planning the national territory as a whole, thus giving equal attention to cities and villages, rather than reducing the countryside to the "hinterland" of an urban center—an approach that he attributed to the impact of Western planning tradition on Ghana.[51]

Pál Virágh, Hungarian architect and author of *Town Planning in Hungary* (1968), took a step further along the path of socialist planning imagination, and discussed Hungarian agrarian towns in which "everybody is an urban citizen" as an inspiration for socialist urbanization.[52] Increases in income and car ownership under socialism would allow agricultural workers to live in towns fully equipped with social facilities and, repeating the historical rhythms of agrarian towns, would permit them to work in industrialized state farms during the summer, while taking on industrial jobs in the winter.[53] The reality was less appealing, and some of the major challenges of the country's development, in particular the dominance of Budapest, stemmed from temporary migrations to urban centers by a population that retained part-time agricultural work. Yet to Virágh and other planners, that challenge confirmed that rural and urban areas in Hungary needed to be planned together in both spatial and economic terms.[54]

Polónyi had extensive experience with regional planning in Hungary, and he agreed with Richert and Virágh that regional planning in Eastern Europe was useful for West Africa. However, he rejected their attempts at opposing "socialist" and "capitalist" planning, and argued that the difference between a radical and a gradual change resulted not from political systems, but from specific conditions on the ground and tasks at hand. Along those lines, when writing with John Falconer and J. Max Bond Jr., his colleagues at UST, Polónyi argued that the development of Ghana might require both a radical change (which they called "newformation"), as in the construction of Tema New Town, and a gradual one ("transformation"), as in the development of the Bolgatanga region.[55]

Accordingly, and in distinction from Polish planners in Ghana, Polónyi did not import specific tools from Eastern European regional planning to West Africa. Rather, he translated his experience from Hungary into a broader rethinking of the role of architecture and planning in the conditions of underdevelopment. This rethinking originated from Polónyi's contributions to two projects in rural Hungary: the Mohács Island Regional Restoration Plan (1956) and the Balaton Regional Outline Plan (1957). Both projects were central to the institutionalization, legislation, and implementation of regional planning in the country: the former was the first practical attempt at regional planning in Hungary, while the latter shaped the method and the implementation machinery of Hungarian regional planning.[56]

The Mohács Island Plan proposed a new settlement network for an area in southern Hungary that had been destroyed by a flood in 1956 (figure 3.8). Plans were prepared by the City Planning Bureau (VÁTERV) in Budapest, with Tibor Farkas as chief architect, and detailed plans for particular settlements were provided by various planning institutions supported by an interdisciplinary team, including civil engineers and agriculture experts. Among the bigger settlements was Újmohács (New Mohács), planned by Polónyi and István Bérczes together with a team from the postgraduate course of the Association of Hungarian Architects, taught by Polónyi. Distribution and subdivision of land was at the core of the design process, and the resulting land pattern followed the medieval settlement layout, as Polónyi later discovered, with the fields in walking or biking distance. Prepared by on-site research and interviews focused on the traditional housing layouts, the lifestyle of their inhabitants and their expectations, and reusable materials, the design consisted of 260 brick houses with supporting facilities. The houses were built according to standard designs prepared by the planning office IPARTERV (1955), inspired by vernacular typologies.[57] The housing areas, which Polónyi compared to prewar discussions on "Garden Hungary," were divided into zones with unified typologies,

3.8. Mohács Island Regional Restoration Plan (Hungary), 1956. VÁTERV (Hungary). Tibor Farkas and Charles Polónyi, "Beszámoló a délmagyarországi árvízsújtotta területek újjáépítéséről," *Magyar Építőművészet* V, no. 9 (1956): 266.

resulting in a coherent village-scape. New health, education, and social services, which inhabitants had no access to previously, were designed as larger buildings that formed communal spaces. The construction work was done by brigades assembled by the Ministry of Construction, skilled workers, and craftspeople recruited from across the country, while unskilled work was provided by a youth organization and the army.[58]

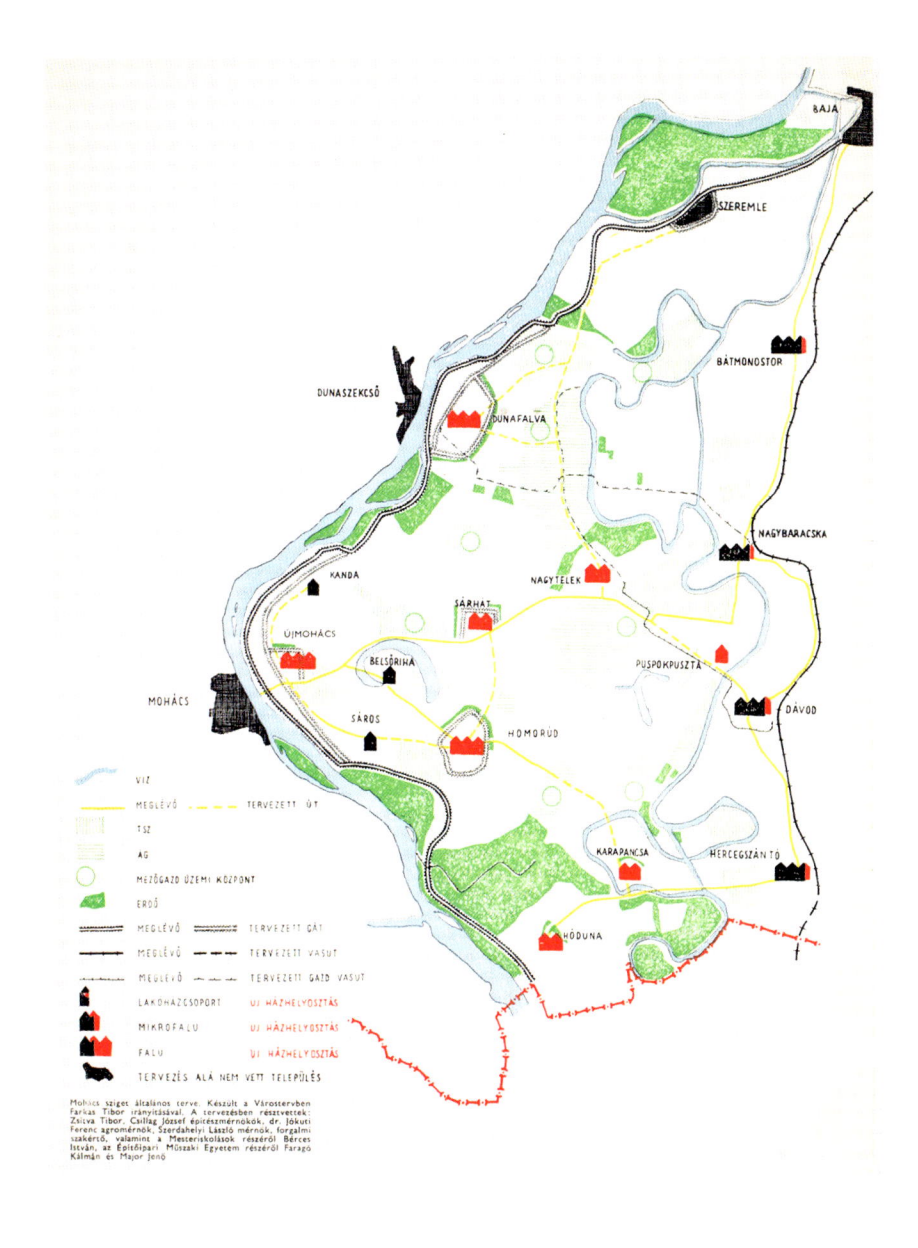

The experience of the Mohács Island Plan fed into the planning of the Lake Balaton area. Its regional plan was prepared by VÁTERV, with Tibor Farkas as head, and with Polónyi and Bérczes as chief architects of local offices on the south and north shores of Lake Balaton, respectively. The area, with fine examples of historic architecture and vernacular buildings, had been a favorite holiday destination for the Hungarian elite since the turn of the century, and had become a hub of the emerging international tourist industry in socialist Hungary.[59] In the plan for Lake Balaton, facilities for visitors and inhabitants were carefully programmed and differentiated into centers for weekend visitors, tourists, health-resort guests, and backpackers. As with the earlier plan for Mohács, and as later utilized in West Africa, the plan connected the layout of a settlement network, landscape design, and infrastructure, with architectural designs "adapted to our inheritance and our possibilities."[60] Polónyi was in charge of a range of architectural projects, for which he designed a system of standardized construction elements in reinforced concrete, prefabricated in workshops during winter, then assembled by unskilled workers. The supporting structure of a single type of column and a single type of beam was inspired by vernacular architecture, with external walls made of local stone, and partitioning walls of brick and wood. The structure was designed as independent of any specific program; thus, it could be used for various purposes (restaurants, stores, changing rooms, social centers, hotels) (figure 3.9). Ventilation was based on natural air movement between sunny and shaded parts of the building, while some buildings, including a hotel, used simple passive solar-energy systems to heat the water—technologies Polónyi returned to in his African projects. He designed twenty-eight buildings in this system, which was also the basis for designs by other architects (figure 3.10).[61]

The Balaton plan received the Abercrombie Prize (1965) by the International Union of Architects, and Polónyi's architecture—open-ended, flexible, designed to be appropriated for a variety of uses, and integrated into larger planning scales—was presented and appreciated during Team 10 meetings.[62] This visibility facilitated Polónyi's appointment at UST in Kumasi, as Dean Lloyd knew the Lake Balaton plan from French and British architectural journals.[63] That project was celebrated by Hungarian authors, too, with some of them hailing it as an example of the modernizing potential of socialism's powerful planning machinery.[64] However, this was not Polónyi's view, and he argued that, far from being a typical example of socialist planning, the project benefited from a short-lived combination of the centralized planning framework with a temporary power vacuum on lower administrative levels in the wake of the 1956 revolution in Hungary.[65] Furthermore, his Balaton designs did not rely exclusively on state intervention but, rather, envisaged a mixture of state provisions with a mobilization of local materials, technologies, knowledge, and labor power.

On his arrival in Ghana, Polónyi continued working along these lines. In his article with Falconer and Bond, he argued that "no government…has the resources to finance all the needed projects, nor the power or wisdom to effectively regulate human performance."[66] This comment reflected dissatisfaction with Nkrumah's planning, but it also might have referred to Polónyi's experience on the Balaton project, which after a temporary relaxation of political control over architectural design, had become increasingly bureaucratized, resulting in his withdrawing from the team.[67] In their account, Polónyi, Falconer, and Bond agreed that while a government needs to provide future inhabitants with land, social and technical infrastructure, engineering, sanitation, and town planning, these were to be complemented by other "resources," to which he included "ambition, energy, organizing capacity, and even the limited purchasing power of the lower income groups."[68]

While differing in training and experience, Polónyi, Falconer, and Bond found as the common denominator for their approach the tradition of self-help construction, supported by the authorities in West Africa since the late-colonial period. It could involve owner-built housing, mutual-aid programs in building, and publicly assisted self-help programs in which the government provided builders with planning, training, specialized labor, loans, or parts of a house that were difficult to obtain. Polónyi, when he arrived in Ghana, studied self-help projects in rural and urban areas of the country, including the roof-loan scheme by the UN (1954) and the "core housing" programs applied in the Volta River Resettlement Project.[69] As explained by Charles Abrams, an advisor on those programs and a frequent visitor to UST in Kumasi, self-help programs not only provided shelters but also brought about numerous "collateral dividends," including the general amelioration of construction methods and skills, the construction of roads

> 3.9. Service pavilion at Lake Balaton (Hungary), 1958. Charles Polónyi. Oscar Newman, *CIAM '59 in Otterlo* (Stuttgart: Krämer, 1961), 46.

> 3.10. Variants of assembling standardized structural elements, Lake Balaton (Hungary), 1958. Charles Polónyi. Oscar Newman, *CIAM '59 in Otterlo* (Stuttgart: Krämer, 1961), 43.

WORLDING EASTERN EUROPE

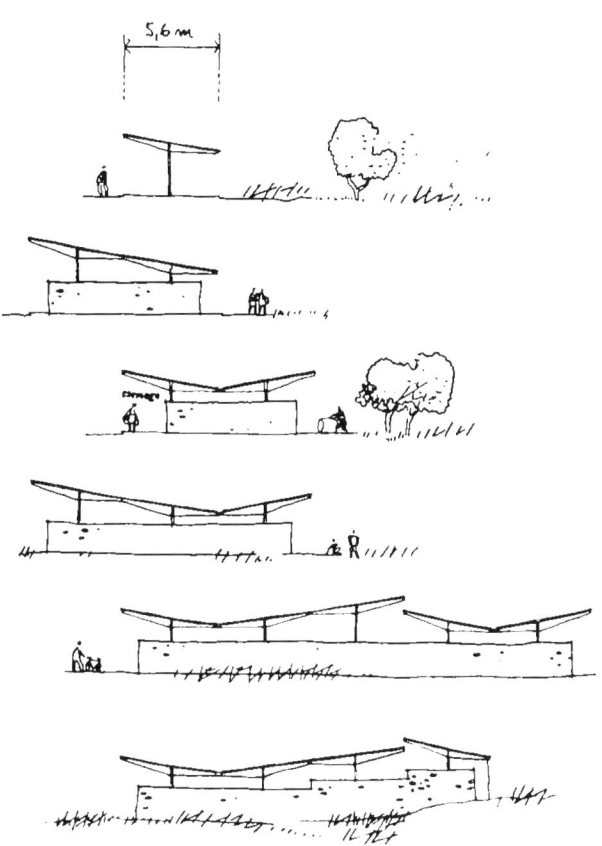

and infrastructure, promotion of literacy, and societal cooperation (figure 3.11).[70]

This way of thinking informed the Bui Resettlement Study (1966), which focused on an area in western Ghana around the proposed hydroelectric scheme designed by Soviet Union's Gidroproekt. Straddling all scales, from the region to individual buildings, the study was developed by the Research Department at UST. It was one of the department's "live projects," in which teachers and students worked together on actual design commissions received from the authorities (figure 3.12). The Bui Study was commissioned by the Ministry for Fuel and Power, and was headed by anthropologist David Butcher and planner Laszlo Huszar, a Hungarian émigré to Britain, with Polónyi in charge of the urban and architectural design.[71] The task of the project was to resettle people affected by the proposed dam, and to provide those communities with tools that improved living conditions, skills, and their economic prospects.

Like Polónyi's Hungarian projects, the Bui Study was carried out by a multidisciplinary team, which accounted for the social composition of the population, local chieftaincy, land tenure, occupancy patterns, and economic activities (largely subsistence economy), as well as village and house forms, house ownership, and social structure of households. Drawing on the surveys, the study proposed grouping inhabitants in three new villages (New Bui, New Jama, New Battor) according to the paramount chieftaincy from which inhabitants came, proximity to areas from which farmers and fishermen derived their livelihood (farmlands or the lake that the new dam would create), and by respecting differences in traditional culture between various ethnic groups. Program requirements for individual houses were defined by the daily routine of communities, and respected customary rules about sharing a room within a kinship group. The surveys also identified actors involved and resources at their disposal on local, regional, and national levels.[72] The surveys made use of data collected by the UST Research Department. For instance, the department documented construction details of vernacular buildings and traditional solutions for thermal comfort, lighting, acoustics, soil stabilization, and self-help building methods. The "Manual of Building Technology," prepared by Kumasi's School of Architecture, compiled those technologies and complemented them with instructions concerning concrete technologies and products of Ghana's emerging construction industry (aluminum roofs, plywood). These materials were used in rationalization studies of type designs, which improved colonial typologies of educational and health facilities, and combined them with a critical evaluation of large-scale governmental development projects, in particular the Volta River Resettlement Project.[73]

3.11. "Filling in the Walls of a Core House in the New Town of Ajena," Ghana. Charles Abrams, *Man's Struggle for Shelter* (Cambridge, MA: MIT Press, 1964), 181.

The Bui Study learned from the latter. While in the Volta River Project housing was the biggest expenditure, in the Bui scheme the largest share of resources would be allocated to support economic activities of inhabitants by building on their existing skills and occupations. Next in line were expenditures for improved services (education, health, water supply), roads and transportation, housing and compensation, and administration and planning. The involvement of the community was encouraged by means of a system of incentives, with the state granting additional financing for skilled labor and house-building material dependent on meeting minimum design standards.[74] These decisions were supported by the urban layout provided by Polónyi, which defined fixed elements in a settlement (compact central spine of infrastructure and public facilities) and in houses (narrow frontages of uniform width). Other elements and their fitting was left to communities and individuals, who were to receive appropriate training.[75] This approach, in which the main design decision was the delineation and distribution of actors, resources, and tasks on a variety of scales, advanced the lessons from the Lake Balaton project. At the same time, it responded to the calls of Max Bond and the Ghanaian architect John Owusu-Addo, who urged architects working in Ghana to leave behind disciplinary boundaries and to "assume a broader place in society as consolidators, innovators, propagandists, activists, as well as designers."[76]

Designing across the Rural-Urban Continuum

The Bui Dam and its supporting investments were constructed several decades after the study and in a changed form.[77] However, the methodology of the Bui Study was absorbed and advanced in the master plan Polónyi's team delivered for Calabar. That plan was produced by the Budapest-based Design Institute for Public Buildings (Közti), which had been active abroad since the late 1950s, first in Syria (hospitals) and then in Algeria, where the commission of the 5 July 1962 Stadium in Algiers (1965–72) was followed by a significant number of hospitals, schools, and residential districts.[78] The contract was mediated by Tesco, the Hungarian foreign trade organization (FTO).

Közti's master plan, which resulted from a tender competition, was the first comprehensive plan for Calabar, a city where subsequent planning attempts during the colonial period were hindered by the traditional land-tenure system, negligence of colonial administrators, opposition of local elites, and a chronic lack of funding.[79] Since the seventeenth century, Calabar was an important trading port, first for the slave trade and then since the early nineteenth century for "legitimate" trade, in particular palm oil. As a missionary and educational center, Calabar became an administrative capital for British rule in Nigeria and the capital of the British protectorate (1894), but by the early twentieth century it had lost importance to Port Harcourt, the new railway terminus and the port serving northern Nigeria.[80] A new beginning was promised when Calabar became the capital of the South-Eastern State after the reorganization of independent Nigeria into a federation of twelve states (1967). The Közti master plan returned to those ambitions, interrupted by the civil war, which left the South-Eastern State, including Calabar, with staggering damage to the economy.[81] Accordingly, the plan combined the task of reconstruction and consolidation of social facilities with provisions for economic development, and infrastructure for the newly acquired functions of the city as capital.[82]

The planning process began with comprehensive surveys carried out by the Hungarian team assisted by Nigerian students. The surveys revealed Calabar as a rural-urban continuum, "neither a city nor a village" in the words of Tayo Olafioye, a professor at the University of Calabar.[83] Its most numerous occupational groups were sales workers, farmers, fishermen, hunters, and loggers, followed by craftsmen, and other workers, with industry too limited to offer occupation to a significant group of inhabitants.[84] Polónyi was well positioned to operate within such a rural-urban continuum, which had been the basic condition of his earlier work: in Hungary, where the idealization of traditional agrarian towns clashed with the reality of rural-urban workers, and then in Ghana, where large cities were interfaces between the "jet age" and "subsistence economy."[85]

As in his earlier work, regional planning provided the appropriate scale for designing across that continuum (figure 3.13). The plan proposed an overarching settlement structure connecting the territory around Calabar in order to facilitate balanced economic development of agriculture, craftsmanship, trade, and services, and to provide the basis for future industry. The backbone of this structure was a network of roads, including the road that linked Calabar with the west of Nigeria via a newly planned bridge, and along which a string of service nuclei was planned. These were to combine administrative, educational, and health services with commercial functions, connected by buses.[86] The road network was to be complemented by water-transport infrastructure linking the riverine settlements, which would be visited at regular intervals by floating cinemas, libraries, and clinics on barges—an idea explored in one of Polónyi's design studios at Kumasi.[87] The urban core of Calabar was divided into three parts: the western zone with business, governmental, and industrial functions; the residential zone in the center; and the eastern zone with hospitals, higher-education institutions, and other large-scale amenities (figure 3.14).[88]

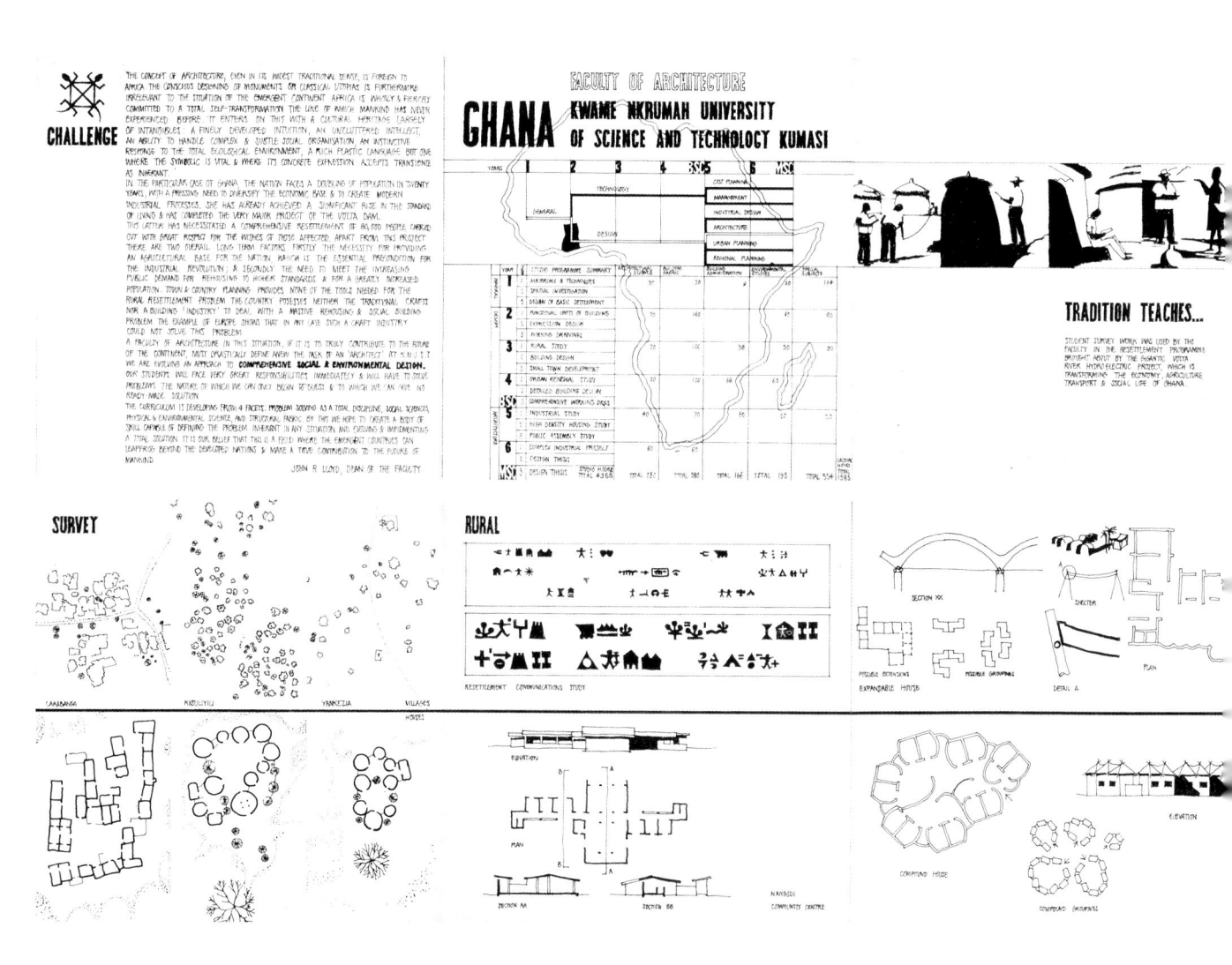

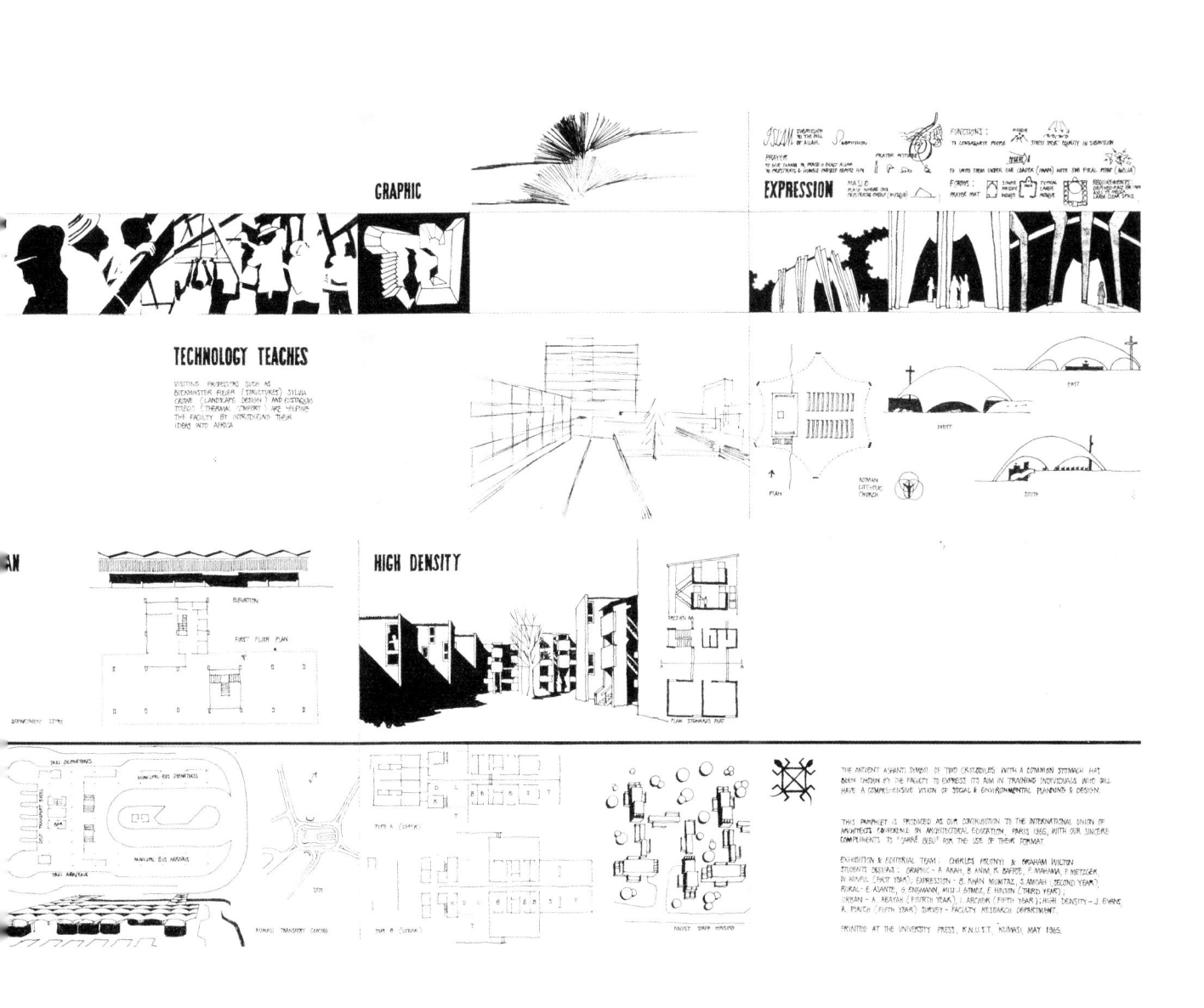

3.12. Summary of the curriculum of the Faculty of Architecture, UST, Kumasi, 1965.

3.13. "Calabar Metropolitan Area. Possible Saturation of the Metropolitan Area," 1969. Közti (Hungary). "Survey and Development Plan for Calabar" (Calabar: Tesco-Közti Consulting Engineers [NIG], 1969), 4.4.

> 3.14. Structure Plan of Calabar, 1969. Közti (Hungary). "Survey and Development Plan for Calabar" (Calabar: Tesco-Közti Consulting Engineers [NIG], 1969), 5.4.

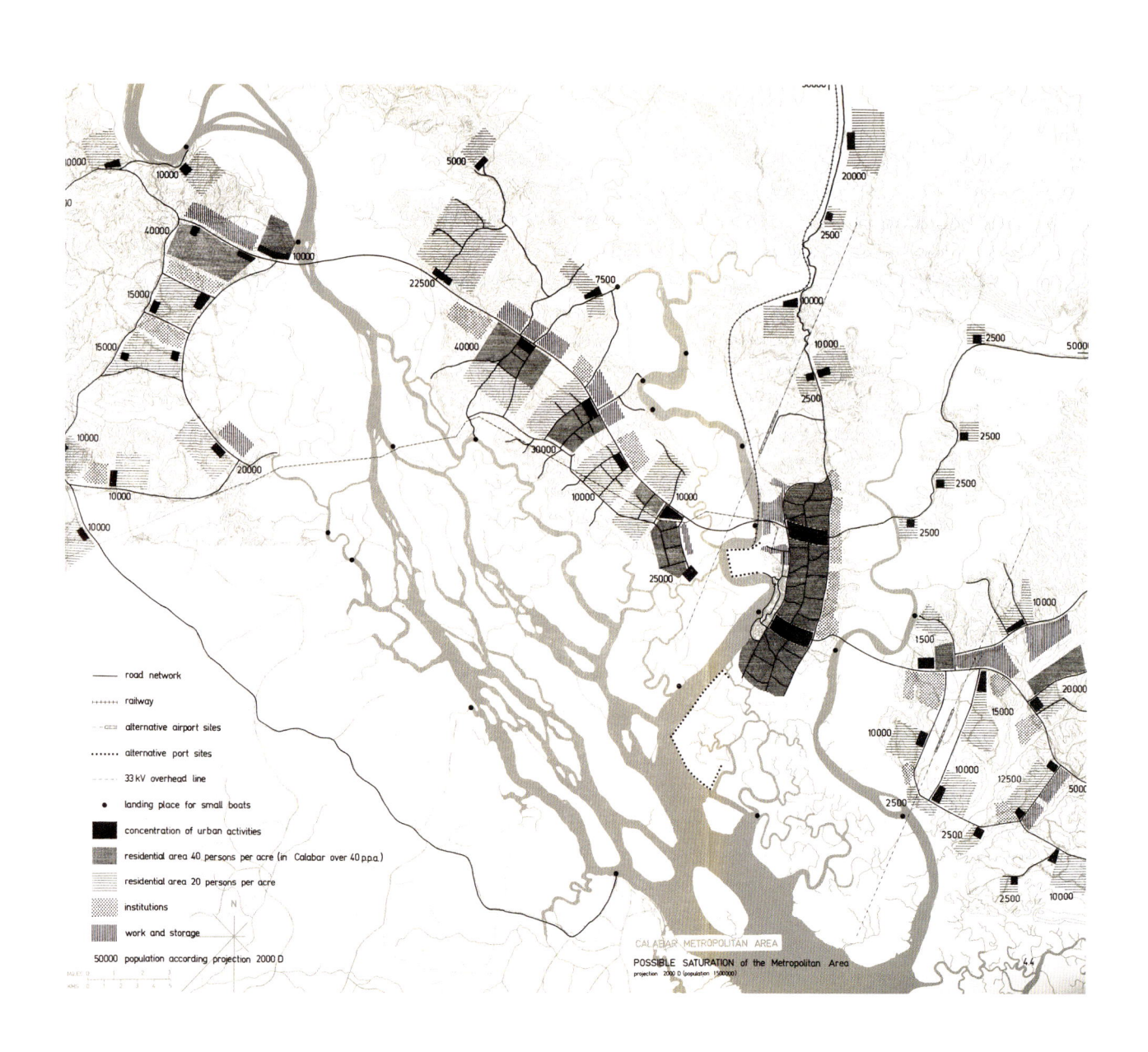

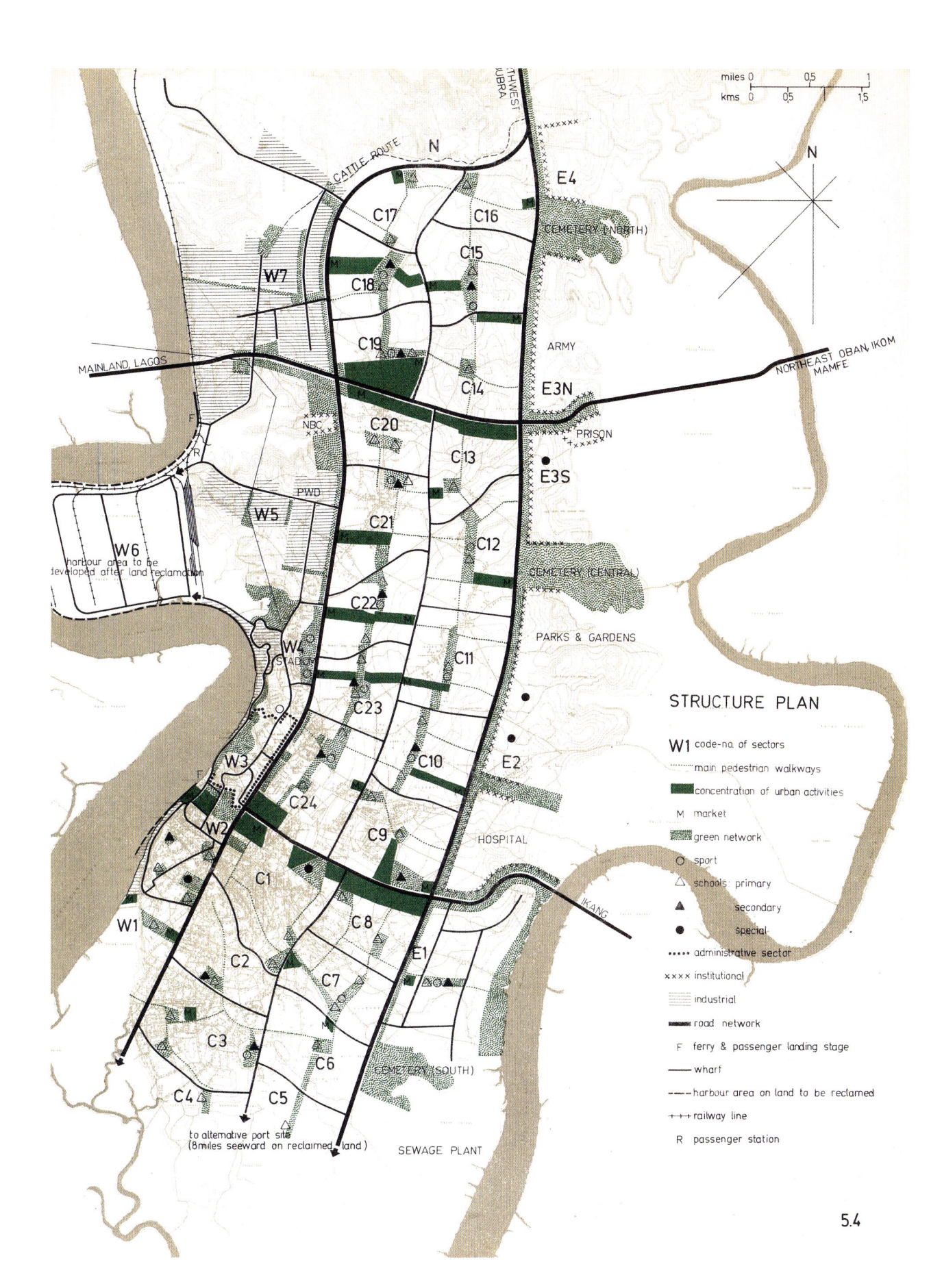

STRUCTURE PLAN

- **W1** code-no. of sectors
- ········ main pedestrian walkways
- ▓ concentration of urban activities
- M market
- ▒ green network
- ○ sport
- △ schools: primary
- ▲ secondary
- ● special
- ···· administrative sector
- ×××× institutional
- ▥ industrial
- ▬ road network
- F ferry & passenger landing stage
- — wharf
- --- harbour area on land to be reclaimed
- +++ railway line
- R passenger station

5.4

The housing typologies were fine-tuned according to the rural-urban continuum in Calabar, and rethought not solely as a welfare provision but also in terms of collateral dividends: stimulation of the construction industry, employment possibilities, and opportunities for training (figure 3.15). On the rural end of Calabar's urbanization processes, the designers proposed a distribution of standard-size plots of developed land, grouped around service nuclei, which would be made available for self-help construction, supported by agriculture, home industry, trade, and wage employment. Moving toward the central areas, Közti planners suggested the distribution of plots with sanitary units for self-help houses, which were designed as extendable and able to accept various functions, from the accommodation of owners and their families through rental accommodation to workshops.[89] A more developed typology of low-rise, high-density units for low-wage earners were the so-called earth scrapers, which continued Polónyi's proposal for the Bui project (figure 3.16).[90] Their layout was based on narrow, priority-for-pedestrians streets equipped with storm and wastewater infrastructure, flanked by a wall carrying electricity and water pipes. The wall had openings for all required functions (doors, windows, vents, entrances to commercial facilities), and from there each house could grow by adding new rooms to the nucleus that was planned as a service core and a covered terrace for cooking and living. The materials (aluminum sheeting

3.15. "Housetypes and Densities," 1969. Közti (Hungary). "Survey and Development Plan for Calabar" (Calabar: Tesco-Közti Consulting Engineers [NIG], 1969), 2.9.

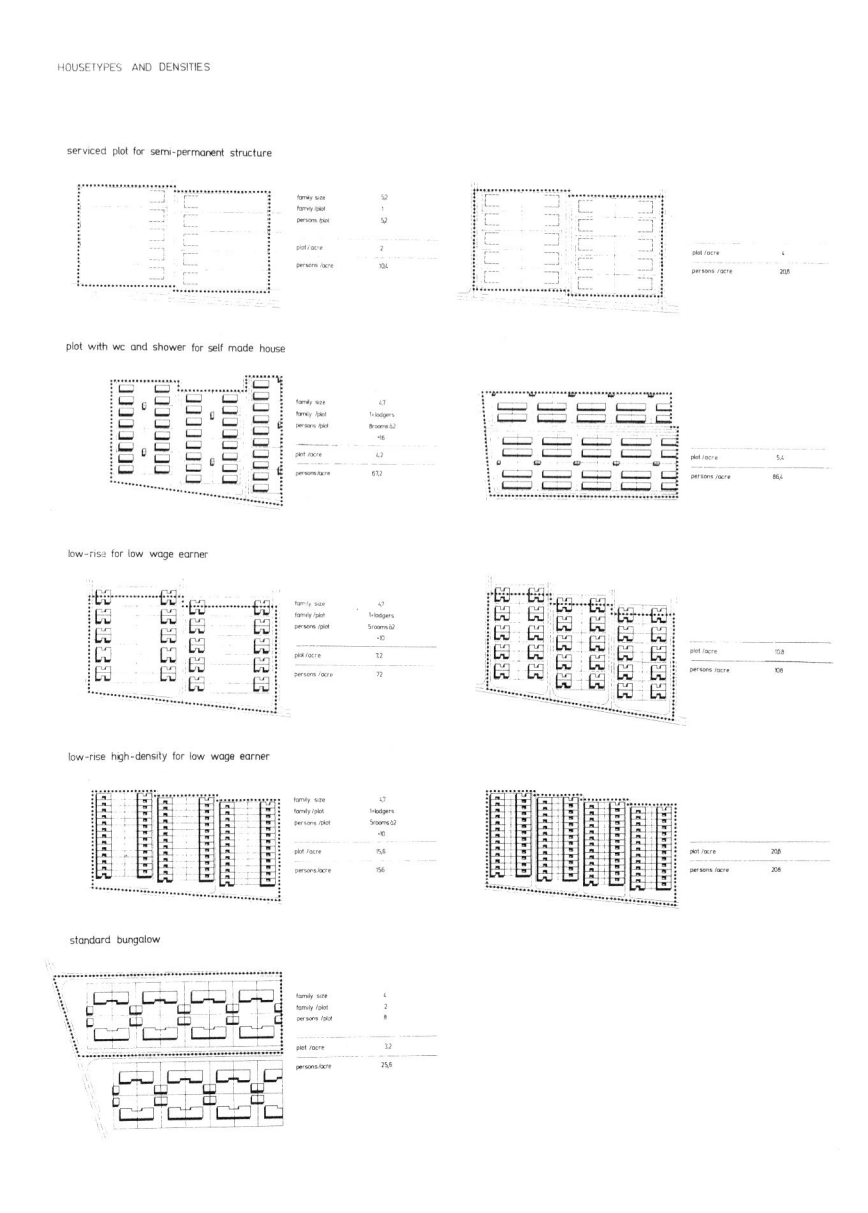

3.16. Calabar, model of low-rise, high-density housing ("Earth scrapers"), 1969. Közti (Hungary). "Survey and Development Plan for Calabar" (Calabar: Tesco-Közti Consulting Engineers [NIG], 1969), 2.13.

3.17. GNCC bungalow type 100, Roman Ridge, Accra, 1964. GNCC, Vic Adegbite (chief architect), Charles Polónyi (project architect).

3.18. Flagstaff House housing project, Accra, 1964. GNCC, Vic Adegbite (chief architect), Charles Polónyi (project architect).

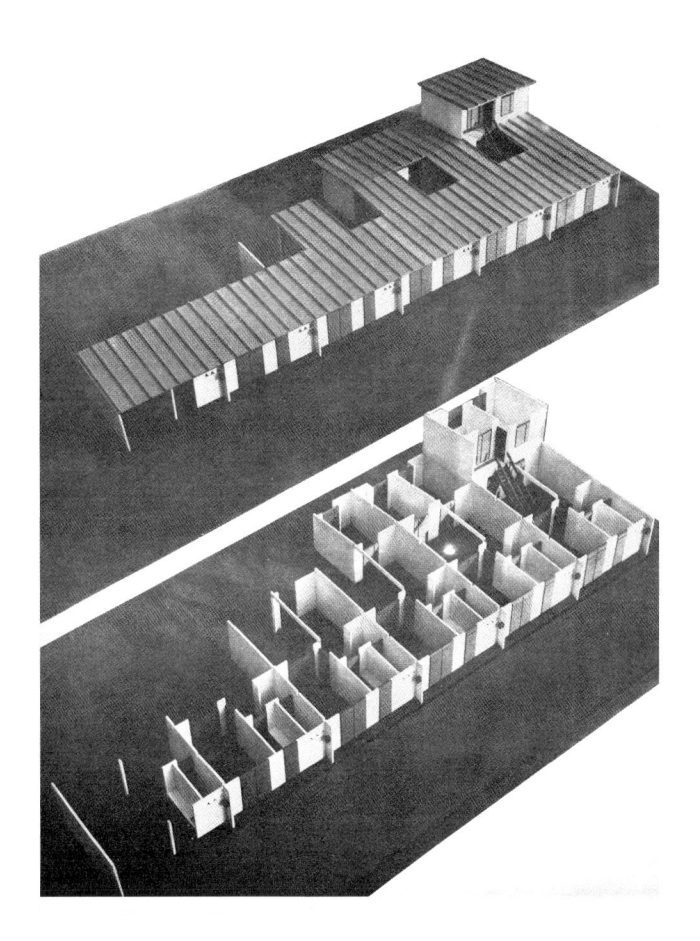

WORLDING EASTERN EUROPE

and concrete blocks) were expected to be supplemented by future industrial production in Calabar, including the existing plywood factory.

The typologies for higher-income groups were building on Polónyi's housing designs at the Ghana National Construction Corporation (GNCC), including detached and semidetached bungalows, such as those constructed in the Roman Ridge neighborhood in Accra (1964) (figure 3.17).[91] Multistory apartment buildings, foreseen as "landmarks, as tools of urban identification, as symbols of urban life," were similar to the six blocks of apartments on Independence Avenue in Accra (1964) (figure 3.18).[92] The housing blocks in Calabar were conceived as flexible and adaptable, and the design was confined to a layout of floor slabs, columns, stairs, and infrastructure as fixed elements that would accommodate multiple functions. As in Accra, the ground floor would be left open, protected from sun and rain, to be used for meetings, preparation of food and other domestic work, play areas for children, and spaces for small traders, craftsmen, and hawkers.[93] "Instead of prohibiting and persecuting the 'partisan architecture' normally produced by such people, our intention is to encourage it," wrote the authors.[94]

Unlike his earlier projects in Ghana, the Calabar plan was directed by Polónyi from Budapest, where he had returned from Kumasi to work as city architect.[95] During his occasional visits to Calabar, he worked in Tesco-Közti's temporary office at the Old Residency, one of the prefabricated colonial houses that were included in the Hungarian study of historic landmarks in the city.[96] From there, the preliminary report was consulted with the advisory committee in Calabar and its subcommittees, local chiefs, and various social associations, and then the final report was submitted in 1970 and approved the next year by the government. One member of the Hungarian team would stay in Calabar with the role of the chief architect, to oversee implementation of the plan and to support the chief town-planning officer of the South-Eastern State, as well as the Calabar Area Planning Authority and the Master Plan Implementation Committee.[97]

The plan became the basis for building permits and governmental-investment decisions in Calabar, including road infrastructure, with the Murtala Mohammed Highway and the mainland link (moved northward to comply with plans for the Trans-African Highway).[98] Benefiting from the oil boom, a large number of buildings were constructed over the course of the 1970s, with a stadium and a swimming pool, a new culture center, and buildings for higher education, administration, military, commerce, healthcare, and industry. With the exception of several governmental buildings, most of those new structures were broadly located in zones foreseen in the master plan, but rarely in the positions specified by Közti's Detailed Action Plan, and only sporadically supported by adequate road infrastructure (figure 3.19).[99] Investment in housing for high-middle and for low-income groups followed the master plan, too, with the neighborhood in Ikot Ansa by the South-Eastern State Housing Corporation among the first to be completed (figure 3.20).[100] The predominant housing typology was one-family bungalows, while the "earth scrapers" were considered to be at odds with the preferences of inhabitants and abandoned.[101]

The plan was implemented by combining federal and state investment in infrastructure, including roads, and self-help projects, supported by the state government with direct payments and distribution of construction materials.[102] The results were highlighted in the series "Calabar Yesterday, Today and Tomorrow" published by the city's daily newspaper *Nigerian Chronicle* (1974), which celebrated the "birth" of Calabar as a "modern city" in the wake of the civil war, and acknowledged the role of the master plan in this process.[103] Other voices were less enthusiastic. Writing in 1980, Anam E. Ntukidem of the University of Calabar took issue with the layout proposed by the plan for hindering the growth of residential areas between

3.19. "Action Area (No. 2): Business Centre, Residential Sector C24," 1969. Közti (Hungary). "Survey and Development Plan for Calabar" (Calabar: Tesco-Közti Consulting Engineers [NIG], 1969), 6.5.

the two service zones; he also considered the road network inefficient, and criticized the location of the governmental and business centers.¹⁰⁴

The plan provided lessons for subsequent designs by Tesco-Közti in Nigeria, including plans for four towns west of the Calabar River, prepared by the team of Polónyi, László Szabados, and Gergely Pantó.¹⁰⁵ The latter two would join the Tesco-Közti team that delivered the master plan of Makurdi (1977–78), while Polónyi moved to his new position in Algeria and then later in Ethiopia.¹⁰⁶ A Hungarian team also designed the master plan for Kano and a district center of sixty thousand inhabitants in Abuja, the new Nigerian capital (1982), to which several teams from socialist countries contributed, along with numerous architectural projects in Kano and other cities in northern Nigeria.¹⁰⁷

Unlike blueprints produced by Polish planners in Nkrumah's Ghana, the documentation of these master plans did not refer to the experience of overcoming underdevelopment in postwar Eastern Europe. Nor did other planning documents coproduced by Eastern Europeans in 1970s Nigeria, including the master plan of Zaria, prepared by a team of the Department of Urban and Regional Planning at Ahmadu Bello University in Zaria, led by the department head, Polish architect and planner Stanisław Juchnowicz (1979); and master plans for seven cities in Kano state, prepared by Yugoslavia's Energoprojekt in collaboration with the Institute for Town Planning and Housing in Belgrade (1973) (figures 3.21 and 3.22).¹⁰⁸ Similarly, when Romanian architects prepared the "Ten Year Federal Housing Development Scheme" for Nigeria (1976–85), they avoided direct references to the Romanian postwar experience of translating vernacular typologies into urban housing layouts for rural migrants, despite numerous parallels with their work in Nigeria (figures 3.23 and 3.24).¹⁰⁹

In retrospect, some of the architects involved did connect their West African work to their earlier projects in underdeveloped areas of their home countries. For instance, Zoran Bojović, head designer at Energoprojekt, recalled that his work on the master plans in Kano State drew upon his previous experience in Kosovo, one of the least developed regions of Yugoslavia, which he saw as similar to Kano in terms of economic, social,

3.20. A new housing estate in Calabar, 1970s.

> 3.21. "Zaria Master Plan. Proposed Land Use," 1978. Ahmadu Bello University, Department of Urban and Regional Planning, Stanisław Juchnowicz; Ministry of Land and Surveys, Kaduna State, Kaduna, "Zaria Master Plan—2000" (Zaria: Gaskiya Corporation, 1979).

> 3.22. "Dambatta. Purpose of Town Surface Area from 1978 to 1986," 1973. Energoprojekt (Socialist Republic of Serbia, Yugoslavia). Energoprojekt; Kano State Government, Ministry of Works and Survey, "Danbatta [sic]. Master Plan. 25 Year Development Plan," 1973.

WORLDING EASTERN EUROPE

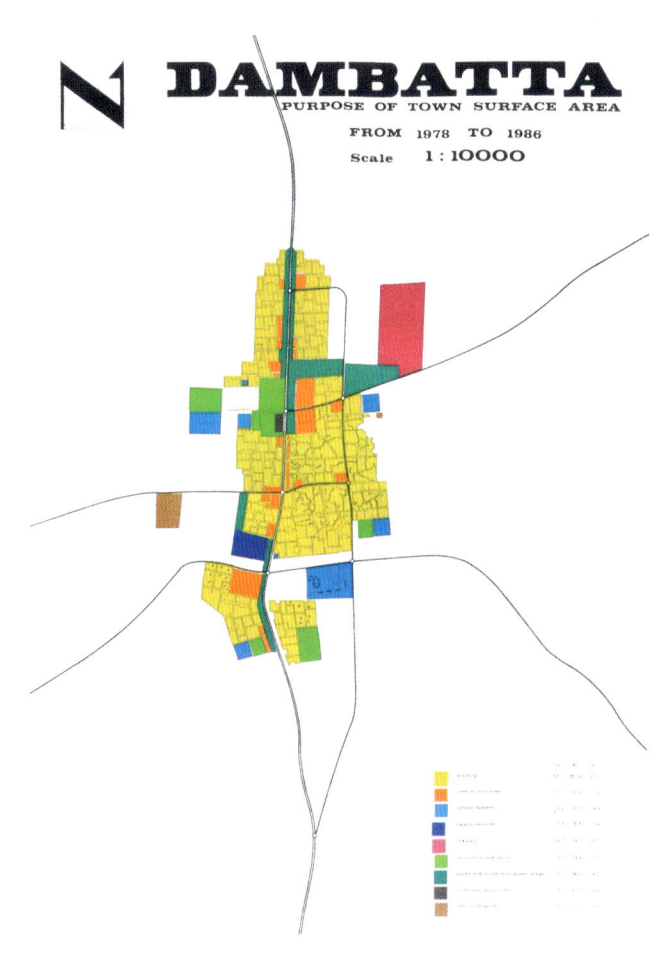

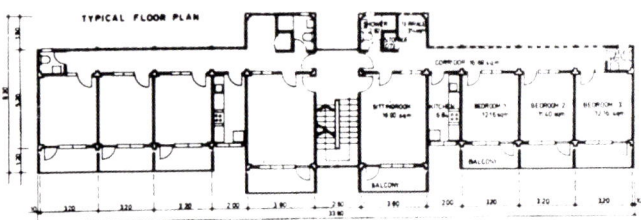

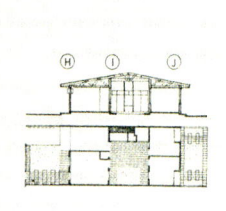

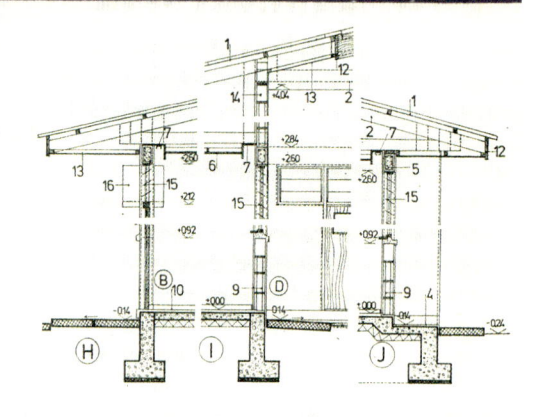

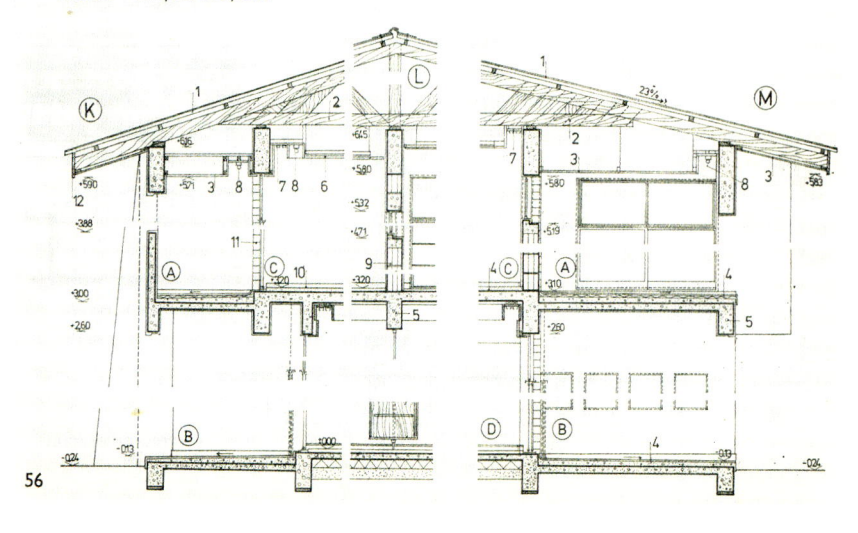

3.23. Housing for northern Nigeria. Romconsult (Romania), Design Institute for Housing and Urban Technical and Social Infrastructure (ISLGC, Romania), Ana Solomon and others. Ana Solomon, "Proiecte tip destinate programului național de locuințe din Republica Federală a Nigeriei," *Arhitectura* 5 (1980): 16.

3.24. Technical fiche for two housing projects in Festac Town, Lagos. Romconsult (Romania), Design Institute for Housing and Urban Technical and Social Infrastructure (ISLGC, Romania). *Arhitectura* 6 (1980): 56.

and cultural factors.¹¹⁰ However, the marketing materials of Hungarian, Bulgarian, East German, Romanian, Polish, and Yugoslav firms in 1970s Nigeria presented them as conveyors of "internationally accepted basic principles and methods of present-day architecture and engineering," as it was put in a brochure prepared by Tesco-Közti's regional office in Kano.¹¹¹ Rather than reading that statement as a pledge to conform with Western models, Polónyi's trajectory in Ghana and Nigeria suggests that it may be read as a claim to Eastern Europe's worlding.

ZBIGNIEW DMOCHOWSKI AND THE DECOLONIZATION OF NIGERIAN ARCHITECTURE

Eastern European economists of the late nineteenth century, who commented on their region's backwardness, often pointed out its structural similarity with colonies of Britain, France, and other Western European powers. As occupied parts of neighboring empires, the pursuit of large-scale industrialization in Eastern Europe was hindered, as in the colonies, by the lack of capital and external markets, and Eastern European territories were exploited by Western capital with the effect of proletarizing the local workforce and transferring abroad the wealth thereby accumulated.¹¹² Yet such parallels did not end with economic domination, and extended to the application of an entire range of military, administrative, and cultural technologies that were performed by the occupying empires. Eastern Europe and the Balkans, discovered during the Enlightenment as the "other" of Western Europe, and its "first Orient," were subjected to Austro-Hungarian civilizing missions in Galicia and Bosnia and, in particular, to Prussian-German settlement projects.¹¹³ Continuities that remain to be studied in depth include those between late eighteenth-century Prussian settlements in annexed Eastern European territories, German settler colonies in Africa in the nineteenth century, and Nazi genocide during World War II that aimed at clearing *Lebensraum* in the East for German colonists.

In the interwar period, analogies became widespread between the Mandate system and the new nation-states emerging or expanding in Eastern Europe from defeated empires. British imperial figures such as Jan Smuts called for the Mandates to be used in Eastern Europe, claiming that those nations needed to be shepherded toward self-rule, too. As scholars have observed, such a way of thinking was commonplace at the League of Nations, which was granted the right to intervene into minority affairs in Eastern Europe, as well as in financial matters. Racialized visions of superiority stemming from the imperial rule were a returning rhetoric: Smuts referred to Poles as "kaffirs," and for other British politicians they were "orientalized Irish."¹¹⁴

By the late nineteenth century, some Eastern European intellectuals were already drawing affinities between Eastern Europeans and Africans. For instance, the Polish writer Henryk Sienkiewicz condemned atrocities of the Boer Wars along with Prussian violence on Polish lands, and Joseph Conrad's anticolonialism was inspired by his family history, as son of a resistance fighter in one of Poland's numerous nineteenth-century uprisings.¹¹⁵ After the rise of fascism in interwar Europe, the Italian invasion of Abyssinia (1935), and the German occupation of Czechoslovakia (1938), intellectuals in places as varied as Poland, Trinidad, and India pointed to similarities between Eastern Europe and the colonized world, and at the interdependence of their fates.¹¹⁶ This claim was reiterated after World War II, when the socialist propaganda argued that Eastern European struggles against the empires prefigured anti-imperialist struggles in Africa and Asia. The promotion of the socialist development path in Central Asian republics was typically accompanied in Soviet discourse by an account of the "moslems [*sic*] masses who suffered from dual oppression—that of local feudals and Tsarist colonialists."¹¹⁷ Soviet scholars compared favorably these republics with European colonies both in terms of economic progress and cultural development.¹¹⁸ Anti-imperialist discourse was adapted by the satellites, and Poland's representatives would present the country to the Nigerian public as "a state that has never been a colonial power but during the thousand years of its existence often confronted hostile invaders," and hence "acknowledged with sympathy and friendliness the foundation of independent Nigerian state in 1960."¹¹⁹

Such a narrative was myopic about the violence of Poland's own eastward expansion since the late Middle Ages, and its "internal colonization" up to the interwar period of territories of today's Lithuania, Belarus, and Ukraine. During its Second Republic (1918–39), colonial fantasies drove mass organizations including the Maritime and Colonial League to demand overseas colonies for Poland (figure 3.25). Nnamdi Azikiwe, who would later become Nigeria's first president, commented that "now that Poland which, by 1914, was a colonial territory of three different States has been allowed to exercise the Wilsonian right of self-determination, Poland needs colonies, not in Europe but in Africa. . . . The former servant . . . now wants to be the master of an African country."¹²⁰ Poland's colonial fantasies were paralleled by a concentrated settlement program of Polish settlers in the eastern territories of the country, underdeveloped and inhabited by a heterogeneous population including Lithuanians, Belarusians, Ukrainians, and Jews. On those territories, called "borderlands" in Polish, the state allocated plots of land to its officials and military personnel, and the typology of a classicist, Polish-gentry country house was turned into a formal reference for designs of schools, military barracks, railway stations, and housing neighborhoods. Many among the most talented Polish architects between the wars started their careers in the "borderlands" in the service of the military, including architects who contributed decisively in the reconstruction of Poland after World War II.¹²¹

Other countries in the region pursued programs of internal colonization, too, including Austria-Hungary in Transylvania, and expressed colonial fantasies, including interwar Czechoslovakia.¹²² Polónyi's memoirs conveyed this ambiguity of the Eastern European experience of colonialism: he sympathized with Africans and quoted Senegalese poet and theorist Léopold Sédar Senghor to liken Hungarian and African relations to France as a source of both inspiration and disappointment. Yet he saw Hungary as a "result of several successive colonisations," and praised Austrian colonization in the Danube River region after Turkish rule, while condemning the Soviet subjugation of Hungary, which he called "colonization," too.¹²³

3.25. Poster of the Maritime and Colonial League in Marcinkowice (Poland), 1936.

The ambiguities of Soviet anticolonialism were particularly evident to the elites of Central Asian republics who were sent to the Global South to promote the success of Soviet decolonization of the tsarist Empire. They became increasingly disillusioned by what they considered a colonial pattern in the social-spatial composition of the republics, where a largely European urban elite was surrounded by a native population engaged in agriculture. By the 1980s, Central Asian intellectuals began to question the possibility of anticolonialism in the Soviet Union, sometimes borrowing the language of resistance that Moscow had encouraged them to use against Western powers.[124]

Cultural Emancipation of the Postcolony

Such ambiguities did not make it to official communiqués of Eastern European diplomats and reports of West African journalists, which focused instead on the shared experience of foreign domination as a source of solidarity between the two regions. For instance, a Ghanaian journalist accompanying Nkrumah on his trip to Eastern Europe observed that Bulgarians, who "for 500 years were under the Turkish rule, also understand the African and are very sympathetic with her struggle for the liberation of his [sic] continent from foreign domination."[125] For that journalist, similarities of historical fate went beyond overcoming economic backwardness, and included cultural emancipation; consequently, he argued that Eastern European states such as Bulgaria, by reclaiming their national cultures, demonstrated that "in the field of culture, there are no big and small nations, no superior and inferior peoples."[126]

Cultural emancipation was high on the agenda of leaders of newly independent countries in 1960s West Africa, and this expectation was often communicated to architects arriving from socialist Europe.[127] When confronted with such tasks, they could draw on the architectural culture in their region, including the search for national styles since the late nineteenth century and the recasting of modernism as nationalism during the interwar period in contested territories such as Silesia, Moravia, and the Balkans. Radically modern buildings in Brno, Katowice, and Zagreb were cases in point since they demonstrated the rupture with German or Habsburg historicism, and the emergence of the new states: Czechoslovakia, Poland, and the Kingdom of Yugoslavia.

Such visual differentiation from the prevalent architectural production of the past was sought by modern buildings produced in Accra and in Lagos on the cusp of independence. This was also the tone of the dossier "Changing Face of Lagos," published in the Lagos-based newspaper *Daily Times* in anticipation of the independence of Nigeria (1960) (figure 3.26).[128] With images of newly planned or recently constructed high-rises, such as the Independence House (Federal Ministry of Works and Surveys or FMWS, 1961), the General Post Office (Charles C. Stevenson and others for FMWS, 1960), the Co-operative Bank (Fry, Drew, Drake & Lasdun, 1958), and the Investment House (Architects Co-Partnership, 1961), the newspaper predicted that Lagos might become "a skyscraper city like Manhattan," or at least on par with the new modernist capitals of Brasilia and Chandigarh, both of which the dossier discussed and illustrated.[129] Aerial photographs of Lagos Island approximated the view that future users would have of a city with new office buildings, including the Hanbury House (Godwin and Hopwood, 1957) and Barclays Bank (Walker, Harwood and Cranswick, 1960), as well as new public buildings including the National Museum (William Jack for FMWS, 1957) and the National Hall (K.A.R. Purdom for FMWS, 1960). The population from the island's dilapidated areas was being relocated to new housing districts on the mainland, such as Surulere, a neighborhood built according to British models, with detached homes and blocks of flats along wide streets, and schools designed by Oluwole Olumuyiwa, and John Godwin and Gillian Hopwood.[130] The *Daily Times* account emphasized the architects' young ages and included an article by Olumuyiwa, representing the tiny group of Nigerian architects.[131]

In West Africa, as in interwar Eastern Europe, modernist forms offered a white canvas on which the desire for new beginnings could be projected. But they were also useful in what they did not communicate. In particular, these forms avoided any references to the various ethnic cultures in Nigeria, a society that emerged from the colonial period divided along ethnic lines that were feared to be, and proved to be, a major challenge for its future. In this way, these buildings distinguished themselves from the colonial practice of naturalizing vernacular traditions into the system of indirect rule, or the governance of West Africa through traditional kings and chiefs, which often referred to local rituals and ornaments.[132] In Nigeria, this practice was first introduced in the north of the country, where architects in service of the Northern Region Public Works Department designed public buildings with references to regional forms, such as the Law Courts (J. E. Evans, J. C. Hames) and State House (J. E. Evans, J. Greer), both at Kaduna (figure 3.27).[133]

However, with the waning of post-independence enthusiasm after the 1966 putsch and the civil war, modern architecture in Nigeria came

3.26. "Changing Face of Lagos." *Daily Times*, May 11, 1960, 24.

3.27. State House at Kaduna. Ministry of Works, Northern Region Public Works Department, J. E. Evans (chief architect), J. Greer (architect in charge). "State House Kaduna," *West African Builder and Architect* 2, no. 5 (1962): 93.

under fire, too. When journalists revisited the Surulere housing estate a few years after its completion, they found rapidly deteriorating apartments and put the blame on its architects, who had "designed western-type flats" inadequate for average Nigerians and their extended families. Rather than continuing to "disregard our culture and develop for us concrete jungles with utterly unsuitable facilities," planners were urged to account for traditional and cultural norms.[134] While architects such as Olumuyiwa continued to be committed to the abstract forms of the modern movement, the climate of opinion was changing.

The journal *New Culture*, edited by Demas Nwoko, artist, stage designer, director, architect, a founding member of the Zaria Art Society, and member of the Mbari Club, provided a platform for this critique. Authors writing for *New Culture* argued that "tropical architecture" unfavorably compared with vernacular buildings, as it failed not only in respect to inhabitants' needs, but also in terms of climatic comfort, the declared objective of Drew, Fry, and other "tropical" architects.[135] Among the journal's authors writing most eloquently on architecture was David Aradeon, a Nigerian architect, scholar, and educator.[136] Writing in 1981, Aradeon argued that "European transplants...have dominated both rural and urban Nigerian landscapes for the past twenty years."[137] If this architecture added a few concessions to security, ventilation, and shade in the tropical climate, it did not account for the multiple ways of life in the Nigerian society undergoing profound transition and change. Addressing Surulere specifically, Aradeon showed how the single-space concept of eating and living disregarded the cultures of inhabitants, as did the abrupt entries into apartments. He urged architects to acknowledge Nigerian traditions in their heterogeneity and variety, and to study vernacular buildings as evolving spaces rather than ossified forms.[138]

Aradeon argued that such study required the rejection of "ignorant, prejudiced, and ethnocentric" interpretations of African vernacular architecture by Europeans that had been absorbed by educated African elites, "as though African houses neither fulfill the functions of a house or home nor conceptually define architectural spaces."[139] Consequently, his call to uncover "the spatial concepts of our traditional house forms" required that architects confront the epistemic violence inflicted on Africans by colonial occupation.[140] In particular, such a return required undoing the colonial system of prestige and value that contrasted European and indigenous cultures according to dichotomies of maturity and immaturity, civilization and barbarism, modernity and backwardness. The devalorization of indigenous cultures along those oppositions resulted, according to Aradeon, in "our refusal or inability to explore fully and exhaustively" the possibilities offered by traditional forms and technology.[141] Aradeon argued that it was only through the undoing of the colonial hierarchy of cultural value that Nigerian architects could recognize the structural, functional, and economic thinking in vernacular buildings. He urged that these be seen according to the same criteria that had been the basis for modern architecture, rather than prolonging colonial discourse that opposed European modernity and African tradition.[142]

This shift in perspective was the purpose of the exhibition "African Architectural Technology," which Aradeon curated as part of FESTAC. The principle of the show was summarized by Nigeria's head of state, General Obasanjo, who opened FESTAC with the call to recognize that the "subtle and complex designs of African traditional architecture" were at the origins of modern technology and were thus an inspiration for "restor[ing] the link between culture, creativity, and the mastery of modern technology and industrialism."[143] In particular, the exhibition featured examples of structural thinking in West and Central African buildings, including thin shells and tensile structures, thus the very principles that underlay the cutting-edge structures of 1960s Western engineering.¹⁴⁴ It was through the appreciation of such technologies, Aradeon argued, and the ways in which they allowed creation of spaces appropriate to the various and changing lifestyles of their communities, that Nigerian architects could learn how to design appropriate architecture for the independent nation.¹⁴⁵

Aradeon's call for a return to the indigenous culture to relaunch modernity as distinctively black and African closely subscribed to the overarching aims of FESTAC. The festival was not a nostalgic revival of the precolonial past, since Nigerian intellectuals were fully aware that much of the "traditional" culture that survived the colonial period was in itself invented over the course of the colonial encounter and instrumentalized within the system of indirect rule. Rather, the aim of FESTAC was to recuperate these cultural forms. The Durbar, the choreographed public spectacle honoring emirs, governors, and district officers in northern Nigeria, was a case in point. Adapted from India by British officials to naturalize the policy of indirect rule, the Durbar was staged as part of FESTAC to purge it of the very colonial history in which it developed and took shape. In so doing, the festival put the emphasis on creativity rather than authenticity, and responded to the colonial violence by taking over, nationalizing, and indigenizing Africa's invented traditions.¹⁴⁶ In the words of anthropologist Andrew Apter, FESTAC "performed a cultural exorcism, casting out the colonial ghosts and demons that continued to afflict African hearts and minds."¹⁴⁷

Eastern European architects in post-independence Nigeria were instrumental in performing this exorcism. A case in point is the work of Polish architect and scholar Zbigniew Dmochowski, the first director of the Museum of Traditional Nigerian Architecture (MOTNA) in Jos and author of the monumental, three-volume *Introduction to Traditional Nigerian Architecture* (1990) (figure 3.28).¹⁴⁸ This work was at once a comprehensive documentation of vernacular architecture in Nigeria and a resource for the creation of a "modern school of Nigerian Architecture."¹⁴⁹ The concept of space, which Aradeon urged to be uncovered in vernacular forms, was the main tool in this respect. Initiated in service of the colonial administration in the 1950s and completed over the course of the 1970s with the support of institutions in Poland, Dmochowski's work in Nigeria shows the instrumentality of Eastern Europeans in the indigenization of colonial knowledge by the postcolonial state. It also points at the mediating function assumed by Eastern Europeans in the process of the decolonization of Nigerian architecture. At the same time, this work was haunted by Poland's own colonial past, and the first test of Dmochowski's project was his ability to exorcise those ghosts, too.

3.28. Zbigniew Dmochowski, *An Introduction to Nigerian Traditional Architecture* (London: Ethnographica; Lagos: National Commission for Museums and Monuments, 1990), 3 vols., covers.

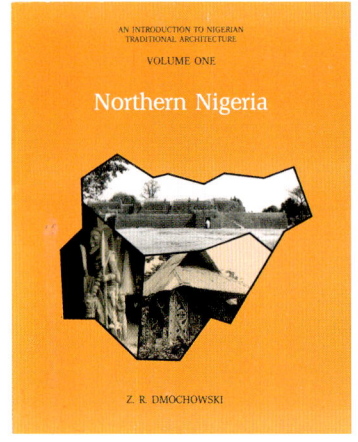

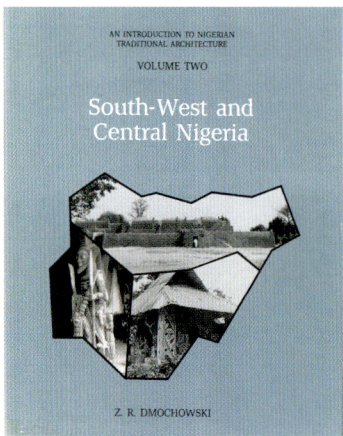

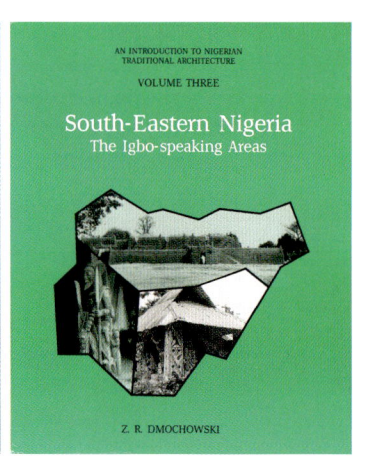

3.29. "House of T. Leśko in Olhomle," 1934. Drawings and photograph by Zbigniew Dmochowski and students of the Institute of Polish Architecture, Warsaw University of Technology (Poland). Zbigniew Dmochowski, "Sprawozdanie ze studjów nad poleskiem budownictwem drzewnem w r. 1934/5," *Biuletyn historji sztuki i kultury* III, no. 4 (June 1934): 317.

The Politics of Drawing in Independent Nigeria

Dmochowski's work in Nigeria was building on his previous research at the Institute of Polish Architecture at Warsaw University of Technology during the 1930s. Established in 1923 and headed by architect and scholar Oskar Sosnowski, the institute carried out extensive surveys of historic architecture in Poland seen as a preserve of national heritage, threatened during the division of the country among neighboring empires through the long nineteenth century. Along with gothic cathedrals, renaissance townhouses, baroque synagogues, and military architecture, the buildings studied included vernacular wooden architecture, widely seen since the late nineteenth century in Poland and across the region as a repository of national identity (figure 3.29).[150] A graduate of Warsaw University of Technology (1932), Dmochowski was employed at the institute, where he carried out surveys of wooden architecture in Polesie and elsewhere in the then-eastern territories of Poland.[151] The surveys were incorporated into the curriculum of the School of Architecture, and they resulted in the documentation of over six hundred villages, presented in standardized dossiers. Each dossier included descriptions, photographs, drawings of the general plan of the village, and characteristic plans, sections, and elevations of its main components (the oldest building and typical structures).[152]

After the German invasion of Poland in 1939, Dmochowski fled to England and took up a teaching position at the Polish School of Architecture in Liverpool. That institution was established to prepare Polish architects for the tasks of postwar reconstruction, including the reconstruction of historic ensembles destroyed in planned demolitions by the German occupiers.[153] His lectures in the history of Polish architecture, including vernacular wooden buildings, resulted in the book *The Architecture of Poland*, published in London in 1956 (figure 3.30).[154] After the war, Dmochowski taught at a number of Polish institutions of higher education in Britain, and worked at the Historic Buildings Section of the London County Council, where he conducted surveys of historic buildings in the British capital.[155]

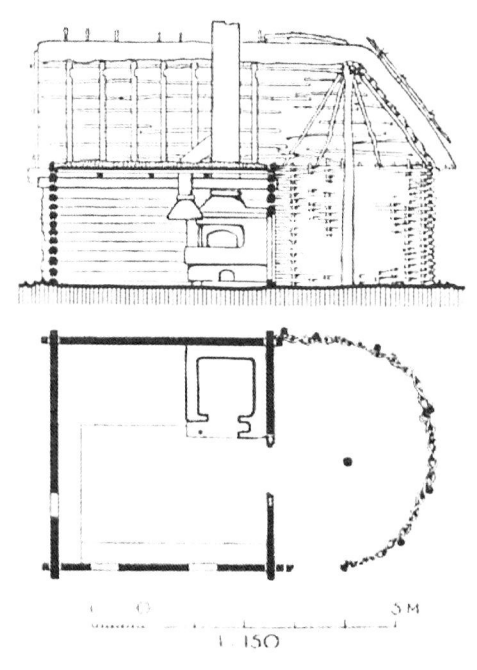

In 1958, he left for Lagos, where he was appointed to the Department of Antiquities, joining an already sizable group of Polish émigré architects and engineers who arrived in colonial Nigeria after the war and who often stayed in the country after independence, as Dmochowski would.[156] Within the remit of the department to study and preserve material culture of the diverse peoples of Nigeria, Dmochowski worked closely with the department directors, Bernard Fagg (1957–63) and Kenneth Murray (1963–68), succeeded by its first Nigerian head, Ekpo Eyo (1968–79).[157] On his arrival, Dmochowski was put in charge of design work required by the department's program of establishing regional museums in Nigeria.[158] Along with designing the extension of the Lagos museum and detailing museum projects delivered by other architects, Dmochowski drew layouts of museums in Owo and in Benin City, both based on vernacular typologies specific for the regions (figure 3.31).[159] This design work benefited from his second remit at the department: that of surveying vernacular architecture, which reflected the increasing acknowledgment of vernacular buildings as part of Nigerian heritage. At times, both tasks were intertwined—for instance, when a surveyed building was restored and transformed into a museum, as was the case with Gidan Makama, a historical palace in Kano. Apart from the latter, on Nigeria's independence the department succeeded in opening museums in Jos (1952), the Nigerian Museum in Lagos (1957), Ife (1954), Oron (1959), and temporary museums in Esie, Benin City, Kaduna, and Argungu.[160]

In 1965, Dmochowski left his position at the department as well as his recent appointment as reader at the School of Architecture at Ahmadu Bello University in Zaria (1964), the first architectural school in Nigeria.[161] He returned to Poland to assume the position of professor of the history of architecture at the School of Architecture at Gdańsk University of Technology, where he founded the Institute of Tropical Architecture.[162] At the institute, his team of up to six architects and graphic designers redrew to scale the materials gathered in Nigeria.[163] Between 1965 and 1967, Dmochowski traveled twice to Nigeria, and in 1972 he assumed the position of principal architect with the Federal Department of Antiquities in Jos, where he was put in charge of the construction of MOTNA, thus reanimating the project initiated by Bernard Fagg, founder of the Jos museum, which had opened in 1952.[164] With the help of members of his Gdańsk team, and of scholars at the Ahmadu Bello University, Dmochowski translated his surveys of vernacular buildings into designs for full-scale replicas, typically replacing fragile materials with modern and durable ones.[165] This procedure followed his earlier adaptation of the Gidan Makama, which was measured, dismantled, and rebuilt on a secure foundation of masonry, reinforced concrete, and sheet copper as a termite-proof course. As with this building in Kano, which was rebuilt by the emir's chief builder under

3.30. "Cottages in Podhale," isometry by Bolesław Fidali at the Polish School of Architecture, University of Liverpool (UK), early 1940s. Bolesław Szmidt, ed., *The Polish School of Architecture, 1942–45* (Liverpool: Birchall, 1945), 53.

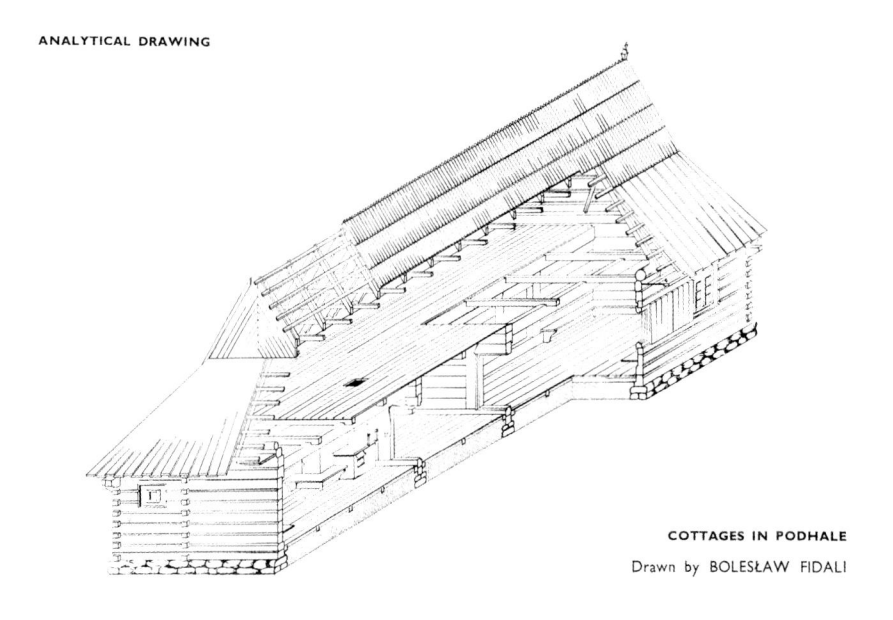

3.31. The Benin Museum, design 1959, plan. Zbigniew Dmochowski and others at the Department of Antiquities, Lagos. Bernard Fagg, "The Museums of Nigeria," *Museum International* 16 (1963): 129.

3.32. Plan of the Jos Museum, including the Museum of Traditional Nigerian Architecture, 1978. *25 Years of Jos Museum* (Jos: National Museum, 1978).

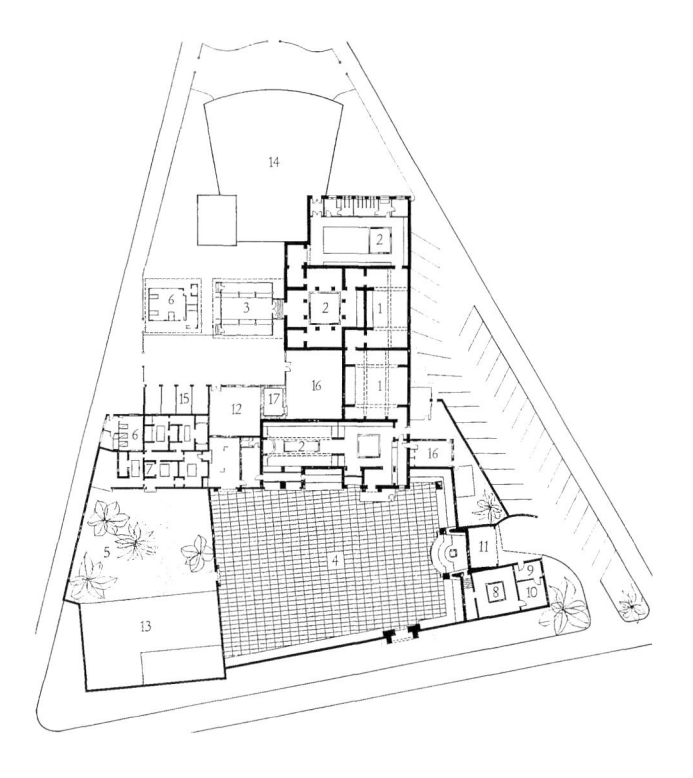

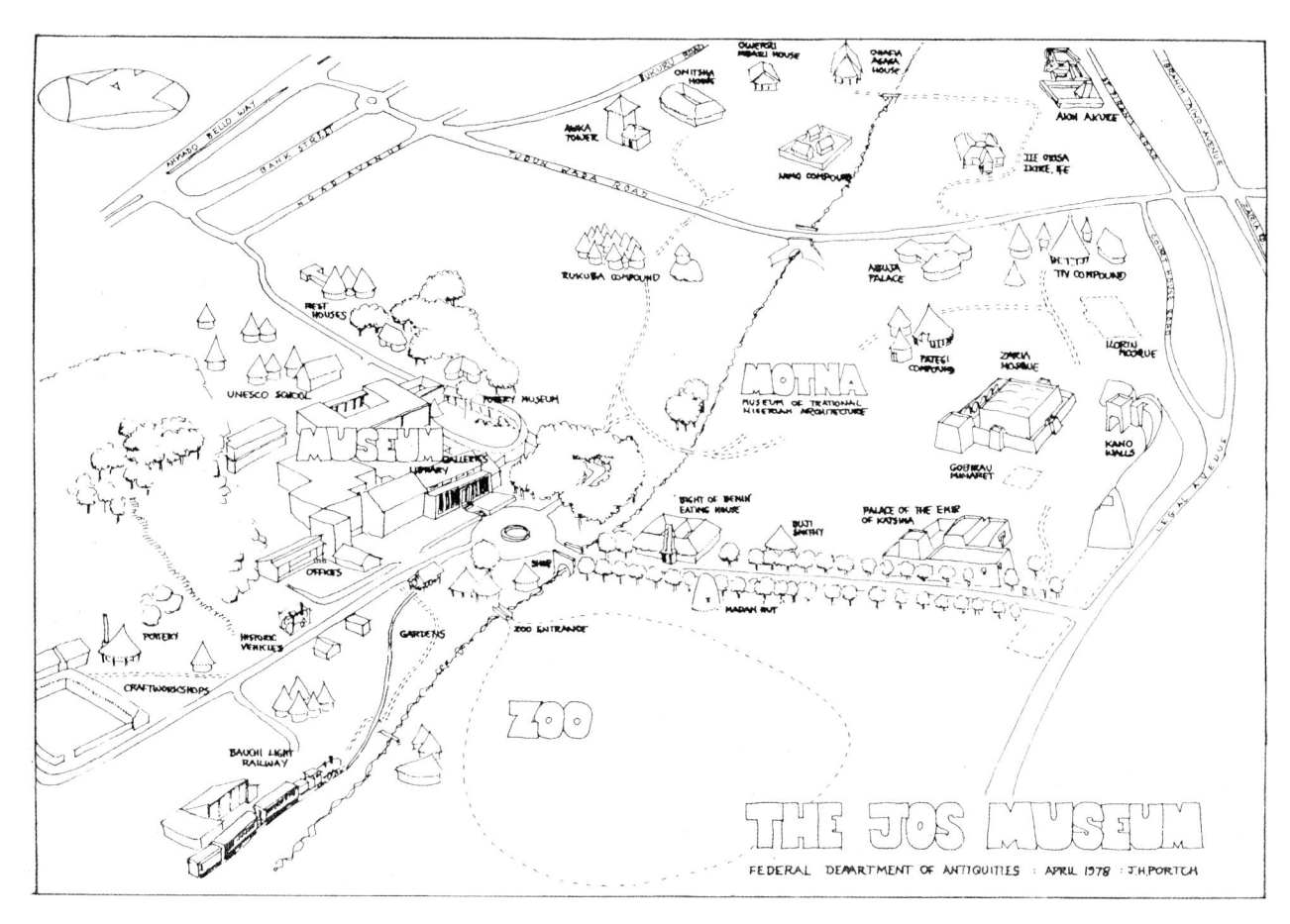

WORLDING EASTERN EUROPE

Dmochowski's supervision, the buildings at MOTNA were constructed by craftsmen from the respective regions, who used traditional construction techniques, including *tubali*, cone-shaped, sun-baked bricks used by Hausa builders (figure 3.32).[166] In line with his previous design experience at the Department of Antiquities, and following the example of Bernard Fagg, Dmochowski designed accommodations for the expanding Jos museum in structures inspired by vernacular buildings, including the Pottery Museum in the form of a traditional Nupe house.[167]

Dmochowski's failing health forced him to leave Nigeria in 1981, and he died the following year, before the *Introduction to Nigerian Traditional Architecture* was published in 1990 by the London-based publisher Ethnographica and the National Commission for Museums and Monuments in Lagos.[168] Based on sixteen hundred drawings, thousands of photographs, and texts written by Dmochowski since the 1970s, the book is an unfinished work. Some sections lack commentary, and the structure of the published work is a container for sections drafted by the author (such as "Hausa Building Technology" and "Muslim Religious Architecture"), distributed over three volumes according to broad geographic locations (Northern Nigeria; South-West and Central Nigeria; and South-Eastern Nigeria).[169]

While initiated by the colonial administration, Dmochowski's project explicitly targeted the systematic devalorization of indigenous culture in Nigeria under colonial rule. The main addressees of the *Introduction* were African postcolonial elites who saw in vernacular African architecture "a bunch of mud huts," wrote Ekundayo Adeyinka Adeyemi, Nigerian architect, scholar, and educator, Dmochowski's collaborator, and later head of the Zaria School of Architecture. Adeyemi argued that Dmochowski's aim was to challenge this perception.[170] In his own words: "all over the world familiarity with the architectural achievements of one's country, an understanding and appreciation of its traditions and development through the ages, [is] now almost universally considered to be an elementary means towards the formation of national consciousness and self-assertion. The aim that is sought by these means is to create deference and regard, and finally love, for one's own traditions."[171]

This argument, which closely followed Dmochowski's lectures to his Polish students in Liverpool, was repeated in the first guidebook to MOTNA (1978). Its author—probably Dmochowski himself—added that the museum responded to the "lack of respect" for vernacular buildings in Nigeria.[172] By preserving them as part of "national culture," it aimed at liberating Nigerian students of architecture from "the unjustified sense of inferiority…with respect to foreign achievements." In contrast to the often degraded state of such buildings as Nigerian visitors would have known them from their towns and villages, the guidebook demonstrated to those visitors "how extremely rich is their own architectural heritage; how ingenious in construction, how functional in planning and beautiful in general composition and decoration."[173] Sensitive to Nigeria's interregional rivalries, both the guidebook and the *Introduction to Nigerian Traditional Architecture* emphasized the unique value of each of the country's building cultures represented by structures in the museum's compound, which in this way became a miniature map of Nigeria.[174] In spite of this attempt, after the construction of MOTNA some among its visitors took issue with what they perceived as the dominance of Islamic architectural monuments on the museum grounds.[175]

While being a comprehensive documentation of buildings and building cultures in Nigeria, Dmochowski saw his work as more than that. Just as the MOTNA guidebook addressed "Nigerian students of architecture," so was the *Introduction* dedicated to the "architectural youth of Nigeria" who "[t]hrough the intense study of the functional planning, remarkable construction and splendid form created by their ancestors…will develop an instinct, an almost subconscious capacity for shaping space in a way that would be their own continuation of the work done by their forebears."[176] Similar to Demas Nwoko and British architect Alan Vaughan-Richards, Dmochowski's interest in vernacular architecture did not translate into an encouragement of reviving traditional crafts.[177] Rather, he advised Nigerian architects to accept "tradition as the starting point of their creative, independent thinking" and to develop it toward "a modern school of Nigerian Architecture."[178]

Dmochowski argued that the privileged tool for such a task was the architectural drawing. As with his previous engagements in Warsaw and Liverpool, the drawing was understood not only as a common denominator for architectural practice at large, but also as a specifically architectural mode of thinking.[179] The *Introduction* contains a range of drawings, including plans, sections, and elevations, but among them Dmochowski favored isometries, or parallel projections. The most elaborate were drawn with axes in 60-degree angle to each other, among them the cutaway isometry of Masallaci Juma'a (Friday Mosque) in Zaria (figure 3.33).

In the *Introduction*, isometries were used to synthesize information gathered by various techniques. Their bases were measured drawings, produced by means of plane-table surveys for measuring horizontal projections and three-dimensional triangulations for sections and elevations.[180] These survey techniques were introduced at the interwar Institute of Polish Architecture by Jerzy Raczyński, Sosnowski's first assistant, who adapted to architectural purposes the military photogrammetric methods that he had learned during his studies in Germany (1913–14). In particular, Dmochowski applied the "radial" technique, which consisted of measuring the directions and distances from a chosen focal point, and that allowed for measuring distances to inaccessible points starting from already surveyed ones.[181] This technique resulted in precise measurements of vernacular buildings in Nigeria produced in a timely manner by a small team guided by one qualified surveyor (figure 3.34). The team members were recruited from the Department of Antiquities, sometimes assisted by students of the Zaria School of Architecture, who were trained by Dmochowski on site.[182]

Measured drawings were complemented by historical sources and secondary literature and, in particular, by photographs. Taken by Dmochowski, who registered the location of the camera in the field notes, these carried information about materials and details, both structural and decorative, and conveyed the general atmosphere of the buildings. When possible, Dmochowski photographed the complete construction process, step by step, and documented the organization and division of labor, both social and technical, as well as the training of the builders, the commissioning procedure, and remuneration (figure 3.35). He paid particular attention to building materials, including those provided by the emerging construction industry (cement, steel), which were sometimes combined with traditional ones. This information was recorded in the field notes, together with the quantities and origins of materials, the process of their preparation and tools needed for it, as well as interviews with house owners, master builders, and workers.

Yet Dmochowski's isometries were far from mere additive collections of data. Rather, they were instrumental in his attempt to uncover what he saw as specifically architectural values of the studied buildings. He explained this ambition in a report to the Department of Antiquities, where he wrote that his study was "deliberately confined to the architectural analysis of the building's virtues.... Information concerning natural, social and religious setting is provided where it was thought necessary for fuller appreciation of artistic and technological aspects."[183] Accordingly, Dmochowski stressed the expression by architectural means of climatic, social, and religious conditions of the building surveyed, rather than seeing them as determinants of the building's form. For instance, he did not hesitate to call Zaria's Masallaci Juma'a a "classical" monument, "the

3.33. "Zaria. Masallaci Juma'a. Isometry of Interior." Drawing by Zbigniew Dmochowski and collaborators. Published in Zbigniew Dmochowski, *An Introduction to Nigerian Traditional Architecture* (London: Ethnographica; Lagos: National Commission for Museums and Monuments, 1990), vol. 1, 2.19.

> 3.34. Measured drawing of a house in Bida by Zbigniew Dmochowski and collaborators.

> 3.35. "Kano. The Rebuilding of Gidan Makama. Stages in the Construction of a Domed Roof." Photograph by Zbigniew Dmochowski. Published in Zbigniew Dmochowski, *An Introduction to Nigerian Traditional Architecture* (London: Ethnographica; Lagos: National Commission for Museums and Monuments, 1990), vol. 1, 1.50.

> 3.36. "Benin. Oba's Palace. Plan." Drawing by Zbigniew Dmochowski and collaborators. Published in Zbigniew Dmochowski, *An Introduction to Nigerian Traditional Architecture* (London: Ethnographica; Lagos: National Commission for Museums and Monuments, 1990), vol. 2, 1.18.

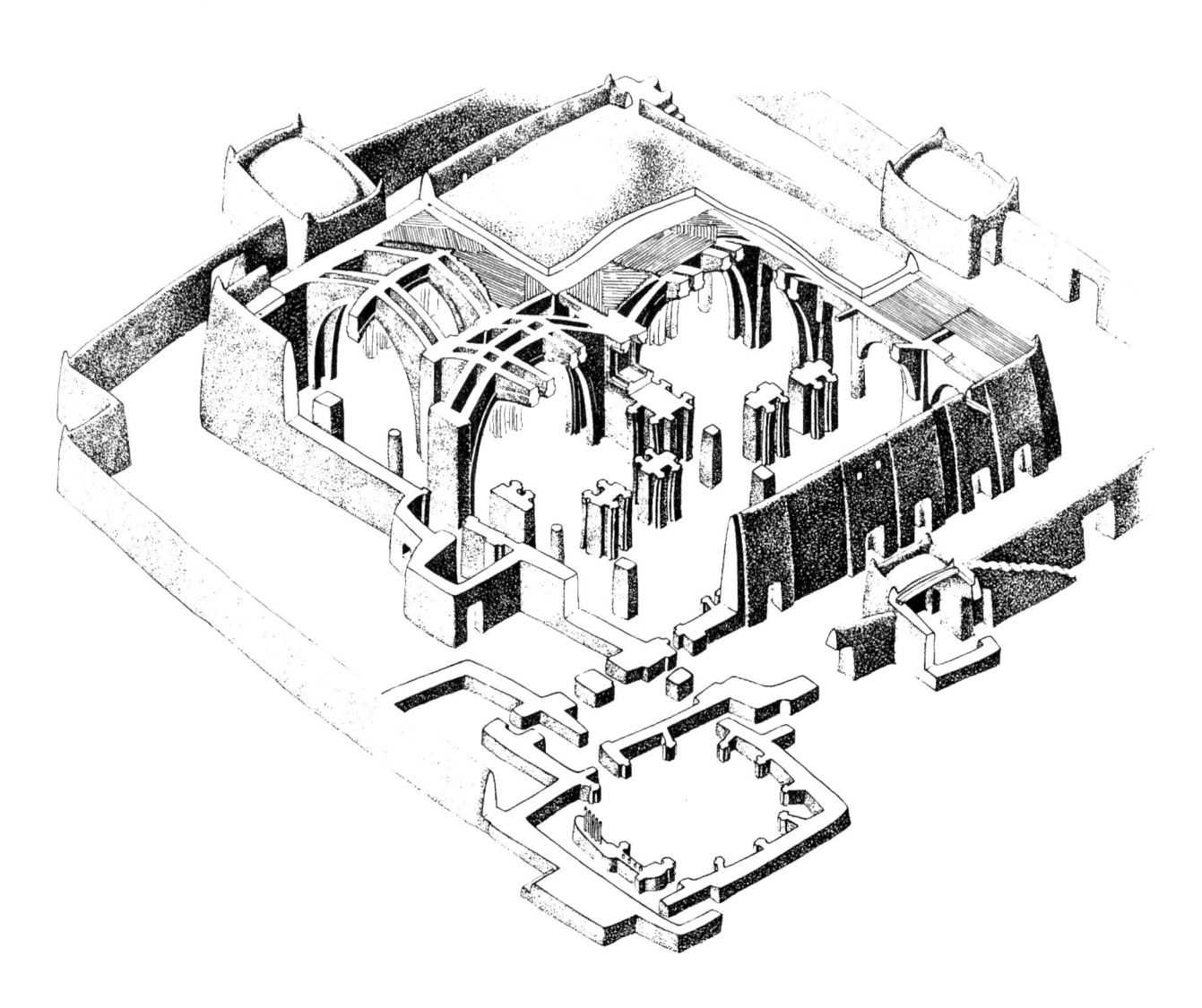

WORLDING EASTERN EUROPE

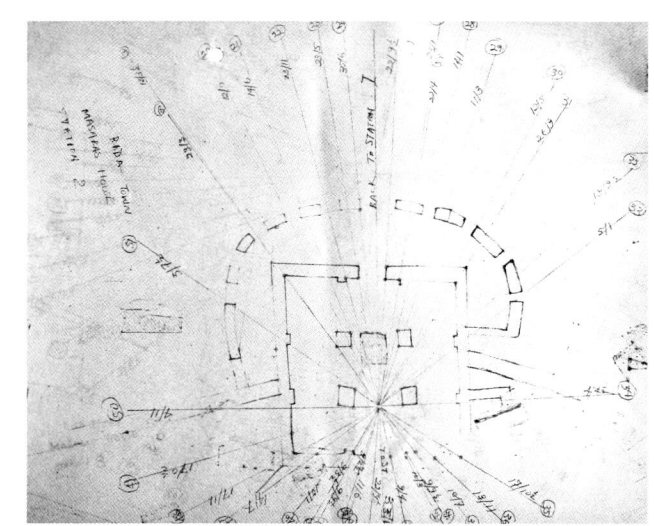

word classical being used to express the ultimate achievement possible within given technological limits."[184] Discussing Benin architecture, he was interested in the composition of individual interiors and their relations to each other that negotiated the spheres of the personal, the social, and the sacred (figure 3.36).[185] Describing a *katamba* (entrance building) in Pategi, he admired the "subtly obtained contrast between the mass of the roof and the delicately screened base of carved posts" (figure 3.37).[186] When commenting on the village of Bahit in the Central Plateau, he praised the ways in which its "spatial composition" offered "picturesque views" and "alleviated the impression of confinement within the walled compound."[187]

Dmochowski's photographs, and in particular the drawings, convey these observations. As Sosnowski had emphasized to his collaborators at the Institute of Polish Architecture, a drawing could, "for the sake of a clear vision, eliminate later additions, reconstruct…what was once produced and today is concealed or disfigured, sometimes delineate the presumed shapes or…emphasize only some features while leaving out others or at least weakening them."[188] This approach was conveyed by the isometries produced at the institute. Having learned this approach in Warsaw, Dmochowski perfected it in Liverpool, applied it in the illustrations in *Architecture of Poland*, then employed it in Nigeria.[189] Accordingly, the differentiation of the thickness of lines in the section of a building in Awka Nimo emphasized the contrast between the load-bearing wood parts and

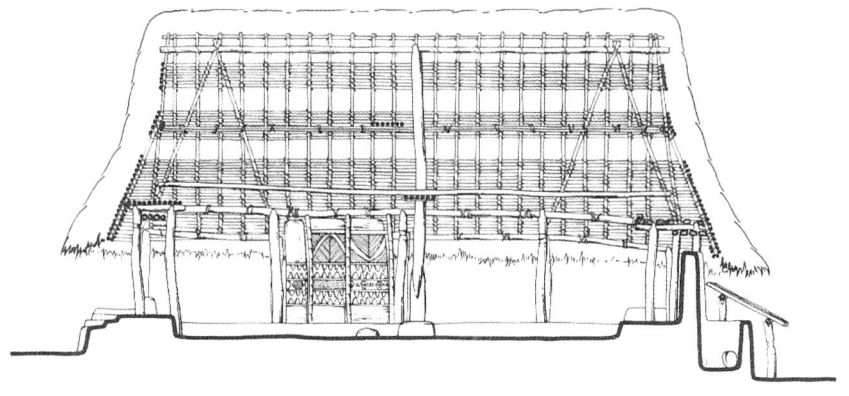

3.37. "Pategi. The Katamba of Etsu Pategi." Photograph by Zbigniew Dmochowski. Published in Zbigniew Dmochowski, *An Introduction to Nigerian Traditional Architecture* (London: Ethnographica; Lagos: National Commission for Museums and Monuments, 1990), vol. 2, 3.41.

3.38. "Compound of Isiebue Nwakwa, House 1," section. Drawing by Zbigniew Dmochowski and collaborators. Published in Zbigniew Dmochowski, *An Introduction to Nigerian Traditional Architecture* (London: Ethnographica; Lagos: National Commission for Museums and Monuments, 1990), vol. 3, 92.

> 3.39. Regional Museum in Esie, design 1969, model. Federal Ministry of Works and Housing, Lagos; Augustine Egbor (director), Marian Łyczkowski (project architect).

> 3.40. Regional Museum in Esie, design 1969, plans and sections. Federal Ministry of Works and Housing, Lagos; Augustine Egbor (director), Marian Łyczkowski (project architect).

> 3.41. Regional museum in Kaduna, design 1968, model. Federal Ministry of Works and Housing, Lagos; Augustine Egbor (director), Marian Łyczkowski (project architect).

WORLDING EASTERN EUROPE

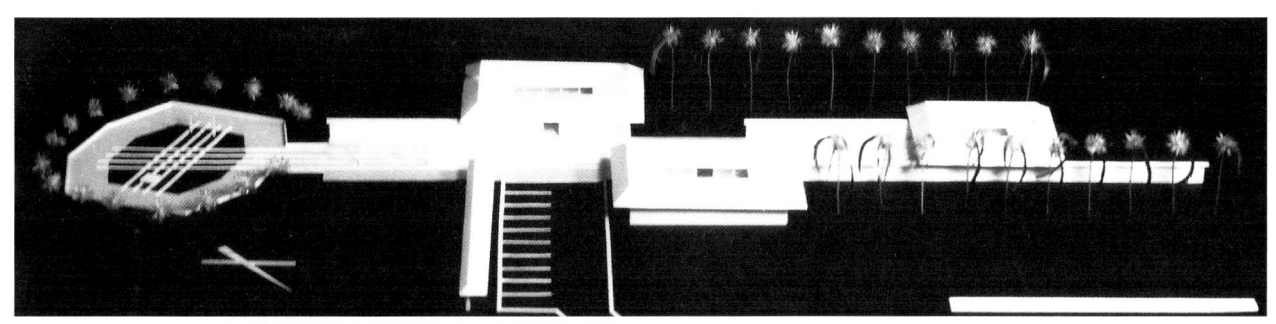

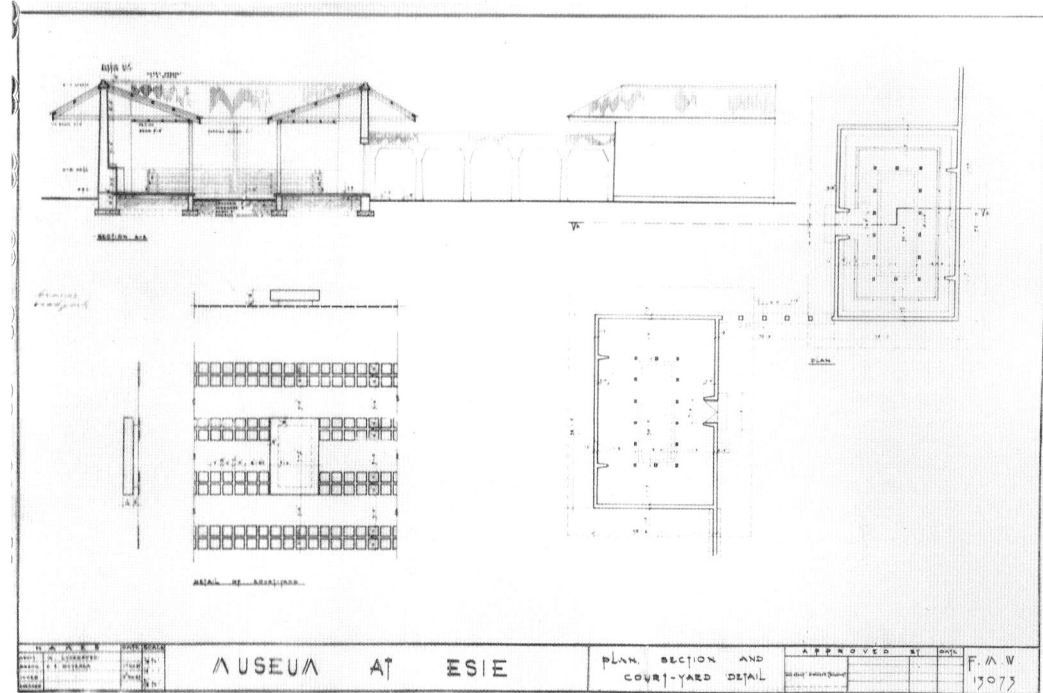

the loam walls, which did not have a structural function but which framed the living space, shaped the interior, and provided a visual screen (figure 3.38). The continuity between walls, floor, and surroundings was emphasized in the drawing by means of a continuous line, while the hierarchy of wooden structural elements was reflected by the gradation of the lines' thicknesses.[190] In this way, the drawing showed the building as a composite of two materials characterized by specific structural logic: the stereometry of mud and the tectonics of wood.

That such drawings provided a bridge to architectural practice is proven by the designs by the Federal Ministry of Works and Housing in Lagos, where Polish architect Marian Łyczkowski was put in charge of the program of national museums after independence (1964–70). Dmochowski's surveys, which Łyczkowski received from Kenneth Murray, were translated into the blueprints of the museum in Esie, constructed in 1969. Designed as an ensemble of three pavilions (exhibition, workshop, social facilities) around open courtyards, the museum's details conveyed the contrast between the masonry and the roof structure in Yoruba architecture, emphasized in Dmochowski's survey drawings (figures 3.39 and 3.40). Similarly, Dmochowski's studies of Hausa architecture, its materiality and indigenous technologies of climatic control, were the basis for Łyczkowski's project for the museum in Kaduna (unrealized, 1968) (figure 3.41).[191]

Dmochowski's "architectural analysis" of the "virtues" of particular buildings culminated in his emphasis on the "excellence in shaping splendid forms in space," and "spatial composition" in vernacular buildings in Nigeria.[192] In his work, space could mean many things, and his drawings showed those possibilities: from an additive composition of volumes, as in the rendering of the Emir's Palace in Potiskum; through a sequence of planes, as in the drawing of the Masallaci Juma'a in Zaria; to an isometric container, as in the Kano market stalls; to the sense of bodily enclosure in his renderings of the Nok house (figure 3.42).[193] Dmochowski posited such

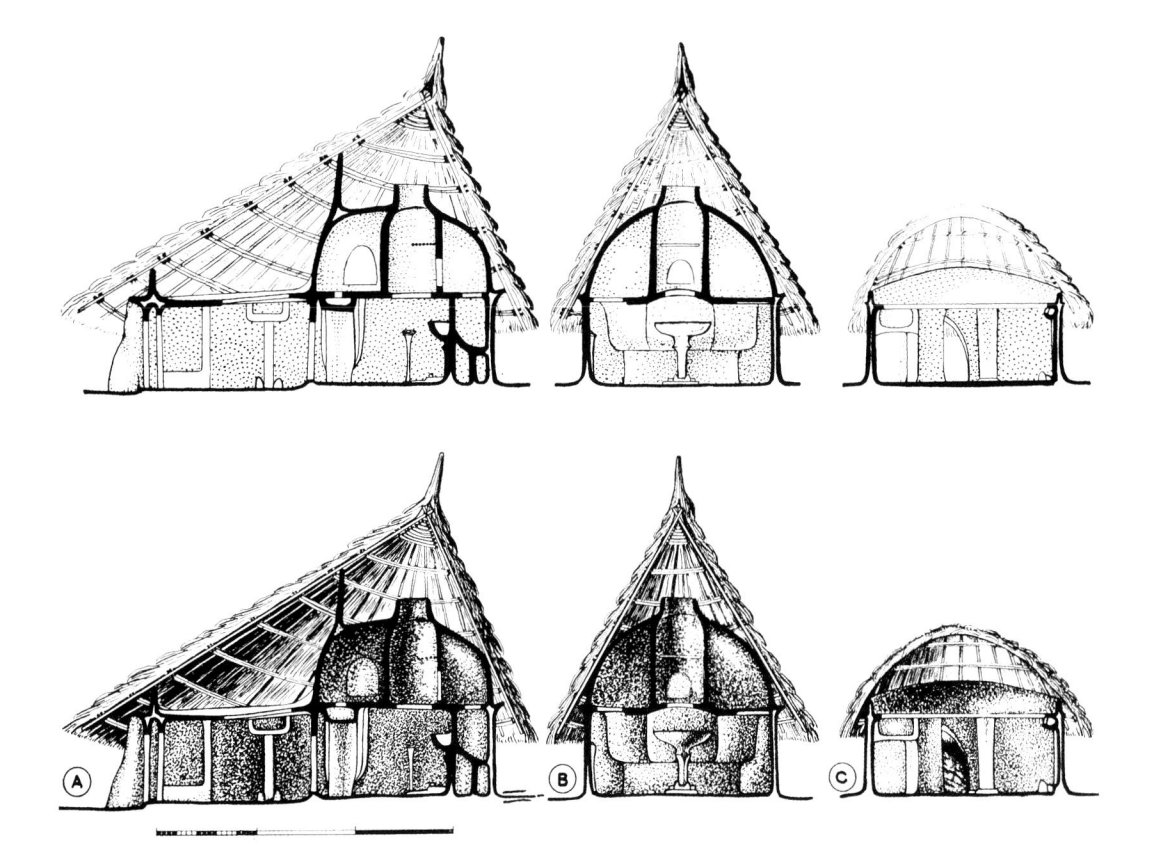

3.42. A house in Nok, two variants of rendering of the sections. Zbigniew Dmochowski and collaborators.

understanding of architecture as "three-dimensional art" as the common feature of Nigerian architecture, and at times he attributed distinct spatial features to specific ethnic building cultures.[194]

These statements suggest that Dmochowski's project was deeply informed by the modernist vision of "architecture as space," and its performative historiographies, from Sigfried Giedion to Christian Norberg-Schulz, for whom the modernist "discovery" of space allowed architecture to be seen as always-already spatial.[195] This pedigree is consistent with Dmochowski's multiple meanings of space, which in European modernism was far from a unified concept, and with his use of isometry, privileged by architects of the modern movement.

This dependence on European modernism may appear as an imposition of foreign categories onto West African material culture, thus seemingly undermining Dmochowski's ambition to decolonize Nigerian architecture. Yet as pointed out by art historian Chika Okeke-Agulu, modernist concepts and formal tools were part of artistic practice in Nigeria since the late-colonial period, and they were put to highly divergent purposes and associated with opposing political positions. They could be employed to institutionalize professional artistic practice in Nigeria, as was attempted in the early twentieth century by painter and nationalist Aina Onabolu, who applied perspective and landscape painting to contemporary African topics. But they could be also used to revive traditional crafts as envisaged by Kenneth Murray, a sympathizer with indirect rule.[196] In post-independence Nigeria, the debate about the uses of European modernism was advanced by Ulli Beier and the members of the Zaria Art Society, including Nwoko and artist Uche Okeke.[197] The latter applied the mode of perception shaped by modernist experiments to vernacular cultures as sources of new formal solutions, and not just of subject matters. For Okeke, this meant embracing the ambiguity between the mimetic, symbolic, and expressive functions of the line in the drawings of the Igbo-Uli, which he explored in his graphic work.[198] Like Okeke, Dmochowski appropriated a modernist concept, that of space, and a modernist tool, that of isometry, in order to expand the precedence of contemporary architectural practices toward the Nigerian vernacular.

This centrality of the concept of space distinguished Dmochowski's Polish and Nigerian work, in spite of numerous continuities between them discussed earlier. The discourse of space was absent from his writings from the 1930s, which focused instead on the evolution of construction systems in response to material, technological, and sometimes economic concerns in rural settlements in the Polesie region.[199] In these studies, Dmochowski had little concern for aesthetic intentions of individual builders: he revised specific buildings as test cases for hypotheses about the overarching evolution of structural solutions, and his interlocutors were other scholars rather than indigenous builders or professional architects. On rare occasions when Dmochowski noted the aesthetic qualities of a building ("the barn…is a strong accent among monotonous buildings"), he attributed their forms to utilitarian concerns and assured the reader that "there is no reason to assume that it was consciously used for the purpose of an [aesthetic] composition."[200]

This denial of aesthetic intentions reveals Dmochowski's orientalist gaze at the Polesie peasant, which was characteristic for the metropolitan elite in interwar Poland vis-à-vis inhabitants of territories targeted by internal colonization. That discourse closely followed dichotomies between the colonial and colonized cultures, and conveyed the paternalism and civilizing mission of the Polish state, with the gentry country house as the center of civilization, culture, and progress, as opposed to the backwardness, superstition, and exoticism of the local population, sometimes explicitly compared with Africans.[201] That gaze was denounced by the journalist Ryszard Kapuściński, born in Polesie: when traveling around West Africa in the 1960s on behalf of the Polish Press Agency, Kapuściński retrospectively discovered Polesie as a "colonized" territory.[202]

On his arrival in Lagos, Dmochowski might have drawn similar parallels between the colonization of Nigeria and Poland's internal colonization programs. Whether that was the case or not, in contrast to his writings about Polesie, the *Introduction to Traditional Nigerian Architecture* would forcefully emphasize the aesthetic intentions of builders from the past, whether collective or individuals such as Mallam Mikhaila, who had been in charge of Zaria's Masallaci Juma'a. Spatial representations of vernacular buildings became for Dmochowski a tool on this path, and he projected his understanding of spatial concepts as intentions of their creators: products of an intellectual labor that was specifically architectural. For instance, commenting about Gidan Makama in Kano, he wrote that by "resign[ing] from using pillars," the architect provided "as large a space as possible, architecturally elaborate and brilliant, giving an unimpaired view on the whole interior."[203] However speculative this projection might have been, Dmochowski's interpretation needs to be seen as a contribution to the decolonization of Nigerian architecture. Dmochowski used the modernist claim to a trans-historical concept of space in order to connect his ideal readers—"the architectural youth of Nigeria"—and the builders of the past. In this way, he imagined a reunited community that had been torn by the violence of colonial epistemologies.

Decolonization of Architectural Education

Dmochowski's work debunked colonial oppositions that had served to devaluate colonized cultures: it emphasized the aesthetic and technological creativity of indigenous builders (rather than attributing innovations to European influence), and it showed vernacular buildings as part of an evolving society (rather than seeing them as ahistorical and immutable). It was in architectural education, and specifically in the curriculum building of the Zaria School of Architecture, that this potential of Dmochowski's surveys for the decolonization of Nigerian architecture came most forcefully to the fore.

Established in 1952 as part of the Nigerian College of Arts, Science, and Technology and relocated to Zaria in 1954, the Faculty of Architecture was the first to offer architectural education to Nigerians who, until then, could be trained in the country only as draftsmen and needed to go abroad for an architectural degree. In this way, the school in Zaria ushered in the way for the profession's establishment in a country where, on gaining independence, there were only two Nigerian private offices, including Oluwole Olumuyiwa (educated at the University of Manchester) and Alex Ekwueme with S. I. Kola-Bankole (educated at the University of Washington and the University of Minnesota, respectively). The rest of the tiny group of Nigerian architects, educated in Britain or the United States, went into public service, including Michael Olutusen Onafowokan (University of Glasgow) and Adedokun Adeyemi (Architectural Association in London), the older brother of Ekundayo Adeyemi (himself educated at Zaria).[204]

The School of Architecture was organized according to the British model by the predominantly British teaching staff, and at independence they secured the accreditation of the Board of Architectural Education at the Royal Institute of British Architects (RIBA).[205] That accreditation followed complex negotiations in which the board at first resisted deviations from RIBA's standard curriculum. In the end, the board yielded to political pressure, notably that of the Colonial Office in London, and accepted that the curriculum in Zaria could include courses specific for Nigeria as long as they were introduced in addition to RIBA standard requirements.[206]

By the mid-1960s, this curriculum became a bone of contention, with tension escalating between students, the university administration, and the (mainly British) staff. The students saw the curriculum as unsuitable for an African school, and challenged the lecturers on the very high attrition rate.[207] As an example of the latter, Ekundayo Adeyemi recalled that in his cohort of twenty-five fellow students enrolled in the 1958/59 academic year, only six graduated in 1963.[208] In response to the situation, students accused British lecturers of blocking access of Nigerians to the British-dominated profession. In this way, they were hurting the economy of the independent nation, which was in dire need of professionals—a concern echoed by Nigerian officials.[209] The lecturers countered that the drawing skills of the majority of students did not match RIBA requirements, which centered on "the ability to observe or think in three-dimensions and reproduce this in drawing."[210] W. J. Kidd, the British head of school (1965–69), offered an explanation and argued that the "lack of three-dimensional appreciation" of Nigerian students resulted from "a lack of playthings and mechanical contacts during childhood."[211] Accordingly, and in spite of university-wide protests, high rates of students continued to be removed from the course.[212]

One consequence of Kidd's reasoning was to plead tolerance for the students and call on the teachers to lower their expectations. Such a call was made by Ishaya Audu, the university's vice chancellor, who repeated after Kidd that Nigerian students were "obviously disadvantaged" since they "did not normally grow up with three-dimensional toys and therefore might not grasp complex three-dimensional problems."[213] Evidently, this would not have been Dmochowski's conclusion. His isometric drawings, which revealed spatial concepts in vernacular Nigerian architecture, eloquently refuted the purported lack of spatial imagination among Nigerians. Dmochowski's core argument about the country's vernacular architecture as a product of three-dimensional thinking would reverberate in the School of Architecture's newly revised curriculum, which followed recommendations of a panel headed by Augustine Egbor of the Federal Ministry of Works and Housing (1969). Revisions to the curriculum were initiated by the international team of lecturers headed by Robert R. Ferens, visiting professor from the University of Oregon (1969–71), and were implemented by Adeyemi as head of school (1974–86) and his team, the majority of which consisted of Polish, Hungarian, and Czech architects.[214]

In the framework of the new curriculum, studies of vernacular buildings became a way of introducing students to "architectural and three-dimensional thinking."[215] Such studies were included in the freehand drawing course, led by Ewa Oleszkiewicz, and the introductory course, first conceived by Ewa Podolak and developed by Hubert Dąbrowski, three lecturers coming from Poland.[216] The new focus conformed with the call from prominent Nigerian architects to give vernacular buildings a predominant place in the training of architects, and was then followed in the curricula of newly opened architectural schools in Nigeria, modeled on the School of Architecture in Zaria, including Nsukka (1963) and Lagos (1970).[217] The inclusion of Ibo, Yoruba, and Benin buildings to the Zaria curriculum was praised by governmental officials, one of whom, at the opening of an exhibition of students' designs at Zaria (1972), called for buildings that would be "architecturally satisfying, culturally harmonious and economically within the reach of ordinary man."[218] Building on the work of the first generation of British lecturers at the School of Architecture, and in line with the Egbor panel's recommendations to introduce research-led teaching that would respond to the needs of the Nigerian economy, vernacular building traditions were studied at Zaria. These surveys straddled both architectural and urban scales, and paid particular attention to technological solutions.[219]

In addition to the introductory and freehand drawing courses, surveys of vernacular architecture also became integrated into design modules at

Zaria. During Dmochowski's employment at the Faculty of Architecture in the early 1960s, his research already included "experimental designs...for buildings that would combine modern technology and planning with the traditional Nigerian ways of architectural composition."[220] A decade later, such an approach can be seen in the "Climatic Comfort Design Guide" (1979), which Hungarian-born architect and artist Nick Hollo developed during his teaching at the school in Zaria (by then renamed Department of Architecture at the Faculty of Environmental Design). Hollo used the guide to teach his Building Science course, as well as in the Rural Development Module, which he cotaught together with Hungarian architect Peter Magyar (figure 3.43).[221] While many of the lecturers actively studied vernacular architecture in the region, it was Dmochowski's drawings that were used as teaching aids, as Magyar recalls.[222]

More generally, drawings were the main unit of the circulation of Dmochowski's work before the posthumous publication of the *Introduction*, and that circulation facilitated the continuous infiltration of his work into architectural practice in Nigeria. His drawings were disseminated among students at Zaria and other Nigerian architectural schools.[223] They infiltrated public design offices, such as the Ministry of Works and Housing in Lagos, where they impacted on the work of Łyczkowski and his colleagues, as well as private ones established by Zaria graduates, such as Habitat Associates and Triad Associates, whose work was inspired by regional traditions.[224] Dmochowski's drawings were also reproduced in the journal of the Nigerian Institute of Architects, which published numerous articles on vernacular architecture in Nigeria.[225]

This introduction of vernacular buildings into architectural education in Nigeria was paralleled by the process of indigenization of Nigerian architectural practice. A decisive step in this process was the replacement of the colonial-era, British-dominated Society of Professional Architects in Nigeria by the Nigerian Institute of Architects, founded in the mid-1950s by the small group of Nigerians educated in the UK, and recognized by the government in 1960 with Onafowokan as president and Olumuyiwa as general secretary.[226] Expatriate architects were often blocked from entering the new institute for prolonged periods. Further restrictions were introduced on expat architects in 1969, when the professional title of architect was reserved for Nigerian citizens and members of the Architects Registration Council of Nigeria (ARCON), thus forcing foreign architects to enter partnerships with Nigerians.[227] ARCON was also put in charge of the supervision of architectural education in Nigeria, including the Zaria school, which decided not to continue with RIBA examination and lost the British institute's accreditation (1968).[228]

These changes aimed at undoing the economic and institutional dominance of British architects, and they paralleled Dmochowski's attempts at undoing the Eurocentric hierarchy of value and prestige inherited from the colonial period. Eastern Europeans at Zaria's School of Architecture were instrumental in this process. They provided the workforce that bridged the gap between the departure of British educators, many of whom left in the wake of the student protests, and the period when Nigerians would take over.[229] Supported by the "expatriate staff supplementation scheme" that allowed increasing the salaries of foreign nationals, architects from socialist countries bought time for selected Nigerians, such as Adeyemi, who left for Columbia University in New York City for additional training. On his return, Adeyemi took over from Polish architect Barbara Urbanowicz as the head of school, while working closely with Eastern Europeans who supported him in the implementation of the new curriculum. Most of them worked as designers, too. For example, Hubert Dąbrowski and Jan Gniadzik designed the new building of the Department of Architecture at Zaria, where they taught (1974–80), while the Project Office at Zaria's Department of Urban and Regional Planning was headed by Stanisław Juchnowicz.[230]

Commenting on the large numbers of Eastern Europeans in architectural schools between 1963 and 1979, Nigerian scholar Zanzan Akaka Uji wrote that "Polish and other Eastern European nationals...virtually displaced the British founders."[231] Uji's assessment may be supported by FTO Polservice statistics, which show that in Nigeria between independence and the 1980s, at least 107 Polish architects worked in the country, among them 28 at Nigeria's universities, including Zaria (10), Nsukka (6), Jos (3), and elsewhere.[232] Because of this overrepresentation of Eastern Europeans, Uji calls this period in Nigerian architectural education "semi-colonial."[233]

His qualification was contradicted by Adeyemi, who emphasized that, in their transitory role at Zaria, the position of Eastern European architects was distinct from that of British professionals. Adeyemi recalled that in spite of being in the majority, Polish, Czech, and Hungarian lecturers at Zaria never posed a danger of dominating the School of Architecture in the way British lecturers had in the 1950s and early 1960s.[234] This opinion would have pleased the authors of guidelines issued by socialist FTOs, who contrasted the work of Eastern European professionals with the "neocolonial" motivations of Western professionals.[235] However, and departing from the explicitly postcolonial terms of Dmochowski's work, in the next chapter I will argue that this loyalty might have had less to do with an imagined postcolonial proximity between Eastern Europe and the newly independent nations, and more with the political economy of foreign trade under state socialism and the contractual frameworks of socialist FTOs.

ENERGOPROJEKT: FREEDOM AND POVERTY OF THE PERIPHERY

When Charles Polónyi published in 1992 the memoir of his peripatetic work, *An Architect-Planner on the Peripheries*, the title of his book conveyed a sense of postsocialist melancholy: Hungary's celebrated "return to Europe" after the end of socialism meant the return to Europe's periphery.[236] Such a postsocialist vantage point might have retrospectively sharpened what Polónyi experienced during his travels to 1960s and 1970s West Africa: an imaginary geography shared by Eastern Europeans and Africans at the fringes of centers of knowledge production.

Yet Polónyi's use of the term "periphery" exceeded melancholy: while he took issue with the "false starts" of the periphery, he saw the periphery as an open field where ideas forged in the centers may be questioned, tested, and modified.[237] Such understanding subscribed to a tradition in Eastern European culture that distinguished between periphery and province.[238] According to Croatian archeologist and art historian Ljubo Karaman, provincial cultural production was characterized by an influence of one powerful center; in contrast, a peripheral artist receives influences from many centers, mixes, and develops them, taking advantage of what Karaman called the "freedom of the periphery."[239] Such combinatorics is evident in Polónyi's bibliography, which lists Hungarian, English, French, and German sources, and in multilingual bibliographies of other protagonists of this chapter, including Richert and Dmochowski.[240] Indeed, Polónyi used the term "periphery" similarly to Karaman: the delays, distortions, and echoes that characterized a peripheral mode of cultural reception offered an opportunity for skepticism, relativism, and a pragmatic appropriation of ideas for the specific purposes at hand.[241]

Decolonization transformed West Africa from a province to a periphery—this was the argument underlying Polónyi's imaginary geography. If a reading of Karaman in postcolonial terms would reveal nuance, hybridity, and mimicry in what might appear to be a mere provincial imitation, there is no doubt that the sudden availability of ideas from multiple directions was

3.43. Nick Hollo, "Climatic Comfort Design Guide for Nigeria," 1979. Department of Architecture, Ahmadu Bello University, Zaria.

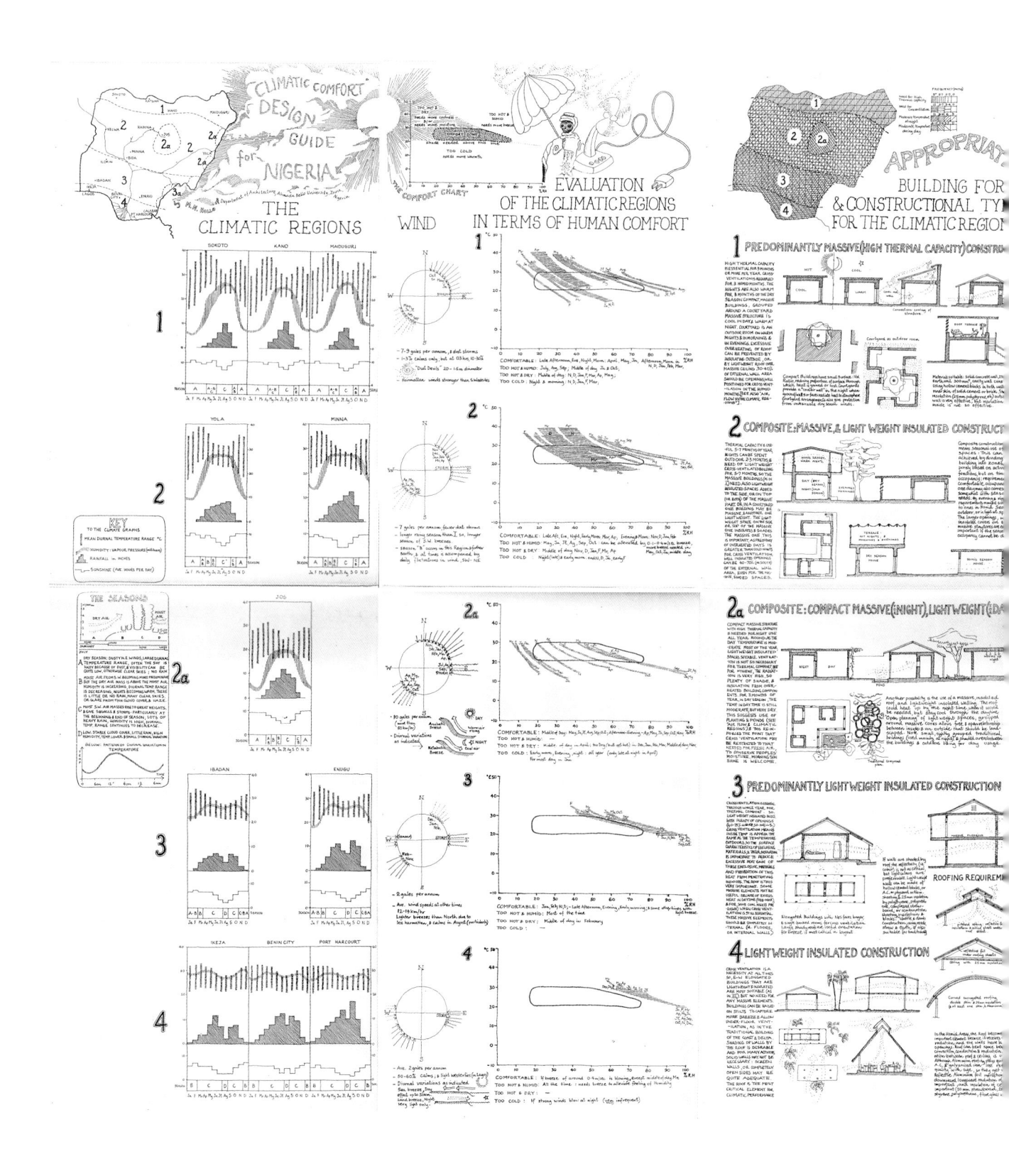

SUN SHADING IN THE CLIMATIC REGIONS

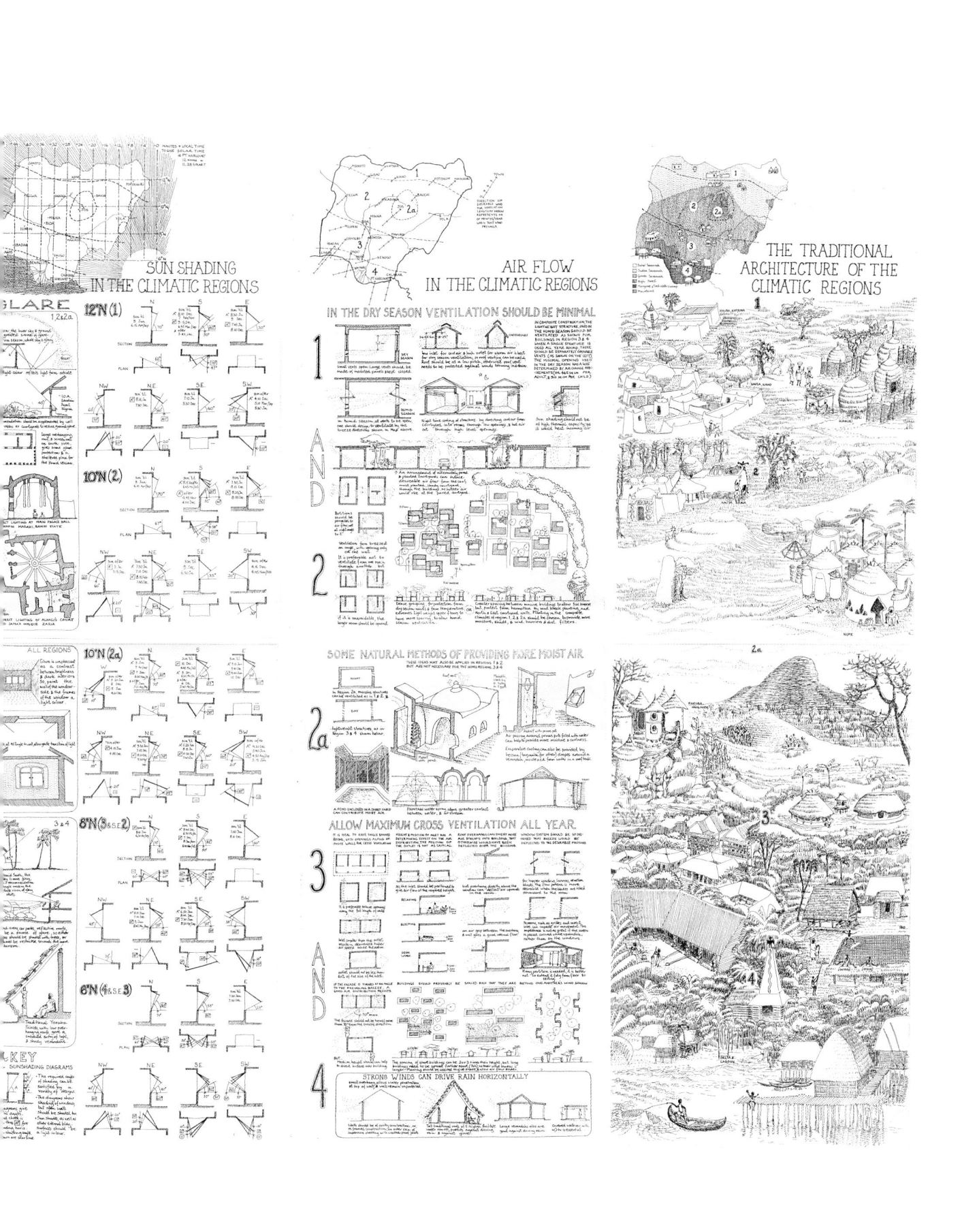

AIR FLOW IN THE CLIMATIC REGIONS

THE TRADITIONAL ARCHITECTURE OF THE CLIMATIC REGIONS

a crucial part of the experience of independence in 1960s West Africa.[242] During their work at UST in Kumasi, Polónyi and Richert themselves contributed to such refraction of what had until then been a largely unilateral flow of knowledge from the colonial metropolis. They insisted on the critical reading of foreign models of architectural and planning practice, on their evaluation according to the needs of Ghana, and on their combination with other sources.[243] Such "freedom of the periphery" was in tune with the geopolitical ambition of Nkrumah to situate Ghana within many worlds: like several other first-generation leaders of independent West Africa, he refused to replace dependency on the colonial metropolis with subordination into the bipolar order of the Cold War.

No country exemplified this refusal better than Yugoslavia, Ghana's ally within the Non-Aligned Movement (NAM). Following Yugoslavia's expulsion from Cominform (1948), the country that had previously been a close ally of Stalin embarked on a path of decentralized socialism and workers' self-management, institutionalized in the 1953 constitution, and followed by an effort at further decentralization and destatization in "market reform" (1965–75). Dependent on Western loans, grants, and technology as much as on political assurances against the Soviet Union, Yugoslavia reformed its economy by yielding to pressures from the United States and from US-based institutions, from the Agency for International Development in the 1960s to the International Monetary Fund and the World Bank in the 1980s. Trade with Western Europe, first with West Germany then with Italy, grew from the 1960s onward, resulting in industrial facilities based on Western technology and a booming tourist industry, primarily geared toward Western vacationers, while Yugoslav "guest workers" traveled to Western Europe and brought back remittances, consumer patterns, and, sometimes, expertise.[244]

After the death of Stalin, the relationship with the Soviet Union and Eastern Europe improved, and at one of its peaks in the mid-1970s, the Yugoslavs pronounced their country a part of the "communist world."[245] While concerns about a possible Soviet intervention never fully subsided, Soviet oil and gas, and Polish coal, played important roles in the Yugoslav economy, often exchanged for manufactured goods within the barter system of the Comecon, of which Yugoslavia had been an associated member since 1964.[246]

Foreign trade with the West and with Comecon were complemented by that within NAM, of which Yugoslavia was a founding member. Following the first NAM congress in Belgrade (1961), NAM networks were used to present the Yugoslav experience as relevant for other nonaligned countries with an emphasis on the maintenance of societal cohesion within a multinational, multilingual, multicultural, and multireligious society, which included a sizable Muslim minority. Some aspects of Yugoslav political and administrative structures were specifically studied by delegates from developing countries, including the commune as the basic unit of production, distribution, consumption, and governance, as well as the principle of self-management and multinational federalism in a one-party state.[247] Yugoslavia was also included in the group of "less developed countries" within UNCTAD, which demanded nonreciprocal concessions granted by developed countries to developing ones.[248] Yugoslav leader Josip Broz Tito advocated for the need of a New International Economic Order (NIEO), formulated by UNCTAD over the course of the 1970s. Nigeria joined this advocacy, even if relations between the two countries were strained in the wake of the civil war, during which Yugoslavia had supported Biafra.

As historians have pointed out, Yugoslavia's multiple affiliations were as much an aspiration as they were a consequence of the country's precarious geopolitical condition after World War II.[249] The unequal pressures resulting from those affiliations and the obligations they triggered led to contradictions in the country's political economy, ultimately contributing to the breakup of Yugoslavia (1990–92). Nevertheless, over the course of the 1960s and 1970s, the ability to "balance" between the three "worlds" in order to secure political independence and exploit economic advantages was part of Yugoslavia's carefully cultivated image of a "country in-between," and another feature distinguishing it from Soviet satellite states.[250] Representatives of Yugoslavia were at pains to communicate to their counterparts within NAM that they did not see their country as a model to follow. Rather, they emphasized the multiplicity of development paths that were to be based on specific experiences, needs, and traditions of each nation.[251]

Belgrade-based design and contracting company Energoprojekt shared this hands-on approach, and it came to the fore in its work in Nigeria. The design and construction of the International Trade Fair (ITF) in Lagos were instances of Energoprojekt's "peripheral" practice facilitated by Yugoslavia's multiple affiliations (figure 3.44). While for Karaman such practice was a cultural one, the study of ITF's construction site will allow the extension of its meaning toward material practices carried by Energoprojekt in collaboration with actors from across multiple worlds. Among those actors was the Yugoslav-Nigerian joint venture Nigerian Engineering and Construction Company Ltd. (NECCO), and the focus on NECCO will allow a reassessment of opportunities and limitations to the "freedom of the periphery."[252]

Architecture across Three Worlds

Energoprojekt was founded in Belgrade in 1951 by a merger of two state companies specializing in the design of power plants. The design of hydro, thermal, and electrical facilities and their supporting buildings was in the focus of activities of the firm during its first decade, when it contributed to postwar reconstruction and infrastructural development of Yugoslavia. By the mid-1960s, Energoprojekt consisted of four departments: water engineering, thermal power plants and industrial facilities, commerce, and construction, to which a department of urban design and architecture was added in 1971, with Milica Šterić as its first director.[253] The firm further expanded over the course of the 1970s to include separate departments of mining, information technology, and surveying. By 1979, all these departments were turned into formally independent, self-managed productive units, the Basic Organizations of Associated Labor. Architecture and urban design were among them, with each divided into several teams headed by individual architects, including Zoran Bojović, the chief designer of ITF.[254] Energoprojekt's multidisciplinary composition facilitated collaboration between various specialists on a given project, and allowed for an internal flow of knowledge. For instance, engineers working on high-end hydro-engineering structures migrated to the architectural units, where they optimized the design of concrete structures.[255] This organizational framework allowed the company to receive large commissions, catapulting Energoprojekt into the group of the world's twenty largest engineering companies in the 1980s.[256]

Such growth was predicated on Yugoslavia's diplomatic links. As with other Yugoslav companies working abroad, Energoprojekt's first commissions were often facilitated by Yugoslav technical-assistance programs and were paid by loans granted by Yugoslavia to other NAM countries. This applied specifically to West Africa, where Energoprojekt's first commissions were signed by the firm's general director, Živko Mučalov, who accompanied Tito in his tour in the region in 1961. Representatives of Energoprojekt, along with other Yugoslav firms, were dispatched to Accra, Bamako, Kpalimé (Togo), and Conakry, and to other West African cities.[257]

Presence on the ground allowed an understanding of local economic and technological requirements, but also cultural and religious ones that, as Energoprojekt's newsletter emphasized, were essential when designing such facilities as slaughterhouses in Muslim countries, an important part in the firm's early activities in the region.[258]

The Hydro Power Plant Kpimé in Togo was Energoprojekt's first commission abroad that included research, design, construction, delivery, and the installation of equipment (1963).[259] This and other complex industrial projects in West Africa were constructed in cooperation with other Yugoslav contractors (including Astra and Ingra from Zagreb) and producers of industrial equipment from various Yugoslav republics.[260] They were complemented by training programs organized in both the recipient countries and in Yugoslavia.[261] Infrastructure projects abroad were often followed by architectural commissions, which contributed to the need for the architectural department established in Energoprojekt in 1971. In sub-Saharan Africa, these commissions included a conference center designed by Dušan Milenković and built for the third NAM conference in Lusaka (Zambia, 1970), followed by conference centers in Kampala (Uganda, 1970–71) and Libreville (Gabon, 1975–76), both according to Milenković's designs. These paved the way for other projects in those cities during the 1970s, including hotels (Kampala), office buildings (Lusaka), municipal buildings (Libreville), and numerous unrealized designs.[262]

Visits to Belgrade within NAM networks were essential in initiating contracts between Energoprojekt and countries that, like Nigeria, were at first hesitant to work with Yugoslav companies and reluctant to accept Yugoslav loans.[263] One such visit in 1965 was that of A.M.A. Akinloye, the Nigerian minister of industry, during which he was presented with a tour of industrial facilities and other projects by Energoprojekt, including

3.44. Nigerian Federal Pavilion at the International Trade Fair in Lagos, 1974–77. Energoprojekt (Socialist Republic of Serbia, Yugoslavia), Zoran Bojović.

irrigation systems and hydroelectric power plants.²⁶⁴ Akinloye was most impressed by the New Belgrade Urban Plan, the new development of the Yugoslav capital. The Nigerian official must have appreciated not only the technological feat of reclaiming marshlands for the capital's extension, but also the symbolic character of the project, which demonstrated the ability of socialist Yugoslavia to develop land that previous regimes had been unable to make use of.²⁶⁵

Competence in land reclamation was the basis for Energoprojekt's first contracts in Nigeria. As a result of Akinloye's visit, Energoprojekt was commissioned to carry out a land-reclamation project in Kano (1966), followed by the construction of irrigation systems in Yola (1977) and Kano (1978), as well as electrification of sixty towns in Nigeria (from 1975) and food-processing facilities.²⁶⁶ Contracts that were already signed with actors in the region facilitated further commissions. For instance, representatives of Zambian-owned construction firms with whom Energoprojekt had collaborated were used as middlemen in the Nigerian market.²⁶⁷ They might have been instrumental in the signing of the first architectural contract of Energoprojekt in Nigeria: the design and supervision of a large school complex in Oshodi (1966), delivered by a team of seven architects and engineers of Energoprojekt working on site in Lagos.²⁶⁸ This commission was followed by the master planning of seven towns in Kano State (1973, with the Yugoslav Institute for Town Planning and Housing), the design and construction of the Ministries Complex in Kano (Milica Šterić, Zoran Bojović, 1978), and an ophthalmology clinic in Kaduna (1981), among others (figure 3.45).²⁶⁹

To maximize its entry points to Nigeria, Energoprojekt collaborated with other actors, including international and Western organizations. In 1963, the firm had registered with the UN Special Fund, which financed

WORLDING EASTERN EUROPE

technical documentation of energy infrastructure, agriculture, water supply, and other investments in developing countries, for which Energoprojekt became eligible to apply as contractor.[270] The firm also cultivated contacts with British, French, and Italian banks, as well as the International Bank of Reconstruction and Development (later the World Bank), and actively brokered loans for African development projects to be executed by Energoprojekt.[271] Those commissions were facilitated by Energoprojekt's subsidiaries in financial centers in Western Europe and the United States, including New York, which had first been established to purchase machinery for the firm's construction sites.[272] Some contracts came with strings attached, including the use of construction materials from the crediting countries. This was also the case when Energoprojekt and other Yugoslav firms collaborated with Comecon countries on commissions in Africa and the Middle East.[273]

The practice of collaborating across multiple networks was formalized in Yugoslavia by means of joint ventures. The establishment of joint ventures in Yugoslavia between Yugoslav and foreign firms was permitted by the 1967 reform preparing the country's shift toward "market socialism." Moving beyond the insistence on import substitution in the postwar decades, the shift included a reorientation toward an export-focused, internationally competitive industry, and the increasing integration of the Yugoslav economy into the world market.[274] Collaboration with Western companies was expected to result in the acquisition of foreign capital, modern technology, and managerial know-how, as well as in easier access to foreign markets and improved export competitiveness.[275] At the same time, the Yugoslav leadership preferred joint ventures over other forms of direct foreign investment, because they did not contravene the principle of workers' self-management.[276] Yet with the development of "market socialism," the removal of barriers to the operation of foreign investors, and accelerated dismantling of state control over the economy, workers' councils in Yugoslav enterprises, including the joint ventures, ceased to play a key role in decision-making, and in many instances became subordinated to enterprise directors and technical experts.[277] Resulting from an attempt

3.45. Ministries Complex, Kano, 1973–78. Energoprojekt (Socialist Republic of Serbia, Yugoslavia), Milica Šterić, Zoran Bojović.

3.46. Federal Secretariat Complex in Ikoyi, Lagos, late 1970s, constructed by Energoprojekt (Socialist Republic of Serbia, Yugoslavia). Federal Ministry of Works and Housing, Lagos; Isaac Fola Alade. John Godwin, "Nigeria. Building in a Boom Economy," *RIBA Journal* 88, no. 7 (1981): 40.

at bringing market pressures to bear on industrial enterprises while preserving the principle of self-management, joint ventures exemplified contradictions resulting from Yugoslavia's "market socialism."

Yugoslavia was not the only socialist country open to Western joint ventures, but it was the most active in establishing interfirm links abroad: of 231 joint ventures of Western firms operating in Eastern Europe by 1980, 199 were set up in Yugoslavia, with the rest in Hungary, Poland, and Romania.[278] Similarly, Yugoslavia and Romania were the two most active socialist countries in establishing joint ventures in Africa, where Yugoslav activities continually expanded since the 1960s.[279]

While familiarity with joint ventures in Yugoslavia helped Yugoslav companies to establish themselves in Africa, those companies often had no choice, as such organizational forms were required by some newly independent countries, including Nigeria. During the 1960s, Nigerian governments introduced restrictions on foreign firms operating in the country. New legal regulations included the indigenization of management in foreign-owned and foreign-controlled companies, which also pertained to architectural offices, and by 1968, all foreign companies doing business in Nigeria were required to be incorporated in Nigeria. This tendency was strengthened by the Nigerian Enterprises Promotion ("Indigenization") Decree of 1972, which entirely excluded foreigners from certain business categories, while others were reserved for Nigerians if the businesses were below a certain size (defined by share capital and annual turnover). Foreign businesses above that size required no less than 40 percent equity participation by Nigerian citizens.[280] In the subsequent reform, announced in 1977, that share was raised to 60 percent in the case of contractors.[281] Restrictions applied also to construction-materials industries (cement, sawn timber, and plywood).[282]

The establishment of joint ventures with socialist countries was an attempt on the part of the Nigerian government to offset the dominance of Western firms in the country's economy.[283] Joint companies between Nigeria and Bulgaria, Hungary, Poland, Romania, and the Soviet Union had already been established in the early 1960s, and during the next decade they became Nigeria's most widespread form of economic cooperation with socialist countries.[284] By the 1970s, joint ventures specializing in design, construction, and technical support included subsidiaries of Hungary's Tesco, and Poland's Polservice and Budimex, Romania's Institute for Technological Studies of Light Industry and Arcom, and Czechoslovakia's Strojexport.[285] Bulgaria's TES, whose projects for FESTAC were directly commissioned by the Nigerian government, established two joint ventures.[286] These companies, along with being contracted to construct industrial facilities coowned by the Nigerian government and that of a respective socialist country, competed for commissions with local firms (such

3.47. International Trade Fair in Lagos, 1974–77, aerial view of the area. Energoprojekt (Socialist Republic of Serbia, Yugoslavia), Zoran Bojović.

as Cappa & d'Alberto, established in Lagos in 1932), as well as subsidiaries of foreign ones. These latter included contractors from the UK, several of them present in Lagos since the colonial period (Costain, Taylor-Woodrow), as well as from West Germany, France, Austria, and Israel.[287]

Energoprojekt's joint ventures in Nigeria extended its previous experience in establishing joint ventures with governments of Zambia and Guinea in the late 1960s.[288] In the wake of signing new contracts in northern Nigeria, and following the requirement of incorporation in the country, the Energoprojekt Engineering and Contracting Company Ltd. was established in Kano (1971).[289] The statute of the company allowed for a range of activities, starting with construction work, including buildings and infrastructure, research and design, as well as the delivery of mechanical equipment, the execution and operation of complete facilities, and activities considered ancillary, such as shipping of goods and machines and their leasing.[290]

Some assets of Energoprojekt Ltd. were transferred to the Nigerian Engineering and Construction Company Ltd. (NECCO), established in Lagos in April 1974, thus after Bojović's team was awarded the tender for ITF in Lagos. According to the agreement, 60 percent of shares in the new joint venture were owned by the Federal Government of Nigeria and 40 percent by Energoprojekt; this ownership structure was reflected in the numbers of Nigerian and Yugoslav members on the board of directors.[291] On the creation of the company, the Nigerian government announced that NECCO had been awarded the contract to construct ITF in Lagos, but the main contractor of the trade fair remained Energoprojekt, with NECCO hired as a subcontractor. Its first task was the construction of the bridge linking the Lagos-Badagry Road with the Trade Fair Area.[292]

A report published in Energoprojekt's newsletter described the responsibilities of the partners and the objectives of the organization. Energoprojekt, as the "technical partner" in NECCO, would lead the enterprise, provide professional staff, and be in charge of the purchase of equipment and materials. The report detailed the agreement on repatriation of profits and on employee salaries and claimed that the Nigerian government agreed to provide the new company with commissions. At the same time, the report pointed out benefits for Nigeria: fast-track construction of modern, high-quality buildings, training of workers, and collaboration with a partner "who values a long-term, mutually beneficial business cooperation over quick profit."[293]

Much of this discourse echoed the statements of the Nigerian side. Speaking in 1976 to the then-reconstituted NECCO board of directors, the federal commissioner for works, O. E. Obada, spelled out ambitions for this "parastatal" company. Obada urged NECCO to participate in competitive tenders, with the focus on the urban development of Lagos, including housing projects. He endorsed the envisaged construction of factories for steel and concrete products that would allow the company to become self-sufficient with regard to the supply of most building components.[294] He also assured the directors of the government's support, already exemplified by then in new governmental commissions for the Administrative Staff College in Badagry and the construction of the twelve-story building of the Federal Secretariat in Ikoyi (Isaac Fola Alade for FMWS), as well as the irrigation systems in Yola (figure 3.46).[295] Ultimately, Obada saw NECCO as the agent of modernization for the Nigerian construction industry. "The reason for entering into partnership with Energoprojekt," the commissioner explained, "was to increase the availability of executive capacity in the building and construction industry." Specifically, Obada expected the company to "operate in such a way as to set standards, in particular in the pricing of contracts, and thus help the government to arrest the inflationary trends which had become noticeable in the construction industry."[296] The

WORLDING EASTERN EUROPE

following review of the work of NECCO and Energoprojekt in Lagos will put those aims to test.

The Trade Fair as an Urban Project

Shortly before the opening of the International Trade Fair in Lagos in November 1977, the area was photographed by Zoran Bojović, its head architect (figure 3.47). Taken from a helicopter, Bojović's photographs show sharply delineated surfaces being filled with sand, gravel, asphalt, and earth to form buildable land, green areas, sports courts, streets, and parking lots. Three permanent pavilions and their supporting buildings, minuscule from the air, are positioned at key points of the landscape's geometry: in the centers of the three circles constituting the ITF layout, at the borders between surfaces, and at points when a line pierces into a plane. Only the photographs' margins reveal what was necessary to produce and maintain this landscape: swamps to be drained, bush to be cleared, and a pumping station, a water-treatment plant, an artificial lake, an electrical substation, storage of equipment and machinery, and housing for workers and staff. With almost no people appearing in the images, Bojović captured a moment of standstill when pipes, drainage, and wiring had disappeared under clean-cut surfaces, but before those surfaces were replenished with temporary pavilions sustained by the infrastructure beneath: generative planes for a city to come.

The power of these images can be appreciated only when read against accounts of the urban crisis that characterized 1970s Lagos (figure 3.48).[297] The urban condition of Nigeria's capital as it was inherited from the colonial period was captured in the 1964 survey by the UN Technical Assistance Programme, headed by Otto Koenigsberger.[298] As in the colonial period, Lagos Island remained the core of the city, with its traditional center around the Oba's Palace and the Central Business District along the marina. The main vector of urbanization was directed toward the north, to the mainland, where it followed the railway line, constructed by the British government since 1895, with new nuclei including industrial estates in Apapa (around the port), Ebute Metta (with the railway corporations), Ikeja, and Mushin. The survey showed a city with an inefficient transportation system and insufficient, often nonexistent public transport, and with an acute housing shortage resulting in vast areas poorly equipped with technical and social infrastructure.[299]

By the time Energoprojekt worked in Lagos, the government's attempts at alleviating this crisis proved to be largely futile, in view of the continuing explosive growth of the city (figure 3.49).[300] As documented by surveys included in the Regional Plan for Lagos State by Doxiadis Associates (1976), only a fraction of inhabitants were accommodated in government-owned housing, including neighborhoods for senior governmental employees in Ikeja and Victoria Island, and in middle-income housing constructed by specialized governmental agencies in Surulere and the Dolphin Scheme (apartments in Festac Town were included into this housing stock after the end of the festival).[301] The majority of middle- and low-income groups depended on an aggressive rental market, which the government tried unsuccessfully to regulate. Traffic jams (or "go slows") were a ubiquitous reality, while public transport remained unreliable. The new system of overarching highways designed and constructed by the late 1970s by the Nigerian subsidiary of West Germany's Julius Berger improved connectivity at the metropolitan level, but links to the rest of the network were inadequate and the needs of pedestrians were largely ignored.[302]

Another major challenge was the access to buildable land. Land was both scarce in the landscape of swamps, marshland, lagoons, and sandbars that characterized Lagos, and contested because of the dual system of

3.48. "Land Use in Lagos, 1974."

3.49. "Lagos—Phases of Growth," 1975. Doxiadis Associates, "Black Arts Festival Village."

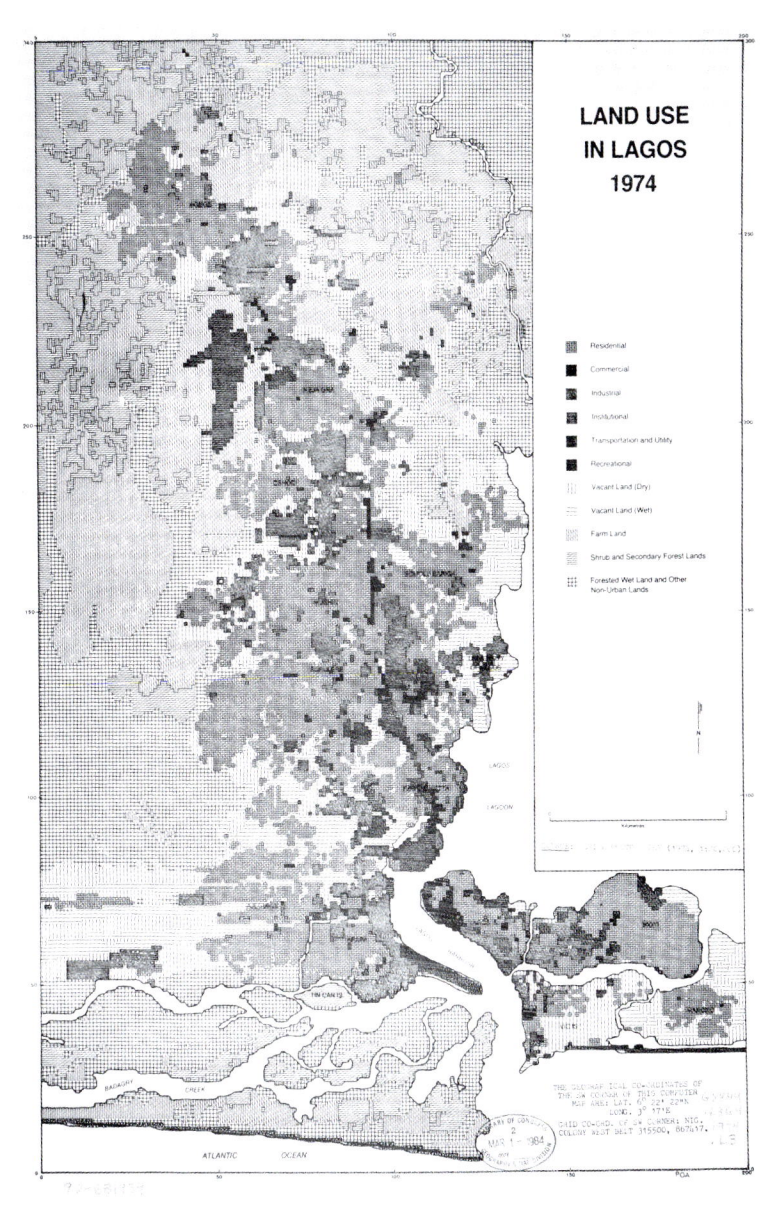

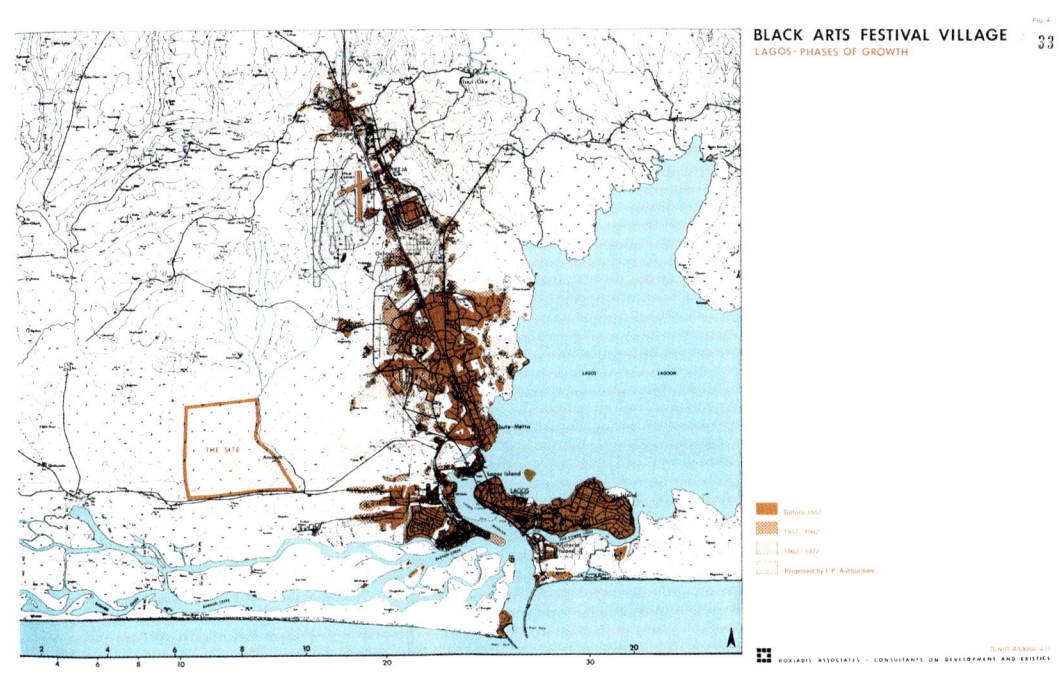

WORLDING EASTERN EUROPE 157

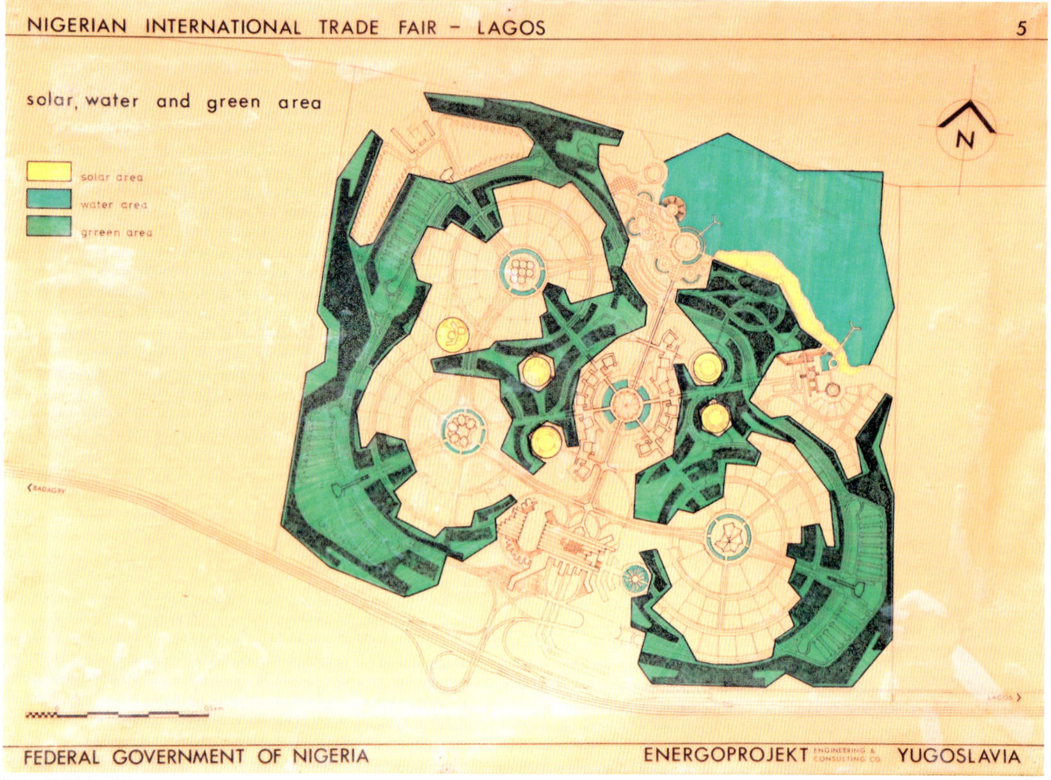
NIGERIAN INTERNATIONAL TRADE FAIR – LAGOS
5
solar, water and green area
solar area
water area
grreen area
N
LAGOS
FEDERAL GOVERNMENT OF NIGERIA
ENERGOPROJEKT ENGINEERING & CONSULTING CO.
YUGOSLAVIA

< 3.50. "Solar, Water, and Green Area," International Trade Fair in Lagos, 1974–77. Energoprojekt (Socialist Republic of Serbia, Yugoslavia), Zoran Bojović.

< 3.51. International Trade Fair in Lagos, 1974–77, model. Energoprojekt (Socialist Republic of Serbia, Yugoslavia), Zoran Bojović.

land ownership, combining family ownership in customary Yoruba law with British-based property law.[303] That legal system made land very expensive and resulted in lengthy court cases, often leaving costly land reclamation as the only way to address the city's needs.[304] The resulting everyday reality in Ajegunle and Apapa districts of Lagos was described in a letter by an inhabitant published in 1972 by the newspaper *West African Pilot*: congested and dilapidated buildings; health services available to expats and senior civil servants but not to other inhabitants; people getting up at 4 am every day to trek for miles on poorly maintained roads to catch an expensive minibus as no other transport was available; and no adequate school buildings and shopping facilities, no drainage, and trash not being collected.[305] Subsequent reports on Lagos, including the master plan by Wilbur Smith (1980), confirmed that by the late 1970s, the daily life of city inhabitants had not improved and, in some cases, had deteriorated further.[306]

ITF appeared to have left all those challenges behind. Its planes of developed land, fully equipped with technical and social infrastructure, were given a layout according to principles of modern urban planning, including functional zoning and division of traffic (figure 3.50).[307] Bojović's team tapped into its knowledge of international design standards and revised the original functional program of the commissioner. The architects suggested four areas accommodating pavilions of the Nigerian Federation and Nigerian states, Nigerian enterprises, foreign governments, and international enterprises (figure 3.51). The network of pedestrian routes connecting the trade fair's circular layout was designed as part of the system of green spaces that, along with their functions of recreation and leisure, were to ventilate the entire area. The plan was supported by comprehensive infrastructure networks, including water, sewage, electricity, telephone, and a drainage system. The design demonstrated an awareness of the haphazard, unstable, and irregular infrastructural provisions in Lagos, as most of the ITF infrastructure networks were planned to function independently if needed.[308]

The trade fair, while designed to perform as a self-contained compound, was also conceived as a kernel of the city's expansion. Attuned with the aims of NECCO spelled out by Nigerian administrators, the designers of the fair extended the initial brief to address broader aims of urbanization in Lagos. In so doing, the master planning of the compound followed and solidified the intention of several post-independence governments to direct urbanization toward the mainland, west of Lagos Island. That decision guided the construction of social facilities (hospitals and schools) and industry, along with investment in rural areas, support for self-help housing schemes, and the construction of the Lagos-Badagry Road (1974), into which the trade fair was plugged.[309] The drawings included with Energoprojekt's tender submission showed this road as the urbanization axis for existing villages and for new developments, including the planned Amuwo Odofin neighborhood.[310] Accordingly, clusters of social and commercial facilities on the trade fair grounds were programmed to be used by inhabitants of nearby settlements. Other functions were envisaged as serving the entire metropolitan region, including a conference center with a restaurant and a hotel, as well as leisure areas around the lake.[311] The concentric layout would lend itself to enlargement in a set of discrete steps, with radial streets securing connection and the concentric ones offering a movable border of the compound.

This vision of ITF as a kernel of urbanization was supported by buildings designed by Energoprojekt as expandable frames in steel and concrete, filled with what would become walls, decks, roofs, and partitions that could receive various programs (figure 3.52).[312] Such a construction system had already been sketched in the winning entry to the tender competition, submitted in June 1973 by Zoran Bojović and his team to

WORLDING EASTERN EUROPE

the Ministry of Works in Lagos, up against two other proposals (one by Hungary's Tesco-Közti and the other by the ministry's planning team). After the contract was signed for delivery of the compound on the "turn-key" principle, Bojović worked out the executive design for the construction system based on seven elements, on a triangular raster of 7.2 meters, to be prefabricated on site (figure 3.53). (As three points define a plane, the triangular grid responded to unstable soil conditions by allowing for some movement of supporting pillars without cracking the plates resting on them.)[313]

This construction system, used by Bojović and his architectural team to design individual pavilions, responded to the challenges of logistics, budget, timing, and labor at the construction site in Lagos (figure 3.54). The system limited the number of components that could be bought in bulk and in advance, thus alleviating the shortage of construction materials in Nigeria (cement, stone, reinforced concrete), their irregular supply from the clogged port of Lagos, and their rising prices because of rampant inflation.[314] Working with a unified system accelerated the design process, with the final drawings produced a month ahead of construction, and approved

3.52. International Trade Fair in Lagos, 1974–77, one of the pavilions under construction. Energoprojekt (Socialist Republic of Serbia, Yugoslavia), Zoran Bojović.

3.53. The mold of the floor elements for the International Trade Fair in Lagos, 1974–77. Energoprojekt (Socialist Republic of Serbia, Yugoslavia), Zoran Bojović.

3.54. International Trade Fair in Lagos, 1974–77, aerial photographs documenting the progress of the construction. Energoprojekt (Socialist Republic of Serbia, Yugoslavia), Zoran Bojović.

on site by Bojović, Energoprojekt's Aleksandar Slijepčević, the technical director of ITF, and L. D. Kataria, the architect at the Ministry of Works in Lagos delegated for the supervision of the trade fair project.[315] The unitary construction system also facilitated the training of Nigerian workers. During the busiest periods, their number surpassed a thousand people, managed by no more than one hundred Yugoslav foremen. Some among the Nigerian workers, upon departing the construction site, were given certificates of professional qualification as carpenters or bricklayers.[316]

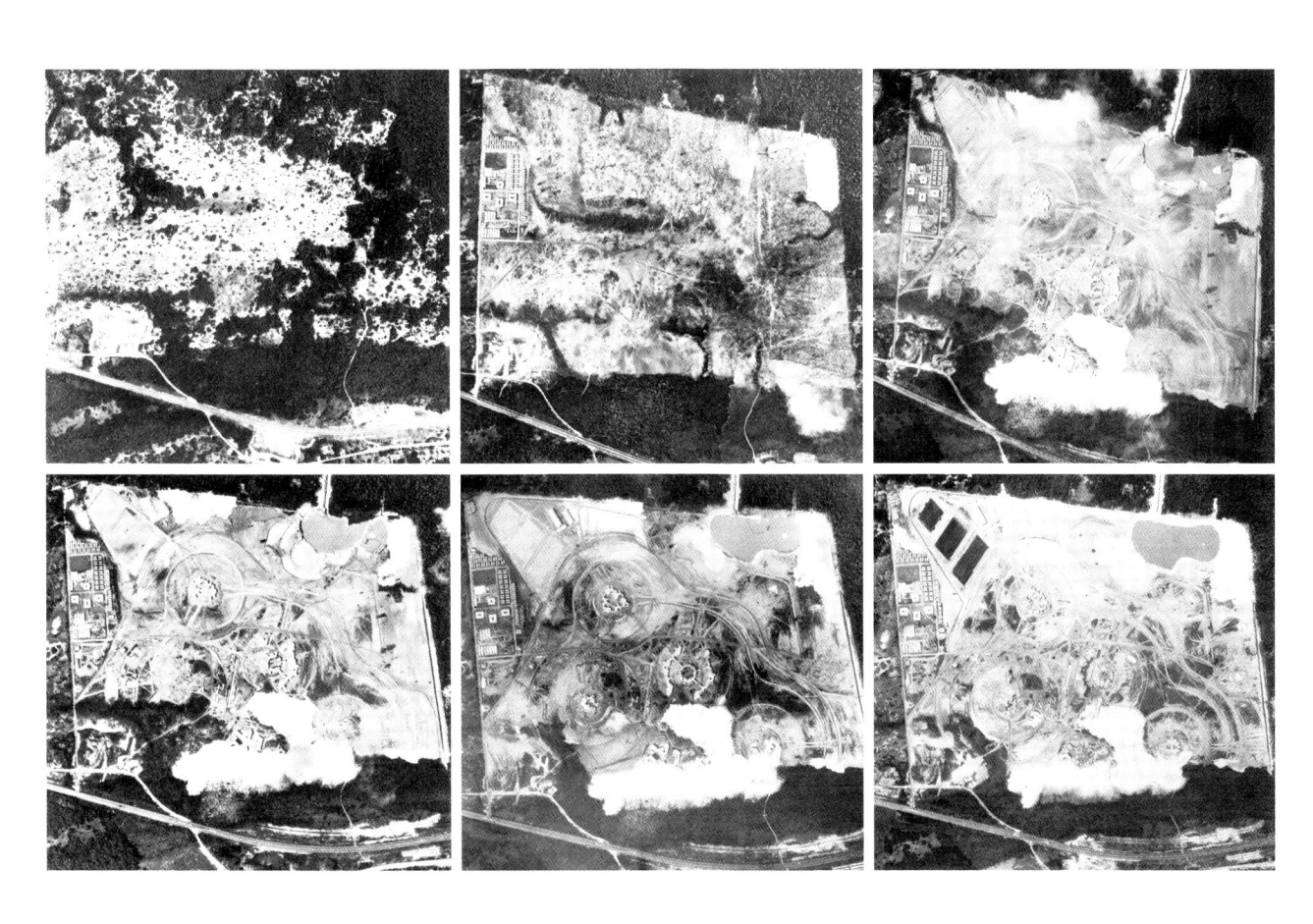

Such training opportunities were among the explicit aims of NECCO. Yet the organization of labor and its remuneration by NECCO points to contradictions that undermined some of the joint venture's envisioned advantages. NECCO, while subjected to decisions by self-management groups at Energoprojekt's headquarters in Belgrade, did not form a self-management group that could help in resolving tensions between Nigerian and Yugoslav workers. (While the creation of self-management bodies in joint ventures abroad was permitted and even encouraged, they included only Yugoslav workers and explicitly excluded foreign workers.)[317] These tensions pertained to differences in accommodation and salaries, with low salaries among Nigerian workers being a source of considerable savings for Energoprojekt. Because of this practice, Energoprojekt appeared to Nigerian commentators as any other multinational company that, in the analysis of Marxist scholar Bade Onimode and his colleagues, had benefited since 1966 from oppressive labor laws, wage freezes, and strike bans in Nigeria.[318] However, that approach backfired in the series of wildcat strikes by Nigerian workers demanding salary increases from NECCO.[319] As a result, the company struggled to hire and retain the Nigerian workforce, which could not be supplemented with Yugoslav workers because of Energoprojekt's expanding international commitments. Consequently, reports from Lagos show an interchange between periods of standstill and frantic activity in three shifts with little Yugoslav supervision.[320] Securing an adequate workforce continued to be a major challenge to the joint venture in the years to come.[321]

Equally apparent was the conflict between the imperative of meeting the delivery deadline of the trade fair complex on one hand and, on the other, long-term aims of developing the Nigerian construction industry. When put under the pressure of tight deadlines, and with a view to the unreliable market for construction materials in Nigeria, Energoprojekt and NECCO managers tapped into the Yugoslav and international supply chains. As a result, a large share of the construction components was shipped from Yugoslav republics. These included Serbia (with steel construction provided by Belgrade's Mostogradnja, and insulating materials from other suppliers), Croatia (with aluminum façade elements produced by Zagreb's Top, already tested in the Conference Hall in Kampala, as well as ceramic tiles and carpet flooring), and Slovenia (with elements of furniture, according to the interior design by Ljiljana Bojović) (figure 3.55). They were complemented by West German, French, British, and US producers of electronic installations, air conditioning, and elevators.[322] Western firms were subcontracted to construct roads and the artificial lake, the latter designed by a specialized British engineering firm.[323] Cranes and other machinery were occasionally borrowed from the construction site of the National Theater, being built by TES.[324]

In this way, the construction of ITF tapped into the various worlds Energoprojekt straddled. But as a consequence, this investment not only failed to contribute to the development of the Nigerian construction-materials industry but also proved to be more expensive than initially expected, since most materials and services needed to be imported. Nigerian critics of foreign joint ventures saw this procedure as an exploitative practice

3.55. International Trade Fair in Lagos, 1974–77. Energoprojekt (Socialist Republic of Serbia, Yugoslavia), Zoran Bojović (project architect), Ljiljana Bojović (interior design).

3.56. Housing and community centers in Festac Town, Lagos. Romconsult (Romania), Design Institute for Housing and Urban Technical and Social Infrastructure (ISLGC, Romania). Mircea Nicolescu, "8 locuințe pentru Festival Town, Lagos," *Arhitectura* 6 (1980): 18.

3.57. One of the community and commercial centers in Festac Town, Lagos, designed by Romconsult (Romania) and Design Institute for Housing and Urban Technical and Social Infrastructure (ISLGC, Romania).

benefiting foreign owners who profited from the sales of construction materials, in particular as they put down those construction materials as their share of the required capital investment in the joint venture.[325] Hence, technology transfer performed by joint ventures in Nigeria was a "myth," argued Onimode, who counted ITF among "prestige buildings" of "imperialist construction companies"—without, however, listing Energoprojekt among them.[326]

Approvals granted by Nigerian authorities to the exploding costs of these projects were widely seen as resulting from governmental officials' corruption, and they became the subject of formal investigations after the overthrow of Gowon in 1975. In parallel to the "Cement Tribunal," investigating the government's purchase of cement in excess of need and of port capacity, the new regime assembled the "Festac Tribunal," which investigated the procurement of buildings for FESTAC.[327] This tribunal recommended the recovery of funds released to contractors of housing in Kaduna and Lagos, the latter including Romania's Romconsult, and for the race course in Kaduna by TES (figures 3.56 and 3.57). The main point of contention was the National Arts Theater in Lagos, which, as the tribunal revealed, had been commissioned to TES as an international contractor (not registered in Nigeria) without competitive tendering (figures 3.58 and 3.59). The report showed that the responsible authorities granted the Bulgarian contractor excessive fees, paid double for the same service, and approved undue tax exemptions. In conclusion, the tribunal recommended scaling back some of the work and renegotiating TES's payments.[328]

In contrast, ITF avoided such controversies.[329] When it opened in November 1977, only minor complaints were raised, with most concerns focusing on future uses of the compound.[330] A new function for the trade fair

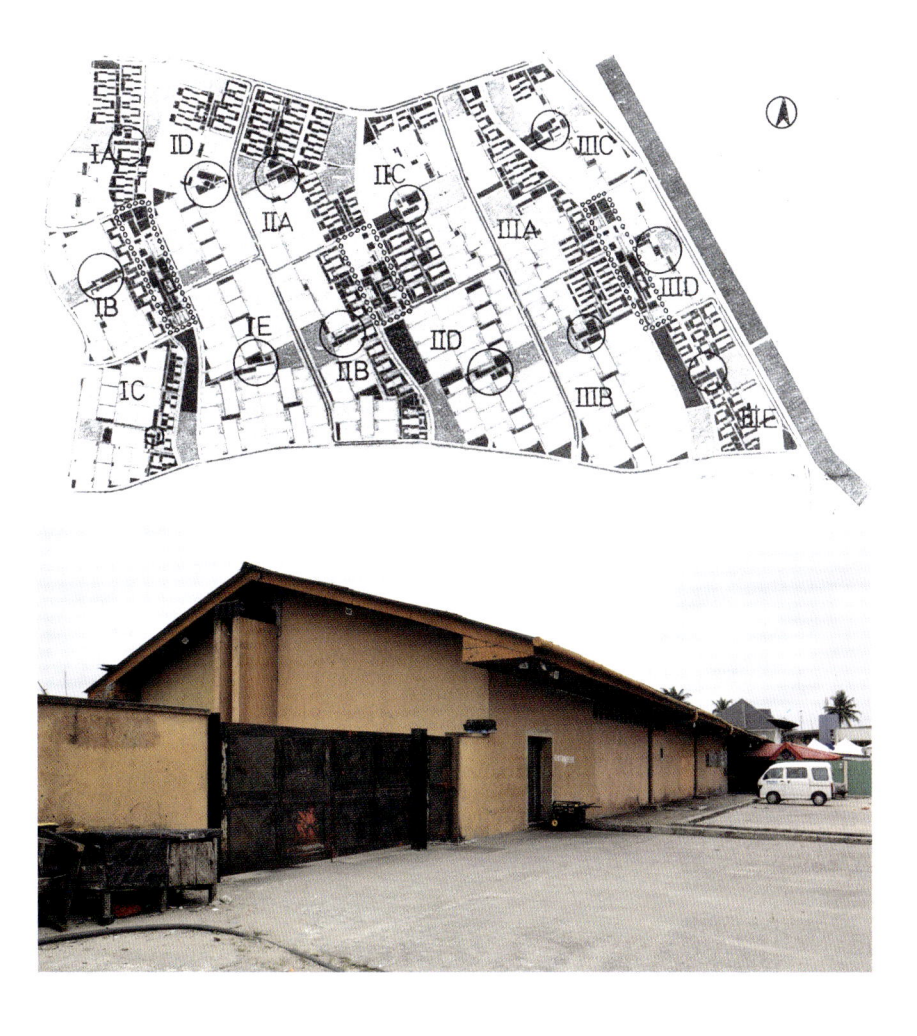

WORLDING EASTERN EUROPE 163

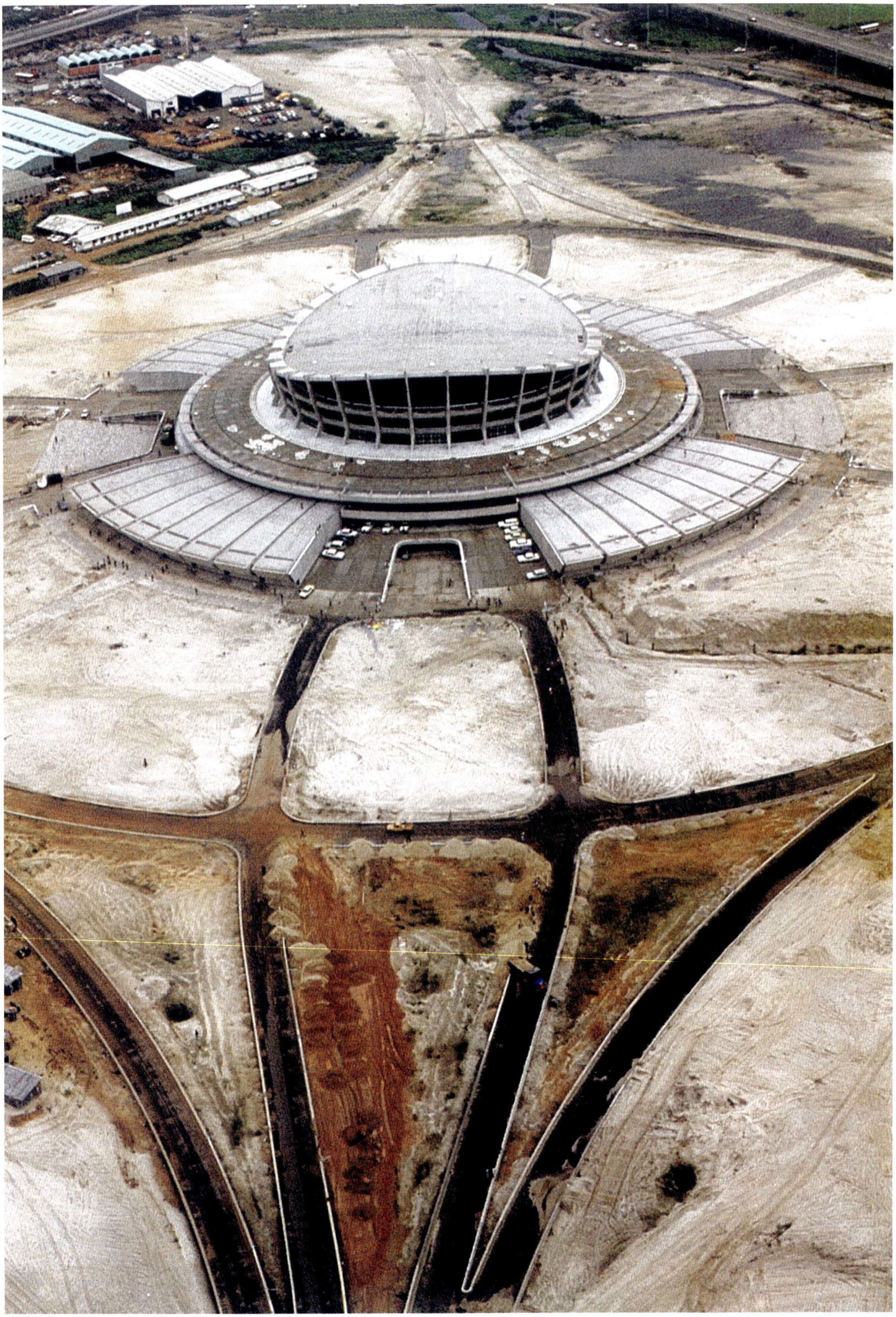

< 3.58. National Arts Theater, Lagos, 1972–77, construction site. Technoexportstroy (Bulgaria), Stefan Kolchev and the Regional Planning Office of the City of Varna (Bulgaria), Building Research Institute (Bulgaria). "Technoexportstroy" (Sofia: Technoexportstroy, n.d.).

3.59. National Arts Theater, Lagos, 1972–77, construction site. Technoexportstroy (Bulgaria), Stefan Kolchev and the Regional Planning Office of the City of Varna (Bulgaria), Building Research Institute (Bulgaria). "Technoexportstroy" (Sofia: Technoexportstroy, n.d.), cover.

was found only a decade later, as the site for the market relocated from Apapa. Today, forty years after its construction, areas designed for temporary pavilions have been taken over by stores and workshops. While the fair's border became permeable to the urbanization processes of Lagos, its original layout continues to function as a system of scale, measure, and visibility. New development makes use of the infrastructural networks of the compound, and it is scaled according to the concentric plan, with plot dimensions defined by distances between the circular streets. Two of the permanent pavilions are rented out to banks, mobile-phone operators, and other services, while two others are closed, their circumferences fenced and policed. Whether in use or not, all four pavilions continue to anchor the flows of people, okadas (motorcycle taxis), and cars, with their golden façades shimmering at the end of narrow passages. Launched as a geometric hypothesis, ITF continues to produce new ones (figures 3.60 and 3.61).

CONCLUSION: WORLDING FROM BELOW

Underdevelopment, colonialism, and peripherality were three explicitly global conditions with which the protagonists of this chapter identified to make sense of their work in Nigeria. They posited those three predicaments as defining moments in a historical experience shared between Eastern Europe and what emerged after World War II as the "Third" world. If the Cold War appeared to some of its contemporaries as a machine that, in a seemingly random manner, connected people and places that were never connected before, these three predicaments became starting points for constructed affinities between Eastern Europeans and West Africans across and beyond Cold War divisions. After their arrivals in Nigeria, Charles Polónyi, Zbigniew Dmochowski, Zoran Bojović, and their colleagues revisited the Eastern European tradition of architectural responses to underdevelopment, colonialism, and peripherality. This tradition furnished them with clues for addressing the concerns of their Nigerian counterparts, including the advancement of rural areas, cultural emancipation, decolonization of architectural institutions, and diversification of resources. This worlding of Eastern Europe allowed for singling out architectural tools and concepts, drawing and survey techniques, and organizational forms to translate them for application in West Africa.

Neither that identification of a shared Eastern European experience nor its extension toward West Africa were watertight. Socialist

3.60. Hall of Nations at the International Trade Fair in Lagos, 1974–77. Energoprojekt (Socialist Republic of Serbia, Yugoslavia), Zoran Bojović.

3.61. Hall of International Organizations at the International Trade Fair in Lagos, 1974–77. Energoprojekt (Socialist Republic of Serbia, Yugoslavia), Zoran Bojović.

countries were hardly homogenous, and few would see East Germany and Czechoslovakia, the two most technologically advanced states in the socialist bloc, on the same trajectory of overcoming "backwardness" as Romania and Bulgaria. Neither did countries in the region share the same history of foreign domination. A successor to the German Empire and the Third Reich, East Germany disavowed its colonial past in both Eastern Europe and sub-Saharan Africa.[331] In turn, Polónyi would not have been alone in seeing the Soviet Union as the successor to the tsarist colonial empire rather than a colonized nation itself—a view sometimes shared not only in Eastern Europe and Soviet Central Asia, but in West Africa, too.[332] For many protagonists of this chapter, apparent correspondences between Eastern Europe and West Africa were fundamentally revised on their arrival in Nigeria. For yet others, trips to Africa exposed ambiguities of the very architectural traditions that they intended to mobilize, including the ambiguities of Eastern Europe's own colonial history. Some among the three conditions seemed to exclude others and, for instance, the postcolonial dependence on the former colonial metropolis directly contradicted a "freedom of the periphery" in choosing impulses from various centers.

These distortions, discrepancies, tensions, and sometimes contradictions made it clear that backwardness, colonialism, and peripherality did not define a stable world. The focus on them as opportunities for encounters between Eastern Europeans and West Africans showed that the contribution to modernization of architects and planners from socialist countries did not follow a unified project in 1970s Nigeria. In their work, modernization was not a package containing a comprehensive offer of economic, political, technological, social, and cultural development—as had been the case, for instance, with Soviet blueprints for Nkrumah's Ghana. Rather, the worlding of Eastern Europe in Nigeria consisted of situated responses to the tasks at hand developed from singular trajectories and instances of problem solving.

4.1. Master plan of Baghdad (1973) by Miastoprojekt-Kraków (Poland) in the offices of the Amanat al-Assima (Mayoralty of Baghdad), Baghdad.

Chapter 4
The World Socialist System
Baghdad, 1958–90

In 2014, the international consulting firm Khatib & Alami submitted the fourth stage of the Comprehensive Development Plan for Baghdad (2030), commissioned by the city's Mayoralty, the Amanat al-Assima. When approved, it will replace the master plans of Baghdad from 1967 and 1973, which had been delivered by the Polish planning office Miastoprojekt-Kraków. Due to Iraq's belligerent history, several attempts to update them over the past forty years have failed. Miastoprojekt's plans thus continue to be the official regulatory documents for Baghdad, in spite of the fact that the 1973 plan was meant to expire by the year 2000 (figure 4.1).[1]

The production of the Baghdad master plans was a part of intense exchanges between socialist countries and Iraq, which included other large-scale commissions of Miastoprojekt—such as the General Housing Programme for Iraq (1976–80)—as well as industrial plants, land-reclamation projects, infrastructure, housing projects, social and educational facilities, and public buildings developed with Romania, Hungary, East Germany, Bulgaria, the Soviet Union, and Yugoslavia.[2] This opening of Iraq toward Eastern Europe followed the 1958 coup led by Abd al-Karim Qasim, which had overthrown the pro-Western monarchy of King Faisal II. In spite of a lapse in political relations after Qasim was toppled by the Baath Party (1963), followed by several regime changes, interaction with socialist countries picked up after the Baathists returned to power in 1968. These exchanges continued until the end of the Cold War, with subsequent Iraqi regimes exploiting East-West rivalries to advance their strategic priorities in security, state building, and industrial development.[3]

Assisted by the Soviet Union and its Eastern European satellites, the Baath authorities proclaimed the development of Iraq as a united Arab state with Islam as the state religion, based on a socialist system of planned economy, state ownership of natural resources and of the principal means of production, and free education and healthcare.[4] Along with military support, the exchange of Soviet and Eastern European equipment, machinery, and know-how were indispensable for key economic decisions taken by the Iraqi government, including agrarian reform followed by large-scale land reclamation and irrigation projects and, in particular, the nationalization of the oil industry (1972).[5] The "National Action Charter of the Baath Party" (1971) favored "noncapitalist development" that focused on the mobilization of resources by the state to generate capital for further investment. It also advocated comprehensive cooperation with the world socialist community—a declaration that did not prevent the Baath Party from persecuting the Iraqi communists.[6]

This rapprochement with the socialist bloc culminated in the Soviet-Iraqi Treaty of Friendship and Cooperation (1972), followed by an intensification of Soviet and Eastern European trade with Iraq.[7] The latter was financed by Iraq's skyrocketing revenues in the wake of the 1973 oil embargo imposed by the Organization of the Petroleum Exporting Countries (OPEC), which resulted in the quadrupling of petroleum prices. Yet by the end of the decade, with the Iraqi market gradually open and attractive to international actors, enterprises from socialist countries working in Iraq were increasingly competing against Western firms that looked for opportunities beyond recession-hit Western Europe and North America.[8]

If Western commentators saw this internationalization of economic exchanges as an instance of the emerging global integration dominated by the United States and Western Europe, socialist countries offered an alternative narrative. They argued in favor of a different type of worldwide economic cooperation, conveyed by the concept of the "world socialist system." In the words of Soviet leader Leonid Brezhnev (1964–82), the world socialist system was "the prototype of the future world community of free nations."[9] As argued by Leon Zalmanovich Zevin at the Institute of Economics of the World Socialist System in Moscow: "for its aims, essence and methods socialist integration differs in principle from integration processes of the capitalist world because these two types of integration are engendered by different modes of production, are motivated by different socio-economic aims and apply different methods of economic policy."[10]

Zevin and others pointed to the specific experiences of socialist countries from which developing countries could benefit, such as state ownership of the means of production and the planned economies. However, different from Soviet technical assistance during the Khrushchev period, Soviet economists did not insist on a specifically Soviet path of development as the basis of the world socialist system. Rather, they claimed that this system was open to "all countries of the world irrespective of their economic and social system." The defining principle of this collaboration was that of "mutual advantage" in foreign trade.[11] Soviet economists foresaw a "new international division of labor" that would replace the bifurcation of the world economy between industrialized countries and producers of raw materials, which had been inherited from the colonial period.[12] Refuting the Maoist narrative of the two superpowers, the developed, and the exploited nations, those economists pointed out that participation in the world socialist system restricted neither political nor economic activities of participating states, all of whom were "genuinely equal."[13] Writing in 1975, a Soviet author argued that "today more than one-third of the world population live in the countries which make up the world socialist system," and when describing the system "in action," he included several examples from Iraq, such as the support of socialist countries in developing Iraqi oil and gas industries, and large-scale farming.[14]

In retrospect, historians have questioned Soviet claims to a global economic system alternative to that of the West, which they regard as covering up the ambition of Soviet leaders at economic inclusiveness in the international community.[15] However, when seen from the point of view of Eastern European architects, planners, and managers working on export contracts, the world socialist system was neither an ideological smokescreen nor a utopian vision. It was, rather, an existing reality of foreign trade between those actors and their partners outside the bloc. This chapter will show how their exchanges facilitated the worldmaking of architecture during détente, or the easing of tensions between the United States and the Soviet Union in the course of the 1970s. I will argue that the global mobility of architecture accelerated not in spite of, but rather because of differences between the political economy of the world socialist system and that of Western capitalist countries then on the cusp of globalization processes.

In the wake of the 1973 embargo, Middle Eastern oil, Western money, and Eastern European goods and services became linked in a cycle that made the three regions more intertwined and interdependent. The profits from oil sales, deposited by Arab governments with Western financial institutions, were lent to socialist countries in need of modernizing their economies and financing their models of consumer societies. Yet the industrial leap that would have permitted paying those debts with a range of newly manufactured goods never materialized, and Hungary, Poland, and East Germany found themselves struggling with huge loans in Western currencies.[16] Debt repayment became a key motivation in stimulating their export of design and construction services, in particular as the range of their marketable products was shrinking and as they did not have fossil fuels to sell to Western Europe, unlike the Soviet Union. In Iraq, these goods and services were often bartered for crude oil, badly needed by energy-hungry Eastern European economies as the Soviet Union curtailed subsidized oil supplies for its satellite states over the course of the 1970s and 1980s. In addition, socialist countries sold that crude oil to the West to provide supplementary income for debt repayment.

The economic practices of actors from socialist countries in such transactions, and in transactions within the world socialist system more generally, were based on instruments introduced by the Council of Mutual Economic Assistance (Comecon). Comecon was at the core of the world socialist system, and it was a "real experience of restructuring world economic relations on the principles of equality, interest of all the cooperating countries, and friendly mutual assistance for the sake of common progress," as the official discourse went.[17] Comecon was founded in 1949 by Bulgaria, Czechoslovakia, Hungary, Poland, Romania, and the Soviet Union to organize economic relations between socialist countries. The founding members were joined in 1950 by East Germany. Under Khrushchev, Comecon expanded to Mongolia and, under Brezhnev, to Cuba and Vietnam, as well as numerous associated countries. The latter included Iraq, admitted to Comecon as an observer in 1975 with the purpose of stimulating multilateral economic, scientific, and technical cooperation.[18]

It was only after the death of Stalin in 1953 that Comecon developed an institutional profile. Under Khrushchev, its structures were used to pursue an economic integration of socialist countries based on coordination of national short-term and long-term economic planning. Within the fundamental principle in state socialism of state monopoly on foreign trade, and with the inconvertibility of national currencies of socialist countries, the main instruments of foreign trade within Comecon were intergovernmental agreements concerning the supply of specific goods on a barter basis. These agreements were intended to induce the production of selected goods in one or more countries, which in turn would result in a "socialist international division of labor" benefiting from the economies of scale across the entire bloc.[19] Under Brezhnev, the Soviets put pressure on the Eastern European satellites to stimulate economic integration through joint planning, industrial specialization, and cooperation in science, technology, and production.[20] While few of those objectives were realized—they were often thwarted by the satellites—the political economy of Comecon did create a specific set of tools, institutions, and practices for economic actors from socialist countries, including those in charge of the export of design and construction services.

In what follows, I will study these tools, institutions, and practices as frameworks of architectural mobilities from socialist countries to Iraq between the Qasim coup in 1958 and the first Gulf War in 1990. While Comecon did use architecture to represent itself, most prominently in its headquarters building in Moscow (Mikhail Posokhin and others, 1963–70), questions of representation are secondary in this chapter (figure 4.2).[21] Rather, by focusing on such issues as legal forms of contracts, exchange rates between currencies, and the barter system, I will argue that the political economy of the world socialist system was not only a principle of distribution of architecture but also the principle of architectural production. In other words, it not only defined where architects and planners from socialist countries worked but also how they worked and what they produced.

4.2. The Comecon building in Moscow (USSR, today Russian Federation), 1963–70. M. V. Posokhin, A. Mndoiants.

As has been the case in the previous chapters, the focus on labor will be the guiding line, starting with the discussion of the master plan of Baghdad. The legal framework of the contract for the plan, stemming from the principles of socialist foreign trade, resulted in the specific conditions of work for the Polish planners in Baghdad, and conditions for their collaborations with Iraqi administrators, planners, architects, and scholars. In turn, those working conditions made possible the activation of earlier Polish planning experiences, resulting in what distinguished the master plan from earlier planning documents in Baghdad: its embedded, empirical, interdisciplinary, collaborative, and scenario-based character. These features facilitated the absorption of the master plan in Baghdad, and its overarching impact on the development of the city. This impact of the master plan was further strengthened by individual architects and planners from Poland who continued to work in Baghdad, directly employed in municipal-planning departments, state administration, educational institutions, and private architectural offices.

Design commissions, such as the master plan, and individual employment contracts were not the only conveyors of architectural labor from socialist countries to Iraq. This labor also traveled as part of larger packages, in particular within design-and-build contracts. The focus on buildings designed and constructed by East German and Romanian companies in Iraq will show how the political economy of the world socialist system profoundly impacted those buildings' design procedures, construction technologies, and materiality. Eastern European designers and contractors in Iraq aimed at exploiting the opportunities and avoiding the hindrances that resulted from operating at the intersection between the state-socialist foreign trade and the emerging, increasingly global and Western-dominated market of design and construction services. In order to do so, architects, planners, and managers employed and adapted specific architectural tools and procedures. They included type designs that were used to facilitate the collaboration between various East German companies and their subcontractors, and the procedure of "technological adaptation," or of redrawing third-party plans so that they could be constructed by means of Romanian material, technology, and labor, bartered for crude oil. In turn, the focus on the collaboration between East German and Romanian companies in the project of Baghdad's industrial slaughterhouse (1974–81) will put to the test the principle of the "new international division of labor" as the core tenet of Comecon's global vision. Rather than stemming from a coordinated specialization within Comecon, the specific profiles of actors from socialist countries in Iraq were shaped by path-dependent adaptation to the conditions on the ground.

PLANNING BAGHDAD FROM WITHIN: MIASTOPROJEKT IN IRAQ

In 1967, the Kraków-based newspaper *Dziennik Polski* published an extensive account about Miastoprojekt's planning of Baghdad. The article imagined an "air bridge" linking the Miastoprojekt headquarters in Kraków with a private villa in Baghdad, its Iraqi base, where, at the time of the journalist's visit, seven engineers were working. They were part of a group of twenty-one planners, architects, sociologists, economists, Arabists, and climatologists who had been passing through the villa since it had been rented to the Polish firm two years before. The paper's article gave a fair account of challenges faced by the planners and of the decisions taken in the master plan. After an optimistic assessment of possible future commissions in Iraq, it ended with a less celebratory statement: "For its work in Baghdad, Miastoprojekt did not receive even the smallest amount of convertible currency, which could be used, for instance, to buy current professional literature. The engineers are told that their work falls under the export of propaganda, and hence they should address the Ministry of Foreign Affairs, but there they are advised that it is commerce, rather, and they are redirected to the Ministry of Foreign Trade."[22]

This account offers a glimpse into the political economy of Miastoprojekt's work in Iraq. If Miastoprojekt planners addressed Polish state institutions rather than the Iraqi commissioner for their fees, it was because the planning office had not signed the contract for the master plan directly with the Iraqis. It was foreign trade organizations (FTOs) and ministries of foreign trade rather than companies and individuals that were in charge of imports and exports in socialist countries. In the case of Poland, the FTO in charge of the export of labor was Polservice, created in 1961 as a spin-off from the Foreign Trade Organization for Complete Industrial Plants (Cekop).

Polservice had negotiated the contract with Iraqi governmental institutions, including the Mayoralty of Baghdad and the central government, and those negotiations were monitored by the Polish Ministry of Foreign Affairs. At the same time, the passage from *Dziennik Polski* reveals that, along with geopolitical concerns, a crucial motivation for architectural export was the acquisition of "convertible currency"—that is "hard" currency exchangeable on international markets, such as US dollars, as opposed to the Polish currency and that of other socialist countries, which were not exchangeable. If the Polish economic press in the 1960s pointed out that Poland's foreign trade with developing countries aimed both at supporting those countries and at securing raw materials for national industry, ten years later that same press was clarifying the fundamental aim of those export activities as the acquisition of convertible currency.[23] This new priority stemmed from the need to repay foreign loans, combined with the easing of international tensions after the recognition by West Germany of Poland's western border (1970), changed in the wake of World War II. Yet Miastoprojekt did not see any of the convertible currency paid for the master plan. The fee that the planning office received from Polservice was paid in Polish currency, according to the exchange rates regulated by state institutions. This is why Miastoprojekt's planners often shared a sentiment of getting a rough deal, and feared that the lack of funding undermined their ability to keep up to date with international professional debates.

Technical Assistance as Entry Point

The sobriety of the article from *Dziennik Polski* contrasts with the enthusiasm shared by most accounts in the Polish press, which reported, for example, on how "Baghdad, the City of Thousand and One Tales, Is Modernized by Kraków Architects."[24] Yet Polish planners arriving in Baghdad soon realized that it had been decisively shaped during the twentieth century and had little to do with the city of the Abbasid caliphs, whether of Abu Jafar al-Mansur's eighth-century round plan or Harun al-Rashid's palatine city, the latter among the protagonists of the fabled tales (figures 4.3 and 4.4). The seeds for the city's development in the twentieth century were laid by Ottoman governor Midhat Pasha (1869–72). The city walls were demolished and replaced with a dike (called a "bund") to which another, "Eastern" bund was added, to mitigate the effect of annual flooding of the Tigris River, thus opening the possibility of the city's eastward expansion. British occupation during World War I began the period of the UK's influence in Iraq, which was established as a British mandate in 1920, then declared a constitutional monarchy a year later, and became formally independent in 1932.[25]

Up to 1958, British architects, urban planners, and engineers had a decisive impact on the urbanization of Baghdad. In the city's commercial heart on the east bank, Rusafa, new streets parallel to the Tigris were constructed. These pierced the fabric of two-story courtyard houses, most

4.3. View of Baghdad (Kadhemiya), 1960s.

4.4. View of Baghdad, 1960s.

constructed in the nineteenth century, separated by meandering alleys and occasionally a mosque and a souk.[26] On the right bank of the Tigris, within and around the old settlement called Karkh, the city had expanded westward. In that area, new civic and governmental buildings were designed by British architects in a classical manner and often overlaid with Islamic details, such as Baghdad's (Western) Railway Station (James M. Wilson and Harold C. Mason, 1946–51).[27] Kadhemiya, the third historic node of the city, built around a revered Shia shrine, had hardly changed since the Ottoman period. Along with Adhamiya, the fourth historic settlement in Baghdad, the Rusafa, Karkh, and Kadhemiya districts were surrounded by an archipelago of British-era garden suburbs, government-sponsored neighborhoods for its employees, and housing constructed by professional cooperatives (for lawyers, doctors, engineers) and by private enterprises or individual landowners.[28] New roads were built to connect these to the historic centers, and along these *sarifas* emerged, slum settlements with little or no infrastructure. They housed migrants arriving from the countryside, often dispossessed peasants.[29]

Baghdad's development accelerated in 1950, when the renegotiated agreement with the British-controlled Iraqi Petroleum Company transferred half of the oil profits to Iraq's government. Seventy percent of them were allocated to the Development Board, put in charge of the modernization of the country. During the first six-year plan (1951–56), the board directed most funding to irrigation and flood protection, indispensable for agriculture, but also for urbanization. In particular, the construction of the Wadi Tharthar reservoir and diversion project, on the Tigris north of Baghdad (1956), allowed the development of the city to the east. The next plan (1955–60) allocated significant funds for social needs, including a nationwide housing program commissioned from Doxiadis Associates, along with the urbanization of Baghdad, including transportation, public buildings, housing, healthcare, education, and culture. The Development Board invited prominent Western architects to design signature buildings (Le Corbusier, Alvar Aalto, Willem Marinus Dudok, Gio Ponti, Walter Gropius, and Frank Lloyd Wright); few of those buildings were constructed and even fewer in their intended forms.[30] The first-generation Iraqi architects were returning from their educations abroad, mainly in the UK and the United States, to assume positions in the state administration and to receive their first commissions. These included Mohamed Makiya (educated in Liverpool and Cambridge), Hisham Munir (the American University in Beirut, the University of Texas), Hazim Namiq (Cardiff), Abdullah Ihsan Kamil (Liverpool), and Rifat Chadirji (Hammersmith University, London).[31] All of them would become important counterparts of Eastern Europeans arriving in Iraq after 1958.

The coup led by Qasim—called the 14 July Revolution by its protagonists—brought about a decade of instability, with four regime changes between 1958 and 1968. But it also ended the grip of the landed and the urban wealthy classes over the political system, placed the new middle class in power, and installed policies of egalitarianism and broader distribution of wealth.[32] The change of priorities was reflected in the replacement of the Development Board by the Economic Planning Board, whose first plan (1959–60) shifted the government's priorities from agriculture to industry.[33] The biggest growth of investment was, however, in public buildings and housing, and on several occasions Qasim pronounced that "in the near future no one will be without a house."[34]

Baghdad, the capital and the center of the political, economic, and cultural life of the country, was the principal scene of these operations. The daily press reported on the bustling construction activities, with Qasim frequently inspecting new housing districts. The houses were typically distributed among junior officials, police, and the military, including Officers City in the east and, on the other side of the river, al-Hurriyah, al-Salam, and West Baghdad, the latter under construction according to the design by Doxiadis Associates.[35] Doxiadis's planning also impacted the largest new settlement: the Madinat al-Thawra, or City of Revolution, east of the newly constructed seventeen-kilometer Army Canal (1961), which served mainly for irrigation and created an axis for the city's expansion to the northeast.[36] Many new inhabitants of al-Thawra, as well as Sabiyat and Daura, were former sarifa dwellers, the areas that, according to various estimates, contained almost half of all buildings in Baghdad and housed up to a third of the population of the entire city.[37] The eradication of sarifas was the explicit aim of Qasim. Plots of land, including *miri* land (state land) and nationalized land of the royal family and some larger private estates, were distributed by various governmental bodies to factories, trade unions, and state-housing cooperatives, with the purpose of constructing houses for their employees or members.[38] Most of those new neighborhoods, however, lacked water and electricity supplies, sewage networks, and social facilities (schools, mosques), as well as public transport.

Several buildings designed before the revolution by Western architects went ahead, including two buildings at the Baghdad University campus designed by Walter Gropius and The Architects Collaborative (TAC);

4.5. Master plan of Baghdad, 1954–56. Minoprio, Spencely & Macfarlane (UK).

other structures of the university were constructed until 1985. The Iraq Museum in Karkh, on which the German Werner March (designer of Berlin's Nazi-era Olympic Stadium) had worked since the 1930s, was opened in 1966. The Development Board Building, designed by Gio Ponti, was constructed in Karkh in 1961, and the extension of the Rafidain Bank by Philip Hirst was added to the earlier building in Rusafa by the same architect (1953).[39] Western architects continued to be invited to Baghdad, with the UK's Alexander Gibb put in charge of the new airport, constructed by Bulgaria's Technoexportstroy (TES).[40] Josep Lluís Sert was considered for the design of the Civic Center, following the opening of his widely admired US Embassy (1961).[41] Architectural competitions, whose outlines were distributed by Iraqi diplomatic outposts in Western and Eastern Europe (along with New York City and several Arab countries) attracted participants from both sides of the Iron Curtain. Swiss architect William Dunkel (who had designed the Central Bank of Iraq, 1955–56) won the competition for the Electricity Board in 1961, in which Bulgarian and Polish architects also participated.[42] Demolition in several parts of Rusafa and Karkh continued in order to make space for new buildings constructed by private and public companies and institutions, in particular the Department of Awqaf, the Sunni endowments foundation.[43] New squares were constructed, including Tahrir Square with the monument for the 14 July Revolution, by sculptor Jewad Salim and architect Rifat Chadirji (1961), along with parks, followed by attempts to redesign the Tigris banks, in particular in Kadhemiya, as well as new hospitals, governmental buildings, and sports facilities.[44]

This intense construction program contrasted with the lack of a comprehensive master plan at the disposal of the Amanat al-Assima. The plan in use had been delivered in 1956 by British planners Minoprio, Spencely & Macfarlane, whose main credential for working in the Middle East was their master plan of Kuwait City (1952) (figure 4.5).[45] The Amanat's commission for the British planners was restricted to the specification of the main road system, land use and zoning, and a "diagrammatic" allocation of public buildings.[46] Accordingly, the plan proposed a "broad framework" for

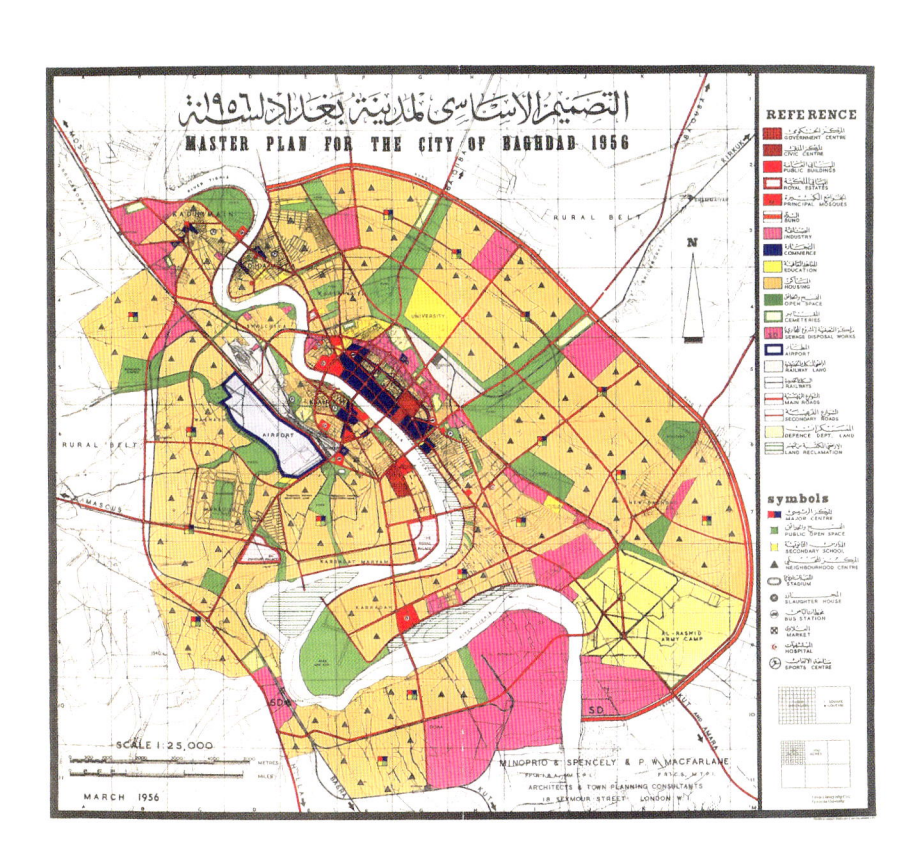

THE WORLD SOCIALIST SYSTEM

Baghdad's future development, captured in one color drawing, explained and extended by an accompanying twenty-three-page text. This included rudimentary urban standards (such as the distribution of various school types and medical facilities according to population numbers), whose use was impaired because of the incompleteness of the demographic data. The plan's main decision was to encourage the east-west development of the city along a new axis, perpendicular to the "untidy ribbons" along the Tigris, which the plan wanted to restrict. The new ovoid shape would encompass all neighborhoods constructed over the course of the 1950s, to which new housing districts were added, designed on the principle of neighborhood units. These were intended to rehouse sarifa dwellers and a portion of the inhabitants of Rusafa and Karkh, districts that were considered overpopulated and whose parts were to be cleared for the civic and governmental centers, respectively. The city, envisaged as "compact," would be delineated by an outer rural belt, and interconnected by new roads and bridges, a reorganized railway network, rezoned industry, new open spaces, green wedges, and an extended eastern bund that would protect the city from flooding.[47]

Until 1966, the Amanat's policy of urban localization was based on the Minoprio plan, complemented by the schematic plan that Doxiadis Associates produced as a spin-off of its Housing Program (1958).[48] However, according to Iraqi professionals and decision makers, the Minoprio plan was not based on empirical studies or surveys, and it contained "many errors" that prevented its implementation. It did not account for the city's expansion, such as the Army Canal and the area around it, nor for new squares and streets in the center.[49] Critics pointed out that the plans preceding Miastoprojekt's did not allow control of the growth of the city, leading to chaotic and scattered development that prevented an appropriate distribution of services among the population.[50] The Poles arriving in Baghdad, too, were highly critical of the Minoprio master plan, even if their future planning would confirm several of its decisions. They argued that the main fallacy of the plan was the threefold extension of the urbanized areas, without its proper phasing. Accordingly, the master plan contributed to the exacerbation of a "scattered city" (and, hence, of rising costs of infrastructure and public transport), which it had intended to prevent in the first place.[51] The Polish planners also questioned the lack of a mediating spatial element positioned between the neighborhood unit and the large district, which is how Doxiadis's plans were implemented in al-Thawra.[52] They took issue with the proposal of razing large parts of Rusafa to create vast blocks for governmental functions and a civic center, as proposed by Minoprio in a subsequent commission.[53]

Their critique of the Minoprio plan was formulated from within their experience of working for Baghdad's planning authorities as part of the technical-assistance program granted to Iraq by the Polish government. Shortly after the revolution, Iraq signed treaties of technical cooperation and assistance with the Soviet Union (1958), followed by Poland, Bulgaria, Hungary, and Czechoslovakia.[54] The USSR took upon itself to help in expanding Iraqi heavy and light industries, including the machine-building and chemical industries, along with extensive military support. Soviet experts, estimated to number seven hundred in 1961, were to plan the expansion of Iraqi irrigation systems and to carry out geological and hydrographic surveys; they also worked on railway construction of the Baghdad-Basrah line.[55] These industrial projects and those that followed were to change Iraqi cities in the long run. Accordingly, the Iraqi press, when listing Soviet-assisted projects, reported that "Kut will be a town of textile workers; Iskanderiya a town of engineering workers; Samarrah a drug producing center."[56]

Baghdad received Soviet projects as well, including the broadcasting station on the outskirts of the capital at Salman Pak, in front of which

Qasim celebrated the third anniversary of the revolution.[57] It was designed by the Design Institute of the Ministry of Communication in Moscow (Giprosviaz) in accordance with technical requirements submitted by the Iraqi side. Prommashexport, an FTO at the Soviet Ministry of Foreign Trade, supplied equipment and supervised its installation.[58] Other Soviet-constructed structures in Baghdad under Qasim included a modern slaughterhouse, silos, and water towers, though the Soviet-designed TV tower remained unbuilt.[59] As shown by the memorandum sent in August 1963 by Soviet advisors working at the Ministry of Works in Baghdad, these activities faced many problems. Designs were not sufficiently typified and standardized, which resulted in higher costs, delays, and technological difficulties; the financial calculations and specifications of construction materials were often inaccurate; the work of Soviet design institutes was not sufficiently coordinated; and the delivered design documentation was often incomplete.[60]

The assistance of socialist countries was particularly strong in education, seen as an integral part of the modernization process. The Soviet Union was by far the most generous country in offering scholarships, and by 1959, nearly eight hundred Iraqis studied in the Soviet Union at Soviet expense; the following year, this number reached more than thirteen hundred.[61] These included architectural students, and over the next two decades at least thirty-six Iraqis graduated from the Moscow Architectural Institute (MARKhI), among them five women, with the vast majority (thirty-one) arriving in Moscow between 1960 and 1962.[62] In the years to come, fellowships were offered by other socialist countries, too, including a significant number of Ph.D. placements.[63] The case for education in socialist countries was made through a concentrated propaganda effort, with movies and books imported to Iraq in the framework of cultural cooperation, and numerous articles planted in the Iraqi press discussed the "phenomenal" progress in the Soviet Union.[64] Reports on the Soviet space program were complemented by others on the postwar reconstruction of Eastern Europe, both topics showcased at Baghdad's International Trade Fair in the early 1960s.[65]

The first group of Polish planners came to Iraq following the trade treaty between the two countries in 1959. In the early 1960s, there were already fifty Polish engineers working on the construction sites of a sugar plant in Mosul and other industrial plants, along with a bridge in Tikrit and multiple water-engineering and irrigation works. By that time, several architects from Poland were working for Iraqi institutions.[66] Their first group of eight arrived in Baghdad in mid-1959, and in the next year it was extended by seven more.[67] At the Ministry of Works and Housing and the Ministry of Municipalities, they worked along with and sometimes together with Soviet and, later, East German advisors, designing public facilities, including hospitals and schools. They also programmed and designed urban housing districts and parks in Baghdad and other cities, and supervised design work, consulting and coordinating it with other planning departments, and prepared tender documentation (figure 4.6).[68] Previous planning documents in Iraq, including housing projects by Doxiadis Associates and their master plan for Kerbala and other cities, as well as British master plans for Mosul by Raglan Squire (1955) and Basrah by Max Lock (1958), were adjusted or replaced by Polish planners, with Stanisław Jankowski among them (figure 4.7).[69] Other architects from Warsaw visited for short periods, including Jerzy Hryniewiecki, who traveled twice to Baghdad between 1960 and 1962, where he designed the Ministry of Foreign Affairs building.[70] The fact that Poland was sending architects of such high profile as Jankowski and Hryniewiecki, both of whom held leadership positions in Warsaw's planning and academic institutions, testified to the importance attributed by the Polish authorities to the cooperation with Iraq.[71]

Together with the representative of Polservice, members of this group prepared the submission to the two-stage tender competition for the Baghdad master plan, announced by the Amanat in 1961.[72] Their previously acquired knowledge of conditions on the ground allowed them to win over proposals from four Western European countries, including West Germany, Sweden, and Switzerland, in the second phase of the tender procedure.[73] In turn, their personal acquaintance with Iraqi planners helped during long negotiations with the Amanat.

Technical-assistance projects in Iraq also set a precedent for negotiating the financial conditions of the Polish offer. Along with a few gifts, most Eastern European assistance to Iraq was delivered by means of concessional lending mechanisms and trade preferences.[74] This is why Western commentators often classified socialist development assistance

4.6. Office building, Samarra, 1963. Ministry of Municipalities, Directorate General of Planning and Design, Baghdad; Jerzy Baumiller (chief architect and project architect).

4.7. Master plan of Basrah, 1962. Ministry of Municipalities, Directorate General of Planning and Design, Baghdad; Stanisław Jankowski (chief engineer town planning).

as commercial exchange.[75] Even if that had been the case, the financial conditions of this exchange were favorable to the Iraqis when compared with those offered by Western economic actors. Soviet theorists of the world socialist system claimed that technical-assistance projects were delivered without profit. For example, the fee requested by the Soviets for technical documentation of an industrial facility already built in the Soviet Union amounted to compensation for the costs of adapting that documentation to specific conditions of a recipient country.[76] Favorable conditions offered by socialist countries were praised by Qasim, who argued that Soviet equipment was sold to Iraq "at the lowest international prices."[77] When technical-assistance projects were funded by Soviet and other Eastern European credit, the interest rate was typically 2.5 percent, which was both lower than commercial Western credit and lower than the rate of return on capital invested in the Soviet Union.[78]

This blurred distinction between aid and trade from socialist countries pointed to the principle of "mutual advantage," which theorists of the world socialist system placed at the system's core. Similar language was used by Eastern European leaders. For example, Romania's head of state Nicolae Ceaușescu argued that Romania, a developing country itself, could not afford to offer gifts, but could provide help to other developing countries by "cooperation...on mutually advantageous bases."[79] A similar point was made by the booklet *Rights and Obligations of an Expert* (1972), distributed among Polish professionals going abroad by the FTO Polservice. When discussing their remuneration in foreign countries, Polservice argued that, even if their work was paid, it should be considered "assistance" because "this remuneration is not fully equivalent to the actual value of the work of Polish experts in these countries," which is to say the "remuneration for similar work in the framework of commercial contracts."[80]

This statement also applied to the financial conditions of Baghdad's master plan, which were favorable to the Iraqis when compared to the four proposals offered by Western competitors. The ability to offer those conditions stemmed from Polservice's exploitation of a fundamental characteristic of Comecon economies: the fact that they were based on unconvertible currencies. Actors from Comecon countries working in Iraq were typically operating in two monetary systems: the Iraqi dinar, pegged to the US dollar, and inconvertible Eastern European currencies—the Polish zloty, in the case of Polservice. The exchange rates between these two currencies for Polish contractors were decided by Polish state institutions, and these rates were multiple, depending on the type of transaction and the actors involved. In this sense, when the Polservice brochure argued that the remuneration of Polish experts was "not fully equivalent" to that requested by Western experts, this statement could be read as pertaining not simply to a lower price, but, more fundamentally, to the incommensurability of the two financial regimes.

This incommensurability was reflected in the contracts offered by Polservice. Like most FTOs in other socialist countries, Polservice distinguished between "collective" contracts, signed with a foreign institution, and "individual" contracts, signed by individual experts and their foreign employers, whether private or public.[81] Both types of contracts became conveyors of labor from socialist Poland to Iraq. The collective contracts combined two agreements, and the master plan of Baghdad provides a case in point. It consisted of, first, an agreement between Polservice and the Amanat, formulated in convertible currency (Iraqi dinars); and, second, the contract between Polservice and Miastoprojekt, in unconvertible currency (Polish zlotys). After the subtraction of Polservice's fee, a part of the dinars paid to Polservice by the Amanat was used to cover operating costs of the office Miastoprojekt set up in Baghdad, with another part changed into zlotys and transferred to Miastoprojekt. Exchange rates for the latter transaction were subject to fierce negotiation between the two Polish companies.[82] In order to substantiate a lower exchange rate offered to Miastoprojekt, Polservice representatives could have quoted from the *Rights and Obligations of an Expert* booklet and argued that "the difference between the conversion rate [used in Polservice's transactions] and an average cost of earning one US dollar by means of export is to be seen as compensation owed to the state for the reduction of the national income caused by the deployment of a number of specialists to work in institutions and enterprises abroad."[83] Yet while economists tried to estimate the value of Polish currency by generalizing the costs of earning one US dollar in particular export contracts, such generalizations proved highly problematic.[84] In this sense, the agreed exchange rate was more a question of political leverage than economic calculation, which was the case with the negotiations with Miastoprojekt, whose work was closely monitored by the political authorities in Poland.[85]

At the same time, the modifiable exchange rate allowed Polservice to be more flexible vis-à-vis the Amanat. For instance, at one point in the negotiations, Polservice yielded to Amanat's demand to extend the range of the services offered. The FTO compensated for the resulting additional costs by imposing a lower exchange rate for the US dollar on Miastoprojekt in calculating the planning office's fees (hence a lower payment in the Polish currency to Miastoprojekt).[86] In so doing, Polservice was able to offer the Amanat conditions that Western competitors were not able to match, including the large size of the Polish team stationed in Baghdad, along with the recruitment of experts from numerous scientific institutions in Poland. In other words, when competing with Western companies in Iraq, Polservice benefited from its monopolist position as a mediator between the closed socialist economy and the emerging global market in design services. More generally, the negotiations around the master plan exemplify the structurally weak position of Polish planners vis-à-vis their own state leadership, which was eager to sign the contract with the Iraqis in order to gain US dollars and, by extension, the planners' weak position vis-à-vis the Iraqi commissioners.[87] This weakness was also translated into individual contracts that, for example, obliged the experts to pay the expenses incurring to Polservice in case the experts were dismissed by a foreign institution for fault.[88] While the Miastoprojekt staff expressed frustration about these dynamics, they defined the conditions of work of the Polish team in Iraq, which in turn shaped the character of the master plan.

Thinking Baghdad through Warsaw

In a 1974 interview, the director of Polservice recalled that the master plan of Baghdad "was for us the first big consulting commission, which we have won in an international tender in spite of strong competition." He pointed out that financial conditions played a considerable role in winning the contract, but added that the "reputation of Polish planners" was just as decisive.[89]

Much credit for the fact that this reputation reached Iraq needs to be attributed to Adolf Ciborowski, a member of the planning team of the city of Warsaw and its head architect from 1956 to 1964. Ciborowski advised the Amanat during his trips to Baghdad between 1962 and 1964, in parallel to his work as head of the Polish technical-assistance team and as UN project manager for the reconstruction of Skopje after the 1963 earthquake, and in addition to his consultancy work in Asia and Africa.[90] During his 1962 visit, Ciborowski gave a public lecture in which he expressed his enthusiasm for the construction activities under Qasim. To Ciborowski, Baghdad appeared as a city of "one thousand and one construction sites." However, he urged the coordination of those building activities within a new master plan, and argued that the experience of Polish planners could be useful for this task.[91]

What Ciborowski told his Iraqi audience may be approximated from his booklet *Town Planning in Poland, 1945–55* (1956). It presented the main tasks of Polish architecture and urban planning during the first postwar decade in a way that seemed closely attuned to the aims of the Iraqi government. In Poland, those tasks had included the expansion and development of existing cities and the construction of new towns as part of the intertwined processes of urbanization, industrialization, and modernization.[92] These processes were to be guided by urban planning as part of spatial and economic planning on regional and national levels, which in the case of Warsaw spanned back to the urban analysis of Warsaw presented during the Fourth CIAM Congress (1933) and the Functional Warsaw scheme (1934).[93] The postulate of uniform housing standards for all residents reverberated with Qasim's speeches, just as Ciborowski's examples of workers' neighborhoods fully equipped with social services and planned alongside industrial facilities were paralleled by similar ambitions in Iraq.[94] Increasing attention under Qasim to Baghdad's history, expressed during the official celebrations of the city's twelve-hundredth anniversary, corresponded with the postwar rebuilding of Warsaw's historic Old Town.[95] The reconstruction of the Polish capital's "spatial proportions" and "general atmosphere" from wartime destruction was combined with infrastructural modernization that included an east-west thoroughfare tunneled under the Old Town.[96] This approach offered an alternative to demolitions being practiced in Baghdad.

Ciborowski's lecture in Baghdad, which took place shortly after the short-listing procedure of the master plan competition, must have worked in favor of the Polish proposal. It was Ciborowski who was first approached by the Amanat to head the Polish team in Baghdad. However, other obligations prevented him from accepting the commission. Accordingly, in early 1964, the Polish Ministry of Construction approached architect and planner Tadeusz Ptaszycki, director of the state-planning office Miastoprojekt in Kraków in southern Poland.[97]

Miastoprojekt was responsible for another internationally visible postwar project: the planning of Nowa Huta, "the first socialist city in Poland," for a hundred thousand inhabitants. Looking back at that experience, Kazimierz Bajer, longtime head of Miastoprojekt's export department, in charge of all Iraqi projects, recalled that "the planning of Nowa Huta was for us an experience of designing a city as a whole—and it was the same in Baghdad."[98] Over the course of the late 1950s and 1960s, the size of Miastoprojekt stabilized (with three hundred seventy to four hundred employees), and so did its profile, which included urban planning as well as civil and industrial architecture. With commissions growing scarce in the Kraków region, Miastoprojekt was on the lookout for new markets, both in Poland and abroad, which included exporting technical documentation of industrial plants to China (1955) and Iraq (1962), followed by offers and competition entries in the USSR, Tunisia, Israel, and Syria.[99] The contract with the Amanat (1965), and those that followed in Iraq, secured Miastoprojekt's high employment levels.

Miastoprojekt's commission in Baghdad unfolded in three phases. After the first phase (1965–68), the firm delivered the Basic Map ("Zoning and Land Use"), as well as its supporting drawings, designs for model residential districts, and outlines for detailed plans (figure 4.8). This master plan was promulgated by the Revolutionary Command Council in 1970 and declared as legally binding for all public institutions in Iraq by law no. 156 (1971).[100] Upon its delivery, Sayed Shafi, an Indian urban planner and UN expert delegated for consulting the master plan, considered it a "workable framework" for further development of the city.[101] However, Shafi was critical of the deficient survey, inadequate financial calculations, and insufficient involvement of Iraqi planners in the production of the plan.¹⁰² This criticism was taken into account in the outline of the second commission (1971–73) by the new Baath government.¹⁰³ This commission resulted in the Comprehensive Development Plan, which was approved by the appropriate authorities shortly after its submission (1973) (figure 4.9).¹⁰⁴ The third installment of the commission (1973–74) included detailed plans for selected areas of the city, and an implementation and action plan. At all three stages, the contracts stipulated the training of Iraqi planners. In parallel, Miastoprojekt was commissioned to deliver the street-naming and plot-numbering scheme for Baghdad.¹⁰⁵

The design of the master plan was a consultative process. At each stage, the work of the Poles was presented to, discussed with, and accepted by the authorities and professionals in Iraq. The body in charge was the Consulting Board for the Affairs of the Master Plan, nominated by the Amanat. Its members included, among others, Naman al-Jalili, architect and head of the Technical Section of the Amanat, and Abdullah Ihsan Kamil, architect and cofounder of the newly established Department of Architecture at the University of Baghdad (1959).¹⁰⁶ Sayed Shafi remained involved at all stages, with social and demographic questions consulted with a team of UN experts in Beirut.¹⁰⁷ The Amanat also nominated an Iraqi team of at least seven specialists who worked with Miastoprojekt's office in Baghdad; four of them went to Poland for a six-month training course at the International Postgraduate Course of Urban and Regional Planning for Developing Countries in Szczecin.¹⁰⁸ The consultation of the plan included its presentation to professionals at the Department of Architecture, the Association of Iraqi Architects, and the Union of Iraqi Engineers, and to

4.8. "Master Plan of Baghdad. Zoning and Land Use," 1967. Miastoprojekt-Kraków (Poland).

4.9. "Inner City—Structure in 2000." Miastoprojekt-Kraków (Poland). Miastoprojekt-Kraków, "Baghdad 2000—Comprehensive Development Plan for Baghdad," 1973.

the broad public by means of an exhibition at the Gulbenkian Museum in Baghdad (1966).[109] As one of the Polish architects recalled: "Baghdad was like Warsaw: everything we produced was showcased and people flocked to see the plans."[110] In the wake of the second agreement, feedback and objections were processed by the Consulting Board and passed on to the planners. In parallel to the work on the plan, members of the Miastoprojekt team participated in the Amanat's Committee on Planning, which decided on the localization of new buildings in the city.[111]

On the Polish side, the work was divided between Miastoprojekt's office in Baghdad and the firm's headquarters in Kraków, along with external specialists, including architects and planners from the Town Planning Office at the Department of Architecture at the Kraków University of Technology. Planners from the Warsaw planning office were included, too, as were experts from state-planning offices in various cities (Lublin, Częstochowa, and Wrocław) and research institutes, including Łódź

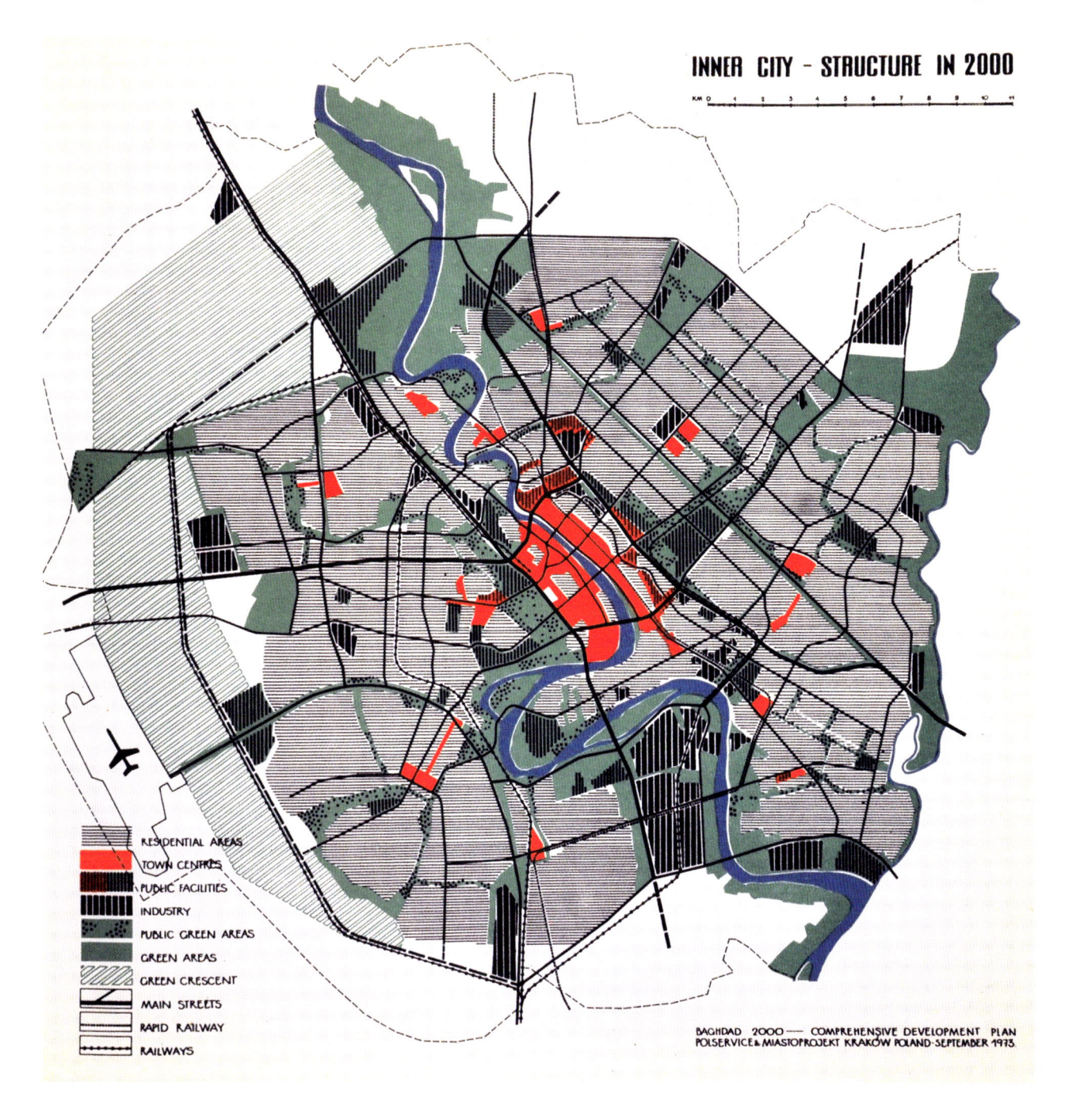

THE WORLD SOCIALIST SYSTEM

University, which cooperated on the climatological study. In total, thirty-six people worked on the master plan, including fifteen Miastoprojekt employees, five additional Polish collaborators, and five Polish consultants, as well as seven Iraqi experts.[112] Such a wide range of professionals allowed the team to activate what Ciborowski praised as the key characteristic of Polish planning: its empirical character, based on extensive interdisciplinary surveys, which takes stock of the existing conditions and builds the design decisions upon them.[113]

Taking stock was the first task for Miastoprojekt planners in Baghdad (figure 4.10). Surveys carried out in the framework of the first agreement included interviews with four hundred families and traffic studies. They were extended by the analysis of selected social and economic problems, conditions of ownership, and extent of development.[114] Polish planners mapped Baghdad's urban fabric with the help of Iraqi architects and students from the Department of Architecture. The maps in the 1967 submission included a study of the historical development of the city, its social-spatial stratification, and geological, hydrographical, and climatological surveys, in particular in relation to flood risk and flood protection. The maps also included a survey of infrastructure (sewerage, water supply, electricity networks, and garbage disposal), detailed traffic and transportation studies, and land use.[115] Strikingly, the religious significance of Baghdad, though given attention in the accompanying text, was not reflected in the drawings. In the decades to come, these studies became indispensable sources for understanding Baghdad's development in the 1960s and early 1970s.[116]

Following the second agreement, planners carried out a systematic survey of the city. It included detailed maps in all categories listed earlier, extended by studies at the scale of the region and the country. This survey allowed the planners to correct and refine their data, and, along with the experience of the implementation of the 1967 plan, it resulted in a more flexible application of planning categories in the final plan, differentiated according to conditions on the ground.[117] Detailed surveys of particular districts, including Kadhemiya, were based on systematic interviews with inhabitants ("together with Iraqi architects we have surveyed thirty-five hundred houses, and the sociologists interviewed households in every tenth house," recalled one member of the Miastoprojekt team).[118] Measured drawings of buildings in Kadhemiya were complemented by an assessment of their use, ownership, technical condition, and historical value.

Based on these surveys, the planning of the growth of the city, its environmental impact, and transportation networks were embedded in regional and national planning, in consultation with Piotr Zaremba, the head of the Postgraduate Course in Szczecin. Zaremba advised the Iraqi Ministry of Planning on the organization of spatial-planning institutions in Iraq and, along with a colleague from Szczecin and a scholar from Baghdad University, consulted on the planning of the Baghdad Metropolitan Region, sometimes taking issue with Miastoprojekt's decisions (figure 4.11).[119] On a regional scale, Miastoprojekt's 1973 plan distinguished between four zones. The "inner city," with a radius up to fifteen kilometers, was followed by the "suburban zone" with a radius of twenty-five kilometers, including a "green crescent" (a system of strips of high trees shielding the city against dust from the desert), agriculture, and two linear-urbanization areas on the north-south axis. Next followed a buffer zone of a sixty-kilometer radius, reserved for agricultural functions, and then two urban centers located outside the buffer zone, one in the north and the other in the south. The phasing of the master plan pertained to the development of each of these four zones, with a population of six million foreseen for Greater Baghdad (the inner city and the suburban zone) in the year 2000.[120]

The inner city was conceived as consisting of three "belts": the central "Tigris belt" flanked by two residential belts (figure 4.12). The Tigris belt was

> 4.10. Urban analysis, Baghdad. Miastoprojekt-Kraków (Poland). Miastoprojekt-Kraków, "Plan ogólny Bagdadu," 1967.

> 4.11. "Baghdad Metropolitan Region—Strategy of Development," 1972. Sketch by Piotr Zaremba.

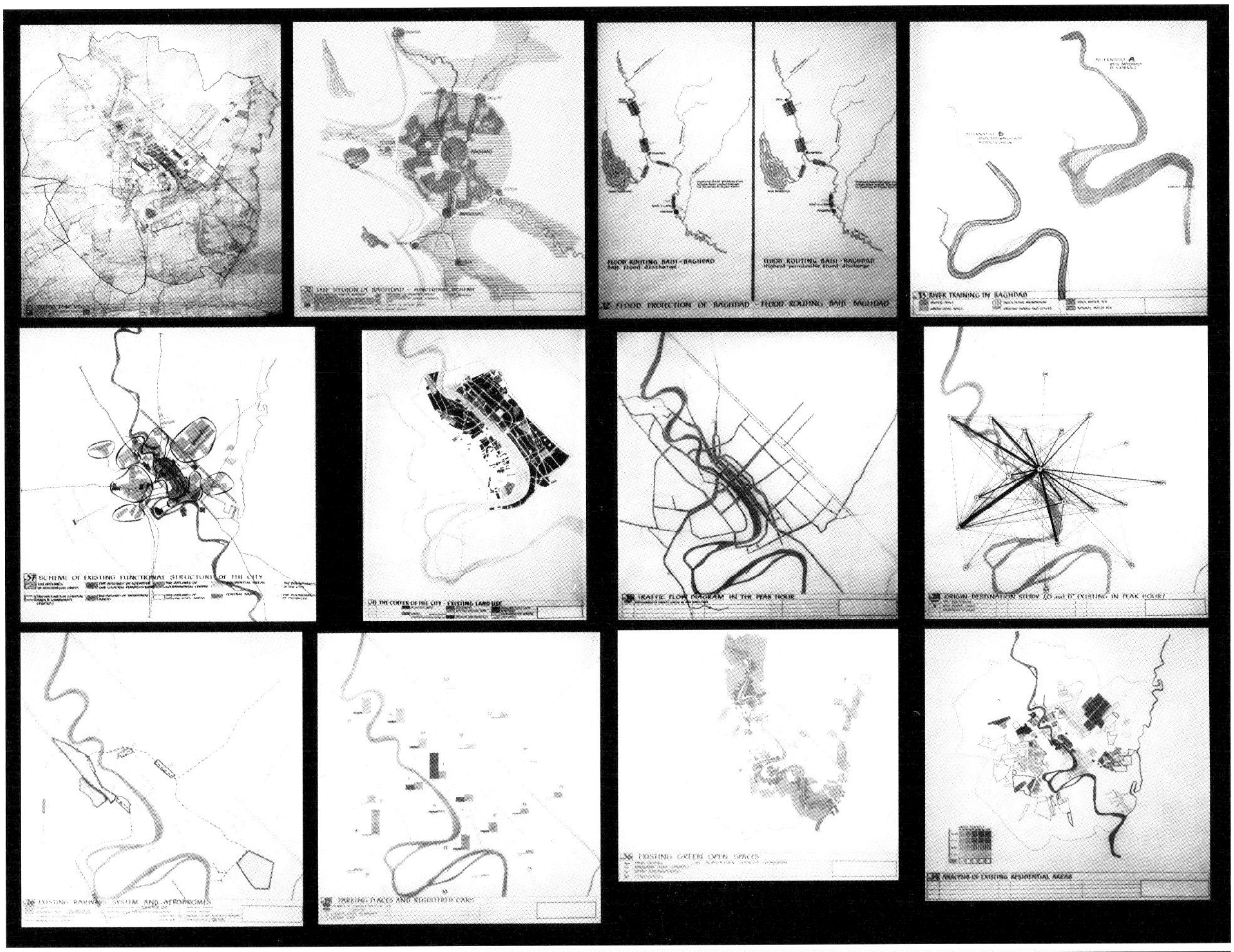
THE REGION OF BAGHDAD - FUNCTIONAL SCHEME
FLOOD ROUTING BAIJI - BAGHDAD
FLOOD PROTECTION OF BAGHDAD - FLOOD ROUTING BAIJI BAGHDAD
RIVER TRAINING IN BAGHDAD
SCHEME OF EXISTING FUNCTIONAL STRUCTURE OF THE CITY
THE CENTER OF THE CITY - EXISTING LAND USE
TRAFFIC FLOW DIAGRAM IN THE PEAK HOUR
EXISTING RAILWAY SYSTEM AND AERODROMES
PARKING PLACES AND REGISTERED CARS
EXISTING GREEN OPEN SPACES
ANALYSIS OF EXISTING RESIDENTIAL AREAS

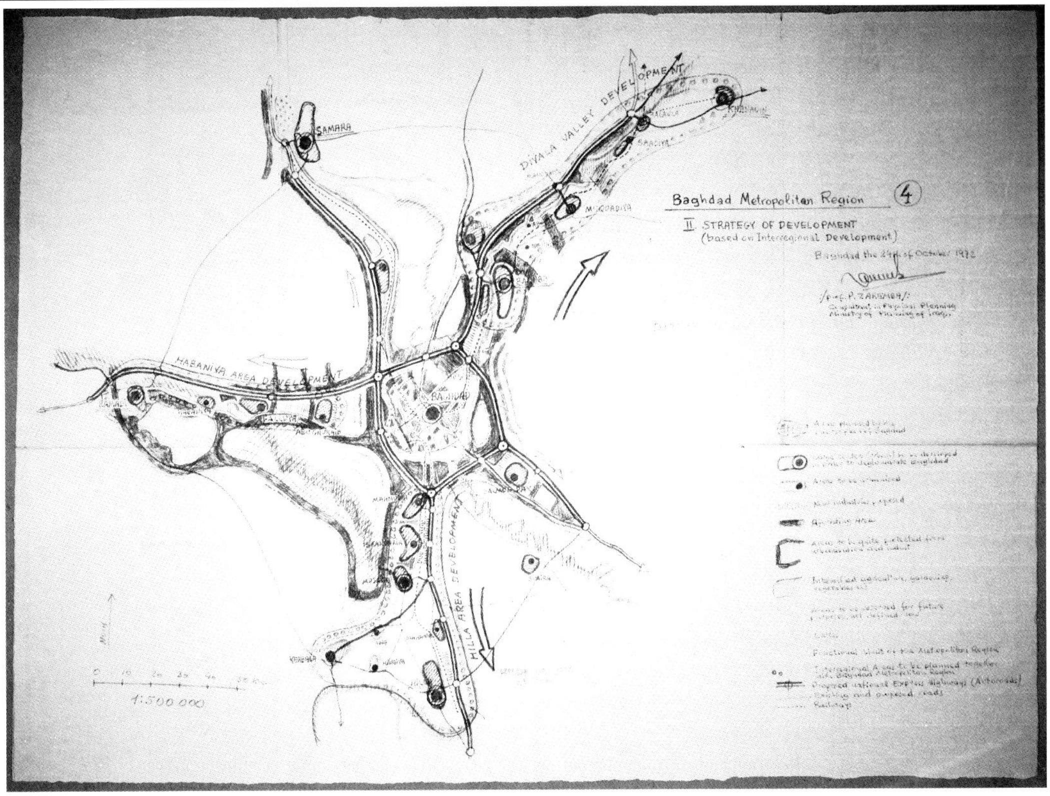
Baghdad Metropolitan Region
4
II STRATEGY OF DEVELOPMENT
(based on Interregional Development)
DIYALA VALLEY DEVELOPMENT
HABANIYA AREA DEVELOPMENT
HILLA AREA DEVELOPMENT
SAMARA
1:500 000

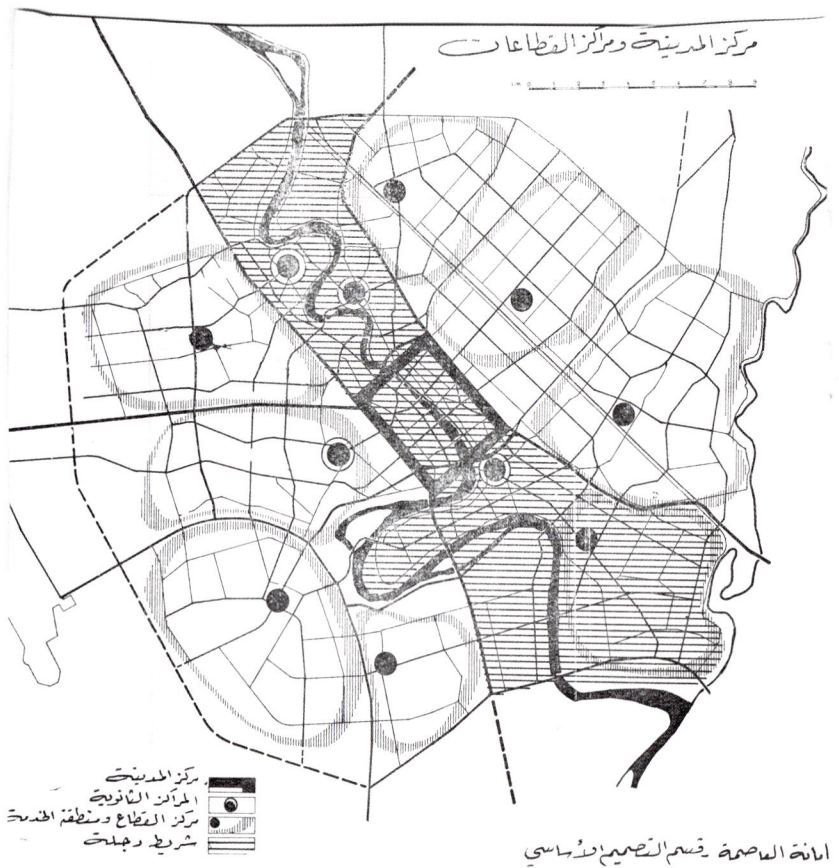

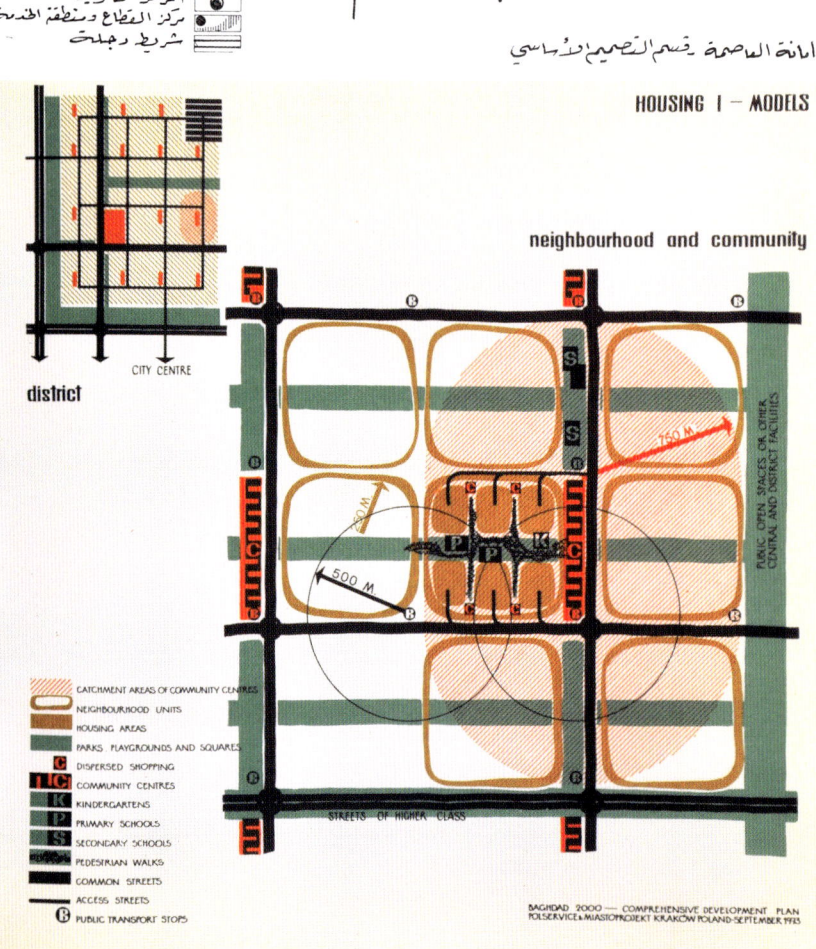

4.12. City and district centers. Miastoprojekt-Kraków (Poland). Miastoprojekt-Kraków, "Baghdad 2000—Comprehensive Development Plan for Baghdad," 1973.

4.13. "Housing I—Models. District, Neighborhood, and Community." Miastoprojekt-Kraków (Poland). Miastoprojekt-Kraków, "Baghdad 2000—Comprehensive Development Plan for Baghdad," 1973.

4.14. "City Centre Rusafa, Civic Centre—Visual Composition." Miastoprojekt-Kraków (Poland). Miastoprojekt-Kraków, "Rusafa—Karradah City Centre. Outlines for Detailed Plans. Short Report," 1967.

envisaged as a polycentric urban landscape along the river, with business and commercial districts and the new Civic Center in Rusafa; the National Governmental Center in Karradat Maryam; a cultural, business, and commercial center in Karkh; religious centers around the Golden Mosque in Kadhemiya and the Abu Hanifah Mosque in Adhemiya; and the university on the Karrada peninsula. These functions were combined with tourist facilities, housing, and their supporting programs.

Each residential belt consisted of three or four residential districts, conceived as self-sufficient and envisaged to serve all needs of the inhabitants, including employment (such as services and light industry). Each district was subdivided into communities, scaled according to pedestrian accessibility to each center (figure 4.13). The communities were divided in turn into neighborhood units, and these into housing areas. The units were served by two primary schools, one for boys and one for girls. Inhabitant numbers in these subordinate residential units, fixed in the 1967 master plan, were relaxed in the 1973 plan.[121]

The housing areas were designed as socially homogenous according to three income classes distinguished by Iraqi scholar Abduljabbar Araim, and their projected development was based on the assumption of growth of the higher- and middle-income groups, the decline of the average size of a household, an increased number of professional women, and the increase of non-work-related needs.[122] As with the plan of Doxiadis Associates, the combination of various socially homogenous housing areas for specific income groups resulted in socially heterogeneous communities, expected to intensify social contacts and act as tools for "democratization" of Iraqi society.[123] This phrasing, left without explanation, could have related to "popular democracies" in Eastern Europe—authoritarian regimes, in fact—or to equally questionable declarations of democracy under Qasim and those regimes that followed, or to mainstream Western planning discourse: an ambiguity that might have been intentionally employed by Miastoprojekt planners.

The master plan proposed single-family houses of medium density as the main typology for the residential belts, along with a few areas of low-density housing (mainly existing neighborhoods), and multifamily housing. The latter was foreseen to increase to 20 percent of the housing stock by 1990. The planners considered such development necessary to overcome the housing crisis and the sprawl of the city, despite the fact that interviews demonstrated the overwhelming preference of the population for a single-family house.[124] Suggestions from the 1967 plan to concentrate high-rises in Rusafa were abandoned, and the 1973 plan allocated multifamily housing more evenly among housing estates, areas of single-family houses, and district centers (figure 4.14). For single-family houses, the plan defined minimal plot sizes and aimed at reducing the number of large plots, while restricting plot sizes in new subdivisions to three categories, with recommended sizes of 150, 300, and 600 square meters.[125] That

THE WORLD SOCIALIST SYSTEM

classification would allow the estimate and control of the number of inhabitants in residential areas, thus making possible the application of urban standards proposed by the planners, in line with the emphasis of the Baath Party on welfare distribution.

In terms of architectural designs, the planners encouraged courtyard houses, as opposed to the free-standing villas that they saw in British-era middle- and upper-class neighborhoods, such as those built in Adhamiya and al-Mansour. Two such models were included in the 1967 plan: one by Miastoprojekt, and the other by the team led by Tomasz Mańkowski at the Chair of Residential Architecture at Kraków University of Technology (figure 4.15). The former design consisted of a composition of pavilions in wood and brick, while the latter focused on volumetric studies of strict geometric compositions, influenced by Mańkowski's fascination with Louis Kahn, his teacher at the University of Pennsylvania.[126] The planners suggested a number of incentives for private-housing developers, including the provision of infrastructure networks and favorable credits, yet they also emphasized that housing production as foreseen by the master plan would require major state intervention.

According to the master plan, various parts of the city would be connected by means of a differentiated traffic system. The plan introduced a uniform classification of roads, including radial roads extended into principal directions (to Mosul, Kirkuk, Basrah, Ruthba), which were joined in the "Motorway Box," a quadrangle ring road around Rusafa and Karkh.[127] This new traffic system required tripling the number of bridges over the Tigris. Networks for the railway, water transport, buses, and vans were redesigned. Furthermore, the master plan proposed a system of green spaces, which had the double function of recreation and climatic protection, with the green crescent complemented by transversal belts airing the city and green areas (public and private) linked to housing districts.[128] The planners argued that elements of the city should constitute not only a functional but also a visual whole, a coherent "townscape." Accordingly, the Tigris River was to become a "large architectural interior," in which civic and governmental centers were displayed on the background of historical settlements and new districts with a "modern architectural expression."[129] The differentiated character of particular streets was to be maintained and enhanced, with Rashid Street as a "high street," Abu Nuwas as a "main promenade," and the 14th Ramadan and Karrada Streets as "shopping streets."[130] The outer belts would gradate the atmosphere from bustling activities in the centers to a more intimate atmosphere in the residential parts.

The attention to Baghdad's architectural heritage distinguished Miastoprojekt's plans from the Minoprio master plan. While the latter acknowledged the architectural value of historic mosques, it insisted that their surroundings should be cleared. The planners recommended that the old areas of Rusafa, Karkh, and parts of Adhamiya and Kademiya, "dense mass of congested buildings...[with] the most rudimentary sanitary arrangements," should be demolished.[131] In contrast, the Miastoprojekt plan stressed the scientific, aesthetic, and touristic potential of "traditional Iraqi buildings" in Kademiya, Adhamiya, Rusafa, Karkh, and Karrada Old Quarters. Following the arguments about the reconstruction of Warsaw's Old Town, the planners wrote that those buildings were "a school for educating the Iraqi nation in the spirit of studying and appreciating their great national heritage."[132] Writing before the oil boom, they estimated that the complete preservation of Rusafa and Karkh would exceed the financial possibilities of the Iraqi state; hence they suggested a differentiated approach to those areas. The 1973 plan confirmed and extended the list of most valuable building complexes, and it introduced several categories of preservation, from complete preservation of individual buildings and their groups, through the integration of archaeological sites into the system

4.15. Housing Models, "Group and Single House." Miastoprojekt-Kraków (Poland), Władysław Leonowicz, Tadeusz Suwaj. Miastoprojekt-Kraków, "Model Housing Unit Baghdad, Iraq," 1966.

4.16. "Kadhemiyah Old Town." Miastoprojekt-Kraków (Poland). Miastoprojekt-Kraków, "Kadhemiyah Central District. Outlines for Detailed Plan. Short Report," 1967.

of public spaces, to the replacement of groups of dilapidated houses by "structures modern in standards but traditional in scale and character."[133] Areas around selected monuments in Rusafa, Karkh, and Adhamiya were to be preserved as "vicinity zones" interlinked by pedestrianized spaces. Old souks in Rusafa, several historic streets, and some alleys connecting vicinity zones were to be preserved, too.[134]

In contrast, the urban fabric around the mosque of Kadhemiya was to be preserved (figure 4.16). The plan suggested new legal and financial tools to regulate the transformation of individual buildings between the historic core around the mosque and outer neighborhoods. Recommended measures included visual correlation of new and historical façades, and the creation of modern social facilities and parking spaces for a limited number of vehicles inside the blocks (cleared of dilapidated buildings deemed of little historical value). The plan proposed a new organization of traffic of religious pilgrims, including two parking areas outside the district, and a partial pedestrianization of the access road to the Eastern Gate, transformed into a souk.[135] In general, the master plan required that new architectures in the protected complex do not interfere "with the principles of the traditional town-planning system."[136]

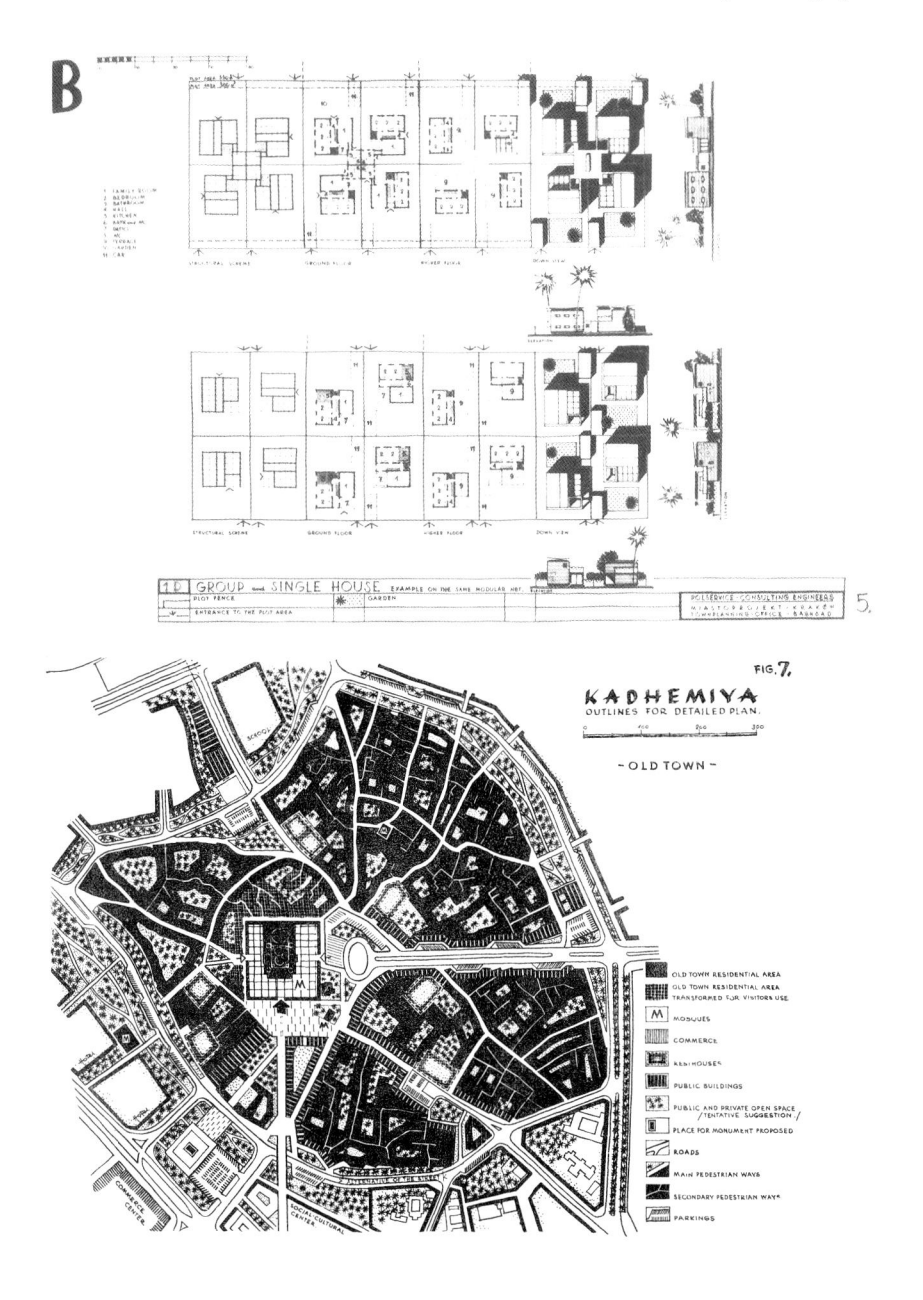

THE WORLD SOCIALIST SYSTEM

The planners suggested an extension of the powers of the Amanat, which they deemed necessary for the implementation of the master plan. They revised Iraqi building law and planning standards and suggested the creation of new administrative units responsible for development and implementation of urban planning.[137] While legislative suggestions had been part of the Minoprio plan, too, Miastoprojekt went much further and proposed that the Amanat be granted substantial powers to expropriate land. These were direct lessons from the reconstruction of Warsaw, for which the nationalization of land had been a precondition. Some of these recommendations were already being implemented during the work on the master plan.

Yet perhaps the most striking difference between the Minoprio and Miastoprojekt plans was their length. The contrast between the twenty-three pages of the British plan and the four volumes of the Miastoprojekt plan stemmed from the latter's mode of presentation. Rather than communicating a set of final decisions, the Miastoprojekt plan documented the planning process itself. For instance, the presentation of each element in the city's functional program followed the same pattern: quantification of its existing condition, estimation of its future growth as a function of the increase of population and employment, and the distribution of the functional element in the city. Since at every stage of these procedures the planners were working with uncertain and incomplete data, conclusions were presented as alternative scenarios and then prioritized. When suggesting urban standards (such as, for instance, surface requirements for particular programs), the planners substantiated them by comparing them with British and American sources, as well as French, German, Italian, Polish, Soviet, Swedish, and Swiss ones. In order to choose the appropriate solution, the results of the surveys were matched with experiences of other countries that were deemed comparable, such as postwar Poland (including Nowa Huta), post-independence India, or neighboring Syria and Kuwait.[138]

The transparency of this procedure was necessary for the acceptance of Miastoprojekt's planning decisions by the Consulting Board, but it can also be attributed to the project's origin in Polish technical assistance to Iraq. Reflecting about the role of foreign experts, Piotr Zaremba argued that they should not "elaborate the whole plan of the city or of a region, as this job must be carried by nationals." He recommended that foreign experts provide training in methodology, present case studies of selected problems, and support local planners in producing alternative plans of spatial development and establishing criteria for evaluating them.[139] While Miastoprojekt planners took a much more direct role in the planning of Baghdad than the one recommended by Zaremba, their embedded, empirical, collaborative, interdisciplinary, and scenario-based planning approach may be read as an attempt to train Iraqi planners, and to prepare them to take over in the planning process.

This planning approach was facilitated by the conditions of work on the collective contracts of Polservice, which allowed them to employ a large interdisciplinary team in the field office, their prolonged stay in Baghdad, and their "weak" position vis-à-vis their Iraqi counterparts and authorities (figure 4.17). In turn, this approach resulted in an unprecedented impact of the master plans on Baghdad's transportation network, housing development, and heritage preservation in the wake of the oil boom (figure 4.18). Iraqi reviewers emphasized that the survey-based character of the plans allowed them to account for Baghdad's historical, social, and economic reality in a way that previous plans had failed to do.[140] Furthermore, the empirical character of Miastoprojekt's plans allowed for fine-tuning the plans to conditions on the ground, and for avoiding large-scale demolition. The plans' use of urban norms and standards furnished Iraqi planners and administrators with design instruments applicable beyond the areas

4.17. Miastoprojekt Office in Baghdad, early 1970s.

4.18. "Bagdad: Irak, gubernatorstvo Bagdad," 1976. Sovetskii Armeiskii General'nyi Shtab (USSR).

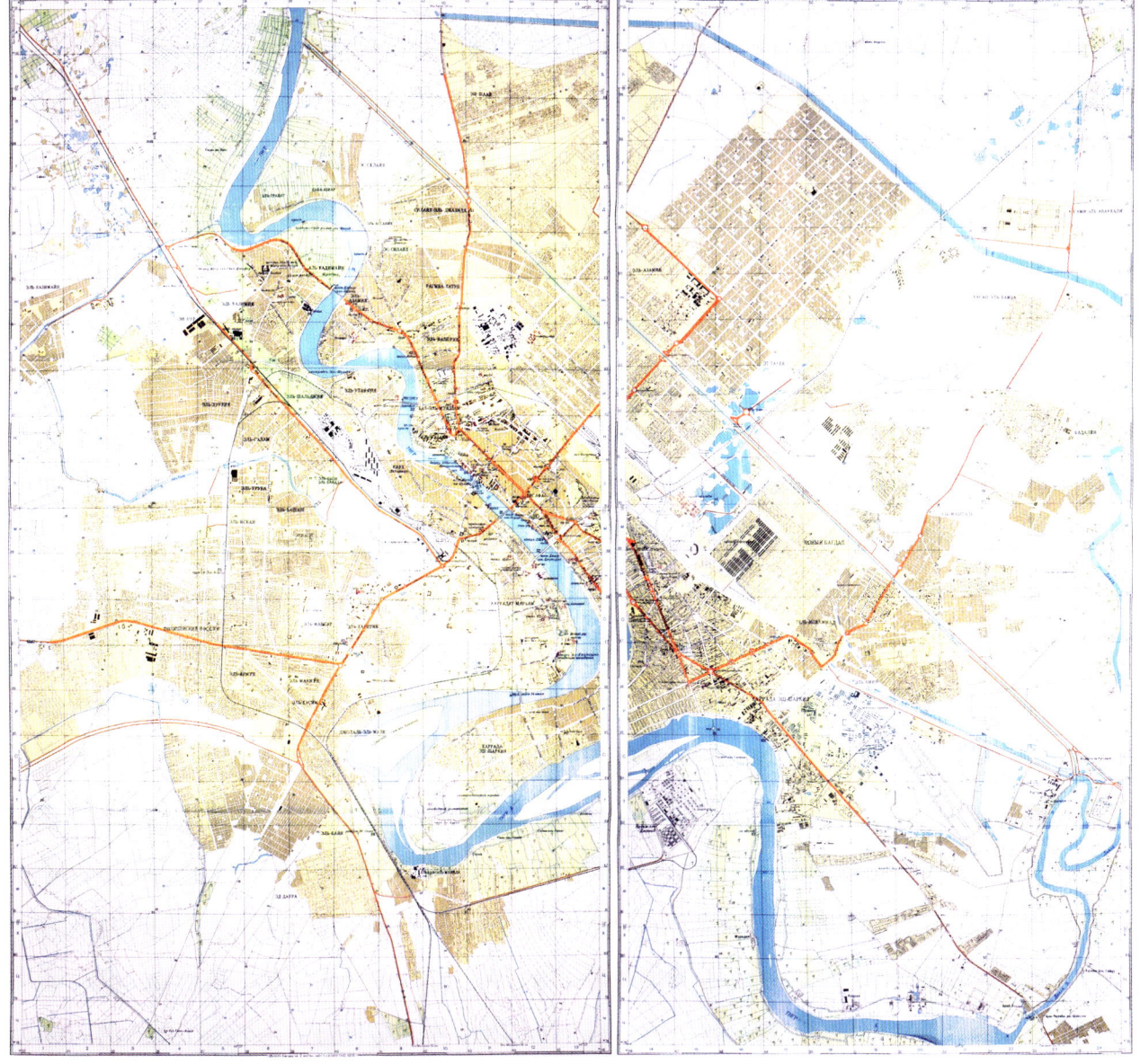

THE WORLD SOCIALIST SYSTEM

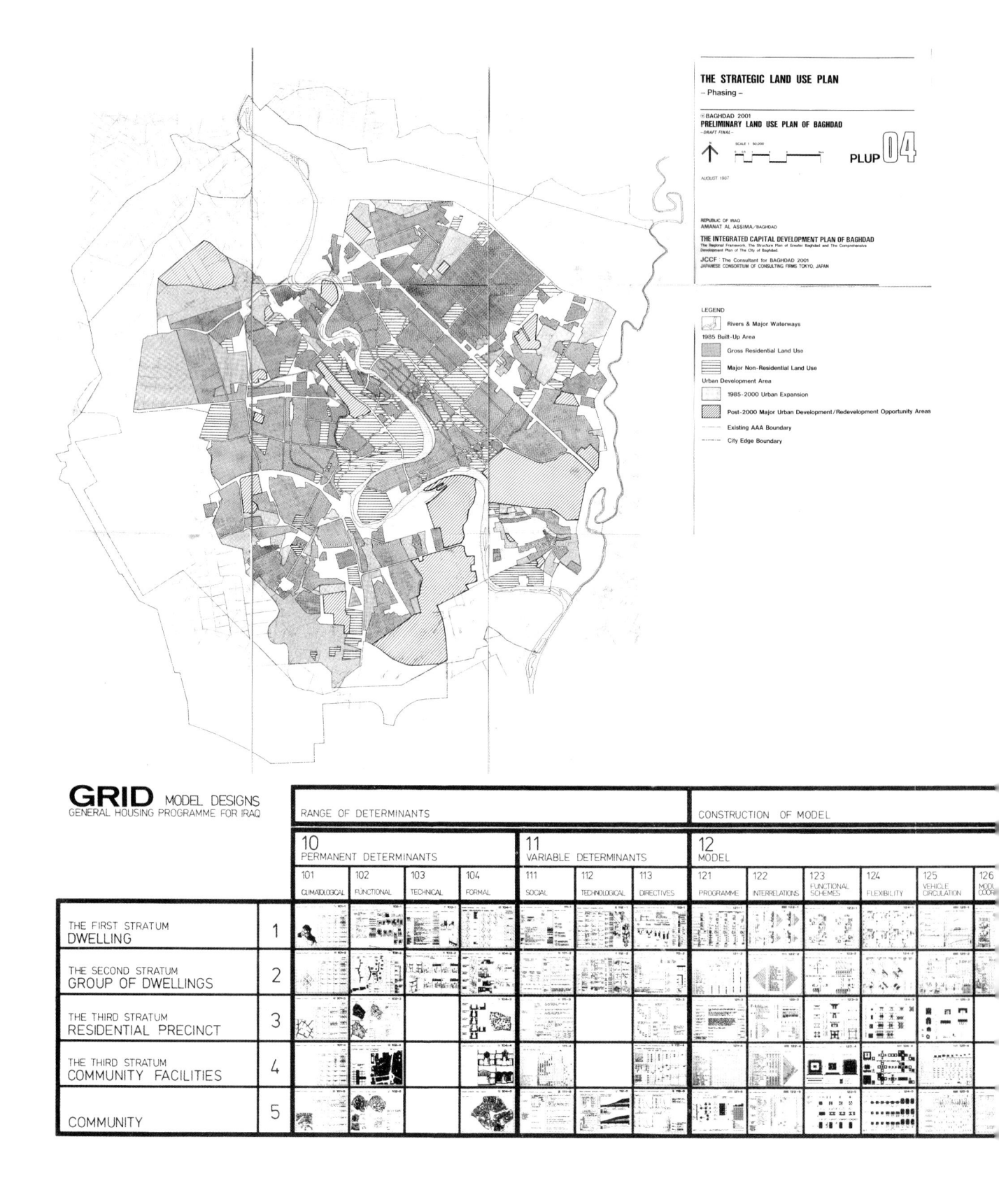

THE STRATEGIC LAND USE PLAN
— Phasing —

BAGHDAD 2001
PRELIMINARY LAND USE PLAN OF BAGHDAD
- DRAFT FINAL -

SCALE 1: 50,000

PLUP 04

AUGUST 1987

REPUBLIC OF IRAQ
AMANAT AL ASSIMA/BAGHDAD

THE INTEGRATED CAPITAL DEVELOPMENT PLAN OF BAGHDAD
The Regional Framework, The Structure Plan of Greater Baghdad and The Comprehensive Development Plan of The City of Baghdad.

JCCF The Consultant for BAGHDAD 2001
JAPANESE CONSORTIUM OF CONSULTING FIRMS TOKYO, JAPAN

LEGEND
- Rivers & Major Waterways
- 1985 Built-Up Area
- Gross Residential Land Use
- Major Non-Residential Land Use
- Urban Development Area
- 1985-2000 Urban Expansion
- Post-2000 Major Urban Development/Redevelopment Opportunity Areas
- Existing AAA Boundary
- City Edge Boundary

GRID MODEL DESIGNS
GENERAL HOUSING PROGRAMME FOR IRAQ

		RANGE OF DETERMINANTS							CONSTRUCTION OF MODEL					
		10 PERMANENT DETERMINANTS				**11** VARIABLE DETERMINANTS			**12** MODEL					
		101 CLIMATOLOGICAL	102 FUNCTIONAL	103 TECHNICAL	104 FORMAL	111 SOCIAL	112 TECHNOLOGICAL	113 DIRECTIVES	121 PROGRAMME	122 INTERRELATIONS	123 FUNCTIONAL SCHEMES	124 FLEXIBILITY	125 VEHICLE CIRCULATION	126 MODUL COORD
THE FIRST STRATUM DWELLING	1													
THE SECOND STRATUM GROUP OF DWELLINGS	2													
THE THIRD STRATUM RESIDENTIAL PRECINCT	3													
THE THIRD STRATUM COMMUNITY FACILITIES	4													
COMMUNITY	5													

< 4.19. Strategic Land Use Plan of Baghdad, late 1980s. Japanese Consortium of Consulting Firms (Japan). Japanese Consortium of Consulting Firms, "The Integrated Capital Development Plan of Baghdad," n.d.

4.20. "Grid. Model Designs." Miastoprojekt-Kraków (Poland). Miastoprojekt-Kraków, "General Housing Programme for Iraq. Report no. 3. Model Design," 1978.

specified in the original commission. The fact that the 1973 master plan offered variants of development made it malleable and correctable when new data was gathered. As Sayed Shafi recalled, the practice of reviewing several thousand cases of building applications against the background of the master plan provided training for the Amanat's planning staff and officials, and accustomed them to the master plan before its official acceptance.[141] In Shafi's view, the plan's "approach…and the overall climate it has created for initiating planning for other towns and cities of Iraq" were among Miastoprojekt's main achievements.[142] At the same time, the master plan set up a number of tasks for Iraqi architects in the years to come, in particular multistory housing and building in historical context, and changed the ways in which the city was conceived by architects.

Capillary Urbanization

When in 1987 Japanese urban planners surveyed Baghdad, its geography was very different from the one that the Polish planners had encountered when they started to work in the city (figure 4.19). Rather than an archipelago of urban islands, Baghdad's shape was largely consistent with that foreseen by Miastoprojekt's master plan: a continuous figure, with most of the land available for development located at the fringes of the fifteen-kilometer radius from the center.[143]

Miastoprojekt's planning approach was instrumental for this impact, and the implementation of the plan was facilitated by the continuous involvement of Polish architects and planners in Baghdad after the plan was delivered. This involvement consisted of subsequent collective contracts of Miastoprojekt in Iraq, including the biggest among them: the General Housing Programme for Iraq (GHPI, 1976–80) (figure 4.20). GHPI assessed housing stock and housing needs nationwide and suggested comprehensive housing policies and implementation strategies through the year 2000.[144] Like the master plan, GHPI involved hands-on research produced by a large team of fifty-nine employees of Miastoprojekt and fifty-three external experts from various universities in Poland, Iraq, and other countries, including the UK. Following Iraqi regulations that required foreign enterprises to collaborate with a local partner, Miastoprojekt worked on the GHPI with the Baghdadi office Dar al-Imarah, headed by Kahtan Madfai. The program was closely consulted with the commissioner, the State Organization for Housing (SOH), and was discussed with the authorities and professionals by means of seminars and exhibitions (figure 4.21).[145] The GHPI authors were explicit that the program was a "methodological instrument," rather than a set of operational plans. It was delivered by means of variants and models, and followed by the "Complementary Study of Housing Standards for Iraq" (1982), which was approved as binding for architectural practices in Iraq.¹⁴⁶

Along with collective contracts such as the Baghdad master plan and GHPI, the involvement of Polish professionals in Baghdad's urbanization also proceeded in a capillary way, wherein individual architects, planners, and engineers from Miastoprojekt and other Polish design institutes were employed by Iraqi administrative and planning institutions, universities, and private offices. These professionals were employed on the basis of Polservice's individual contracts. The Polish FTO claimed to have been the first to introduce such contracts among socialist countries, followed by Bulgaria and Czechoslovakia. An individual contract was signed by an expert for a limited period of time (usually for three to six years), after which they needed to spend a period of time in Poland (three years) before being allowed to leave again. Such contracts consisted of three separate but interdependent agreements. First, an employment contract with the foreign employer. Second, a contract with Polservice, according to which the expert paid a portion of salary received to the FTO in foreign currency (from 15 to 30 percent and sometimes more). In return, Polservice paid a fixed sum of Polish zlotys to the expert's bank account in Poland, organized and financed the trip (sometimes also the trip of the family), and covered the expert's health insurance, pension fund, and other social expenses in Poland. After signing the contract, the expert was granted an official passport and a customs status equal to that of employees of Polish diplomatic missions. Experts were also guaranteed unpaid leave from their Polish employer and the opportunity to return to the same or equal position after the end of the foreign contract. At times, the contract was complemented by specific instructions concerning the tasks to be performed, as well as general comportment. An employment contract with a Polish employer was necessary for an agreement with Polservice; hence it was considered the third component of the deal. Distinct from collective contracts, individual contracts required proficiency in a language used professionally in the receiving country, typically English or French.¹⁴⁷

4.21. Design of a rural settlement al-Zuhairi, 1980. Miastoprojekt-Kraków (Poland), Wojciech Obtułowicz (master plan), Wojciech Obtułowicz, Danuta Olęcka (housing design), in the framework of the General Housing Programme for Iraq.

4.22. Al-Qadisiyah neighborhood in Mahmudiyah. Miastoprojekt-Kraków (Poland), in the framework of the General Housing Programme for Iraq, 1976–80.

4.23. Hostels in al-Qadisiyah neighborhood, Mahmudiyah, 1978. Miastoprojekt-Kraków (Poland), Dar al-Imarah, in the framework of the General Housing Programme for Iraq.

Most individual contracts with Polish architects and planners were signed by state and municipal administrative and planning institutions in Baghdad, which were in charge of the implementation of the master plan. Among those professionals were transport engineers, who were hired by the Amanat to oversee the implementation of the plan's traffic system, including the introduction of the east-west and north-south thoroughfares and the modernization of roads and construction of bridges, including the al-Sinak Bridge.[148] This road-construction program, already initiated in the late 1960s in parallel to the work on the plan, was complemented by a system of flyovers and multistory parking facilities.[149] In line with the detailed outlines for particular districts, several public spaces were built, including the development of Tahrir Square, with a tunnel constructed in the early 1970s, and the leisure areas at the Abu Nuwas.[150] In the early 1970s, Zawra Park was created on former military grounds in Karkh, as well as the linear park along the Khir River. The first sections of the green belt were implemented, too, even if doubts were raised about its feasibility.[151]

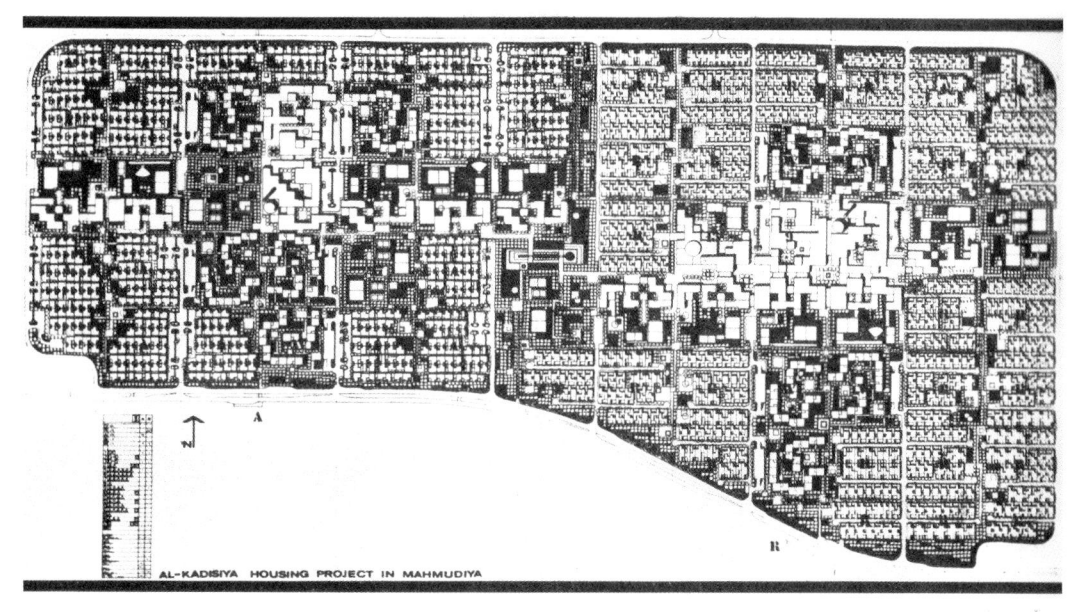

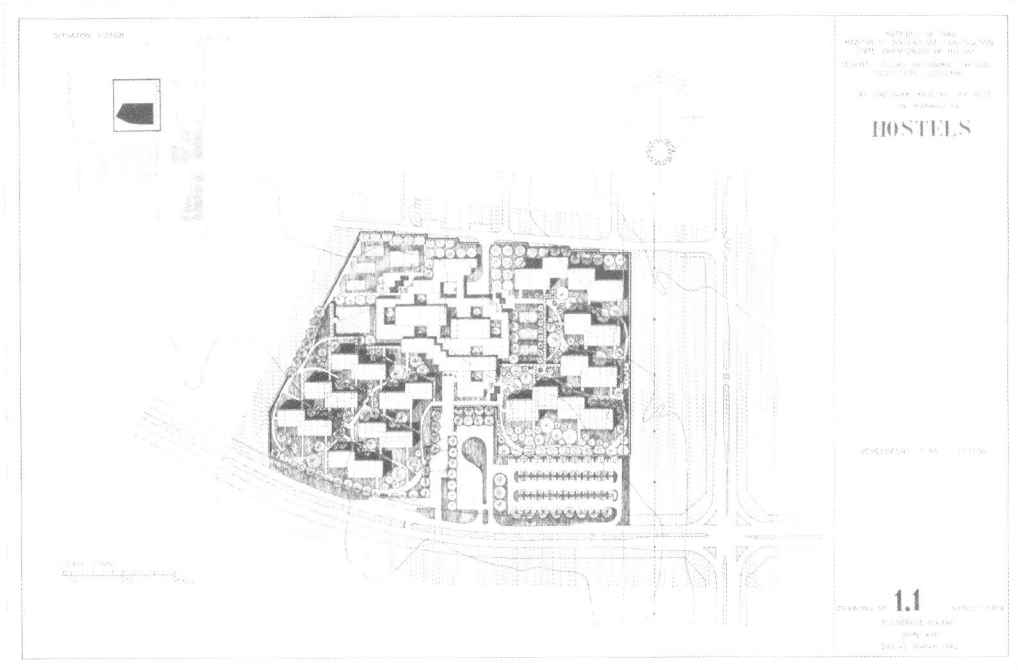

One of the most consequential decisions of the master plan was the allocation of housing areas and the specification of their standards. The authorities in Baghdad followed the master plan's decision to fill gaps between existing housing districts. The government continued to build single-family houses in Baghdad West, al-Thawra (its name was changed to Saddam City in 1979), and embarked on new worker-housing projects in East Baghdad and elsewhere.[152] Furthermore, the construction of the al-Qadisiyah neighborhood in Mahmudiyah started as one of six pilot neighborhoods of the GHPI in Iraq (figures 4.22 and 4.23).[153] Al-Qadisiyah was part of the linear urbanization south of Baghdad along the planned rapid-rail line, as foreseen by the master plan. It became a test site for type projects of social facilities designed by Danuta Mieszkowska and her team according to urban norms introduced by the master plan. These included a kindergarten, a primary school, two secondary schools, and a souk, designed with particular attention to the everyday practices of its users (figures 4.24 and 4.25). Those layouts were typified and constructed in other cities in Iraq, too.[154] The plan for a neighborhood of fifteen-thousand inhabitants in Mahmudiyah, realized only to a small extent, reflected the diversity of housing typologies proposed by GHPI, from row and atrium houses to multifamily estates, grouped around a dense sequence of squares and streets flanked by building volumes and vegetation.

The design of multistory housing in al-Qadisiyah followed the decision of the master plan to introduce such a housing typology on a large scale in Baghdad. Since the late 1960s, officials from various institutions embraced multistory housing as quicker to construct and more economical in terms of the cost of a single unit, services, and infrastructure.[155] While multistory buildings, including apartment buildings, had been constructed in Baghdad since the 1950s, their inclusion in the 1967 zoning plan as a specific category was a game changer for Iraqi architecture, and it staked out the field

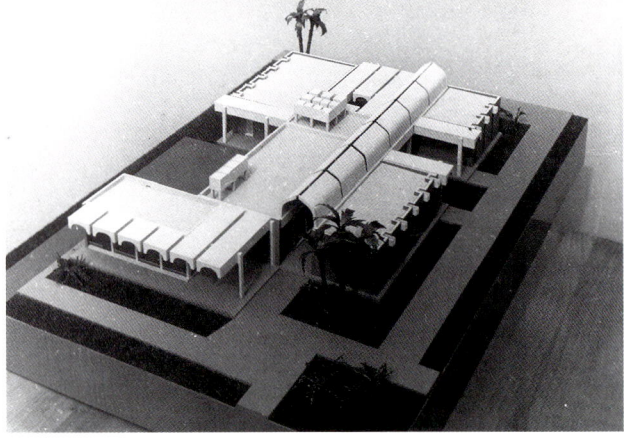

4.24. Elementary school for the al-Qadisiyah neighborhood, Mahmudiyah. Miastoprojekt-Kraków (Poland), Dar al-Imarah, Danuta Mieszkowska, in the framework of the General Housing Programme for Iraq, 1976–80.

4.25. Souk for the al-Qadisiyah neighborhood, Mahmudiyah. Miastoprojekt-Kraków (Poland), Dar al-Imarah, Danuta Mieszkowska, Zdzisław Gołąb, in the framework of the General Housing Programme for Iraq, 1976–80.

4.26. Housing for the al-Qadisiyah neighborhood, Mahmudiyah. Miastoprojekt-Kraków (Poland), Dar al-Imarah, Tadeusz Myszkowski, in the framework of the General Housing Programme for Iraq, 1976–80.

of debate and experimentation for Iraqi architects.[156] Some of these designs, including housing projects by Rifat Chadirji and Kahtan Madfai, were used by planners at the Amanat to defend the master plan, and to show that apartment buildings could suit Iraqi occupants.[157] Following the 1973 master plan, multistory buildings were built in differentiated typologies and for various social classes. These ranged from social housing projects up to five stories in the Zayona area in east Baghdad, the Saydeya area in south Baghdad, al-Dora in the south, and in al-Thawra, as well as luxurious vertical apartment buildings built in Rusafa and Karkh.[158]

The construction of the first multistory housing was an opportunity to address the widespread argument that such buildings were incompatible with Iraqi climate and Islamic culture.[159] Local and foreign experts in Baghdad debated the advantages and drawbacks of apartment buildings, and weighed them against each other.[160] The architect Salam Sim'an admitted that such buildings clashed with the desire for a private garden and the custom of sleeping on the roof during summer, but argued that those disadvantages were offset by the availability of services and more intense social contacts with neighbors.[161] An attempt to combine the best of both worlds was the design of three-story housing for a neighborhood in Mahmudiyah, by Miastoprojekt's Tadeusz Myszkowski. Each of the apartments was designed to be experienced as a detached house. The staircase leading to apartments on the second and third floors was separated from the building, and the night part of each apartment was furnished with a private terrace located on a higher floor, linked by an internal staircase. This layout was supposed to convey the experience of a private roof, and gave the volumes a recognizable silhouette (figure 4.26).[162]

In continuation of the master plan, GHPI argued that the construction of multifamily housing needed to be supported by the creation of a domestic industry of construction materials.[163] Accordingly, the State Organization for Housing (SOH, created in 1974), contracted the construction of four factories for prefabricated housing elements based on the French Camus-Setap system (in Baghdad, housing districts of two to three stories were constructed with this system). SOH was also experimenting with small-scale prefabrication systems, one of them delivered by Miastoprojekt.[164] The organization hired several Polish architects to oversee implementation of the prefabrication systems, including Włodzimierz Gleń (employed between 1979 and 1981). His task at SOH was to review housing designs that had been submitted to SOH by external parties, and to revise them in cooperation with contractors specializing in prefabricated systems from France, the UK, West Germany, South Korea, and Spain. This included the

4.27. "Permanent Determinants—Formal—Group of Dwellings." Miastoprojekt-Kraków (Poland). Miastoprojekt-Kraków, "General Housing Programme for Iraq. Report no. 3. Model Design," 1978, plate 104-2.

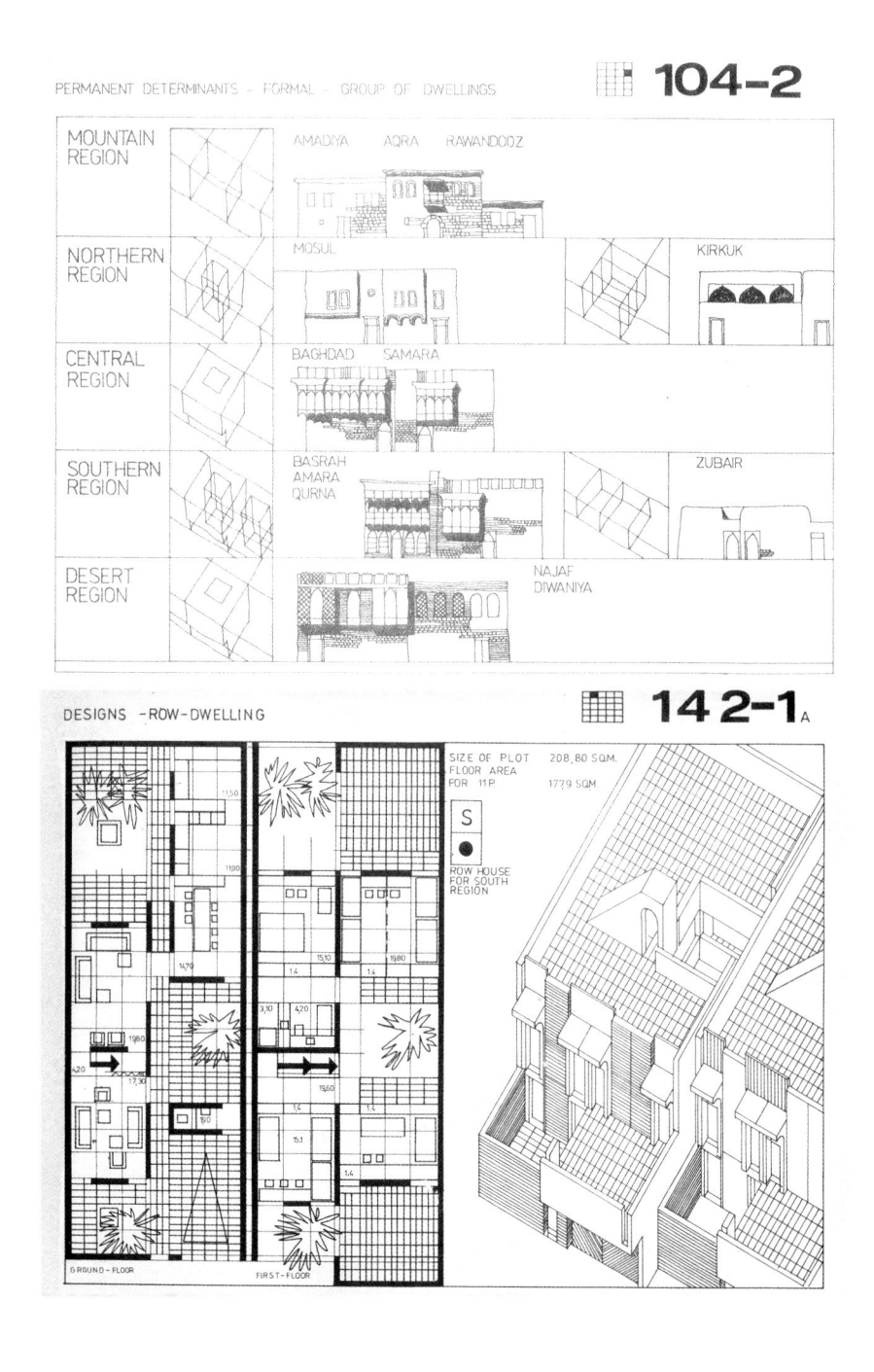

4.28. "Designs—Row-Dwellings." Miastoprojekt-Kraków (Poland). Miastoprojekt-Kraków, "General Housing Programme for Iraq. Report no. 3. Model Design," 1978, plate 143-1A.

4.29. Office building on Jumhuriyah Street, Baghdad, early 1960s. Kahtan Awni, Aleksander Markiewicz, Jerzy Staniszkis.

design of neighborhoods for military officers in northern Iraq, constructed with the large-scale prefabrication system delivered by France's Dumez (with K. Hassan, 1980). As a member of various teams, Gleń was also responsible for designing housing districts in several Iraqi cities, along with delivering standards for urban and rural housing at SOH.[165]

The task of designing multifamily housing became an opportunity for Iraqi architects to negotiate traditional customs with imported technologies, lifestyles, and forms.[166] While such negotiation had been part of architecture in Iraq for a long time, its antagonisms appeared sharper in the 1970s. The rapid urbanization of Baghdad was paralleled by a rising interest in the city's history, with discussions in the Iraqi press on historic souks and caravanserais (such as the Khan Murjan, restored by 1977), educational institutions (such as the Abbasid Mustansiriyah madrasah), coffeehouses, traditional transportation, and daily life more generally.[167] Several traditional Baghdadi houses were restored and studied as possible precedents for architectural and urban designs.[168] For example, GHPI architects built on Miastoprojekt's Kadhemiya study, and documented the interplay between a monument and urban texture in the historical fabric; they also took cues from historic façades and street profiles differentiated by regions (figure 4.27).[169] This research was translated into Miastoprojekt's proposals for regionally specific housing typologies and urban morphologies for selected Iraqi cities (figure 4.28).[170] The plan's requirement of protecting and conserving historical buildings in their "shape, scale, urban pattern, skyline and architectural forms, both in general, and in detail" pointed to design strategies of fine-tuning modern architecture to the Baghdadi context: an ambition shared by leading Iraqi architects of the 1960s and 1970s, including Kahtan Awni, Kahtan Madfai, Mohamed Makiya, Rifat Chadirji, and Hisham Munir.[171]

These protagonists of Iraqi architecture, at various points in their careers, were either employed by governmental or municipal authorities or commissioned by them. In this capacity, they often met architects from socialist countries, which resulted in multiple collaborations, whether sanctioned by FTOs or not. The work of the office of Berkeley-trained architect Kahtan Awni is a case in point. One of Awni's large projects in Baghdad from the early 1960s was an eight-story office building for the Department of Awqaf, on Jumhuriya Street (1963), which resulted from a winning competition proposal submitted by Awni with Polish architects Aleksander Markiewicz and Jerzy Staniszkis, both employed at that time by the Ministry of Works and Housing (figure 4.29).[172] While only a few projects of Awni and Markiewicz departed from the idiom of international modernism, since the late 1960s, Awni argued for a "local" Baghdadi architecture that would learn from both Islamic-Arabic culture and the Western experience of cultural modernization.[173] Some of Awni's best-received projects were perceived along these lines, including the campus of Mustansiriyah University in Baghdad, an institution founded in 1963 and named after the thirteenth-century madrasah in Rusafa. The ensemble, consisting of several meandering volumes, was praised by an Iraqi newspaper for its "Islamic design" and as one of the city's modern landmarks. Rifat Chadirji listed it among Baghdadi buildings that successfully "combined the past and the present" (figures 4.30 and 4.31).[174]

Polish architect Lech Robaczyński had a key influence on the design of this ensemble, from its urban layout to the details. Robaczyński worked

4.30. Mustansiriyah University, Baghdad, Assembly Hall, ca. 1968. Kahtan Awni, Lech Robaczyński.

4.31. Mustansiriyah University, Baghdad, ca. 1968, plan.

> 4.32. Mustansiriyah University, Baghdad, ca. 1968, façade under construction. Kahtan Awni, Lech Robaczyński.

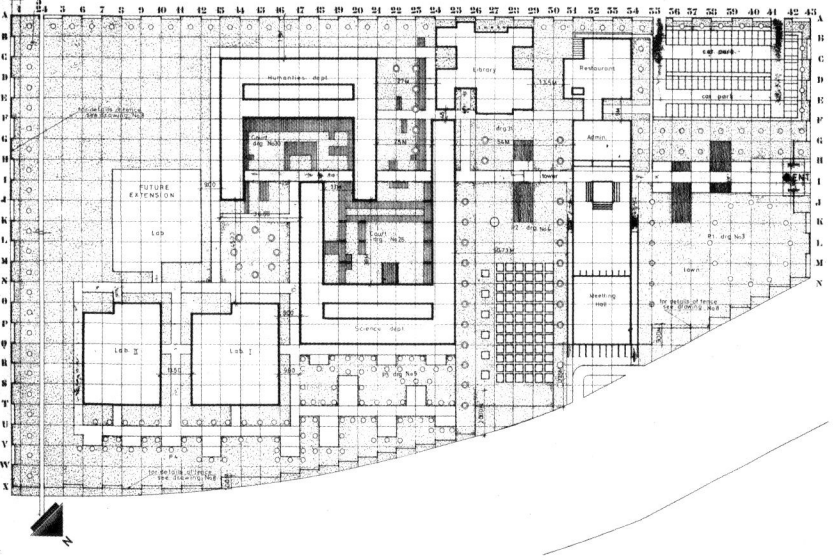

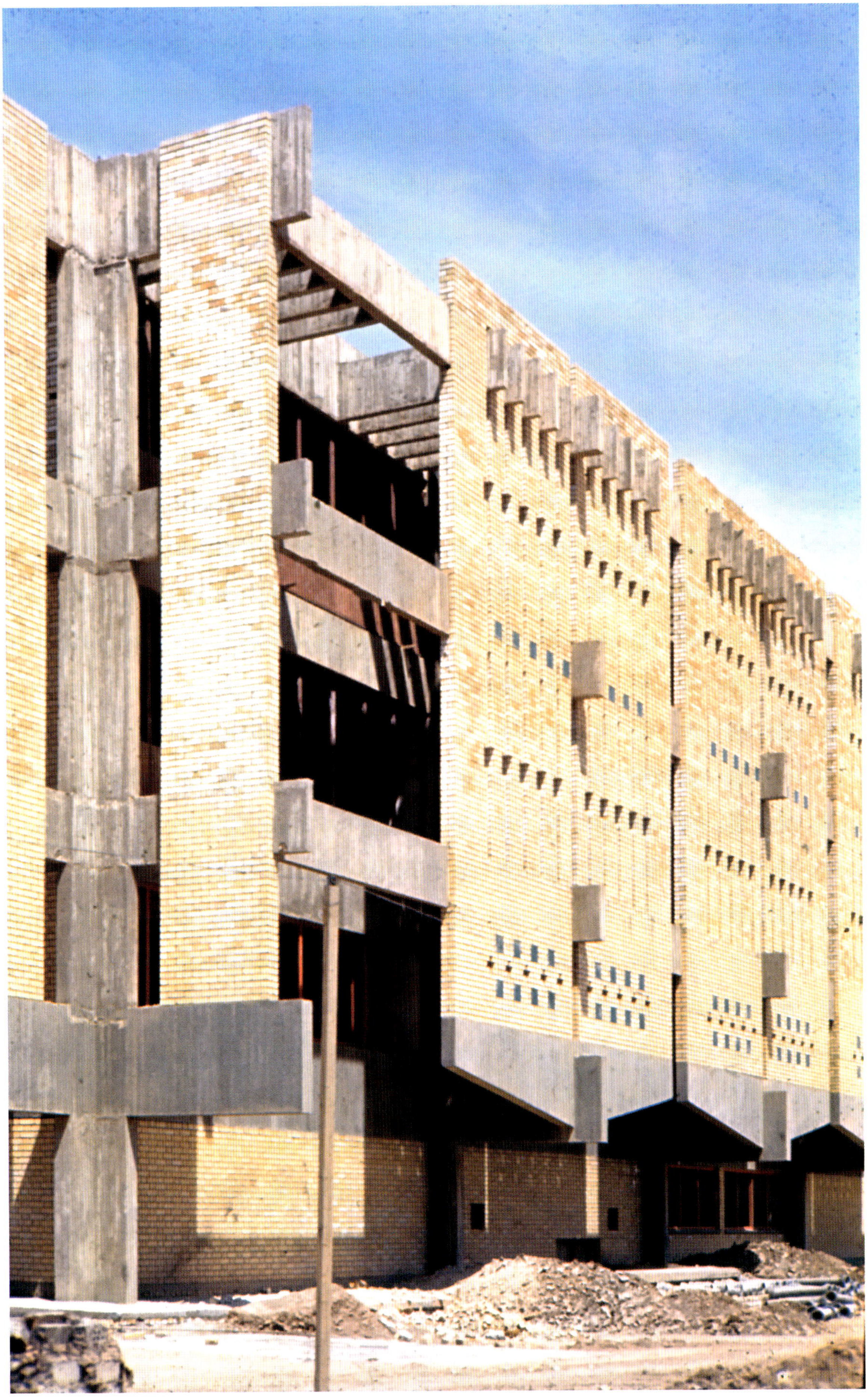

in Awni's office between 1962 and 1969, in parallel with his employment at the Ministry of Works and Housing. His designs for the ministry included hospitals in Kufah and Mosul; type designs of secondary schools for central, northern, and southern Iraq; and court buildings and offices in various Iraqi cities, among them the Central Income Tax Office Building in Baghdad.[175] Those experiences were reflected in Robaczyński's detailing of Mustansiriyah University, including brick screens consulted with craftsmen with whom he had worked on earlier governmental projects—yet another instance of the embedded character of architectural work on Polservice contracts (figure 4.32). The collaboration between Robaczyński and Awni also resulted in other major buildings in Baghdad, among them the Girl Students' Hostel of the University of Baghdad, the National Electricity Board Building, and the Trade Administration Building (figure 4.33). These were complemented by designs for state and private clients in Baghdad and elsewhere in Iraq, and also in Kuwait, India, and the UK.[176] Some of these buildings were designed in collaboration with Jerzy Baumiller, who returned to Baghdad in the late 1960s, after his earlier appointment as chief architect at the Ministry of Municipalities.[177]

4.33. National Electricity Board Building, Baghdad, 1960s. Kahtan Awni, Lech Robaczyński.

4.34. Vaclav Bašta, lecture notes, history of architecture course at the Department of Architecture, College of Engineering, University of Baghdad, 1960s.

Baumiller, along with working with Awni, was teaching at the Department of Architecture at the University of Baghdad—another key venue where professionals from socialist countries contributed to the urbanization of Baghdad, in that context as educators of future Iraqi architects.[178] The foundation of the department in 1959 by Mohamed Makiya, Hisham Munir, and Abdullah Ihsan Kamil opened a new chapter for the architectural profession in Iraq, where until then all architects had to be educated abroad.[179] Fuad Uthman, architect and educator at the department in the 1960s, recalled it as a vibrant venue, with the faculty consisting of Iraqi architects educated in the United States and the UK, American guest professors, and Eastern Europeans.[180] Besides ten Poles, the latter group included the Czech architects Vaclav Bašta, who taught drawing and descriptive geometry (1962–71), and his wife, Miroslava Baštova, who taught history of architecture, including a course on Islamic architecture (1969–71) (figure 4.34).[181] The Baštas were joined by others, including Jan Čejka from Prague, who was teaching design and history of architecture (1964–70). These architects worked in Baghdad on contracts with Polytechna, the Czechoslovak FTO offering individual contracts similar to those of Polservice.[182]

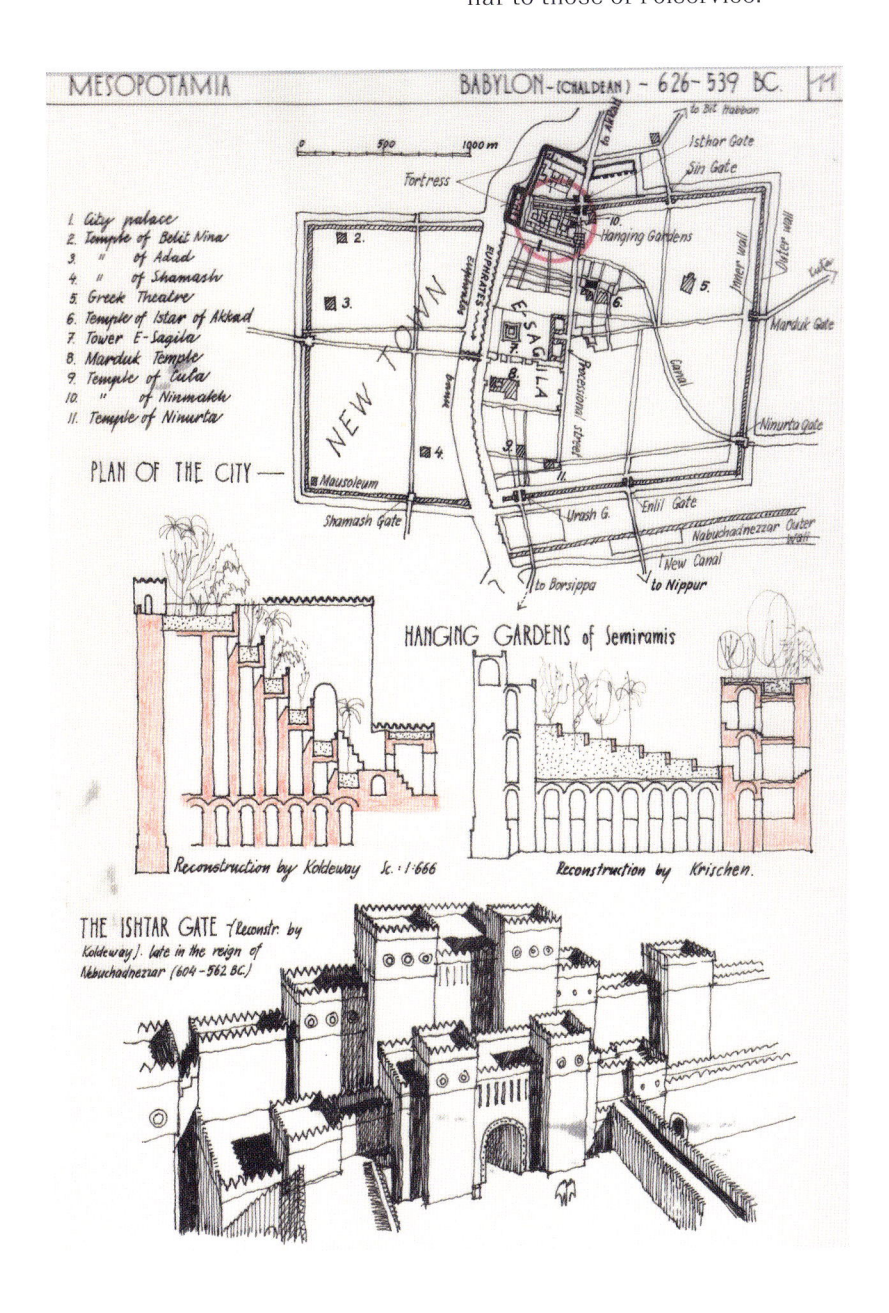

THE WORLD SOCIALIST SYSTEM

Under the deanship of Makiya (1959–68), the Department of Architecture aimed at furnishing a new generation of Iraqi architects with the breadth of skills required by tasks at hand. Accordingly, the curriculum included courses in community and regional planning, architectural design, and interior design, supported by extensive training in architectural history, building technology, and architectural representation. The variety of references and ambitions is conveyed by a booklet produced by Bašta, which shows the work of the first cohort of students (1966). The booklet combined Corbusian slabs with a diagram of Mansour's ancient round plan of Baghdad, juxtaposed row houses in the Miesian manner with survey drawings of ornate Baghdadi houses, and set exercises in Bauhaus aesthetics side by side with arabesque patterns (figure 4.35).[183]

The experience of working on the master plan reverberated in debates in the design studios, which revolved around questions of social-spatial justice, including the persistence of traditional land ownership, rural-urban migration, and housing shortage. As with Mohamed Makiya and Lorna Salim, who were encouraging their students to study old buildings by the Tigris, traditional alleys, and historic monuments, the Baštas, Čejka, and the Polish architects insisted on learning from the past, whether from housing typologies, such as the courtyard house, or from structures inspired by Bedouin tents and Madan reed houses.[184] Recalling these exercises, Polish architect and educator Lech Kłosiewicz emphasized that he insisted on teaching architecture beyond a singular building. He related this approach to an emerging planning culture, exemplified by the master plan, that put pace to the privileging of "individual interest over social interests."[185] More generally, the master plan contributed to the shift in

4.35. Vaclav Bašta, booklet presenting the curriculum of the Department of Architecture, College of Engineering, University of Baghdad, 1966.

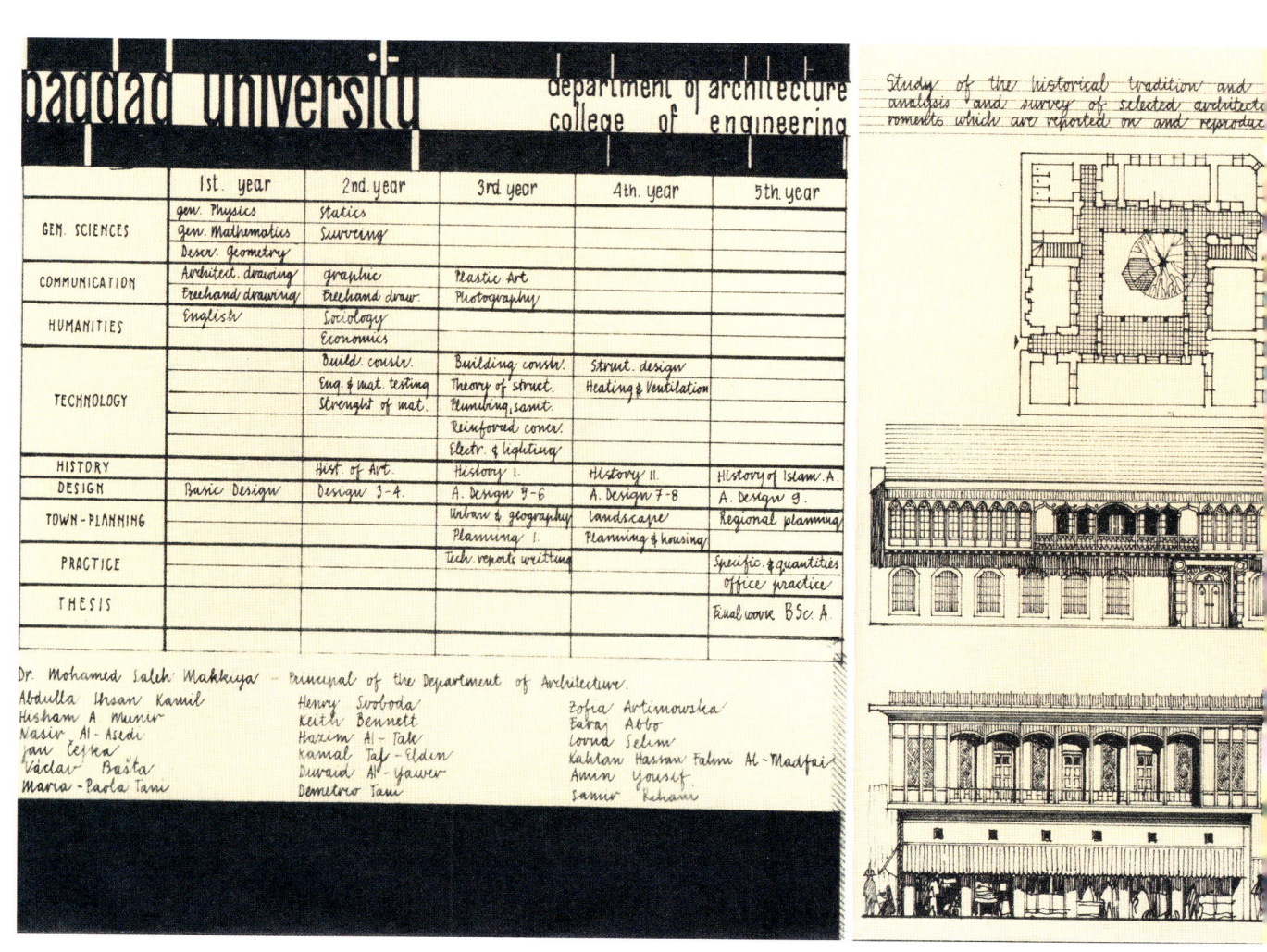

architects' way of thinking about Baghdad. For example, in 1972, Kahtan Madfai argued that a "contemporary city" depended less on a "building style," and more on what was in the center of the master plan: transport, economic factors, distribution of public spaces, and availability of industrialized technologies of construction.[186]

These discussions continued in private architectural offices, where lecturers hired graduates of the department, and sometimes invited their Eastern European colleagues to collaborate. This included Bašta's collaboration with Fuad Uthman and Jan Čejka on the Ministry of Foreign Affairs design (for Makiya, Munir, Madhloom Associates, 1966).[187] In turn, Čejka worked on a competition design for the Shorja area in Rusafa (with Rifat Chadirji and Uthman, 1969).[188] Those projects confirm that the master plan became the framework for architectural competitions in Baghdad. For instance, the latter competition entry followed Miastoprojekt's detailed plan for Rusafa by integrating mosques, churches, and clusters of historic buildings into one megastructure combined with parking lots and with the monorail foreseen by the 1967 master plan (figures 4.36 and 4.37).

This overview shows that individual contracts of socialist FTOs facilitated the absorption of the master plan across various registers, from design work to administration, education, and research. By the late 1970s, however, architects traveling to Baghdad on such contracts became aware that some of Miastoprojekt's designs were no longer up to par with international design culture, nor with the changing climate of opinion in Baghdad. This change was reflected in the discourse of the Amanat. If the arrival of the first planners from socialist countries to Baghdad coincided with

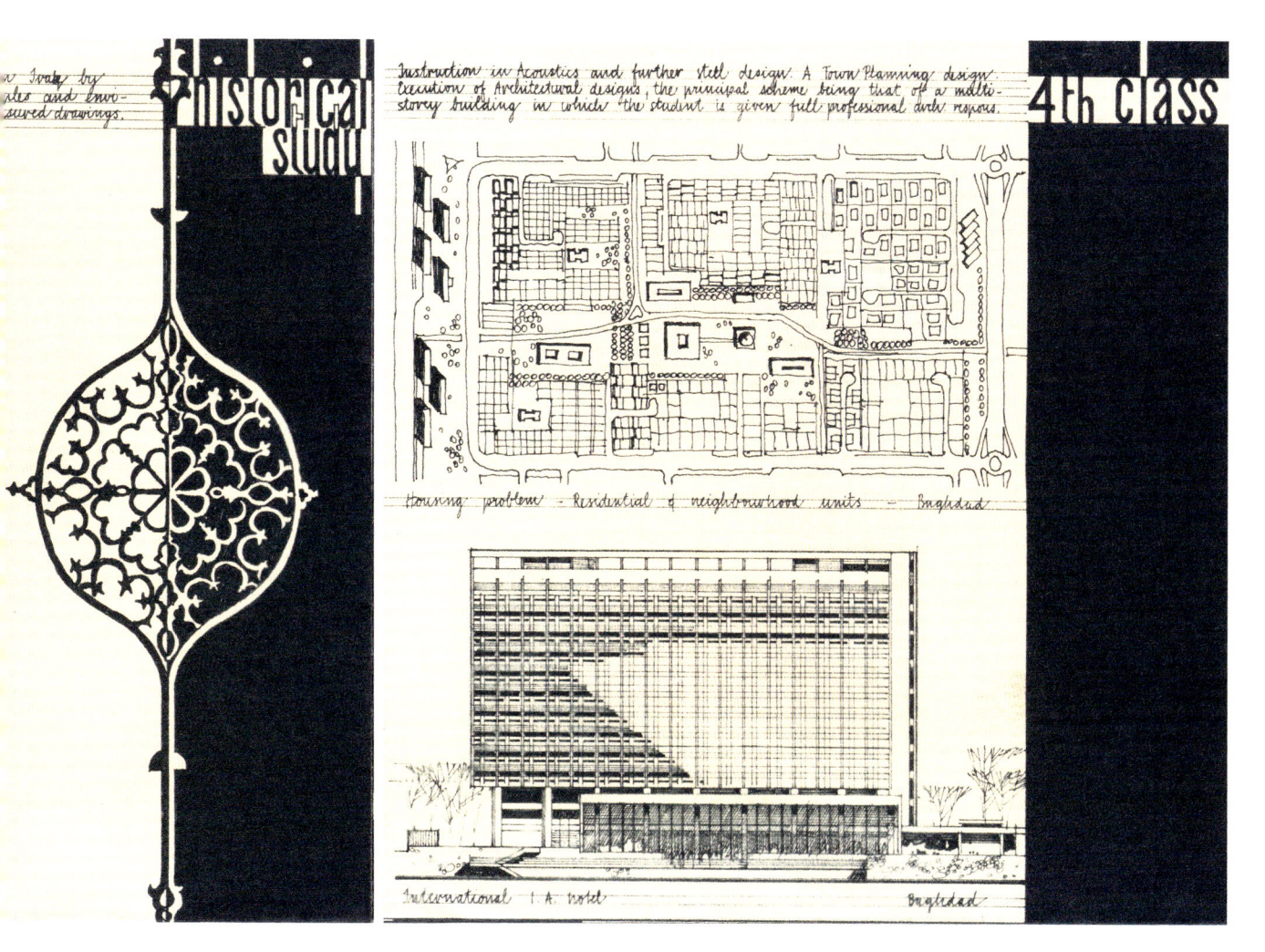

THE WORLD SOCIALIST SYSTEM

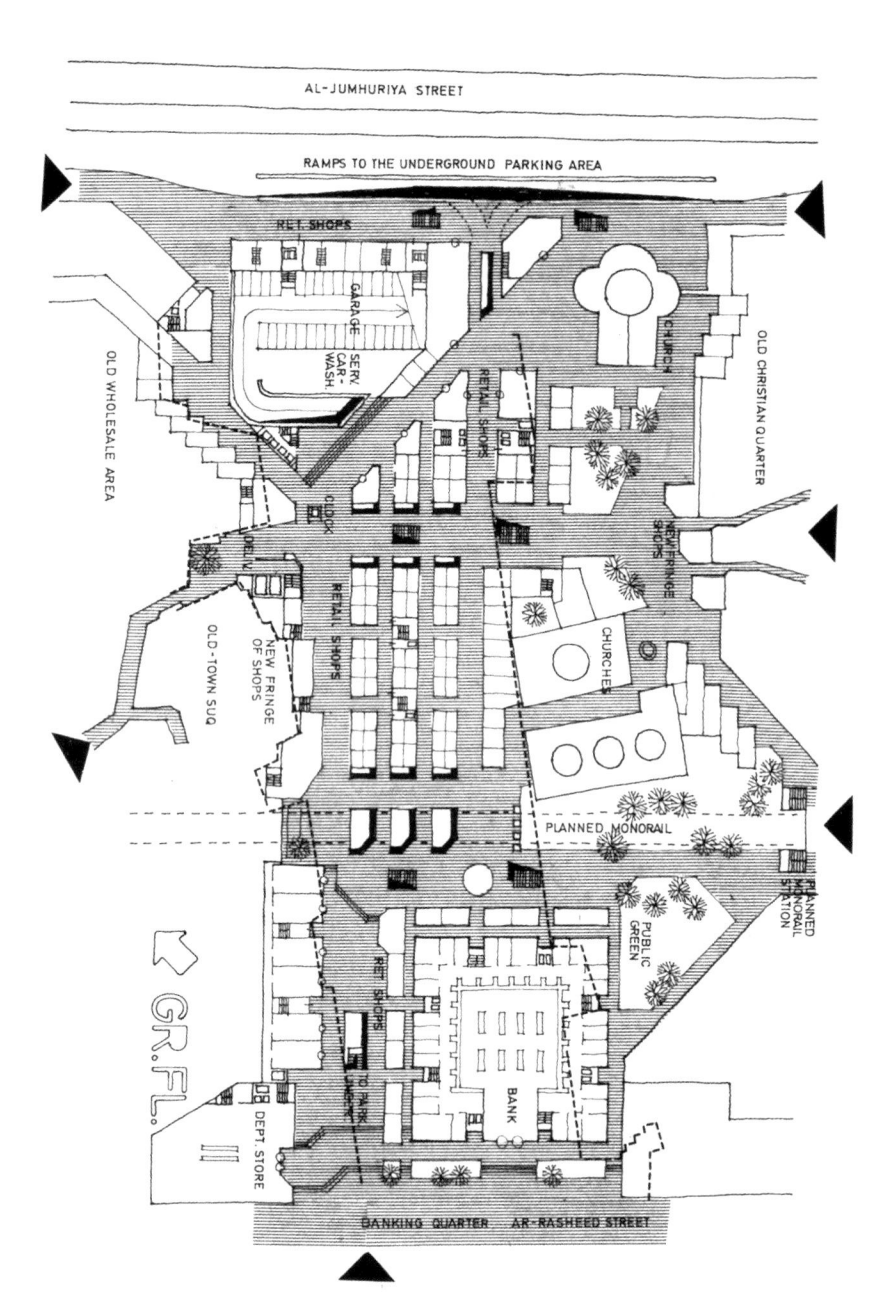

4.36. Shorja area competition, 1969, plan. Jan Čejka, Rifat Chadirji, Fuad Uthman.

4.37. Shorja area competition, 1968, model. Jan Čejka, Rifat Chadirji, Fuad Uthman.

4.38. Baghdad International Airport, façade design by Vaclav Bašta, design 1980.

Amanat's ambition to transform the city into a modern metropolis, twenty years later Amanat's work was described as developing the capital "in a manner to be on the same level of its golden ages."[189]

The point of reference was nothing less than "Baghdad's Abbasid glory," and the ambition was to link "the golden era of Baghdad in the Abbasid period with the equally bright contemporary era of President Saddam Hussein."[190] Accordingly, historical references were included to the National Theater, new housing projects, and the new international airport with an arched façade designed by Bašta in 1980 (figure 4.38).[191] Allusions to Islamic architecture were mixed with those to Iraq's Mesopotamian heritage, as was the case with the Babylon Hotel, an iteration of a design by the Yugoslav (Slovenian) architect Edvard Ravnikar.[192] Historical references also populated designs by Iraqi and Western architects who had been invited by Rifat Chadirji, in his new position as councilor to the Amanat, to design buildings in four urban-development sites: on Khulafa Street (master-planned by TAC), in Bab al-Sheikh, in Abu Nuwas (master-planned by Arthur Erickson), and on Haifa Street in Karkh.[193] Several of those architects, including protagonists of postmodernism such as Ricardo Bofill, Denise Scott Brown, and Robert Venturi, participated in the international competition for the State Mosque, envisaged as extending the new monumental landscape of Baghdad with the Unknown Soldier Monument (Khalid al-Rahal, Marcello D'Olivo, 1982) and the Martyrs' Monument (Ismail Fattah al-Turk and others, 1983).[194] For architects from socialist countries, that competition and others in 1980s Iraq offered opportunities to experiment with postmodern forms.[195]

What was common for this rethinking of Baghdad was a shift away from Miastoprojekt's modernist tradition.[196] While Arthur Erickson's master plan of Abu Nuwas broadly followed Miastoprojekt's decisions concerning land use and circulation, the break with the 1973 master plan was most evident in historical areas, where the plan's proposals had been under fire from Iraqi scholars since the 1970s.[197] Accordingly, decisions in the master plan for developing a central business district in the Haifa Street area were explicitly rejected for the sake of redeveloping that area in continuation of its historical fabric. In turn, architects deplored Rusafa's dissection into isolated fragments by the road network, and suggested restoring pedestrian routes between those fragments.[198] In this climate, Miastoprojekt was not invited by Chadirji to contribute to the new vision of Baghdad.[199]

COLLABORATION IN THE WORLD SOCIALIST SYSTEM: ROMANIA AND EAST GERMANY

Among the impulses for the reconstruction of Baghdad in the early 1980s were preparations for the seventh Summit of the Non-Aligned Movement, scheduled in Baghdad for 1982 (in the end, the summit was moved to New Delhi because of Iraq's war with Iran). Iraq's rapprochement with NAM resulted in a friendly atmosphere toward Yugoslav companies. Among these was Energoprojekt, which was put in charge of eight eleven-story multifunctional buildings on Khulafa Street, built as part of the reconstruction of Rusafa, overseen by Chadirji (1983).[200] Energoprojekt won the tender (1980) for the construction of this ensemble according to the design of Iraqi architects, but after the approval of a new master plan of the area (TAC, 1981), the Yugoslavs were requested to deliver a new design (figure 4.39). It was drawn by Zoran Bojović and then built by Energoprojekt in collaboration with a number of Western European companies (1981–84) (figures 4.40 and 4.41).[201]

If such extension of the commission from construction to design was unusual, the combination of both was not. By the time of the Khulafa Street commission, Energoprojekt had acquired significant experience in such design-and-build commissions, and so had other Yugoslav companies in Baghdad. Those included the Belgrade-based contractor Rad, which constructed the headquarters of the Baath Party (Radmila Vučković, 1979), and the Skopje-based company Beton, in charge of the Ministry of Oil building (Nako Manov, from 1980) (figure 4.42).[202]

Over the course of the 1970s, the design-and-build procedure became the most important vessel for mobilizing architectural labor from socialist countries abroad.[203] Already the Qasim administration had applied this procedure for the acquisition of fully equipped and operational ("turn key") industrial plants as part of the industrialization program pursued by the Iraqi government.[204] Socialist countries seemed perfectly placed to carry out such tasks because of their centralized economies that allowed them to coordinate large-scale projects. In the following decades, this procedure was extended from industrial facilities to other programs.

Yet if the design-and-build procedure was privileged both by state companies from Eastern Europe and by Iraqi commissioners, it was also because it allowed them to take advantage of the political economy of the world socialist system. This will be clear in the following reading of a rather unspectacular ensemble: an industrial slaughterhouse designed and constructed by East German and Romanian companies in the southern suburbs of Baghdad, an area envisaged by the master plan for industrial

4.39. Al-Khulafa Street Development Project, 1981. Amanat al-Assima, The Architects Collaborative (US).

> 4.40. Al-Khulafa Street Development Project no. 2, 1981–84. Energoprojekt (Socialist Republic of Serbia, Yugoslavia), Zoran Bojović.

> 4.41. Al-Khulafa Street Development Project no. 2, 1981–84, structural system. Energoprojekt (Socialist Republic of Serbia, Yugoslavia), Zoran Bojović.

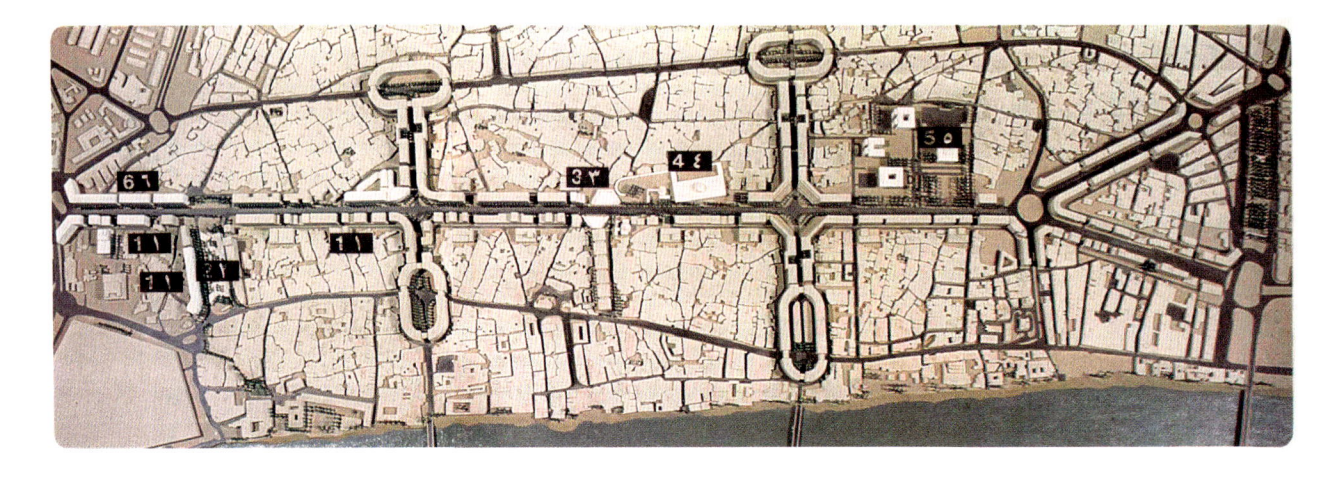

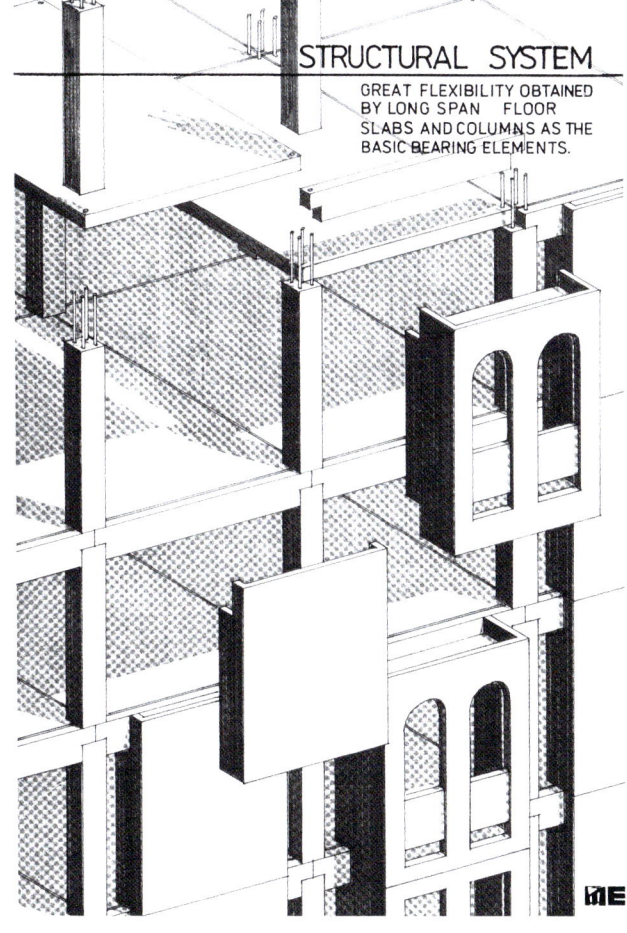

STRUCTURAL SYSTEM

GREAT FLEXIBILITY OBTAINED BY LONG SPAN FLOOR SLABS AND COLUMNS AS THE BASIC BEARING ELEMENTS.

THE WORLD SOCIALIST SYSTEM

development (1976–81) (figure 4.43).²⁰⁵ On the construction site in Baghdad and in the drafting rooms in East Berlin and Bucharest, architects, engineers, and managers practiced the world socialist system by negotiating the division of labor between the companies involved and by adapting to the principle of barter, which was employed in most construction export from socialist countries. Much of this negotiation and adaptation was mediated by specific design tools and procedures from Eastern European architectural practice.

The slaughterhouse project brought together two countries that were at opposite ends of the economic spectrum in socialist Europe: East Germany (German Democratic Republic, or GDR) and Romania. While East Germany's aspirations to an economic *Weltniveau* (world class) were warranted for only very few branches of its industry, it belonged to the most advanced industrial countries of the Eastern bloc. In contrast, Romania was among the least developed. At the same time, both countries, until the end of the Cold War, insisted on their special relationship with the developing world. In the 1970s and 1980s, when most socialist states were cutting their aid programs, East Germany continued to support socialist regimes abroad, in particular in Africa.²⁰⁶ In the 1980s, it emerged as the biggest donor

4.42. Ministry of Oil Building, Baghdad, early 1980s. Beton (Socialist Republic of Macedonia, Yugoslavia), Nako Manov (project architect), and others.

4.43. Modern slaughterhouse Baghdad, 1974–81, model. Ipro Dessau (GDR). "VEB Industrieprojektierung Dessau: Betriebschronik," vol. 2, n.d.

among socialist countries—for example, it funded development projects in Tanzania in continuity with housing projects gifted in the mid-1960s by the GDR to Zanzibar, shortly after that island's independence.[207] In contrast, Romania sought to forge its relationship with African and Asian countries by proclaiming itself a "socialist developing country."[208] Nicolae Ceaușescu, Romania's head of state from 1965 to 1989, imagined himself to be a leader of the developing world, and recruited Romanian construction and design firms in this diplomatic offensive. Along with a long series of housing facilities and infrastructure in Africa and Asia, these firms constructed a few high-profile buildings, such as the Parliament of Khartoum in Sudan (Cezar Lăzărescu and the Design Institute Carpați, 1972–78).[209] Different from the close allegiance of East German leadership to the Soviet Union, Romanian suspicion of Soviet hegemony resonated with a number of developing countries who were wary of Soviet influence.[210] Along these lines, Romania became a strong supporter of the New International Economic Order (NIEO), with its insistence on sovereignty, noninterference, mutual advantage, and self-control of each country's own resources.[211]

During the 1970s, foreign debt skyrocketed in both East Germany and Romania, and their need for convertible currencies became increasingly difficult to satisfy by means of export to the West, due to the diminishing competitiveness of their industrial production and the rising cost of fossil fuels. The latter was further exacerbated when the Soviet Union reduced its oil and gas deliveries and raised their prices. In this context, trade with Iraq grew in importance. As other socialist countries had, both East Germany and Romania had initiated exchanges with Iraq a few months after Qasim's coup, but those exchanges took off less vigorously than with other countries in the bloc. In the case of East Germany, Iraq's aversion stemmed from the Hallstein Doctrine of West Germany (1955), which announced that the recognition of East Germany by third states would be considered a hostile act and would result in diplomatic and economic sanctions. Only when Iraq broke off contacts with West Germany after its recognition of Israel (1965) were East German-Iraqi relationships upgraded and expanded.[212] Trade played an increasingly important role in these contacts, in particular from the 1970s, when East Germany became gradually recognized internationally (including the treaty of 1972 with its western neighbor).[213] While Romania had already established diplomatic relations with Iraq in 1958, its refusal to sever contacts with Israel, as the Soviet Union demanded of its satellites in the wake of the Six-Day War (1967), was an impediment to the intensification of economic relationships with Arab countries until the mid-1970s.

Following the practice of foreign trade among Comecon countries, the outlines of Iraqi trade contracts with East Germany and Romania were decided within joint-intergovernmental committees.[214] These committees identified potential areas of bilateral trade and issued trade protocols, according to which Iraqi enterprises and governmental agencies signed agreements with FTOs from the GDR and Romania. The majority of them were barter agreements, by which Iraqi crude oil was exchanged for East German or Romanian goods and services. The value of these transactions was denominated in US dollars or in Iraqi dinars and was cleared on a periodic basis.

With crude oil as Iraq's dominant export product, the main task of the joint committees was to identify goods and services that Iraq could import. Industrial plants featured prominently in the export offers of both East Germany and Romania, in particular those for construction materials and the oil industry. In the case of the GDR, their offer was extended to design and construction services in many areas, including housing, transport, infrastructure, and agriculture. As a result, by the 1970s East Germany was Iraq's second biggest economic partner among socialist countries, after the USSR and before Czechoslovakia.[215] The war with Iran opened new possibilities for military exports from the GDR, which the country took advantage of, despite its declared neutrality.²¹⁶ In turn, Romanian exports to Iraq included cement plants, land-reclamation and irrigation projects, electricity networks for Baghdad and other cities, roads, housing projects throughout the country, and other construction commissions, among them the Baghdad abattoir.²¹⁷

Tools of Collaboration

The tender for the Baghdad slaughterhouse was prepared by the West German engineering firm Fritz Thier and announced by the Iraqi Ministry of Agriculture and Agrarian Reform in April 1974.²¹⁸ The construction of this facility, which was complemented by four other modern slaughterhouses in Iraq, was part of the modernization of the country's agriculture. The decision of the East German authorities to participate in the tender stemmed from the ambition of the government in East Berlin to expand the export of industrial plants. The government also intended to intensify economic and technical ties with Iraq, in anticipation of the first session of the GDR–Iraqi joint committee and the forthcoming visit of Saddam Hussein, deputy chairman of the Baath Party and deputy head of Iraq's Revolutionary Command Council (May 1975). In response to the tender announcement, the FTO Transportmaschinen sent an offer on behalf of the company Ascobloc, a producer of food and meat processing machinery, which answered to the Ministry of General and Agricultural Machinery and Vehicles. The East German offer was the second most expensive in comparison to four others sent to Baghdad. After the intervention of the Iraqi government, this offer was modified, and the requested price was reduced. This modified bid was accepted by the Iraqis in September 1975, and the contract was signed after it was given a green light by the chairman of the Council of Ministers of the GDR, Horst Sindermann.²¹⁹ Soon afterward, Transportmaschinen appointed Arcom, a Romanian contractor with an FTO license, as the subcontractor for construction. Arcom replaced an Iraqi contractor with which Transportmaschinen had entered the bid but that withdrew in the course of the negotiations. Besides Arcom, at the time of signing the contract with the Iraqi authorities, Ascobloc planned to collaborate with around 30 specialized companies from the GDR (figure 4.44).

The organization of the collaboration between these numerous enterprises was based on East German procedures. Foreign trade regulations in the GDR foresaw a tripartite functional framework for construction export. This framework included, first, an FTO, and second, the FTO's contractual partner, called the "general supplier," who, third, appointed the "general contractor."²²⁰ The general contractor, in turn, appointed the subcontractors. After several months of negotiation and multiple reviews of East German controlling bodies, the function of the general supplier on the Baghdad abattoir project was given to the East Berlin–based state enterprise Rationalisierung und Projektierung Berlin (RaPro), with Transportmaschinen keeping its role as the FTO.²²¹ RaPro was chosen because of its experience as the general supplier of an abattoir in the East German town of Eberswalde, then-recently delivered by a West German contractor.²²² Acquaintance with West German companies was advantageous given that Thier continued to represent the Iraqi commissioners, and it specified Western standards, norms, and parameters of performance and construction, often unfamiliar to companies in the GDR and incompatible with their standards.

The crucial function of the general contractor for construction was assumed by the firm Industrieprojektierung (Ipro) Dessau.²²³ Ipro specialized in the design of industrial facilities for the production of construction materials, in particular of cement factories, and it acted as general contractor

4.44. "Time schedule for complete execution 'Modern Slaughterhouse Baghdad,'" 1977.

for East German construction companies since 1972.[224] The Baghdad abattoir was its first foreign project in this capacity, and Ipro's tasks included the delivery of the architectural design and the supervision of the construction work, as well as the supply of building materials (with the exception of those to be delivered by the Iraqi side). The remit of Romania's Arcom was defined as a subcontractor for construction. Ascobloc became the general contractor for equipment, in continuation of its original remit, and it hired ten other subcontractors. Thirteen other contractors for specific tasks were hired from the GDR, and complemented by a Yugoslav supplier of insulation and elevators, and a West German supplier of waste-water systems.[225]

This organizational scheme mirrored the East German construction practice. The function of the general contractor was introduced for the first time in the GDR during the construction of a petrochemical plant in the town of Schwedt in the early 1960s. In Schwedt, the remit of the general contractor was to implement the "complex line production" by matching sequences of the delivery of materials, construction activities, and their coordination within a detailed plan.[226] (The term "complex" was used in the architectural discourse in socialist countries in the sense of "comprehensive," and "complex construction" integrating all aspects of architecture,

THE WORLD SOCIALIST SYSTEM 215

urban design, transport, and construction, was posited as an aspiration and specialty of East German building culture.)²²⁷ That coordination entailed a close collaboration with the commissioner, from the stage of concept design through the elaboration of the preliminary design, the selection of contractors, delivery of the final design, the construction process of the plant and its equipment, on to the start-up phase of the facility.²²⁸

Such organization of work was not restricted to industrial plants, and it included all areas of East German construction export, among them military infrastructure, housing, and social facilities. The institutionalization of this organizational scheme was part of the cooperation within the Comecon, as Schwedt's petrochemical factories were the end point of the Druzhba ("friendship") pipeline, a major Comecon infrastructure project constructed in order to deliver crude oil from the USSR to Poland, Czechoslovakia, the GDR, and Hungary (figure 4.45). In the years to come, the East German organizational scheme was promoted as a model to follow by Comecon's Permanent Commission for Construction, created in 1958 in East Berlin and headed by German architect Gerhard Kosel.²²⁹ By the early 1970s, construction export in several other socialist countries was reorganized along similar lines.²³⁰

The ability to coordinate a large number of specialized actors in the construction process was presented by theorists of the world socialist system as a key feature of centrally planned economies and a major advantage for countries on the path of state-led modernization, such as Iraq.²³¹ That argument was conveyed by offers sent abroad by East German FTOs, which listed all design and construction companies participating in the offer, and which made a point of spelling out their specific competencies and contributions to be coordinated by the general supplier.²³²

A crucial role in this coordination was played by type designs. Type designs were core instruments for architects in the GDR and in socialist countries more generally, as typification allowed the construction of buildings by means of a small number of mass-produced elements and thus it was a precondition of industrialized construction. Yet for East German architects, typification was more than a technical question: it was a way to distinguish socialist architecture from that of the West. For instance, speakers at the 1957 congress of East German architects contrasted the cosmopolitanism of the Inter-Bau exhibition in West Berlin, with housing designed by leading Western architects (1957); and socialist internationalism, which informed the collective work on types.²³³ The bulk of the

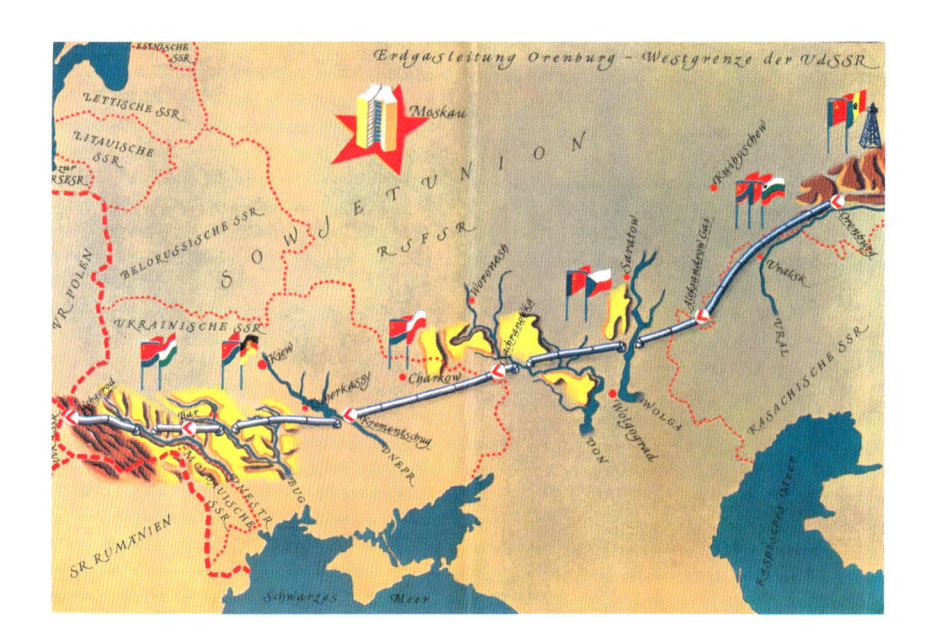

4.45. The Druzhba pipeline. Thomas Billhardt and Peter Jacobs, *Die Drushba-Trasse* (Berlin: Verlag Neues Leben, 1978).

4.46. Aircraft shelter for Iraq, early 1980s. Bauakademie der DDR (GDR).

activities of the PCC focused on the exchange of type projects, too. East German construction industry benefited from such exchanges, drawing in particular on industrialized housing from Czechoslovakia, the Soviet Union, and Poland; in turn, those countries imported East German prefabrication systems.[234]

Type designs were distinctively advantageous for export contracts. Such designs were attractive to clients by allowing them to consult earlier iterations of a particular program and to inspect and compare them with their needs. For instance, before commissioning in the GDR the construction of a cement plan in Ethiopia (New Mugher) in the late 1970s, an Ethiopian delegation inspected a plant of the same type that East Germans had constructed in Cuba.[235] Type designs allowed clients to benefit from the economies of scale in the construction process, since building materials could be bought and shipped in bulk. A case in point was several investments of the Directorate of Military Works in Baghdad that, during the war with Iran, commissioned various East German firms to deliver sixteen hundred sheds, along with a military camp for a thousand soldiers, and aircraft shelters, all based on type designs (figure 4.46).[236] Furthermore, the use of type designs guaranteed a unified standard of equipment, as East German tender offers pointed out.[237]

By the 1980s, the reuse of type designs was expected to economize on the architectural labor of institutes in the GDR and to optimize the design solutions for export.[238] At that time, the task of compiling databanks of type designs for export and their optimization was assigned to the Pilot and Experimental Project Office at the Academy of Architecture (Bauakademie) in East Berlin, the country's central research institution in architecture and construction.[239] In particular, the Project Office offered to East German companies the service of adapting type designs to the requirements of a specific export commission, from climatic, social, and material conditions of the site to the economic and legal framework of the contract. Furthermore, the Project Office issued guidelines for specific countries, including Iraq, and produced catalogues of type projects adapted to climatic, social, and technological specificity of particular locations, among them the study *Housing in Developing Countries* (1985).[240] Several of those proposals foresaw large-scale prefabrication technology, and suggested the construction of factories for prefabricated elements based on East German systems.[241] However, attempts at persuading leaders in the region to purchase housing factories in the GDR bore little success.

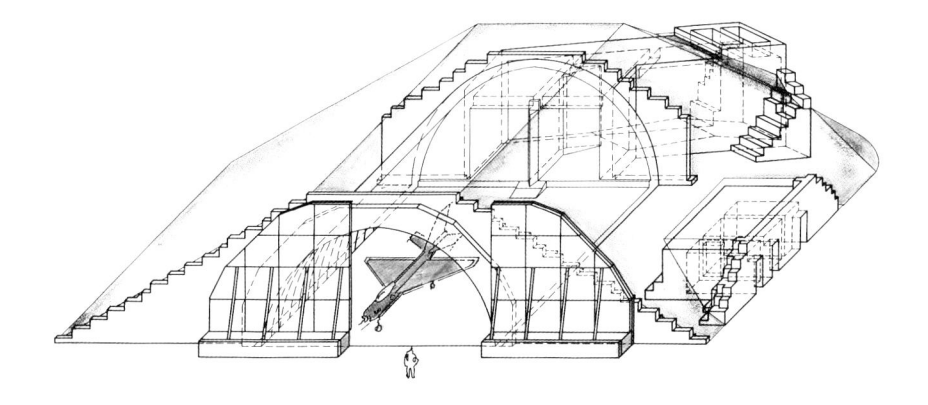

HANGAR COUVERT DE TERRE

THE WORLD SOCIALIST SYSTEM

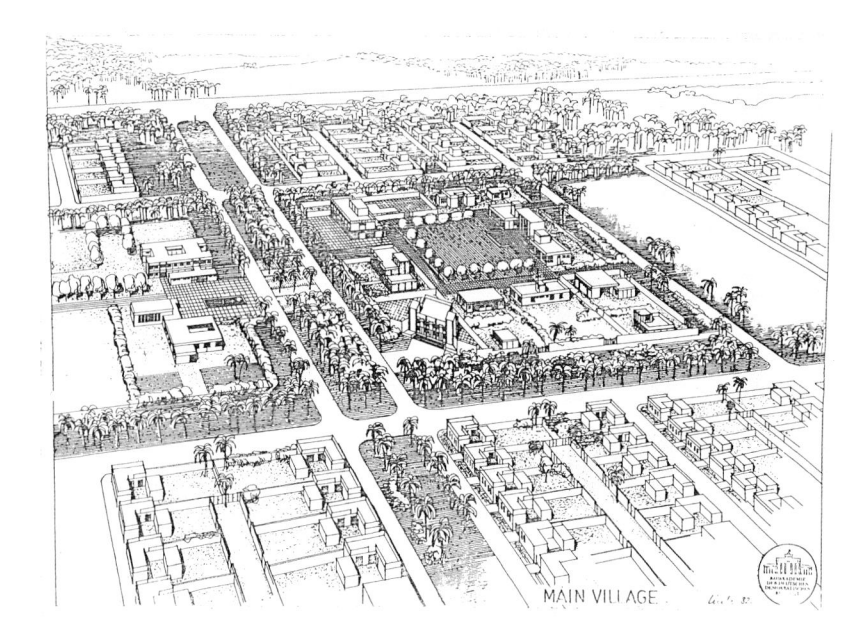

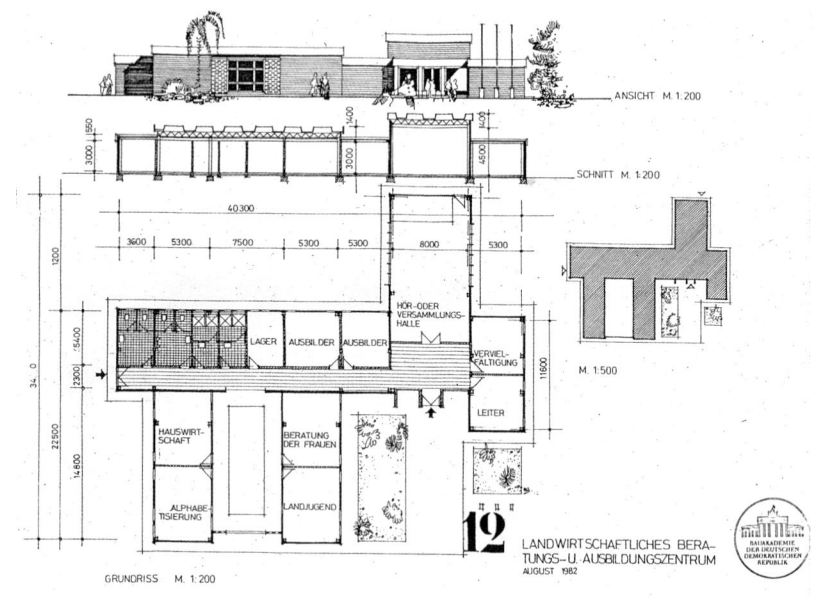

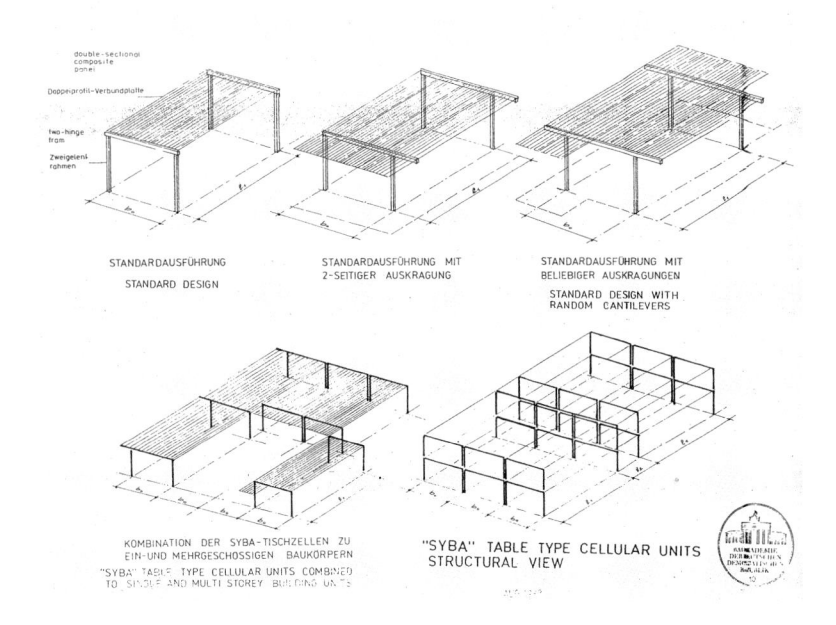

4.47. "Main village," Iraq, 1982. Bauakademie der DDR (GDR).

4.48. Agricultural consulting and training center, Iraq, 1982. Bauakademie der DDR (GDR).

4.49. "'Syba' Table Type Cellular Units. Structural View," Iraq, 1982. Bauakademie der DDR (GDR).

4.50. Planetarium in Tripoli (Libya), 1976–80, general view and plan. Carl Zeiss Jena (GDR), Gertrud Schille. *Jenaer Rundschau/Jena Review* 6 (1981), cover.

More successful were attempts at implementing "intermediary" technologies, which were based on prefabricated typologies but foreseen to be constructed by means of traditional, labor intensive techniques; and lightweight steel structures, as planned for the project of six villages in Iraq (figures 4.47, 4.48, and 4.49).[242]

The latter design was produced by the Project Office, which coordinated the work of other partners, including two other institutes of the Academy of Architecture (one specialized in climatic design, the other in buildings for agricultural uses), along with a combine specializing in wood and light-metal construction, a contractor, and the FTO Limex. This points to a crucial role of type designs in the coordination of the work of several increasingly specialized East German design institutes and contractors that participated in export contracts. During negotiations concerning tender proposals or particular commissions, the parties involved used type designs to compare the required tasks with their capacities, and to estimate costs and profitability of a project, from design to construction. Type designs were used in negotiations between East German design institutes and contractors to subdivide and manage their work, and to define areas where additional design work would need to be commissioned.[243]

One highly visible case of using type designs for the division of work in export contracts was the planetarium in Tripoli (1976–80), a building that was often used to advertise East German design and construction services abroad (figure 4.50). That turn-key commission was awarded to the state combine Carl Zeiss from the city of Jena, specializing in optical instruments and equipment. Building on its prewar experience, traditions of craftsmanship, and integration of research into production, some thirty companies of the combine had a significant share in East German exports.

Carl Zeiss established its own FTOs, technical, and commercial offices in about forty countries (including one in New York City), and joint-venture companies abroad, including several in Western Europe.[244] The company also had its own architectural office, which was in charge of designing planetariums, one of its most successful export products, which Carl Zeiss exported to Stalingrad (now Volgograd), Beijing, Katowice, and Calcutta, followed by Prague, Colombo, Cairo, Jakarta, Bogota, Riga, and Kuwait City.[245] In its Tripoli commission, the architectural design was delivered by Carl Zeiss's architectural section, with Gertrud Schille as project architect, and with the design institute Spezialbetonbau Binz, headed by engineer Ulrich Müther, in charge of the calculations (figure 4.51). Their collaboration is visible in the constructed ensemble, which consisted of two segments. The first was a double dome in steel-bar structure with a concrete shell, surrounded by a ring-formed service area in reinforced concrete. Schille used this typology in her other designs of Zeiss's planetariums in North Africa and West Germany. The second was an annex with educational and cultural functions accommodated within a thin-shell structure: a signature form of Müther's Spezialbetonbau, which was in charge of its construction.[246]

Coordination and Competition in the Comecon

After its completion in 1980, the Tripoli planetarium was widely reproduced in the marketing materials to promote construction export from the GDR. Yet while East Germany's architectural culture of specialization and typification looked impressive in the offers of the FTOs, reports from the construction site of Baghdad's slaughterhouse revealed that their application in Iraq was far from smooth. The postponed appointment of the general supplier and the general contractor, and the prolonged negotiation about their remits, resulted in delays in the signing of contracts with subcontractors. Accordingly, the "chain of subcontractors" was "closed" only in 1978.[247] Negotiation of the specific tasks between multiple, highly specialized East German companies took a lot of time. In spite of RaPro's experience with the slaughterhouse typology constructed in collaboration with West German firms, Thier often rejected the design solutions and machinery proposed by the East Germans, and required their substitutions

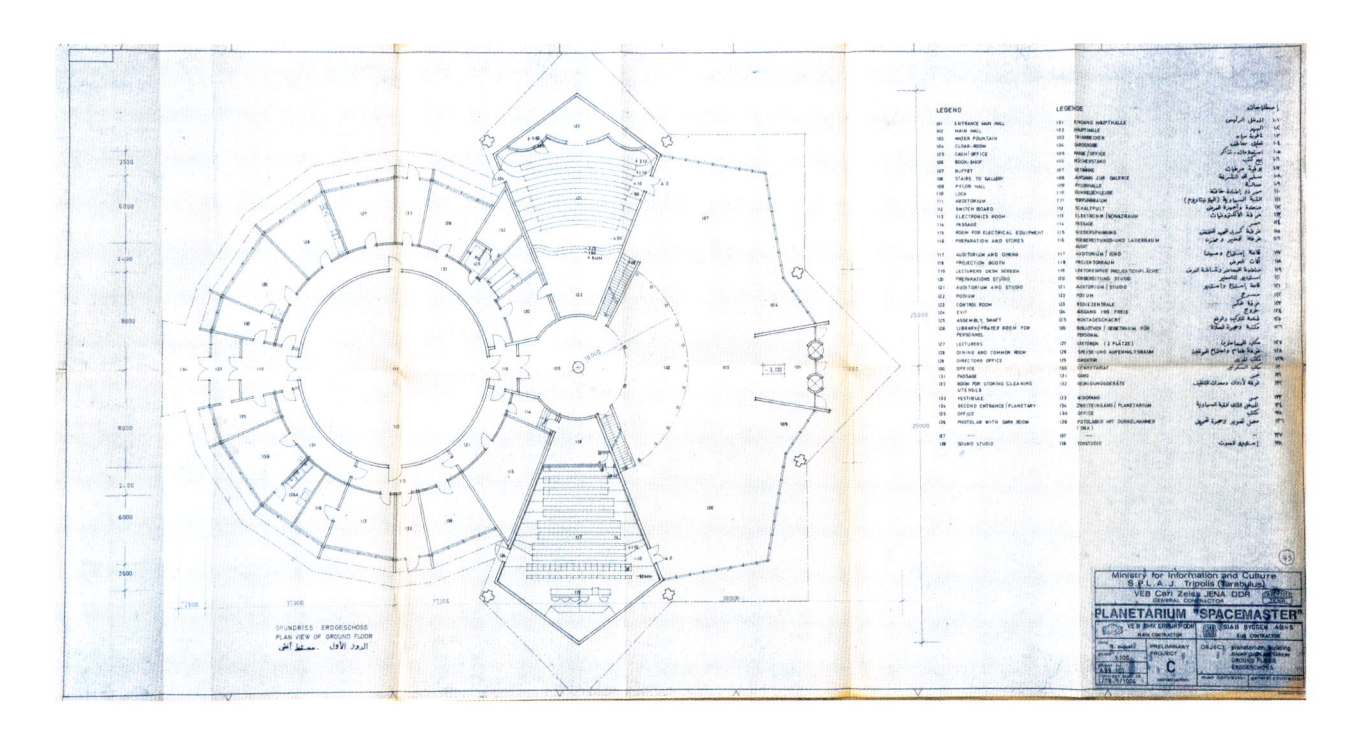

4.51. Planetarium in Tripoli (Libya), 1976–80, plan, 1978. Carl Zeiss Jena (GDR), Gertrud Schille.

with Western products.[248] These imports caused additional costs and further delays.[249] The shortage of people who were allowed to travel abroad, and the long vetting process that accompanied the application for a GDR passport, also restricted the operation in Baghdad. Further delays were caused by the requests of the Iraqi side concerning changes to the design. Iraqi authorities were behind with the agreed periodical payments, and failed to deliver on their obligation to provide construction materials such as concrete and steel. Furthermore, in autumn 1980 the construction was put on hold because of the war with Iran, which also interrupted the supply chains.[250] The prolonged decision-making processes in East Berlin, from where management personnel were only gradually and partially transferred to the construction site, made it difficult for East German actors to respond to the quickly changing situation on the ground.[251]

Among the most important reasons for the delays of the project was what was supposed to be its asset: the collaboration between East German companies and Arcom. Conflicts between these two parties were not only economically damaging but also politically embarrassing, since collaboration between enterprises from socialist countries both within the bloc and on third markets was part of Comecon's vision of the world socialist system. At the same time, the conflicts on the construction site in Baghdad were indicative of fundamental controversies around the economic integration of Comecon countries that originated in the 1950s and were not resolved until the end of the Cold War.

The economic integration of the Comecon was high on the agenda of the Khrushchev leadership, which broke with Stalinist-type autarkic national economies. The new Soviet leader argued that full industrialization of Comecon countries required planned harmonization of their economies and their mutual complementarity that would lead to economies of scale. Accordingly, Soviet economists envisaged an international division of labor based on existing industries and specific resources within each country, even if such a division would reinforce the uneven development of their economies. In these debates, Romania was specifically cited as an example of a country that would need to lay aside its attempts at developing an electronics industry, and to import electronics from the GDR instead. Romanians rejected that principle, which, they argued, would have conserved the backwardness of their country. They opted for a division of labor within production branches rather than between them, and anticipated a fine-grained network of suppliers of industrial goods from all socialist states.[252] Faced with the Romanians' opposition, Khrushchev's attempt to introduce supranational economic planning was abandoned. Instead, socialist leaders agreed on the "basic principles of the international socialist division of labor," including the coordination of national economic plans, clearing agreements meant to promote specialization of production in the member states, and joint projects based on pooled resources.[253]

The stimulation of such international division of labor in architecture, engineering, and construction-materials industries among Comecon countries was the aim of the Permanent Commission for Construction (PCC). The PCC consisted of five sections: building materials and elements; building industry; design solutions, type designs, and standards; regional and urban planning; and economics of construction. The activities of the commission included comparative surveys of construction materials and procedures in member countries, followed by the selection of those performing best, and their recommendation for implementation elsewhere. For example, the commission recommended prestressed concrete procedures from Romania and the USSR for implementation across the entire bloc. It also participated in the coordination of design and the construction of pilot and experimental buildings, and organized trips for experts to study them.[254]

The PCC's explicit aim was the standardization of construction materials, products, nomenclature, and norms so that blueprints from one country could be reused elsewhere and the supply of materials could be internationalized. By the early 1960s, the commission launched a program for the unification of design norms, recommending standardized structural solutions in industrial facilities and unified tolerance provisions. Based on an analysis of a large number of designs from member states, a unified modular system was proposed as the basis for typification and standardization of industrial and other designs, equipment, machinery, and several construction elements (figure 4.52). According to an internal review (1967), the majority of the standardizing recommendations of the PCC were incorporated into members' national standards and normative documents. In cooperation with other permanent Comecon commissions, type projects were developed, including projects for silos and other agricultural facilities.[255] Among the implemented procedures was a standard methodology of urban planning for border areas, which became the basis for bilateral and multilateral agreements among Comecon countries.[256] The commission coordinated the work of national research institutes related to architecture and construction, and it produced and circulated hundreds of map sheets showing type projects of industrial and social facilities (figure 4.53). It also surveyed the terminology in architecture, industrial design, and urban and traffic planning, and published a unified dictionary of those terms in twelve languages of Comecon members.[257]

This extensive work of normalization, standardization, and typification was in tune with general tendencies in architecture and construction in Comecon countries, and could have been used as the basis for coordinating their projects abroad. Remits from Comecon agreements created at times the basis for export activities, with sugar mills, of which Poland was the specialized exporter within Comecon, becoming that nation's major export product within the world socialist system.[258] Precedents for coordination of the bloc's construction activities outside Europe could also be found in technical assistance jointly offered to less developed Comecon members. For instance, within the first ten years since the creation of the PCC, Mongolia reported that it received catalogues and type projects for housing districts, and that groups of experts from Comecon countries advised the government in Ulaanbaatar on the design of industrial facilities.[259] In the next decade, the PCC coordinated Comecon's technical assistance to the construction industry in Mongolia and provided technical standards for the design of objects constructed in that country by Comecon members.[260] By the 1970s, the PCC coordinated Comecon's assistance to the construction and construction-materials industries in Cuba.[261]

In contrast, commercial projects such as the Baghdad abattoir were not coordinated within the commission. Rather, East German and Romanian firms found themselves competing against each other in the original tender for the abattoir, when Transportmaschinen in cooperation with an Iraqi contractor was bidding against Romania's Arcom partnered with a West German firm. It was only after the tender was awarded and the withdrawal of the Iraqi partner that Transportmaschinen invited Arcom to join as a subcontractor.[262] The resulting collaboration was far from smooth. The East German side considered much of the Romanian-produced design documentation to be of poor quality and thus required multiple amendments. These were particularly onerous because of the complex process of acceptance of the drawings: Arcom's drawings were sent from Bucharest to East Berlin to be checked, then to Munich to be approved by Thier, then back to Bucharest to include possible changes, then back to East Berlin, and finally to the construction site in Baghdad.[263] Decision makers from East Berlin repeatedly requested that Arcom double the number of its

> 4.52. Representation of the modular system recommended by Comecon's Permanent Commission for Construction. Gerhard Kraft, *Die Zusammenarbeit der Mitgliedsländer des RWG auf dem Gebiet der Investitionen* (Berlin: Akademie-Verlag, 1977), 54.

> 4.53. Type project of a cinema-theater for 1,200 people, distributed by Comecon's Permanent Commission for Construction, 1965. Gerhard Kraft, *Die Zusammenarbeit der Mitgliedsländer des RWG auf dem Gebiet der Investitionen* (Berlin: Akademie-Verlag, 1977), 63.

THE WORLD SOCIALIST SYSTEM

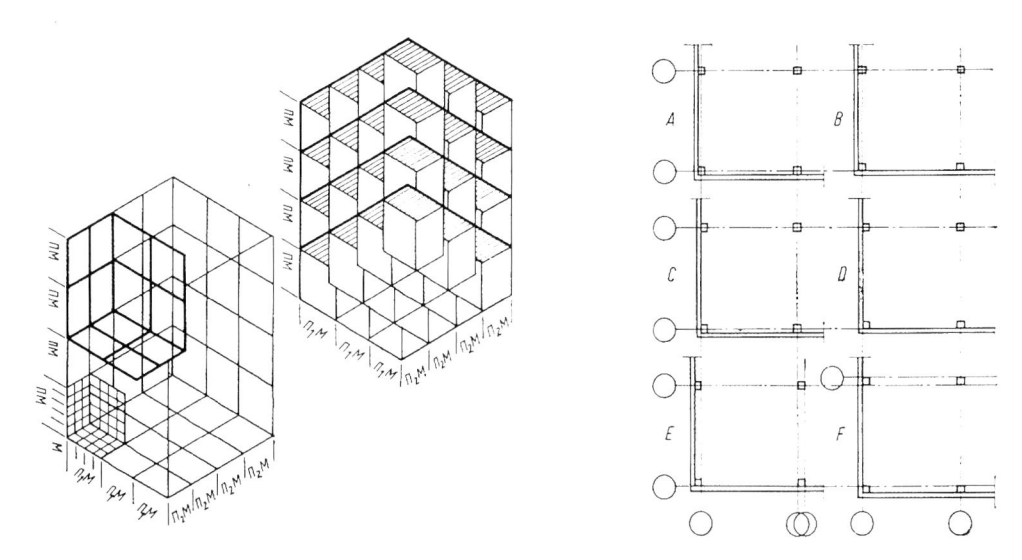

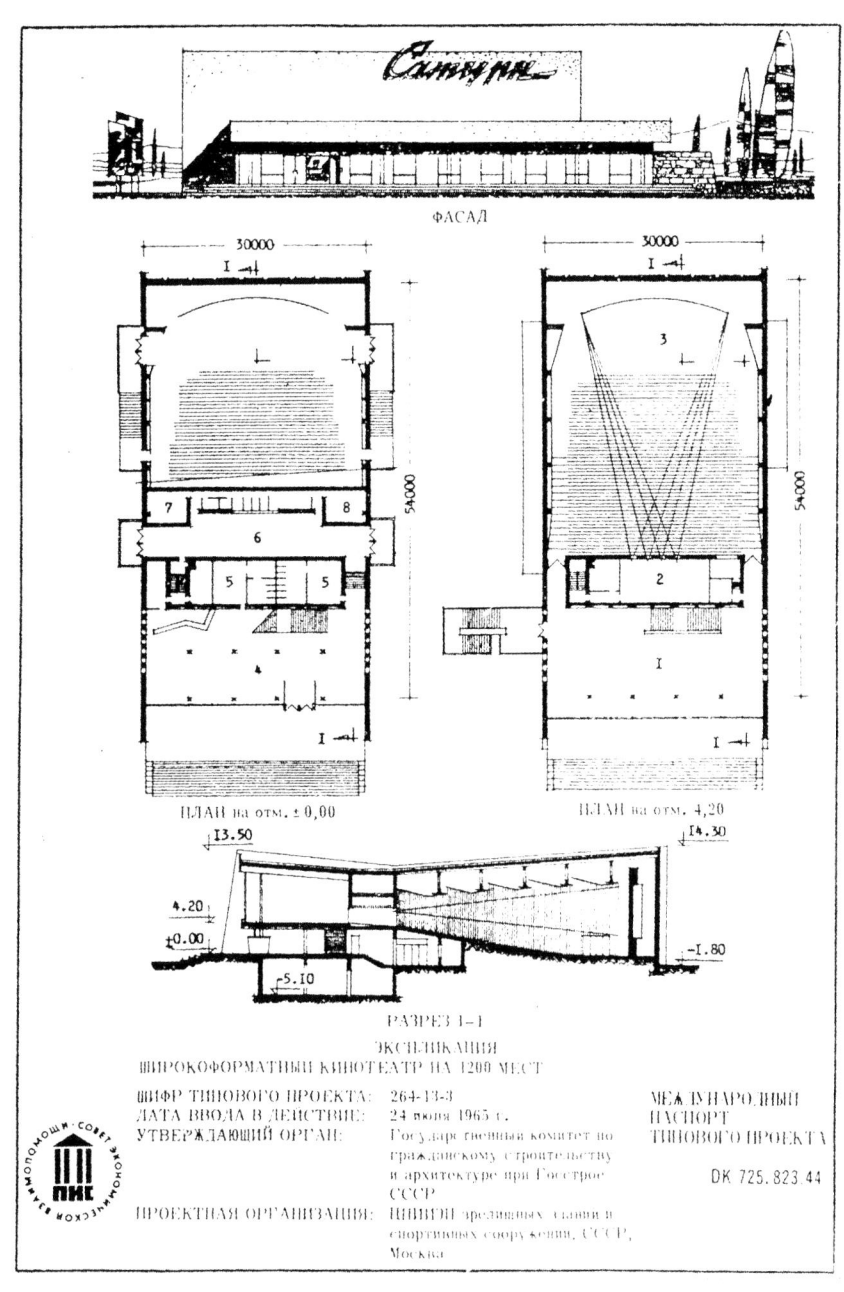

construction workers in Baghdad (over six hundred in early 1979) in order to catch up with the work, a request that Arcom resisted.[264]

In view of constant disagreements with Arcom, managers in East Berlin frequently considered replacing the Romanian contractor. No East German company was ready to take over, however. The estimation of costs and benefits, and in particular the fear of the project being taken over by a West German firm, repeatedly confirmed that keeping Arcom on board was the least-bad scenario.[265] The disputes between GDR firms and Arcom could have been rarely resolved on the construction site in Baghdad. Yet the archival materials do not suggest any attempts to involve Comecon institutions to resolve these disputes, and in case of another, equally troubled collaboration between GDR and Bulgarian companies in Syria, the East Germans explicitly aimed not to involve such institutions.[266] Rather, disputes around the slaughterhouse projects were addressed on a bilateral level. The double chains of command of the party and the state, with East German and Romanian companies responding to the ministries in East Berlin and Bucharest, respectively, opened communication channels and possibilities of leverage for both sides. Given the "political and economic significance" of their collaboration, of which representatives from East Berlin reminded their Bucharest counterparts, the companies involved found ways to muddle through, even if concessions from Arcom required additional payments from the GDR, and financial disagreements were not resolved until the mid-1980s.[267]

By that time, East German decision makers tried to learn from the disappointing experience of the abattoir. Reports sent from the Middle East to East Berlin pointed out that GDR design institutes and contractors needed to improve their performance along the lines of "flexibility, variability, and risk-taking."[268] However, the addressees were rarely able to follow such recommendations, and both the specialization of the contractors and the organizational procedures of East German construction export were among the main reasons. The time necessary for the coordination of the highly specialized GDR enterprises effectively prevented them from meeting deadlines in tenders in the Middle East, in particular in the Gulf region, which had emerged as an attractive market. The fact that many East German companies specialized in a particular technology further diminished their flexibility when rising import tariffs on steel, for example, undermined the economic rationale of steel-based projects.[269] The aversion of East German management to spending convertible currency often prevented firms from improving their products with components from the West, and the management sometimes blocked necessary last-minute changes to designs (for which local draftsmen needed to be hired), causing commissions to fall through.[270] On the demand side, further constraints stemmed from the depletion of Iraqi monetary reserves since the early 1980s and the fact that payments in crude oil were often deferred for several years (as a result, unified Germany inherited over 1 billion German marks in Iraqi debt to the GDR).[271] In turn, East German companies found more lucrative commissions in West Germany, which subsidized its eastern neighbor in exchange for political concessions.

Architecture and Petrobarter

A key reason for the trials and tribulations of the East German architects, engineers, and managers involved in the slaughterhouse project was the unfavorable contract signed between the FTO Transportmaschinen and the Iraqi government in November 1975. Besides the lack of relevant experience, preparation, and capacity of the FTO and Ascobloc, the financial conditions to which East Germans agreed practically precluded financial profits. To the consternation of subsequent controllers, the initial price requested by the FTO was reduced by 43 percent in the amended offer, and this reduction was not supported by any calculations.[272] Furthermore, the FTO agreed to pay Arcom for the construction of the buildings more than it would receive from the Iraqis for that part of the contract. The necessary imports from the West had not been correctly assessed by the planners in East Berlin, and neither were taxes, shipping costs, and insurance taken into account. In consequence, a report from the State Bank of the GDR argued already in spring 1976 that the benefits of the East German companies were problematic, and the bank's controllers hinted that the contract might end with a loss.[273]

In retrospect, several reviewers in East Berlin pointed to the political motivations of the GDR to enter and to pursue the project, in spite of its bleak economic prospects. And yet the conventional wisdom that socialist leadership would accept economic losses because of envisaged political gains does not fully capture the motivation of the decision makers in East Berlin. Economic calculations in themselves were complex, and the economists in the State Bank, after pointing to the uncertain gains for the companies involved ("operational benefits"), discussed the prospective "benefits for the national economy" brought about by the abattoir project. These included the facilitation of further economic cooperation with Iraq, the valuable experience in delivery of abattoirs, the inclusion of the GDR into the international market of turn-key abattoirs that would open the path to further commissions, and the availability of hard currency on the State Bank accounts.[274] This latter point was constantly on the minds of the architects, engineers, and managers of the slaughterhouse project, as by the 1970s profit in convertible currencies was a key reason for construction export projects from socialist countries. This is why the substitution of East German materials and equipment by Western ones, as requested by Thier, were defeating the purpose of the project.

In order to maximize the income of convertible currencies and to minimize their expenditure, decision makers in socialist countries favored barter, or the exchange of goods and services without the mediation of money. Barter agreements were not unique to socialist countries. For example, since the late 1950s, the Soviet Union had signed barter agreements with Italian state-owned companies, and Iraq signed oil-for-weapons agreements with France in the 1980s. However, barter dominated trade between socialist countries, and played a crucial role in the trade between them and countries in Africa and Asia.[275] Under Khrushchev, the bartering of raw materials from developing countries was considered a temporary measure, to be replaced by industrial goods produced by factories constructed with socialist assistance. Under Brezhnev, however, most of those attempts at fast-track industrialization in developing countries were deemed disappointing, and the Soviets encouraged these countries to capitalize on their traditional role as suppliers of raw materials.[276]

The privileging of barter in socialist foreign trade can be traced back to the immediate postwar period, when it was introduced in response to the shortage of convertible currencies in socialist countries. After the death of Stalin, clearing agreements concerning the supply of goods became the basic tool of economic integration within Comecon. These allowed enforcement of the balance of trade between countries through offsetting exports with imports and through minimizing the use of monetary transactions. Attempts at introducing multilateral clearance between Comecon states, for which the "transfer ruble" had been introduced as a unit of calculation (1963), were considered unsuccessful, and the final decade of the Cold War witnessed the return to bilateral agreements.[277]

In agreements between Comecon countries, prices were periodically adjusted according to those on the world market but did not play a primary role in negotiations. What was central, rather, was the balancing of "baskets" of goods exchanged. Relations between "hard" and "soft" goods in these baskets were key: hard goods were those easily sold on capitalist markets for convertible currency, or those badly needed and difficult to obtain, while soft goods were those produced in surplus in the seller country, or nonessential for that country, or difficult to sell on the capitalist market. This system introduced a specific set of incentives and aversions for economic actors in Comecon countries. In their negotiations, representatives of each country aimed at minimizing the hard goods that they gave away, and the soft goods that they accepted, while maximizing the hard goods that they accepted, and the soft goods that they gave away.[278]

Since the late 1960s, barter became the dominant mode of transactions between Comecon countries and Iraq, which, in the next decade, emerged among oil-producing countries as the main recipient of Eastern European trade, and as the main source of crude oil for socialist Europe.[279] This "petrobarter," or the exchange of goods and services for crude oil, was seen by commentators from socialist countries as an exemplification of the principle of "mutual advantage" by which they characterized the world socialist system. Petrobarter circumvented the need for convertible currency, and offered an outlet for goods of limited marketability, including machinery, equipment, arms, and services from Eastern Europe. For example, the barter of Eastern European military equipment for Iraqi oil in the 1960s and early 1970s allowed the governments in socialist countries to receive a strategic resource while saving on convertible currency. In turn, Iraqis could acquire equipment that the Western countries were not willing to sell them at that time, while paying with oil that they feared would be difficult to sell to the West, due to international tensions after the nationalization of the Iraqi oil industry.[280] Long-term contracts, which often accompanied barter agreements, shielded those in the transactions from the fluctuation of prices on the world market. For example, by the second half of the 1970s, the Soviet Union continued to exchange its military equipment for Iraqi oil based on prices from before their spike (1973). Consequently, when the Soviets started to resell this oil to the West, and to profit from the higher prices, relations with Iraq became strained.[281] This latter practice was common, and the bulk of oil imported from the Middle East to most Eastern European countries was not used for domestic consumption but for reexport to Western Europe in exchange for convertible currency. This procedure was practiced by the Soviet Union, Bulgaria, Czechoslovakia, East Germany, Poland (after 1980), and Hungary.[282]

In contrast, Romania along with Yugoslavia used all or most imported oil for domestic consumption.[283] The Romanian insistence on barter intensified over the course of the 1980s, in the wake of Ceaușescu's decision to fast-track the repayment of the country's massive foreign debt. Minutes of meetings held by the Romanian leadership with directors of institutions responsible for construction export and with Iraqi officials show that Ceaușescu insisted on expanding barter transactions. When discussing a report about the delivery of Romanian cement plants to Iraq and several projects for Libya in July 1981, for example, Ceaușescu emphasized the need to use Romanian materials in projects abroad: "we get involved in these contracts to export [building] materials, designs, and intelligence.... This is where money is made. I'm not going abroad to pour concrete!"[284] During another meeting (1982), he reiterated that commissions abroad should be accepted only when all materials, machinery, and labor, both manual and intellectual, were delivered from Romania. Foreign currency needed to be saved; therefore, he considered it unacceptable that 60 percent of the income of projects in Libya and Iraq was spent on the import from third countries of construction materials, machinery, and consumer goods for Romanian workers on site. Managers responsible for those decisions were to be dismissed. Ceaușescu emphasized that everything needed to be sent

4.54. Airport Road Housing under construction, Tripoli (Libya), 1974–78. National Housing Corporation, Edward Wysocki (chief and project architect).

from Romania, including barracks for workers and their equipment: "we shouldn't be buying a needle from abroad."[285]

Romanian actors in charge of construction and design export had to comply. Among them was Arcom, established in 1969 with the remit of studying, designing, engineering, executing, building, and assembling structures, in particular industrial buildings. It was followed by the Romanian Institute of Consulting (Romconsult), created in 1971, which recruited architectural institutes from Bucharest for designs abroad, along with individual architects for direct employment in foreign planning offices and universities. In 1981, several design institutions, with a total workforce of five hundred architects, engineers, economists, and technicians, were merged into the Center for Studies and Design Abroad (Romproiect), which answered to the Department of Constructions Abroad at the Ministry of Industrial Constructions. Romproiect's first design engagements included Arcom's construction commissions in Libya, and land-reclamation and irrigation works in Iraq carried out by the Romanian contractor Arcif.[286]

The barter principle was implemented at the largest scale in Arcom's projects in Libya, which was the most important market for Romanian construction services in the 1970s and 1980s. These included contracts for industry, housing, and cultural, sports, health, and educational amenities. Arcom specialized, in particular, in a long series of type-designed buildings, including 125 schools, 44 culture and sports centers, as well as health facilities.[287] Some of those projects were designed by Romanians, but most were based on third-party designs. At times, they were delivered by local institutions, often employing foreign architects. This was the case with the housing estate by Airport Road in Tripoli (first phase), designed by Edward Wysocki, a Pole employed as chief architect by the National Housing Corporation in Libya (1974–78) (figure 4.54).[288] Other buildings were planned by foreign offices, either from the West, with type schools designed by Alexander Gibb & Partners, or from the East, with the type design of a cinema-theater delivered by a group of Polish architects on contract with Polservice.[289] Arcom was also commissioned to complete unfinished buildings by Egyptian contractors in Libya, who left the country after the

THE WORLD SOCIALIST SYSTEM

short Libyan-Egyptian War (1977), as well as a sports center near Tripoli, designed by Bulgaria's TES.

In most cases, third-party designs underwent a procedure called "technological adaptation" by Romanians, which included redrawing blueprints and rewriting specifications in such a way that they fit the capacities of Romanian companies. This practice had multiple precedents in Romania since the 1960s. They included, for instance, the government's directive to replace steel construction with reinforced concrete in order to save steel needed for machine-building plants, and the directive to replace wood roof structures with typified, prefabricated concrete elements that, even if more expensive and heavy, allowed wood to be saved for export.[290]

In Libya and elsewhere, technological adaptation was a translation procedure aimed at maximizing competitive advantages made available to Romanian firms by the petrobarter system. Among these was the cheap labor of Romanian workers: a 1981 report, for example, accounted for seventy-seven hundred people on Arcom building sites in Libya, with two thousand more scheduled to come; in Iraq their number was expected to reach four thousand by the end of the year.[291] To make use of that labor force, buildings designed by third parties in large-scale prefabrication technology were redrawn as structures cast on site, complemented by smaller prefabricated elements. Romanian FTOs did offer prefabrication systems to foreign governments, including the "spatial" (three-dimensional) Brasov system, which was used to construct almost five thousand apartments in the Libyan desert town of Sebha. A large-scale prefabrication system was also applied in the construction of housing districts in Saida (Algeria, completed in 1987) (figure 4.55).[292] In most cases, however, Arcom worked with labor-intensive technology. In such projects, the Romanian workforce was employed not only on the construction sites but also in supporting facilities, including quarries for aggregates, asphalt plants, and workshops for the prefabrication of concrete, metal, and wood and ceramic elements (figure 4.56). Such produced materials allowed non-Romanian

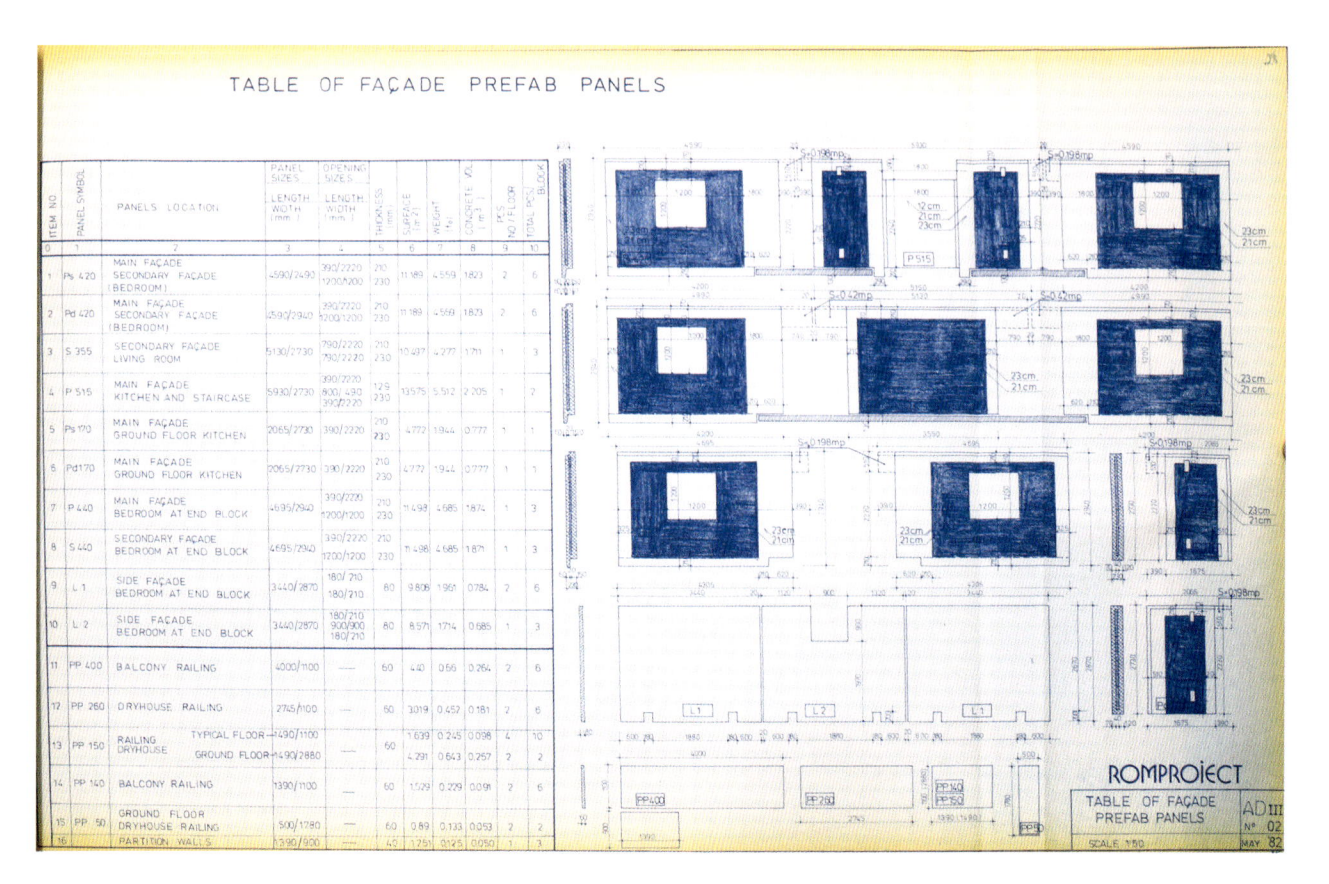

4.55. "Table of Façade Prefab Panels," 1982. Romproiect (Romania).

4.56. Factory of prefabricated panels in Saida (Algeria), 1980s. Romproiect (Romania). "Romproiect" (catalogue), n.d.

4.57. Diagram showing the development process of a design offer for export, 1984. Romproiect (Romania).

THE WORLD SOCIALIST SYSTEM

purchases to be avoided, and also bypassed import taxes and licenses required by the Libyan authorities and others in the region.

In line with the regime's aversion to spending convertible currency, Arcom aimed at importing from Romania materials it could not produce on site. In this regard, a core task of "technological adaptation" was redrawing designs to replace the materials specified in the original contract with others, produced in Romania (figure 4.57). Rewriting specifications became a central task for Romanian architects working on export projects. Dan Agent, head of one of the four architectural teams in Romproiect (1972–77) and the man in charge of many Libyan operations, recalls that all materials for a Polish-designed cinema-theater in Aljmail had to be changed. The adaptation of the specifications in Romproiect's branch office in Tripoli was subject to lengthy negotiations involving Libyan clients, directors of Romanian factories commissioned to produce replacement materials, the leadership of Arcom, and ministries in Bucharest (figure 4.58).[293]

Romanian architects sometimes needed to "adapt" their own designs. A case in point was the designs of six technical and agriculture institutes and three pedagogical institutes, commissioned from Romconsult by the Iraqi Ministry for Higher Education. The individualized and differentiated designs from the tender phase contrast with the rigid grid and unified technology of the construction designs. As the Romanian journal *Arhitectura* commented, "the new solution, much more clear and with a better technical approach, has the disadvantage of making the architectural object less prominent."[294] When interviewed in the present day, several Romanian architects point out that architectural labor on export contracts often moved from design labor (producing "architectural objects") toward a different set of activities. In the words of Dan Agent: "the bulk of my job [in Libya] was to write specifications, including production standards, quality conditions, handing over procedures, substitution materials, and so on."[295]

At times, the insistence on barter brought about losses—for example, when entire shipments of wood joinery or tiles were damaged on their way from Romania and rejected by the client.[296] In general, though, the procedure of technological adaptation proved effective, and a 1981 report about Arcom's work in Libya registered that 58 percent of materials came from Romania, which also included industrial products, such as lamps, cables, bathroom fixtures, ironware, and pumps. Materials purchased or obtained locally (32 percent) were mostly aggregates for concrete, stone, fuel, lubricants, bitumen, and masonry materials. The remaining 10 percent was bought from third parties, such as West Germany, France, Sweden, the UK, and Italy, and included finishing materials, equipment, and, for example, aluminum joinery that were requested by the clients not satisfied with Romanian products.[297]

"Libya was constructed by Arcom," quipped Nicolae Besnea, the Arcom resident architect on the construction site of the abattoir in Baghdad.[298] While Arcom was paid for the construction of the main buildings of the ensemble directly by the East Germans, this construction was based on the procedure of technological adaptation as developed within the petrobarter system. This procedure was performed by architects from the Institute of Technological Design for Light Industry (IPIU) in Bucharest and from Arcom, with the support of a number of other engineering institutes from Bucharest (figure 4.59).[299] These architects redrew large prefabricated elements foreseen by the East German design so that the buildings could be cast on site by Romanian workers, housed in on-site barracks. Smaller concrete elements, such as railings and parapets, were prefabricated on site.[300] Romanian architects redesigned the execution plans for all buildings in reinforced concrete frame, while complying with strict requirements related to thermal insulation, as well as plumbing and sanitation equipment, according to specifications given by East German

4.58. Housing project for Libya. Romproiect (Romania).

4.59. Modern slaughterhouse Baghdad, 1974–81, administrative building. Ipro Dessau (GDR). "VEB Industrieprojektierung Dessau: Betriebschronik," vol. 2, n.d.

companies. Those norms were the basis for the execution and the acceptance of materials and the final reception of the work.[301] With the exception of cement and steel, for which Iraqis were in charge, other construction materials were brought from Romania, and they were tested on the construction site and approved by Thier.

The same procedures were applied to the design of the canteen for six hundred people, commissioned by the Iraqis directly from the Romanians (Arcom and IPIU), and constructed by Arcom. The two-story building was executed in reinforced concrete, cast on site with elements of on-site prefabrication, in compliance with East German norms and equipped with machinery from the GDR.[302] In addition, Besnea designed four identical villas for management on the Tigris River bank, in the middle of a date and orange grove (figure 4.60). Each villa was organized around a patio, which the architect wanted to see as a reference to the traditional Baghdadi

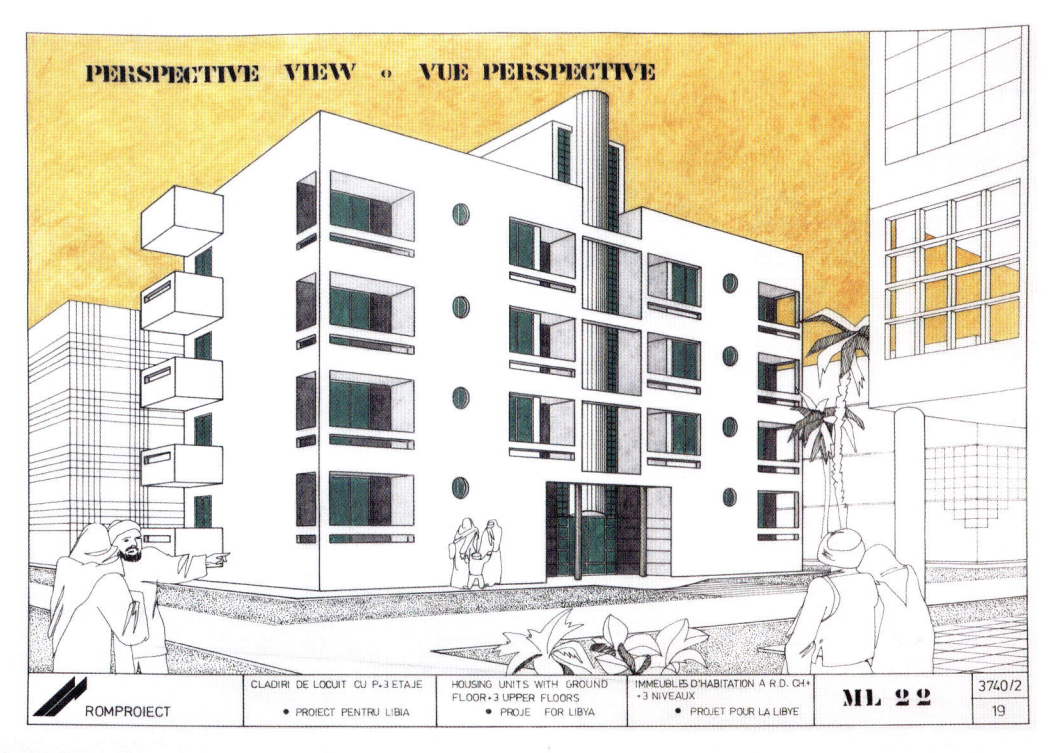

THE WORLD SOCIALIST SYSTEM

house. The villas were strikingly luxurious in finishes and in program (the living rooms, of thirty-six square meters, were larger than a standard two-room apartment in Romania).[303]

The abattoir project shows how the pressure to maximize the use of Romanian materials and labor impacted the materiality and design of Romanian-constructed buildings. In the years following the project, these pressures intensified within the attempts of the Romanian leadership to expand on its construction export to oil-producing countries. Housing projects delivered by Arcom in Iraq during the 1980s were a case in point. Not unlike the regionally specific type projects by East Germany's Pilot and Experimental Project Office, Romanian contractors made a point of adapting the housing layouts to climatic regions and the "traditional way of living" of the local populations. That adaptation included designs provided for specific locations, and type designs that Romanian firms offered to the authorities in the Middle East and North Africa. To make its offer more attractive, Romproiect commissioned type projects of "Arab housing" from architect Dorin Ștefan, an educator at the Ion Mincu University of Architecture in Bucharest (1980). Foreseen for construction in the Brasov prefabricated system, their layouts paid particular attention to cross-ventilation and privacy by means of a split-level section or a courtyard plan. Each apartment was designed with a small garden and a roof terrace for sleeping outdoors, equipped with a kitchen and a toilet.[304]

While these blueprints showed a personal architectural approach, most Romanian export catalogues conveyed an understanding of design as a result of decisions concerning norms, standards, and technology.[305] For instance, the catalogue *Housing Buildings for Export*, issued by Romproiect for Iraq, Libya, and Algeria (1984), presented the commissioners with an entire gamut of choices about standards of finishing, ventilation, air-conditioning, heating, sanitation, equipment, and plumbing. These choices resulted in specific plans, sections, and construction systems (load-bearing walls or concrete frame), as well as type details (figure 4.61). They were complemented by country-specific guidelines, which included options for spatial arrangements of the apartments and their zoning, and decor, such as arches and ornamental railings.[306] A case in point was the housing project for the al-Zafraniya area in Baghdad (1984) (figure 4.62).[307] As was the case with the procedure of technological adaptation, these catalogues testify to the mutation of architectural labor within the petrobarter system. During the postwar decades, the adaptation of imported technologies to local conditions was celebrated as the creative core of architectural labor by critics subscribing to various postwar idioms, from tropical architecture to critical regionalism.[308] In contrast, such adaptation in Romanian export contracts was a distributive procedure, performed by means of flow charts showing possible choices derived from urban norms and budgets of welfare programs of Middle Eastern and North African authorities.

Besides individual apartment buildings, this planning procedure was applied also to larger ensembles composed by Romproiect from type projects of housing and social facilities, all to be built with the same construction system.[309] They included neighborhoods attached to cement plants in al-Qaim and in Sinjar, designed by Romania's Research and Design Institute for Building Materials Industry, commissioned by the Iraqi Ministry of Industry and Minerals, with Arcom as the contractor (figures 4.63 and 4.64). The planning documentation for both projects, delivered in 1982, contained designs of various typologies of housing, from semidetached to apartment buildings, as well as restaurants, shopping centers, kindergartens, primary and intermediary schools, sports grounds, and bomb shelters.[310]

An even more extensive program was foreseen in Romproiect's design for a neighborhood in Mosul with thirty-five hundred housing units

> 4.60. One of the four villas constructed next to the slaughterhouse, Baghdad, early 1980s. Arcom (Romania), IPIU (Romania), Nicolae Besnea. Nicolae Besnea, "Vile în Baghdad," *Arhitectura* 6 (1984): 78.

> 4.61. Housing designs for export (Algeria, Libya, Iraq), comparative analysis of roof and wall details, 1984. Romproiect (Romania), Dan Agent (chief architect), Albert Naiman (project architect).

> 4.62. Housing designs for export (Iraq), 1984. Romproiect (Romania), Dan Agent (chief and project architect).

THE WORLD SOCIALIST SYSTEM

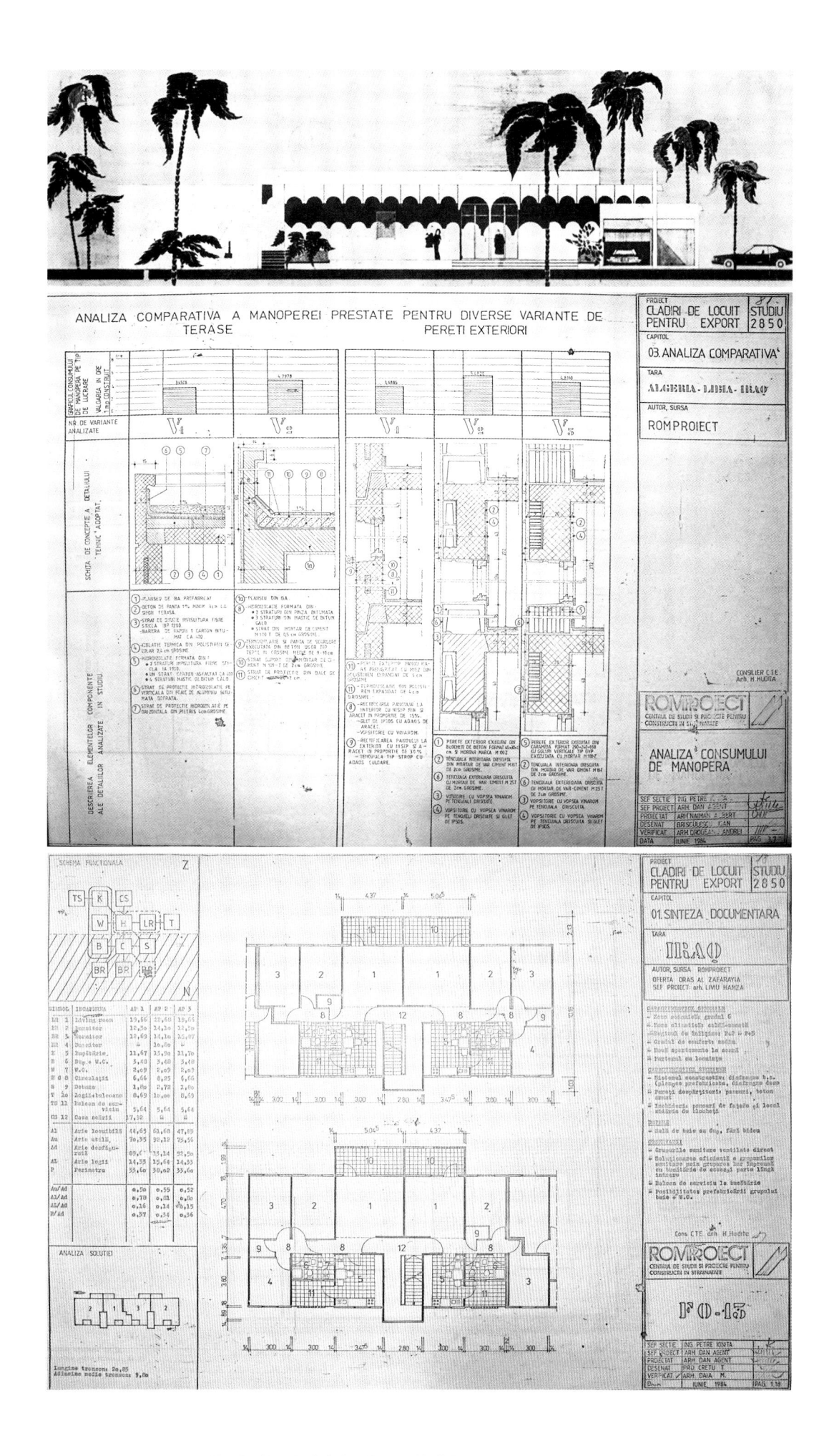

234 CHAPTER 4

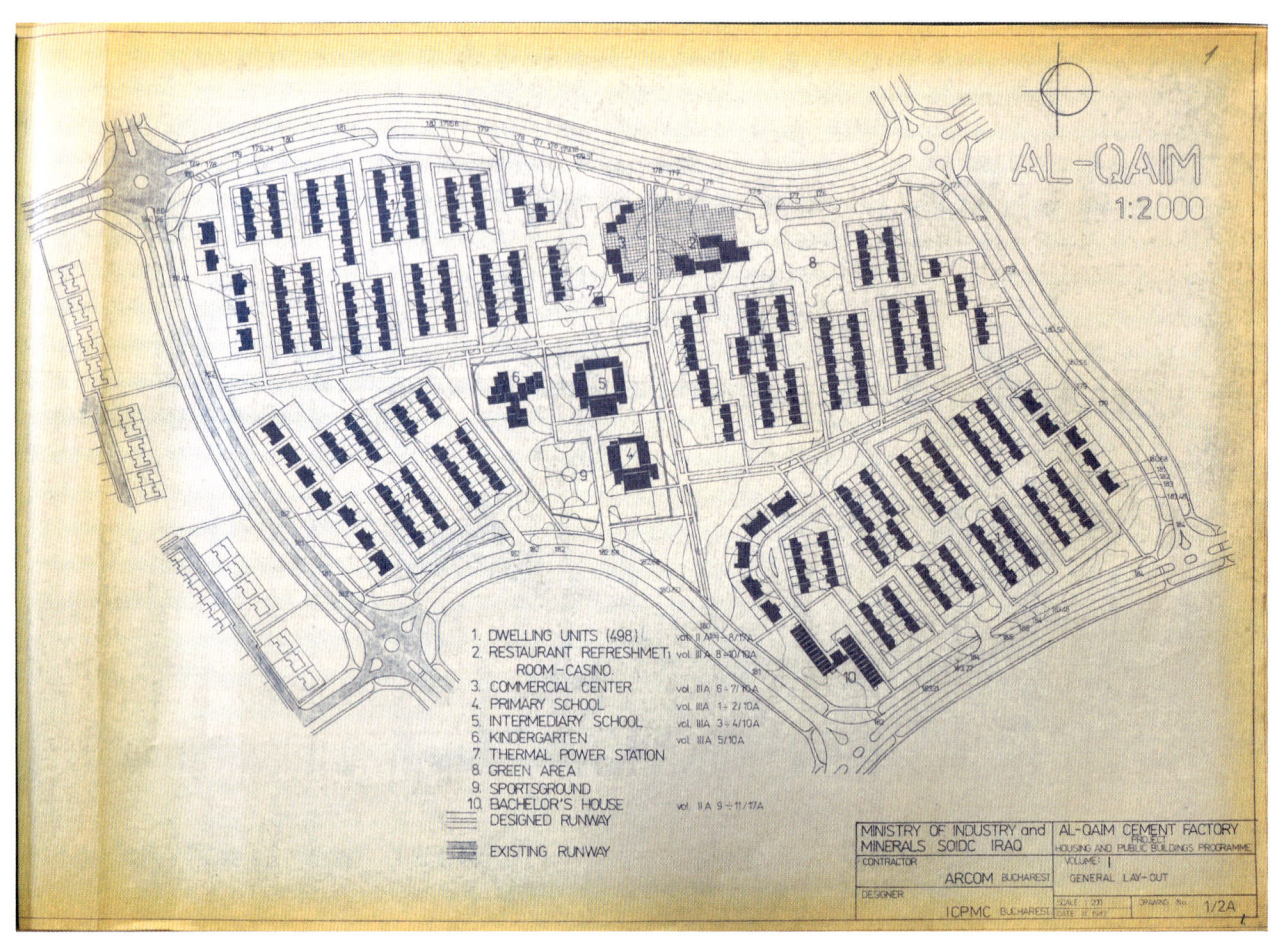

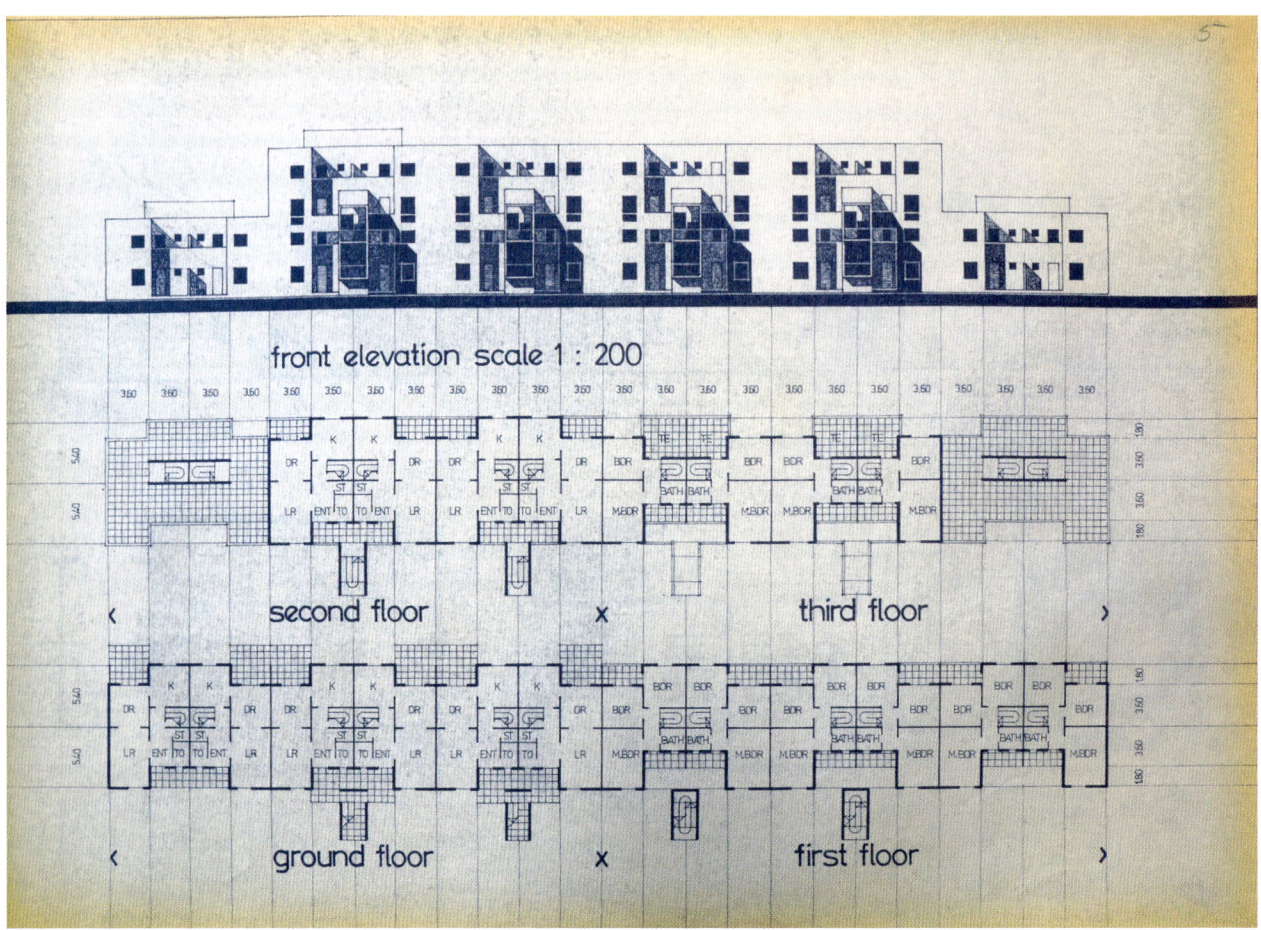

< 4.63. Layout of a residential district in al-Qaim, 1982. Arcom (Romania), Research and Design Institute for Building Materials Industry (ICPMC, Romania).

< 4.64. Housing in al-Qaim, 1982. Arcom (Romania), Research and Design Institute for Building Materials Industry (ICPMC, Romania).

in apartment blocks (1983). They were grouped along streets and squares, in line with the mid-1970s Romanian "Streets Law," which prescribed front alignments of buildings to economize on land and break with the monotony of housing estates that had been constructed during the previous decade.[311] The largest Romanian project for Iraq, on the territorial scale, was the design of twenty-three small urban centers at the perimeter of the Hillah-Kafel region by the Institute of Studies for Land Improvement from Bucharest. Within comprehensive environmental and economic planning, each settlement combined industry and social facilities, programmed according to Romanian norms.[312] In this way, the project supported the program of the Baath Party to equalize life conditions in cities and villages that were to characterize a "flourished socialist society" in Iraq.[313] It also gave credence to Cezar Lăzărescu's explanation of Romanian architectural export as a response to the demand by the "so-called Third World" for the "right to an urban life."[314]

During the war with Iran, Arcom's engagements in Iraq focused on industrial projects, some with military significance, and irrigation and land reclamation works, while other projects were delayed or remained unbuilt.[315] Romproiect's largest housing district in the Arab countries during the 1980s was built in Saida, Algeria, which included thirty-two hundred apartments and social facilities, completed by 1986 (figure 4.65).[316] "For Saida, everything was imported from Romania: design, workers, shuttering, trucks, cranes," recalled Gheorghe Radu Stănculescu, Romproiect's resident architect in Libya in the 1980s. Stănculescu called Saida a "turn-key city," which consisted of three distinct areas, designed according to the master plan by the municipal planning office of Saida.[317] Connected by green spaces, these areas were fully equipped with water, sewage, telecommunication, electricity, and gas infrastructure. They were built by the Romanian contractor together with streets and parking spaces (with streetlamps), kindergartens, schools, playgrounds, and sports facilities.[318] In comparison to Iraqi and Libyan housing layouts, the Algerian apartments were generally foreseen in lower standards, on par with apartments typically built in Romania. As in Romania, the number of variants of the layouts was small, and the construction system was simple and repetitive (although in Saida the corner apartment was changed to introduce a variation in volumes). The ensemble was also based on Romanian seismic norms, formulated in the wake of the devastating earthquake in Bucharest (1977), which became the basis for the seismic code for Algeria.[319] The apartments were designed for large families, as required by Algerian officials, and adorned with decorative elements, derived from local patterns.

Saida was one more example of how Romanian contractors applied the procedure of technological adaptation in order to exploit the opportunities that stemmed from the petrobarter system. Yet it also testified to the fact that this "exploitation" included the exploitation of Romania's own population. When interviewed today, several Romanian architects recalled that they resisted going to the North African construction sites, where they were housed in camps far away from cities, with little else to do than work. More generally, the gearing of Romania's economy toward export since the early 1980s resulted in drastic cuts on imports and a severe austerity program resulting in blackouts, freezing homes and workspaces, and food rationing.[320] This approach, again, contrasted with that of East Germany: while sharing with Romania the pressures of debt repayment, authorities in East Berlin resisted the diversion of resources from internal consumption. The consequences could be seen in the Tripoli planetarium project, which was largely constructed by a Swedish contractor because contractors in the GDR, that had been approached by Carl Zeiss, were tied to the execution of housing programs at the home market.[321]

CONCLUSION: A GENEALOGY OF ARCHITECTURE'S GLOBALIZATION

Had the Permanent Commission for Construction decided to organize a session about the three decades of engagements of Comecon members in Baghdad, the tone would likely have been celebratory. The Soviet delegation would have shown how Soviet-assisted industry provided the economic basis for city and country, and Hungarians, Czechs, Slovaks, and East Germans would have presented industrial facilities of their own. Poles would have showcased Baghdad's master plans and residential districts resulting from the GHPI, including those designed and constructed by Romanian firms. Bulgarians would have shown the Baghdad airport and water infrastructure for the capital, complemented by infrastructure projects by other Comecon countries. Picking up on the tone of Soviet publications about the world socialist system, a press release might have discussed the urbanization of Baghdad as one more example of the world socialist system "in action," based on the socialist international division of labor.

The reality on the ground was rather different. By the 1980s, Eastern European companies were competing against one another on the Iraqi

4.65. Technical fiche, prefabricated façade elements for Saida (Algeria), 1984. Romproiect (Romania), Arcom (Romania). *Arhitectura* 3 (1984): 53.

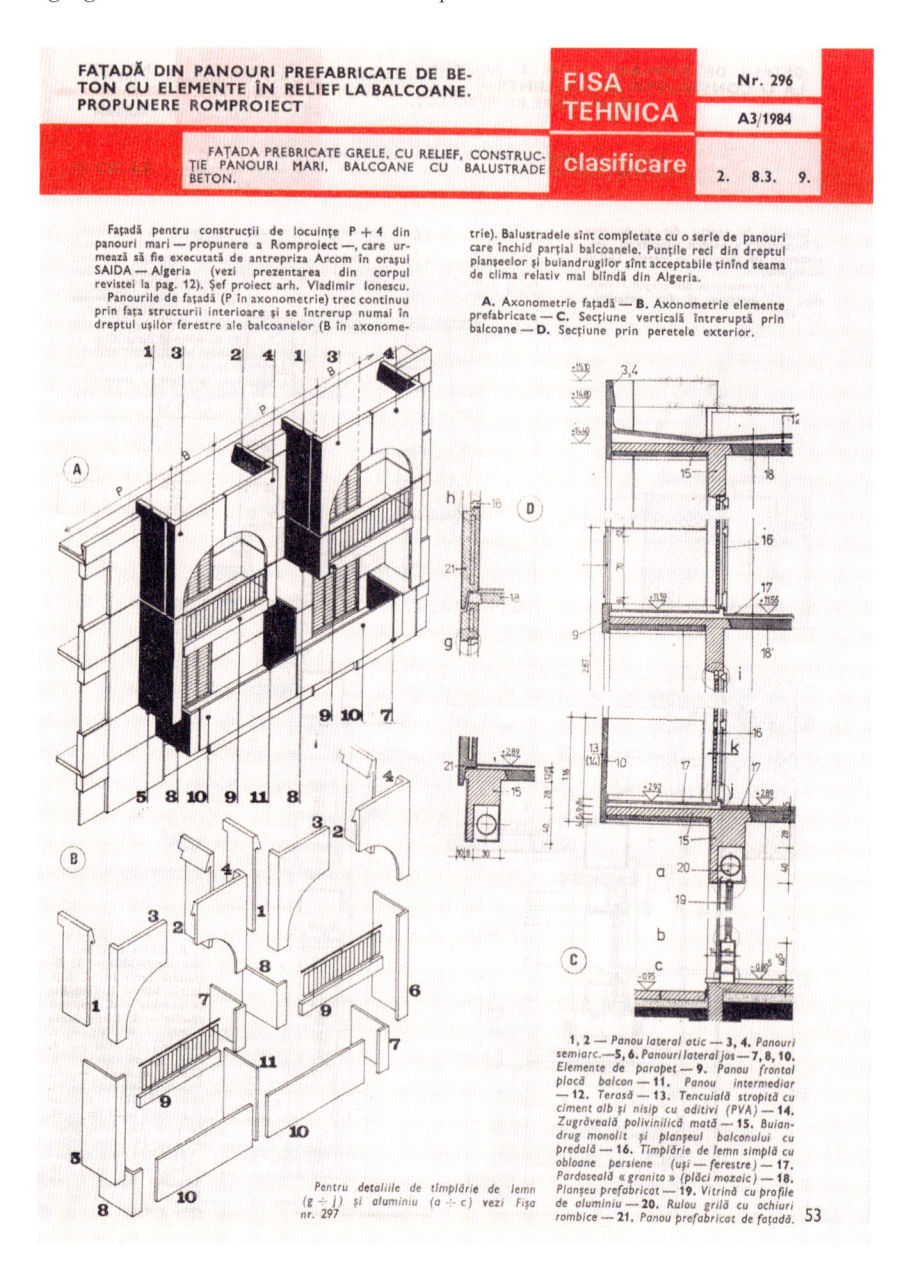

market, instead of coordinating their operations. However, the absence of a formal division of labor did not preclude the specificity of engagements of Polish, East German, and Romanian design institutes and contractors in Iraq. That specificity was very much on the mind of the protagonists of this chapter: thus the Poles reported on the impact of "Polish town planning methodologies" in Iraq, while GDR experts sent to the region assessed the demand for East Germany's "complex construction," and Romanian decision makers advocated their experience with economical prefabrication systems.[322] Such continuities may be seen in the work of other Eastern European actors in the Middle East, where Bulgarians drew on their experience in tourist urbanization, Czechs and Slovaks referred to their traditions of heritage conservation, and Hungarian firms advocated light prefabrication systems, whether developed in Hungary or adapted from Western systems.[323] At times, the entrance point for construction commissions lay in other types of expertise—in particular, in machinery and equipment that, when imported from the GDR to Baghdad or Tripoli, resulted in building commissions for East German contractors.

Rather than seeing these specific national experiences as ready-made for export and application abroad, this chapter has argued that they were actualized and reshaped when mobilized in the framework of the political economy of the world socialist system. This political economy, when translated into working conditions for the Polish team in Baghdad and their conditions of collaboration with their Iraqi counterparts, provided opportunities that planners took advantage of in order to apply the lessons of Polish urbanism. Similarly, Romanian and East German practices of typification, industrialization, and specialization of design and construction labor were mobilized, advanced, and modified in the framework of barter agreements, resulting in the procedure of technological adaptation and in bespoke type designs.

At the same time, export activities were path-dependent upon exporters' trajectories within the networks of the world socialist system. Those networks provided entry points to Iraq for the protagonists of this chapter, while opening further possibilities. A case in point was the chain of commissions linking Polish technical-assistance projects in Iraq with the Baghdad master plan, the GHPI, and individual contracts in Baghdad. Design-and-build commissions often started with complete industrial plants, which opened opportunities for other turn-key projects. Infrastructure commissions created economic advantages, at times unrelated to the original task. For instance, when constructing the Baghdad airport, Bulgarian companies used their machinery, construction materials, and labor, which they had already employed in Iraq on their construction sites of Soviet-designed military infrastructure. Each new commission was predicated upon decisions of Iraqi governmental and other actors who, in this way, shaped patterns of specialization for Eastern European enterprises in the Middle East. In turn, familiarity with specific technologies and compatibility with already acquired systems provided incentives for the Iraqi authorities in choosing technologies from socialist countries, even when knowing they were outdated.[324]

By the final decade of the Cold War, little remained of the emancipatory discourse of the world socialist system. However, the twenty years of experience that had been gained by then by several state-socialist actors in Baghdad offered them a head start in the opening of the Middle East to the global market of design and construction services. In particular, as I will argue in the next chapter, those actors benefited from previous experiences with local commissioners and international firms—experience that they had gained in the networks of the world socialist system. In that sense, rather than a failed project of architecture's globalization, the world socialist system needs to be seen as one of its pedigrees.

5.1. Municipality and Town Planning Department, Abu Dhabi, 1979–85. Tayeb Engineering, Bulgarproject (Bulgaria), Dimitar Bogdanov.

Chapter 5
Socialism within Globalization
Abu Dhabi and Kuwait City, 1979–90

Despite its seven stories, the building of Abu Dhabi's Municipality and Town Planning Department appears horizontal (figure 5.1). Its planes evoke permanence and cachet, while the taller structures around it stand for change and speculation, with office buildings, housing, and hotels being cyclically demolished and rebuilt at height to extract more revenue from the plots. Some structures in the vicinity have undergone such cycles more than once since the Municipality Building was opened in 1985, built as a result of an architectural competition won by Bulgarproject, the design branch of Technoexportstroy (TES).[1] The Bulgarian office had entered the competition for the Municipality Building as a joint venture with the Abu Dhabi–based firm of the Sudanese architect al-Tayeb Rabei Abdul Kareem (Tayeb Engineering). By the late 1970s, such collaboration between actors from socialist countries and local firms in the United Arab Emirates (UAE) and Kuwait had become widespread, with professionals from Bulgaria, East Germany, Czechoslovakia, Hungary, Poland, Romania, and Yugoslavia increasingly present on construction sites and in design offices in the Gulf.

This architectural production differed from what has been described thus far in this book. While previous chapters have focused on commissions resulting from political rapprochement with socialist countries, this was not the case with the UAE, which was a monarchy based on competitive markets and on Islam. At the time when TES and Tayeb participated in the Abu Dhabi tender, the UAE, independent since 1971, was a member of the Non-Aligned Movement (NAM), but it did not have diplomatic relations with Eastern European countries, which would be established only in the mid-1980s. Kuwait, independent since 1961, did maintain diplomatic exchanges with socialist countries; it set up joint intergovernmental committees with several among them, and accepted Soviet military assistance after the British military left the region in 1971.[2] However, the country's diplomats took pains to emphasize its neutrality in respect to Cold War confrontations. Kuwait joined NAM (1964), while it relied on Western powers in both economic and political terms, and secured its economic interests as a founding member of the Organization of the Petroleum Exporting Countries (OPEC). Along these lines, in a 1983 interview, a Kuwaiti diplomat specifically referred to the country's building industry when he argued that "Kuwait is a completely open market, no political consideration is given as far as the tender is concerned."[3]

That market was a lucrative one. Since independence, the governments of Kuwait and the UAE invested much of their soaring incomes from state-owned oil industries into urban development. Managers of Eastern European companies were eager to join other international actors in profiting from this construction boom. At that time, those companies had hardly been successful in their efforts to gain better access to Western European markets, because of policies of socialist countries themselves and because of the defensive reactions of the West.[4] In response, economic and political leaders in Eastern Europe hoped to offset such setbacks with an economic expansion toward North Africa and the Middle East, including the Gulf.

While engagements in Kuwait and the UAE in the late 1970s and 1980s were only a fraction of the export of construction and design services from socialist countries—the bulk of which continued to be received by Iraq, Libya, and Algeria—the focus on the Gulf shows a new type of global dimension in the work of Eastern European architects abroad. That dimension was not informed by a vision of the socialist path of development as an alternative to that of the West, nor by the project of reorganizing global economy within the world socialist system. This chapter shows instead the integration of architects, planners, and contractors from socialist countries into the emergent, Western-dominated, and increasingly globalized market of design and construction services by the end of the Cold War. This integration was facilitated by a set of adjustments and adaptations by professionals and firms from socialist countries to the Western technological, financial, legal, and aesthetic regimes that in large part regulated the design and construction markets in the Gulf. Those adjustments allowed individual and aggregate actors from Eastern Europe to compete against and collaborate with international actors in the UAE and Kuwait of the 1970s and 1980s.

Design labor was at the forefront of these processes. The previous chapter has shown that by the end of the Cold War, the main competitive advantage in the Middle East of contractors from socialist countries consisted of price differentials, mainly those of construction materials. However, such advantages were rarely transportable to the Gulf, either because of successful import-substitution policies, which resulted in the emergence of regional construction industries protected by import tariffs, or due to competition from South and East Asian contractors. By contrast, economists at socialist foreign trade organizations (FTOs) and managers of state design institutes argued that "intellectual" or "immaterial" export was better suited for Gulf markets, particularly since it came with a "low level of investment expenditure."[5]

In turn, architects, planners, and engineers were eager to embrace an emerging era in which "territorial boundaries that had kept most architects tied to a small set of national markets no longer make much sense for design firms capable of operating in the dynamic economies of the Gulf and China."[6] This is how one author recently described the globalization of architecture, for which Kuwait and the UAE have been paradigmatic examples. However, such accounts to date have largely focused on two groups of actors: migrant workers, whose daily practices constitute a "globalization from below," and an architectural elite shaping urban icons. The latter group has included large corporate offices from Western Europe and North America, international boutique firms, architects belonging to the emerging star system, and signature designers of "Arab" architecture, based in the region or elsewhere.[7] In this chapter, I extend this spectrum by discussing actors from socialist countries: contractors including TES, design institutes such as Bulgarproject, joint ventures between Eastern European companies and Gulf entrepreneurs, and individual architects employed in private design offices and governmental planning institutions in the region. In reviewing their work in the Gulf, this chapter takes issue with accounts of scholars who have reduced the agency of Eastern Europe in architectural globalization to a "new market," that was "created" for Western firms after the end of the Cold War.[8]

More fundamentally, this chapter inscribes socialist worldmaking into the genealogy of architectural globalization since the late twentieth century. While actors from Eastern Europe working in the Gulf did not refer to ideas of socialist solidarity, the work of many among them benefited from their earlier experience, expertise, personal contacts, and professional reputations gained during the commissions in countries of North Africa and the Middle East since the late 1950s. Over the course of those exchanges, individual and aggregate actors from socialist countries were exposed to and acquired operative knowledge of Western design and construction regimes that, by the 1970s, were being widely imported to the Gulf. These included American and British building norms and specification standards, financial frameworks recommended by international institutions, increasingly computerized design environments, building-management systems, and construction materials, technologies, and machinery from Western Europe and North America. By highlighting these continuities, I argue that the integration of Eastern European actors into the global architectural market during the late Cold War ought to be seen as part of a longer history of socialist solidarity and worldwide cooperation.

In the case of the Gulf, such integration was based on yet another lesson that architects, planners, and contractors from Eastern Europe had learned in the Arab world. During their earlier exchanges in North Africa and the Middle East, they were confronted with the requirement to account for "Arab" or "Islamic" culture. These requirements were also written into regulations and competition briefs in the Gulf in the 1970s and 1980s, such as the brief for the Abu Dhabi Municipality Building competition. Bulgarian designers' response to that brief resulted in an architecture that differed from what was described in this book's previous chapters. Arches, ornamental decoration in the conference hall, and the historical silhouette of the mosque in the Abu Dhabi building hardly fit the tradition of the modern movement—however modified and "adapted"—to which most of the buildings discussed earlier had subscribed. Similar motives can be found in TES's other designs in the UAE, in particular in the Municipality Building in Al Ain, finished in the early 1980s. Housing districts, social facilities, and public buildings that architects from other socialist countries designed in Kuwait offer even more exuberant examples. These designs included elements borrowed from the historical architecture of the Arab world, such as a *mashrabiyya*, lattice work used on balconies or bay windows, and a *muquarnas*, a pointed niche projecting over those below and often used in vaults.

SOCIALISM WITHIN GLOBALIZATION

Those buildings conformed to the expectations of Gulf elites disenchanted with urbanization patterns in the region since the 1950s. Two decades later, Emirati and Kuwaiti elites continued to see Western technological expertise as indispensable for the urbanization of the Gulf. However, they were increasingly critical about ways in which architectural and planning concepts had been applied in the region after World War II. While destruction of the vernacular urban fabric and the waning of inherited forms of sociability were a consequence of overarching social changes instigated by Gulf elites after the oil boom, by the late 1970s, many in the region attributed this loss of pre-oil urbanity to the import of foreign architecture, sometimes associated with the modern movement and with the urbanism of the International Congresses of Modern Architecture (CIAM). In response, officials, journalists, and scholars, as well as private and public clients, demanded architectural designs reflecting "Arab" or "Islamic" culture and tradition.

This double demand of modern technology and cultural specificity puzzled commentators, both contemporary practitioners on the ground and scholars writing retrospective accounts. Some among them identified these seemingly contradictory requirements with the opposed vectors of "homogenization" and "localization," which they saw as intrinsic to global urbanization processes.[9] However, the reading of the Municipality Building in Abu Dhabi in the first part of the chapter will bring to the fore an entanglement—rather than an opposition—between the technological and cultural expertises of TES. I will argue that this work was not informed by a dichotomy between the global and the local, the universal and the specific, but rather by a simultaneous movement of deterritorialization and reterritorialization of knowledge gained during previous TES work in Arab countries.

By the final decade of the Cold War, such ability was explicitly required from experts on foreign contracts, as I will show in the second part of the chapter, which focuses on Eastern European architects in Kuwait. By the 1980s, professional profiles specified by socialist FTOs privileged portable knowledge over place-bound experiences, such as those of postwar reconstruction of Eastern Europe, which legitimized earlier export projects from socialist countries. Such a profile remains in demand today in architectural offices around the world, including offices in which some of this chapter's protagonists work, either in the Gulf or in Eastern Europe, to which they returned after the end of the Cold War.

REFLEXIVE URBANIZATION IN THE GULF

The double requirement of cultural and technological competence comes to the fore in the brief of the competition for the design of the Municipality and Town Planning Department Building in Abu Dhabi, issued in April 1979. In addition to the detailed functional program and the list of documents to be submitted for the competition, that brief included a more general statement about the envisaged ensemble, which was "supposed to play an important role in the visual organization of the site and of the city."[10]

In particular, the design was expected to express "two important ideals." First, it was to reflect the city's "growing importance on both the political and commercial grounds."[11] In this way, the brief hinted at the rising political role of Abu Dhabi as the capital of the UAE, and the city's economic potency benefiting from the export of oil since 1962. The requirement to match the scale of the expanding city was reflected in the brief's expectation of a plaza (with a "flag site" and possibly a "festival area") and in the sheer scale of the building, which foresaw an increase of the municipality's staff to around fifteen hundred employees.[12] This large and complex building required, according to the brief, the application of "international technology," such as modern filing equipment and computerized systems.[13] Second, the "contemporary image" of the city conveyed by the building was supposed to be "framed in the values inherited by the Arab-Islamic culture:" a postulate that reflected the desire of Abu Dhabi's elites to correct patterns of post-oil urbanization in the region.[14]

Disenchantment with Post-Oil Urbanization

The double postulate of technological modernity and "Arab-Islamic culture" was conveyed already in the master plan of Abu Dhabi, delivered by the Egyptian planner Abdulrahman Makhlouf during his tenure as director of the city's Town Planning Department (1968–76).[15] In contrast to previous master plans, including that by British planners William Halcrow & Partners (1962), Makhlouf foresaw accelerating growth of the city, and adjusted the projected population from a hundred thousand inhabitants in the Halcrow plan to a quarter of a million. This size, argued Makhlouf, would create economies of scale that would allow the financing of large infrastructural projects, including the airport, desalination and electricity plants, new bridges, the Corniche, or the promenade around the sea, as well as new administrative buildings and public transport facilities (figure 5.2).[16]

Many of them, including the Main Bus Terminal designed by TES (1980–91), were foreseen in the central, mixed-use spine of the city, along which housing and industrial areas were allocated. In the years to come, the plan became a tool for implementing the state policy of redistribution of oil-generated wealth among citizens of Abu Dhabi who were entitled to three and in some instances four pieces of land, to be used for residential, commercial, and industrial purposes. These fast-paced, real estate-driven urbanization processes in the city were overseen by the Khalifah Committee, the body set up in 1976 to distribute state-owned land to Emirati citizens, to develop the land on their behalf, and to approve commercial and residential building projects.[17] The designation system for street names and building numbers for the expanding city was provided by Poland's Miastoprojekt-Kraków (figure 5.3).[18]

This ambitious vision of Abu Dhabi's growth was complemented in the master plan by attention paid to the city's cultural specificity. The Bahrain-based *Gulf Weekly Mirror* reported shortly after the delivery of the plan that "as well as being as up to date as possible and purely functional, it was decided at a very early stage that Abu Dhabi should uphold the more traditional Arab characteristics."[19] In Makhlouf's recollections, his appointment resulted from the wish of Sheikh Zayed, installed as the Emirate's ruler in 1966, to work with an "Arab planner," rather than with designers with whom he would need to communicate by means of translators.[20] Educated in Cairo and Munich, and experienced as a UN expert for town planning in Saudi Arabia and as a planner in Cairo, Makhlouf rethought the modernist concept of a neighborhood unit according to Islamic principles. In particular, he defined the size of an "Islamic neighborhood unit" by the catchment area of the mosque, located within a walking distance of the residents, and clustered with a souk.[21]

Makhlouf's master plan shows that upon the announcement of the Municipality Building competition, there was nothing new in the juxtaposition of an enthusiasm for Abu Dhabi's growth and the desire to shape it according to an "Arab-Islamic tradition." UAE's accelerating urbanization over the course of the 1970s confirmed to the elites of the Emirate that this was the right direction. The contemporary development of Dubai, with its thirty-nine-story World Trade Centre (John Harris & Partners, 1979), and tall buildings around the Creek, found little appreciation in the UAE capital.[22] The difference between Abu Dhabi and Dubai comes to the fore in the comparison of two office buildings, each designed in 1979 in the two cities by

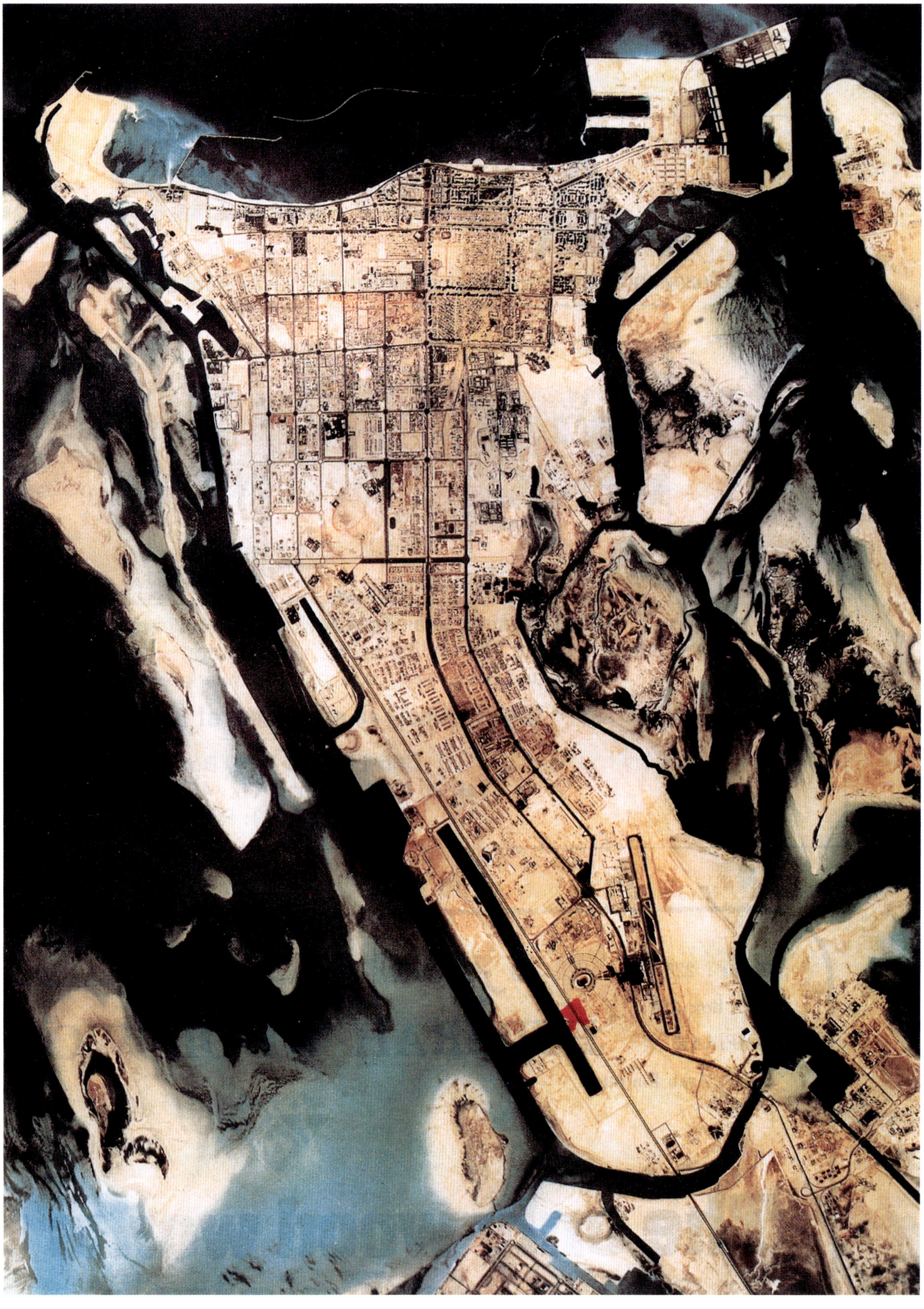

< 5.2. Aerial view of Abu Dhabi, early 1980s.

5.3. System of street names and building numbers, Abu Dhabi, early 1980s. Miastoprojekt-Kraków (Poland). "System nazewnictwa ulic i numeracji budynków w Abu Dhabi," n.d.

the same architect (Gibb, Petermuller & Partners) and for the same client (the UAE Currency Board), and constructed from the same materials. While the façade of the building in Abu Dhabi (currently the Central Bank of the UAE) is composed of monumental ogee arches clad in travertine and filled with decorative aluminum grilles, the building in Dubai is an orthogonal structure with curtain walling of aluminum and solar control glass.[23] When presented with spectacular designs such as an offshore tower with a museum and a revolving restaurant, Abu Dhabi's elites decided to reject them and to invest in a new marina instead.[24]

Even clearer warnings came from Kuwait. The Abu Dhabi government followed closely, and critically, the tendencies of post-oil urbanization in the city-state up north. Kuwait's fast pace of urbanization since the growth of the export of crude oil in the early 1950s intensified after independence. In the course of the 1960s, its government embarked on state-led and centrally planned urban development (including housing, schooling, health, and technical infrastructure) and the creation of social welfare for citizens.[25] The ruler, Abdullah al-Salem, bought the previously powerful merchant elite out of politics by means of generous land acquisition schemes and by privileging Kuwaitis in the economy at the expense of foreign nationals.[26]

Over the course of the 1970s, Kuwait was often the first to receive new architectural typologies entering the Gulf. Luxury hotels combined with other programs continued to pop up; governmental complexes reached a new scale; high-rise housing blocks were tested; and large-scale commercial centers were introduced (following the example of Qatar).[27] Announcing the end of the "all work and no play" lifestyle in Kuwait, public beaches, new restaurants, museums, and a theater were built on the redeveloped waterfront, as well as an amusement park.[28] In order to accommodate the building boom, the ten-floor ceiling was abandoned in Kuwait in 1977 (until then surpassed only by special permission), ushering in the way to the first generation of high-rises, some of which were co-designed by architects

SOCIALISM WITHIN GLOBALIZATION

from socialist countries (figure 5.4).[29] These populated the skyline along with telecommunication towers, bank headquarters, including that of the National Bank of Kuwait (Arne Jacobsen, 1976), new spaces of representation such as the new parliament building (Jørn Utzon, 1985), the Ministry of Foreign Affairs (Reima and Raili Pietilä, 1983), and the State Mosque (Mohamed Makiya, 1983), as well as new international institutions, such as the Kuwait Fund for Arab Economic Development in Kuwait City (The Architects Collaborative, or TAC, with PACE, 1973 and 1978).[30]

When photographed for international journals, these buildings conveyed the image of a "new Eldorado" for architects, as the ironic title of a *Domus* report on Gulf architecture put it (1979).[31] For a pedestrian, the view was entirely different, however, and a visitor to Kuwait wrote in 1983 that these buildings were "free-stand[ing] among parked cars, the ruins of what remains of Kuwait's stock of single-storey courtyard family houses and the dusty walk-ups from the 1950 building boom."[32] This landscape resulted from the combination of the state policy of land acquisition and state-sponsored resettlement programs, which followed the spatial reorganization of Kuwait foreseen in the master planning by Minoprio, Spencely & Macfarlane (1951). Under this policy, the state was buying land from property-owning families within the old town walls at purposely inflated rates, both to distribute oil revenue among citizens and to open these areas for the construction of a commercial and business "city center" foreseen by the master plan. Around the green belt, which replaced the old town walls, the master plan allocated a fan of new residential suburbs, equipped with social facilities and linked by a system of radial and ring roads. By the 1970s, most of the pre-oil urban population of the city center was relocated to suburban houses built on government-distributed land, or to government-built housing for lower-income Kuwaitis. In this way, the city center was left for development, which then did not occur, however, since the inflated land values made speculation more profitable. The areas cleared of old courtyard houses in Sharq and Jibla were largely left empty, used as parking lots for commuters from the suburbs who worked in the few realized parts of the master plan, such as Fahad al-Salem Street (figure 5.5).[33]

Already in the mid-1960s, Palestinian architect and urban planner Saba George Shiber, employed by the Kuwait Municipality, regretted the missed opportunities in the city-state.[34] If several designers in the 1950s and 1960s had pledged allegiance to an "oriental character" of architecture or an "Islamic-Arabic approach" in design, such statements rarely amounted to more than the use of ornamental sunshades or colonnaded passages.[35] Shiber characterized the ten previous years in Kuwait by "economically wasteful" land-use planning, "visually dubious" architectural and aesthetic design, and disappointing master-planning and programming.[36]

Some of this criticism was taken into account by the next master plan, commissioned from British consultants Buchanan & Partners in 1968, which aimed at giving the city a new framework of development and at correcting its perceived hindrances of growth. Revised in 1977 and endorsed by the Municipal Council, the plan suggested a linear development following the coast (figure 5.6). Housing districts as well as two new towns envisaged in the south and in the north of Kuwait City directed discussions among professionals toward questions of urbanity specific for the city-state. These discussions were behind some of the more innovative architectural designs of the decade.[37]

By that time, architects, journalists, and intellectuals called for the preservation of the little that was left of historical Kuwaiti architecture. The 1981 revision of the master plan of Kuwait declared the Behbehani compound, the American Mission, the traditional souk, and part of the Sharq area frontage to be conservation areas. The plan singled out several buildings, including the Naif Palace, that were to be preserved, together with all

5.4. Al-Fintas towers, Fintas, 1982–84. Arabi Engineers Office, Włodzimierz Gleń (project architect), J. Damija, N. Fatteh.

5.5. View of Kuwait City with the Audit Bureau Headquarters Building, 1986–96. KEG, Wojciech Jarząbek, Edward Lach.

SOCIALISM WITHIN GLOBALIZATION

mosques.[38] Some of the work that followed, including the reconstruction of the city gates, new programming of several historic houses, and the reconstruction of Kuwait's first police station at Safat Square, was done by Czech and Slovak architects in collaboration with Kuwaiti offices (figure 5.7).[39] Nostalgia for traditional ways of life was expressed, for instance, in the rebuilding of the heritage Seaman's Day Village (1986).[40] As scholars have pointed out, these commodified spaces were a far cry from the intertwined, mixed, integrated spaces of the pre-oil town.[41]

Similar efforts took place elsewhere in the Gulf, including the UAE, where professionals compiled lists of buildings and ensembles to be preserved, among them the Bastakia Quarter on the southern side of Dubai Creek.[42] New institutions emerging in the region and beyond granted support to these efforts, including the Arab Urban Development Institute in Riyadh (since 1980), new UNESCO initiatives, and the Aga Khan Foundation.[43] By awarding prizes to the Water Towers in Kuwait (Sune and Joe Lindström of VBB and Malene Bjørn of Bjørn & Bjørn Design, 1977) and the Hajj Terminal (Skidmore, Owings & Merrill, or SOM, 1981), the Aga Khan Foundation set influential examples of what it considered an "Islamic architecture that successfully retains traditional character and identity, while clearly expressing the demands, social aspirations and, where appropriate, the technology of the 20th century."[44]

The border between preservation and design became increasingly fluid in the work of architects practicing in the Gulf, whether local or foreign. This included the designs of Mohamed Makiya and Rifat Chadirji in Iraq, Kuwait, and the UAE.[45] Kuwaiti architect Ghazi Sultan worked both on the renovation of the Old Kuwait Courts (1983–87) and on a number of designs that aimed at introducing an intermediary scale into the enormous spaces of Kuwait's Waterfront Project (1988).[46] Hassan Fathy, Egyptian architect of international renown, designed the Beit al-Reihan house around four courtyards, a project praised in the Saudi-based architectural journal *Albenaa* (Construction) as following "the pattern of the Arabian palaces which observe the Arabian Kuwaiti environment characteristics."[47]

By far the most extensive attempt in Kuwait to "reflect and combine the progressive traditions of Arabic and Islamic cultural heritage with the creativity of modern technology" was the design of the Amiri Diwan, an ensemble housing the ruler's new palace, the crown prince and prime minister's office, the council of ministers offices, and the secretariat (figure 5.8).[48] The complex was located on the waterfront adjacent to and in front of the historic Sief Palace, which was integrated into the ensemble. The design was delivered by the Kuwait-based office Archicentre, founded by Iraqi architect Akram Ogaily in partnership with Kuwaiti engineer Jasem Qabazard, and with a number of collaborators from abroad.[49] Besides Finnish, British, and American experts, they included a large team of architects from Czechoslovakia, employed by Archicentre. This group was headed by Vaclav Bašta, Ogaily's former professor at the University of Baghdad (figure 5.9).[50]

Bašta's teachings from Baghdad were reflected in the design of the Amiri Diwan, which employed "elements and components of Arab-Islamic architecture" from Asia, Africa, and Europe. Among them, the designers listed the principle of an integrated urban scale, gradation of privacy, contrast between juxtaposed spaces, the typology of courtyards and porticos, and the use of decorative bricklaying, tiles, and screens. These elements were depicted in numerous collages included into the documentation, and the new ensemble was itself conceived as a collage containing a heterogeneous collection of structures constructed within the boundaries of the Sief Palace through the twentieth century (figure 5.10).[51] Beyond the compound, the designers saw their work as aiming at a restoration of an "organic" connection between the palace and the city, from which it was separated by the Arabian Gulf Road.[52]

> 5.6. "Metropolitan Structure Plan Map," 1977. Municipality of Kuwait, Shankland Cox Partnership (UK).

> 5.7. "Al-Shaab Gate. Preliminary Field Survey." State Institute for the Restoration of Historic Towns and Monuments (SURPMO, Czechoslovakia). Ministry of Public Works, Kuwait; Strojexport (Czechoslovakia); SURPMO (Czechoslovakia), "Preservation of Kuwaiti Historic Monuments," 1985.

METROPOLITAN STRUCTURE PLAN MAP 1977

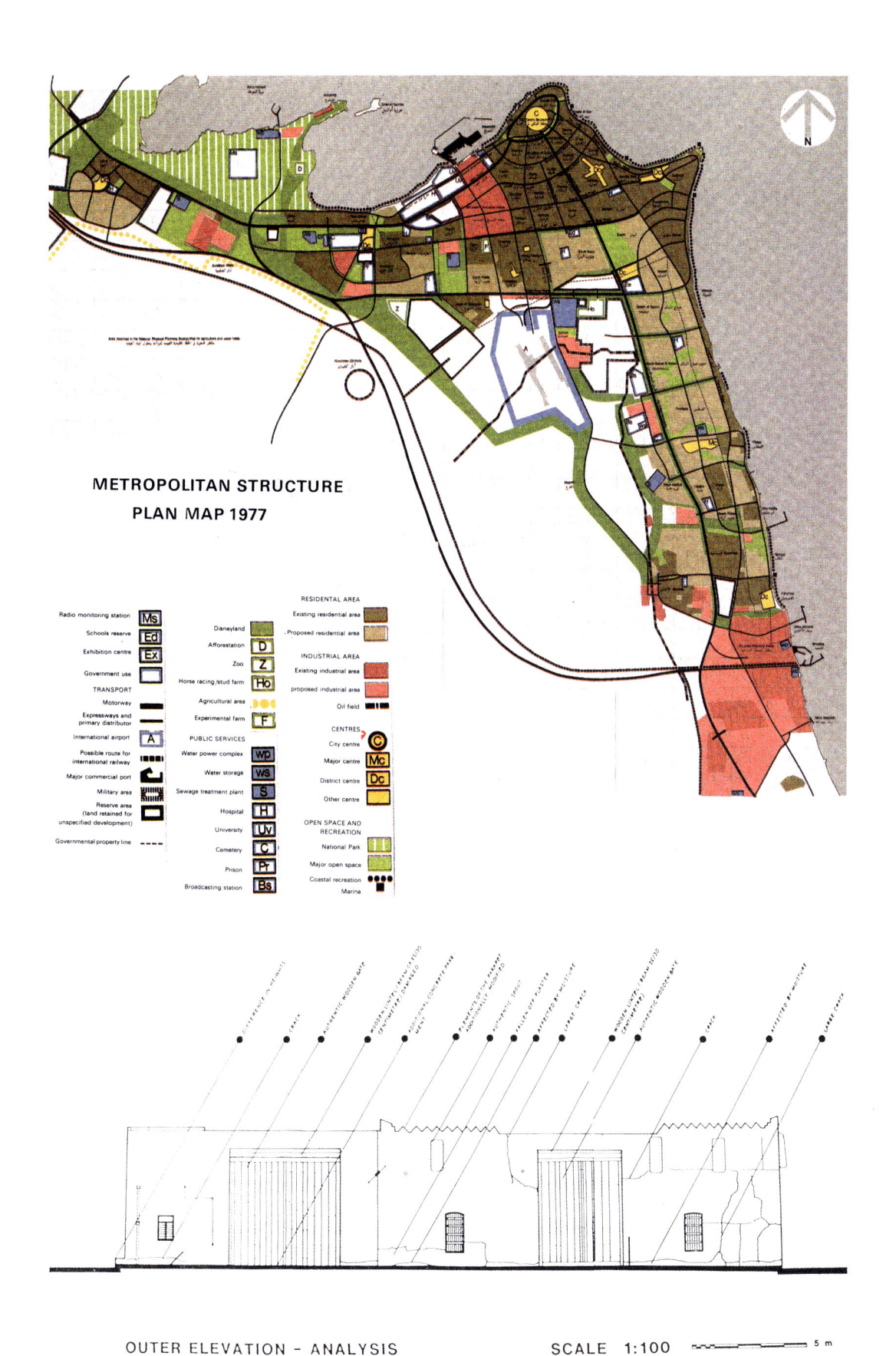

OUTER ELEVATION - ANALYSIS   SCALE 1:100

SOCIALISM WITHIN GLOBALIZATION

250 CHAPTER 5

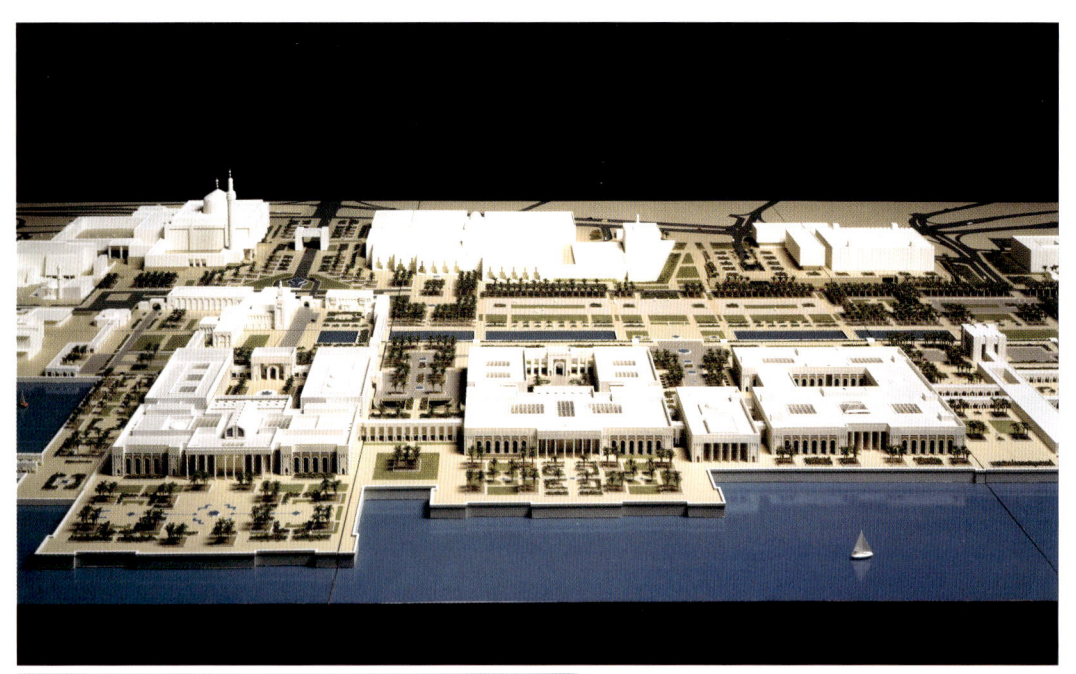

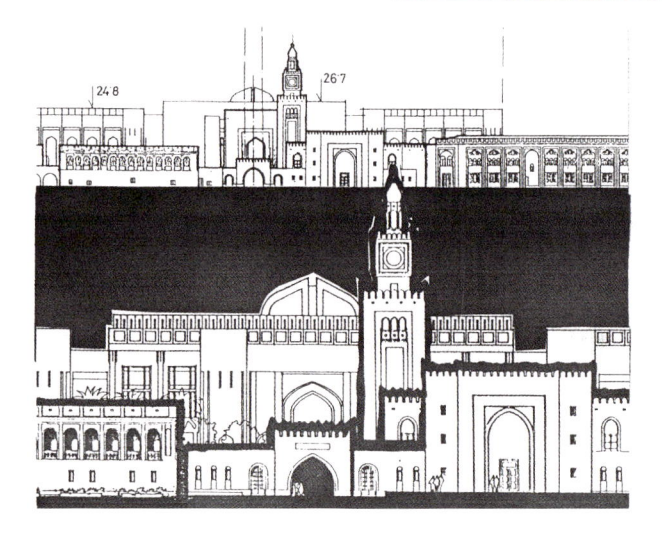

< 5.8. Amiri Diwan and Council of Ministers, Kuwait, model photograph. Archicentre. Ministry of Public Works, Kuwait; Archicentre, "Amiri Diwan and Council of Ministers. Predevelopment Study. Conceptual Design Stage 4. Technical Report," vol. II-A, n.d.

< 5.9. Amiri Diwan and Council of Ministers under construction, 1980s. Archicentre.

< 5.10. "Architectural Design—Sief Palace." Archicentre. Ministry of Public Works, Kuwait; Archicentre, "Amiri Diwan and Council of Ministers. Predevelopment Study. Conceptual Design Stage 4. Technical Report," vol. II-A, n.d., 2–37.

While in the case of the Amiri Diwan such connection would be merely visual, the recommendation to restrict traffic, to give more attention to pedestrians, and to slow down the pace of Kuwait's inner-city spaces was in tune with the "decelerated growth" in the 1980s Gulf and the more reflexive mood that followed. The crash of Kuwait's unofficial stock exchange, the souk al-Manakh (1982), and falling oil prices, which hit municipal budgets in the UAE, were followed by a slowdown in construction activities. In turn, clients started to pay more attention to operating and maintenance costs, and to the quality of construction and materials.[53] The architecture of the postwar decades was revisited too, often very critically. A case in point was the Kuwaiti documentary film *Kuwaiti Architecture: A Lost Identity*, which built up a contrast between traditional architecture, including that of the British protectorate, and post-oil development when "an attack on tradition and Kuwait's architectural identity was launched." The offscreen narrative pointed out that the destruction of courtyard houses in the 1950s had been paralleled by the construction of villas around the ring roads, "designed by architects, complete strangers to the architectural identity of Kuwait." According to the documentary, they were "odd in form and structure," "unsuitable to the needs of the inhabitants," and included balconies "only to be filled with dust and sand."[54] Local critics, among them Huda al-Bahar, condemned these buildings as an "architectural extravaganza, a carnival, a showroom of copied styles and motifs."[55]

By the 1980s, such a tone became widespread in the general and professional press in the Gulf, which lamented that the cities in the region were becoming "a dumping ground" for "alien architectural landmarks."[56] Karim Jamal, a planner in Kuwait, argued that the only expertise that could be passed on by "Japanese, East European and, above all, Western firms" working in the Middle East was "how not to do it."[57] A younger generation of municipal planners and officials pointed out that while the planning legislation was often based on UK regulations, the British framework of enforcement was lacking, while conservation policies adapted from abroad were hardly applicable to vernacular architecture in the Gulf, and Western standards in traffic planning sometimes turned out to be inadequate.[58] This critique was complemented by the observation that foreign architects and planners unaware of the cultural and environmental settings of the region were not the only ones to blame. Local clients who demanded fashionable international forms ("at all costs, but with little taste") were also responsible for the widely deplored condition of Gulf cities.[59]

At times, this critique was explicitly directed at "modern architecture" as it was introduced to the region during the post-oil era. Some of those voices consciously echoed the postmodern discourse, and professionals in the region closely followed the planning of Baghdad, where Rifat Chadirji, together with Denise Scott Brown, Robert Venturi, Ricardo Bofill, Arthur Erickson, and Martin van Treeck were rethinking the city's urbanity.[60] Authors writing for *Albenaa* targeted forms that they considered alien to the Gulf, including apartment blocks with oversized spaces between the buildings ("similar to the theory of Le Corbusier"), private villas with large spaces around them, the car-oriented city, and the gridiron plan.[61] The appreciation of the courtyard house as a flexible and multipurpose space was opposed to the reductive understanding of the division and separation of functions attributed to modern architecture.[62] Initial enthusiasm for designs such as the al-Sawaber estate in Kuwait City (Arthur Erickson, 1981) as "modernistic" and a "complete break-away from the stereotyped, impersonal, rectangular blocks of brick and cement" was quickly juxtaposed with reservations concerning high-rise blocks, as not allowing for privacy and hence against Islamic tradition.[63]

Occupants of state-funded housing in Kuwait and the UAE concurred. Interviewed for the first time in the mid-1970s by Kuwait's National Housing

Authority (NHA), many expressed the wish to maintain continuity with the traditional uses of dwelling spaces. The interviewees opted for one-story courtyard houses with a usable roof space, and a paved courtyard with some area for planting. The *diwaniyya* (plural: *diwawin*), a reception room for male visitors, accessible from both inside and outside the dwelling unit, was requested, too.[64] While in pre-oil Kuwait only the wealthy could afford a diwaniyya, the construction of bigger houses meant that such rooms could be also included for middle- and lower-income classes.[65]

Similar studies were carried out in the city of Al Ain in the UAE. Interviews with inhabitants determined that the open plan was inappropriate and inefficient. They suggested including a separate service quarters and setting apart a visitors area (called *majlis* in the UAE), with an independent entrance so that guests could be received without affecting the household.[66] The Town and Planning Department in Al Ain began to account for such preferences in its designs, and the department's architect argued that "it is up to a new generation of local architects to frame a response to people's expectations, and develop a local style which can give clear expression to cultural identity."[67]

The Labor of Mediation

These discussions convey the sentiment that clients and the broad public in the Gulf wanted the best of both worlds. Commenting on the designs of Falah al-Salman of Atkins' Dubai office, a journalist explained that a "historic-reference approach to architectural design is proving attractive to those clients whose preferences are for buildings that are modern in terms of function and equipment but which, nevertheless, retain links with the local past."[68] The confidence of al-Salman in his ability to deliver upon such expectation contrasts with the uncertainty of many Western architects no longer believing in modernism's global remit; in the words of Paul Andreu, French designer of Abu Dhabi's International Terminal (1982), "building in a foreign country became more problematic since modernism has gone wrong."[69]

In response, a Los Angeles-based consultant advised architectural and construction firms working in the Gulf to have two designs at hand: one that "harmonizes with the physical and historical environment," and a second that was "Western."[70] Such versatility in design approaches was also offered by Peter Mlodzianowski, who in 1977 became the head of the newly established Abu Dhabi branch of London's Fitzroy Robinson Partnership.[71] Within the contextual approach of this firm, expressed in its high-quality buildings in the City of London, Mlodzianowski was "equally at ease composing in either modern or traditional vernacular styles of architecture." The latter referred to the design of the Ministry of Foreign Affairs in Muscat (Oman, 1985), which, at the explicit request of the client, was given the appearance of the white stucco architecture of Muscat's Old Town. The former referred to the Bank of Credit and Commerce International in Dubai (BCCI, 1979) and several buildings in Abu Dhabi, including the BCCI building (1978) and the building of the Arab Monetary Fund (1982), both at the Corniche, as well as the Bank of Oman (1985) (figure 5.11).[72]

Yet this opposition between "modern" and "vernacular" style proved to be hardly clear-cut, and Abu Dhabi's BCCI building was a case in point. Described by the designer as "uncompromisingly international late-twentieth century style," the twelve-story office building with a penthouse on top stood out as the highest structure in late-1970s Abu Dhabi. It was also cutting-edge in terms of building technology, with careful concrete details, an innovative façade, and a sophisticated air-conditioning system.[73] At the same time, the building conveyed the taste of Abu Dhabi clients for decoration. Making use of the Emirate's bylaws, which allowed for a meter-and-a-half

5.11. The BCCI (1978) and the Arab Monetary Fund (1982) buildings, Abu Dhabi. Fitzroy Robinson Partnership (UK), Peter Mlodzianowski. "The Buildings and Projects of the Fitzroy Robinson Partnership in the Middle East," n.d.

cantilever above the mezzanine level, Mlodzianowski designed arches connecting the mezzanine of the building with the cantilevered upper floor.[74] Together with sculpturally formed corners and arabesque ornaments on the cornice, these details identified three spots where architectural decoration would not diminish rentable space, and all three were widely copied in the decade to come, shaping the image of today's Abu Dhabi.

The new building code of the Abu Dhabi Emirate (1981), which allowed a protrusion of the façade for "architectural decoration," prepared the formalization of the requirement for "Islamic" or "Arabic type architecture."[75] While such a requirement had been included in competition briefs for governmental and prestige buildings in Abu Dhabi since the 1970s, the Emirate's elites saw the need to inscribe it into the building law.[76] The personal proclivity of Sheikh Zayed for traditional forms found its expression in the "Islamic Decree," signed by the ruler in 1984. The decree obliged the municipality, city-planning, and works departments to ensure that "the designs of public and private buildings and services premises—whether done by your apparatuses or assigned to consultants—reflect the Arab, Islamic character and the history of the civilization of the region." Failure to comply would result in the refusal of building licenses for private or public investors.[77]

Following the decree, architectural designs submitted to the Khalifah Committee needed to be approved by the Heritage Section of the Town Planning Department.[78] The municipality of Al Ain followed suit, and in 1987, the city introduced the requirement that plans for buildings in the city

SOCIALISM WITHIN GLOBALIZATION

"reflect the Islamic style of design."[79] One year later, the Committee for the Preservation of the Arab Islamic Architectural Style was created.[80] These regulations were not accompanied by specific bylaws, and an architect working in Abu Dhabi since the late 1970s recalls only one governmental commission accompanied by stylistic guidelines, which consisted of patterns of arches.[81]

Nor was much explanation given to the request for "Arab-Islamic culture" in the competition brief of the building for the Abu Dhabi Municipality and Town Planning Department. The twenty-four architects invited to the competition were encouraged to "put...inspirations from Islamic architecture...in the contemporary abstract formal organization."[82] Such ambiguous juxtapositions were characteristic for the discourse of Abu Dhabi officials assessing new buildings in the city, journalists reflecting upon architectural designs and completed structures in the region, and several historians seeking to provide design guidelines to prevent both "imported vulgarity" of generic Western architecture and "copied vernacular."[83] This was also the preferred discourse of architects of otherwise disparate design credos, who jumped upon the opportunity to explain their own work to the broader public and to the clients as that of "mediation" between "Islamic" or "Arab" culture, and its various "others."[84] Whether educated in and committed to the modern tradition, or subscribing to postmodernism as the new architectural mainstream, architects in the Gulf of the 1970s and 1980s widely presented their work as the production of images, experiences, and regulations that would perform such mediation. Some among them speculated about trans-historical forms derived from a sequence of time-specific appearances to be used as operative diagrams for new spatial organizations.[85] Others suggested ways in which trans-historical urban experiences, reconstructed by means of a phenomenological rhythm-analysis, can be respected and sustained by contemporary means.[86] Yet others proposed to normalize the envelope of the building as a recognizable shape, or to project historical images on the façade, to alleviate the shock of the increasingly unfamiliar urban landscape.[87] The following focus on the work of architects from socialist countries in the Gulf will challenge this imagination of architectural labor as a labor of mediation.

5.12. Municipality and Town Planning Department, Abu Dhabi, construction site, early 1980s. Tayeb Engineering, Bulgarproject (Bulgaria), Dimitar Bogdanov.

TWO INTERNATIONALISMS: TECHNOEXPORTSTROY IN THE UNITED ARAB EMIRATES

The ambition expressed by the competition brief for the building of the Abu Dhabi Municipality and Town Planning Department became fully clear to the project architect, Dimitar Bogdanov, when he traveled to Abu Dhabi for the first time, in 1980. Only after his design won the competition was Bogdanov able to see the site for which it was destined.[88] It was located in the vicinity of Abu Dhabi's downtown and was defined by an oblique pattern of streets within the gridiron layout set out in the Makhlouf master plan. The site was neighbored to the north by the growing business center of the city, with buildings populating streets parallel to the Corniche, and to the west by Zayed Town, a residential neighborhood with mixed-use buildings on the perimeter. Taking advantage of the recently liberated height restrictions, some of these buildings reached up to thirteen stories.[89] In the south, residential buildings were taking over what had previously been an area designated for industrial uses. New structures were under construction to the east of the site, left blank on the tourist map the Bulgarian team had received along with the competition brief.[90] The land use for this area was a subject of debate among planners since the early 1960s, from the plan by Halcrow & Partners to various versions of Makhlouf's plan.[91] The decision to locate the new administrative center of the city was an attempt to create "a service hub" that would revitalize the entire area.[92] On a larger scale, it conveyed the ambition to extend Abu Dhabi to the east, including the al-Reem and Sadiyat Islands, as formalized in the 1988 master plan by the Abu Dhabi Town Planning Department.[93]

After ground was broken for the Municipality Building, its construction site reflected the hectic development to which a variety of international actors contributed (figure 5.12). As recalled by Georgi Anastassov, chief resident architect of TES in Abu Dhabi in the early 1980s, the Bulgarian supervisors and the assistant resident engineer of Tayeb, Mohammad Abul Sham, and Tayeb's two other employees, met every day on the construction site with representatives of the client, the execution section of the Town Planning Department, and the contractor, Consolidated Contractors International Company. The latter was a Lebanese-Palestinian firm with headquarters in Athens, which employed Palestinian and British engineers, as well as Greek and Lebanese workers and a number of subcontractors from various countries in the region and from the UK.[94]

The supervisory team consisted of Bulgarian structural, electrical, and mechanical engineers, supported by Tayeb's engineers and technicians, several of them Sudanese engineers educated in the Soviet Union. They held weekly meetings, during which materials and details proposed by the contractor were approved, possible changes of specifications were accepted, and work progress was discussed. The architectural part was the responsibility of Anastassov, who also designed the interiors of the building, including the patterned marble and granite floor with a fountain, marble-clad balconies, and the dome in the entrance hall with a star-shaped glazed finish and an opulent chandelier.[95] Technical specification and bills of quantities were issued in both English and Arabic (Tayeb was in charge of the latter), while site meetings were conducted in Arabic with technical matters discussed with Bulgarian engineers in English. The landscaping, the open-air theater, and the fountains were designed by a Bulgarian architect, as were the decorative ceramic tiles.[96] Construction materials unavailable in the UAE were imported from the region and from Europe, including furniture designed by Anastassov and assembled in Italy.[97]

The construction sites of other projects of the Tayeb-TES partnership in the UAE, all supervised by Anastassov, also gathered a large number of international actors. The building of the Abu Dhabi Main Bus Terminal, a 1980 competition project won by Kuno and Stanka Dundakov, was completed in 1991 by the Abu Dhabi–based Zakum Construction Company, supervised on behalf of the client, the Transportation Department, by architect Mohamed Abusham (figures 5.13, 5.14, and 5.15). Zakum hired workers from India who were housed on the construction site.[98] Besides the terminal, this contractor was also responsible for two bus stations in Abu Dhabi, designed by the Dundakovs (1981) (figure 5.16).[99]

The Municipality Building in Al Ain, the first project won on behalf of Tayeb and TES in the UAE, was designed by Vasil Petrov of the Bulgarian state office Sofproekt. It was constructed by the contractor al-Muhairy from

5.13. Main Bus Terminal, Abu Dhabi, 1980–91, mini bus stands. Bulgarproject (Bulgaria), Kuno Dundakov, Stanka Dundakova.

5.14. Main Bus Terminal, Abu Dhabi, 1980–91. Bulgarproject (Bulgaria), Kuno Dundakov, Stanka Dundakova.

5.15. Main Bus Terminal, Abu Dhabi, 1980–91, interior of the main hall. Bulgarproject (Bulgaria), Kuno Dundakov, Stanka Dundakova.

SOCIALISM WITHIN GLOBALIZATION

Al Ain, with several subcontractors from abroad. As the former project manager of al-Muhairy recalls, Tayeb and TES met regularly on the construction site with the general contractor and representative of the client. Along with the approval of changes to the design, those meetings also involved testing samples of building materials in a lab set up at the construction site.[100]

From Socialist to Capitalist Internationalism

The glances into these construction sites show that the work of TES in the UAE was predicated on its ability to work with a large number of international actors. This collaboration was prepared by earlier experiences of TES in design-and-build commissions based on international agreements signed by the Bulgarian government with "progressive" countries in Africa and Asia. Their geographic distribution reflected the more general patterns of Bulgarian foreign trade with Arab countries, 77 percent of which went to countries with political links to the Eastern bloc, including Algeria, Iraq, Libya, and Syria.[101] Key clients of TES were governmental institutions such as the Libyan Ministries of Defense, Public Buildings, and Housing, as well as the Iraqi Ministry of Transport and the Algerian Ministry of Planning.[102]

By the late 1970s, however, Bulgarian and other Eastern European exporters were facing new challenges. Local governments in many Middle Eastern countries put restrictions on operations of foreign firms; they started to block working permits of foreign workers and demanded the employment of their own citizens. They insisted on the use of locally produced building materials, often delivered by factories that had been designed and (sometimes) built by Eastern Europeans. These challenges were particularly strong in the Gulf, as reported by socialist FTOs. For example, representatives of East Germany's Limex assessed that the export of simple construction materials to the Gulf was not profitable for the firms involved, given the transportation costs. In turn, when advanced materials

5.16. Bus Station, Abu Dhabi, 1981. Bulgarproject (Bulgaria), Kuno Dundakov, Stanka Dundakova.

were concerned, state-socialist firms struggled to meet the expectations of technical and design quality. According to one report, clients in the UAE were interested in East German steel products, but only for roof construction, since GDR wall panels were considered "aesthetically unsatisfying and internationally outdated."[103] Eastern European actors in the Gulf struggled with short delivery times, competed with companies from other socialist countries, the Middle East, Western Europe, North America, and South and East Asia, and faced high import tariffs on construction materials such as steel.[104] Further constraints included the necessity to comply with British and American norms, the requirement to deliver building documentation in English and Arabic, and the privileging of Arab firms by private and public commissioners. Such constraints complicated not only the export of construction services, but also of design activities.[105]

This tendency was worrying for managers of Bulgarian state-socialist contractors, who were expected by the party and the state administration under the long-time leader Todor Zhivkov to contribute to the country's debt repayment. By the early 1980s, these managers anticipated the exhaustion of commissions, which until then had benefited from bilateral diplomatic relations with Arab countries, and the Eastern European reputation for low-cost construction.[106] Bulgarian projects in the Emirate of Abu Dhabi differed in both respects: they were not prepared by intergovernmental treaties, and they were high-quality representational buildings. Consequently, collaboration with local partners was indispensable because of the requirement of a local "sponsor" in the Emirate, while alliances with international firms allowed the satisfying of the expectation of a high-quality building.[107] By entering these collaborations, TES focused its Gulf operations on design services, contrary to its earlier design-and-build commissions in the Middle East and North Africa.

In this sense, TES's activities in the Gulf can be seen as following the advice of an economic commentator who, writing in 1985, urged Bulgarian firms to "improve the quality of our goods to the level of international standards, so that they will be suited to the specific climatic conditions of the Arab world."[108] This statement may appear counterintuitive within the postwar architectural discourse, which challenged the presumed universality of "international standards" and was invested in adapting such standards (typically stemming from Western Europe and North America) to climatic and other conditions of the recipient countries. However, the following review of the work of TES will show that by the 1980s, it was cutting-edge technologies that facilitated a situated response to local conditions and client requirements in the Gulf. This argument will point to the shift in emphasis on the "international" character of TES. At the time when the firm was entering the UAE, its marketing materials increasingly downplayed its allegiance to socialist internationalism and stressed another type of internationalism of TES: its integration into the globalizing construction market.

These two were not necessarily exclusive, however, and the 1963 book *Bulgarian Engineering Achievements in Foreign Countries* is a case in point. Printed in Bulgarian and English, the book documents the first experiences of Bulgarian building export since the 1950s. The book claims an affinity between Bulgaria and the Arab countries based on geographic proximity, a common historic experience of foreign domination, and "sincere feelings of friendship harbored by Bulgarians for the Arab peoples, as well as their common aspirations for peace and progress in the world."[109] The ability to assist Arab countries in fast-track modernization was illustrated by Bulgaria's own experience on this path, and supported by images of postwar cities in Bulgaria, large-scale infrastructure, and modern factories. References to Orthodox churches and mosques served not only as a contrast to the modern development but also as a proof of Bulgarian competence in preservation of historic Islamic architecture: a message that in the years to come would be planted in the Middle Eastern press (figure 5.17).[110] Color images of resorts at the Black Sea drew attention to the modernized Bulgarian tourist industry. Based on those experiences, Bulgarian architects planned several Syrian towns with tourist development in view, and their layouts were reproduced in the book (figure 5.18).[111]

However, in addition to such worlding of Bulgaria, the editors of the book made a point of stressing the entanglement of Bulgarian firms with international planning culture and construction industry. In the case of the master plans of Syrian cities, this included the employment of up-to-date design tools, such as detailed urban norms, comprehensive traffic-planning systems, and the concept of a neighborhood unit. The editors stressed that the work of Bulgarian architects complied with standards of international professional organizations, including the International Union of Architects (UIA).[112]

In particular, the book documented at great length the ability of Bulgarian companies to work with a range of diverse actors, including local administrators and Western designers and contractors. A case in point was the presentation of the Rastan Dam in Syria, one of TES's early commissions (1961), a collaboration between TES as the contractor, the Board of Large Works in Damascus as the commissioner, and the Swiss firm Gruner as the designer. The book detailed the procedures that linked all parties involved:

> A monthly record was kept of the work done. At the end of each month bilateral measurements of the work done were made by the contractor and the Engineer [the representative of the commissioner and the designer]. In accordance with these measurements, the contractor drafted the monthly certificates, always including the work done from the very beginning of the construction period to the end of the given month.... The monthly certificates consisted of quantitative bills, protocols, price schedule, orders of the Engineer in case of additions or modifications in the blueprints, and the executive drawings showing how the different quantities were determined. The monthly certificate was checked and signed by the Engineer in original. Then it was typewritten in nine copies. The blueprints were prepared in five copies.... These materials [all written in English], signed by the contractor and the Engineer, were sent to Damascus for approvement [sic] by the administration and payment by the Bank.[113]

With such descriptions, the editors demonstrated to prospective clients that TES was a reliable partner and one able to collaborate with actors with vastly different experiences and cultures. Knowledge of such procedures was useful already on the stage of the tender submission when, in the case of the Abu Dhabi competition, a technical offer (with drawings of the building and the site, perspectives and models) needed to be complemented by a financial offer, including a timetable of the design process and the fees requested, a timetable of construction, and costs estimation. *Bulgarian Engineering Achievements* provided guidelines in all these respects, and its account of the Rastan Dam was complemented by a detailed description of the timing of each subcontract, the list of people employed, the composition of the materials and their logistics, and problem-solving procedures. Easy to overlook, because placed in a different section of the book, was a brief account about facilities in the city nearby to the dam, which were designed by the Bulgarians as "a modern ensemble with pronounced Oriental features."[114]

Hovering between a coffee-table book with lavish photographs and a technical report with engineering calculations, *Bulgarian Engineering*

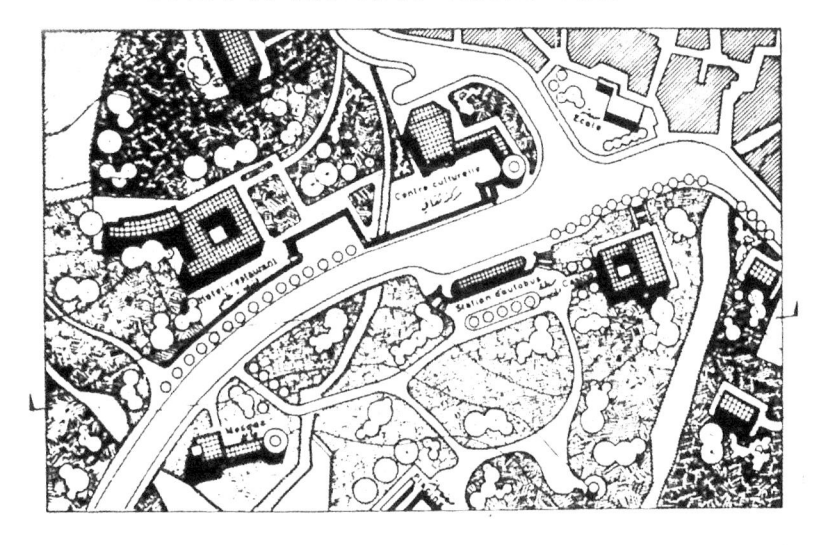

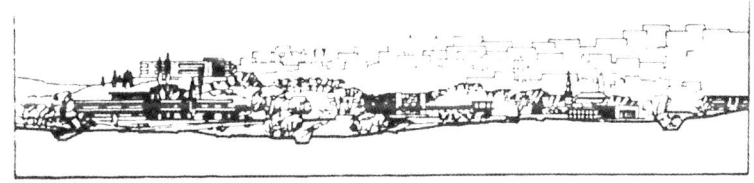

5.17. "Bulgaria Preserves Its Mosques as 'Monuments of Culture,'" *Kuwait Times*, November 13, 1978, 6.

5.18. Plan for the city center of Kessab (Syria). Technoexportstroy (Bulgaria). Mincho Chernev, Georgi Malchev, and Mitre Stamenov, *Dela na bulgarskite stroiteli i arkhitekti v chuzhbina/ Bulgarian Engineering Achievements in Foreign Countries* (Sofia: Tekhnika, 1963), 136.

SOCIALISM WITHIN GLOBALIZATION

Achievements shows two coexisting practices of internationalism: socialist and "capitalist" ones. Both practices prepared TES's projects in the UAE. The partnership with Tayeb, which opened the door for TES to the Emirati market, was based on a personal connection stemming from socialist technical assistance: it came about through a Sudanese architect who had completed his studies in Sofia, funded by the Bulgarian government, suggesting to Tayeb that they sign a partnership with TES.[115] Previous projects by TES in the Arab world, most of which were facilitated by friendly relations between Bulgaria and countries embarking on a "noncapitalist path of development," allowed the firm to fulfill the high eligibility requirements for the participants in the Abu Dhabi competition, which concerned the size, value, volume, and program of completed commissions. These requirements were not met by Tayeb, which, until its collaboration with TES, had worked mainly on small projects, mostly private villas.[116] At the same time, the demonstrable professionalism and the capacity of TES to collaborate with Western actors gained during earlier engagements allowed it to secure the commission and to execute it.

This collaborative capacity was emphasized by the TES catalogues from the 1970s and 1980s, distributed among the contractor's current and prospective clients (figure 5.19). Printed in West Germany, they showed large color photographs of constructed projects accompanied by short descriptions in Bulgarian, English, French, and Arabic. These were arranged in groups, from public buildings and hotels to hospitals, sports facilities, industrial projects, roads, bridges, railroads, water dams, and irrigation networks, through to decorative wood carving on walls and ceilings (most of the latter executed by TES in Arab countries).[117] Some catalogues included detailed lists of projects specifying clients, external designers (including Snam Progetti and Italconsult of Italy, and Alexander Gibb of the UK), supervision (often carried out by the designers themselves), the period of execution, contract value, and list of main works carried out by TES. They were complemented by maps of their geographic distribution ("over 20 countries in Africa, Asia and Europe"), the location of workshops and factories, and the firm's local branches in North Africa and the Middle East.[118] The list of the equipment and machinery owned by TES showed that most of them were produced in Western Europe, and the contractor's credibility among Western partners was certified by Western-based international prizes and by recommendation letters from British, Italian, and West German firms that had supervised works completed by TES.

The catalogues were silent about ideological issues to an extent that the reader may forget that TES was a state company from a socialist country. The presence of the Bulgarian state was manifested only in occasional reproductions of the 1964 decree of the incorporation of TES under the Bulgarian Ministry of Foreign Trade, a certificate from the Bulgarian Chamber of Commerce, and a register of assets from the Bulgarian Foreign Trade Bank. However, while issued by state-socialist institutions, these documents emphasized the firm's embeddedness into the international regime of financial and legal guarantees.[119] This impression was further enhanced by the fact that the firm's financial accounts were held in a commercial bank in West Germany.

"We were like a Western company," insisted the former technical director of TES when I interviewed him in 2015.[120] The experience of working with Western standards, specifications, machinery, materials, institutions, and firms was primarily gained throughout TES's engagements in the Middle East and North Africa. It included collaborations with local administrators, governmental officials, local and international businessmen, and professionals on every stage of the investment process, from assessment of the tender through design, construction, and delivery. (The firm was also commissioned for projects in Europe,

5.19. "Buildings and Hotels," designed and constructed by Technoexportstroy. "Technoexportstroy" (Sofia: Technoexportstroy, n.d.).

including West Germany, but fewer and later.) To appear as a "Western company" was also vital for the recruitment of personnel in Bulgaria, where the prestige of the firm was an important incentive, as was the higher salary and the ability to travel abroad. The engineers and foremen were trained in Western Europe, and European and American experts were invited to Sofia to train staff in the use of equipment applied in TES commissions, in particular industrial ones.[121]

While TES would hire Arab graduates of Bulgarian universities as supervisors of projects in their countries of origin and place them in charge of contacts with local administrators, the decision makers at higher governmental levels were, more often than not, educated in the West, in the UK and, increasingly, in the United States. They required that TES comply with Western-based legal and financial regimes, and they often included Western materials and machinery into building specifications, thus forcing TES to reinvest much of its profit into equipment bought in West Germany, Italy, and France.[122]

Already the creation of Bulgarproject, separated in 1969 from TES as a formally independent company (yet fully controlled by TES), was itself an adaptation to the British legal system adhered to by the former British colonies and protectorates, which required a separation of the roles of contractor and architect. Accordingly, design contracts by TES were signed by Bulgarproject, as was the case with the projects in the UAE.[123] Western regulations were used by the company in North Africa and the Middle East, when building norms were missing or incomplete. At times, local regulations were combined with foreign norms: in Libya, TES worked with British norms (also applied in UAE buildings by Tayeb-TES), and with French norms in the former French North Africa. Through contracts with Western companies,

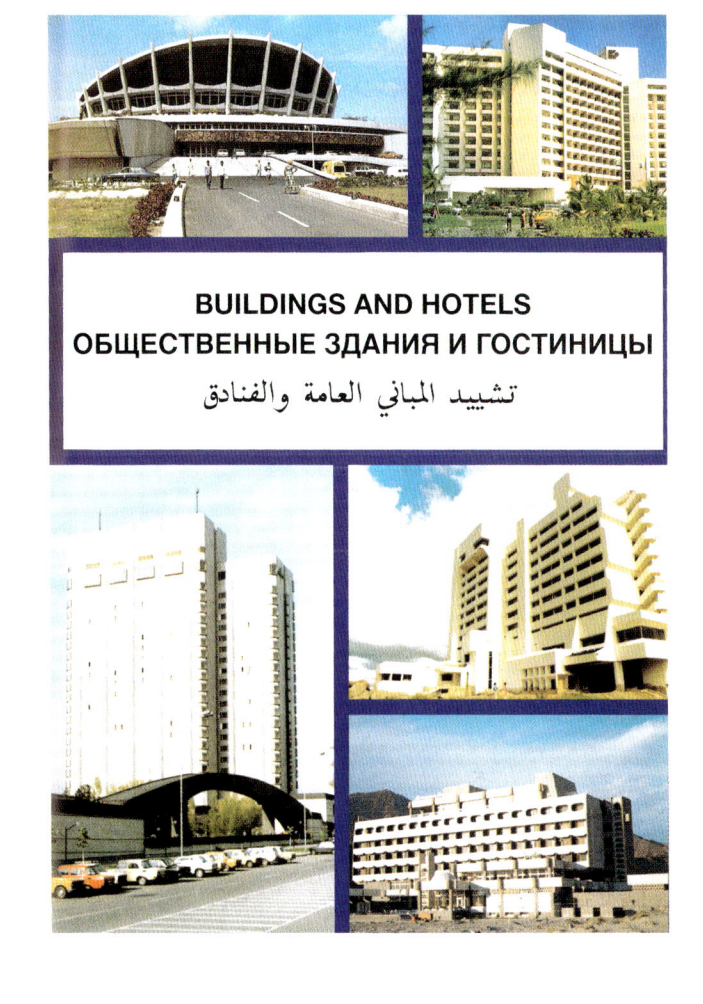

SOCIALISM WITHIN GLOBALIZATION

TES managers taught themselves standard international construction contracts, as recommended by the International Federation of Consulting Engineers (FIDIC), as well as specification standards.[124] In emerging markets in the Gulf, with multiple international producers and contractors on the spot, there was a strong preference for performance specifications that spelled out the desired result and verification procedures (typically associated with US practice) over prescriptive specifications, which described material and workmanship requirements (associated with the British tradition). TES worked with either, according to the wishes of clients. Standard contracts and specifications, country-specific building norms, and catalogues of materials were gathered in the archive of TES in Sofia and used during competition and tender submissions, and the commissions that followed. As one architect in TES recalls, "we sometimes participated in competitions just to get the tender documentation and to learn from it."[125]

A key role in this process of acquiring site-specific knowledge went to local branches and local sponsors. Such partnerships, if successful, tended to continue for several projects and resulted in an accumulation of local experience. This was the case with the collaboration between TES and Tayeb in Abu Dhabi, where Tayeb, as the local sponsor, was constantly on the lookout for new commissions. During their work in the UAE in the 1980s, TES architects participated in several competitions for hospitals, office complexes, and other facilities in the UAE and in Kuwait.[126]

Much credit for this collective learning process of TES needs to be given to the head designers and leaders of the design teams into which the architectural section of TES in Sofia was divided. They included Dimitar Bogdanov, designer of the Abu Dhabi Municipality Building and from 1977 director of the company's architectural section. Bogdanov graduated in architecture in Sofia, and his first employer was the design office of the state railways in the Bulgarian capital. In this capacity, he was delegated to the Ministry of Transport in Tunis (1965–69), after which he began working for TES. His built projects at the company included urban parks, twelve technical schools, and administrative buildings in various cities in Algeria; a coal factory in East Germany; and a silo, residential buildings, and a multifunctional shopping complex in Libya. Bogdanov also submitted many tender projects for Libya: sports complexes, health facilities, hotels, and culture centers. After winning the competition in Abu Dhabi, he continued to work on a number of other projects for the region, including a tourist complex and administrative buildings in Yemen, and he won the competition for the Administration Center Hamma in Algiers, for which the National Library and the hotel were realized by an Italian firm (figure 5.20).[127]

The trajectories of other designers of major TES projects in the UAE were similarly international. After graduating in architecture from Sofia

5.20. Dimitar Bogdanov (third man standing from the left) and his colleagues discuss the model of the Administration Center Hamma, Algiers (Algeria), mid-1980s.

University of Technology (1955), Kuno Dundakov was hired by the Ministry of Communication and the Union of Sport and Physical Education. In 1960, Dundakov joined the design office Sofproekt, where, together with his design partner and future wife, Stanka Lozanova (Dundakova), he won the competition for the extension of the Vasil Levski National Stadium in Sofia. During that period, he began to specialize in designing sports facilities. These included the Olympic Sports Complex in Tunis (one of the main projects that TES constructed in the 1960s), the award-winning competition entry for the 5 July 1962 Stadium in Algiers (eventually constructed according to a design by Hungary's Közti), and the Olympic Sports Complex in Khartoum. Based on those experiences, TES hired Dundakov as a team leader in 1969. At TES, he and Lozanova designed the sports complex of Ilorin in Nigeria and other buildings in Nigeria, Lebanon, Ethiopia, Libya, Iraq, Vietnam, and Morocco, some of which resulted from won competitions. The Dundakovs' designs in Abu Dhabi, including the bus terminal and both stations, shared with their previous work the expressive structure in reinforced concrete. Their other competition projects in UAE from the 1980s, all unrealized, included a theater in Abu Dhabi, a palace for the ruler of Dubai, and the Main Bus Station in Al Ain.[128]

In turn, Vasil Petrov, designer of the Al Ain Municipality Building, was employed by Sofproekt, where he collaborated with Kuno Dundakov on the Olympic Sports Complex in Tunis. As an employee of Sofproekt, Petrov was contracted by TES to deliver the winning competition entry for the Al Ain municipality, and the layout of the headquarters of UAE's armed forces in Abu Dhabi. He also won third prize for his design of the Ministry of Foreign Affairs in Abu Dhabi.[129]

The paths of Bogdanov and the Dundakovs, which connected most of TES's projects in the Arab countries, contrasted with, for instance, the trajectories of Polish architects on Polservice contracts in the Middle East, who typically stayed in one country, and would make one, if any, geographic leap during their careers. When working with governmental clients, head designers of TES were often directly negotiating with high-level governmental officials in Arab countries. During those negotiations, the affiliation of these architects with the communist party in Bulgaria opened additional possibilities of communication and leverage through state and party channels.[130] Those were tapped into when, for instance, governments in Arab countries were delaying payments for TES. For some decision makers in the Middle East, this close relationship of the Bulgarian architects to their state and the party was also a guarantee of professionalism. As the resident engineer from Tayeb in the UAE put it: "Since there were no private design firms in Bulgaria, the cooperation with TES meant cooperating with the Bulgarian government. It was a major opportunity for Tayeb to benefit from the best architects that they had, most of whom were university professors."[131]

Technological and Cultural Competence

Learning from their earlier experiences in North Africa and the Middle East, Bogdanov and the Dundakovs got to know the requirements of governmental clients in Arab countries, including that of cultural specificity. In the words of Georgi Anastassov: "We got accustomed with the Arab character of architecture during our practice in North Africa and the Middle East since the late 1950s."[132] The criteria of such "Arab character" were communicated by trial-and-error during negotiations with the commissioners, when particular versions of a project would be discussed, accepted, modified, or declined.

This deliberative procedure comes to the fore in the Bulgarian designs for the UAE. In the presentations to their Emirati clients, TES architects closely combined the claim to cultural expertise with that to technological competence (figure 5.21). This combination was conveyed by the Bulgarian entry to the Al Ain competition (1976), as recalled by Bedri Omar Elias, a Sudanese architect employed in the late 1970s by the Town Planning Department of Al Ain and, in that capacity, in charge of the competition: "Among sixty-five offices that participated in this open competition, the jury unanimously agreed that the Bulgarian project, submitted with Tayeb, was the best. It had a clear functional and spatial organization, and it reflected Islamic tradition. By this I mean the form of Iraqi arches, the white color, the courtyards, and the general volumes, which were presented to us in the final round by the designer, Mr. Vasil Petrov."[133]

The contributors to the debate about "Arab" architecture in the Gulf since the 1970s would have taken issue with this statement, wondering, for instance, why Iraqi arches were applied in the southern Gulf. This was, however neither a concern of TES nor, more importantly, of its client. What is striking about Bedri's recollection is that each element singled out by him as "reflecting Islamic tradition" allowed Petrov to argue the firm's technological competence (figure 5.22). The repetitive arches, emphasized in the drawings of the competition entry, demonstrated the advanced prefabrication techniques foreseen for the building. The courtyards, shaded arcades, large spaces for circulation, conversation, and lingering under the lateral wings, as well as generously sized corridors, allowed for flexibility and extendibility of the building, which was then taken advantage

5.21. Municipality Building, Al Ain, 1976–85. Tayeb Engineering, Bulgarproject (Bulgaria), Vasil Petrov.

5.22. Municipality Building, Al Ain, 1976–85, situation plan. Tayeb Engineering, Bulgarproject (Bulgaria), Vasil Petrov.

> 5.23. Municipality Building, Al Ain, 1976–85, plan of the entrance level. Tayeb Engineering, Bulgarproject (Bulgaria), Vasil Petrov.

> 5.24. Municipality Building, Al Ain, 1976–85, interior of the entrance hall. Tayeb Engineering, Bulgarproject (Bulgaria), Vasil Petrov.

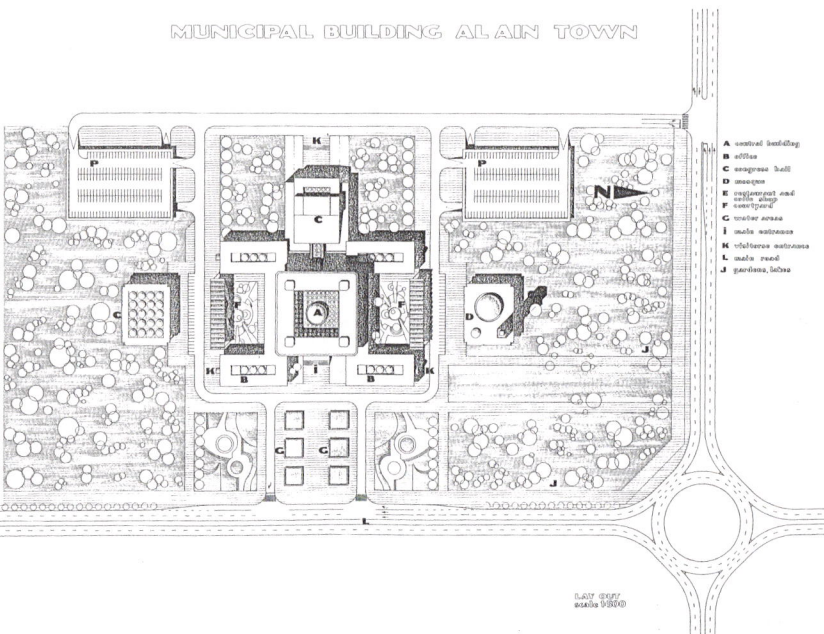

MUNICIPAL BUILDING - AL AIN TOWN

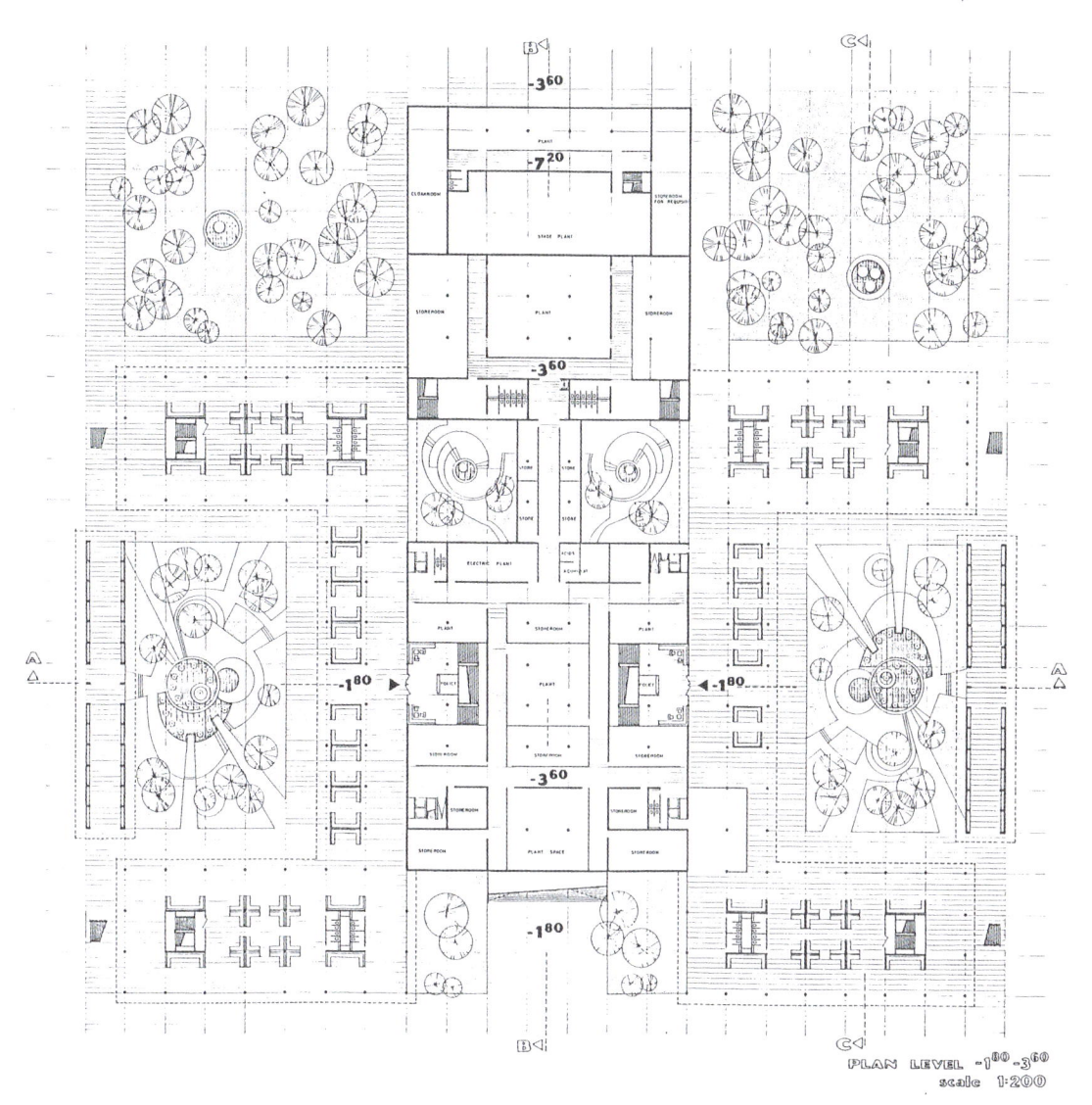

PLAN LEVEL -1⁸⁰-3⁶⁰
scale 1:200

SOCIALISM WITHIN GLOBALIZATION

of in its subsequent expansions (figures 5.23 and 5.24). To a trained eye, these opportunities were evident from the drawings submitted to the competition. Even the white color of the prefabricated concrete elements, mentioned by Bedri, implied the ability of TES to master advanced concrete technology with white cement, a particularly challenging task in the hot climate of the Gulf.[134]

The same strategy of using cultural references in order to emphasize technology, modularity, flexibility, and economy can be seen in the Abu Dhabi Municipality project, a "fine example of Islamic architecture" according to a booklet published by the Municipality (figure 5.25). The author of the booklet argued that this building "reflect[ed] the country's Islamic character by having arches and arcades, domed halls and a mosque. The octagon features as a repeated motif in all the plans, façades, decorative elements, fountains, etc."[135] This was not an isolated opinion and, upon its opening in 1985, the building was described by the Emirati press as "combining the features of modern buildings as well as the historical qualities of the Arabic and Islamic cultures."[136]

Not unlike Bedri's recollections, all elements listed in this account drew attention to the technological expertise of the designers. The arched elements were attached to the façade in a way that emphasized their modular, prefabricated character, and the arcade with ogee openings stressed the possibility of an extension of the office space within the building's envelope, which was undertaken a few years after the completion of the building (figure 5.26). The octagon elements, including the conference and the entrance halls, and the mosque divided the building into segments in which the jury would have recognized the organizational chart provided by the competition brief; they sit within a modular plan that allows for a flexible distribution of volumes and voids (figure 5.27).[137]

5.25. Municipality and Town Planning Department, Abu Dhabi, 1979–85. Tayeb Engineering, Bulgarproject (Bulgaria), Dimitar Bogdanov.

5.26. Municipality and Town Planning Department, Abu Dhabi, 1979–85, north-east elevation. Tayeb Engineering, Bulgarproject (Bulgaria), Dimitar Bogdanov.

> 5.27. Municipality and Town Planning Department, Abu Dhabi, 1979–85, situation plan, 1980. Tayeb Engineering, Bulgarproject (Bulgaria), Dimitar Bogdanov.

> 5.28. Municipality and Town Planning Department, Abu Dhabi, 1979–85, working drawings of the mosque, 1984. Tayeb Engineering, Bulgarproject (Bulgaria), Dimitar Bogdanov.

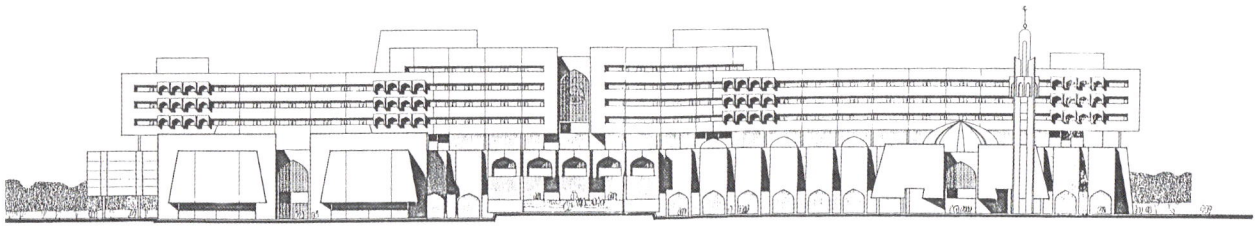

NORTH·EAST ELEVATION /TO AL SALAM STREET/

SOCIALISM WITHIN GLOBALIZATION

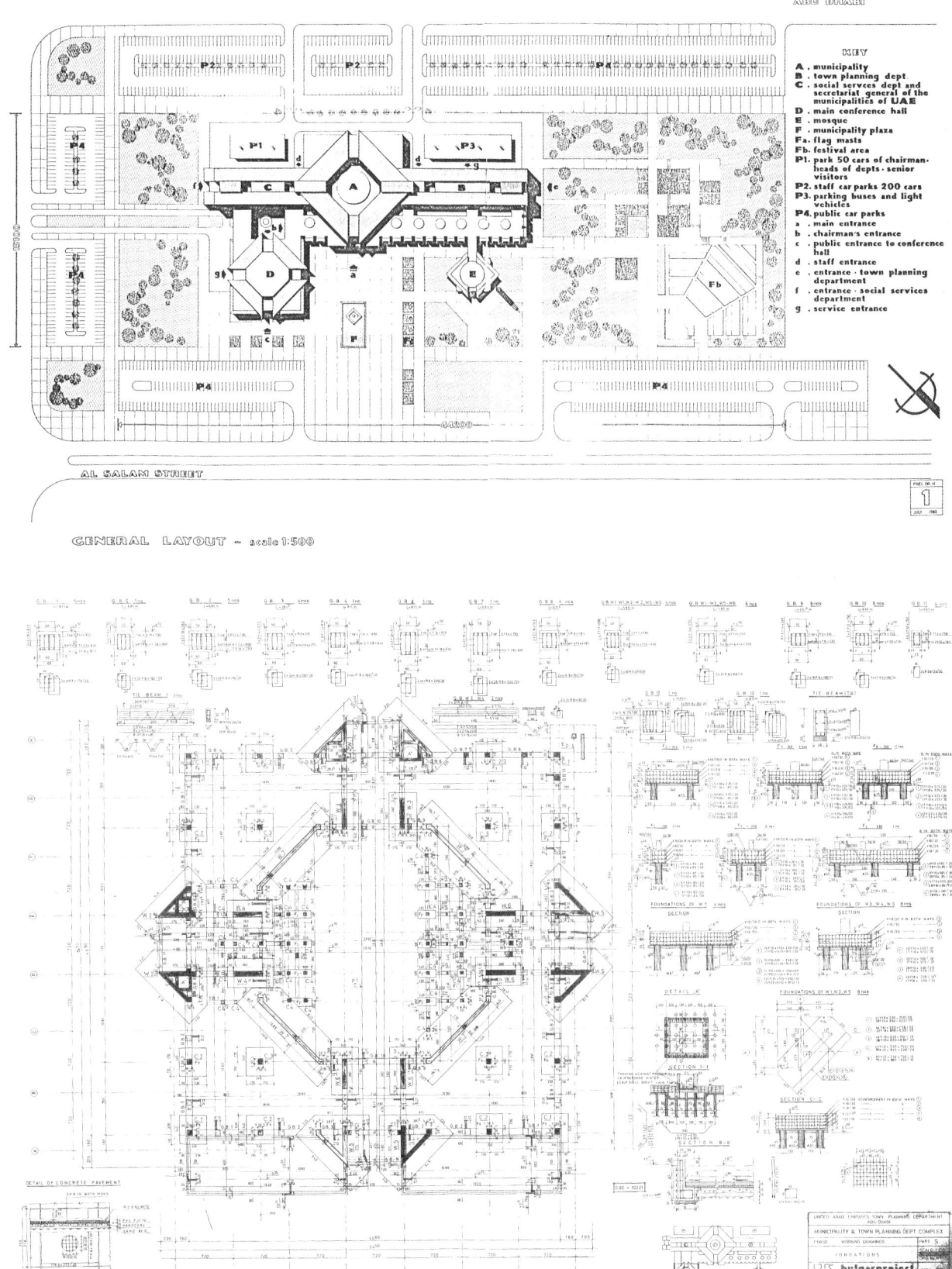

Maybe the best example of TES's strategy to use cultural references not in order to compensate for technological means employed but, rather, to draw attention to them, can be seen in the mosque of the Municipality Building (figure 5.28). In spite of its traditional silhouette, the mosque was the most challenging element of the building in terms of engineering.[138] The dome sits on a ring beam supported by a slab cantilevering in from the internally inclined buttress walls, which in turn sit on the four main triangular support walls. The shuttering for the complete structure had to remain in place until the last of the concrete had reached its twenty-day strength. The dome and the upper parts of the minaret were clad with bronze-colored glass tiles that, when seen from distance, gave the impression of sheet bronze while retaining their sparkle.[139]

The mosque was also the key part in the urban layout proposed by the Bulgarians. The building framed the entrance plaza, was a focal point of the public park planned nearby, and was visible in long vistas, in particular from the axis of the yet to be constructed al-Reem Street. The prominent location of the mosque in the urban layout was the main element distinguishing the Bulgarian submission from other competition entries. This singularity would spring out in an array of models, which was how the finalist projects were presented to Sheikh Zayed, who selected the winner, and in this sense the urban layout might have been decisive for the victory of TES.[140]

In particular, the Bulgarian urban design contrasted with the entry awarded the second prize, won by the Kuwaiti office Shiber Consult and co-designed by two Polish architects, Wojciech Jarząbek and Edward Lach (figure 5.29).[141] While they designed a walled compound, the Bulgarians envisaged an ensemble within an urban system visually connected with the park and the surrounding city. The drawing methods in both submissions reinforced this contrast. The most evocative perspective submitted by Shiber Consult showed a vast interior of the building as a hotel-like lobby with nondirectional, lingering space adorned with water, plants, and furniture (figure 5.30). In turn, the Bulgarian submission stressed the external view that put to the fore the mosque and the conference center, on a background of the office wings. The renderers at Shiber Consult worked with deep shadows that emphasized the enclosed character of the building,

5.29. Entry to the competition for the Municipality and Town Planning Department, Abu Dhabi, 1979, external view. Shiber Consult (Kuwait), Wojciech Jarząbek, Edward Lach.

5.30. Entry to the competition for the Municipality and Town Planning Department, Abu Dhabi, 1979, interior. Shiber Consult (Kuwait), Wojciech Jarząbek, Edward Lach.

stressed the articulation of the mass and the void as the basic architectural syntax, and alluded to relief from the harsh Gulf sun. In turn, the Bulgarian drawings accentuated the module, with its connotation of prefabrication technology, flexibility of distribution, and logics of construction. Their modular background emphasized the octagons of the auditorium, the entrance hall, and the mosque: all elements identified by the Municipality's marketing materials with Islamic inspirations. In this sense, the Bulgarian proposal was more than a piece of architecture: rather, it was a vision of an expandable, efficient, and open-ended urban system punctuated by characteristic elements that lent themselves to being read as cultural references.

A NEW ARCHITECTURAL WORKER: EASTERN EUROPEANS IN KUWAIT

The competition entry of the Abu Dhabi Municipality Building submitted by Shiber Consult was one among many designs coproduced by Polish architects employed in architectural offices in late 1970s and 1980s Kuwait. While the Bulgarian head designers traveled to the Gulf as employees of TES, Polish architects entered private Kuwaiti offices on individual Polservice contracts. These working conditions provided them with a specific set of constraints and opportunities that they used to respond to the dual requirement of technological and cultural competence in the Gulf. In particular, their response to this requirement conveyed their own disenchantment with postwar modern architecture in socialist Poland, which resulted in their interest in reorienting urbanism toward contextual forms.

Jarząbek and Lach, along with Krzysztof Wiśniowski, Andrzej Bohdanowicz, and most other Polish architects in 1980s Kuwait, were of a younger generation than Bogdanov and other head architects of TES. They had graduated in the second half of the 1960s from Wrocław University of Technology, and some of them went on to teach and research Silesian vernacular architecture at the University's Institute of History of Architecture, Art, and Technology.[142] By the early 1970s, several architects of the future Kuwait group were employed in the state office Inwestprojekt-Wrocław, a design office with state housing corporations as its primary clients.

During the decade that preceded their arrival in Kuwait, they engaged in a critical rethinking of "real existing modernism," or modern architecture as it actually existed in 1960s and 1970s Poland.[143] A privileged medium for these engagements was architectural competitions, including the winning competition design for the City Center Housing Estate in Łódź, B Area (1969), then followed by others.[144] Feeding into modernization efforts of the regime of Edward Gierek, first secretary of the Polish communist party (1970–80), these designs provided Jarząbek, Lach, and their colleagues with an opportunity to reimagine the urban experience. For example, for the town center of Racibórz, they proposed a pedestrian landscape of pavilions that retrofitted empty spaces between modernist slabs (1969), and for the universities' district in Łódź, they laid out a dense sequence of urban interiors (1973). For centers of medieval Silesian cities and towns damaged in World War II, the architects foresaw buildings in the scale of a historical urban fabric, adapted to topography and to the silhouettes of pitched roofs, which harmonized with gothic and baroque monuments (Lwówek Śląski, 1975). Their design for a neighborhood adjoining the convent in Trzebnica (1977) returned to the typology of a street with explicit references to the

5.31. Residential district in Trzebnica (Poland), 1977. W. Brzezowski, S. Medeksza, E. Niemczyk, K. Wiśniowski.

scale, section, and tectonics of historic buildings, while leaving no doubt about the modern technology and materials employed (figure 5.31).[145]

This decade-long exploration of contextualized urbanities shaped the interests of these architects in ways that were to resonate with their work in the late 1970s and 1980s Gulf. Yet their work in Poland was also an experience of the limits to the state-controlled building industry. The award-winning competition entry for the Kozanów neighborhood in Wrocław (1974) was a case in point.[146] Breaking with the undifferentiated and homogenous blocks of flats that had populated Poland since the early 1960s, Kozanów was designed as a "small city within a big city."[147] Its design was a topographically sensitive composition of diverse housing typologies, linked by a low, dense part with social facilities. In spite of the fact that the project won first prize in a national competition, it was rejected by the Ministry of Construction, which did not accept the prefabrication system designed by the architects. As one of them recalled, "I had to go back to designing the very same blocks of flats which, as we were told during our studies, don't work."[148] This disenchantment was further aggravated by a new regulation that banned academic staff from working in design offices outside the university, as well as the increasingly apparent economic and political crisis in Poland of the late 1970s.[149]

Eastern European Labor in Kuwait

In this context, the invitation to Kuwait mediated by a Palestinian alumnus of Wrocław University of Technology offered a welcome change.[150] In contrast to the extensive foreign experience of TES designers, there was little that prepared the Wrocław architects for their work abroad, except for one commission in Italy and a competition design of the National Library in Damascus (both in 1976).[151] The first group from Wrocław to go to Kuwait, in 1976, included Lach and Daczkowski, who were employed in the Gulf Engineering Office (GEO). Wiśniowski and Bohdanowicz were hired in 1977 by Shiber Consult, and after a year they were replaced by others, including Jarząbek. These architects also cooperated with the Industrial and Engineering Consulting Office (INCO).[152] According to INCO's director, Mohammad al-Sanan, in early 1980s there were eighteen Polish architects and engineers working in this office, which employed about two hundred people, including technicians, supervisors, architects, and engineers.[153]

While the architects arrived in Kuwait on tourist visas (and on leave from Inwestprojekt, where they were still formally employed), the competition won for Site C of the Sabah al-Salem district (1977) allowed them to legalize their work in Kuwait. They signed a contract with Polservice, and recommended other architects, among them their wives and partners.[154] Architects from other Polish cities arrived as well, including Janusz Krawecki, who was invited by his former student at the School of Architecture at Kraków University of Technology, and Włodzimierz Gleń of Kraków's state office Miastoprojekt, who, unlike other Polish architects in Kuwait, already had extensive work experience in the region (Iraq).[155] Professional links with Poland were rarely severed, and Jarząbek, for example, sent drawings from Kuwait for the church of St. Mary Queen of Peace in Wrocław-Popowice, the details of which resemble those of the al-Othman Center he co-designed in Hawally (with Lach for Kuwait Engineering Group, KEG, 1995). Other members of the group were participating in competitions in late 1980s Poland.[156] After the imposition of martial law in Poland (1981), most decided not to return, and found employment in various Kuwaiti offices, with or without Polservice contracts: INCO, SSH, KEO, KEG, and GEO (later Gulf Consult).[157]

Work in these offices, all of which had been established in the 1960s and early 1970s by ambitious Kuwaitis educated in the UK and the United

States, offered Polish architects an opportunity to rethink their disciplinary and professional identities. As Sabah al-Rayes of Pan Arab Consulting Engineers (PACE) recalled in the early 1980s, the foundation of PACE in 1968 had aimed at raising architectural and construction standards in Kuwait "from the cheap and cheerful mentality of the 1960s to the high quality projects that are the hallmark of the latest wave of Kuwait's development."[158] The employment of expat architects was one way of achieving this goal. Besides British, Western European, and American architects, these included Egyptian, Iraqi, Lebanese, and Palestinian professionals, as well as Indians and Pakistanis.[159] Another way to tap into foreign expertise were joint ventures with foreign offices, increasingly required for larger projects by both the authorities and private clients. Cooperation by Kuwaiti offices with prestigious US firms, such as TAC and SOM, complemented traditional links with British offices. During their work in Kuwait, Eastern Europeans cooperated with those Western architects and companies, and sometimes competed with them. For example, the project by Wiśniowski and Bohdanowicz for INCO was selected along with one by Denys Lasdun as finalists in the Kuwaiti National Theater competition (1978).[160]

Yet over the course of the 1980s, recruitment of Western Europeans for positions in Kuwait became increasingly challenging: few agreed to come, and those who did demanded higher salaries than employers were willing to pay.[161] In contrast, the salaries of architects from socialist countries were significantly lower than those of professionals from the West. "We have chosen Eastern European architects because of the combination of their competitive salaries, their commitment to work, and their competence," recalls Akram Ogaily, a partner at Archicentre.[162] Besides at least fifteen Czech and Slovak architects on contracts from Czechoslovak FTO Polytechna, Archicentre hired also engineers from Poland and Yugoslavia.[163] External consultants recruited for the work on Amiri Diwan included Kuwaiti landscape architects and infrastructure planners; British quantity surveyors and water engineers; Finnish engineers responsible for mechanical, electrical, and plumbing services; and US architects for furniture, fitting, and equipment.[164]

A similarly international team was gathered by Archicentre for its design of the Conference Center Complex at the Bayan Park, a project that shows yet another modality of work for architects from socialist countries in 1980s Kuwait (figure 5.32). The head designer of the complex was Stojan Maksimović, director of the Institute of Design and Planning of the city of Belgrade and the architect of the Sava Center in the Yugoslav capital. Originally built for the 1977–78 Conference on Security and Cooperation in Europe, the ensemble impressed the Kuwaiti delegation, which appreciated its flexibility.[165] Following the conference, the Kuwaiti government invited Maksimović to participate in the 1982 competition for a conference center in the city-state. His award-winning project kept the spatial and functional disposition of the Sava Center and added several additional buildings in response to the competition brief.[166]

After the competition results were announced, Maksimović signed an agreement with the Kuwaiti Ministry of Public Works on behalf of the Yugoslav (Serbian) construction firm Rad, which already had projects in the region. This agreement resulted in the creation of a joint venture with Archicentre, and the Yugoslav-Kuwaiti team produced the full tender documentation.[167] However, when the building opened for the Fifth Islamic Summit Conference (1986), only the general layout of the ensemble resembled the plan by Maksimović and Archicentre.[168]

Maksimović was introduced to Archicentre by the staff of Energoprojekt, which by the early 1980s was completing the construction of a military hospital in Kuwait, the Ministries Complex, infrastructural projects (including power stations), and other commissions (figure 5.33).[169]

5.32. General view of the Bayan Park Conference Center, Kuwait, 1982–86. Archicentre, Stojan Maksimović. Ministry of Public Works, "Kuwait Conference Centre Complex and Master Plan of Bayan Park. Report," n.d.

5.33. Ministries Complex, Kuwait City, 1978–81. Ministry of Public Works, Kuwait, constructed by Energoprojekt (Socialist Republic of Serbia, Yugoslavia).

5.34. Bedouin housing, Kuwait, 1969, ground floor and roof plan. Energoprojekt (Socialist Republic of Serbia, Yugoslavia), Milica Sterić, Dragoljub Bakić. "Beduinsko naselje u Kuvajtu (Housing—Kuwait)," *Architektura Urbanizam* 58 (1969): 25.

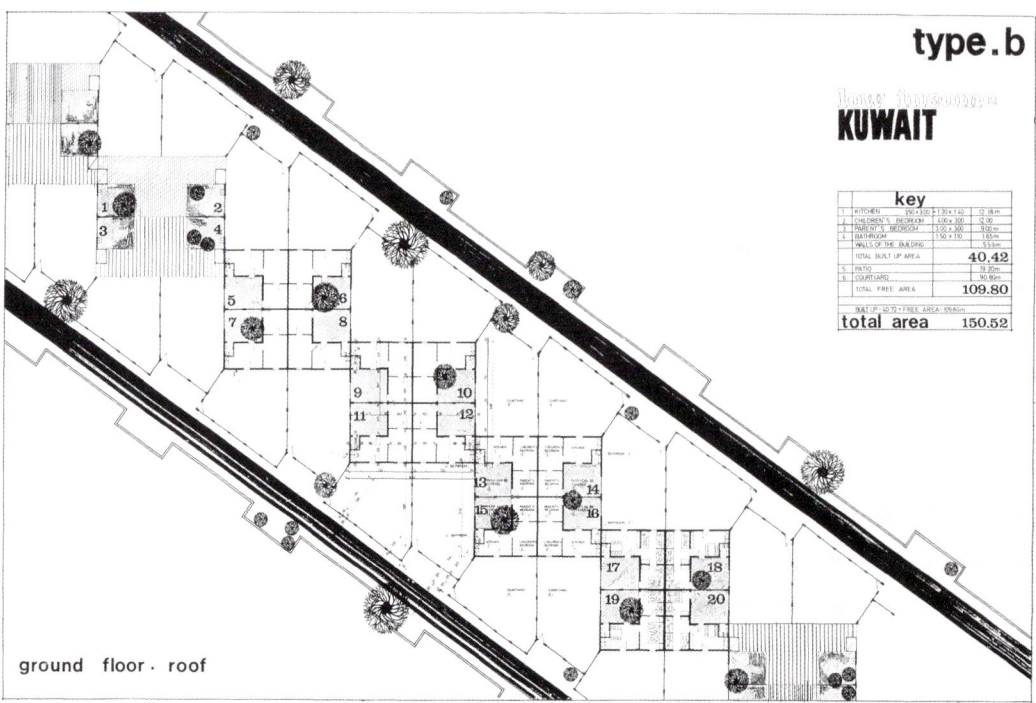

Energoprojekt's engagements in Kuwait originated from the early 1960s. Already in 1964, architect Dragoljub Bakić had come to Kuwait to work in the newly opened branch office of Energoprojekt, set up as a joint venture with the local company Kharafi, the sponsor required by Kuwaiti law. The acquisition of commissions was a major task of the architects, and Kharafi was supposed to help with networking among the elite of the city-state. In contrast to governmental projects designed and built by Energoprojekt in Africa, such as the International Trade Fair in Lagos, Bakić's projects in Kuwait were mainly private villas, including one for the rector of the University of Kuwait (1965). He was soon joined by his wife, architect Ljiljana Bakić, who was hired by a private Lebanese office in Kuwait. During their stay in Kuwait (1964–66), she designed several private villas, rental-housing complexes, and schools.[170]

These direct commissions allowed the Bakićs to become acquainted with requirements of Kuwaiti clients concerning layout and privacy, as well as technology, materials, and contractors available in the city-state. They tapped into this knowledge in their subsequent projects, including their successful entries to competitions called by the Kuwaiti government in the framework of the resettlement programs for Bedouin nomads (figure 5.34). In response to the brief, which requested an economical house for a Bedouin family, the architects proposed a layout with a diwaniyya, a family area, and a courtyard, part of which could be isolated for animals. In collaboration with Kharafi, Energoprojekt constructed three thousand such units in Mina Abdullah in the course of the late 1960s and 1970s.[171] Ljiljana Bakić returned to Kuwait several times in the 1970s in order to supervise this project, and to draw new ones, including a villa neighborhood for university professors.[172]

This structure of a small, joint-venture office was repeated by Energoprojekt in Dubai, where Ivan Pantić was in charge of the branch office opened in 1976, with Dragoljub Bakić as the head of Energoprojekt's Middle East operations. Consisting of four architects, the team designed two mosques and residential buildings in Dubai, all constructed by local firms, and participated in competitions in the region, including the competition for a conference center in Abu Dhabi (1976). However, problems with acquisition of projects and with the execution of payments from local clients, and the slowdown of the UAE economy resulted in the closure of the office in 1981.[173]

Similar challenges of running joint-venture offices in the Gulf were experienced by Hungarian architects Tibor Hübner and Attila Emődy. They worked on a contract with the Hungarian FTO Tesco in an office set up in Kuwait by a Kuwaiti engineer and an Egyptian architect, where they designed sectors of the Coastal Strip Development Project, a large housing district with complete social facilities, according to the master plan provided by Miastoprojekt-Kraków.[174] In their recollections, working conditions in 1980s Kuwait were marred by misunderstandings with international collaborators without a shared professional culture, by lack of commitment of external parties, and by unhelpful public officials. Hübner remembers more fondly his work in the UAE in the second half of the 1980s, where he benefited from knowledge about the region gained in Kuwait. In Al Ain, he designed the extension to the International Hotel, and he was part of a Hungarian team that contributed to several hospital designs in Abu Dhabi.[175]

In contrast, several architects from Romania on Romconsult contracts traveled only for short stays to private offices in Abu Dhabi over the course of the 1980s, where they worked on designs of palaces for the royal family, residential neighborhoods, interiors for hotels (including the Meridien Hotel), and on competitions.[176] Others were not allowed to travel at all, and architect Anca Oțoiu recalls that she and her colleague working at Romproiect's Bucharest office were requested to design several villas for Al

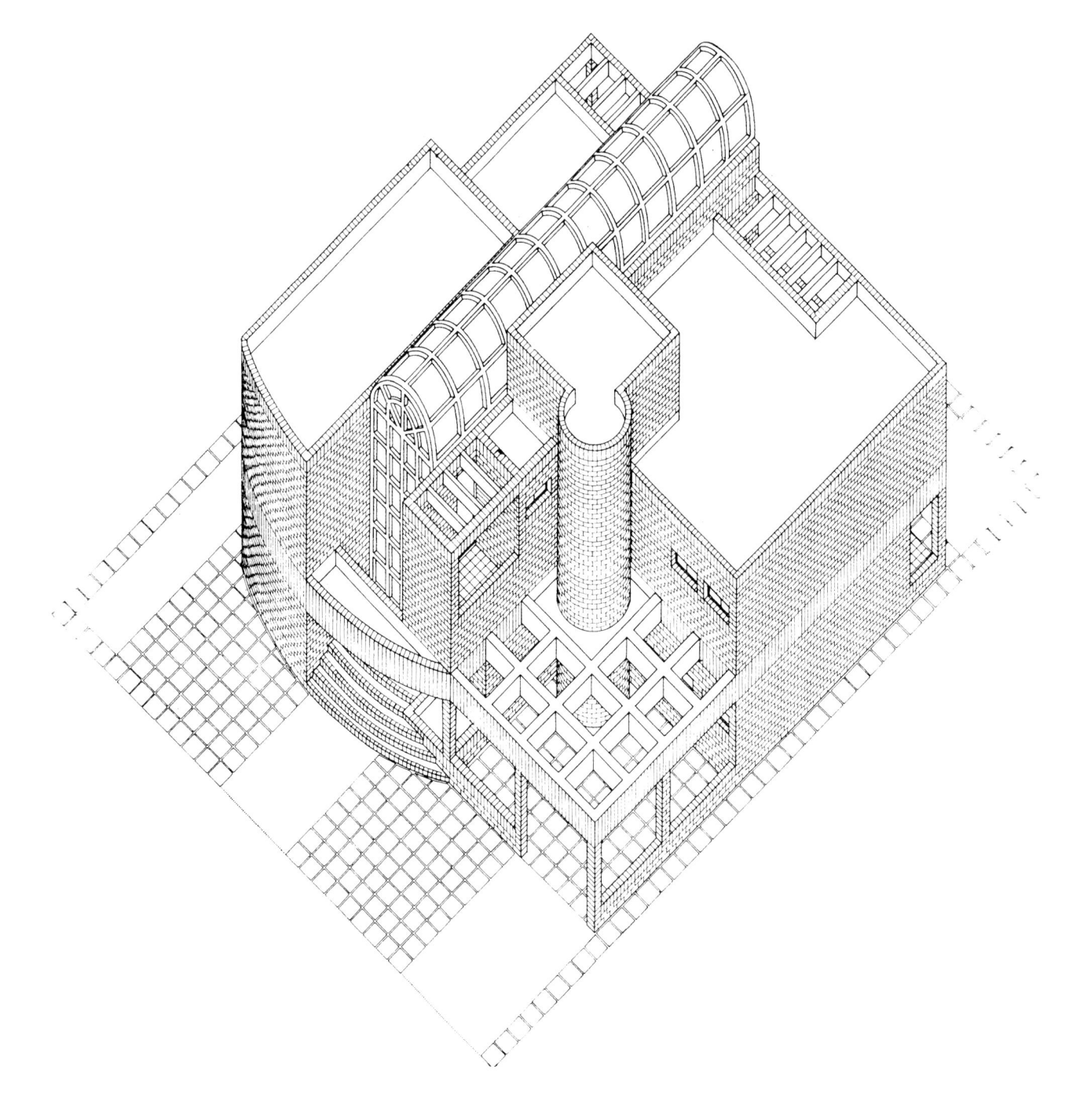

5.35. Villa in Abu Dhabi. Romproiect
(Romania), Viorel Trocan, Anca Oțoiu.

5.36. Diwaniyya for H.H. Emir of Kuwait—Cabinet for State Affairs, Kuwait City, 1980–82. Ministry of Public Works, Kuwait, Design Section, Jan Amos Havelka (deputy chief and project architect).

Ain without the opportunity to visit the site and with little information about the location (figure 5.35). The architects made the most of this commission and designed a complex geometry of volumes from glass and brick. Against all odds, Oțoiu recalls this work as "an experience of freedom," which contrasted with the usual routine of designing type projects in Romania.[177]

This overview shows differentiated modalities of work by architects from socialist countries in Kuwait: from employment by state contractors and design institutes in their home countries, through state-sponsored joint ventures, to individual contracts. Polish, Czech, Slovak, Hungarian, and Yugoslav professionals in Kuwait tended to change employers frequently, which also included state institutions. For instance, after his arrival in Kuwait on a Polytechna contract with KEG (1975), Czech architect Jan Amos Havelka moved to the Ministry of Public Works, where he became Deputy Chief Architect of the Design Section (1977–80) (figure 5.36).[178] In turn, Slovak architect Ján Strcula arrived to work for the National Housing Authority (1979), before moving to a number of private Kuwaiti offices.[179]

During their work in Kuwaiti offices, several architects from socialist countries were promoted to project leaders, in particular when the heads of the offices were engineers. Some of them became chief designers in major firms, including Janusz Krawecki at Gulf Consult.[180] Their authority was strengthened by their broad training in Eastern Europe, which prepared them to cover the design process from urban planning to the structure of the building, rather than leaving the latter to the office's engineers.[181] Al-Sanan, trained as an engineer, recalled about his office in the 1980s: "the architect was the authority; I was not interfering."[182] Eastern European architects negotiated directly with clients, and consulted on a whole range of projects, from opulent private villas to office towers, university campuses, and governmental buildings.[183]

When interviewed today, many among them recall ambitious contractors, eager to improve the quality of construction and interested in exchanges with architects. In turn, architects from socialist countries valued the opportunity to learn about cutting-edge technologies and construction materials, often unavailable in Eastern Europe.[184] In so doing, they learned to anticipate the capacity of contractors in Kuwait, where South Korean, Indian, and Pakistani contractors were receiving commissions for which cheap labor provided a competitive advantage, while European, Japanese, and American firms were typically commissioned for technologically challenging projects, increasingly joined by Kuwaiti and Saudi contractors.[185] Companies from socialist countries were part of the latter segment, either individually or as subcontractors. Besides the commissions of Energoprojekt, they included Yugoslavia's Union Inženjering as well as Strojexport and Armabeton of Czechoslovakia; the latter two were the contractors of Kuwait Towers (1977) which won the Aga Khan Award for Architecture in 1980.[186] In turn, the contractor Ivan Milutinovic (PIM) from Belgrade built several sections of the waterfront development.[187] East Germany's Spezialbetonbau Binz supplied the structure of Kuwait's planetarium (1985) and other East German companies supplied aluminum windows, door screens, and façade elements for the Bayan Park Conference Center.[188] The steel sections of the new telecommunications tower (1993) were provided by Poland's Mostostal-Zabrze.[189]

Supervision of the building sites, where many final details were drawn up, contributed to the quality of buildings while encouraging the architects to rediscover their vocation. In the words of Lach, "after my experience in Poland of a complete impotence of architects, I felt empowered by the architectural supervision in Kuwait, and I regained my confidence as a designer."[190] It was also in Kuwait that these architects became exposed to Western European and North American postmodernism. The Western architectural press (not always available in Poland and never affordable), was a major source of inspiration. By reading the *Architectural Review* in Kuwait, Jarząbek discovered the work of James Stirling, his ferryman to postmodern architecture, which had an impact on his Kuwaiti work and later Polish designs.[191] Exhibitions organized by the Society of Engineers, the NHA, and the Special Projects Department at the Ministry of Public Works provided further opportunities to learn about new ideas. Above all, it was by visiting buildings designed at that time in Kuwait by such American offices as SOM and TAC, along with their local counterparts, that these architects became directly acquainted with contemporary international architectural culture, construction, and technology.[192]

Kuwaiti Urbanities

Maybe the most relevant discovery the Wrocław group made after arriving in Kuwait was that their previous interests in contextual urbanity tuned in to the new climate of opinion in the city-state and in the Gulf in general. This does not mean that the requirement to reflect "Arab" and "Islamic" tradition did not puzzle them. In responding to this requirement, Eastern European professionals could rely on little that was specific to the Gulf from their training, unlike graduates of the University of Baghdad, where Mohamed Makiya and Vaclav Bašta lectured on monumental and vernacular building traditions of the region. The one source that could have been useful, namely publications about architecture in Soviet Central Asian Republics, did not seem to have served as a reference. The reason might have been the broadly modernist language of the buildings that were published in Eastern Europe, such as the Karl Marx State Library in Ashgabat, the capital of Turkmen Soviet Socialist Republic (Abdullah Akhmedov, 1964–75).[193] More generally, by the late 1970s Soviet Central Asia ceased to be the go-to example for socialist development in a non-European and an Islamic context, both because of the evidence of the social and environmental costs to Soviet industrialization in the region and, in particular,

> 5.37. Senior Citizens Housing, late 1970s, Kuwait City. Wojciech Jarząbek, Edward Lach.

> 5.38. Sabah al-Salem Neighborhood Site C, Mubarak al-Kabeer, 1977–82, general plan, 1978. Shiber Consult and INCO, Andrzej Bohdanowicz, Wojciech Jarząbek, Krzysztof Wiśniowski.

SOCIALISM WITHIN GLOBALIZATION

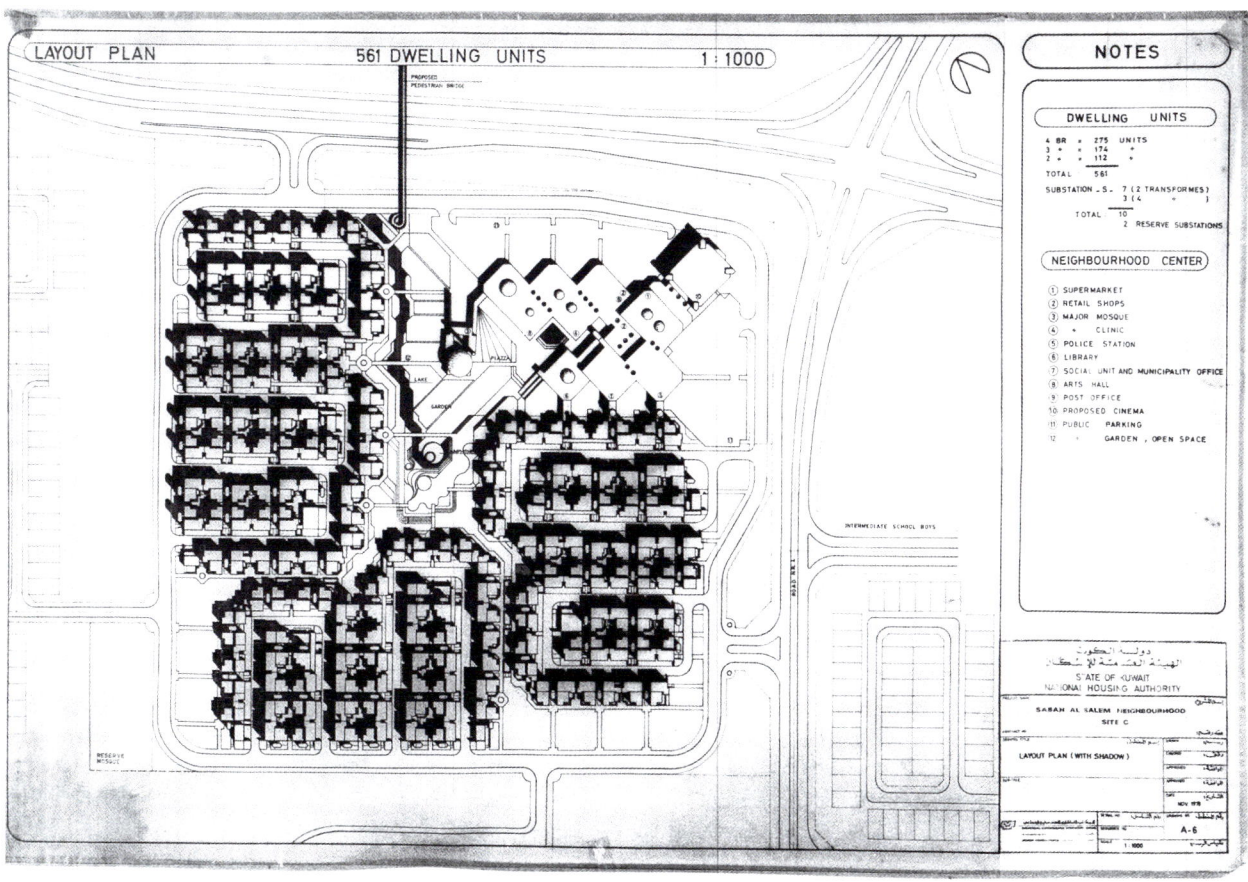

because of the damage of Soviet reputation in the wake of USSR's invasion of Afghanistan (1979).[194]

In order to produce type designs of schools (Mieczysław Rychlicki and Zdzisława Daczkowska for Gulf Consult), mosques (Anna Wiśniowska), and housing districts, these architects had to gather references elsewhere. Some of them walked in the city with a sketchbook, others studied the few available books, in particular Saba George Shiber's *Kuwait Urbanization* (1964), and followed debates in professional journals in the region, such as *Middle East Construction*.[195] In this way, the Wrocław architects extended their interest in traditional urban typologies in Silesia toward the Gulf region.

The blueprint of senior-citizens housing in Sharq by Lach and Jarząbek shows how these interests impacted their design work (figure 5.37). The project's scale, disposition, sequences of spaces, materials, and details directly referenced the disappearing courtyard typologies. This unrealized design from the early 1980s consisted of sixty one-story units grouped in nine compounds, opened to gardens on one side and facing on the other a pedestrian street with restaurants, coffee shops, diwawin, and shops, with a mosque and a polyclinic in the center. The housing compounds assembled residential units around a courtyard with common dining and living rooms, and facilities. Only several details, including large windows and shades, construction methods, air conditioning, and parking places for visitors attached to the compounds differed from the old courtyard buildings, photographs of which were included on the presentation drawings. Social contacts were in the center of the project, with elaborate perspectives showing residents in traditional urban situations: a narrow street, a diwaniyya, a garden, and a courtyard.

In contrast, direct quotations of historic buildings were avoided in the design of Site C in the Sabah al-Salem neighborhood (1982), a result of a competition won in 1977 by Bohdanowicz and Wiśniowski for Shiber Consult, and developed together with Jarząbek and INCO (figure 5.38).[196] The requirements of "Arab design" in both urban layout and floor plans that sustain traditional customs were included to the competition brief by the NHA. Together with the Ain Baghze project, the Sabah al-Salem was the biggest district laid out in 1970s Kuwait within the linear urbanization scheme proposed by the Buchanan master plan. Combining housing for lower and average income groups, the district was laid out in neighborhoods of approximately three thousand units with schools, community facilities, and a shopping center. Each of the neighborhoods was further divided into "sites" of three hundred to five hundred housing units grouped around a community center.[197]

In the Site C project, the requirement of the "Arab character" of architecture was conveyed by the interpretation of Kuwaiti courtyard typology (figure 5.39). The designers explained the courtyard structure of the apartment buildings by particular attention to privacy, enhanced by a split-level disposition, with the day part below and the night part above (figure 5.40). The day part included two larger rooms, one of which could be separated from the rest of the apartment and used as a diwaniyya, while the other would be used as a living room for the whole family. This followed the recommendation of the NHA, as did the possibility of transforming the terrace into an additional bedroom in the family part of the apartment.[198] The ground-floor apartments included a small garden or patio, to which several rooms were open, separated by a wall from carefully landscaped public spaces. The ensemble was constructed in sand brick and cement blocks, with structural elements in reinforced concrete cast on site, and later retrofitted with elevators (figures 5.41 and 5.42).

Differing from other neighborhoods in Sabah al-Salem, and from districts for average income groups designed by the Wrocław architects, Site

C was furnished with a network of pedestrian-only pathways.[199] Inspired by the dense urban fabric of Sharq, these pathways linked houses to the local community center with a mosque, kindergarten, and shops, situated diagonally in the neighborhood. Perpendicular to the pedestrian paths, a grid of roads for vehicle traffic was introduced, with parking spaces shaded by the overhangs resulting from the split-level section of the apartments.

The negotiation between car accessibility and pedestrian movement was given much attention by architects and planners in the 1970s and 1980s city-state. If in the 1960s, Saba Shiber had written that walking "has... become a lost and dead art" in Kuwait, over the next decade the revisions of the master plan paid particular attention to pedestrian zones.[200] The traditional souk was renovated as a pedestrian-only area, and underground passages at Safat Square and the al-Kuwait souk were constructed (SOM with SSH, 1976).[201] These interventions were intended to improve pedestrian areas in a city where most pavements were discontinuous, poorly surfaced, and cluttered with parked cars, in contrast to roads that complied with or surpassed US and Western European standards.[202]

Relations between the pedestrian and the car were recognized in Kuwait as a key challenge for an intended "Arab urbanism." Such considerations had already been in the focus of the brief of Kuwait's urban-development study commissioned from four European design offices: BBPR, Candilis-Josic-Woods, Reima Pietilä, and Alison and Peter Smithson (1968). The Smithsons suggested replacing the landscape of individual buildings standing in the midst of car parks with a mixed-use mat building, limited in height and punctuated by minarets, accessible on foot from parking garages distributed equidistantly.[203] A typology that took hold was a reinterpretation of the souk as a multistory structure combining parking garages, shops, offices, and cafes, equipped with an up-to-date air-conditioning system, elevators, and telecommunication facilities. The potential of this "modern souk" typology was demonstrated in the souk al-Kuwait, which included a double atrium, and in the souk al-Wataniya (TAC with PACE, 1979), with a "village" of duplex courtyard houses on the roof, among others.[204] Architects from Wrocław designed the souk Dawliyah, consisting of a multistory parking garage, partially open to the arcade surrounding the building on the street level, combined with offices around an atrium, and a separate office block on top (Daczkowski and Lach for GEO, late 1970s) (figures 5.43 and 5.44).[205] This typology, which accommodated a car-based lifestyle, responded to climatic concerns, and provided places for social interaction, was seen by many architects as an opportunity to redefine Kuwait's post-oil urbanity.

However, typologies that negotiated car users and pedestrians also brought complexities and contradictions to the fore that characterized urbanization processes in Kuwait. A case in point is the al-Othman Center, a commercial and residential complex in Hawally, designed by Jarząbek and Lach for Kuwait Engineering Group before the Iraqi invasion in 1990 but finished only in 1995 (figures 5.45 and 5.46). It consists of three floors of shopping and offices areas, twin ten-floor residential towers, and a multistory parking garage for three hundred and fifty cars. The department store groups several small shops around a narrow central atrium with escalators, extended onto two passages, connected by staircases.

The building is located at the intersection of al-Othman and Ibn-Khaldoun Streets, to which it opens by means of an arcade and four entrances on the external ends of the allotment. Yet in spite of a rhetorical opening to the street, the building is introverted. Shops were designed not as opening directly to the arcade, but instead to a passage shielded from the streets by a set of kiosks with stairs between, to accommodate the slope of Ibn-Khaldoun Street (figure 5.47). While these kiosks were eliminated in

CHAPTER 5

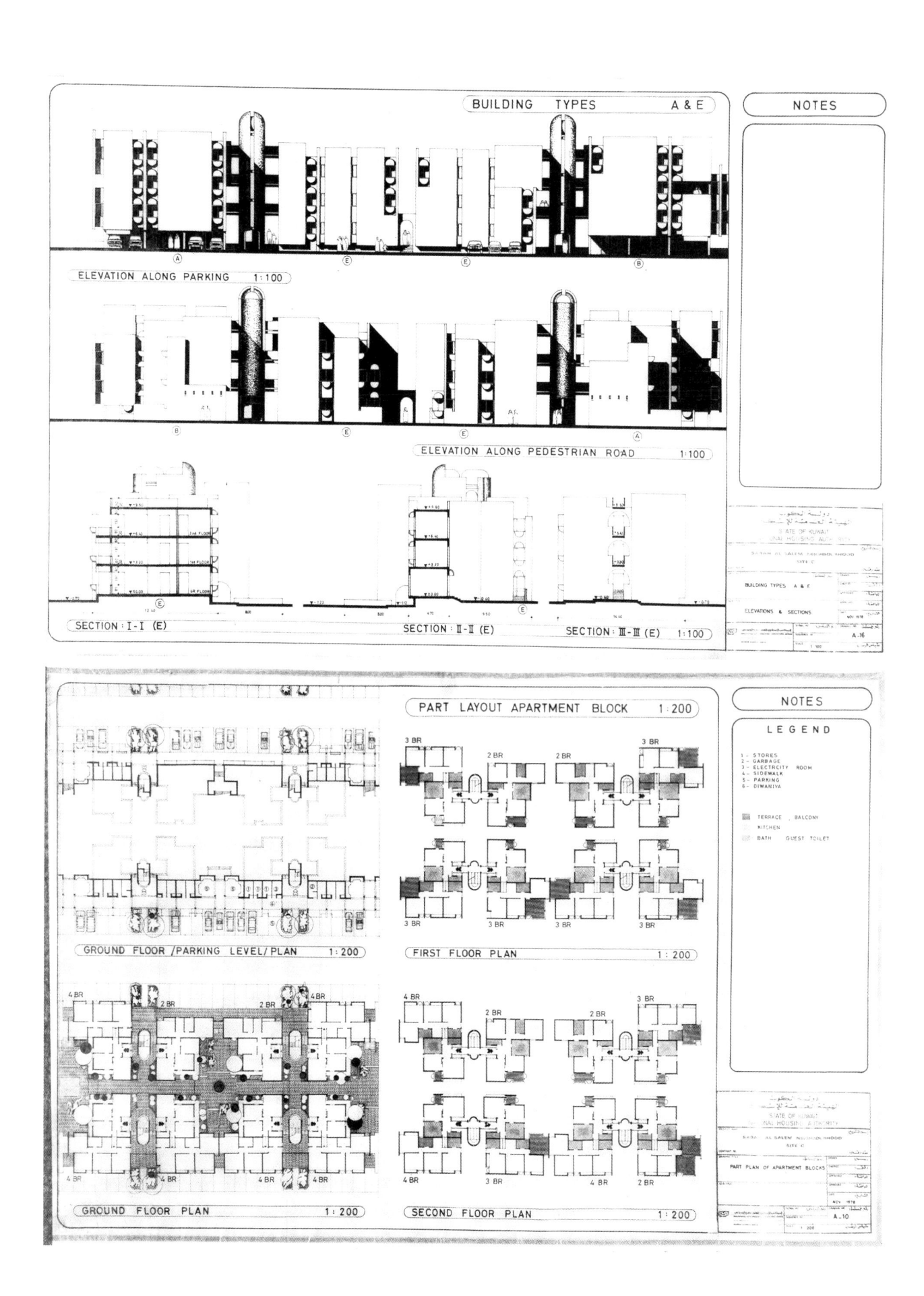

< 5.39. Sabah al-Salem Neighborhood Site C, Mubarak al-Kabeer, 1977–82, façades, 1978. Shiber Consult and INCO, Andrzej Bohdanowicz, Wojciech Jarząbek, Krzysztof Wiśniowski.

< 5.40. Sabah al-Salem Neighborhood Site C, Mubarak al-Kabeer, 1977–82, plans, 1978. Shiber Consult and INCO, Andrzej Bohdanowicz, Wojciech Jarząbek, Krzysztof Wiśniowski.

5.41. Sabah al-Salem Neighborhood Site C, Mubarak al-Kabeer, 1977–82. Shiber Consult and INCO, Andrzej Bohdanowicz, Wojciech Jarząbek, Krzysztof Wiśniowski.

5.42. Sabah al-Salem Neighborhood Site C, Mubarak al-Kabeer, 1977–82. Shiber Consult and INCO, Andrzej Bohdanowicz, Wojciech Jarząbek, Krzysztof Wiśniowski.

SOCIALISM WITHIN GLOBALIZATION

5.43. Souk Dawliyah during construction, Kuwait City, late 1970s. GEO, Ryszard Daczkowski, Edward Lach.

5.44. Souk Dawliyah, Kuwait City, late 1970s. GEO, Ryszard Daczkowski, Edward Lach.

5.45. Al-Othman Center, Hawally, 1995. KEG, Wojciech Jarząbek, Edward Lach.

5.46. Al-Othman Center, Hawally, 1995. KEG, Wojciech Jarząbek, Edward Lach.

the realized building, the stairs were built according to the initial design. They are sparsely distributed and narrow, at odds with the image of the arcade. Long stretches from the entrance area to the atrium contrast with the short connection between the atrium and the parking garage at the point when the two buildings, based on skewed construction grids, touch each other (figure 5.48).

A similar hiatus between an image of urban space and its uses can be seen in three apartment buildings constructed in Salmiya in 1978 according to the design by Andrzej Bohdanowicz for Shiber Consult (figure 5.49). They stand out among the neighboring structures, distinguished by their careful sequencing of transition spaces between apartment and street. However, these shared spaces are hardly maintained, and this is also the case with the streets nearby, which often have no sidewalks. This poor maintenance of Salmiya resulted from the neighborhood's structure of inhabitants with apartment buildings, including those designed by Bohdanowicz, rented to lower-income immigrants. According to the 1980 census, over three-fifths of the population in Kuwait and three-quarters of the labor force consisted of immigrants, which held true both for those in skilled occupations and for those with intermediate and manual jobs.[206] At the same time, only citizens were entitled to housing provisions (and to ownership of property). As a result, housing districts in Kuwait were divided into low-density villa neighborhoods within gardened avenues, for citizens, and areas inhabited by *bidun* (stateless people) and migrants. The latter ranged from upper-grade apartments rented by better-paid professional groups, to overpopulated workers' apartments, surrounded by poorly cared for streets.[207] While Kuwaitis expected the government to maintain their neighborhoods and provide social services, noncitizens had few instruments to put pressure on the authorities and landlords. They could, at best, associate in district

288 CHAPTER 5

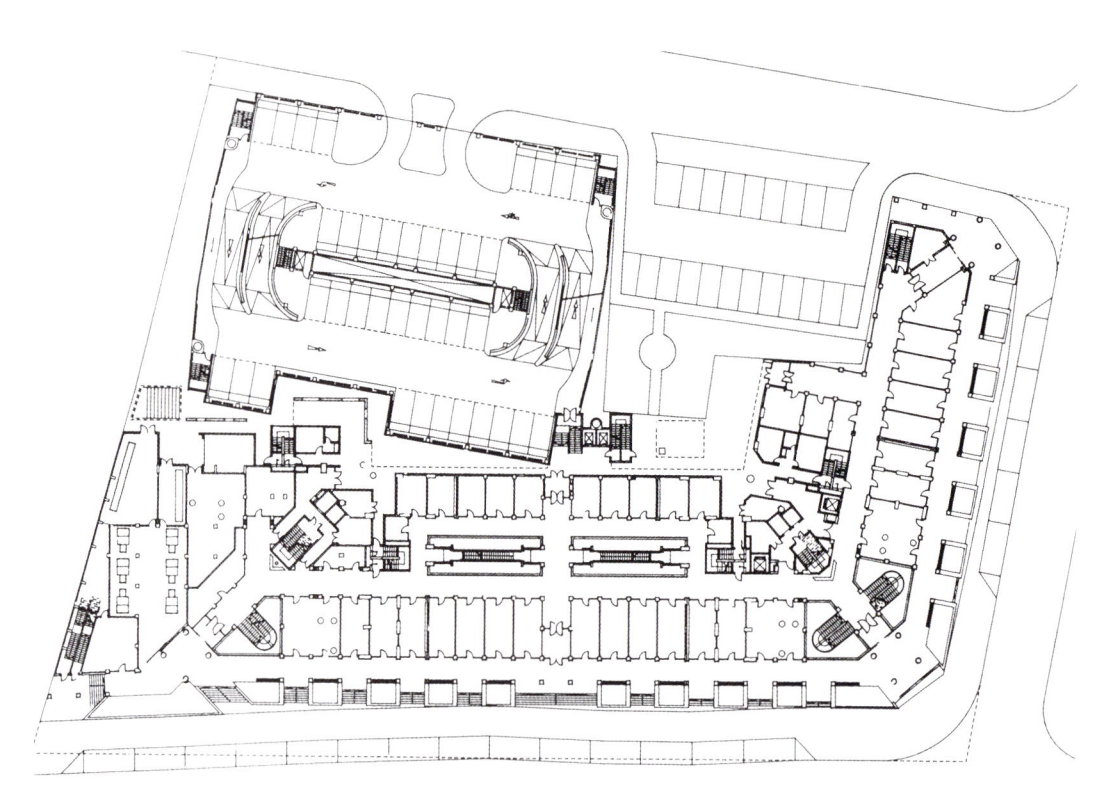

< 5.47. Al-Othman Center, Hawally, 1995, ground floor plan. KEG, Wojciech Jarząbek, Edward Lach.

< 5.48. Al-Othman Center, Hawally, 1995, interior. KEG, Wojciech Jarząbek, Edward Lach.

5.49. Residential building in Salmiya, 1978. Shiber Consult, Andrzej Bohdanowicz.

neighborhood councils, which mobilized self-help efforts designed to raise the standard of a district's welfare and to petition representatives of the central government.[208]

The application of urban typologies that projected an image of spatial practices that were generally absent in Kuwait, such as those in the al-Othman Center and the Salmiya apartments, did not simply stem from the architects' formalist approach. Rather, these typologies were often explicitly demanded by the commissioners themselves, as the design of the Baloush bus station shows. This ensemble resulted from a competition won by INCO (Wiśniowski, Wiśniowska, L. Chyczewski, 1984) (figure 5.50). The program of a bus station implied that its users would be mainly low-income, non-Kuwaiti residents, who were the main users of buses according to studies carried out in the 1980s.[209] After the competition, the Kuwait Public Transport Company changed the functional program and replaced commercial spaces proposed by the architects with openly accessible "public" spaces without commercial use, which is how the building was constructed in 1988.[210] In spite of the building's multiple gestures toward public space—pronounced eaves, two open entrance pavilions, and the basilica section of the main hall—it could not have become a space where people of different backgrounds meet, and it was unable to fill the gap of such spaces depleted during the process of post-oil urbanization (figure 5.51).[211]

The Baloush station and other designs by Wrocław architects responded to the climate of opinion in Kuwait in the 1980s by reimagining the pre-oil urban fabric (Sabah al-Salem), by alluding to images acculturated in the Middle East by colonial urbanism (al-Othman Center), or by reinterpreting the 1970s souk (souk Dawliyah). However, it was against the background of these more familiar images that the "other within" appeared: the migrant, the noncitizen, and the bidun. This is also the case in the landscape of stairs and ramps of the Port Complex in Shuwaikh, another won

5.50. Baloush Bus Terminal, Kuwait City, 1984–88. INCO, L. Chyczewski, Anna Wiśniowska, Krzysztof Wiśniowski.

5.51. Baloush Bus Terminal, Kuwait City, 1984–88, interior. INCO, L. Chyczewski, Anna Wiśniowska, Krzysztof Wiśniowski.

competition project (Bohdanowicz, Wiśniowski for INCO, 1982–92).[212] The only pedestrians I met around this building when I visited in 2014 were immigrant blue-collar workers trying to catch a minibus. They needed to wait for it on the artificially watered lawn next to the expressway since there was no other place where the bus could stop without disturbing private-car traffic of white-collar employees (figure 5.52).

Such sites qualify the statements of Polish architects who, when interviewed today, often emphasize that they saw their work in the Gulf as apolitical. By this, they mean not only their lack of belief in the socialist system, which they were representing according to Polservice guidelines, but also their refusal to attribute any type of political instrumentality to their designs. However, the politics of an architecture is distinct from the politics of its architects, and the neighborhoods, commercial spaces, and office buildings that they designed in Kuwait contributed to the redistribution of places and times in the city-state according to categories of class, occupation, gender, and nationality. In this way, their work was part of the negotiations and conflicts that, since the late 1970s, revolved around questions of citizenship, societal modernization, political representation, welfare entitlement, and national identity in the Gulf.

The Profile of an Expert

The ways in which Eastern European architects reimagined Kuwaiti urbanities might be interpreted as a confirmation of the narrative of architecture's role as a cultural "mediator" of imported typologies and international technologies, which was a dominant rhetoric in the 1980s Gulf. The technologies of the car, the escalator, the elevator, air conditioning, and prefabricated construction systems appear to be moderated by floor plans inspired by courtyard houses or covered by details abstracted from pre-oil monuments. However, rather than insisting on the opposition between foreign technologies and local culture, a closer focus on imported building materials, management procedures, and computerized design environments employed in Kuwait shows that they facilitated, rather than hindered, the recontextualization of Kuwaiti architecture.

As was the case with TES in the Abu Dhabi Emirate, cultural and technological expertise reinforced each other in the work of Eastern Europeans in Kuwait. However, while the head designers of TES tapped into their previous, extensive experience with Arab clients and Western enterprises, for the Czech, Slovak, Hungarian, Polish, and Yugoslav architects the absorption of both types of expertise was part of their overarching learning process in the Gulf. This ability to learn was not just an individual virtue but rather it was part of the profile stipulated by socialist FTOs for professionals leaving on export contracts by the last two decades of the Cold War.

An entry point to this discussion can be provided by controversies around the single construction material most strongly associated with the modern movement: reinforced concrete (figure 5.53). By the late 1970s, the Kuwaiti press noted that while most buildings in the city-state were less than twenty to thirty years old, the concrete often displayed an appalling level of deterioration.[213] Its decay in the hot, salty, humid, dust-laden climate of the Gulf became hard to overlook when the cracked and spalled concrete of the boom-era buildings became a familiar sight in Kuwait and elsewhere in the region.[214] The oil boom in the early 1970s brought about rising costs of land, construction, and rents, followed by the shift among main investors in real estate from individuals to developers and governmental agencies. If that shift contributed to the professionalization of the building industry and to tighter supervision, the rapid pace of

5.52. Port Authority, Shuwaikh, 1982–92. INCO, Andrzej Bohdanowicz, Krzysztof Wiśniowski.

5.53. Anwar al-Sabah Complex at the Fahad al-Salem Street, Kuwait City, 1960s.

construction during the boom period had an adverse impact on the quality of construction.[215]

While in Kuwait the poor quality of these buildings often resulted from the procedure of automatically accepting the lowest tender for all development work, some participants in the debate argued that foreign architects specified products, technologies, and standards unsuitable in the Gulf, including those pertaining to reinforced concrete.[216] Professional journals reported that in Bahrain, "collapsing balconies are not uncommon" and that governmental schools had their lifespan dramatically shortened because of rebar corrosion. Office buildings, a hotel, a major shopping center, and the concrete causeway linking Bahrain with the Saudi mainland became a subject of concern.[217] A study discussed in the professional press (1987) estimated the life expectancy of a concrete building in Saudi Arabia at ten to fifteen years (in comparison to sixty to eighty years in less tiring environments). Another study for an unnamed Gulf city extended this span to twenty-seven years, hardly an optimistic estimate either, meaning that buildings constructed during the boom years would need to be demolished by the end of the century.[218]

In response, private investors and governmental agencies introduced a number of preventive measures. These were tested in regional building-research laboratories, discussed at professional conferences, and popularized in the technical press.[219] They included epoxy coating of steel reinforcement (the Gulf's first coating facility was established in Abu Dhabi), dense concrete (impervious to the salts that threaten the rebar), pulverized fuel ash as an alternative to cement, and surface coating that sealed the concrete against chlorides and other contaminants.[220] A new generation of concrete technologies, either imported or locally produced on foreign license, promised to dispense with technical problems associated with post-oil concrete buildings. But these materials also offered new

SOCIALISM WITHIN GLOBALIZATION

possibilities for expressing the cultural specificity of the region. For example, producers offered large-scale prefabricated elements with openings in the shape of ogee arches, and "ornamental" rubber molding for precast façade panels that, when used on a building in Abu Dhabi, were accepted by an architectural critic as giving the high-rise "a local vernacular feel."[221]

Eastern Europeans were eager to apply these new technologies and embraced their potential in order to accommodate the demand for a visual environment into which collective identities could be projected. For example, in his design of the Bayan Park complex, Maksimović specified white-cement concrete for all main visible structural elements, solid external walls, and mashrabiyya sun breakers. The project description made a point of stressing that these elements allowed the achievement of a "special regional identity of a modern building."[222] Austenitic stainless steel as well as careful specification of the components of concrete and their treatment became necessary for constructing details that were both decorative and technically challenging. Among them was the complex floor plan of the al-Mazidi building in Fintas, designed by Andrzej Bohdanowicz in the shape of an eight-pointed star, which he described as an "Arab" geometry (1982, demolished).

Other materials entering the market included glass-reinforced concrete (GRC) produced on foreign license by numerous factories in the region. This was the very material that Lach and Jarząbek foresaw for the decorative elements in their entry to the Abu Dhabi Municipality Building competition.[223] GRC's light weight, good thermal properties, chemical resistance, and the fact that it could be cast into virtually every profile made it a favorable refurbishment and cladding material across the Gulf in the 1980s.[224] Along with other cladding systems, often presented by their producers as "reflect[ing] Arabesque aesthetic values," these materials were used by architects charged with the task of redesigning buildings' envelopes.[225] This was an increasingly widespread design commission in view of the newly introduced requirements of thermal insulation of governmental and other buildings in the UAE and elsewhere.[226]

The introduction of these construction technologies and materials was paralleled by an advancement of building management procedures. They included the organization of building sites and, over the course of the 1970s, the NHA argued against large housing projects, which proved to be too difficult to manage. The construction site of the Sabah al-Salem neighborhood was a case in point, when thirty-five hundred workers went on strike in October 1980 because their employer, the Pakistani government–owned National Construction Company, had not paid their wages for two and half months. This was a consequence of the inability of the contractor to accommodate inflation and the rise in prices of materials that were underestimated when the contractors had submitted the tender application two years before.[227] Other projects of the NHA became notorious when inhabitants publicly complained about technical failures, which they associated with inexperienced workers, notably by Korean firms ("no more than army conscripts without the necessary skills").[228]

With such glitches becoming increasingly common in the highly competitive market in Kuwait, the NHA declared that no single contractor was to be given more than five hundred housing units to build, and opted for increasing the share of contracts going to locally registered joint ventures. While the main aims included the diversion of profits back to the country, the provision of more efficient procedures of capacity control and risk management, as well as enhancement of the knowledge and expertise of local firms, the regulations also set an end to large, uniform housing projects.[229]

At the same time, the NHA introduced the requirement of computerization of the design and construction process. The objective was

5.54. Fintas Center, Fintas, 1980, model. Arthur Erickson (Canada). Kuwait Municipality, KEG, Dar al-Handasah (Lebanon), "Fintas Centre. Eastern Block Development. Summary Report," 1987.

acceleration of information flow between all actors involved, the optimization of risk management, the facilitation of communication between them, and ensuring their accountability within the design-and-build procedure.[230] For many architectural and construction firms from the United States and the UK, the Middle East became one of the first places to implement computer-aided design (CAD), on a commercial scale. This technology, used by the Bechtel Group and SOM in Saudi Arabia, and by John Bonnington and Ove Arup in Kuwait, dramatically accelerated the production of tender documentation, the coordination of architectural and engineering drawings, possibilities of visualization and designing in variants, and the ability to respond to contract program updates and forecasts.[231]

For most architects from socialist countries, the projects in Kuwait offered the first opportunity to work with CAD. This included those working for Archicentre, which introduced CAD for the Bayan Park complex and Amiri Diwan projects. With CAD files transferred by modem overnight, the computerization of the design work allowed for its division and integration among Archicentre's subdesigners in England, West Germany, Finland, and Kuwait, resulting in an acceleration of the production of the extensive documentation for both projects.[232] Orlin Ilinčev, one of the Czech architects who taught themselves and then operated CAD software for Archicentre, recalled that CAD-produced layouts of grids, columns, and perimeter walls were combined with manual drawings. By the mid-1980s, CAD was also used for 3D presentation renderings of the Amiri Diwan.[233]

Other offices invested in CAD, too. KEG bought the General Drafting System (GDS) especially for the working drawings of the Fintas Center project, prepared by a group of architects from Poland according to the design by Arthur Erickson (figure 5.54).[234] The use of GDS was necessary because of the size and the short timing of the project, but also because

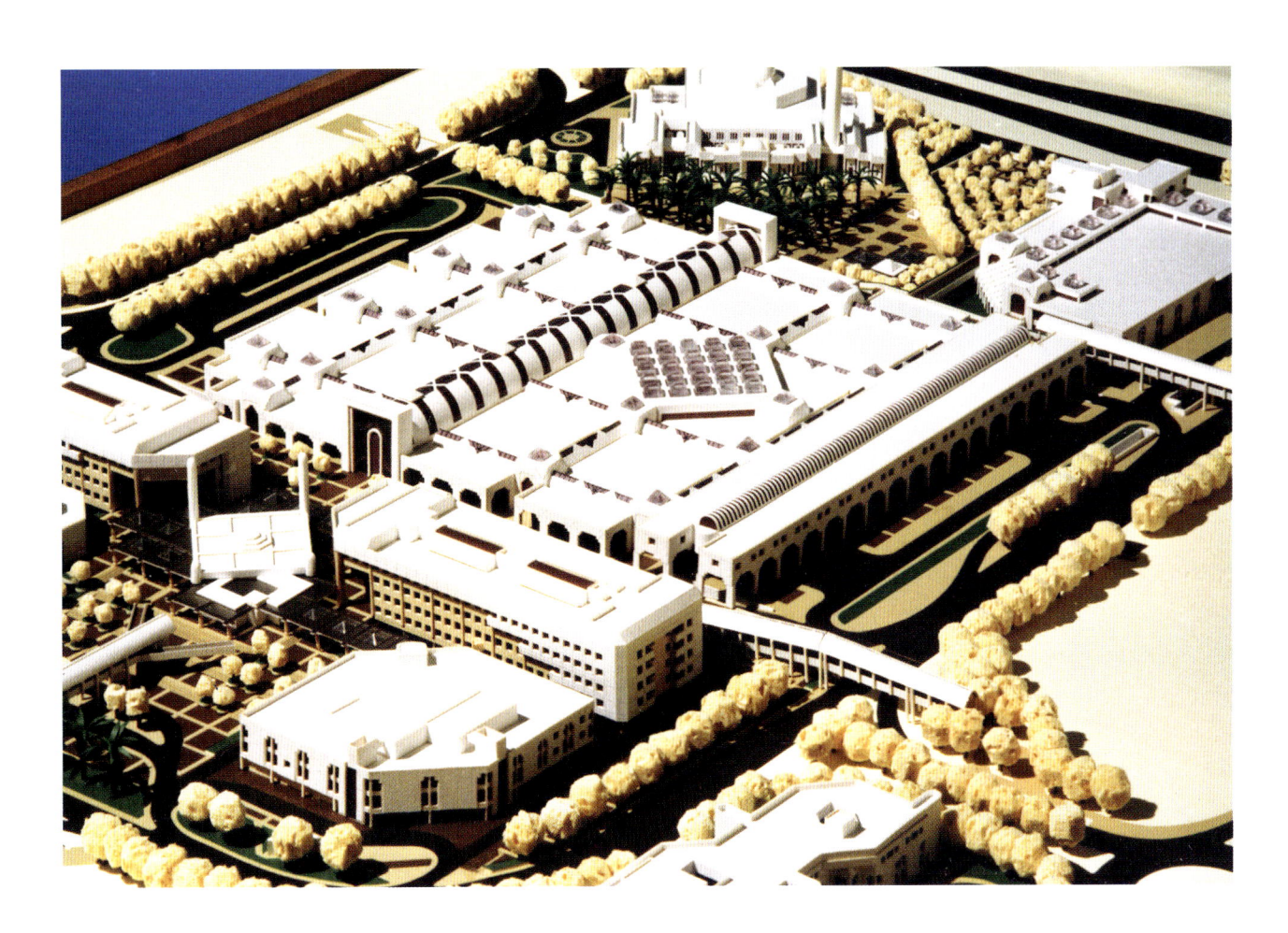

SOCIALISM WITHIN GLOBALIZATION

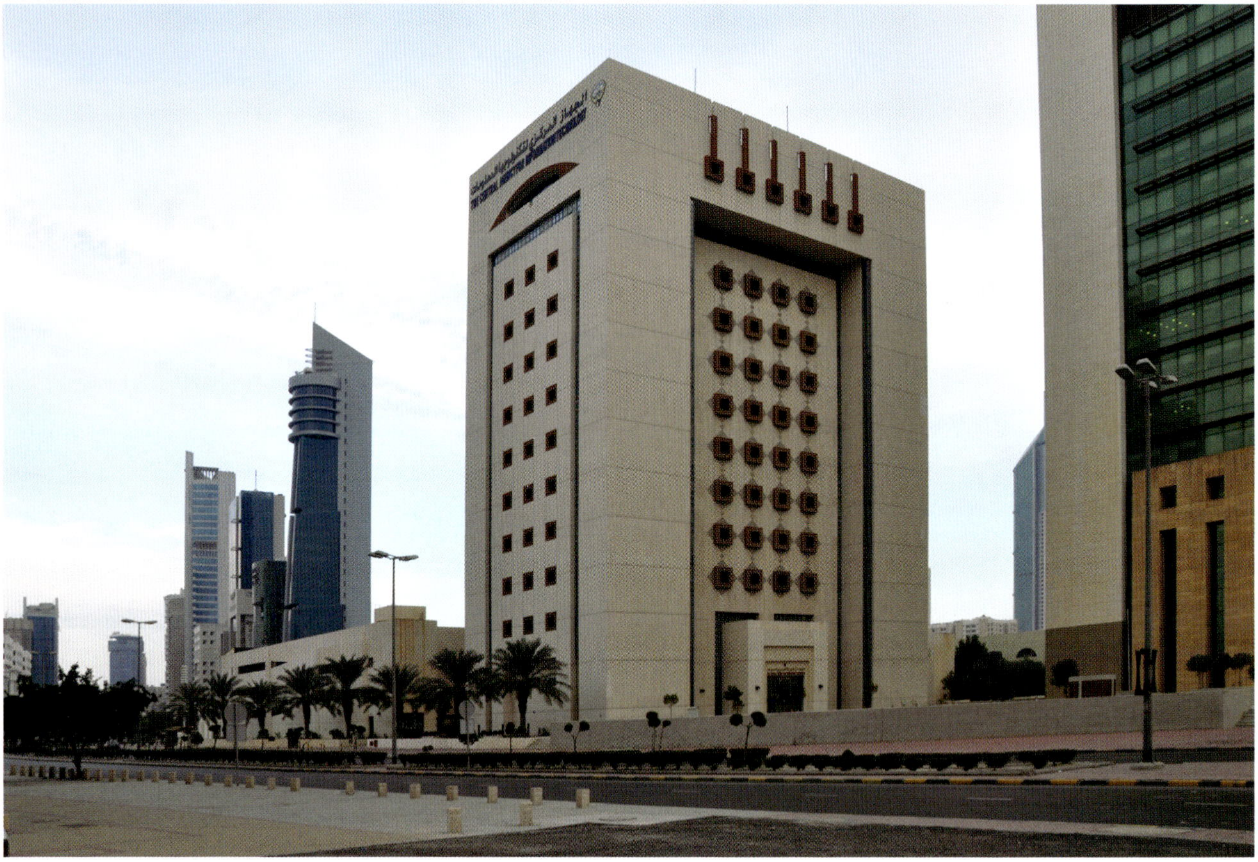

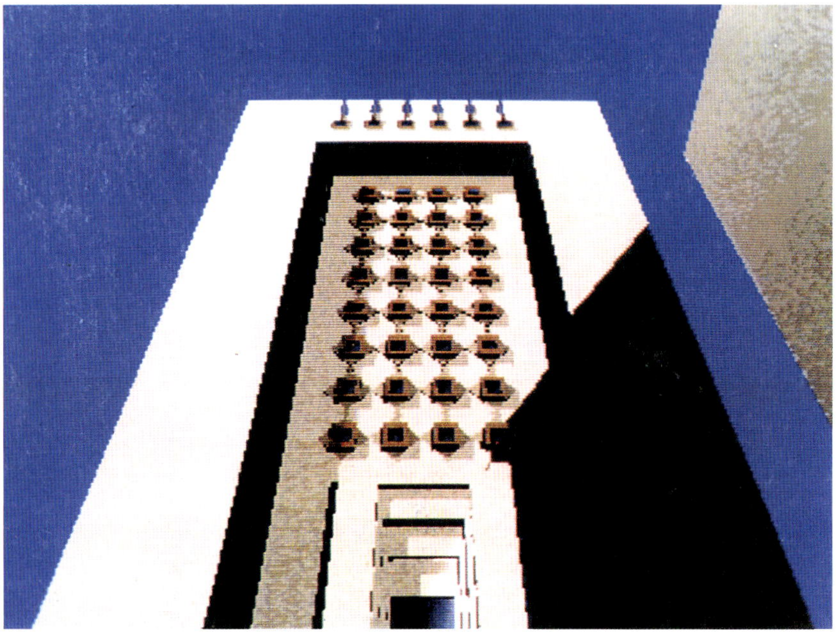

< 5.55. Audit Bureau Headquarters Building, Kuwait City, 1986–96. KEG, Wojciech Jarząbek, Edward Lach.

< 5.56. Audit Bureau Headquarters Building, Kuwait City, 1986–96, CAD rendering. KEG, Wojciech Jarząbek, Edward Lach.

of the complexity of the design, which included air-conditioned pedestrian malls clustered with offices and community facilities, and one section designed as a souk.[235] In the wake of this (unrealized) project, CAD technology was used by architects from Wrocław in other projects of KEG, and soon became a new standard, applied in the al-Qurain neighborhood and the Baloush bus station designs.[236]

The increasing computational capacity of CAD sped up the design and construction of ornamental details, too. This can be seen in the façades and interiors of the Audit Bureau, designed by Jarząbek and Lach in Kuwait City before the invasion but finished only in 1996 (figure 5.55). The building is prominently located at Ahmad al-Jaber Street in Kuwait City and consist of office spaces, a conference hall, a library, a safety shelter, and a parking garage. The building was designed without historical references in its silhouette and volume, and ornaments were restricted to elaborate, three-dimensional decoration of the windows, a distant reference to a mashrabiyya, all drawn by CAD (figure 5.56). This technology was also used in the design of the al-Othman Center that, as with the Audit Bureau, was finished after the Iraqi invasion. The building's careful details, including the complex geometry of ceramic tiles drawn with software provided by their West German producer, were exceptional within the general drop of building expertise in 1990s Kuwait.

The implementations of CAD and other imported technologies in Kuwait through the 1980s were instances of deterritorialization and reterritorialization of expert systems across diverse social and cultural situations. Such instances have been discussed by Science and Technology Studies (STS) scholars in their analyses of global knowledge transfers. In line with these studies, construction sites and architectural offices in the Gulf may appear as "technological zones" where international actors agreed upon standards and norms, negotiated the application of construction materials by interpreting building specifications, and conducted experiments concerning the performance of building materials to be applied.[237] However, while STS scholars writing about technological zones described them as places where the separation between "global" (or "Western") and "local" regimes are forged, the protagonists of this chapter engaged in a different type of negotiation.[238] They demonstrated that the use of imported prefabrication methods, CAD software, and other expert systems did not clash with the demand for cultural specificity but, instead, allowed for its accommodation.

By the 1970s, this capacity to deterritorialize knowledge from previous conditions of its implementation and to reterritorialize it in new contexts was emphasized by state-socialist FTOs, such as Polservice, Polytechna, and Tesco. While architects from Wrocław arrived in Kuwait without previous experience in the Arab world, they fully subscribed to the profile of "our specialists abroad" stipulated by Polservice in the brochure *Rights and Obligations of an Expert* (1972). Polservice expected Polish experts to be flexible, open-minded, and willing and able to learn and to implement innovations, whether in architectural culture, building technology, or construction management.[239] Polservice's managers required from candidates high professional qualifications, efficiency, dedication, and an ability to adapt to the new environment, while prohibiting them any "involvement in political or religious debates" in host countries.[240] By the 1970s, this profile took precedence in Polservice's recruitment procedures and marketing efforts over involvements into postwar reconstruction, which had been showcased by the previous generation of Polish professionals. The expertise implied by this profile—generalist rather than specialist, portable rather than place-bound—had been supported by the training of the Wrocław architects, straddling engineering, architecture, and urban planning, which was valued in Kuwaiti offices, all the more so as it came with a modest price tag.

SOCIALISM WITHIN GLOBALIZATION

Professional competence, imagination, leadership, and organizational skills had been required since the 1950s from conveyors of socialist technical assistance.[241] However, in the final two decades of the Cold War, socialist FTOs expanded their expectations of experts sent to the increasingly competitive markets in the Middle East and North Africa. For example, in a 1980 issue of *Magyar Építőművészet* (Hungarian Architecture) the author argued that professional competence was not enough, since the commission needed to be "won, defended, and kept." The offer "becomes palpable and acceptable to the commissioner by the person of the architect, their eloquence, culture, appearance, humor, and trustworthiness," behind which the commissioner "can sense professional competence on the highest level." According to the author, "men of such profile" were the pivot of "Hungarian intellectual export."[242] Most protagonists of this chapter embraced such a profile and imagined themselves as autonomous, self-realizing, flexible in relations, open to change and risk, and critical of the past—a subjectivity that announced that of twenty-first-century architectural workers.[243]

Not everybody was thrilled, however, by this overidentification of architects from socialist countries with the subjectivity of their Western competitors. For example, in her 1987 report from the Gulf, East German architect Maria Gross wrote that "design labor became cheap in Kuwait"—both because of the increasing use of computers and because local consultants hire "cheap labor" from abroad.[244] While informed by a professional ethics that belonged to a world that was about to disappear, Gross also sensed a new one emerging. This world comes to the fore in her list of suppliers of "cheap labor," which included "Bangladesh, India, the Philippines, Poland, Yugoslavia, and Egypt"—a new geography of architectural workers beyond Cold War dichotomies.[245]

CONCLUSION: GLOBALIZATION BY WEAK ACTORS

The 1990 Iraqi invasion of Kuwait was followed by the exodus of foreign professionals from the city-state. The invasion coincided with the end of socialism in Eastern Europe, and most Wrocław architects returned to Poland. On their arrival, they became known by the nickname "Kuwaitis," and they helped shape the urban landscape of 1990s Wrocław. For example, Jarząbek designed the first department store in the city center after 1989 (Solpol, 1993) (figure 5.57), by using CAD technology that he had previously utilized in the Audit Bureau and al-Othman Center projects. Lach was responsible for the Dominikańska department store alongside the medieval town (1999), among other commissions.[246]

In general, the experience of working in the Gulf, the Middle East, and North Africa in the final decade of the Cold War was a decisive career step that prepared a large number of architects from Eastern Europe for practicing architecture after the end of socialism. By the 1980s, with economic crises in most socialist countries and with exchanges with the West being restricted, filtered, and unequal, it was the experience of working in Asia and Africa that furnished many Eastern European architects with learning opportunities and testing grounds for new ideas. After their return to Eastern Europe, they distinguished themselves by their professional knowledge and familiarity with functional programs with which architects who had practiced only in state socialism had little experience, from underground parking garages and middle-class housing to office parks and shopping malls.[247] Architects from Czechoslovakia, Bulgaria, Hungary, Poland, Romania, the Soviet Union, and Yugoslavia benefited from their experience with cutting-edge technologies from CAD software to construction technologies and advanced materials. While some among them had already had experience with private commissions, which in the final

5.57. Solpol Department Store, Wrocław (Poland), 1991–93. Studio A+R, Wojciech Jarząbek.

two decades of the Cold War were increasingly tolerated by the authorities in several Eastern European countries, in the Gulf they learned about the organization of large private offices and became acquainted with local entrepreneurs, and international developers and contractors.

No less important was the acquaintance with postmodernism, which was embraced by investors, authorities, and the broad public in postsocialist Eastern Europe. While Eastern European architects were aware of and engaged with postmodern debates since the 1970s, it was only after the end of socialism that postmodern forms were turned into a new mainstream, facilitated by imported programs, materials, building technologies, and capital.[248] This included not only the imports of Western models, tested in the Middle Eastern "laboratories of postmodernism," but also the rediscovery of traditional forms of urbanity, whether the casbah of Algiers, or colonial transplants of European nineteenth-century urbanism in the Maghreb and the Levant. For instance, Andrzej Ryba, the designer of the first office block in the center of postsocialist Warsaw (the Atrium Complex, 1994–2002), saw it as a return to Warsaw's historic urbanity, in continuation with his contextual designs in 1980s Syria.[249] Reversing the vectors of knowledge transfers discussed in this book, Eastern European architects returning from export contracts thought Warsaw through Damascus, Prague through Kuwait City, and Sofia through Abu Dhabi.

The Atrium Complex in Warsaw also testifies to the importance of contacts with international firms that Eastern European architects made during their work abroad: Ryba received this commission from Swedish contractor and developer Skanska, based on the firm's previous acquaintance with Polish architects in 1980s Syria and Libya.[250] Based on their previous contacts and their experience with international markets, several architects returning from the Middle East to postsocialist Europe set up joint ventures with Western firms. Among them was Prague architect Orlin Ilinčev, who entered into collaboration with the UK's Wilson Mason.[251] Others, including Jan Amos Havelka, did not come back to design practice. Instead, they were hired by the state administration and tapped into their previous experience with Western firms that, by then, were encouraged to invest in the Czech Republic.[252]

The sense of pride with which Eastern European architects recall their ability to integrate into the new capitalist market in postsocialist Europe needs to be understood against the backdrop of the overarching dissolution of design institutions and contractors, the breaking up of professional networks and standards, and the general dilapidation of buildings and infrastructures in postsocialist countries. This creative destruction, brought to Eastern Europe by the economic shock therapies of the 1990s, was paralleled by destruction *sans phrase* by military action in Yugoslavia, and by wars in Libya, Syria, and Iraq, which largely interrupted the engagements of Eastern European contractors in these countries. The counterpart of that pride might have been a tendency by my interviewees to retroactively emphasize the confluence, rather than divergence, between their export work during socialism and that of Western actors. This tendency came to the fore in several recollections quoted in this chapter. But those recollections also point to the fact that the continuities in architectural practice between socialist and postsocialist periods had nothing to do with an inert persistence, and everything to do with a frantic adaptation to new realities in order to "survive," a word used quite often in the interviews.

"Romproiect survived because of our acquaintance with the construction process in the conditions of a competitive market," Gheorghe Radu Stănculescu told me, when I interviewed him in his Bucharest office in 2015. Stănculescu had been Romproiect's resident architect on its export contracts in 1980s North Africa, then the firm's head manager in the 2000s. After being privatized in the mid-1990s, Romproiect offered its services to investors from the UK, France, and Israel who were keen to enter Romania.[253] Energoprojekt, too, benefited from its contracts outside Europe when the contractor's operations were undermined by the war in Yugoslavia and Western sanctions against Serbia. As recalled by its former employees, the contractor was able to continue its operations because of commissions received in Vietnam (which was itself under US sanctions), Malaysia, and other countries in Southeast Asia.[254] For Energoprojekt and other companies from the former Yugoslavia, such as Macedonia's Beton, the Russian market and that of the former Soviet republics, in particular Ukraine, provided a lifeline, as was the case with Romproiect, Miastoprojekt, and TES.

In the new millennium, some of these firms returned to North Africa and the Middle East, and sometimes reengaged with the tasks on which their predecessors had worked in previous decades. Warsaw Development Consortium (WADECO) delivered master plans for Libya in the 2010s, in continuation of its planning projects from the 1980s, and Hungarian firms are currently bidding to participate in the renovation of the 5 July 1962 Stadium in Algiers, designed by Közti.[255] TES, too, continues to receive commissions in North Africa and the Middle East, and its manager pointed out that the Bulgarian firm typically works on midsize contracts, while smaller contracts are operated by local firms, and bigger ones are granted to Western companies. Individual architects who stayed in Arab countries after 1989 often occupy a similar middle ground on their labor markets, expressed in the range of architects' salaries, in particular in the Gulf countries, where salaries are related to the passport of the employee.

The current positions of Eastern European actors in these processes have been path-dependent upon their original placements in the Middle East and North Africa since the late 1950s by means of state-socialist networks. Those placements concerned both institutional affiliations, in public or private offices, but also the "weak" bargaining position of non-Soviet actors. That weak position was typically shared by a state-socialist company, under pressure to fulfill the compulsory "hard currency plan," and by individual architects employed by a local planning agency, for whom a dismissal would inhibit their career prospects and deprive them of the opportunities that came with overseas contracts. This "weakness" was structural, hence independent of personalities and abilities of the individuals involved, including such exceptionally skilled designers as Dimitar Bogdanov of TES and Zoran Bojović of Energoprojekt. Yet it was precisely this "weakness" and its corollaries, such as flexibility and adaptability, that made these actors highly instrumental, and sometimes indispensable, within development roadmaps of local administrators, planners, and decision makers. This instrumentality resulted in an impact on urbanization processes around the world that constitutes one of the most relevant legacies of twentieth-century socialism's global visions.

Epilogue and Outlook

Many of the interviews for this book took place in the homes of its protagonists. Quite often, these were sizable detached houses, located in suburbs of Belgrade, Bucharest, Budapest, Prague, Sofia, Warsaw, and Wrocław. Districts of such individual houses added up to new patterns of urbanization emerging since the 1970s at the peripheries of Eastern European cities.[1] I was told several times by my interviewees that "this house was paid for by [their] work on export projects." This suggests that suburbanization in Eastern Europe during the Cold War needs to be understood through the lens of decolonization and the subsequent cooperation between the developing countries and the Comecon that resulted not only in the remittances sent home, but also in other flows: crude oil bartered for export projects, expertise and technologies acquired on construction sites abroad, and consumption patterns interiorized when living in foreign countries.

This is one of the possible lines of research that could follow from this book. Initiated as a contribution to the historiography of twentieth-century architecture, its first step was to reverse the research focus on architectural mobilities from their points of departure in the Global North to their points of deployment in the Global South. From such a recalibrated perspective, this book challenged capitalist triumphalism that, in the wake of the Cold War, reduced architecture's globalization to Westernization or Americanization, and retroactively extended these narratives into a teleological development path of architecture after World War II. Against the Cold War propaganda and its afterlives, the preceding chapters showed that West African and Middle Eastern countries were no Soviet "proxies" or "pawns," and neither was Eastern Europe a homogenous "Soviet bloc." Rather, the view from the South allowed showing how architectures coproduced by Eastern Europeans, West Africans, and Middle Easterners were part of complex and uneven negotiations between parties with different and evolving geopolitical ambitions, state-building aims, economic motivation, and cultural agendas.

This vantage point from the South contributes to the current effort of historians of modernism by showing that modern architecture's worldwide emergence was a fundamentally antagonistic and heterogeneous process, informed by competing visions of global collaboration in the Cold War. When seen from West Africa and the Middle East, modern architecture appears as always-already on the move, and its history is that of resources circulating at various scales and with various speeds, their capturing and appropriation. This appropriation included a reactivation of the modern movement's "other" traditions, in particular Central European, but also contributions from countries that have been less studied by architectural historians, such as Bulgaria and Romania. New types of institutions were instrumental in this process, including foreign trade organizations in Eastern Europe and municipal planners and state contractors in West Africa and the Middle East. The process of revising, challenging, and abandoning modern architecture was equally heterogeneous, and among its many sources was the encounter between the experience of "real existing modernism" in Eastern Europe with an equally disappointing experience of post-oil urbanization in parts of Asia and Africa.

The preceding mapping of architectural collaboration between Eastern Europeans, West Africans, and Middle Easterners did not start with a normative definition of what architecture is but rather with a nominalist study of what architects did as architects. Such an ostensibly limited entrance point revealed that the deployment of architectural labor on export contracts was not restricted to design work but included also construction management, supervision, administration, legislation, teaching, and research. The preceding chapters studied these engagements in specific locations: state design institutes and private architectural practices, construction sites, municipalities and ministries, and architectural schools and research centers. The review of such deployments showed that architectural labor often traveled as part of larger packages: aggregated with other types of labor, including that of planners, engineers, technicians, managers, scholars, and workers, and associated with other things. They included Soviet prefabrication systems and machinery, Bulgarian engineering tables and building materials, East German type designs and legislation schemes, Hungarian planning concepts and research methodologies, Polish conservation methods and drawing techniques, Romanian design guidelines and seismic norms, Czechoslovak teaching curricula, Croatian façade systems, Slovenian furniture, and Serbian steel. The architects' job was not just to bring these things to their destinations but also to manipulate them in order to adjust their performances to the conditions on site or, by contrast, to maintain their original performance in the new locations.

This book reconceptualized these deployments of architectural labor as part of urbanization processes. Its protagonists participated in the production of all functional programs, from housing to infrastructure, and on all scales, from buildings to landscapes. They assisted local professionals in setting up construction-materials industries, in modernizing traditional building technologies, and in implementing mechanized construction procedures. They contributed to the formulation and promulgation of professional guidelines, building codes, architectural standards, urban norms, and territorial regulations, including principles of land use, transportation, land tenure, and governance. Their drawings and models, even when left unrealized, provided impulses to envisage new urban futures in the territories where they worked. They contributed to the formation of professional, research, and educational institutions in architecture and planning, thus preparing the ground for local production of knowledge and pedagogy. By thinking Accra through Tashkent and Baghdad through Warsaw, they diversified the conceptual references of urbanization, while specialized research institutes in Weimar, Szczecin, Gdańsk, Prague, Budapest, and Moscow began to provincialize Western imperial capitals as centers of knowledge production about urbanization. While neither the only nor the most dominant actors in these processes, architects contributed to them in ways that often transgressed their initial remits and redefined the consensual understanding of what architects do as architects.

Eastern European architectural labor in West Africa and the Middle East was both postcolonial and socialist. It was postcolonial in the sense that independence fundamentally changed the conditions of architectural production in Ghana, Nigeria, Iraq, and the Gulf, the continuities with the preceding period notwithstanding. This meant the establishment of new and reorganization of old institutions, but also the emergence of new clients, new programs, new discourses, and new ambitions that defined the parameters and stakes of architectural production. For many, the arrival of Eastern Europeans promised to break the vicious circle of underdevelopment in which the damage inflicted by the colonizers on the colonized could be undone only with the resources and knowledge of the former colonial center. While these dynamics have rarely been done away with, the arrival of these architects complicated them, not the least by disrupting the division of spaces and times assigned to non-Europeans and Europeans in a design institute, an administrative office, or an architectural school. In the wake of independence, their engagements were considered a temporary measure and conceived as a bridge between colonial dominance and the period when the local cadres would take over, even if the latter often turned out to be postponed for decades.

Eastern European officials wanted to see these working relationships as specifically socialist and fundamentally different from Western attempts at exploitation of the former colonies. Such claims were used in diplomatic offensives of the socialist countries in Africa and Asia and by foreign trade organizations to discipline the professionals they sent on export contracts. At times, Eastern European architects and planners themselves referred to the discourse about socialist labor. For a few among them, this discourse helped to make sense of their deployment abroad, while others used it to secure new commissions or to claim more resources from the authorities back home. When interviewed today, some architects contrast the professionalism of the traveling personnel from Eastern Europe with the negative selection of their Western counterparts ("Failed in London, try Hong Kong," as a British saying went). Such statements might convey their frustration with the unequal treatment they sometimes experienced from local commissioners in comparison to Western professionals, combined with pressures from state-socialist institutions. Most, however, saw themselves on par with their Western peers, either as members of the international architectural culture or, later, as part of the worldwide mobile workforce: liquid, contingent, and "free" to be deployed everywhere. These various and evolving readings notwithstanding, the export of architectural labor from socialist countries was consistently conditioned by the political economy of state socialism, from the organization of architecture and construction in Eastern Europe, to the state monopoly on foreign trade.

The controversies around socialist labor point to what might be the main dilemma of this book: the relationship between the studied architectures and the project of socialism. This relationship was addressed by means of the concept of socialist worldmaking, or visions of global cooperation practiced by actors from socialist countries against the delineations of the world inherited from the colonial period and in competition with other projects of global cooperation after World War II. Socialist worldmaking included, but was not limited to, the claim to the worldwide applicability of the socialist path of development; the worlding of Eastern Europe, or the sharing with the developing countries of the Eastern European experience of overcoming underdevelopment, colonialism, and peripheriality; and collaboration within the world socialist system. So understood, socialist worldmaking informed the changing geographies, volumes, speed, distribution, and programs of architectural resources that were moved between Eastern Europe and the Global South.

In several of these locations, architectural resources were deployed in programs of socialist modernization. This was the case in Ghana under Nkrumah, where architecture and the construction-materials industry were reorganized with an aim to become integrated into a centrally planned apparatus put in charge of state-led industrialization, collectivization of agriculture, and an egalitarian welfare provision. This architectural production contributed to the undermining of inherited spatiotemporal divisions of the Ghanaian society and their redistribution according to the new socioeconomic order envisaged by the Convention People's Party. In the Ghanaian mass media, this architecture was often acknowledged as a signifier of what a socialist everyday meant, thus staking out a field of debate that was relevant and meaningful for actors operating on the ground, who sometimes remember its empowering effects.

However, the review of the Soviet engagements in Ghana showed the limits to the country's socialist modernization, in particular in terms of implementing the principles of central planning. Similarly, the emancipatory targets of the worlding of Eastern Europe were challenged both by the increasingly mercantile motivations of the socialist countries in their exchanges with the Global South, and the ambiguities of Eastern Europe's own colonial past. In turn, some of the core ideas of the world socialist system, including that of the socialist international division of labor, were directly undermined by the competition in the Global South between Comecon countries themselves. By the end of the Cold War, the export of socialism was rarely within the remit of architects, planners, and contractors from Eastern Europe, as exemplified by Energoprojekt's instruction not to involve foreign workers on export contracts in self-management procedures.

Some readers may draw conclusions in the manner in which Western Marxists assessed the urbanization in state-socialist Europe: as a failure to fulfill the socialist promise of a new type of space.[2] However, such wholesale critique of the engagements discussed in this book would obscure their specificity and their emancipatory potential. What the preceding chapters showed was that the mobilities of architecture from Eastern Europe made a difference in West Africa and the Middle East: both in the sense of having a huge impact on people's everyday lives, and in a more literal sense, of differentiating urbanization processes beyond the consequences of the colonial encounter with Western Europe and the hegemony of global capitalism.

This book can be read as a history of such differentiated urbanization in Accra, Lagos, Baghdad, Abu Dhabi, and Kuwait City. In the preceding chapters, differences were understood not as essentialized particularities of a specific place that lend themselves as candidates for cooptation into the colonial (or neocolonial) system of governance, or as opportunities for capitalist value-extraction and commodification. But neither were they theorized as resulting from grafting an original Eastern European technology or a design concept in Africa or Asia, nor from adapting such technologies and concepts to the ontological irreducibility of these territories.[3] Rather, difference was understood as divergence, contrast, disparity, and sometimes incommensurability or contradiction between the economic, financial, ideological, logistical, regulatory, and cultural regimes within and across which Eastern Europeans, West Africans, and Middle Easterners worked.

By aiming to make the most of such relational differences, the protagonists of this book practiced worldmaking—for example, by negotiating the entrance protocols and gatekeeping procedures of competing networks of architectural resources. Among such differences, I paid particular attention to those between the political economy of foreign trade in Comecon countries and the emerging global market of design and construction services dominated by Western enterprises. Working across both systems provided incentives for the use of barter agreements, which resulted in the Romanian practice of redrawing plans so that they could be constructed by means of materials, technologies, and labor from Romania bartered for crude oil. In turn, Polservice exploited the inconvertibility of the Polish currency in a way that shaped the working conditions of Miastoprojekt's team in Baghdad. These conditions differed from those of previous foreign planners in Iraq, both in terms of the size of the team, its composition, and time spent in Baghdad, and in terms of their relationship to the Iraqi authorities and collaborators. These working conditions provided the Polish and Iraqi planners with resources to produce a master plan that was embedded, empirical, interdisciplinary, consultative, and scenario-based.

Few in Baghdad attributed this character of the master plan to socialism, and even fewer would so describe its consequences, including the ways in which the plan was negotiated, implemented, modified, and, ultimately, how it guided the urban development of Baghdad. In other locations revisited in the preceding chapters, too, differences that resulted from socialist worldmaking continue to be reproduced beyond their original association with socialism, and often in unexpected ways. Sometimes they result in accelerated development—for example, when a factory built by Eastern Europeans in Ghana brought about training opportunities into remote locations and expanded the skills of the local people they could draw upon long after the factory was closed in the wake of Nkrumah's fall. At other times, they result in slowdowns and obstacles to rapid urbanization—for example, at the International Trade Fair in Accra, where Nkrumah's nationalization policies led to still unresolved conflicts around land ownership. Elsewhere, they lay out distinct vectors of urbanization, as has been the case with the infrastructural grid of the International Trade Fair in Lagos. In turn, the wide area around the National Theater continues to inspire new ways for imagining the future of Lagos, its transportation networks, and its everyday economies. The concept of socialist worldmaking provided a way to account for the genealogy of these differences, but the understanding of their reproduction requires new methods, new hypotheses, and new concepts: as much a theoretical as a political task.

A Note on Sources

The diversity of sources used for this book conveys the heterogeneity of urbanization processes described by it. I studied the archives of individual architects, design institutes, contractors, professional organizations, and research centers from Eastern Europe and their clients, collaborators, and employers in Ghana, Nigeria, Iraq, the UAE, and Kuwait. In successor countries to Cold War's Eastern Europe, I queried private and public archives in Bulgaria, Germany, Hungary, Poland, Romania, Russia, and Serbia, and I carried out targeted research in Croatia, the Czech Republic, Macedonia, and Slovakia. Eastern European state and party archives, straddling diplomacy, foreign trade, and construction, were essential to understand how the political economy of architectural export worked. The organization of this trade and its dynamics was followed in repositories of national institutions, such as foreign trade organizations (FTOs), and transnational ones, such as Comecon's Permanent Commission for Construction. These surveys were complemented by archives in the United Kingdom, which continued the political, economic, cultural, and educational engagements in the former British colonies and protectorates; and the United States, which closely monitored Eastern European activities in West Africa and the Middle East.

The most urgent to consult were private archives of professionals, since they are under threat of dispersion after their owners pass away. In Eastern Europe, I consulted archives of architects, planners, and engineers who worked abroad either as employees of design institutes and construction companies, or on individual contracts. These archives were compiled in a highly selective manner, as architects tended to take with them documents that were easier to transport and that they expected to be more useful for advancing their careers. Accordingly, they preserved letters of reference from foreign employers and clients, contracts with FTOs, and samples of designs that could be integrated into their professional portfolios. When compiling such a portfolio, architects typically preferred evocative renderings over technical drawings, and photographs of constructed buildings over bulky Ozalid copies of plans and sections. Design documentation was often confidential, and many architects complied with the ban on taking copies with them. Such restrictions applied sometimes to research work too, as Zbigniew Dmochowski experienced when copies of his surveys of Nigerian vernacular architecture had been confiscated at the Lagos airport before he boarded the plane back to Poland. I complemented queries in Eastern Europe by studying personal archives of West African and Middle Eastern professionals, both preserved in the regions in question and donated to Western-based institutions.

When preserved, archives of design institutes and contractors are more complete. The largest among state-socialist design institutes had specialized departments in charge of archiving the design documentation and other materials, including minutes of negotiations, tender agreements, and country-specific building norms and standards, catalogues of suppliers of construction materials, and lists of contractors. However, these archives were often dispersed in the wake of the institutes' privatization after the end of socialism. Repositories of West African and Middle Eastern design institutes and contractors are often confidential, but I was granted permission to use the archive of Architecture and Engineering Services Limited in Accra, the successor of the Ghana National Construction Corporation, and the Development Office of the

A. This diagram shows the periodization of foreign designs by the members of the Society of Polish Architects (SARP), on the basis of 417 dossiers of architects that cover the period between 1958 and 1989. The vertical axis represents the number of designs abroad and the horizontal axis the number of the countries in which these designs were located. Each point in the diagram represents both numbers in a given year. The diagram suggests that the period of geographic expansion with a relatively modest number of designs until the early 1960s was followed by a period of quantitative expansion during the 1970s. Data source: Stowarzyszenie Architektów Polskich (SARP). Software: Tableau.

Kwame Nkrumah University of Science and Technology in Kumasi. In all three regions, design documentation rarely made it to public repositories. Notable exceptions discussed in this book include the Soviet designs of neighborhoods in Accra and Tema stored at the Russian State Archive of Scientific and Technical Documentation (Moscow), and the Russian State Archive of the Economy (Moscow and Samara), as well as the files of Romproiect stored at the Romanian National Archives (Bucharest).

Professional organizations, including the Architectural Chamber of Bulgaria in Sofia and the Society of Polish Architects (SARP) in Warsaw, gathered materials about the work of their members. These are typically self-curated collections, as they were compiled by their protagonists, often as part of an application for a particular professional status or distinction. For example, the dossiers in the SARP Archive were submitted by individual architects who applied for the status of "architect-creator" that came with specific benefits in socialist Poland, such as access to scarce commodities and working spaces. The application process required demonstrating the applicant's creative labor and, accordingly, its core part was a portfolio of architectural work. Among them, 417 dossiers include references to foreign projects. However incomplete, when considered as a whole set, these dossiers allow for an overview of the general patterns of international engagements of the Society's members. After its transcription into a digital database, I used this data to speculate about the periodization of Polish architectural export. These hypotheses, assisted by data visualization software and supported by additional documents, were explored in chapter 1 (figure A). In turn, the study of this data by means of social networks analysis software revealed the biggest recipients of architectural labor from socialist Poland. I used force-directed graphs to develop a taxonomy of the mobilities of this labor, applied throughout this book (figure B). The juxtaposition of the dossiers from the SARP Archive with datasets reconstructed on the basis of archival materials of Romania's Romproiect and Bulgaria's Technoexportstroy informed the comparative arguments in the preceding chapters (figure C).

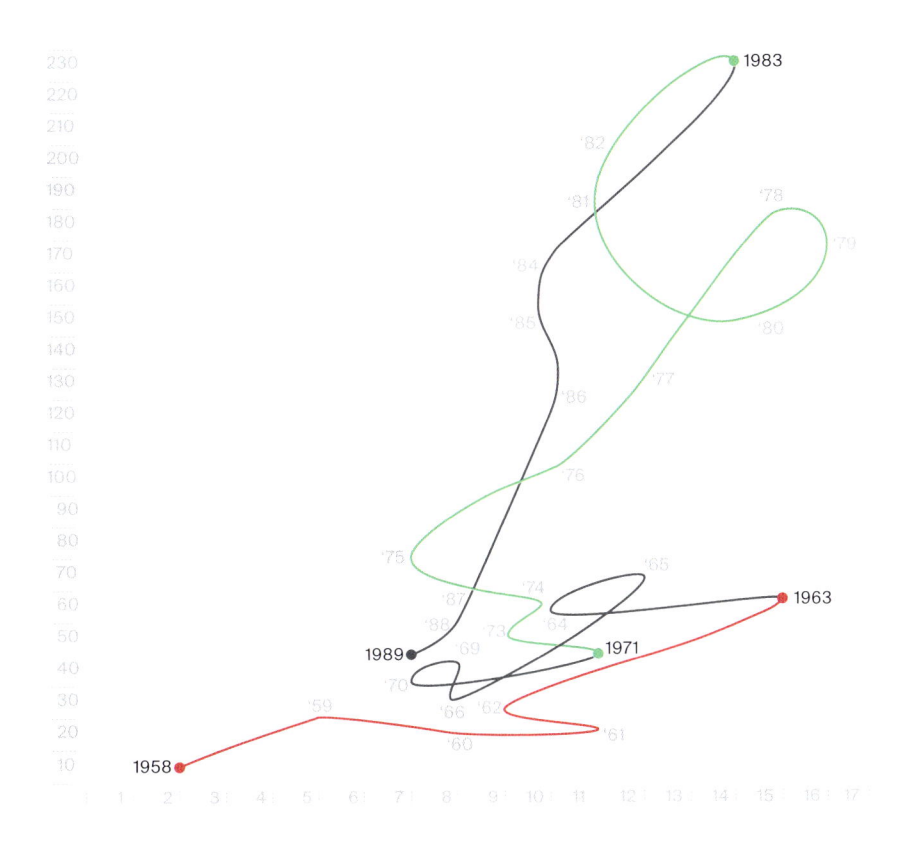

A NOTE ON SOURCES

During the socialist period, Eastern European architectural journals published special issues about designs produced by "our architects abroad," and regularly included such designs into reviews of current work. I undertook queries of full runs of Bulgarian, Czechoslovak, East German, Hungarian, Polish, Romanian, Soviet, and Yugoslav architectural journals. In the same way, I reviewed professional journals in West Africa and the Middle East, among them the *West African Builder and Architect*, published in English in Accra, and *Albenaa*, published in Arabic with English summaries in Riyadh. I also studied more ephemeral publications, including those issued by West African and Middle Eastern institutes of architects, universities, and governmental agencies such as the Department of Antiquities in Lagos. As it was the case with other written materials, I was assisted by translators to research publications in languages that I did not read—in particular, large amounts of materials were translated from Arabic, Bulgarian, Hungarian, Romanian, and Serbo-Croatian.

In order to understand the economic conditions of architectural export, particularly useful were Eastern European journals that specialized in foreign trade and newsletters of design institutes and contractors, among them Energoprojekt's. Market surveys of design and construction services in West African and Middle Eastern countries were prepared by specialized research institutions in Eastern Europe. Among these, the studies by East Germany's Academy of Architecture were comprehensive, but largely based on Western sources. By contrast, dissertations about architecture and urbanization of West African and Middle Eastern countries written by

B. This graph identifies the destinations of foreign designs by the members of the Society of Polish Architects (SARP), on the basis of their 417 personal dossiers, which cover the period between 1958 and 1989. The nodes of the diagram represent individual architects; the edges represent the countries of their designs. Two nodes representing two architects are connected by an edge representing a particular country if each of them worked on at least one design destined for that country. This graph shows the twelve biggest recipient countries of architectural designs by SARP members, starting with Iraq, Libya, and Algeria. Most architects worked in a limited number of countries (one or two); those who are represented in the graph as connected to a larger number of countries were typically experts of international organizations, designers in charge of international tenders, or authors of competition designs. The named nodes identify people discussed in this book, but only two-thirds of Polish architects discussed in this book submitted a dossier to SARP. Data source: Stowarzyszenie Architektów Polskich (SARP). Software: Gephi.

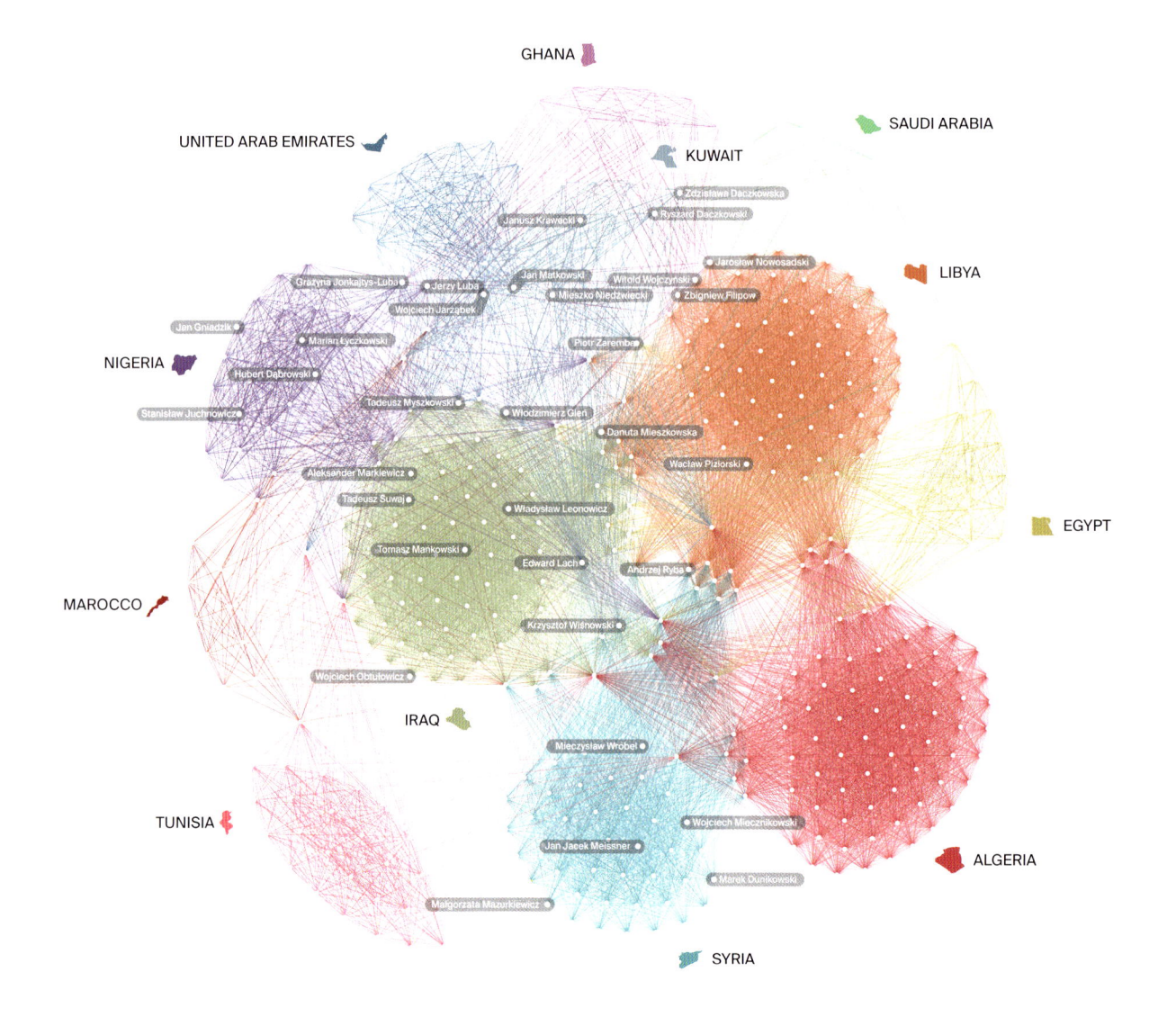

C. This diagram shows the geographic distribution of 973 realized and unrealized designs by Romproiect (Romania) between 1979 and 2009. The areas in red indicate designs drawn during the Cold War; the areas in blue indicate designs drawn afterward. In the wake of the end of socialism, Romproiect's commissions shrank in North Africa and the Middle East and were largely replaced by commissions in Romania and countries of the former Soviet Union (Russia, Ukraine). Data source: Arhivele Naționale ale României. Software: Tableau.

doctoral students from these regions at Eastern European institutions were often based on original primary sources. Urban surveys were sometimes a component of larger planning commissions for particular cities, and increasingly subjects of independent commissions. Some of them, prepared by social scientists, conveyed the voices of local inhabitants, and today they offer time-specific glimpses into the social reality of the cities discussed in this book. Such studies were also carried out by architects and planners who were teaching at the architectural schools in Kumasi, Zaria, Baghdad, and elsewhere, and their lecture notes and readers that they compiled for their students were critical sources of this book, as were the scholarly and popular publications that they produced after their return to Eastern Europe.

Besides professional publications, I surveyed full runs of Ghanaian, Nigerian, Iraqi, Emirati, and Kuwaiti daily newspapers. West African newspapers were published in English, and the Middle Eastern ones in English and Arabic. Some of them, such as Ghana's *Evening News*, were party organs, and others were under varying levels of political control. While they privileged the official narrative about the cities in question, they also conveyed opinions of planning professionals, historians, and, occasionally, more ordinary voices. By reading these texts and looking at the hundreds of photographs that accompanied them, I was able to follow discussions and controversies about buildings and master plans, and to study the ways in which they were part of the self-presentation of the regimes.

These voices were complemented by interviews with architects, planners, administrators, educators, and managers in Eastern Europe, West Africa, and the Middle East. In a few cases, I was assisted by translators, but in general I was able to carry out these interviews myself in English, French, German, and Polish. (Professionals in West Africa and the Middle East during the period covered by this book typically communicated in English and French; in turn, while larger Eastern European teams included

A NOTE ON SOURCES

translators, knowledge of a relevant foreign language was required from professionals who applied for individual contracts abroad.) The interviews provided important clues for further archival queries and crucial insights into individual motivation of Eastern Europeans to work abroad and of West Africans and Middle Easterners to hire them. They also provided accounts of the working conditions, everyday life, and professional and personal relationships between those involved and their families.

I understood many of these conversations as narratives connecting the past and the present, as they were shaped by current debates, in particular about the legacy of socialism in Eastern Europe, Nkrumah's Ghana, and Baathist Iraq. Many of my interlocutors addressed what they thought might be my preconceptions about the period discussed: some of them defended their involvement with the socialist regimes, while others made a point of claiming that they resisted them, either from within or from without the communist party. The fact that I was born in Poland but spent much of my childhood in Germany, that I was employed by a Swiss, American, or British institution during this study, and that I spoke French with a Polish accent and English with a German one (as I am told), often added to the confusion. When the conversations stalled, it was helpful to return to the drawings, photographs, and amateur movies, which my interlocutors generously presented to me and commented on.

Images were among the core sources for this book. They included drawings in all formats, from small sketches to large technical drawings; of all types, from evocative perspectives to engineering schemes of concrete reinforcement; and in all scales, from details of children's playgrounds for Accra to regional plans of Iraq. Some of these drawings were preserved in larger packages that documented the entire design and construction process of a building or an ensemble, from initial sketches, through variants of the designs that testified to the negotiation of the programs, layouts, technologies, and materials employed, to the execution drawings used at the construction site. More often, however, the drawing sets were incomplete and sometimes as little as a photograph of a model or a perspectival rendering of the envisaged building could be found. The primary purpose of these drawings was to negotiate and guide the construction processes, but they also took on a life of their own, circulating among professionals and educators and in the daily press. The latter were used as promises of the future to come and evidence of the goals achieved.

Assembling images into series was an important part of researching this book. This procedure showed that the same image could take an instrumentality specific to a circumscribed community of practice. For example, a photograph of an industrial plant in Benghazi (Libya) could be used as a claim to individual creative labor of an architect when included

D. This diagram compares the street layout for Kadhemiya in the 1956 master plan of Baghdad (Minoprio, Spencely & Macfarlane), the 1973 master plan (Miastoprojekt-Kraków), and a 1976 map of Baghdad. In contrast to the invasive traffic planning in Kadhemiya in the Minoprio plan, the 1973 plan supported the preservation concept of Kadhemiya by lowering the intensity of traffic in and around the area. This scheme was not fully implemented, as the 1976 map shows. Data source: Map and Geospatial Information Center, Peter B. Lewis Library, Princeton University, Princeton, NJ (US); private archive of Kazimierz Bajer, Kraków (Poland); Library of Congress, Washington, DC (US). Software: QGIS.

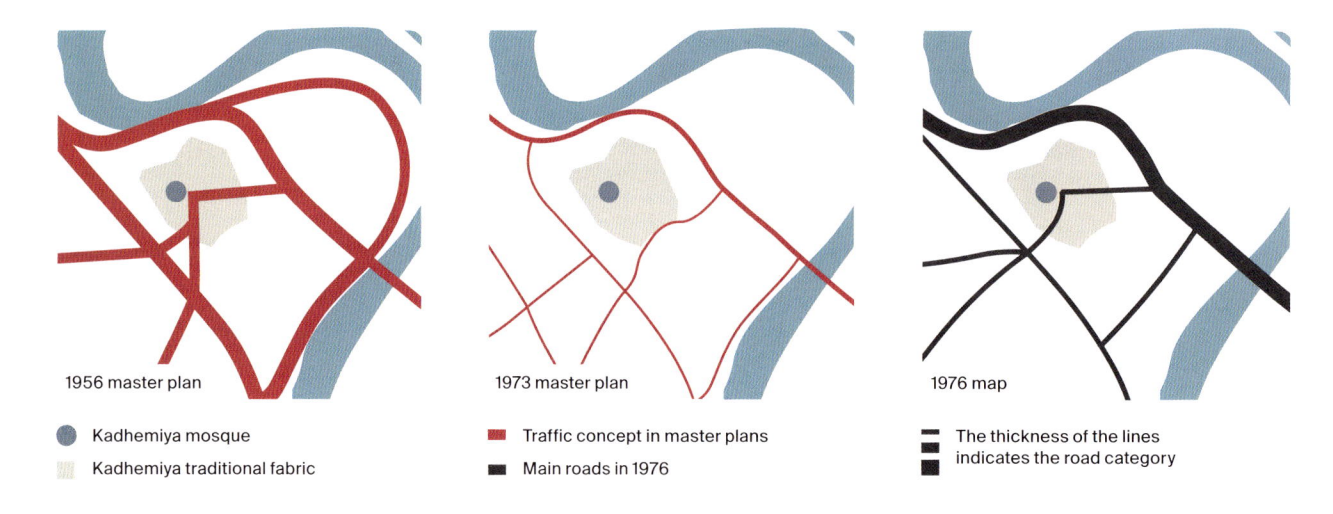

1956 master plan | 1973 master plan | 1976 map

- Kadhemiya mosque
- Kadhemiya traditional fabric
- Traffic concept in master plans
- Main roads in 1976
- The thickness of the lines indicates the road category

E. This diagram compares the residential areas in Baghdad surveyed in 1985 (by the Japanese Consortium of Consulting Firms) with the housing layouts foreseen by the 1973 master plan (Miastoprojekt-Kraków). It shows that the master plan guided the allocation of housing in Baghdad until the mid-1980s—in particular, in the west and in the northeast of the city. The diagram confirms that the urbanization of Baghdad within the municipal boundary followed the basic structure proposed by Miastoprojekt's plan: a multifunctional Tigris Belt flanked by two belts of residential districts. Data source: Private archive of Ghada al-Slik, Baghdad (Iraq); private archive of Kazimierz Bajer, Kraków (Poland). Software: QGIS.

in a portfolio sent to SARP. But when published in an engineering journal, it was put forward as a proof of collaboration between professionals; when included in a daily newspaper, it could represent socialist assistance to Libya; and when reproduced in a catalogue of an FTO, it was supposed to evidence the integration of socialist contractors into the international construction market.

In turn, arraying images related to a particular location in Accra, Lagos, Baghdad, Abu Dhabi, or Kuwait City allowed an understanding of the development of these locations through the years. Some of these documents, including cartographic material about Baghdad and its master plans, were digitized, geo-referenced, and vectorized by means of Geographic Information System (GIS) software. This spatial database facilitated a comparison of the master plans with other cartographic materials. In this way, I was able to understand the specific principles of Miastoprojekt's plans—for example, the distribution patterns of social facilities or the relationship between transportation planning and heritage preservation (figure D). I used geo-referenced cartographic material to test and evidence the argument about the capillary impact of the 1973 master plan on the development of Baghdad, in particular on housing development and transportation networks (figures E and F). The plan's impact on architectural practice was tested by redrawing selected neighborhood projects in the GIS environment in order to calculate the urban standards underlying their designs (inhabitants' density, green space per capita, distance to public transport) and to compare them with the standards that had been

■ Residential use in the 1973 master plan
■ Gross residential land use in 1985
  Tigris belt (1973 plan)

A NOTE ON SOURCES

set by the master plan. By overlaying the land use planning with specific sites of architectural competitions, I was able to study the ways in which architectural discussions in Baghdad responded to the master plan.

More generally, references to the same location were the primary means for interrelating the documents studied. Their comparison across archives brought to the fore omissions and discrepancies. Sometimes, they resulted from mistakes, sometimes from tailoring the message for a specific community of practitioners, but sometimes they reflected the confusing reality on the ground. For example, when Romanian and Polish architects claimed authorship over the same housing neighborhood in Algeria, these competing claims reflected the often-temporary involvement and the limited control of Eastern European architects over their foreign projects, the distributed authorship of these collectively produced designs, and little precedence for referencing such collaboration. At times, divergence in assessment of urbanization processes stemmed from competing conceptual frameworks conveyed by surveys carried out by planners from socialist countries, by various United Nations agencies, or by Western offices. In turn, comparison across archives showed economic, ideological, and professional conflicts. I was explicitly looking for materials produced by rivals of Eastern European architects, including organizations such as the Royal Institute of British Architects and the Commonwealth Association of Architects, which documented competition among practitioners in post-independence West Africa and the Middle East. The juxtaposition of Eastern European archives related to the same commission showed rivalry among the institutions involved, as discussed in the study of the Baghdad abattoir, and allowed reading them against the grain. Such rivalry, both real and exaggerated, was reported by US embassies with great detail, as documented by the State Department Central Files. By bringing these conflicting sources into conversation through the spaces they related to, this book aimed at a study that was both transnational and situated.

F. This diagram compares the road network in a 1991 map of Baghdad and its foreseen layout in the 1973 master plan (Miastoprojekt-Kraków). It shows that by 1991, the road network in the city generally followed the master plan. Because the 1991 map does not allow a conclusive assessment of the classification of the roads, the functional coherence of the realized network requires further study. Data source: Private archive of Kazimierz Bajer, Kraków (Poland); Library of Congress, Washington, DC (US). Software: QGIS.

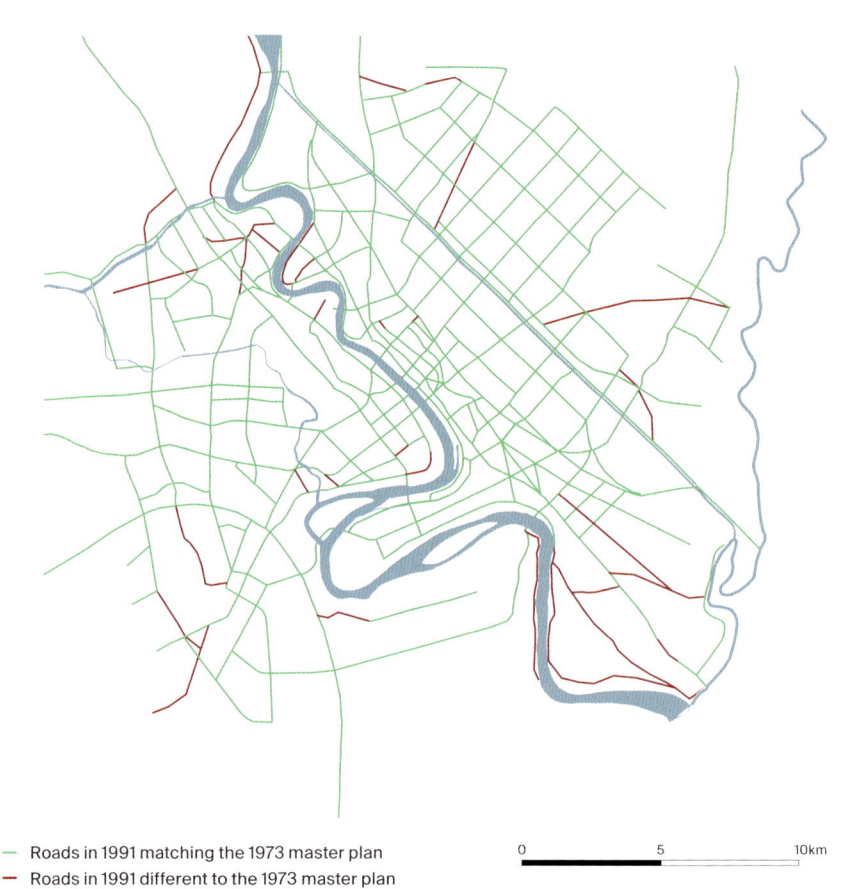

— Roads in 1991 matching the 1973 master plan
— Roads in 1991 different to the 1973 master plan

Acknowledgments

This book has had many starting points. Perhaps the first among them was my study about Nowa Huta, a new town in Poland planned by Miastoprojekt-Kraków, during which I learned that Miastoprojekt's subsequent commission comparable in size was the master plan of Baghdad. I came back to Miastoprojekt in 2009, when I was invited to curate an exhibition at the Museum of Modern Art in Warsaw. The exhibition *PRL™* (2010)—PRL being the Polish-language acronym of People's Republic of Poland—documented the architectural transfers from socialist Poland to Iraq, Syria, Libya, Algeria, Nigeria, Ghana, the UAE, and Kuwait. It was followed by a second exhibition, *Postmodernism Is Almost All Right* (2011, curated with Piotr Bujas), which argued that the experience of working in oil-producing countries in Africa and Asia during the last two decades of the Cold War shaped architecture as a profession and as a discipline in postsocialist Poland.

The archival surveys and interviews that prepared these exhibitions resulted in a very rich historical material, but they also made it clear to me that the phenomenon of architectural mobilities from socialist countries can be fully appreciated only in a comparative manner. This resulted in two major shifts in the research perspective: its extension from Poland to other European socialist countries, and the relocation of the vantage point from Europe to West Africa and the Middle East.

I have tested this approach in a number of formats and venues, among them several graduate seminars at the Department of Architecture, Swiss Federal Institute of Technology (ETH) in Zurich (2009–11); Harvard University Graduate School of Design (2012); and the Manchester School of Architecture at the University of Manchester (2012–18). Other venues included sessions that I coorganized at the International Meeting of the European Architecture History Network (2012, with Rachel Kallus) and at the Conference of the Society of Architectural Historians (2013, with Max Hirsh), as well as conferences that I co-conveyed: "Mobilities of Design," at the ETH Zurich Future Cities Laboratory in Singapore (with Max Hirsh, 2013); and "Identity, Sovereignty, and Cold War Politics in the Building of Baghdad," at Harvard University Graduate School of Design (with Diane Davis and Phillip Baker, 2014). The topic of architectural mobilities from socialist countries was also at the center of two themed journal issues that I edited: "Cold War Transfer: Architecture and Planning from Socialist Countries in the 'Third World,'" *Journal of Architecture* 17, no. 3 (2012, with Tom Avermaete); and "Socialist Networks and the Internationalization of Building Culture after 1945," *ABE Journal* 6 (2014).

I presented this research in numerous institutions, academic and others, and I am grateful to their participants for the feedback that I received. Parts of this research were also included in several exhibitions: *Africa: Big Change, Big Chance*, at the Triennale di Milano (2014, curated by Benno Albrecht); *After Year Zero: Universal Imaginaries—Geographies of Collaboration*, at the Museum of Modern Art in Warsaw with Haus der Kulturen der Welt in Berlin (2015, curated by Annett Busch and Anselm Franke); *Radical Pedagogies: Reconstructing Architectural Education*, at the Museum of Modern Art in Warsaw (2015, curated by Beatriz Colomina and Evangelos Kotsioris); and *Architectural Ethnography: Portraits on Livelihood*, at the 16th Venice Biennale of Architecture (2018, curated by Momoyo Kaijima with Laurent Stalder and Yu Iseki). Preliminary results and working hypotheses of this research were presented in the *Journal of*

Architecture, the *Journal of the Society of Architectural Historians*, and the *International Journal of Islamic Architecture*.

This research has been supported by grants that I received from the ETH Zurich; the Center of Advanced Study in the Visual Arts (CASVA) at the National Gallery of Art, Washington, DC; Casco (Utrecht); the Adam Mickiewicz Institute in Warsaw; and the University of Manchester.

I am very grateful to people who assisted me with this work, and who often became collaborators on projects that followed. The original team at the Museum of Modern Art in Warsaw included Piotr Bujas, Alicja Gzowska, and Aleksandra Kędziorek. I would like to thank my research assistants: Ahlam Sharif in Abu Dhabi, Stefan Nešić in Belgrade, Diane Barbé and Phuong Phan in Berlin, Miruna Stroe in Bucharest, Balint Tolmar and Mária Klagyivik in Budapest, Elena Balabanska in Sofia, Alicja Nowak in Kraków, Jeremy Lecomte in Manchester, Nikolay Erofeev and Florid Mahmutov in Moscow, and Jana Pavlová in Prague. Hajir Alttahir, Fadi Shayya, and Zain Toma helped me with the Arabic materials. I also am very grateful to several people whose assistance was invaluable during my travels to West Africa and the Middle East: Margaret Asare and Kofi Asare in Accra, Rexford Assasie Oppong in Kumasi, Ayodele Arigbabu and Marc-André Schmachtel in Lagos, Yasser Elsheshtawy in Al Ain, and Roberto Fabbri and Farah al-Nakib in Kuwait City.

This book would not have been possible without the assistance and support of its protagonists, their families, and scholars who granted me interviews and shared with me their personal archives. Among them, I would like to mention in particular: A. W. Charaway, E.G.A. Don Arthur, Nat Nuno-Amarteifio, and H. Nii-Adziri Wellington in Accra; Ghada al-Slik in Baghdad; Peter Dew, Hashem al-Hassan, and Abdulrahman Makhlouf in Abu Dhabi; Talal M. Abdullah and Bedri Omar Elias in Al Ain; Danilo Udovički-Selb in Austin, Texas; Dragoljub Bakić, Ljiljana Bakić, Zoran Bojović, Mario Jobst, Nina Pantić, Zorica Savičić, and Aleksandar Slijepčević in Belgrade; Dan Agent, Nicolae Besnea, Mircea Ochinciuc, Anca Oțoiu, Radu Serban, Romeo Simiras, Gheorghe Radu Stănculescu, and Maximilian Zielinski in Bucharest; Peter Mlodzianowski in Bucks; Zoltán Boór, Attila Emődy, Ildikó Halmágyi, László Herald, Tibor Hübner, Miklós Marosi, and Anikó Polónyi in Budapest; John Godwin and Gillian Hopwood in Cheltenham; Akram Ogaily in Dubai; Jacek Popek and Maria Sołtysik in Gdańsk; Jerzy Baumiller in Greenport, New York; Jerzy Bajer, Kazimierz Bajer, Marek Dunikowski, Włodzimierz Gleń, Stanisław Juchnowicz, Władysław Leonowicz, Janusz Krawecki, Danuta Mieszkowska, and Krystian Seibert in Kraków; Mohammad al-Sanan, Andrzej Bohdanowicz, Salah Salama, and Krzysztof Wiśniowski in Kuwait City; Ekundayo Adeyinka Adeyemi and Otunba 'Segun Jawando in Lagos; Mikhail Tsyganov in Moscow; Jan Čejka in Münster; Mirjana Maksimović and Stojan Maksimović in Nahant, Massachusetts; Miroslava Baštova, Alexander Gjurič, Jan Amos Havelka, Orlin Ilinčev, and Ján Strcula in Prague; Andreja Ivanovski in Skopje; Georgi Anastassov, Encho Balukchiev, Borislav Bogdanov, Detchno Detchev, Stanka Dundakova, Georgi Goshev, Lyudmil Leonidov, Evlogi Raichev, Lyubomir Shinkov, and Tacho Tachev in Sofia; Zdenka Ciko and Nick Hollo in Sydney; Jacek Chyrosz, Sławomir Gzell, Grażyna Jonkajtys-Luba, Marian Łyczkowski, Wacław Piziorski, Lech Robaczyński, Henryk Roller, Andrzej Ryba, Stanisław Rymaszewski, and Witold Wojczyński in Warsaw; Wojciech Jarząbek and Edward Lach in Wrocław; and Nebojša Weiner and Zvonimir Žagar in Zagreb.

Elke Beyer, Neil Brenner, Owen Hatherley, Max Hirsh, Iain Jackson, Johan Lagae, Caecilia Pieri, Christian Schmid, Quinn Slobodian, Eric Verdeil, and Albena Yaneva have read the manuscript or parts of it, and I am very grateful for their comments. I would also like to thank the two anonymous reviewers for their insightful and generous comments. This research has also benefited from conversations with Lucia Allais, Richard Anderson, M. Christine Boyer, Hilde Heynen, Sandrine Kott, Vladimir Kulić, Neil Levine, James Mark, Małgorzata Mazurek, Ákos Moravánszky, Cole Roskam, Oscar Sanchez-Sibony, Dubravka Sekulić, Mercedes Volait, and Kimberly Elman Zarecor. I would also like to thank my colleagues at the Manchester Architecture Research Group, the University of Manchester, where I presented this research on several occasions: Isabelle Doucet, Deljana Iossifova, Alan Lewis, Ray Lucas, Leandro Minuchin, Léa-Catherine Szacka, Stephen Walker, and Albena Yaneva, as well as Ola Uduku, my colleague at the Manchester School of Architecture.

I am very grateful to Michelle Komie at Princeton University Press for her enthusiasm and support for this complex project.

Special thanks goes to Paul van Lange for supporting this project all the way.

Notes

Chapter 1

1. Conversation with author, June 2012, Accra.
2. In this book, I understand "Eastern Europe" in the political sense that this term received during the Cold War. I use the term "Central Europe" to refer to the cultural space of the former Habsburg Empire.
3. Interview with E.G.A. Don Arthur, Accra, June 2012.
4. Interview with H. Nii-Adziri Wellington, Accra, June 2012.
5. Interview with Otunba 'Segun Jawando, Lagos, July 2015.
6. Interview with Said Jassim Mohsen Alsaady, Cambridge, MA, September 2014; telephone conversation with Ghada al-Slik, February 2015.
7. Interview with Akram Ogaily, Cambridge, MA, September 2014; interview with Bedri Omar Elias, Al Ain, March 2015.
8. Busch, Franke, eds., *After Year Zero*.
9. For exceptions, see Ward, "Transnational Planners"; Kultermann, *Contemporary Architecture*. By contrast, scholars from the Global South have been aware of these exchanges; see, for example, Adeyemi, *Making*; Fethi, "Contemporary Architecture"; Huwysh, *al-'amārat al-hadithat fi al-'iraq*.
10. Verdeil, "Expertises nomades"; Lagae, Toulier, "De l'outre-mer"; Lagae, de Raedt, "Global Experts."
11. Bremner, *Imperial Gothic*; Celik, *Empire*; Cody, *Exporting American Architecture*; Crinson, *Modern Architecture*; Glendinning, *Robert Matthew*; Healey, Upton, eds., *Crossing Borders*; Lee, "Negotiating Modernities"; Masey, Morgan, *Cold War Confrontations*; Nasr, Volait, *Urbanism*; King, *Bungalow*; Osayimwese, *Colonialism*; Wright, *Politics of Design*. See also notes 26–35 in this chapter.
12. Prakash, *Chandigarh's Le Corbusier*; James-Chakraborty, "Reinforced Concrete."
13. James-Chakraborty, "Beyond Postcolonialism"; Karimi, *Domesticity*; Volait, *L'architecture moderne*; Hein et al., eds., *Japan*; Scriver, Prakash, *Colonial Modernities*.
14. Chang, *Genealogy*; Bozdogan, *Modernism*; Nitzan-Shiftan, "Contested Zionism."
15. Isenstadt, Rizvi, eds. *Modernism*; Jackson, Holland, *Fry and Drew*; Glendinning, *Robert Matthew*; Adams, *SOM*.
16. Wright, *Politics of Design*; Wright, "Tradition"; Vacher, "Planification."
17. Avermaete et al., eds., *Colonial Modern*; Osayimwese, *Colonialism*.
18. King, ed., *Urbanism*; Soja, Kanai, "Urbanization."
19. For overviews, see Engerman, "Second World's Third World"; Mark, Slobodian, "Eastern Europe."
20. Stanek, "Accra"; Stanek, "Architects from Socialist Countries"; Stanek, *Postmodernism*; Stanek, "PRL™"; Stanek, "Second World's Architecture"; Stanek, "Socialist Networks"; Stanek, "Mobilities"; Stanek, ed., "Socialist Networks"; Stanek, Avermaete, eds., "Cold War Transfer." Research publications on Eastern European architects abroad include Alonso, Palmarola, "Panel's Tale"; Branczik, "Exporttervezési munkák"; Butter, "Showcase"; Dolinka et al., *Bojović*; Hirsh, "Post-Modern Architectural Exchanges"; Hong, "Through a Glass"; Nowakowska, "Osiągnięcia"; *Razvojna*; Sekulić, "Energoprojekt"; Schwenkel, "Traveling Architecture"; Schwenkel, "Affective Solidarities"; Schaefer, "Socialist Modernization"; Sit, "Soviet Influence"; Souami, Verdeil, eds., *Concevoir et gérer*. See also Antoniak, *Polska twórczość*.
21. Brenner, Schmid, "New Epistemology"; Schmid et al., "New Vocabulary"; Schmid, "Specificity."
22. Ong, "Worlding Cities."
23. *Daily Graphic* (later: *DG*), November 6, 1965, 6–13; *West African Pilot*, February 5, 1972, 3.
24. *DG*, November 6, 1965, 6–13.
25. Ibid., 11.
26. Crinson, *Modern Architecture*; Chang, *Genealogy*; Le Roux, "Networks"; Livsey, "Lodgings"; Isenstadt, Rizvi, eds., *Modernism*; Jackson, Uduku, "Sub-Saharan Africa"; King, *Bungalow*; Scriver, *Scaffolding*.
27. For the transition between colonial and postcolonial architecture, planning, and construction in French, Portuguese, Belgian, and Dutch colonies, see Avermaete, Casciato, *Casablanca Chandigarh*; Avermaete et al., *Colonial Modern*; Beeckmans, "Adventures"; Beeckmans, "Architecture of Nation-building"; Culot, Thiveaud, *Architectures françaises*; Cunha Matos, "Colonial Architecture"; Lagae, Laurens, *Laurens*; Akihary, *Architectuur*; Lu, *Third World Modernism*; Silva, *Urban Planning*; Verdeil, *Beyrouth*; Vellut, ed., *Villes*; Vaz Milheiro, *Nos trópicos*; Yetunde, "Systemic Shifts."
28. De Raedt, "True Believers"; De Raedt, "Policies, People, Projects: School Building as Development Aid in Postcolonial Sub-Saharan Africa," Ph.D. dissertation, Ghent University, 2017; M. Iljal Muzaffar, "The Periphery Within: Modern Architecture and the Making of the Third World," Ph.D. dissertation, MIT, Boston, MA, 2007; Bjažić Klarin, *Weissmann*.
29. Le Roux, "Networks."
30. Jackson, Holland, *Fry and Drew*; Glendinnig, *Matthew*.
31. Levin, "Imperial Modernity"; Feniger, Kallus, "Building a 'New Middle East'"; Yacobi, *Israel and Africa*; "Forms of Freedom: African Independence and Nordic Models," Nordic Pavilion, Venice, June 7–November 23, 2014, 14th International Architecture Biennale.
32. Quoted in Yacobi, *Israel and Africa*, 24.
33. Matsubara, "Banshoya."
34. Bremner et al., "Intersecting Interests"; Nasr, "Shiber."
35. Westad, *Global Cold War*.
36. Haefele, "Rostow's Stages"; Gilman, *Mandarins*.
37. Cody, *Exporting American Architecture*; Franch i Gilabert et al., *OfficeUS Atlas*.
38. Quoted in Cody, *Exporting American Architecture*, 127.
39. Westad, *Global Cold War*; Mazower, *Governing the World*.
40. Sanchez-Sibony, *Red Globalization*.
41. Raedt, "Policies," 149; see also Mitchell, "Econometality."
42. Prashad, *Darker Nations*.
43. Cooper, Packard, eds., *International Development*.
44. Mazower, *Governing*, 287, 299–300.
45. Arndt, *Development*; Bockman, "Socialist Globalization."
46. Mark, Slobodian, "Eastern Europe."
47. Möller, *DDR*, 4.
48. Mark, Slobodian, "Eastern Europe."
49. Mëhilli, *From Stalin to Mao*.
50. Quoted in Walters, *Aid*, 30.
51. Engerman, "Second World's Third World"; Westad, *Global Cold War*.
52. Kalinovsky, *Laboratory*.
53. Sit, "Soviet Influence"; see also Ren, *Building Globalization*.
54. Butter, "Showcase"; Hong, "Through a Glass"; Shin, Jung, "Appropriating"; Kim, Jung, "Planning of Microdistricts."
55. Westad, *Global Cold War*.
56. Boden, "Cold War Economics," 118–19; "Stadion v Dzhakarte," *Arkhitektura SSSR* 9 (1960), 14–17.
57. Sanchez-Sibony, *Red Globalization*; Kaftanov, "From International Architecture."
58. Mark, Slobodian, "Eastern Europe."
59. Sanchez-Sibony, *Red Globalization*, 247–48.
60. Quoted in Chen, "China," 145.
61. Ding, Xue, "China's Architectural Aid."
62. Deluz, *Urbanisme*; Jałowiecki, *Procesy*; Peter Beňuška, "Územný plán hlavného mesta Alžíra," *Projekt* 3 (1990): 8–9.
63. Interview with Mircea Ochinciuc, Bucharest, May 2015.
64. Rudner, "East European Aid."
65. From the end of World War II until the fall of the USSR, the total value of Soviet aid roughly equaled that offered by the United States to Israel; Sanchez-Sibony, *Red Globalization*, 138.
66. See the housing projects for Conakry in the archive of Vyacheslav Egorov, Moscow (Russian Federation).
67. Stone, *Satellites and Commissars*.
68. The USSR was an exception; Wentker, "Für Frieden."
69. Gawlik, "Eksport," 1.
70. Kotkin, "Kiss of Debt."
71. "Rozwój eksportu budownictwa," AAN z. 2350, s. 1/113, 2–3.
72. ANR f. C. C. al P.C.R., s. Relații Externe, p. 14/1972, n. 672, 7–8.
73. Kaftanov, "International Architecture."
74. Master plan of Tripoli (Libya), 1979–83, Warsaw Development Consortium, Poland, archive of Wacław Piziorski, Warsaw (Poland); Zagreb, Urbanistički institut, "Conakry"; Oldřich Kolář, František Přikryl, "Rozvoj cestovního ruchu v Tunisku," *Architektura ČSSR* 5 (1967): 282–89.
75. Scheffler, "Himmelskuppeln."
76. Chernev et al., *Dela*; "Czechoslovak Architects"; Zachwatowicz, *Protection*; Gzowska, "Exporting Working Patterns"; "Study of the Planned National Sports Centre of the Proposed New Capital City Abuja," July 1981, BA DH2/13881.
77. Seibert, *Rozważania*; Seibert, *Urbanizacja Syrii*; Syrian Arab Republic, General Organization of the Euphrates Project; Krystian Seibert and Claude Dagher, "Tabqua Town: Final Report on the Plan of the Town," Damascus, June 1968, archive of Krystian Seibert, Kraków (Poland).
78. Lorenzini, "Comecon."
79. Ferkai, ed., *Közti*.
80. TES's only Bulgarian commission was the Vitosha hotel in Sofia, a case of "internal

319

export" (a commission paid by convertible currency); "Technoexportstroy," catalogue, n.d. [1980s].
81. *35 godina*; "Technoexportstroy"; "S.C. Romproiect S.A.," catalogue, n.d. [2000s].
82. Zevin, *Economic Cooperation*, 59.
83. Rimsha, *Gorod*.
84. Beyer, "Competitive Coexistence."
85. Lorenzini, "Comecon."
86. See also Stanek, "Image."
87. Piotr Bujas, Alicja Gzowska, Hou Li, and Łukasz Stanek, "Planning Transition beyond Socialism: From Poland to China and Back," talk at the IPHS conference (July 15–19, 2018), Yokohama. I would like to thank Alicja Gzowska and Piotr Bujas for making available to me parts of their ongoing archival research financed by the National Science Center (Poland), "Piotr Zaremba (1910–1993): The Oeuvre and Impact of Urban Planner and Scholar in the Age of Globalized Competence," no. 2015/19/N/HS2/03406.
88. Compare Armstrong, *Tyranny*; Mëhilli, *From Stalin to Mao*.
89. Hamilton, "Conclusion," 189–90.
90. "Polytechna," catalogue (Prague: Polytechna, 1973). Commissions of the UN were part of architectural and engineering engagements from other socialist countries too, including Yugoslavia and Hungary.
91. "Stavoprojekt Liberec, Atelier 2," catalogue (Prague: Polytechna, n.d.).
92. For architectural history from the perspective of labor, see Jaskot, *Architecture of Oppression*; Deamer, ed., *Architect as Worker*; Amhoff et al., eds., *Industries*.
93. Quoted in Butter, "Showcase," 249.
94. Anderson, *Russia*; Wakeman, *Practicing Utopia*.
95. Kalter, *Discovery*.
96. Amin, "Challenge of Globalization," 227.
97. Lefebvre, "Worldwide Experience"; Madden, "City Becoming World"; on Lefebvre's concept of concrete abstraction, see Stanek, *Lefebvre on Space*, ch. 3.
98. Glissant, *Poetics*, 195; see also Obrist, Razā, *Mondialité*.
99. Lynn, "Globalization"; Sayward, "International Institutions"; Spaulding, "Trade."
100. Obrist, Razā, *Mondialité*; Nancy, *Globalization*; see also Elden, "Mondialisation."
101. Pons, *Global Revolution*; see also Kott, "Cold War Internationalism."
102. Khrushchev, *Memoirs*; Mëhilli, *From Stalin to Mao*, 10–12.
103. Polónyi, *Architect-Planner*, 12. Károly Polónyi often used the English version of his first name (Charles).
104. Dmochowski, *Introduction*, vol. 1, ix.
105. Compare Simone, "Worlding," 17.
106. I owe this comment to a conversation with Quinn Slobodian, Hong Kong, March 2017.
107. Schmid et al., "New Vocabulary"; Brenner, Schmid, "New Epistemology."

Chapter 2

1. "Main Report: The First International Trade Fair, 1–19 February 1967," Accra, 1967; Stanisław Rymaszewski, "Handing Over Notes: Ghana International Trade Fair," Accra, May 27, 1967, both in archive of Stanisław Rymaszewski, Warsaw (Poland).
2. Interview with Nana Kwame Ofori-Amanfo, Accra, June 2012.
3. Ahlman, *Living*.
4. Quoted in ibid., 126.
5. d'Auria, "More than Tropical?" 196.
6. "The Kingsway Street Map of Accra," 1958, LC G8854.A2 1958.H3; "Accra: Compiled, Drawn, and Photo-lithographed by the Survey of Ghana," 1965, LC G8854.A2 1965.G5. The latter plan was drawn by German architect Hannah Schreckenbach in the service of the GNCC.
7. *Daily Graphic* (later: *DG*), March 25, 1958, 1; *DG*, May 19, 1961, 18; *DG*, May 19, 1961, 19; *Evening News* (later: *EN*), September 30, 1961, 8; *EN*, January 18, 1965, 3. See also Yacobi, *Israel*.
8. Yacobi, *Israel*; Feniger, Kallus, "Israeli Planning."
9. *DG*, May 19, 1961, 19; *EN*, September 30, 1961, 8.
10. *EN*, June 11, 1966, 1.
11. See, for example, *Nigeria Public Works*; Agg, *Handbook*; *Information Book*; *A Building Guide*; Drew et al., *Village Housing*; Alcock, Richards, *How to Plan*.
12. Interviews with Jacek Chyrosz and Grażyna Jonkajtys-Luba, Warsaw, June 2011. For an overview, see Jackson, Uduku, "Sub-Saharan Africa."
13. See "Staff List of Administrative, Professional, Senior Executive and Senior Technical Appointments" for the fiscal (financial) years 1956–57, 1957–58, 1959–60, 1960–61, 1961–62, PRAAD ADM 38-2-35 to 40 and 8-3-34 to 35; Crinson, *Modern Architecture*, 127–56; Okoye, "Architecture"; Hess, "Imagining Architecture," I and II; Jopp, *Ghana*; Ghana Ministry, *Ghana*.
14. *EN*, April 2, 1960, 13; "Faculty Profile—Victor Adegbite," *Matrix*, n.d., 30–31.
15. Interview with A. W. Charaway and E.G.A. Don Arthur, Accra, June 2012; card index of the students' files, MARKhI.
16. Le Roux, "Networks"; Chang, *Genealogy*.
17. Drew, Fry, *Tropical Architecture*; Jackson, Holland, *Architecture of Fry and Drew*.
18. *DG*, August 8, 1958, 14; *EN*, December 9, 1960, 9; *EN*, July 8, 1964, 5; "Volta River Authority—Offices," *WABA* 4, no. 4 (1964): 66–69. The hospital was designed in collaboration with William F. Vetter.
19. Nickson, Borys & Partners, National Archives Building in Accra, drawings, 1959, AESL. Other designs by Nickson, Borys & Partners in the AESL archives include Kumasi Technical Institute (1958), Accra Technical Institute (1959), Memorial Library in Accra (1960), Magistrates Courts in Accra (1960), Central Library Extension in Accra (1961), School for Librarians in Accra (1961), Survey Headquarters (1961), and schools in several cities.
20. *DG*, February 29, 1960, 7; *DG*, May 11, 1960, 9; *DG*, May 11, 1960, 13; Tipple, *Development*, 23–25; Danby, *Grammar*.
21. The designs by Gerlach & Gillies-Reynburn included the Great Hall at the UST (ca. 1964; see Crinson, *Modern Architecture*, 146) and the Achimota Primary School (1961), AESL. See also Barnes, Hubbard & Arundel Architects and Town Planning Consultants, Wiawso Teachers Training College, drawings, 1961, AESL.
22. A. Gilmour, designs of private bungalows, 1960–62, AESL.
23. Carmichael, *Together*; *Ghanaian Times* (later: *GT*), August 30, 1960, 2; *GT*, March 10, 1961 (supplement); Jones, *Arup*, 141, 155; *DG*, October 5, 1962, 9.
24. *DG*, May 11, 1960, 13.
25. "Main Report."
26. Ibid.
27. "Commonwealth in Action," *Ghana Review* 7, no. 1 (1967): 3–6; *EN*, April 11, 1962, 1, 6.
28. The authors were Valle, Angrisani, and Pacello, "Ghana." Renato Severino with his office Comtec designed the University College in Cape Coast (1967); Severino, *Equipotential Space*, 16–19.
29. The contractor was Sodefra, the architect was Pierre Dufau, *DG*, August 17, 1964, 12; *DG*, July 15, 1965, 1.
30. *GT*, February 3, 1961, 5.
31. *EN*, July 27, 1966, 1; "Einfamilienhäuser"; "Neue Heimat."
32. Uduku, "Bolgatanga Library"; Max Bond, Studio and Practice Hall for the National Orchestra, drawings, 1964, AESL.
33. *DG*, October 21, 1961, 8–9.
34. "Accra-Tema-Akosombo"; "Kwame Nkrumah Commercial Area"; d'Auria, de Meulder, "Unsettling Landscapes"; d'Auria, "Tropical Transitions."
35. *DG*, August 6, 1959, 10.
36. Mazov, *Distant Front*; *DG*, March 5, 1962, 5.
37. "Projects to Be Undertaken by Communist Countries," September 1, 1960; "Report on Sino-Soviet Bloc Politico-Economic Relations," December 23, 1960; both in CCF, Ghana 1960–January 1963, reels 10 and 5, respectively; see also *EN*, June 3, 1962, 4.
38. *DG*, March 5, 1962, 5.
39. Attwood, *Reds and Blacks*.
40. "Semi-Annual Report on Sino-Soviet Bloc Politic-Economic Relations with Ghana," December 22, 1959, CCF, Ghana 1960–January 1963, reel 10.
41. Mazov, *Distant Front*; *Sovetsko-ganskoe*; "Utro respubliki Gana," 1963, dir. Alexandr Medvedkin.
42. Morris, "Soviet Africa Institute."
43. Rosen, *Development*; Kret, "We Unite with Knowledge."
44. They included the Institute for African Studies (Leipzig, 1960), the Research Center of the Economy of Less-Developed Countries (Warsaw, 1961), and University of the 17th of November (Prague, 1961); Mark, Slobodian, "Eastern Europe."
45. Legvold, *Soviet Policy*; Mazov, *Distant Front*; Iandolo, "Rise and Fall."
46. Quoted in Iandolo, "Rise and Fall," 685.
47. Ibid., 684.
48. *GT*, September 4, 1961, 5.
49. *EN*, June 27, 1961, 4; *EN*, July 11, 1961, 6; *EN*, July 27, 1961, 4; *EN*, July 27, 1961, 6; *EN*, August 9, 1961, 6; *EN*, May 24, 1962, 4; *EN*, November 16, 1962, 2; *EN*, November 26, 1962, 5; *EN*, August 23, 1963, 4–5; *EN*, October 31, 1963, 4; *DG*, January 17, 1964, 7; *DG*, April 4, 1964, 5–6; *DG*, November 6, 1965, 10–11.
50. Kalinovsky, 201–2.

51. Iandolo, "Rise and Fall," 692.
52. Quoted in Kalinovsky, 201–2.
53. *GT*, September 4, 1961, 5.
54. Robinson, "Thinking Cities"; Robinson, "Comparative Urbanism."
55. Rimsha, *Gorod*; Rimsha, *Town Planning*. See also Rimsha, *Osnovy*; Rimsha, *Gradostroitel'stvo*.
56. Rimsha was the co-designer of the master plan of Kabul (1962–64), and he took part in UNESCO's International Mission for the reconstruction of Skopje after the 1963 earthquake; see Beyer, "Competitive Coexistence."
57. Rimsha, *Town Planning*, 33–36.
58. Ibid., 142–44.
59. Kirasirova, "Sons of Muslims."
60. Demchenko, "Decentralized Past."
61. Voronina, *Narodnye traditsii*; Voronina, *Narodnaia arkhitektura*; Voronina, *Opyt proektirovaniia*; Voronina, *Arkhitekturnye pamiatniki*; Voronina, *Narodnoe zhilishche*; Voronina, *Sovremennaia arkhitektura*.
62. Anderson, *Russia*, 198–99, 222.
63. Rimsha, *Town Planning*, 200–203.
64. Chukhovich, "Orientalist Modes of Modernism"; Kalinovsky, *Laboratory*, 16.
65. Rimsha, *Gorod*, 193; Beyer, "Competitive Coexistence."
66. Gocking, *History of Ghana*.
67. Quoted in Iandolo, "Rise and Fall," 695.
68. Ahlman, *Living*.
69. *DG*, January 3, 1963, 3.
70. Ginsburgs, Slusser, eds., *Calendar*, 107.
71. *GT*, September 29, 1961, 9; *EN*, November 16, 1962, 1; *EN*, February 19, 1963, 1; *EN*, May 13, 1964, 1; "Polish Firm to Build Cement Factory," *WABA* 2, no. 5 (1962): 108.
72. "Czech Factories for Ghana," *WABA* 1, no. 4 (1961): 107; "Transfúzní stanice pro Ghanu," *Architektura ČSSR* 6 (1963), 351; "Bus Assembly Plant for Accra" (1963), archive of Attila Emödy, Budapest (Hungary); "Ghana. Regierungsdruckerei in Tema," *Deutsche Architektur* XIII (September 1964): 540–43; "Sugar Factory Combine at Asutsuare," AAN z. 2309, 1/104.
73. *EN*, October 1, 1965, 5; *DG*, February 12, 1966, 6–7; Miescher, Tsikata, "Hydro-Power"; "Tamale/Kumbungu," 56–57.
74. Hartmetz et al., "East-South Relations."
75. *Yugoslav Investment Works*, 11, 14, 17.
76. Brautigam, *Dragon's Gift*, 32.
77. Roskam, "Non-Aligned Architecture," 274.
78. Ginsburgs, Slusser, eds., *Calendar*, 147, see also 288; *DG*, August 9, 1961, 1.
79. *DG*, June 20, 1964, 1.
80. *EN*, April 13, 1964, 1; "Sporten kompleks v Akra-Gana," *Arkhitektura* 9–10 (1963): 12–17; "Kompleks 'kraibrezhna zona' v Akra-Gana," *Arkhitektura* 7 (1964): 34–37; Encho Balukchiev, personal dossier, KAB.
81. Interview with Chyrosz; interview with Stanisław Rymaszewski, Warsaw, June 2011.
82. *DG*, March 5, 1962, 5.
83. Ibid.
84. Compare Slobodian, "Uses of Disorientation."
85. Moravánszky, "Peripheral Modernism"; telephone interview with Anikó Polónyi, February 2013.
86. The drawings of designs by Charles Polónyi as project architect (Vic Adegbite as chief architect) in the AESL archives include Bungalow Allocation Housing in Accra, Airport Estates (1964), Garden of the Ghana News Agency (1964), Extension to the Old Chapel Wing of the Osu Castle (1964), and Osu Castle Mausoleum (1965). See also Polónyi, *Architect-Planner*, 53–80.
87. Telephone interview with Zvonimir Žagar and Nebojša Weiner, February 2013; I. C., "In Memoriam," 323.
88. In 1962, Ciko left for Kumasi, where he became university architect (1962–67) and senior architect in charge of the Development Office of the university (1967–68); Niksa Ciko, CV, archive of Zdenka Ciko, Sydney (Australia).
89. Interviews with Evlogi Raichev and Encho Balukchiev, Sofia, July 2014; Ivan Naidenovich, personal dossier, KAB. Other Bulgarian architects working at the GNCC included Evlogi Raichev, S. T. Ploskov, T. I. Todorov, and Z. Doytchev. See also Doytchinov, "Pragmatism."
90. Jacek Chyrosz and Stanisław Rymaszewski, "Międzynarodowe Targi w Akrze," *Architektura* 4 (1969): 143–46.
91. Interview with Chyrosz and Rymaszewski.
92. After the coup in 1966 that ousted Nkrumah, that number quickly declined to thirty (1971), while Nigeria was at top on the list (ninety-four), ahead of Algeria (ninety-one), Grzywnowicz, Kiedrzyński, *Prawa i obowiązki*, 21–22.
93. See, for example, projects for the Accra High School (1967); Extension to the School of Hygiene, Korle Bu Hospital (1970); New Laboratory C.R.I. (n.d.); Ghana Academy of Sciences (1964); Prison Headquarters, Accra (n.d.); drawings, AESL. See also SARP d. 623.
94. Rymaszewski, "Handing Over Notes."
95. Drużyński was in charge of the hotel, Wojczyński of the two symmetrical halls, SARP d. 770, interview with Wojczyński, Warsaw, June 2011.
96. Kapuściński, *Gdyby Cała Afryka*, 248–49; see also Sanders, "Nkrumah." Wojczyński recalled: "I was very uneasy about buying windows in Switzerland and elevators in [West] Germany. My wife, who traveled with me to Ghana, was a doctor, she worked at a hospital in Accra, and I was perfectly aware of the misery in this country.... But we had no choice but to rely on these expensive foreign firms, since the deadlines given us by the government were incredibly tight." Interview with Wojczyński.
97. For the list of projects and designers, see Stanek, "Architects from Socialist Countries," 440.
98. "Pomnik"; *GT*, May 18, 1965. The monument was demolished after the 1966 coup.
99. E-mail correspondence with Hannah Schreckenbach, December 2012; Schreckenbach, Abankwa, *Construction Technology*.
100. Interview with Chyrosz.
101. Interview with Polónyi; Stanek, ed., *Team 10 East*.
102. Interview with Chyrosz; Kaniewski, *Polska Szkoła*.
103. Correspondence with Schreckenbach.
104. Polónyi, *Architect-Planner*, 25–34, 55–59; see the drawings of the Kwame Nkrumah Institute in Winneba (1964), and the Extension to Ghana's Parliament (1965), both in AESL.
105. Hasty, *Press*.
106. *DG*, May 19, 1961, 14–15.
107. *DG*, July 9, 1965, 6–7; *DG*, September 27, 1965, 5; *EN*, July 25, 1963, 6.
108. *DG*, May 20, 1961, 12–13; *DG*, January 11, 1962, 4; *DG*, April 23, 1962, 6–7; *EN*, August 6, 1963, 6.
109. Standard schools and colleges, single story, four classrooms, n.d.; Accra Academy (1967), drawings, AESL.
110. *DG*, August 7, 1962, 7.
111. *GT*, June 21, 1961, 3; *GT*, June 21, 1961, 6; *GT*, June 22, 1961, 3; *GT*, June 24, 1961, 4; *GT*, June 28, 1961, 3; *EN*, September 30, 1961, 5; *EN*, May 17, 1962, 5; *EN*, June 28, 1963, 6; *EN*, January 2, 1964, 4; *EN*, February 19, 1964, 6; *DG*, March 16, 1963, 6–7; Regal Cinema, Accra (1970), drawings, AESL.
112. *EN*, June 8, 1962, 8.
113. Ibid.
114. *EN*, May 17, 1963, 8; *EN*, May 21, 1963, 6; *EN*, October 4, 1963, 6; *EN*, October 21, 1963, 6; *EN*, June 19, 1964, 5; *GT*, June 29, 1961, 9; *DG*, October 22, 1963, 4.
115. *EN*, March 7, 1960, 1; *EN*, May 5, 1960, 2; *EN*, July 9, 1960, 7; *EN*, February 19, 1964, 6; *EN*, June 22, 1964, 5.
116. Interviews with Žagar and Weiner. See the following drawings of buildings at the UST campus in the Development Office, UST, Kumasi: John Owusu-Addo (architect in charge), Miro Marasović (senior architect), Unity Hall (Hall of Residence 5), 1963–68; K.M.G. Kirkbride (architect in charge), Miro Marasović (chief university architect), Faculty of Architecture, 1963; Niksa Ciko (architect in charge), Miro Marasović/John Owusu-Addo (chief university architect), Senior Staff Club, 1964; B. Kalogjera (architect in charge), Miro Marasović (chief university architect), Vice-Chancellor's Bungalow, 1964; John Owusu-Addo/Miro Marasović (chief university architect), Niksa Ciko (architect in charge), Africa Hall (Women's Hall 6), 1964–65; Nebojša Weiner (chief university architect), N. Weiner, W. S. Asamoah, K. Odonfrah-Annoh (architectural team), Faculty of Pharmacy Extension, 1970; Jan Skokánek (chief university architect), Administration Block 1 Extension, 1974.
117. *EN*, June 22, 1964, 5.
118. *EN*, October 21, 1963, 6.
119. *EN*, December 11, 1961, 2–7.
120. *EN*, July 16, 1966, 1; *EN*, December 10, 1966, 2; *DG*, March 5, 1966, 5; *DG*, March 11, 1966, 1; *DG*, April 1, 1966, 1; *DG*, June 13, 1966, 1.
121. *EN*, May 21, 1963, 6.
122. *EN*, September 30, 1961, 5.
123. *EN*, February 17, 1966, 5.
124. *DG*, May 26, 1960, 8–9; *DG*, August 26, 1960, 8–9; *DG*, June 6, 1961, 8–9; *DG*, January 6, 1962, 6–7; *DG*, June 19, 1963, 7; *DG*, December 8, 1965, 8–9; *EN*, October 25, 1961, 6; *EN*, August 6, 1963, 6.
125. *DG*, November 6, 1961, 9.
126. *EN*, July 18, 1962, 1.
127. *EN*, December 6, 1963, 6.

128. *EN*, January 13, 1966, 1.
129. Rymaszewski, "Handing Over Notes," 5; Stanisław Rymaszewski, CV, n.d., Rymaszewski archive.
130. *EN*, May 17, 1962, 3; *EN*, July 18, 1963, 1; *EN*, March 11, 1964, 5; *EN*, July 15, 1964, 5; *EN*, August 21, 1964, 5; *EN*, October 9, 1965, 5.
131. *EN*, July 11, 1964, 5; *EN*, July 15, 1964, 5.
132. *DG*, November 24, 1960, 10–11.
133. *DG*, June 29, 1961, 15; *DG*, March 18, 1963, 1, 3.
134. *DG*, March 16, 1960, 7; *DG*, August 7, 1962, 7.
135. *GT*, July 27, 1961, 5; *EN*, April 13, 1962, 1; *EN*, April 14, 1962, 1.
136. *EN*, December 6, 1963, 1.
137. *DG*, October 12, 1965, 5.
138. Armah, *Beautyful Ones*, 12.
139. Ahlman, *Living*, 78–79.
140. *GT*, August 25, 1960, 1; *DG*, May 20, 1961, 9; *DG*, January 5, 1963, 1; *EN*, March 22, 1963, 5–6.
141. Kumasi bungalows (drawings); R. B. Nunoo, "Testimonial to Mr. S. H. Rymaszewski"; January 17, 1974; National Register of Historic Buildings and Sites, Accra 1972; all three in Rymaszewski archive; Moggridge, "Farmhouse."
142. *GT*, August 1, 1961, 1; Osu Castle, Extension to the Offices of the Prime Minister, n.d., drawings, AESL. For Polónyi's projects for the Osu Castle, see note 86 in this chapter.
143. *GT*, July 27, 1961, 5; *DG*, June 2, 1961, 7.
144. *DG*, September 14, 1959, 5; *EN*, June 19, 1961, 5. Architects: J. G. Halstead and D. A. Barratt.
145. *DG*, July 19, 1961, 7; see also *DG*, August 2, 1961, 7.
146. Residence in Bolgatanga, drawings, 1962, AESL.
147. *EN*, September 30, 1961, 7; *EN*, September 30, 1961, 6, 9; *DG*, August 7, 1962, 9.
148. Interview with Chyrosz.
149. *EN*, May 14, 1964, 1; *EN*, July 9, 1964, 5.
150. Veronika Leonidovna Voronina, "Zametki ob arkhitekture Gany," *Arkhitektura SSSR* 8 (1964): 46–51; Irina Nikolaevna Filippovich, "Sovremennoe zhilishche Gany," *Arkhitektura SSSR* 8 (1964): 52–55.
151. The names of British architects were consistently omitted in both articles, which, by contrast, mentioned Vic Adegbite and Ghanaian artist Kofi Antubam; Voronina, "Zametki," 51; Filippovich, "Sovremennoe zhilishche," 52.
152. Voronina, "Zametki"; Filippovich, "Sovremennoe zhilishche."
153. Filippovich, "Sovremennoe zhilishche," 52.
154. The authors were B.A.W. Trevallion and Alan G. Hood under the direction of W. H. Barrett, "Accra: A Plan."
155. Konadu-Agyemang, "Housing," 69.
156. "Accra: A Plan"; see also "Accra–Tema–Akosombo."
157. "Accra: A Plan."
158. Konadu-Agyemang, "Housing," 83–84.
159. Arku, "Economics," 284.
160. "Accra: A Plan," 53; Schmitter, *Wohnungsbau*, 35–36.
161. Quoted in Arku, "Economics," 288.
162. Arku, "Economics."
163. *DG*, November 6, 1965, 11.
164. United Nations, "Report of the Study Tour." Joseph Henry Mensah, chief economic officer and executive secretary of Ghana's National Planning Commission, participated in the study trip to the USSR focused on Soviet planning, "Report of the United Nations Seminar."
165. United Nations, "Report of the Study Tour," 4–5. For recent discussions on the "socialist city," see Zarecor, "What Was So Socialist"; Hirt et al., "Conceptual Forum."
166. United Nations, "Report of the Study Tour."
167. Meuser, Zadorin, *Towards a Typology*, 164.
168. Anderson, *Russia*, 222.
169. Roskam, "Non-Aligned Architecture." See also Ding, Xue, "China's Architectural Aid."
170. "Raboty Giprovuza za rubezhom," *Arkhitektura SSSR* 9 (1976): 50–57.
171. RGAE f. 5, op. 1, d. 339, 11.
172. RGAE f. 5, op. 1, d. 142, 22–23.
173. Walters, *Aid*, 30.
174. Elke Beyer, "Die Produktion sozialistischer Urbanität. Stadtzentrumsplanungen in der Sowjetunion in den 1960er Jahren," Ph.D. dissertation, ETH Zürich, 2017, 241.
175. For discussion, see Westad, *Global Cold War*; Sanchez-Sibony, *Red Globalization*.
176. Ssorin-Chaikov, "Heterochrony."
177. Kott, *Communism*, 211–29; Crowley, Reid, eds., *Pleasures*.
178. *EN*, 9 July 1960, 7.
179. Ssorin-Chaikov, "Heterochrony," 371; see also Ssorin-Chaikov, ed., *Dary*.
180. Ssorin-Chaikov, "Heterochrony," 362.
181. Ruth Prince, "Modernist Dreams: Hospital Architectures, Soviet Aid, and Medical Modernisms in Cold-War Kenya," talk at the conference "Forms of Freedom. Legacies of African Modernism," Oslo, March 27, 2015; *SSSR i strany Afriki: 1963–1970*, vol. 1, 169–74.
182. RGAE f. 5, op. 1, d. 338, 41–45.
183. Ginsburgs, Slusser, eds., *Calendar*, 310.
184. See also Łukasz Stanek, Nikolay Erofeev, "African Housing in Soviet Gift Economies," talk at the SAH Annual Conference (Glasgow, UK), June 8, 2017.
185. RGAE f. 5, op. 1, d. 338, 41–45.
186. RGAE f. 5, op. 1, d. 339, 11.
187. RGAE f. 5, op. 1, d. 338, 3–4.
188. Iandolo, "Rise and Fall," 699; Boden, "Cold War."
189. Prince, "Modernist Dreams."
190. RGAE f. 5, op. 1, d. 338, 3.
191. See Crawford, "Soviet Planning."
192. "Edinye tekhnicheskie usloviia na proektirovanie predpriiatii i drugikh ob"ektov stroiashchikhsia v Gvineiskoi Respublike pri tekhnicheskom sodeistvii SSSR" (Moscow, 1961); "Edinye tekhnicheskie usloviia na proektirovanie predpriiatii i drugikh ob"ektov stroiashchikhsia v Respublike Gana pri tekhnicheskom sodeistvii Sovetskogo Soiuza" (Moscow, 1962).
193. "Edinye tekhnicheskie usloviia … v Respublike Gana."
194. Prince, "Modernist Dreams."
195. Brautigam, *Dragon's Gift*, 57.
196. *SSSR i strany Afriki: 1946–1962*, vol. 2, 441–43.
197. *DG*, March 5, 1962, 5.
198. Iandolo, "Rise and Fall," 694.
199. d'Auria, "Tropical Transitions."
200. "Accra–Tema–Akosombo."
201. RGANTD f. R-850, op. 9–4, d. 38.
202. One such visit is depicted in the newsreel "Utro Respubliki Gana."
203. Beyer, "Produktion," 139–41.
204. In the design of the system, Giprostroiindustriia was advised by TsNIIEP zhilishcha, the Central Research and Design Institute for Housing Construction.
205. RGAE f. 5, op. 1, d. 140; RGAE f. 5, op. 1, d. 334.
206. RGAE f. 5, op. 1, d. 140; RGAE f. 5, op. 1, d. 334.
207. RGAE f. 5, op. 1, d. 334, 66–67. The Soviets were measuring the drawings in the metric system, but the Ghanaians were working with the imperial system.
208. RGAE f. 339, op. 3, d. 2318, 133–37.
209. RGAE f. 5, op. 1, d. 334, 93–96.
210. *EN*, May 29, 1964, 6; *West Africa* (later: *WA*), February 8, 1964, 162; Asamoah, *Ghana*, 76. According to the Ghanaian press, in summer 1965 concrete elements produced by the factory were used to construct an "experimental house" in Accra, but the accompanying photograph shows a one-floor structure, rather than a multistory one; *EN*, July 17, 1965, 6. In the mid-1970s, the factory was reactivated with the help of Soviet experts; *WA*, March 21, 1977, 577.
211. RGAE (Samara) f. R-150, op. 2–1, d. 433, 1–38; RGAE (Samara) f. R-150, op. 2–1, d. 414; RGAE f. 5, op. 1, d. 334, 57–58.
212. RGAE (Samara) f. R-150, op. 2–1, d. 414, 5.
213. Ibid., RGANTD f. R-850, op. 9–4, d. 66; RGANTD f. R-850, op. 9–4, d. 77.
214. RGAE f. 5, op. 1, d. 334, 57.
215. RGAE (Samara) f. R-150, op. 2–1, d. 414.
216. Rimsha, *Town Planning*, 148–59.
217. There was a precedent of an attempt at large-scale prefabrication in Ghana: the Dutch system Schokbeton (which consisted of wall slabs). It was rejected following the advice of a 1956 UN report because of its poor adaptation to climatic conditions and its uneconomic character. Abrams et al., "Report"; Arku, "Economics," 290.
218. "Report of the Study Tour," 24–31.
219. Meuser, Zadorin, *Towards a Typology*.
220. RGANTD f. R-850, op. 9–4, d. 43 and d. 46. The main difference between the I-464 system and system designed for Accra was the replacement of the room-sized façade elements with smaller, L-shaped blocks.
221. RGAE f. 5, op. 1, d. 140, 4–5.
222. RGAE f. 5, op. 1, d. 140, 52–53; RGAE f. 5, op. 1, d. 140, 94; RGAE (Samara) f. R-149, op. 1–1, d. 1102, 1–63.
223. The comparison with buildings constructed at that time in Accra and discussions with GNCC architects, with local contractors, and with the team of Doxiadis led to the removal of the sound insulation (deemed unnecessary) and to the modification of the waterproofing materials. RGAE f. 339, op. 3, d. 2318, 159–65.
224. Meuser, Zadorin, *Towards a Typology*.
225. The most widespread would be four-story houses with three-room apartments (60 percent of the factory output), consisting of one, two, or three sections.
226. RGANTD f. R-850, op. 9–4, d. 46.

227. Meuser, Zadorin, *Towards a Typology*, 169.
228. Danby, *Grammar*.
229. "The Town of Tema," 165; Rimsha, *Town Planning*, 156–57.
230. Meuser, Zadorin, *Towards a Typology*, 168.
231. RGANTD f. R-850, op. 9–4, d. 46.
232. RGAE (Samara) f. R-149, op. 1–1, d. 1102, 1–63; RGAE f. 339, op. 3, d. 2318, 168.
233. d'Auria, "Tropical Transitions," 55.
234. d'Auria, "Laboratory," 344–48.
235. RGAE f. 5, op. 1, d. 140, 71–73.
236. *WA*, December 2, 1974, 1466.
237. The design of the fair was modified after the inauguration of Greater Accra in 1963 as new administrative entity; *DG*, October 7, 1963, 1.
238. *DG*, January 23, 1965, 1.
239. Large parts of La were foreseen for demolition by the 1958 master plan as overcrowded and lacking adequate services and roads; "Accra: A Plan," 46–47. The authorities explained the postponing of the opening of the fair by the need to develop this area; "Trade Fair Postponed," *WABA* 5, no. 1 (1965): 19. The urban design of La by Grażyna Jonkajtys-Luba and Jerzy Luba at the TCPD preserved places of traditional cult, which resulted in the irregularities of the realized road network.
240. Compare Stanek, "Accra"; Tourist Hotel Castle Road (1963), drawings, AESL.
241. *DG*, April 1, 1966, 13; *DG*, February 2, 1967, 6.
242. *DG*, February 2, 1967, 6.
243. Chyrosz, Rymaszewski, "Międzynarodowe Targi."
244. By contrast, a pavilion for Taiwan was built; *DG*, January 17, 1967, 8–9; *DG*, January 18, 1967, 1; *DG*, February 1, 1967, 1; *DG*, February 16, 1967, 10.
245. *EN*, March 17, 1966, 1.
246. "Ghana's Economic Prospects," 12; *DG*, February 2, 1967, 6.
247. *EN*, July 7, 1966, 8.
248. Roskam, "Non-Aligned Architecture."
249. Drew, Fry, *Tropical Architecture*, 23; compare Drew et al., "Deux études"; Drew, Fry, *Village Housing*.
250. Le Caisne, "Les conditions"; Johan Lagae, "'Kongo zoals het is': Drie architectuurverhalen uit de Belgische kolonisatiegeschiedenis 1920–1960," Ph.D. dissertation, Ghent University, 2002, 316–17.
251. Chyrosz, Rymaszewski, "Międzynarodowe Targi."
252. "Konkurs dla Konga Belgijskiego," *Architektura* 10 (1959): 463; SARP d. 401, 852.
253. Interview with Chyrosz.
254. "Ghana Factory for the Production of Weather Proof Plywood," *WABA* 1, no. 2 (1961): 45–46; "Czech Factories for Ghana"; "Structural Use of Exterior Grade Plywood in West Africa," *WABA* 5, no. 2 (1965): 41; "Low Cost Housing in Nigeria," *WABA* 7, no. 6 (1967): 171–72.
255. "Schedule of various overseas orders for Ghana International Trade Fair," August 10, 1966, AESL. Of particular importance for the construction of the ITF were the firms A. Lang, J. Monta, and E. Tonone; interviews with Chyrosz and Weiner.
256. Drew, Fry, *Tropical Architecture*, 24.
257. See Crinson, *Modern Architecture*, 139–41;

Drew, "Recent Work."
258. Maciej Ziółek, "Budownictwo w warunkach klimatu tropikalnego," *Inżynieria i budownictwo* 7 (1965): 216–20; Ziółek, "Problemy"; see also "Dylematy tropiku," *Fundamenty* 1 (1968): 13; Jerzy Romański and Zenon Zieliński, "Pawilon tropikalny z aluminium," *Inżynieria i budownictwo* 8 (1962): 281–84.
259. Ziółek, "Problemy," 3–4.
260. Ibid.; Ziółek, "Budownictwo."
261. The publications quoted include George A. Atkinson and B. Artch, "Housing Construction in Countries with a Tropical Climate," paper delivered at First Congress of the International Council on Construction, Rotterdam, 1962; Aronin, *Climate and Architecture*; Drew, Fry, *Tropical Architecture*; Danby, *Grammar*; Olgyay, Olgyay, *Solar Control*; among others. For Soviet publications, see notes 55 and 61 in this chapter, and Firsanov, *Arkhitektura*; Punagin, *Tekhnologiia*; Mironov, Malinskii, *Osnovy*; Kiselevich et al., *Zhilishchnoe stroitel'stvo*; Filippovich, *Osobennosti*.
262. Winid, "Centre," 151–58.
263. "Naco Louvre Windows" advertisements in *WABA* 8, no. 1 (1968): A5, and *WABA* 8, no. 3 (1968): A5.
264. "International Trade Fair to Be Held in Accra," *WABA* 3, no. 6 (1963): 116; "Special Import Licenses for Trade Fair," *WABA* 4, no. 2 (1964): 42; "International Trade Fair," *WABA* 4, no. 4 (1964): 86; "Trade Fair Postponed."
265. *Ghana Review* 7, no. 2 (1967).
266. A similar bias was displayed in Richards, *New Buildings*; see also Lagae, Toulier, "De l'outre-mer," 51.
267. Design authorship seemed to have been the criterion for publication in the *West African Builder and Architect*, since the journal presented buildings designed by RIBA architects even if they were constructed by the GNCC; "Volta River Authority."
268. That commission, not realized, went to Wojczyński, as he recalls. Witold Wojczyński, interview with author, Warsaw, June 2011.
269. Interviews with Chyrosz and Rymaszewski. For example, among nineteen architects present at the GIA meeting in Accra on September 29, 1964, eleven were from socialist countries (ten of them from Poland); see "Minutes of the General Meeting of Ghana Institute of Architect[s] Held on Tuesday 29/9/64," Max Bond Papers 1951–2009, 2009.015, Box 26, Avery Drawings and Archives Collection, Columbia University, New York. The GCSA merged with GIA in 1965.
270. Pletsch, "Three Worlds."
271. See also Kott, "Forced Labor."
272. Drew, Fry, *Tropical Architecture*, 24.
273. By the 1970s, the journal relaxed its gatekeeping regime, and it reproduced the design of the Kaduna Museum (Nigeria, 1968) by Polish architect Marian Łyczkowski, employed by the Ministry of Works and Housing in Lagos; "Kaduna Museum," *WABA* 9, no. 3 (1969): 87.
274. Interview with Chyrosz.
275. AAN z. 1154, sygn. 25/526, 42.
276. Interview with Rymaszewski.
277. Interviews with Jonkajtys-Luba and

Rymaszewski. However, other specialists complained about the accommodation, AAN z. 1154, sygn. 25/526, 44–49.
278. Interviews with Chyrosz and Rymaszewski. See also: "Report on Sino-Soviet Bloc." Another difference between the everyday of Soviet and other Eastern European experts was that the former refused to hire domestic staff, a common practice in Ghana. Consequently, bungalows built for Soviet technicians in Tamale had no "servant quarters" (they were added when the bungalows were redistributed among Ghanaians after the Soviets left); "Tamale/Kumbungu," 57.
279. AAN z. 1154, sygn. 25/526, 384.
280. O. J. Ludlam, "Letter of Reference for Stanisław Rymaszewski," January 24, 1972, Rymaszewski archive.
281. Interviews with Chyrosz, Rymaszewski, Żagar, and Weiner.
282. Dalton, "Colony."
283. Rimsha, *Town Planning*.

Chapter 3

1. Stefan Kolchev, "Natsionalniiat teatur na Nigeriia v Lagos—Delo na bulgarskite arkhitekti i stroiteli," *Arkhitektura* 4 (1977): 13–22.
2. Ibid.; *West African Pilot* (later: *WAP*), April 26, 1973, 1.
3. TES, catalogue (Sofia: Technoexportstroy, 1998). The Eko hotel was designed by Nigerian, Lagos-based architect Oluwole Olumuyiwa in collaboration with Warner, Burns, Toan & Lunde of New York; TES's construction was supervised by the Bechtel Corporation; *West Africa* (later: *WA*), October 14, 1974, 1267.
4. *35 godina*; Mircea Nicolescu, "8 locuințe pentru Festival Town, Lagos," *Arhitectura* 6 (1980): 18–21; Mircea Nicolescu, "Spații comerciale în Lagos," *Arhitectura* 6 (1980): 26–28.
5. Apter, *Pan-African Nation*; Falola, Heaton, *History of Nigeria*, 181–95.
6. Ogunbadejo, "Nigeria's Foreign Policy"; Ojo, "Nigerian-Soviet Relations."
7. Prashad, *Darker Nations*.
8. See "Studie über den Baumarkt der BR Nigeria" (1983), BA DH/23020.
9. Polónyi, *Architect-Planner*, 82.
10. Ibid.
11. The only Eastern European country besides (East) Germany that had significant economic experience in sub-Saharan Africa before World War II was Czechoslovakia; see Muehlenbeck, *Czechoslovakia in Africa*.
12. Ong, "Worlding Cities"; McCann et al., "Assembling," 584–86. For a formative understanding of the concept of worlding, see Spivak, "Rani of Sirmur."
13. Ong, "Worlding Cities."
14. Simone, "Worlding."
15. Polónyi, *Architect-Planner*, 49.
16. Ibid., 12.
17. Bond et al., *Transformation*, n.p.
18. "Survey and Development Plan," 0.7–0.9; see also "Master Plan of Calabar (Nigeria)," *Magyar Építőművészet* VI (1980): 8–9.
19. Polónyi, *Architect-Planner*, 82.
20. Moravánszky, "Peripheral Modernism."

21. Sachs, "Revisiting Development," 6; see also Szlajfer, ed., *Economic Nationalism*.
22. Sachs, "Revisiting Development."
23. Mazurek, "Co się stało"; Leszczyński, *Skok*.
24. Rosenstein-Rodan, "Problems"; Leszczyński, *Skok*, 111–26.
25. Sachs, "Revisiting Development."
26. Kula, "Między wspomnieniami"; López, Assous, *Kalecki*, 18–19; Mazurek, "Polish Economists."
27. Chmielewski, Syrkus, *Warszawa funkcjonalna*.
28. Kohlrausch, "Poland"; Mumford, *CIAM Discourse*.
29. Platzer, "From CIAM to CIAM-Ost."
30. Moravánszky, "Peripheral Modernism"; Moravánszky, ed., *Das entfernte Dorf*; Wiebenson, Sisa, eds., *Architecture*.
31. Virgil Bierbauer, "Les bases de la reconstruction rurale en Hongrie," GTA Archive, dossier "5 Kongress: Andere Beiträge."
32. Held, *Modernization*, 294–300.
33. Mazurek, "Co się stało"; Arndt, *Economic Development*.
34. Bierbauer, "Les bases."
35. Wiebenson, Sisa, *Architecture*, 212.
36. Bierbauer, "Les bases."
37. Bierbauer, "A magyar építészet"; Bierbauer, "Nagy feladatok"; Wigand, "A magyar parasztház"; Győrffy, "Az alföldi parasztház"; Viski, "A dunántúli parasztház"; Gulyás, "Heves megyei kisházak"; Koós, "Az erdélyi magyar parasztház."
38. Moravánszky, "Peripheral Modernism," 337.
39. Friss, "Underdevelopment."
40. Richert, *Przestrzenne planowanie*, 5.
41. Ibid., 96–97.
42. Zaremba, "Outline."
43. Ibid.; Zaremba, "Niektóre problemy urbanistyki afrykańskiej," *Architektura* 3 (1962): 109–14.
44. "Seven-Year Plan"; "National Physical Development Plan."
45. "National Physical Development Plan."
46. "Seven-Year Plan," 5; "National Physical Development Plan," iii; Malisz, "Urban Planning Theory," 66–70.
47. "National Physical Development Plan," v; "Seven-Year Plan," Appendix B. For Hungarian economists involved in the Seven-Year Development Plan, including József Bognár, see Ginelli, "Experts." In the services of TCPD, Jerzy Luba and Grażyna Jonkajtys-Luba delivered the first master plans of the regional centers in Ghana, their central areas and extensions, including Ho, Bolgatanga, Big Ada, and Paga; archive of Grażyna Jonkajtys-Luba, Warsaw (Poland). Like Polónyi, Luba and Jonkajtys-Luba moved from Ghana to Nigeria, where they worked in the Lagos-based office of Egbor Associates (1976–79), SARP d. 711.
48. "National Physical Development Plan," 21.
49. Richert, *Przestrzenne planowanie*, 57–59; Waterston, "Program."
50. Richert, *Przestrzenne planowanie*, 74.
51. Ibid., 75; see ibid. 67–69 for Richert's comments on Grove, Huszar, *Towns of Ghana*.
52. Virágh, *Town Planning*, 9.
53. Ibid., 26–27.
54. Moseley, Smith, "Hungary."
55. Bond et al., *Transformation*, n.p.
56. Wettstein, "Balaton Region"; Virágh, *Town Planning*.
57. Compare Hadik, "Nationale und volkstümliche Einflüsse."
58. László Mányoky, "Tervek és valóság Újmohácson," *Magyar Építőművészet* VII, no. 6 (1958): 169–79; Tibor Farkas, Károly Polónyi, "Beszámoló a délmagyarországi árvízsújtotta területek újjáépítéséről," *Magyar Építőművészet* V: 9 (1956): 262–76; Polónyi, *Architect-Planner*, 22–23; Moravánszky, "Peripheral Modernism."
59. Polónyi, *Architect-Planner*, 25–34; Moravánszky, "Peripheral Modernism."
60. Polónyi, "Development."
61. Polónyi, *Architect-Planner*, 25–34.
62. Newman, *CIAM '59*, 42–47; "Aménagements." The Hungarian team shared the prize with the team of British planner Colin Buchanan.
63. Interview with Anikó Polónyi, Budapest, February 28, 2013.
64. Virágh, *Town Planning*, 25.
65. Polónyi, *Architect-Planner*, 26–27.
66. Bond et al., *Transformation*, n.p.
67. Polónyi, *Architect-Planner*, 32–33.
68. Bond et al., *Transformation*, n.p.
69. Abrams, *Man's Struggle*.
70. Ibid.
71. Butcher et al., "Bui."
72. Ibid.
73. Compare the issue of *Arena, the Architectural Association Journal* focused on Kumasi, July–August 1966; and "Volta Resettlement Symposium Papers: Papers Read at the Volta Resettlement Symposium, Held at Kumasi, 23–27 March, 1965," Kumasi, Faculty of Architecture, 1965.
74. Butcher et al., "Bui."
75. Ibid., 61–62.
76. Bond, Owusu-Addo, "Aspirations."
77. Miescher, Tsikata, "Hydro-power."
78. Branczik, "Exporttervezési munkák."
79. Uyanga, "Perspective."
80. Ibid.; Nwaka, "Land Administration."
81. Uyanga, "Perspective"; "First State Development Plan," 9–10.
82. "First State Development Plan," 11; "First Progress Report," 35.
83. *Daily Times* (later: *DT*), July 16, 1977, 20–21.
84. "Survey and Development Plan," 7.9.
85. Polónyi, "Kumasi 2000," 54.
86. "Survey and Development Plan," 4.1–3.
87. Ibid., 4.2; Bond et al., *Transformation*, n.p.
88. "Survey and Development Plan," 5.1–4.
89. Ibid., 2.3–5.
90. Ibid. 2.4–5; see also Butcher et al., "Bui," 61–62.
91. Polónyi, *Architect-Planner*, 55–56.
92. "Survey and Development Plan," 6.2; Polónyi, *Architect-Planner*, 56–59.
93. Polónyi, *Architect-Planner*, 57.
94. "Survey and Development Plan," 6.2.
95. Polónyi, *Architect-Planner*, 81–119.
96. "Survey and Development Plan," 7.11–14.
97. Polónyi, *Architect-Planner*, 94.
98. *Nigerian Chronicle* (later: *NC*), January 21, 1974, 1; Polónyi, *Architect-Planner*, 95–98; *NC*, June 30, 1975, 19–20; "Transportation and Communication."
99. *NC*, April 15, 1974, 6–7; *NC*, April 22, 1974, 6–7, *NC*, April 29, 1974, 6–7; *NC*, May 6, 1974, 13; *NC*, June 18, 1974, 14–15; *NC*, June 28, 1974, 1, 16; *NC*, August 6, 1974, 9; *NC*, September 10, 1974, 15; *NC*, November 8, 1974, 7; *NC*, December 5, 1974, 16; *NC*, April 6, 1975, 15; *NC*, June 3, 1975, 11; Ntukidem, "Calabar Master Plan," 63–64, 78; Polónyi, *Architect-Planner*, 97–98.
100. *NC*, April 15, 1974, 6–7; *NC*, September 27, 1974, 9.
101. Polónyi, *Architect-Planner*, 97.
102. *WAP*, July 25, 1973, 2; *NC*, May 31, 1974, 5; *NC*, July 27, 1974, 11.
103. *NC*, April 15, 1974, 6–7; *NC*, April 22, 1974, 6–7, *NC*, April 29, 1974, 6–7; *NC*, May 6, 1974, 13.
104. Ntukidem, "Calabar Master Plan."
105. The cities were Abak, Ikot Ekpene, Itu, and Uyo. Branczik, "Exporttervezési munkák," 451; *NC*, April 23, 1975, 3; Polónyi, *Architect-Planner*, 98–101; "Presentation of Tesco-Közti consulting engineers (NIG) Ltd," n.d., archive of László Herald, Budapest (Hungary).
106. Polónyi, *Architect-Planner*; László Szabados, "Master Plan of Makurdi (Nigeria)," *Magyar Építőművészet* VI (1980): 10.
107. Tassilo Neiber, "Abuja—die neue Hauptstadt Nigerias," *Architektur der DDR* 2 (1983): 107–12; Barth et al., eds., *Vom Baukünstler*, 206; Łazowski et al., *Polacy w Nigerii*, vol. 3, 33–72; László Mányoky, "The Export of Hungarian Architectural Consultancy Service," *Magyar Építőművészet* VI (1980): 2–3; Ferenc Ulrich, "Export Jobs of the Architectural Consultants for Public Buildings (Közti)," *Magyar Építőművészet* VI (1980): 12.
108. Ahmadu Bello University, Zaria, Department of Urban and Regional Planning; Ministry of Land and Surveys, Kaduna State, Kaduna, "Zaria Master Plan—2000" (1979), archive of Stanisław Juchnowicz, Kraków (Poland); Energoprojekt Engineering and Consulting; Kano State Government, Ministry of Works and Survey, "Danbatta [sic]. Master Plan. 25 Year Development Plan," 1973, archive of Danilo Udovički-Selb, Austin, TX (US).
109. Ana Solomon, "Proiecte tip destinate programului național de locuințe din Republica Federală a Nigeriei," *Arhitectura* 5 (1980): 14–16; ANR f. Romproiect, 5662 and 5758.
110. Zoran Bojović, interview with the author, Belgrade, October 9, 2015.
111. "Közti," n.d., archive of László Herald, Budapest (Hungary).
112. Boatcă, *From Neoevolutionism*.
113. Wolff, *Inventing Eastern Europe*; Todorova, *Imagining the Balkans*; Maner, *Galizien*; Blackbourn, *Conquest of Nature*.
114. Mark, Slobodian, "Eastern Europe."
115. Uffelmann, "Buren und Polen"; Najder, *Conrad*.
116. Mark, Slobodian, "Eastern Europe."
117. *DG*, November 6, 1965, 13.
118. Kalinovsky, *Laboratory*.
119. *New Nigerian* (later: *NN*), July 22, 1975, 7.
120. Azikiwe, "Poland Wants Nigeria." Azikiwe's text was published as a reprint from *African Morning Post* (Ghana); see also Białas, Liga, 221.
121. Wiśniewski, "Po majątki."
122. Verdery, "Internal Colonialism"; Born, Lemmen, "Einleitende Überlegungen," 26.
123. Polónyi, *Architect-Planner*, 11, 25, 46–47.
124. Kalinovsky, *Laboratory*.
125. *Ghanaian Times*, September 4, 1961, 5.

126. Ibid.
127. Enwezor, ed., *Short Century*.
128. *DT*, May 11, 1960, 8–31.
129. Ibid., 9; "General Post Office, Lagos, Nigeria," *WABA* 2, no. 2 (1962): 35–37; "Investment House," *WABA* 2, no. 6 (1962): 112–16.
130. D. J. Vickery, "Contemporary Nigerian Architecture," *Nigeria* 73 (1962): 44–52, 61–62; "Modern Architecture in Lagos," *Nigeria* 73 (1962): 53–60; Godwin; Hopwood, *Sandbank City*, 239; Akinsemoyin, Vaughan-Richards, *Building Lagos*, 69; Immerwahr, "Politics of Architecture"; Marris, *Family and Social Change*.
131. *DT*, May 11, 1960, 9, 20–21.
132. Falola, Heaton, *History of Nigeria*, 110.
133. Vickery, "Contemporary Nigerian Architecture"; "State House Kaduna," *WABA* 2, no. 5 (1962): 93–96; "Law Courts Kaduna," *WABA* 2, no. 5 (1962): 97–98.
134. *DT*, February 15, 1975, 7.
135. "The Functioning of a House," *New Culture: A Review of Contemporary African Arts* 1, no. 2 (1979): 27–28.
136. David Aradeon, "Views and Opinions on Nigerian Architecture and Environmental Design," *New Culture: A Review of Contemporary African Arts* 1, no. 5 (1979): 29–35; Aradeon, "African Architectural Technology."
137. Aradeon, "Space," 25.
138. Ibid., 27. Aradeon's negative example of referencing vernacular architecture was a design by Robin Atkinson constructed within the Kainji resettlement project; see also Gyuse, "Kainji."
139. Aradeon, "African Architectural Technology," 1.
140. Aradeon, "Nigerian Architecture," 27.
141. Aradeon, "African Architectural Technology," 5.
142. Aradeon, "African Architectural Technology."
143. *WA*, January 24, 1977, 172.
144. Aradeon, "African Architectural Technology"; see also Alan Vaughan-Richards, "The New Generation—A View on the Future Building Design by Alan Vaughan-Richards," *WABA* 7, no. 1 (1967): 2–5.
145. Aradeon, "African Architectural Technology"; Aradeon, "Space."
146. Apter, *Pan-African Nation*, 168–99.
147. Ibid., 5.
148. Dmochowski, *Introduction*.
149. Ibid., vol. 1, ix.
150. Dmochowski, "Sprawozdanie z badawczych prac."
151. Dmochowski, "Sprawozdanie z pomiaru"; Dmochowski, "Sprawozdanie ze studjów"; Dmochowski, *Introduction*; Świechowski, Zachwatowicz, *Dzieje*; Kalinowski, "Prace."
152. Lewicki, "Inwentaryzacja," 384–85.
153. Szmidt, ed., *Polish School*, vi; Kaniewski, *Polska Szkoła*.
154. Dmochowski, *Architecture of Poland*; Dmochowski, "Introduction."
155. London Survey, "Survey of London."
156. Łazowski et al., *Polacy w Nigerii*, vol. 1, 158.
157. Fagg, "Museums"; Povey et al.; Fagg; Folorunso, "Eyo"; Dike, *Nigerian Museum Movement*.
158. See the "Annual Reports" of the Antiquities Section/Service in Lagos for 1946, 1947, 1948, 1953–54, 1954–55, 1958–62.
159. "Annual Report 1959–60," in Department of Antiquities (Lagos), "Annual Report 1958–62," 22.
160. "Annual Report 1960–61," in Department of Antiquities (Lagos), "Annual Report 1958–62," 37; Fagg, "Museums."
161. *25 Years*, 54. He continued teaching as visiting professor at Zaria until 1966.
162. "Politechnika Gdańska"; "Skład osobowy," 83.
163. Telephone interview with Jacek Popek, September 17, 2017.
164. *25 Years*. Besides MOTNA, another addition to the museum was a training center for museum technicians, organized by UNESCO.
165. Dmochowski, *Introduction*; "Poznawanie Nigerii. Zabytki, badacze, kultura," catalogue (Gdańsk: Muzeum Etnograficzne w Gdańsku, 2006). Among his collaborators at Zaria was Polish engineer Sylwester Oleszkiewicz.
166. "Annual Report 1960–61," in Department of Antiquities (Lagos), "Annual Report 1958–62," 37; *25 Years*.
167. *25 Years*, 21–22; *WAP*, May 5, 1977, 2–3.
168. Dmochowski, *Introduction*; Barucki, "Dmochowski"; see also Moughtin, ed., *Dmochowski*.
169. Dmochowski planned two volumes. The first included sections on the architectural history and architectural geography of Nigeria, "traditional building materials," "basic constructions," and decoration. The second envisaged sections on the geographical, social, and political conditions of architecture in Nigeria; materials and technologies; and a review of the architecture in specific territories and of specific cultures, followed by conclusions on "traditional architecture of Nigeria as a source of inspiration for modern architectural development"; see "Nigerian Architecture," n.d., ZDA.
170. Ekundayo Adeyemi, "Zbigniew R. Dmochowski: A Review of His Corpus," 1, archive of Ekundayo Adeyemi, Lagos (Nigeria); interview with Ekundayo Adeyemi, Lagos, July 27, 2015.
171. Dmochowski, *Introduction*, vol. 1, v.
172. *25 Years*, 43.
173. Ibid., 43–44.
174. *25 Years*.
175. Suleiman, "Politics of Heritage."
176. Dmochowski, *Introduction*, vol. 1, ix.
177. Vaughan-Richards, "New Generation," 2–6; Alan Vaughan-Richards, "The New Generation (Part II)—A View on the Future Building Design by Alan Vaughan-Richards," *WABA* 7, no. 2 (1967): 24–48; "Architect's Own House," *WABA* 6, no. 1 (1966): 2–6; Godwin, Hopwood, *Architecture of Nwoko*.
178. Dmochowski, *Introduction*, vol. 1, ix.
179. Szmidt, *Polish School*, 51–54.
180. Dmochowski, *Introduction*, vol. 1, vii; Tłoczek, "W sprawie."
181. Lewicki, "Inwentaryzacja," 383–84; Karczewski, "Uwagi."
182. Adeyemi, "Dmochowski."
183. "Report on Chief Nwokolo's House in Ukehe by Z. R. Dmochowski, Architect to the Department of Antiquities," n.d., 1, ZDA.
184. Dmochowski, *Introduction*, vol. 1, 2.2.
185. Ibid., vol. 2, 1.37–39.
186. Ibid., 3.40.
187. Ibid., 4.33.
188. Świechowski, Zachwatowicz, *Dzieje budownictwa*, 5.
189. Compare Szmidt, *Polish School*, 53–54.
190. Dmochowski, *Introduction*, vol. 3, 92.
191. Drawings in the archive of Marian Łyczkowski, Warsaw (Poland); telephone interview with Marian Łyczkowski, July 29, 2017; SARP d. 806. The design for the Kaduna museum was realized (with alterations) in Benin City, thus undermining the intention of regional specificity of the design.
192. Dmochowski, *Introduction*, vol. 1, viii; vol. 2, 1.2.
193. Ibid., vol. 1, 3.4, 2.19, 4.16; vol. 2, 4.7.
194. Ibid., vol. 1, viii–ix.
195. Giedion, *Space, Time, and Architecture*; Norberg-Schulz, *Existence, Space and Architecture*.
196. Okeke-Agulu, *Postcolonial Modernism*.
197. See Ulli Beier, "Changing Face of a Yoruba Town," *Nigeria* 59 (1958): 373–82; Ulli Beier, "Carvers in Modern Architecture," *Nigeria* 60 (1959): 60–75.
198. Okeke-Agulu, *Postcolonial Modernism*, 184–96.
199. Dmochowski, "Sprawozdanie z badawczych prac"; Dmochowski, "Sprawozdanie z pomiaru"; Dmochowski, "Sprawozdanie ze studjów."
200. Dmochowski, "Sprawozdanie ze studjów," 314.
201. Gosk, "Polski dyskurs."
202. Quoted in Domosławski, *Kapuściński*, 24.
203. Dmochowski, *Introduction*, vol. 1, 4.8.
204. Arayela, "Introspection," 94–95; Ihekwaba, "N.I.A."
205. Adeyemi, *Making*; W. J. Kidd, "The Faculty of Architecture, Ahmadu Bello University, Zaria," *WABA* 7, no. 3 (1967): 56–59; and "Overseas Examination Centres," "Board of Architectural Education, November 24, 1964," RIBA Archives, "Board of Architectural Education Committee Minutes, 1950–1965," box 7.1.1.
206. Chang, *Genealogy*, 212–13; on the attempts to regulate the professional standards in the newly independent countries by the Commonwealth Board of Architectural Education (within the Commonwealth Association of Architects), see ibid., 232–33.
207. Thomas Howarth, "Report on the Faculty of Architecture, Ahmadu Bellu University, Zaria, Nigeria, Prepared at the Request of the C.A.A. and the Nigerian Institute of Architects" (1969), CAA, box 12/3; "Report by Dean T. Howarth on a Visit to the School from 22nd to 25th March 1969," CAA, box 12/3.
208. Adeyemi, *Making*, 76.
209. Ibid., 76; *WAP*, May 7, 1973, 5; *WAP*, September 25, 1973, 3.
210. Adeyemi, *Making*, 66–68.
211. Kidd, "Ahmadu Bello University, Zaria, Nigeria," 43.
212. Adeyemi, *Making*, 77; compare Kidd, "Ahmadu Bello University, Zaria, Nigeria."
213. Quoted in Adeyemi, *Making*, 77.
214. Adeyemi, *Making*; see "Prospectus, 1971–72," CAA, box 12/1.
215. Adeyemi, *Making*, 116–18.

216. Adeyemi, *Making*.
217. *NN*, June 30, 1973, 9.
218. *NN*, March 1, 1972, 16.
219. *DT*, January 8, 1977, 20–21; *DT*, January 29, 1977, 20–21; Łazowski et al., *Polacy w Nigerii*, vol. 1, 124–25. See also Cockburn, "Educating."
220. "Ahmadu Bello University," n.d., CAA, box 12/2.
221. Department of Architecture, Ahmadu Bello University, "Climatic Comfort Design Guide for Nigeria," 1979, archive of Nick Hollo, Sydney (Australia); e-mail exchange with Nick Hollo, April 2018.
222. Telephone conversation with Peter Magyar, July 27, 2017; see also Magyar, *Thought Palaces*.
223. Interview with Adeyemi.
224. Adeyemi, *Making*, 174–79.
225. "Nigerian Architectural Heritage in Pix," *NIA Journal* 3 (1982): 1.
226. Ihekwaba, "N.I.A.," 294; Isaac Fola Alade, "The Architectural Profession in Nigeria," CAA, box 12/5.
227. Fola Alade, "Architectural Profession"; interview with Gillian Hopwood and John Godwin, Cheltenham (UK), September 7, 2015. British expat architects alarmed the RIBA and the CAA, but a meeting at the RIBA in London concluded that "little could be done as the intention was clearly that Nigerian architects should take over private practice in the country," "Minutes of the Meeting of the Overseas Relations Committee Held on Friday, 1 October, 1971, at 10.30am," 5, RIBA, "Overseas Relations Committee Papers," 12.2.11, box 1, 1966–73; see also communication on this matter in CAA, box 12.
228. "Note on Discussions with Professor Douglas Jones," July 11, 1969, CAA, box 12/3.
229. Adeyemi, *Making*. The shortages in university staff resulted not only from a small number of trained architects in Nigeria, but also from the fact that during the oil boom most of them preferred lucrative design jobs; see Ihekwaba, "N.I.A.," 295.
230. Hubert Dąbrowski, "Wydział Architektury Uniwersytetu w Zarii, Nigeria," *Architektura* 2 (1981): 16–17; Ahmadu Bello University, "Zaria Master Plan." Other Polish architects whose work in Nigeria straddled education and design practice, and sometimes research, included Andrzej Czerniewski, Marcin Pawlikowski, Lech Radwanowski, Konrad Kaczyński, Marek Czuryło, Janusz Andrzejak, Jan Wysocki, Andrzej Florek, Jan Oleszkiewicz, and Stanisław Kawka; Łazowski et al., *Polacy w Nigerii*, vol. 1, 124–25.
231. Uji, "Beyond," 114.
232. Łazowski et al., *Polacy w Nigerii*, vol. 1, 161–62, 123.
233. Uji, "Beyond," 114.
234. Adeyemi, *Making*.
235. Grzywnowicz, Kiedrzyński, *Prawa i obowiązki*, 16–17.
236. Polónyi, *Architect-Planner*.
237. Moravánszky, "Peripheral Modernism," 335.
238. Ibid., 335.
239. Šerman, "Boris Magaš," 206; Białostocki, "Some Values," 129–36.
240. Polónyi, *Architect-Planner*. This practice was not specific for the Eastern European periphery—for example, Johan Lagae discussed the "selective borrowing" of architectural expertise in the Belgian Congo; see Bremner et al., "Intersecting Interests," 240–41; on "selective borrowing," see Ward, *Planning*.
241. Moravánszky, "Peripheral Modernism."
242. Gandhi, *Postcolonial Theory*; Bhabha, *Location of Culture*.
243. Richert, *Przestrzenne planowanie*, 80.
244. Lampe, *Yugoslavia*.
245. Ibid., 323.
246. Lampe, *Yugoslavia*.
247. Rubinstein, *Yugoslavia*.
248. In a striking case of politics trumping geography, Yugoslavia was also included in UNCTAD's "Afro-Asian group," Rubinstein, *Yugoslavia*, 173.
249. Lampe, *Yugoslavia*.
250. Rubinstein, *Yugoslavia*.
251. Ibid., 196.
252. *WA*, February 11, 1974, 155; *WAP*, January 30, 1974, 1.
253. *Energoprojekt 1951–1996*; Dolinka et al., *Bojović*; Sekulić, "Energoprojekt."
254. *Energoprojekt 1951–1996*, 6.
255. Zoran Bojović, interview with the author, Belgrade, October 9, 2015.
256. *Energoprojekt, 60 Years*, 32, 38.
257. *Energoprojekt* (later: *EP*) 7 (1963), 4.
258. Ibid; *EP* 8 (1963), 6; *EP* 12 (1964), 14.
259. *EP* 8 (1963), 4.
260. *EP* 7 (1963), 4; see also *Yugoslav Investment Works*.
261. *EP* 11 (1963), 3.
262. The names of the designers were Aleksandar Keković (Hotel "Nil" in Kampala); Dušan Milenković; Branimir Ganović (Findeco House in Lusaka); and Radomic Stopić, Mario Jobst, Dušica Maksimović (city hall in Libreville); Mitrović, *Na kraju*, 7; *35 godina*.
263. *EP* 9 (1965), 5.
264. *EP* 12 (1965), 7.
265. Ibid.; Kulić, "National, Supranational, International"; Le Normand, *Belgrade*.
266. *Energoprojekt, 60 Years*; compare Sekulić, "Energoprojekt." Land reclamation commission of the engineering and construction firm Ivan Milutinović (PIM) from Belgrade was also an entry point for urban design of a city extension in Kolkata ("Salt Lake City") by urban planner Dobrivoje Tošković; see Tošković, *Kolkata*.
267. *EP* 9 (1965), 5.
268. *EP* 5 (1966), 3; *EP* 3 (1967), 3; "Školski centar–Nigeria, Lagos-Oshodi," *Architektura Urbanizam* 58 (1969): 36–38. The design, interrupted by the civil war, was reworked after its end and the construction started in 1971; *EP* 1–2 (1970), 7–8; *EP* 4 (1971), 1.
269. Bojović, interview; Dolinka et al., *Zoran Bojović*; *35 godina*; Energoprojekt, "Danbatta."
270. *EP* 9 (1963), 1.
271. *EP* 8 (1967), 3; *EP* 11 (1967), 7; *EP* 11 (1968), 3; *EP* 2 (1969), 6.
272. "How a Yugoslav Company Built."
273. Interview with Aleksandar Slijepčević, Belgrade, October 13, 2015.
274. Artisien et al., *Yugoslav Multinationals*.
275. Ibid., 27–28.
276. Artisien, Buckley, "Joint Ventures in Yugoslavia," 117–18.
277. Artisien et al., *Yugoslav Multinationals*, 35; Artisien, Buckley, "Joint Ventures"; Kirn, "Contradictions."
278. Artisien et al., *Yugoslav Multinationals*, 9.
279. Ibid., 15, 32; see also *EP* 3 (1973), 7.
280. Collins, *Administration for Development*, 140–41; *WAP*, June 30, 1973, 3.
281. "Raport techniczno-ekonomiczny organizacji spółki mieszanej typu kontraktorskiego dla budownictwa w Nigerii," n.d., AAN z. 2350, sygn. 1/115, 4.
282. Collins, *Administration for Development*, 141.
283. "Raport."
284. *WAP*, March 1, 1972, 6; *WAP*, August 23, 1972, 4; *WAP*, July 2, 1973, 2; *WAP*, October 5, 1973, 3; *WAP*, October 13, 1973, 2; *WAP*, April 10, 1975, 2; *WAP*, June 19, 1975, 1; *WAP*, March 30, 1976, 3; *WAP*, March 7, 1977, 1; McMillan, *Multinationals*.
285. McMillan, *Multinationals*.
286. DAA f. 259, op. 44, a.e. 463.
287. Onimode, *Imperialism*, 150; Godwin, Hopwood, *Sandbank City*; Olowo-Okere, "Construction Industry," 309.
288. In Zambia, they included ZECCO, or Zambia Engineering & Contracting Company (1966) and Unico (1967), and Sogeco in Guinea (1969); *EP* 11 (1969), 1; *EP* 4 (1971), 6–7.
289. *EP* 4 (1971), 2; *EP* 2 (1973), 10.
290. *EP* 2 (1973), 10.
291. Carr, *Major Companies*, 205.
292. *WA*, February 11, 1974, 155; *WAP*, January 30, 1974, 1; interview with Bojović and Slijepčević.
293. *EP* 11 (1973), 3.
294. *WAP*, October 26, 1976, 1.
295. Ibid.; *EP* 5 (1977), 5; Godwin, "Nigeria," 40.
296. *WAP*, October 26, 1976, 1.
297. Mabogunje, *Urbanization*, 238–311.
298. Koenigsberger et al., *Metropolitan Lagos*.
299. Ibid., Mabogunje, *Urbanization*, 238–311.
300. Peil, *Lagos*.
301. Doxiadis Associates International, "Regional Plan for Lagos State. Existing Conditions. Report No. 2" (1976), CDA, vol. 1–2, DOX-NIG-A 88.
302. Peil, *Lagos*.
303. Ibid., 142–44.
304. On land reclamation in Lagos, see Godwin, Hopwood, *Sandbank City*, 206.
305. *WAP*, April 1, 1972, 2.
306. "Master Plan for Metropolitan Lagos"; see also "Dossier Lagos"; Gandy, "Planning"; Maier et al., *Lagos*; Tejuoso et al., eds., *Lagos*.
307. Energoprojekt–Yugoslavia/Federal Government of Nigeria, "Nigerian International Trade Fair Lagos," tender documentation, Lagos, June 1973, archive of Zoran Bojović, Belgrade (Serbia).
308. Ibid., interview with Bojović.
309. *WAP*, April 15, 1972, 1; *WAP*, May 12, 1972, 1; *WAP*, August 9, 1972, 4; *WAP*, July 30, 1973, 4; *WAP*, May 21, 1974, 1; interview with Otunba 'Segun Jawando, Lagos, July 28, 2017.
310. Energoprojekt, "Nigerian International Trade

Fair Lagos."
311. Ibid.; Allott & Lomax, Energoprojekt, "International Trade Fair Centre, Lagos, Nigeria. Artificial Lake. Second Report," May 1976, Bojović archive.
312. Energoprojekt, "Nigerian International Trade Fair Lagos."
313. *EP* 7 (1973), 1; *EP* 2 (1974), 6; *EP* 5 (1976), 4; interview with Bojović.
314. Interview with Slijepčević; *EP* 11 (1976), 3.
315. *EP* 6 (1974), 6.
316. Interview with Slijepčević; *EP* 10 (1976), 1, 3; *DT*, November 5, 1977, 3.
317. *EP* 2 (1973), 6; see also *EP* 9 (1974), 3.
318. Onimode et al., *Multinational Corporations*, 62.
319. *EP* 8 (1977), 4.
320. Ibid., 3.
321. *EP* 3 (1979), 5; see also *EP*, April 15, 1982, 3.
322. *EP* 12 (1976), 7; interview with Bojović.
323. Allott & Lomax et al., "Artificial Lake."
324. Interview with Bojović.
325. *DT*, January 23, 1978, 3; "Raport."
326. Onimode, *Imperialism*, 150.
327. Apter, *Pan-African Nation*, 201-3, 214.
328. "Federal Military Government's Views."
329. *DT*, November 26, 1977, 7; *DT* (*Sunday Times*), November 27, 1977 (multiple articles); *DT*, November 28, 1977, 1, 24; *DT*, November 30, 1977, 11; *DT*, December 10, 1977, 18; *DT*, December 11, 1977, 2; *DT*, December 12, 1977, 1, 19.
330. "Lessons from the Fair."
331. Mark, Slobodian, "Eastern Europe."
332. See also Chukhovich, "Orientalist Modes"; Anti-Taylor, "Moscow Diary"; Block, "Capitalism versus Socialism."

Chapter 4

1. In 1990, the Japanese Consortium of Consulting Firms (JCCF) delivered a new master plan of Baghdad, but it was not approved. A planning process initiated in 1998 in Baghdad was stopped by the 2003 US-led invasion. Khatib & Alami were commissioned by the World Bank in the mid-2000s to develop the master plan, but the bank withdrew from the project and the firm was directly commissioned by the Amanat. E-mail from Ghada al-Slik, February 6, 2015; see also JCCF, "The Integrated Capital Development Plan of Baghdad," n.d., archive of Ghada al-Slik, Baghdad (Iraq).
2. For an overview, see "East Europe Increases Share of Arab Market," *Middle East Construction* (later: *MEC*) 12 (1980): 14–15; "East Europe and the Arab World," *MEC* 10 (1981): 53–55; "Hungary: Design and Build," *MEC* 4 (1983): 50–59; "Yugoslav Companies Increasingly Active in the Middle East," *MEC* 9 (1983): 9; "The Hungarian Connection," *MEC* 4 (1985): 19–31.
3. Trentin, "Tough Negotiations"; Marr, *Modern History*.
4. Marr, *Modern History*, 140.
5. Smolansky, *USSR*.
6. Trentin, "Tough Negotiations," 360; *Baghdad Observer* (later: *BO*), February 23, 1972, 7; *National Action Charter*.
7. Smolansky, *USSR*, 16–32.
8. Ferguson, ed., *Shock of the Global*.
9. Yagodovsky, *World Socialist System*, 16.
10. Zevin, *Economic Cooperation*, 25.
11. Ibid., 26.
12. Zevin, *Economic Cooperation*.
13. Yagodovsky, *World Socialist System*, 49–50; Zevin, *Economic Cooperation*, 4.
14. Yagodovsky, *World Socialist System*, 8, 37, 39–43.
15. Sanchez-Sibony, *Red Globalization*.
16. Kotkin, "Kiss of Debt."
17. Quoted in Lorenzini, "Comecon," 189.
18. Smolansky, *USSR*, 22; Schiavone, *Institutions*, 95.
19. Steiner, Petrak-Jones, "Council"; Kaliński, "Rubel transferowy."
20. Stone, *Satellites and Commissars*, 115.
21. Awgustinowitsch, "RGW-Hochhaus."
22. Steinhauf, "Bagdad," 11.
23. *Rynki zagraniczne* (later: *RZ*) 86–87 (1969): 11; *RZ* 9 (1978): 8.
24. "Bagdad–miasto."
25. Levine, *Urbanism*, 334–36; al-Siliq, "Baghdad."
26. Levine, *Urbanism*, 336.
27. Ibid.; Pieri, *Bagdad*; Jackson, "Architecture of the British Mandate."
28. Ahmed, "Morphology"; Hakim, "Co-op Housing."
29. Pieri, *Bagdad*; Marr, *Modern History*, 41.
30. Levine, *Urbanism*, 334–84.
31. Pieri, *Bagdad*, 294.
32. Marr, *Modern History*, 81.
33. Ferhang Jalal, *Role of Government*.
34. *Iraq Times* (later: *IT*), March 20, 1962, 1; see also *IT*, March 27, 1962, 1, 13.
35. "Army Housing Schemes," *New Iraq* 3 (January 1960): 10–11; Government of Iraq, "The Housing Program for Iraq" (Baghdad, March 1957); Government of Iraq, "Experimental Housing Projects" (Baghdad, March 1957); Doxiadis, "Monthly Report no 46"; *IT*, November 28, 1962, 3; Faraidoon Said, "Uprzemysłowione budownictwo jednorodzinne w Bagdadzie (na tle rozwoju miasta)," Ph.D. dissertation, Kraków University of Technology, 1982, 35–37.
36. Huwysh, *al-'amārat al-hadithat fi al-'iraq*, 31; *IT*, March 14, 1962, 2; *IT*, April 2, 1962, 5.
37. *IT*, June 27, 1961, 1–2; *IT*, November 19, 1961, 3; *IT*, February 18, 1962, 3; Jędraszko, "Problemy," 16.
38. *IT*, January 4, 1960, 3; *IT*, February 23, 1962, 1, 13; *IT*, February 26, 1962, 3; Fox, "Baghdad"; Marthelot, "Bagdad."
39. *IT*, March 2, 1961, 1; *IT*, February 22, 1962, 8–9; Levine, *Urbanism*, 334–84; Pieri, *Bagdad*.
40. *IT*, May 14, 1962, 2; *Baghdad News* (later: *BN*), August 30, 1967, 2; "Technoexportstroy" (catalogue, n.d.), 16. At a later stage of the project, Alexander Gibb hired Basil Spence as an architectural consultant; see BSC Acc. No. 2003/101: MS2329/1Q/1/2/1, MS2329/1Q/1/3/1–59, and MS2329/1Q/1/1/1–134.
41. *IT*, January 13, 1961, 3; *IT*, February 9, 1961, 13; Isenstadt, "Faith."
42. *IT*, January 13, 1961, 3; "Internationaler Wettbewerb für das Direktionsgebäude des Werbe- und Informationszentrums in Bagdad," *Deutsche Architektur* 10 (1961): 562–63; "Mezhdunaroden konkurs za sgrada na direktsiiata na osvetlenieto v gr. Bagdad–Irak," *Arkhitektura* 10 (1960) 38–40.
43. *IT*, February 5, 1960, 3; *IT*, February 25, 1962, 3; *IT*, April 29, 1962, 6; *IT*, June 19, 1962, 10.
44. *IT*, January 26, 1960, 5; *IT*, February 7, 1960, 3; *IT*, March 2, 1960, 5; *IT*, April 21, 1960, 6–7; *IT*, March 14, 1962, 2; *IT*, January 4, 1963, 2.
45. Several sources mention a 1930s plan by German planner Joseph Brix (sometimes spelled "Brecks" in Iraq); see Shafi, "Aspects," 4; Huwysh, *al-'amārat al-hadithat fi al-'iraq*, 72. Said also describes a plan of Iraqi planners from 1952; Said, "Uprzemysłowione," 33.
46. Minoprio, Spencely, and P. W. Macfarlane, "The Master Plan for the City of Baghdad. Report" (London, 1956), CCF, Iraq 1955–59, microfilm 95–4564, reel 11, 1.
47. Minoprio et al., "Master Plan"; Levine, *Urbanism*, 340–50.
48. Al-Madfai, "Baghdad," 47; Doxiadis, "Master Plan." Compare Pyla, "Baghdad's Urban Restructuring."
49. Huwysh, *al-'amārat al-hadithat fi al-'iraq*, 19; *IT*, October 11, 1962, 3.
50. "Kānūn raqam 156 li sanat 1971: al-taṣmīm al-'asas li madīnat Baghdād," 1045. http://www.iraq-lg-law.org/en/node/160.
51. Jędraszko, "Problemy"; Olszewski, "Bagdad," parts I and II; Town Planning Office for the Master Plan of Baghdad (later: TPO), "Master Plan of Baghdad," vol. 1, IV-3, archive of Kazimierz Bajer, Kraków (Poland).
52. Olszewski, "Bagdad," p. I, 8; Said, "Uprzemysłowione," 35–37; Sethom, "Quartiers."
53. Levine, *Urbanism*, 350–52.
54. Smolansky, *USSR*; *IT*, February 27, 1961, 3; *IT*, March 2, 1961, 1; *IT*, July 23, 1961, 3; *IT*, January 25, 1962, 2.
55. Ginsburgs, Slusser, eds., *Calendar*; Smolansky, *USSR*; *IT*, January 10, 1962, 2; *IT*, January 18, 1962, 3; *IT*, March 28, 1962, 3.
56. *BO*, September 9, 1969, 3.
57. "Republic of Iraq Enters Year Four," supplement to *IT*, December 31, 1961, 13.
58. *Middle East Record* 2, 1961, 298; *BN*, December 8, 1966, 9.
59. *IT*, June 23, 1960, 3; *IT*, January 5, 1962, 3.
60. RGAE f. 339, op. 3, d. 1819, 109–18.
61. Marr, *Modern History*, 107; *IT*, August 26, 1962, 1; Katsakioris, "Soviet Lessons," 88.
62. Card index of the students' files, MARKhI. The distribution of students from developing countries in socialist countries is conveyed by the statistics of recipients of Comecon's Scholarship Fund for students from developing countries (1974–78): among 1,850 scholarships, the USSR granted 1,259 scholarships, followed by Czechoslovakia (174), East Germany (138), Bulgaria (96), Cuba and Poland (69 each), Vietnam (37), and Mongolia (8). Brzost, Sułkowska-Kusztelak, "Kształcenie," 117; see also Katsakioris, "Socialist Intelligentsia."
63. Compare "Educational Activity."
64. *IT*, April 14, 1960, 3, 9; *IT*, November 7, 1962, 7.
65. *IT*, January 28, 1960, 1; *IT*, February 16, 1960, 7; *IT*, April 6, 1960, 5; *IT*, February 6, 1961, 12; *IT*, July 23, 1961, 7; *IT*, September 8, 1961, 7; *IT*, September 21, 1961, 2; *IT*, November 14, 1962, 12; CCF, Iraq 1960–January 1963, microfilm

2003–8, reel 9.
66. *Fundamenty* 50 (1962): 2; *Fundamenty* 12 (1970): 16; *Fundamenty* 3 (1971): 2; *Fundamenty* 38 (1971): 2; *Fundamenty* 34 (1972): 2; *RZ* 86–87 (1969): 11; *RZ* 135 (1969): 8; *RZ* 105 (1975): 8; *RZ* 119 (1978): 8; Jankowski, "Warszawski architekt," 10–11; Ministry of Municipalities, Directorate General for Planning and Design, "Letter of Reference for Jerzy Baumiller," December 18, 1961, archive of Jerzy Baumiller, Greenpoint, NY (US); Huwysh, *al-'amārat al-hadithat fi al-'iraq*, 45, 148, 154.
67. Jerzy Sobiepan, "Budownictwo mieszkaniowe w Iraku," *Architektura* 11–12 (1961): 477–78.
68. RGAE f. 339, op. 3, d. 1819, 109–18; Gräfe, "Urbanisierung"; Bernhard Gräfe, "Planen und Bauen in der Republik Irak," *Architektur der DDR* 4 (1976): 234–40.
69. Sobiepan, "Budownictwo"; Ministry of Municipalities, Directorate General for Planning and Design, "Letter of Reference for Stanisław Jankowski," August 27, 1962, archive of the Jankowski family, Warsaw (Poland); Stanisław Kawka, "The Future of Mosul" (1967), listed in Shafi, "Aspects," 10. For Doxiadis's planning of Iraqi cities, see Huwysh, *al-'amārat al-hadithat fi al-'iraq*. See also d. 226, 268, 357, 373, 556, 562, 584, 668, 700, 815, 971, 1146 and the dossier of Rafał Chyliński (without number), SARP.
70. *Fundamenty* 50 (1962): 2.
71. Jankowski was the head of the design team responsible for the East-West Thoroughfare in Warsaw, a key element of the capital's reconstruction; and Hryniewiecki, a team leader at the Warsaw Office, was professor at Warsaw University of Technology, and co-designer of the city's new municipal stadium (1955) and the award-winning supermarket in Warsaw (1969).
72. *IT*, November 2, 1961, 3. According to one report, Polish planners in Baghdad were instrumental in formulating the conditions of the tender; *Fundamenty* 51–52 (1968): 21.
73. *IT*, October 11, 1962, 3; *IT*, January 28, 1963, 3.
74. Rudner, "East European Aid."
75. Oprea, "Development," 68.
76. Zevin, *Economic Cooperation*, 54.
77. *Middle East Record* 2, 1961, 297.
78. Ginsburgs, Slusser, *Calendar*; Sanchez-Sibony, *Red Globalization*, 243.
79. Oprea, "Development," 71; compare "Prezențe arhitecturale românești peste hotare," *Arhitectura* 6 (1979): 9.
80. Grzywnowicz, Kiedrzyński, *Prawa i obowiązki*, 16–17.
81. Grzywnowicz, Kiedrzyński, *Prawa i obowiązki*.
82. Kazimierz Bajer, "Sprawozdanie z przygotowań do umowy na opracowanie planu ogólnego Bagdadu oraz z rozmów organizacyjnych z Polservice i Grupą Warszawską," 1964–65, Bajer archive.
83. Grzywnowicz, Kiedrzyński, *Prawa i obowiązki*, 28.
84. Vaňous, "Commercial Exchange."
85. "Urbaniści."
86. Bajer, "Sprawozdanie."
87. The Amanat was advised in the negotiations by French planner Maurice Rotival. Bajer, "Sprawozdanie," 9; Huwysh, *al-'amārat al-hadithat fi al-'iraq*, 81; see also Shafi, "Aspects," 12. On the "toughness" of Arab negotiators with Eastern European countries, see also Trentin, "Tough Negotiations."
88. "Umowa," June 12, 1963, AAN z. 1154, sygn. 25/526.
89. *RZ* 56 (1974): 8.
90. D. 295, SARP; *Fundamenty* 51–52 (1968): 21.
91. *IT*, October 19, 1962, 3.
92. Ciborowski, *Town Planning*.
93. Chmielewski, Syrkus, *Warszawa Funkcjonalna*; Kohlrausch, "Poland."
94. Ciborowski, *Town Planning*; *IT*, February 9, 1962, 1, 13; *IT*, February 27, 1962, 1, 3, 13; "What You Do Not Know about Al-Rashad Town," *New Iraq*, July 1960, n.p.
95. *IT*, December 1, 1962, 3.
96. Ciborowski, *Town Planning*, 39; Ostrowski, *Zespoły*.
97. Kazimierz Bajer, "Szkic historyczny eksportu w BPBO 'Miastoprojekt Kraków' 1955–1984," n.p.; Kraków, 1990, Bajer archive. Stanisław Dylewski of the Warsaw Urban Planning Office was appointed as the first head of the TPO.
98. Interview with Kazimierz Bajer, Kraków, June 2010.
99. Bajer, "Szkic."
100. TPO, "Comprehensive Development Plan for Baghdad 2000" (Baghdad: August 1973), 272, Bajer archive; "Kânūn raqam 156 li sanat 1971."
101. Shafi, "Urban Planning," 48–49.
102. Ibid., 42–48.
103. The second contract was signed with the Polish FTO Budimex, which, in the 1970s and 1980s, continued to work in Iraq on multiple commissions. *BO*, April 18, 1972, 7–8; *BO*, April 19, 1972, 7; Juraszyński, "Budimex."
104. *BO*, December 18, 1973, 4.
105. *Al-'irāq*, July 28, 1977; *BO*, June 15, 1977, 2–3.
106. Miastoprojekt, "Report on the Master Plan of Baghdad," n.d., 17, Bajer archive; TPO, "Master Plan of Baghdad," vol. 1, C-2.
107. Miastoprojekt, "Report," 17; *BN*, April 30, 1967, 6; *BO*, April 21, 1968, 3.
108. "Urbaniści," TPO, "Comprehensive Development Plan," 2–3; "Lista uczestników studium cudzoziemskiego z Iraku i Kuwejtu," n.d., Piotr Zaremba Legacy, Loose Files, No. 800, National Archives, Szczecin.
109. TPO, "Master Plan of Baghdad," vol. 1, 0-2-3; Miastoprojekt, "Report," 16; *BN*, April 30, 1967, 6; *BO*, April 21, 1968, 3.
110. Interview with Lech Robaczyński, Warsaw, June 4, 2013.
111. Miastoprojekt, "Report," 22.
112. *Fundamenty* 51–52 (1968): 21; *Fundamenty* 2 (1968): 13; TPO, "Comprehensive Development Plan," 2–3. Miastoprojekt's field office in Baghdad was called the Town Planning Office for the Master Plan of Baghdad (and variations thereof).
113. Ciborowski, *Town Planning*.
114. TPO, "Master Plan of Baghdad," vol. 1, 0-2-21; Miastoprojekt, "Report," 24–104.
115. "Master-Plan Bagdadu," 1967, Bajer archive.
116. Khalis H. al-Ashab, "The Urban Geography of Baghdad," Ph.D. dissertation, University of Newcastle upon Tyne, 1974; Ihsan Fethi, "Urban Conservation in Iraq: The Case for Protecting the Cultural Heritage of Iraq with Special Reference to Baghdad Including a Comprehensive Inventory of Its Areas and Buildings of Historic or Architectural Interest," Ph.D. dissertation, University of Sheffield, 1977; S. F. al-Rahmani, "Principles for Urban Renewal in Iraq: A Study to Develop Town Planning Principles for the Renewal of the Iraqi Cities with Particular Reference to Baghdad Central Area," Ph.D. dissertation, University of Manchester, 1986.
117. TPO, "Comprehensive Development Plan."
118. TPO, "Kadhemiyah Old Quarters Detailed Plan—Report" (1974); interview with Andrzej Basista, Kraków, June 2010. See also Basista, "Kadhemiya"; Basista, "Plany."
119. Piotr Zaremba, "Sprawozdanie z pobytu naukowego w Iraku, 10.X–13.XI.1972," December 15, 1972; Piotr Zaremba, "Directions for Further Work of the Regional Planning Department of the Ministry of Planning of Iraq," November 10, 1973, Piotr Zaremba Legacy, Loose Files, No. 958, National Archives, Szczecin; Piotr Zaremba, letter to Stanisław Werewka (Polservice), January 25, 1974, 1, archive of the Zaremba family, Szczecin (Poland).
120. TPO, "Comprehensive Development Plan."
121. Ibid.; TPO, "Master Plan of Baghdad," vol. 1.
122. Miastoprojekt, "Report," 47–56.
123. Ibid., 62–63.
124. TPO, "Comprehensive Development Plan," 71–72, 108–9, 121.
125. TPO, "Comprehensive Development Plan," 122–24. Several professionals in Baghdad took issue with these densities as too low; see Department of Architecture, College of Engineering, University of Baghdad, "Urban Development of Baghdad 2015," Baghdad, 1998, Ghada al-Slik archive.
126. Katedra Architektury Mieszkaniowej, "Mieszkaniowa Jednostka Modelowa dla Bagdadu," Kraków: WA, PK, n.d.; Miastoprojekt, "Model Housing Unit," n.d., both in Bajer archive; see also Huwysh, *al-'amārat al-hadithat fi al-'iraq*, 135.
127. TPO, "Comprehensive Development Plan, 208."
128. TPO, "Master Plan of Baghdad," vol. 1.; TPO, "Comprehensive Development Plan."
129. Miastoprojekt, "Report," 207–8; TPO, "Comprehensive Development Plan," 250–59.
130. TPO, "Comprehensive Development Plan," 252–53.
131. Minoprio et al., "Master Plan," 3, 13.
132. Miastoprojekt, "Report," 345; Ciborowski, *Town Planning*, 38.
133. TPO, "Comprehensive Development Plan," 269.
134. Ibid., 262; Polservice Consulting Engineers, Miastoprojekt Design Office, "Rusafah-Karradah City Centre: Outlines for Detailed Plans: Short Report," 1967.
135. TPO, "Kadhemiyah."
136. Miastoprojekt, "Report," 352.
137. TPO, "Comprehensive Development Plan," 272–84.
138. Ibid., 164–66, 304–14.
139. Piotr Zaremba, "Proposal for Training in Coastal Urban and Regional Planning," November 15, 1983, 2, Piotr Zaremba Legacy, Loose Files, No. 1019, National Archives, Szczecin.

140. Ḥuwysh, *al-'amārat al-hadithat fi al-'iraq*; *BO*, August 4, 1970, 7. See also *BO*, April 18, 1972, 7–8; *BO*, April 19, 1972, 7; *BO*, May 9, 1973, 8; *BO*, June 1, 1973, 7, 15; *BO*, April 1, 1975, 2, 15; *BO*, July 10, 1975, 2, 7; *BO*, March 31, 1977, 2; *al-Jumhūrīyah*, December 7, 1971, 12.
141. Shafi, "Urban Planning," 55.
142. Ibid., 49; see also Ḥuwysh, *al-'amārat al-hadithat fi al-'iraq*.
143. The survey was part of the planning of Baghdad by the Japanese Consortium of Consulting Firms (JCCF) that resulted in the Integrated Capital Development Plan for Baghdad. See JCCF, "Capital Development Plan"; see also Shafi, *Urban Planning*, 60; Marthelot, "Bagdad" (1975), 446.
144. "General Housing Programme for Iraq" (later: GHPI), 1976–80, 21 vols., Bajer archive.
145. The documentation of the GHPI included four main reports ("Diagnosis of Existing Situation," "Prognoses and Strategies," "Model Designs," "Final Report"); two appendixes ("Legal Aspects," "Terminology and Criteria"); eight complementary reports; and seven reports on the surveys. Bajer, "Program," 21. See also Kazimierz Bajer, "Szkic"; Miastoprojekt, "Ludność i sytuacja mieszkaniowa w miastach Republiki Irackiej w świetle badań ankietowych," n.d.; Zbigniew Pucek, Kazimierz Sowa, "Rozwój społeczny," n.d.; Bajer et al., *Metody*, all in Bajer archive. For the nine seminars on housing organized in Baghdad in the framework of the GHPI (1975–80), see Said, "Uprzemysłowione," 41–42. See also d. 55, 124, 168, 305, 375, 634, 636, 637, 638, 689, 1023, 1091, 955, 498, SARP; Ali al-Haidary, "Perspektiven des Wohnungsbaus im Irak," *Architektur der DDR* 3 (1983): 172–76; and Ali al-Haidary, "Entwicklungstendenzen der Wohnungsversorgung im Irak. Das Wohnungsbauprogramm 1981 bis 2000," *Architektur der DDR* 9 (1983): 569–73.
146. "GHPI—Final Report," 21. Polservice—Warsaw, Miastoprojekt—Kraków, Poland; State Organization for Housing, "Housing Technical Standards and Codes of Practice. Report Two" (1982); see also Miastoprojekt—Kraków, Budimex, Poland, "Al-Yousufiya Housing Project," all in Bajer archive; Gleń, "Models"; Sowa, "Polskie badania;" and "Housing the Arab Population," *MEC* 1 (1983): 28–29.
147. Grzywnowicz, Kiedrzyński, *Prawa i obowiązki*; "Umowa"; "Instrukcja," AAN z. 1154, sygn. 25/526.
148. *BO*, March 25, 1977, 3; *BO*, May 16, 1979, 2.
149. *BN*, November 16, 1966, 5; *BO*, March 25, 1977, 3; *BO*, July 31, 1982, 2; *al-Ta'akhī*, April 16, 1974, 6.
150. Following the advice of the planners, priority was given to interventions that did not require costly expropriations. *BN*, November 8, 1965, 6; *BO*, April 21, 1972, 5; *BO*, September 3, 1973, 8.
151. *BO*, February 11, 1972, 7; *BO*, September 23, 1974, 11; *BO*, May 21, 1979, 6; *BO*, May 30, 1979, 2.
152. *Al-Jumhūrīyah*, January 24, 1969, 4; *al-Jumhūrīyah*, February 1971, 3; *al-Jumhūrīyah*, June 23, 1972, 8; *al-Jumhūrīyah*, July 13, 1973, 3; *al-Ta'akhī*, June 3, 1974, 6; *BO*, February 23, 1971, 7; *BO*, July 21, 1972, 7; *BO*, September 23, 1974, 2; Jim Antoniou, "New Suburb for Baghdad," *MEC* 8 (1983): 40.
153. Miastoprojekt, "Al Kadisiya Housing Project: Hostels. Short report," n.d.; "Al Kadisiya Housing Project in Mahmudiya: Hostels. Drawings," 1978, Bajer archive. Besides Mahmudiyah, residential districts were designed in Mosul, Amarah, Erbil, Samawah, and the rural settlement al-Zuhairi, "Zestawienie wykonanych opracowań dla program budownictwa mieszkaniowego dla Iraku na 20 lat," n.d., Bajer archive.
154. Co-designer: Z. Gołąb, technical design: A. Reczek; see d. 375, SARP.
155. *Al-Jumhūrīyah*, July 13, 1973, 3; *al-Jumhūrīyah*, December 20, 1973, 3; *al-Ta'akhī*, April 20, 1974, 6; *BO*, April 28, 1976, 2.
156. *BO*, November 26, 1972, 7.
157. *Al-Ta'akhī*, February 5, 1974, 2.
158. *BO*, May 17, 1978, 2; *BO*, June 26, 1978, 2; *BO*, October 15, 1979, 2; *BO*, August 9, 1980, 2; *BO*, December 21, 1981, 2; *BO*, December 22, 1981, 4; *BO*, December 14, 1982, 4; *BO*, March 1, 1983, 4; *BO*, March 24, 1983, 4; *BO*, June 21, 1983, 4; *al-'irāq*, October 20, 1979, 11; *al-'irāq*, September 19, 1979, 7; *al-'irāq*, June 3, 1980, 7. For overview, see Ḥuwysh, *al-'amārat al-hadithat fi al-'iraq*.
159. *Al-Jumhūrīyah*, September 9, 1972, 5; *al-Jumhūrīyah*, December 20, 1973, 3; *al-Ta'akhī*, April 20, 1974, 6; Ḥuwysh, *al-'amārat al-hadithat fi al-'iraq*, 198.
160. Among them was East Germany's Bernhard Gräfe, who worked for the Ministry of Municipalities (1972-73). Gräfe, "Planen"; see also Fox, "Baghdad."
161. *Al-Ta'akhī*, April 15, 1972, 3.
162. D. 689, SARP.
163. *BO*, May 10, 1971, 6, 8; *BO*, September 26, 1974, 2, 7; *BO*, December 19, 1974, 2.
164. Iraqis also tried to adapt a US system (International Housing Ltd.) with limited success; *BO*, August 2, 1975, 4; *BO*, August 23, 1975, 6; *BO*, February 12, 1980, 2; *al-'irāq*, March 18, 1979, 5; *al-'irāq*, October 20, 1979, 11; *al-'irāq*, n.a., July 6, 1980, 7; Said, "Uprzemysłowione," 100–103; Miastoprojekt, "Prefabrication of Small Dimensions Elements for Low Rise (Two Stories High) Buildings to be Implemented within the Territory of Iraq," n.d., Bajer archive; "France," *MEC* 4 (1982): 59.
165. D. 1091, SARP. Before being hired by the SOH, Gleń worked on the GHPI in the Chair of Residential Architecture at Kraków University of Technology; telephone interview with Włodzimierz Gleń, October 2018.
166. Chauhan, "Amanat."
167. *BN*, March 24, 1965, 6; *BN*, March 28, 1965, 5–6; *BN*, October 18, 1965, 6; *BN*, November 8, 1965, 6; *BN*, April 20, 1966, 5; *BN*, July 11, 1966, 6; see the series "Foreign Travellers to Ancient Baghdad," published in *Baghdad News* from November 1966 to April 1967; *BO*, April 10, 1968, 6; *BO*, July 3, 1968, 6; *BO*, September 25, 1968, 6; *BO*, February 4, 1972, 7; *BO*, December 21, 1977, 8.
168. *BO*, April 11, 1981, 2, 8; *BO*, January 16, 1982, 2; *BO*, June 18, 1983, 4.
169. "Report no. 3. Model Design" (November 1978), "GHPI." See also Bianca, *Urban Form*, 248–70.
170. "Report no. 3." Some of this research continued in Poland; see Kozłowski, *Dawny dom iracki*; Zenon Grajek, "Planowanie dla turystyki w północnym Iraku," Ph.D. dissertation, Kraków University of Technology, 1980; Nowakowska, "Metoda." See also Krunić, "Architectural Traditions"; Jan Čejka, "Tonnengewölbe und Bögen islamischer Architektur: Wölbungstechnik und Form," Ph.D. dissertation, Munich University of Technology, 1978.
171. TPO, "Kadhemiyah," 19; Akeel Nuri Huwaish, "Modern Architectural Approaches in Iraq," *Albenaa* 7, no. 37 (1987): 8–11; *al-Jumhūrīyah*, December 4, 1971, 9; *BO*, October 15, 1976, 6. See also "Kahtan Awni: Consultant–Architect," n.d., archive of Lech Robaczyński, Warsaw (Poland); *BO*, May 28, 1970, 6; Makiya, *Post-Islamic Classicism*; Chadirji, *Concepts and Influences*; "Hisham Munir & Assoc. Architects, Engineers and Planners," n.d.
172. Letter of reference by Fadhil al-Bayaty for Aleksander Markiewicz, February 28, 1962. Markiewicz's CV lists 33 designs at the Ministry and 11 in Awni's office; see Aleksander Markiewicz, "Curriculum vitae," archive of Aleksander Markiewicz, New Canaan, CT (US). See also leaflet of the exhibition of Jerzy Staniszkis's work, November 23–December 5, 2004, SARP.
173. *Al-Jumhūrīyah*, March 12, 1970, 3.
174. *BO*, April 15, 1976, 8; *al-Jumhūrīyah*, December 4, 1971, 9; Stanek, "Awni."
175. Ministry of Works and Housing, Directorate General of Buildings, letters of reference for Lech Robaczyński, May 5, 1964, and September 7, 1969. After a conflict with a Polservice representative, Robaczyński defected to Western Europe, from where he returned to Iraq in 1964; interview with Robaczyński, Warsaw, June 2013.
176. Kahtan Awni, "Letter of Reference for Lech Robaczyński," n.d., Robaczyński archive.
177. The contract was signed with the Polish FTO Cekop, Ministry of Municipalities, "Letter of Reference for Baumiller."
178. *Al-Jumhūrīyah*, March 12, 1970, 3.
179. Stanek, al-Slik, "Department of Architecture."
180. Uthman, "Exporting." Among the Americans was Robert Mather from the University of Texas, who taught in Baghdad between 1963 and 1964. Along with Baumiller, Polish architects at the department included artist and educator Zofia Artymowska (in Baghdad between 1963–68), Andrzej Basista (1968–72), and Lech Kłosiewicz (1972–75); the two latter had arrived in Baghdad to work on the master plan and GHPI. Grabski, Macyszyn, *Słońce*; Basista, "Irak." Other teachers at the Department of Architecture from Poland included, in various periods, Hanna Basistowa, Krzysztof Leśniodorski, Andrzej Wojda, Henryk Drzeniecki, Bogusława Drzeniecka, and Mirosław Hrynkiewicz; see Kłosiewicz, "Ucząc"; d. 875, SARP. Artymowska's

husband, artist Roman Artymowski, was teaching at various art institutions in Baghdad (1959–79), including Tahrir College, where Artymowska was also teaching (1960–61); see Dziekan, "Polsko-irackie związki," 15–17. Polish architects from the University of Wrocław contributed to the teaching at the School of Architecture of the University of Mosul, founded in 1977; among them were Zbigniew Bać, Janusz Frydecki, Maciej Hawrylak, and Romuald Pustelnik.

181. Bašta returned to Baghdad to work as a designer at the State Organization of Roads and Bridges (1979–80). Uthman, "Exporting"; Vaclav Bašta, CV; Miroslava Bašťova, CV; Vaclav Bašta, "Iraq in Architectural Sketches," leaflet (Baghdad: Czechoslovak Cultural Centre, 1969), archive of Miroslava Bašťova, Prague (Czech Republic).
182. "Czechoslovak Architects."
183. Vaclav Bašta, "College Day: Architectural Department: 24 March 1966," Bašťova archive.
184. See also Makiya, "Use of Experts."
185. Kłosiewicz, "Ucząc," 52–53.
186. *BO*, November 26, 1972, 7.
187. "Ministry of Foreign Affairs, Baghdad, Iraq," drawings, Bašťova archive; e-mail correspondence with Jan Čejka, October 2016.
188. Archive of Jan Čejka, Münster (Germany); correspondence with Čejka.
189. *BO*, May 30, 1979, 2.
190. *BO*, February 21, 1982, 2; *BO*, May 1, 1982, 2.
191. "Into the 1980s," *MEC* 1 (1980): 38–39; *BO*, August 28, 1980, 2; *BO*, September 10, 1980, 2; *BO*, February 21, 1982, 2; *BO*, June 3, 1982, 2; *BO*, August 4, 1982, 2; *BO*, August 9, 1983, 4; *BO*, August 18, 1983, 2.
192. Al-'irāq, June 2, 1979, 9; al-'irāq, July 7, 1979, 11; *BO*, August 30, 1980, 2; Kulić, "Building"; Pieri, "Editing Out."
193. "Architect of Baghdad," *MEC* 1 (1984): 12–13.
194. Yamada, "Baghdad"; Silivia, Reale, eds., *Marcello D'Olivo*; Makiya, *Monument*.
195. Among others, they included Energoprojekt's Zoran Bojović, who, in collaboration with an international team, submitted award-winning entries to the competitions for the Saddam Hussein palace (1988) and the State Mosque (1989), both in Baghdad (with Tariq al-Jaidah, Alex Cvijanović, and Spasoje Krunić). In 1992, together with Milica Velanac and Zorana Stojnić-Šerbanović, Bojović submitted a design of a residential-conference center (memorial complex dedicated to the victims of the Iraq-Iran War); Dolinka et al., *Bojović*, 147–48; Zoran Bojović, interview with the author, Belgrade, October 9, 2015.
196. Yamada, "Baghdad," 15; see also *BO*, July 12, 1979, 2; *BO*, September 6, 1979, 8; *BO*, November 30, 1979, 2; "Metro for Baghdad Heralds a Revolution in City's Infrastructure," *MEC* 9 (1982): 12–13.
197. "Abu Nuwaz Conservation/Development Project" by Arthur Erickson Associates; CAC, Arthur Erickson Middle East Projects Archive. For a critique of specific aspects of the conservation concepts in Miastoprojekt's master plans, see Fethi, "Urban Conservation"; see also Basista, "Opowieści budynków," 362–65,

367–68.
198. "Haifa Street"; "Conservation"; *BO*, June 18, 1983, 4; The Architects Collaborative, "Khulafa Street Baghdad, Background Information," GSD, UDP 101A, Studio Project, Spring Semester 1983.
199. In a 1983 internal memorandum, Bajer concurred with the critique of some of Miastoprojekt's GHPI designs; Kazimierz Bajer, "Memoriał" (1983), Bajer archive. For Miastoprojekt's designs for Iraq in the 1980s, see Bajer, "Szkic," and d. 788, 691, 668, 375, 692, 789, 790, and the dossier by Anna Agata Kantarek (without number), SARP. For the work of Polish cartographers in Baghdad (1981–86), see Bienek, Kulka, "Mapa Bagdadu."
200. Amanat al-Assima, "Al Khulafa Development Projects Baghdad," n.d.; Energoprojekt "Building Systems"; both in archive of Zoran Bojović, Belgrade (Serbia); *BO*, December 20, 1983, 4.
201. "The Execution"; interview with Aleksandar Slijepčević, October 2015, Belgrade.
202. Perišić, *Građevinarstvo*, 42; "Ministry of Oil, Baghdad," drawing, n.d., archive of Jovan Ivanovski, Skopje (Macedonia); interview with Andreja Ivanovski, Skopje, December 2017; "East Europe and the Arab World," 53–54. Other designs by Energoprojekt for Baghdad included the Central Post Office (1974) and business offices (1985), *35 godina*, 24–25.
203. *RZ* 12 (1978): 8.
204. For Poland, see Liberska, *Polska–Irak*, Obeidat, *Stosunki*; Furtak, "Eksport"; Słoniewski, "Organizacja"; for Bulgaria, see "Technoexportstroy," catalogue, n.d.; for East Germany, see Hartung "Mahnkopf"; for overview, see "East Europe and the Arab World"; "East Europe Increases Share of Arab Market."
205. For overviews, see Butter, "Showcase"; Vais, "Exporting."
206. Wentker, "Für Frieden."
207. "Aufbau des ANC Entwicklungszentrums Dakawa in Tansania," *Architektur der DDR* 9 (1989): 51–54; for the Zanzibar project, see Wimmelbücker, "Architecture."
208. Lawson, "National Independence," 362.
209. Vais, "Exporting."
210. ANR f. C. C. al P.C.R., s. Relații Externe, p. 14/1972, n. 672, 7–8.
211. Lawson, "National Independence."
212. Trentin, "Tough Negotiations," 358–59.
213. Jacobsen, "Strategy."
214. Liberska, *Polska–Irak*, 134–40.
215. VEP Ipro Dessau, "Studie über den Baumarkt des Irak," 1982, BA DH 2/23018; see also DDR Projekt-Bau Berlin, "Kongress-Palast Bagdad" (1978), versions A and B, IRS, personal papers of Josef Kaiser.
216. Möller, *DDR*; VEP Ipro Dessau, "Studie."
217. Nicolae Spătaru, "Realizări ale antreprizei române de construcții montaj," *Arhitectura* 5 (1980): 18–21; ANR f. C. C. al P.C.R., s. Relații Externe, p. 44/1976, p. 108/1977, p. 3/1981; ANR f. C. C. al P.C.R., s. Economică 1979–89, p. 187/1978, p. 192/1981, p. 225/1981.
218. "Information über die Kontrolle…," October 18, 1976, BA DN/10/895.

219. Ibid.; "NSW-Export Schlachthof-Bagdad," March 1, 1976, BA DN/10/895.
220. Enderlein, *Handbuch*, vol. 2, 72; "Stellungnahme," December 6, 1976, BA DG7-818 3 von 3.
221. "Baghdad Modern Slaughterhouse—Gesamtablaufplan," August 5, 1977, BA DG7-748 2 von 2.
222. Nawrocki, "Kombinat."
223. "Baghdad Modern Slaughterhouse—Gesamtablaufplan."
224. "VEB Industrieprojektierung," vol. 2, n.d.; "35 Jahre Dessau."
225. "Baghdad Modern Slaughterhouse—Gesamtablaufplan."
226. Springer, *Verbaute Träume*, 85–86.
227. Palutzki, *Architektur*, 73; see also Murawski, "Actually-Existing Success," 20–21.
228. Waterkamp, *Planungssystem der DDR*, 66–67.
229. Gerhard Kosel, "Das Bauwesen der Deutschen Demokratischen Republik, seine Unterstützung durch die Sowjetunion…," BA N2504 260, 13. Kosel had been a member of the Ernst May brigade in the interwar Soviet Union, where he designed industrial cities; after World War II, he worked on the postwar reconstruction of Soviet cities; Kosel, *Unternehmen Wissenschaft*.
230. "Eksport i import budownictwa w latach 1976–1980" (1976), AAN z. CHZB "Budimex," 1/113.
231. Zevin, *Economic Cooperation*, 59.
232. Pilot and Experimental Design [Muster- und Experimentalprojekt], "Technical Information: Industrialized Housing for the Erection of the Capital 'Abuja'…," BA DH2/13881.
233. Palutzki, *Architektur*, 132–33; Lange, "Form."
234. Palutzki, *Architektur*, 120, 284, 293.
235. Dagne, *Das entwicklungspolitische Engagement*, 54.
236. Möller, *DDR*, 241–42; "Technical Tender for the Project Preparation and Construction of a Camp 1.000…," BA DH2/13971; "Niederschrift über die Beratung BMK Süd—BA zum Vorhaben Militärcamps," July 19, 1982, BA DH2/4845; "Aktualisierung Spezialangebote Irak," BA DH2/13970.
237. "Technical Information," 4.
238. "35 Jahre Dessau"; Muster- und Experimentalprojekt, "Wohnungsbau in Entwicklungsländern," February 1985, BA DH2/5268. For instance, the plans for a housing project for Mozambique reappeared in an offer for Nigeria: "Wohnungsneubau in der Volksrepublik Moçambique," *Architektur der DDR* 8 (1984): 472–75; *Projeté, construit, utilisé*, 37–40; "Technical Information."
239. Muster- und Experimentalprojekt, "Geschäftsbericht 1982," BA DH2/10851.
240. VEP Ipro Dessau, "Studie"; Muster- und Experimentalprojekt, "Wohnungsbau in Entwicklungsländern."
241. "Technical Information."
242. "Wohnungsneubau"; "Wohngebiete im Gouvernorat Abyan, Volksdemokratische Republik Jemen," *Architektur der DDR* 8 (1984): 468–71; "Technical Offer for Construction and Turn Key Supply of Villages in the Republic of Iraq," BA DH2/13884;

"Grobeinschätzung zum Tender über den Bau von 6 Dörfern…," BA DH2/4845.
243. "Auftrag der Bauakademie der DDR—Muster- und Experimentalprojekt—vom 21.7.82…," BA DH2/4845.
244. Möller, DDR, 64–67.
245. Mühlfriedel, Hellmuth, Zeiss.
246. "Raumflugplanetarium in Tripoli," Architektur der DDR 3 (1982): 146–53; Schille, "Designing and Building"; Scheffler, "Himmelskuppeln."
247. "Abrechung," BA DH2/22835-1, 4.
248. Ibid.
249. The import of subcomponents from the West for the most profitable East German companies, such as Zeiss, was facilitated by the Section Commercial Coordination at the Ministry of Foreign Trade, the body in charge of maximizing income in convertible currencies; however, this was not the case with the Baghdad project; Möller, DDR, 67.
250. "Abrechung."
251. "Sonderinformation," June 12, 1979, BA DG7-745 1 von 2.
252. Jonas Flury, "The Idea of a Socialist World System 1950s–1970s: Conceiving an Alternative Global System; Theories of Growing Interconnectedness and Exchange in the Socialist World," talk at the conference "Alternative Encounters: The 'Second World' and the 'Global South,'" Jena, November 3–4, 2014.
253. Steiner, Petrak-Jones, "Council," 243.
254. Kraft, Zusammenarbeit; compare Mëhilli, From Stalin to Mao, 172–76.
255. Kraft, Zusammenarbeit.
256. I. Lérová, F. Vaclávek, "Tematický výzkum ekonomických aspektu hodnocení urbanistických opatření v životním prostředí v členských zemích RVHP," Architektura ČSSR 2 (1982): 91–94; Adam Kotarbiński, "O pracach sekcji planowania regionalnego i urbanistyki stałej komisji budownictwa RWPG," Architektura 11–12 (1962): 474, 480.
257. Kraft, Zusammenarbeit; Schubert, "Bewährte Zusammenarbeit"; Karagozov et al., eds., Dictionary.
258. RZ 45 (1978): 8; "Eksport Cekopu," "Polimex-Cekop oferuje," "Polimex-Cekop oferuje: cukrownie," all three in FN, F. 1130, F. 2819, F. 2820.
259. Kraft, Zusammenarbeit, 21. See also Lhamsurien, "Pomoshch bratskikh stran"; Davaa, "Osnovnoi."
260. "Einheitliche technische Bedingungen für die Projektierung von Betrieben und anderen Objekten, die in der Mongolischen Volksrepublik mit technischer Hilfe der Mitgliedsländer des RGW errichtet werden" (Berlin: Bauakademie der DDR, 1976); "Protokoll der Spezialistenberatung der Mitgliedsländer des RGW…" (Ulaanbaatar, March–April 1973), BA DH1/25038, 2 von 2.
261. "Unterstützung des RGW für Kubas Bauindustrie." Support for Chilean construction industry in the early 1970s, and the reconstruction effort in Vietnam during and after the war (1955–75), were carried out primarily on bilateral basis; see Kosel, Unternehmen Wissenschaft, 321–26.

262. ANR f. C. C. al P.C.R., s. Relații Externe, p. 60/1975, 3; "NSW-Export Schlachthof Bagdad," 3.
263. "Information über den Stand…," January 25, 1978, BA DC/10/895.
264. "Bericht über den Stand…," January 10, 1979, BA DC/10/895; "Bericht," February 1, 1979, BA DH2/22835-3.
265. "Bericht über Probleme…," April 11, 1978, 4, BA DC/10/895.
266. Max Trecker, "The 'Grapes of Cooperation'? Bulgarian and East German Plans to Build a Syrian Cement Industry from Scratch," forthcoming.
267. "Bericht über die Dienstreise nach Bukarest, SRR, von 11.–12.7.1977," 1, BA DH2/22835-3.
268. Dieter Warnke, "Bericht über die durchgeführte Dienstreise in der Zeit vom 18.11.1987–09.12.1987 nach Kuwait und in die V.A.E.," Annex 1, 3; "Einschätzung der bisherigen Bautätigkeit in Kuwait und Schlussfolgerungen für die weitere Arbeit"; both in BA DH1/32777 1 von 2; "Information zur materiell-technischen Basis des Bauwesens der DDR im Staat Kuwait," BA DH1/32777, 2 von 2.
269. Warnke, "Bericht"; "Sonderinformation"; "Kurzbericht über die Dienstreise nach Bukarest und Bagdad vom 9.5. bis 18.5.1979 zum Vorhaben 'Schlachthof Bagdad,'" May 25, 1979, BA DG7/745.
270. "Einschätzung der bisherigen Bautätigkeit in Kuwait"; Maria Gross, "Abschlussbericht zum Auslandseinsatz in Kuwait," August 1987, 8, BA DH1/32777, 1 von 2.
271. Möller, DDR, 247–48.
272. "Information über die Entwicklung…," December 28, 1978, BA DH2/22835-2.
273. "NSW-Export Schlachthof-Bagdad"; "Information über die Kontrolle…."
274. "NSW-Export Schlachthof-Bagdad."
275. Rogers, "Petrobarter."
276. Lorenzini, "Comecon."
277. Steiner, Petrak-Jones, "Council"; Kaliński, "Rubel transferowy."
278. Kornai, Socialist System, 351–53.
279. By the mid-1970s, Iraq was taken over by Libya, and by Iran in the early 1980s; see Vaňous, "Soviet and East European Trade"; compare BO, March 10, 1972, 1; BO, May 10, 1972, 4; BO, October 11, 1972, 5; BO, June 28, 1973, 1, 5; BO, February 20, 1974, 3.
280. Smolansky, USSR.
281. Ibid., 20–21.
282. Vaňous, "Soviet and East European Trade."
283. Ibid., 88.
284. ANR f. C. C. al P.C.R., s. Economică 1979–89, p. 60/1981, 24–25.
285. ANR f. C. C. al P.C.R., s. Cancelarie 1980–89, p. 28/1982, 36.
286. Gheorghe Radu Stănculescu, "A Brief History of Romproiect, 1981–2013," 2013, archive of Gheorghe Radu Stănculescu, Bucharest (Romania); Vais, "Exporting."
287. Stănculescu, "Brief History."
288. D. 573, SARP.
289. Interview with Gheorghe Radu Stănculescu, Bucharest, May 2015; d. 256, SARP.
290. Zahariade, Arhitectura, 35.
291. ANR f. C. C. al P.C.R., s. Economică 1979–89,

p. 60/1981, 29.
292. "Romproiect: Study and Design Centre for Overseas Construction, Romania," n.d.; "S.C. Romproiect, S.A." n.d., Stănculescu archive. Another important project designed and constructed by Romanian companies in Algeria in the course of the 1970s was the School of Architecture of the University of Constantine. The school was staffed by Romanian professors who introduced a curriculum based on their teaching at the Ion Mincu University of Architecture in Bucharest. The traditionally francophone culture of Romania's intelligentsia helped in recruitment for Algeria, where university courses were taught in French; "Proiecte pentru ansambluri universitare în Republica Algeriana Democratică," Arhitectura 6 (1979): 22–40; interview with Mircea Ochinciuc and Radu Serban, Bucharest, May 2015.
293. Interviews with Dan Agent and Maximilian Zielinski, Bucharest, May 2015.
294. Dorin Ștefan, "Consulting în domeniul proiectării arhitectural-urbanistice (II)," Arhitectura 6 (1980): 13.
295. Interview with Agent.
296. Ibid.
297. ANR f. C. C. al P.C.R., s. Economică 1979–89, p. 60/1981, 27–28, 32–34.
298. Interview with Nicolae Besnea, Bucharest, May 2015; see also BO, September 17, 1976, 2; BO, September 27, 1979, 2.
299. The architects were Ion Dumitru, Nicolae Besnea, Ionel Drăgulinescu, Adalbert Naiman, and Constantin Vasile; Miron Măsariu, "Abator în Bagdad—Republica Irak," Arhitectura 5 (1980): 26–27.
300. Interview with Besnea.
301. Ibid.; Măsariu, "Abator."
302. Ionel Drăgulinescu, "Cantina abatorului din Baghdad," Arhitectura 6 (1984): 79–80.
303. Nicolae Besnea, "Vile în Baghdad," Arhitectura 6 (1984): 77–78; interview with Beznea; Stroe, Locuirea.
304. Ștefan, "Consulting."
305. Arcom, Romproiect, "Collective and Individual Dwelling Types," n.d., ANR f. Romproiect, 7254; Romproiect "Proiect tip locuințe pentru export (Iraq)," n.d., ANR f. Romproiect, 7276; Romproiect "Logements/Housing," n.d., ANR f. Romproiect, 7398.
306. Romproiect, "Clădiri de locuit pentru export (II)," ANR f. Romproiect, 7099; see also ANR f. Romproiect 7274, 7282, 7283, and 7288.
307. Romproiect, "Clădiri de locuit pentru export (II)," pr. no. 2850/1984, 1.18.
308. Drew, Fry, Tropical Architecture; Frampton, "Towards a Critical Regionalism."
309. "Romproiect," ANR f. Romproiect, 5709.
310. Romproiect, "Al Qaim and Sinjar Cement Factories: Housing," ANR f. Romproiect, 7256.
311. Romproiect, "Republic of Iraq: Mosul, 3500 Housing Units," ANR f. Romproiect, 7257; Zahariade, Arhitectura, 60–62.
312. Cristina Moscu, "Centre populate în perimetrul Hilla–Kifl, Irak," Arhitectura 2 (1983): 75–79.
313. BO, May 30, 1979, 2.
314. "Prezențe arhitecturale," 10.
315. ANR f. C. C. al P.C.R., s. Economică 1979–89,

p. 2/1987.
316. "S.C. Romproiect, S.A."
317. Interview with Stănculescu; see also d. 1321, SARP.
318. "Algeria—3200 apartments in…ZHUN North 2, Saida," ANR f. Romproiect, 7398.
319. Interview with Stănculescu.
320. Kotkin, "Kiss of Debt," 89.
321. Scheffler, "Himmelskuppeln," 300. The contractor was SIAB Byggen AB. The concrete shells were executed by Spezialbetonbau Binz as subcontractor of SIAB, supervised by Müther.
322. Zaremba, "Sprawozdanie," 2; "Protokoll über die Beratung am 23.1.1987 zum Stand und der weiteren Entwicklung der Bauleistungsexportes in Kuwait…," BA DH1/32777, 2 von 2, 2.
323. Doytchinov, "Pragmatism," 462; "Czechoslovak Architects"; "Hungary: Design and Build," 56.
324. This was the explicit reason for choosing an East German train-signaling system over a West German one in the 1980s; "West Germans Win."

Chapter 5

1. "Pride"; al-Abed et al., eds., *Chronicle*, 250.
2. Casey, *History of Kuwait*.
3. "Kuwait Is an Open Market," *Middle East Construction* (later: *MEC*) 4 (1983): 15.
4. Steiner, "Globalisation."
5. *Rynki zagraniczne* (later: *RZ*) 15 (1980): 8.
6. McNeill, *Global Architect*, 1.
7. Ibid.; Fraser, Golzari, eds., *Architecture and Globalisation*; Elsheshtawy, *Dubai*.
8. McNeill, *Global Architect*, 1.
9. Adam, *Globalisation*.
10. United Arab Emirates, Town Planning Department, Abu Dhabi, "Competition of Design, the Municipality and Town Planning Dept. Complex, Abu Dhabi," April 1979, archive of Borislav Bogdanov, Sofia (Bulgaria), 46.
11. Ibid.
12. Ibid., 11; *al-'itihād*, September 1, 1985.
13. United Arab Emirates, "Competition," 46.
14. Ibid.
15. "Abdel-Rahman Makhlouf."
16. Ibid.; Reisz, "Plans the Earth Swallows"; Saif al-Kaabi, "Towards the Reformation of Abu Dhabi to Be an Environmentally Sustainable City," Ph.D. dissertation, University of Wolverhampton, 2011; telephone interview with Abdulrahman Makhlouf, August 19, 2015.
17. Elsheshtawy, "Cities," 271–72; Damluji, "Brave New Cities," 31.
18. Miastoprojekt, "System nazewnictwa ulic i numeracji budynków w Abu Dhabi," early 1980s. For earlier street naming in Abu Dhabi (1974), see Bani Hashim, *Planning Abu Dhabi*, 148.
19. "Abu Dhabi—The City's on the Move," 9.
20. Reisz, "Plans."
21. The concept of the Islamic neighborhood unit was first introduced in Makhlouf's Ph.D. thesis project at the Munich University of Technology for Giza; ibid. For 1970s and 1980s discussion concerning the possibility of translating the Shari'ah into architectural and urban-planning principles, see Christa Udschi, "International Symposium on Islamic Architecture and Urbanism," *Albenaa* 2, no. 10 (1981): 2–6; Ahmed Farid Moustapha, "Islamic Values in Contemporary Urbanism," part 1, *Albenaa* 7, no. 41 (1988): 18–24, 26–33, and part 2, *Albenaa* 7, no. 42 (1988): 14–19, 16–23.
22. Damluji, ed., *Architecture*.
23. "Dubai Currency Board Building and Abu Dhabi Currency Board Building," *MEC* 9 (1979): 72; "Natural Stone," *MEC* 2 (1982): 49.
24. *Kuwait Times* (later: *KT*), July 1, 1979, 7; *KT*, December 5, 1979, 9; *KT*, February 23, 1980, 6; "Abu Dhabi Starts to Build for Leisure," *MEC* 4 (1981): 11.
25. Al-Nakib, *Kuwait*.
26. Ibid., 92–97.
27. *KT*, June 23, 1977, 2; *KT*, August 4, 1977, 8; *KT*, August 26, 1978, 7.
28. *KT*, September 4, 1980, 1; *KT*, January 12, 1981, 7; *KT*, November 8, 1981, 36–37, 40; *KT*, August 10, 1982, 3; *KT*, April 6, 1983, 2. See also Wojciech Jarząbek, Edward Lach "Amusement Park in Kuwait," n.d., drawings, archive of Wojciech Jarząbek, Wrocław (Poland). The complex was executed according to the design by VTN International; "Kuwait Is an Open Market," 15.
29. *KT*, May 2, 1977, 1. Among the high-rises co-designed by architects from Poland were the al-Fintas towers (Włodzimierz Gleń, J. Damija, and N. Fatteh for Arabi Engineers Office, 1984) and the al-Qibla tower (Krawecki for Gulf Consult, 1988); see SARP d. 1091; Krzysztof Wiśniowski; Wyżykowski, "Zagraniczna twórczość."
30. *KT*, August 4, 1977, 20; *KT*, August 1, 1980, 5; Fabbri et al., *Modern Architecture*.
31. "Il nuovo Eldorado."
32. Neil Parkyn, "Kuwait Revisited," *MEC* 9 (1983): 42.
33. Al-Nakib, *Kuwait*, 124–28; Gardiner, *Kuwait*.
34. Shiber, *Kuwait Urbanization*; Nasr, "Saba Shiber."
35. Fabbri et al., *Modern Architecture*; Fabbri et al., eds., *Essays*.
36. Shiber, *Kuwait Urbanization*, 2.
37. Gardiner, *Kuwait*.
38. *KT*, November 8, 1981, 36–37.
39. "Czechoslovak Architects"; Ministry of Public Works, Strojexport, State Institute for the Restoration of Historic Towns and Monuments (SURPMO), "Preservation of Kuwaiti Historic Monuments," 1985, archive of Miroslava Baštova, Prague (Czech Republic); Ministry of Public Works, M.O.I. Investigation Department, "Building Survey and Preparation of Record Drawings," November 1987, archive of Alexander Gjurič, Prague (Czech Republic).
40. Al-Nakib, *Kuwait*, 160–61; see also *KT*, March 14, 1978, 5; *KT*, May 10, 1978, 5; *KT*, July 16, 1978, 7.
41. Al-Nakib, *Kuwait*.
42. Jim Antoniou, "Conserving the Best of the Past," *MEC* 3 (1980): 18–19; "A Future for the Past," *MEC* 12/1 (1986/87): 13.
43. Jim Antoniou, "The Challenge of Islamic Architecture," *MEC* 10 (1979): 16–17; Jim Antoniou, "Development with Conservation the Way Ahead," *MEC* 2 (1983), 14; see also Abu-Lughod, "Islamic City."
44. *KT*, October 24, 1980, 2; *KT*, October 28, 1980, 7.
45. For Kuwait, see Fabbri et al., *Modern Architecture*.
46. "An Architect from Kuwait," *Albenaa* 7, no. 38 (1987/88): 10–11; Taylor, "Waterfront."
47. "Kuwait, Beit Al-Reihan," *Albenaa* 8, no. 43 (1988): 10.
48. Ministry of Public Works, Archicentre, "Amiri Diwan and Council of Ministers. Predevelopment Study. Conceptual Design Stage 4. Technical Report," vol. II-A, n.d., 0-6-0-7, Gjurič archive.
49. Archicentre was founded in 1970 in Baghdad and registered in Kuwait in 1977; "The New Architects of Arabia," *MEC* 9 (1985): 41–43; "Archicentre," catalogue, n.d.; interview with Akram Ogaily, Cambridge, MA, September 2014.
50. Ministry of Public Works et al., "Amiri Diwan," 0–10. Miroslava Baštova joined Archicentre too. Besides the Amiri Diwan project, during his tenure as project architect and planner in Archicentre, Vaclav Bašta was involved in a number of projects in Kuwait, Iraq, and the UAE. These included the design for the New Headquarters of Building of the Baath Party in Baghdad and the Governmental Guest House in Basrah (second prize in a competition). Realized projects in Kuwait included numerous private residences and a residential complex in Jabriya, Vaclav Bašta, CV, Baštova archive.
51. Ministry of Public Works, "Amiri Diwan," 2-15-2-23; interviews with Alexander Gjurič and Orlin Ilinčev, Prague, May 2017.
52. Ministry of Public Works, Archicentre, "Amiri Diwan and Council of Ministers. Predevelopment Study. Conceptual Design Stage 1. Data Collection Survey," n.d., Baštova archive, 196, 214.
53. "Not Recession but Decelerated Growth," *MEC* 3 (1985): 30.
54. Habib Hussein, dir., *Kuwaiti Architecture: A Lost Identity* (n.d.).
55. Al-Bahar, "Contemporary Kuwaiti Houses," 65.
56. Antoniou "Challenge," 16.
57. Jamal, "Destruction."
58. "Planning to Avoid the West's Mistakes," *MEC* 6 (1983): 22.
59. "What Is Good Architecture?" *MEC* 10 (1983): 5.
60. "Urban Renaissance in Baghdad," *Albenaa* 4: 21–22 (1985): 76–87.
61. Moustapha, "Islamic Values," 1, 23–24.
62. Mohamed Makiya, "Islamic Architecture and Modernism," *Albenaa* 5, no. 26 (1985/1986): 73.
63. *KT*, March 23, 1978, 7; *KT*, August 31, 1980, 10.
64. "Household Interviews," in National Housing Authority (Kuwait), *National Housing Programme*, vol. 4.
65. Al-Nakib, *Kuwait*, 132.
66. Abdullah, "Housing," 140–41.
67. Ibid., 143.
68. "From Airports to Water Supply," *MEC* 9 (1984): 35–37.
69. Andreu, "Points," 30.
70. "Bridging the Culture Gap," *MEC* 10 (1983): 11.
71. Interview with Peter Mlodzianowski, Bucks, UK,

September 2015.

72. "Calling the Tune," *MEC* 8 (1985): 20–21; see also "Fitzroy Robinson International, Middle East," n.d.; "The Buildings and Projects of the Fitzroy Robinson Partnership in the Middle East," n.d. Such offers became increasingly typical for Gulf practices, and Jan Amos Havelka, the Czech architect who worked for the Kuwaiti office KEO in the 1980s, recalled that the office offered both "local" and "international" projects, depending on the wishes of the clients; interview with Jan Amos Havelka, Prague, May 2017.
73. "Calling the Tune," 20.
74. Interview with Mlodzianowski.
75. Town Planning Department, Building License Section Abu Dhabi, "Building Regulations for Commercial, Residential and Industrial Plots," January 1981, 18, archive of Peter Dew, Abu Dhabi (UAE).
76. See also "English Dhabi Winner."
77. *Al-'itihād*, June 17, 1984; see also Damluji, "Brave New Cities," 33.
78. "Abu Dhabi to Ensure Harmony of Buildings," *MEC* 10 (1985): 11.
79. Al-Abed et al., *Chronicle*, 286.
80. Damluji, "Brave New Cities," 36.
81. Telephone interview with Peter Dew, December 2015.
82. United Arab Emirates, "Competition," 46.
83. "Abu Dhabi Central Market Reawakens 'Gulf Architecture,' " *MEC* 6 (1981): 78; Anthony Davis, "Vulgarity versus Vernacular," *MEC* 11 (1984): 5; "Whither Arab Architecture?" *MEC* 4 (1984): 5; *KT*, September 5, 1977, 4; *KT*, June 21, 1978, 1; *KT*, March 13, 1979, 7; "Kuwait Sief Place Area Building," *Albenaa* 1, no. 1 (1979): 20–25; AlSayyad, "Medina."
84. "Design and Consult," *MEC* 3 (1985): 37.
85. "Il nuovo Eldorado," 10; "Clarity of Plan"; "Abu Dhabi Inter-Continental"; "Paradise Gardens."
86. Browne, "Dubai."
87. Hassan El Shishtawy, "Arabesque," *Albenaa* 1, no. 3 (1979), 93–96; Yousef Mahmoud Gholam, "Architectural Arab Decoration" and "Ornamental Concrete," *Albenaa* 1, no. 6 (1979): 4–8 and 9–12; "Analogy in Architecture of the Arab World," *Albenaa* 2, no. 12 (1981): 3–7; "A Future for the Past"; Azara, ed., *City*; see also Martin, *Utopia's Ghost*. Putting different ornamental patterns on buildings based on the same plan economized on the work of architects; such economization was encouraged by the low fees in Abu Dhabi, where architects, engineers, and quantity surveyors received only 4 percent of the building costs of projects managed by the Khalifah Committee; al-Radi, "Constraints," 123.
88. E-mail correspondence with Georgi Anastassov, April–May 2015.
89. Elsheshtawy, "Cities," 270.
90. Town Planning Department, Abu Dhabi, "Key Map of Abu Dhabi Island," 1970, LC G7574.A2 1970.A2; "Abu Dhabi," 1973, LC G7574.A2 1973. A2; Fairey Surveys, Bekshire, "Abu Dhabi," 1979, LC G7574.A2 1979.F3; Geoprojects (Beirut, Lebanon), "Abu Dhabi," 1982, LC G7574. A2 1982.G4. See also "Abu Dhabi," 1972, archive of the Zaremba family, Szczecin (Poland); aerial view of Abu Dhabi, early 1980s, IFA, Fonds Georges Philippe, 390 AA, Box 9.
91. Interview with Makhlouf.
92. *Al-'itihād*, September 1, 1985.
93. The planning process was assisted by the United Nations Development Programme and Atkins, Elsheshtawy, "Cities," 270; Texier, "Abu Dhabi"; Texier, "Villes neuves."
94. "Pride of the City"; correspondence with Anastassov.
95. Ibid.
96. The landscape architect was Mitko Bogdanov, and the ceramic artist was Ivan Ivanov; correspondence with Anastassov.
97. Ibid.
98. "Abu Dhabi's New Bus Terminus," *MEC* 2 (1986): 35; Douglas Watson, "New Bus Station to Offer Inter-city Service," *Emirates News*, February 6, 1982; Technoexportstroy [1] (catalogue), n.d. The structure was designed by Bulgarian civil engineer Vladimir Nedelchev, correspondence with Anastassov; interview with Stanka Dundakova, Sofia, July 2014.
99. Interview with Dundakova; CV Kuno Dundakov, CV Stanka Dundakova, both in the archive of Stanka Dundakova, Sofia (Bulgaria).
100. Interview with Hashem al-Hassan, Abu Dhabi, October 2015 (Ahlam Sharif).
101. Grozdanova, Vale, "Trade."
102. "Technoexportstroy" [1].
103. "Bericht über die durchgeführte Dienstreise in der Zeit vom 18.11.1987–09.12.1987 nach Kuweit und in die V.A.E.," BA DH1/32777 1 von 1.
104. In response, the report suggested that East German firms create a joint venture with a Gulf national and set up a production plant for light steel construction in the free trade zone in Dubai. Such a joint venture would count as a local company and would be able to acquire local commissions and to ship construction elements tariff-free within the Gulf Cooperation Council countries, among them Kuwait; "Bericht über die durchgeführte Dienstreise," 10–12; compare Neveling, "Global Spread."
105. "Bericht über eine Dienstreise in die Vereinigten Arabischen Emirate und in den Staat Qatar vom 15.1.1983 bis zum 9.3.1983," March 14, 1983, BA DH2/4841; "Studie über den Baumarkt der Vereinigten Arabischen Emirate," September 1, 1983, BA DH2/23019; Maria Gross, "Abschlussbericht zum Auslandseinsatz in Kuweit," August 1987, BA DH1/32777, 1 von 2.
106. Nicolas Constantopoulos, "East Europe Increases Share of Arab Market," *MEC* 12 (1980): 14–15.
107. For an example of an agreement between TES and an Abu Dhabi contractor (al-Mansoori al-Omar), see "Sporazumenie," 1977, DAA f. 608, op. 3, a.e. 73; see also "Joint Venture Protocol between Under-signed: Abu Dhabi–Islamic Architecture, Paris–Georges Philippe–Pierre Gregoire," IFA, Fonds Georges Philippe, 390 AA, Box 9.
108. Grozdanova, Vale, "Trade," 126.
109. Chernev et al., *Dela*, 31.
110. Chernev et al., *Dela*; *KT*, November 13, 1978, 6.
111. The cities included Tartus, Baniyas, the Island of Arwad, Kessab, Ericha, Rastan, Jableh, as well as Latakia; Chernev et al., *Dela*, 130–46.
112. Ibid., 160. The 11th congress of the UIA took place in the Bulgarian city of Varna in 1972, and Bulgarian architect Georgi Stoilov was UIA's president between 1985 and 1987, Vago, *L'UIA*; Glendinning, *Matthew*.
113. Chernev et al., *Dela*, 51.
114. Ibid., 140.
115. Interview in Abu Dhabi (interviewee preferred not to be named), October 2015 (Ahlam Sharif).
116. Correspondence with Anastassov.
117. "Technoexportstroy" [1]; "Technoexportstroy" [2], catalogue (n.d.); "Technoexportstroy" [3], catalogue (n.d.). See the documentation in the Bogdanov archive: Technoexportstroy-Bulgarproject, "Public Buildings," n.d.; TES, "Al-Hani Memorial Complex in Tripoli," n.d.; GSPLAJ, TES, "Governmental Complex Syrte," n.d.; Bulgarproject, Tayeb Eng., "Municipal Building Al Ain Town," n.d.; TES, "Ministry of Petrol and Mineral Resources, Sana'a, Yemen Arab Republic," n.d.; TES, "The Municipality and Town Planning Department Complex Abu Dhabi," 1980; Technoexportstroy (Nigeria Ltd), "Federal Republic of Nigeria. Office Building, Motel, and Dwelling Buildings Complex—Abuja," n.d.; Technoexportstroy (Nigeria Ltd), "Kogi State Government—Nigeria. Niger River Tourist Complex—Lokoja," n.d.; TES, "Federal Republic of Nigeria. Mini Sports Complex, Minna," n.d.; Bulgarproject, Tayeb Eng., "United Arab Emirates, Town Planning Department, Abu Dhabi. The Municipality and Town Planning Dept. Complex. Working Drawings," 1981; TES, "Hospital Polivalente—600 camas. Benguela-Angola," n.d.; Bulgarproject, "Ministry of Culture, Public Corporation of Tourism, PDR Yemen. Tourist Complex Gold Mohur," n.d.; Bulgarproject, "Socialist People's Libyan Arab Jamahereya. Tarhouna—Cultural Centre," n.d.; S. N. Technoexportstroy, "République algérienne démocratique et populaire. Centre Administratif du Hamma Alger. Assemblée populaire nationale," 1986. See the following documentation in the Dundakova archive: GSPLAJ, TES, "Administrative Centre Benghazi," n.d.; Technoexportstroy Addis Ababa, "Commercial Bank of Ethiopia. Western Region in Jimma," n.d.; Technoexportstroy Addis Ababa, "Municipal Shopping Center, Addis Ababa," n.d.; Bulgarproject, "National Theatre Abu Dhabi," n.d.; Intermont, TES, Hochtief, "Stade olympique d'Alger," n.d.; "Sports Complex Ilorin, Nigeria," n.d.; "Main Bus Terminal Al Ain," 1991; "Arab Cities Organization Building, Kuwait," 1980.
118. At various times, branches were set up in Rabat, Algiers, Tunis, Tripoli (Libya), Damascus, Addis Ababa, Kuwait and Abu Dhabi, Luanda, Harare, Aden, Ulaanbaatar, Ikoyi (Lagos), but also in West Germany and the USSR, "Technoexportstroy" [1], [2], [3].
119. Ibid.
120. Interview with Tacho Tachev, Sofia, July 2014.
121. Interview with Detchno Detchev, Sofia, July 2014.

NOTES TO CHAPTER 5

122. "Technoexportstroy" [1], [2], [3]; "TES: Construction, Assembly, and Erection (Syria)," catalogue, n.d.; correspondence with Anastassov, interviews with Encho Balukchiev, Borislav Bogdanov, Detchev, Dundakova, Georgi Goshev, Lyudmil Leonidov, Evlogi Raichev, and Lyubomir Shinkov, Sofia, July 2014.
123. "Bulgarproject," catalogue, n.d.
124. Correspondence with Anastassov; interview with Goshev; "Studie über den Baumarkt."
125. Interview with Leonidov.
126. Correspondence with Anastassov, interview with Leonidov; compare "Sporazumenie"; "Doklad," July 2, 1991, DAA f. 608, op. 4, a.e. 52.
127. Dimitar Bogdanov, personal dossier, KAB; Dimitar Bogdanov, CV; "Technoexportproekt. Bulgarproject. Consulting Engineers and Architects. 25 Godini," n.d., the latter both in Bogdanov archive.
128. Kuno Dundakov, Stanka Dundakova, personal dossiers, KAB; CV Kuno Dundakov, CV Stanka Dundakova.
129. Vasil Petrov, personal dossier, KAB.
130. See dossiers of Bogdanov, Dundakov, Dundakova, Petrov, KAB.
131. Interview in Abu Dhabi.
132. Correspondence with Anastassov.
133. Interview with Bedri Omar Elias, Al Ain, March 2015.
134. Bulgarproject, Tayeb, "Municipal Building Al Ain"; correspondence with Anastassov; interview with Mlodzianowski; see also "Tough Times Ahead in UAE," MEC 5 (1986), 25.
135. "New Complex Fine Example of Islamic Architecture," in "Abu Dhabi Municipality. Khaleej Times Special Report," preserved in Bogdanov archive without discernable date, 12.
136. Al-'itihād, September 1, 1985.
137. Bulgarproject, Tayeb, "Abu Dhabi Municipality."
138. Correspondence with Anastassov.
139. "Pride of the City," 21.
140. Interview in Abu Dhabi.
141. Shiber Consult, "The Municipality and Town Planning Dept. Complex Abu Dhabi," 1979, Jarząbek archive; SARP d. 480. The office was owned by Victor Shiber, the brother of Saba Shiber. See also "Hôtel de ville."
142. Among those employed in the Institute were Wiśniowski, Bohdanowicz, and Ryszard Daczkowski.
143. Stanek, ed., Team 10 East.
144. The designers of the Łódź Area B layout were Bohdanowicz, Daczkowski, L. Paperz, M. Sowa, Wiśniowski, Wiśniowski, n.p.
145. City center of Racibórz, designers: Bohdanowicz, Daczkowski, Lach, P. Saternus, Wiśniowski; universities' district Łódź, designers: B. Kardaszewski, W. Nowakowski, A. Wiśniowska; master plan for the old town of Lwówek Śląski, designers: Bohdanowicz, Daczkowski, Lach, Wiśniowski; residential district Trzebnica, designers: W. Brzezowski, S. Medeksza, E. Niemczyk, Wiśniowski; Wiśniowski, n.p.
146. Kozanów Housing Estate, designers: Bohdanowicz, Daczkowki, Lach, Mieszko Niedźwiedzki, Wiśniowski; Wiśniowski, n.p.; e-mail correspondence with Mieszko Niedźwiedzki, November 2011.
147. Interview with Wojciech Jarząbek and Edward Lach, Wrocław, April 2011.
148. Interview with Lach.
149. Ibid.
150. Ibid.; interview with Krzysztof Wiśniowski and Andrzej Bohdanowicz, Kuwait City, January 2014.
151. Leisure Center in Fermignano (Italy), designers: A. Chachaj, Lach, J. Matkowski, Wiśniowski; Library in Damascus, Syria, designers: Bohdanowicz, Chachaj, Daczkowski, Lach, Wiśniowski. The library was realized according to an award-winning design by another Polish team, "Biblioteka w Damaszku," Architektura 375–76, nos. 1–2 (1979): 269–70.
152. During the late 1970s, J. Matkowski and Mieszko Niedźwiecki worked for GEO; and Jan Urbanowicz and Jacek Chryniewicz for Shiber; interviews and e-mail correspondence with Bohdanowicz, Jarząbek, Lach, Mieszko Niedźwiecki, Wiśniowski; d. 279, 282, 351, 353, 363, 480, 533, SARP.
153. Interview with Mohammad al-Sanan, Kuwait City, January 2014.
154. They included Zdzisława Daczkowska, Elżbieta Niedźwiecki, Rudolf and Ewa Staniek, Anna Wiśniowska, and Marian Żabiński.
155. D. 956, 1091, 1138, SARP; interviews with Bohdanowicz and Wiśniowski; telephone interview with Janusz Krawecki, March 2014; Janusz Krawecki, CV, archive of Janusz Krawecki, Kraków (Poland).
156. Wiśniowski, n.p.; Stanek, Postmodernism.
157. Compare Fabbri et al., Modern Architecture; Contemporary Architecture of Kuwait.
158. "No Let-Up in Boom," MEC 3 (1981): 8; Contemporary Architecture of Kuwait, 287.
159. "Manpower and Migration," MEC 3 (1983): 16.
160. Archicentre, n.p.
161. Simon Dunkley, "Stricter Labour Laws," MEC 2 (1981): 11.
162. Interview with Ogaily.
163. Besides the Baštas, architects from Czechoslovakia employed by Archicentre in the 1980s included Miroslav Base, Ivo Bily, Bohumil Blažek, Hana Blažkova, Radim Boháček, Yvona Boháčkova, Alexander Gjurič, Orlin Ilinčev, Paul Ososlobe, Ján Strcula, and Jiří Vít. The firm also employed architect Ljubica Damjanović from Yugoslavia; Ministry of Public Works, "Amiri Diwan"; "Archicentre."
164. Interview with Ogaily; Ministry of Public Works, "Amiri Diwan."
165. Perišić et al., Građevinarstvo, 8–9.
166. Ministry of Public Works, "Kuwait Conference Centre Complex and Master Plan of Bayan Park. Report," March 1983, archive of Stojan Maksimović, Nahant, MA (US); interview with Stojan and Mirjana Maksimović, September 2014, Nahant, MA. The team working for Archicentre in Kuwait included Mirjana Maksimović, Sonja Živković, Branislav Jovin, Jovan Katanic, and Radomir Mihajlović. They collaborated with West German, British, and Kuwaiti consultants; Manević, Maksimović: Stvaralaštvo, 76–78; Ministry of Public Works, "Kuwait Conference Centre."
167. Interview with Maksimović.
168. Interview with Ogaily; Fabbri et al., Modern Architecture, 330–31.
169. Perišić et al., Građevinarstvo, 22–23. See also Fabbri et al., Modern Architecture, 144–45, 388–89.
170. Interview with Ljiljana and Dragoljub Bakić, Belgrade, October 2015; "Naselje 23 dvojne kuće za rentu šeika Duaj Ibrahim al-Sabaha u Kuvajtu," "Šest vila za Mr. Youset al Shaye u Kuvajtu," "Kuće za izdavanje Mr. Abdulatif Al Touenija u Kuvajtu," Architektura Urbanizam 58 (1969): 46–47; Bakić, Anatomija.
171. Interview with Ljiljana and Dragoljub Bakić.
172. "Beduinsko naselje u Kuvajtu (Housing—Kuwait)," Architektura Urbanizam 58 (1969): 23–25; 35 godina, 24; Bakić, Anatomija.
173. 35 godina, 22, 24–25; interviews with Mario Jobst and Nina Pantić, Belgrade, October 2015; Energoprojekt, "Conference City Abu Dhabi, United Arab Emirates," n.d., archive of Mario Jobst, Belgrade (Serbia).
174. The designers were Attila Emödy, Tibor Hübner, and László Szabados; "Közti Középülettervező Vállalat," n.d., Közti Archive, Budapest (Hungary); "Kuwait '85" (drawings), archive of Attila Emödy, Budapest (Hungary); interviews with Tibor Hübner, Attila Emödy, and Miklós Marosi, Budapest, February 2015; "Coastal Strip Development Project," n.d., archive of Kazimierz Bajer, Kraków (Poland); Branczik, "Exporttervezési munkák," 413.
175. Interview with Hübner; Branczik, "Exporttervezési munkák," 413–16.
176. "Arhitectură-tineret-pace," Arhitectura 2 (1983): 21; interviews with Romeo Simiras and Anca Oțoiu, Bucharest, June 2015.
177. Romproiect, "24 villas in Al Ain" (drawing), n.d., archive of Anca Oțoiu, Bucharest (Romania); interview with Oțoiu.
178. Jan Amos Havelka, CV; archive of Jan Amos Havelka, Prague (Czech Republic); interview with Havelka. Havelka combined his work for the ministry with occasional collaboration with other Kuwaiti offices, including KEO and Archicentre.
179. Interview with Ján Strcula, Prague, May 2017.
180. Wyżykowski, "Zagraniczna twórczość," 339.
181. Interview with Bohdanowicz.
182. Interview with al-Sanan.
183. Interview with Salah Salama, Kuwait City, January 2014.
184. Interview with Bohdanowicz and Wiśniowski.
185. KT, August 31, 1980, 5–10.
186. Holod, Rastorfer, eds., Architecture, 252.
187. "Kuwait Waterfront," MEC 9 (1984), 57.
188. Among the subcontractors of the Conference Center was Baufa (with FTO Limex). East German companies sold steel structures for industrial and storage buildings in Kuwait, and they built the structure of a commercial center on Salem Street (BMK Ost, 1987), "Vorlage für die Kommission des Politbüros des ZK der SED…," BA DH1/32777 2 von 2. Among the biggest (unsuccessful) East German bids for Kuwait was the offer to design, construct, and equip Kuwait's Institute of Construction

188. (cont.) Research, delivered by the Academy of Architecture and Limex, "Konzeption für den Aufbau eines Bauforschungszentrum im Staat Kuweit," BA DH2/5181 1 von 2.
189. For an overview, see *RZ* 31 (1986): 6. Furthermore, Bulgarproject designed a slaughterhouse in Kuwait and bid for other projects, including the Arab Cities Organization Building, "Technoexportstroy" [1], "Arab Cities Organization Building."
190. Interview with Lach.
191. Interview with Jarząbek.
192. Interviews with Bohdanowicz and Wiśniowski. A similar learning experience was made by Polish architects Leszek Sołonowicz and Włodzimierz Karczmarzyk in Dubai, who designed for Arenco multifunctional buildings at al-Ghubaiba Road (Sołonowicz, Karczmarzyk, 1983) and al-Sabkha Road (Karczmarzyk, Deepal Patkar, 1983); archive of Włodzimierz Karczmarzyk, Warsaw (Poland).
193. See, for example, the themed issue of *Projekt* (Warsaw) 4 (1977).
194. Kalinovsky, *Laboratory*.
195. Shiber, *Kuwait Urbanization*.
196. Furthermore, the design by Bohdanowicz and Wiśniowski (for INCO) of a low-income group housing neighborhood in the same district won third prize in this competition; *Wiśniowski*, n.p.
197. "Housing the Arab Population," *MEC* 1 (1983): 30; "A Road Network"; *KT*, November 8, 1981, 31.
198. "Household Interviews," 32–33.
199. The designers of the average-income group neighborhood in al-Qurain were Bohdanowicz, R. Singh, and Wiśniowski; *Wiśniowski*, n.p.
200. Shiber, *Kuwait Urbanization*, 391.
201. Fabbri et al., *Modern Architecture*, 220–21, 322–25.
202. *KT*, June 22, 1978, 9; *KT*, December 31, 1978, 3; *KT*, February 25, 1981, 21.
203. "Proposals for Restructuring Kuwait."
204. Fabbri et al., *Modern Architecture*.
205. SARP d. 480.
206. Al-Moosa, "Kuwait," 47.
207. Ibid., 47–48.
208. Ibid.; al-Nakib, *Kuwait*; al-Ragam, "Destruction."
209. Hutchinson, Said, "Spatial Differentiation."
210. Interview with Wiśniowski; *Krzysztof Wiśniowski*; Fabbri et al., *Modern Architecture*, 348–49.
211. Al-Nakib, "Public Space."
212. *Krzysztof Wiśniowski*; Fabbri et al., *Modern Architecture*, 350–51.
213. "Building Maintenance in Kuwait," *MEC* 1 (1980): 51–53.
214. United Nations, "Sulphur-Concrete Demonstration"; "Concrete Trouble in Abu Dhabi," *MEC* 11 (1986): 12.
215. "Building Maintenance."
216. Al-Nakib, *Kuwait*, 108; "Facing Facts," *MEC* 3/4 (1987): 19–20.
217. "Concrete Studies Continue," *MEC* 7 (1986): 31–32.
218. "As Solid as Concrete?" *MEC* 4/5 (1987): 20–21.
219. "Making Good Concrete," *MEC* 5 (1984): 51–53.
220. "As Solid as Concrete?"
221. Al-Radi, "Constraints," 136. The building was the Raisa Bint Darwish Building (Planar, 1991).
222. Ministry of Public Works, "Kuwait Conference Centre Complex," 2.01–2.02.
223. *KT*, November 8, 1981, 40–41.
224. "Versatility of Glass Reinforced Cement," *MEC* 6 (1985): 36–39.
225. "Glasdon International" (advertisement), *MEC* 3 (1984): 33.
226. "Thermal Insulation," *MEC* 6 (1983): 60–71.
227. Simon Dunkley, "Housing Project Runs into Difficulties," *MEC* 12 (1980): 11.
228. "Kuwait Assembly Attacks NHA and Korean Contractors," *MEC* 9 (1981): 10.
229. *Al-Siyāsah*, April 19, 1982, 7; *KT*, November 8, 1981, 30–31.
230. *KT*, November 8, 1981, 30–31.
231. "Design and Build," *MEC* 5 (1984): 29; "Number One for Jubail," *MEC* 5 (1985): 21–23; "Dynamic Management," *MEC* 4 (1986): 32–33; John A. Davison, "Computer Aids in Modern Architectural Practice," *Albenaa* 2, no. 9 (1981): 52–54; "Salhia"; Skidmore, Owings, and Merrill, "Computer Capability."
232. Interview with Ogaily.
233. Interview with Orlin Ilinčev, Prague, May 2017.
234. Interview with Salama.
235. *KT*, November 8, 1981, 38; see also "Updating the Souk," *MEC* 11 (1979): 62–65; "Kuwait's New 'Super City' Takes Shape West of the Capital," *MEC* 4 (1982): 17; "The Changing Suq," *MEC* 11 (1982): 14.
236. Interview with Wiśniowski. Some of these drawings were produced by external firms.
237. Barry, "Technological Zones."
238. Ibid., 249.
239. Grzywnowicz, Kiedrzyński, *Prawa i obowiązki*; interview with Ewa Smolczyńska, Warsaw, June 2011.
240. Grzywnowicz, Kiedrzyński, *Prawa i obowiązki*, 49–50.
241. Hong, "Through a Glass."
242. László Mányoky, "The Export of Hungarian Architectural Consultancy Service," *Magyar Építőművészet* 6 (1980): 3, translation modified.
243. Deamer, "Architectural Work."
244. Gross, "Abschlussbericht," 8, 12.
245. Ibid., 8.
246. Stanek, *Postmodernism*.
247. Ibid.
248. Gzowska, Klein, eds., *Postmodernizm*.
249. Interview with Andrzej Ryba, Warsaw, March 2011.
250. Ibid., interview with Sławomir Gzell, Warsaw, March 2011.
251. Interview with Ilinčev.
252. Interview with Havelka.
253. Interview with Gheorghe Radu Stănculescu, Bucharest, May 2015.
254. Interview with Zorica Savičić, Belgrade, October 2015.
255. Interview with Wacław Piziorski, Warsaw, March 2011; interview with Zoltán Boór, Budapest, February 2015.

Epilogue and Outlook
1. Sutowski, "Gdula."
2. Lefebvre, *Production of Space*, 53–54; see also Murawski, "Actually-Existing Success," 4–5.
3. See also Schmid, "Specificity," 288–89.

Bibliography

Archives and Repositories

Aga Khan Documentation Center, Massachusetts Institute of Technology, Cambridge, MA, US
Architecture and Engineering Services Limited, Accra, Ghana
Archiwum Akt Nowych, Warsaw, Poland
Archiwum Międzynarodowych Targów Poznańskich, Poznań, Poland
Arhivele Naționale ale României, Bucharest, Romania
Bundesarchiv, Berlin, Germany
Canadian Architecture Collection, McGill University, Montreal, Canada
Commonwealth Association of Architects, London, UK
Constantinos A. Doxiadis Archives, Athens, Greece
Development Office, Kwame Nkrumah University of Science and Technology, Kumasi, Ghana
Durzhavna agentsiia "Arkhivi," Sofia, Bulgaria
Filmoteka Narodowa, Warsaw, Poland
Graduate School of Design, Harvard University, Special Collections, Cambridge, MA, US
GTA Archiv, Eidgenössische Technische Hochschule Zürich, Zurich, Switzerland
Institut français d'architecture, Paris, France
Kamarata na arkhitektite v Bulgariia, Sofia, Bulgaria
Közti, Budapest, Hungary
Leibniz-Institut für Raumbezogene Sozialforschung, Erkner, Germany
Library of Congress, Confidential US State Department Central Files, Washington, DC, US
Miastoprojekt-Kraków, Kraków, Poland
Moskovskii arkhitekturnyi institut, Moscow, Russian Federation
Narodowe Archiwum Cyfrowe, Warsaw, Poland
National Archives, Szczecin, Poland
Public Records and Archives Administration Department, Accra, Ghana
Rossiiskii gosudarstvennyi arkhiv ekonomiki, Moscow and Samara, Russian Federation
Rossiiskii gosudarstvennyi arkhiv nauchno-tekhnicheskoi dokumentatsii, Moscow, Russian Federation
Royal Institute of British Architects, London, UK
Sir Basil Spence Collection, Historic Environment Scotland, Edinburgh, UK
Stowarzyszenie Architektów Polskich, Warsaw, Poland
Ulrich Müther Archiv, Hochschule Wismar, Wismar, Germany
Zbigniew Dmochowski–Archiwum, Gdańsk University of Technology, Gdańsk, Poland

Newspapers and Magazines for General Audience
(Full runs reviewed for the time periods in the focus of each chapter)

Al-'irāq, Baghdad
Al-'itihād, Abu Dhabi
Al-Jumhūrīyah, Baghdad
Al-Ta'akhī, Baghdad
Baghdad News, Baghdad
Baghdad Observer, Baghdad
Daily Graphic, Accra
Daily Times, Lagos
Evening News, Accra
Fundamenty, Warsaw
Ghanaian Times, Accra
Iraq Times, Baghdad
Kuwait Times, Kuwait
New Iraq, Baghdad
New Nigerian, Kaduna
Nigeria, Lagos
Nigerian Chronicle, Calabar
West Africa, London
West African Pilot, Lagos

Professional Journals, Corporate Newsletters, and Bulletins
(Full runs reviewed)

Albenaa/Al-Binā', Riyadh
Annual Reports, Department of Antiquities, Lagos
Architektura, Warsaw
Architektura ČSSR, Prague
Architektura Urbanizam, Belgrade
Arhitectura, Bucharest
Arkhitektura, Sofia
Arkhitektura SSSR, Moscow
Deutsche Architektur, from 1974: *Architektur der DDR*, Berlin (East)
Energoprojekt, Belgrade
Inżynieria i budownictwo, Warsaw
Magyar Építőművészet, Budapest
Middle East Construction, Sutton, UK
New Culture: A Review of Contemporary African Arts, Ibadan
Nigerian Institute of Architects Journal, Lagos
Projekt, Bratislava
Rynki zagraniczne, Warsaw
West African Builder and Architect, Accra

Selected Bibliography

Documents from the previously mentioned archives and periodicals are omitted here, as are Ph.D. dissertations, documents from private archives, and documentation of exhibitions; references to these documents are in the notes.

25 Years of Jos Museum. Jos: National Museum, 1978.
35 godina arhitekture Energoprojekta. Belgrade: Energoprojekt, 1987.
"35 Jahre Dessau im In- und Ausland." Dessau: Bauingenieurkombinat für Anlagenexport, 1985.
Abdullah, Talal M. "Housing Development in Al'Ayn." In *The Architecture of the United Arab Emirates*, edited by Salma Samar Damluji, 139–47. Reading, UK: Garnet Publishing, 2006.
"Abu Dhabi Inter-Continental Hotel." *Mimar* 25 (1987): 40–45.
"Abu Dhabi—The City's on the Move." *Gulf Weekly Mirror*, November 25, 1973, 8–9.
Abu-Lughod, Janet L. "The Islamic City—Historic Myth, Islamic Essence, and Contemporary Relevance." *International Journal of Middle East Studies* 19, no. 2 (May 1987): 155–76.
A Building Guide for Self Help Projects. Accra: Ministry of Social Welfare, 1961.
"Accra: A Plan for the Town: The Report for the Minister of Housing." Accra: Town Country Planning Division, 1958.
"Accra–Tema–Akosombo Regional Programme and Plan: Interim Report." *Ekistics* 11 (1961): 235–76.
"Abdel-Rahman Makhlouf: A Passion for Order." *Al-Ahram Weekly Online*, October 20–26, 2001. http://weekly.ahram.org.eg.
Abrams, Charles. *Man's Struggle for Shelter*. Cambridge, MA: MIT Press, 1964.
———. Vladimir Bodiansky, and Otto Koenigsberger. "Report on Housing in the Gold Coast." United Nations: Technical Assistance Programme, 1956.
Adam, Robert. *The Globalisation of Modern Architecture: The Impact of Politics, Economics and Social Change on Architecture and Urban Design since 1990*. Newcastle upon Tyne, UK: Cambridge Scholars, 2013.
Adams, Nicholas. *Skidmore, Owings and Merrill: SOM since 1936*. Milan: Electa Architecture, 2006.
Adeyemi, Ekundayo A. *In the Making of an Architect: The Zaria Experience*. Ota: Covenant University Press, 2012.
Agg, Desmond. *A Handbook on Semi-permanent Housing*. Lusaka: Government Printer, 1947.
Ahlman, Jeffrey S. *Living with Nkrumahism: Nation, State, and Pan-Africanism in Ghana*. Athens: Ohio University Press, 2017.
Ahmed, Ghouse Munir. "Morphology of Baghdad." *Iraqi Geographical Journal* 5 (1969): 1–26.
Akihary, Huib. *Architectuur & stedebouw in Indonesie 1870–1970*. Zutphen: De Walburg Pers, 1990.
Akinsemoyin, Kunle, and Alan Vaughan-Richards. *Building Lagos*. Jersey, UK: Pengrail, 1977.
Al-Abed, Ibrahim, Paula Vine, and Abdullah Al Jabali, eds. *Chronicle of Progress: 25 Years of Development in the United Arab Emirates*. London: Trident, 1996.
Al-Bahar, Huda. "Contemporary Kuwaiti Houses." *Mimar* 15 (1985): 63–72.
Alcock, Alfred, and Helga Richards. *How to Plan Your Village*. London: Longmans, Green, 1956.
Al-Madfai, Kahtan A. J. "Baghdad." In *The New Metropolis in the Arab World*, edited by Morroe Berger, 39–63. New Delhi: Allied Publishers, 1963.
Al-Moosa, Abdulrasool A. "Kuwait: Changing Environment in a Geographical Perspective." *British Society for Middle Eastern Studies: Bulletin* 11, no. 1 (1984): 45–57.
Al-Nakib, Farah. *Kuwait Transformed: A History of Oil and Urban Life*. Stanford, CA: Stanford University Press 2016.
———. "Public Space and Public Protest in Kuwait, 1938–2012." *City: Analysis of Urban Trends, Culture, Theory, Policy, Action* 18, no. 6 (2014): 723–34.
Alonso, Pedro, and Hugo Palmarola. "A Panel's Tale: The Soviet KPD System and the Politics of Assemblage." *AA Files* 59 (2009): 30–41.
Al-Radi, Abbad. "Constraints and Opportunities." In *The Architecture of the United Arab Emirates*, edited by Salma Samar Damluji, 121–37. Reading, UK: Garnet Publishing, 2006.
Al-Ragam, Asseel. "The Destruction of Modernist Heritage: The Myth of Al-Sawaber." *Journal of Architectural Education* 67, no. 2 (2013):

243–52.

AlSayyad, Nezar. "Medina; the 'Islamic,' 'Arab,' 'Middle Eastern' City: Reflections on an Urban Concept." In *Urban Design in the Arab World: Reconceptualizing Boundaries*, edited by Robert Saliba, 17–25. Farnham, UK: Ashgate, 2015.

Al-Siliq, Ghada. "Baghdad: Images and Memories." In *City of Mirages, Baghdad, from Wright to Venturi*, edited by Pedro Azara, 49–72. Barcelona: Universitat Politecnica de Catalunya, 2008.

——— [Al Slik], and Łukasz Stanek. "Department of Architecture, College of Engineering, University of Baghdad." *Volume* 45 (2015): 18–19.

"Aménagements touristiques en Hongrie." *L'architecture d'aujourd'hui* 116 (1964): 98–99.

Amhoff, Tilo, Nick Beech, and Katie Lloyd-Thomas, eds. *Industries of Architecture*. Basingstoke, UK: Taylor and Francis, 2015.

Amin, Samir. "The Challenge of Globalization." *Review of International Political Economy* 3, no. 2 (1996): 216–59.

Anderson, Richard. *Russia: Modern Architectures in History*. London: Reaktion Books, 2015.

Andreu, Paul. "Points de laison." *Mur vivant* 52 (1979): 30–32.

Anti-Taylor, William. *Moscow Diary*. London: Robert Hale, 1967.

Antoniak, Ilza. *Polska twórczość architektoniczna za granicą*. Kraków: PWN, 1972.

Apter, Andrew. *The Pan-African Nation: Oil and the Spectacle of Culture in Nigeria*. Chicago: University of Chicago Press, 2005.

Aradeon, David. "African Architectural Technology Exhibition." Lagos, 1977.

———. "Nigerian Architecture: Tradition and Change." In *Ezumeezu: Essays on Nigerian Art and Architecture: A Festschrift in Honour of Demas Nwoko*, edited by Chika Okeke-Agulu and Obiora Udechukwu, 23–28. Glassboro, NJ: Goldline and Jacobs, 2012.

———. "Space and House Form: Teaching Cultural Significance to Nigerian Students," *Journal of Architectural Education* 35, no. 1 (1981): 25–27.

Arayela, Olatunde. "An Introspection into Forty Years of Architectural Practice in Nigeria (1960–2000)—The Way Forward." In *Architects and Architecture in Nigeria: A Book of Readings in Honour of Professor Ekundayo Adeyinka Adeyemi*, edited by Uche Obisike Nkwogu, 91–107. Akure: Association of Architectural Educators in Nigeria, 2001.

Arku, Godwin. "The Economics of Housing Programmes in Ghana, 1929–66." *Planning Perspectives* 24, no. 3 (2009): 281–300.

Armah, Ayi Kwei. *The Beautyful Ones Are Not Yet Born*. London: Heinemann 1972.

Armstrong, Charles K. *Tyranny of the Weak: North Korea and the World, 1950–1992*. Ithaca, NY: Cornell University Press, 2013.

Arndt, Heinz Wolfgang. *Economic Development: The History of an Idea*. Chicago, London: University of Chicago Press, 1987.

Aronin, Jeffrey Ellis. *Climate and Architecture*. New York: Reinhold, 1953.

Artisien, Patrick F. R., and Peter J. Buckley. "Joint Ventures in Yugoslavia: Opportunities and Constraints." *Journal of International Business Studies* 16, no. 1 (1985): 111–35.

———, Carl H. McMillan, and Matija Rojec. *Yugoslav Multinationals Abroad*. Basingstoke, UK: Macmillan, 1992.

Asamoah, Obed Yao. *The Political History of Ghana (1950–2013): The Experience of a Non-Conformist*. Bloomington, IN: AuthorHouse UK, 2014.

Attwood, William. *The Reds and the Blacks: A Personal Adventure*. London: Hutchinson, 1967.

Avermaete, Tom, and Maristella Casciato. *Casablanca Chandigarh: A Report on Modernization*. Montréal: Canadian Centre for Architecture; Zürich: Park Books, 2014.

———, Serhat Karakayali, and Marion von Osten. *Colonial Modern: Aesthetics of the Past, Rebellions for the Future*. London: Black Dog Publishing, 2014.

Awgustinowitsch, Natalija. "RGW-COMECON-Hochhaus in Moskau/Le Building du COMECON à Moscou." *Werk/Oeuvre* 7 (1974): 854–55.

Azara, Pedro, ed. *City of Mirages: Baghdad, from Wright to Venturi*. Barcelona: Universitat Politecnica de Catalunya, 2008.

Azikiwe, Nnamdi. "Poland Wants Nigeria." *Weekly Mirror* (Liberia), August 28, 1936, 1.

"Bagdad—miasto z baśni 1001 nocy modernizowany przez krakowskich architektów." *Echo Krakowa*, March 24, 1967, 2.

Bajer, Kazimierz. "Program budownictwa mieszkaniowego dla Iraku na 20 lat." *Budownictwo Ogólne* A, no. 11 (1981): 19–23.

———, Jan Bulsza, Tadeusz Grabiński, and Aleksander Zeliaś. *Metody i modele programowania budownictwa mieszkaniowego*. Kraków: Akademia Ekonomiczna w Krakowie, 1989.

Bakić, Ljiljana. *Anatomija B&B arhitekture*. Belgrade: Ljiljana Bakić, 2012.

Bani Hashim, Alamira Reem. *Planning Abu Dhabi: An Urban History*. London: Routledge, 2019.

Barry, Andrew. "Technological Zones." *European Journal of Social Theory* 9, no. 2 (2006): 239–53.

Barth, Holger, et al., eds. *Vom Baukünstler zum Komplexprojektanten. Architekten in der DDR. Dokumentation eines IRS-Sammlungsbestandes biografischer Daten*. Erkner: IRS, 2000.

Barucki, Tadeusz. "Zbigniew Roman Dmochowski, 1906–1982." *Kwartalnik Architektury i Urbanistyki* XL, nos. 3–4 (1995): 245–50.

Basista, Andrzej. "Irak lat siedemdziesiątych." *Autoportret* 4 (2009): 58–63.

———. "Kadhemiya—zespół tradycyjnej zabudowy w Bagdadzie." *Kwartalnik architektury i urbanistyki* XXI, no. 3 (1976): 217–37.

———. *Opowieści budynków. Architektura czterech kultur*. Warsaw, Kraków: PWN, 1995.

———. "Plany przekształcenia Kadhemiyi, zabytkowej dzielnicy Bagdadu." *Kwartalnik architektury i urbanistyki* XXI, no. 4 (1976): 337–58.

Beeckmans, Luce. "The Adventures of the French Architect Michel Ecochard in Post-independence Dakar: A Transnational Development Expert Drifting between Commitment and Expediency." *Journal of Architecture* 19, no. 6 (2014): 849–71.

———. "The Architecture of Nation-building in Africa as a Development Aid Project: Designing the Capital Cities of Kinshasa (Congo) and Dodoma (Tanzania) in the Post-independence Years." *Progress in Planning* 122 (2018): 1–28. https://doi.org/10.1016/j.progress.2017.02.001.

Beyer, Elke. "Competitive Coexistence: Soviet Town Planning and Housing Projects in Kabul in the 1960s." *Journal of Architecture* 17, no. 3 (2012): 309–32.

Bhabha, Homi K. *The Location of Culture*. London: Routledge, 1994.

Białas, Tadeusz. *Liga Morska i Kolonialna: 1930–1939*. Gdańsk: Wydaw. Morskie, 1983.

Białostocki, Jan. "Some Values of Artistic Periphery." *Rocznik Muzeum Narodowego w Warszawie* 35 (1991 [1993]): 129–36.

Bianca, Stefano. *Urban Form in the Arab World: Past and Present*. London: Thames and Hudson, 2000.

Bianco, Silivia, and Isabella Reale, eds. *Marcello D'Olivo: Baghdad*. Udine: Gamud, 2009.

Bienek, Jan, and Jan Kulka. "Mapa Bagdadu." *Roczniki Geomatyki* 7, no. 1 (2009): 37–77.

Bierbauer, Virgil. *A magyar építészet története*. Budapest: Magyar Szemle Társaság, 1937.

———. "Nagy feladatok elött." *Tér és Forma* 2, no. 1 (1929): 1–3.

Billhardt, Thomas, and Peter Jacobs. *Die Drushba-Trasse*. Berlin: Verlag Neues Leben, 1978.

Bjažić Klarin, Tamara. *Ernest Weissmann društveno angažirana arhitektura, 1926–1939*. Zagreb: Hrvatska Akademija Znanosti i Umjetnosti, 2015.

Blackbourn, David. *The Conquest of Nature Water, Landscape, and the Making of Modern Germany*. London: Jonathan Cape, 2006.

Block, Fred. "Capitalism versus Socialism in World-Systems Theory." *Review (Fernand Braudel Center)* 13, no. 2 (1990): 265–71.

Boatcă, Manuela, *From Neoevolutionism to World Systems Analysis: The Romanian Theory of "Forms without Substance" in Light of Modern Debates on Social Change*. Opladen: Leske und Budrich, 2003.

Bockman, Johanna. "Socialist Globalization against Capitalist Neocolonialism: The Economic Ideas behind the New International Economic Order." *Humanity: An International Journal of Human Rights, Humanitarianism, and Development* 6, no. 1 (2015): 109–28.

Boden, Ragna. "Cold War Economics: Soviet Aid to Indonesia." *Journal of Cold War Studies* 10, no. 3 (2008): 110–28.

Bond, Max, John Falconer, and Charles Polónyi. *Transformation—Newformation: A Study, Illustrated by Student Work Selected from the Academic Year 1966–67*. Kumasi: Faculty of Architecture, University of Science and Technology, 1968.

———, and John Owusu-Addo. "Aspirations." *Arena, the Architectural Association Journal* (July–August 1966): 62.

Born, Robert, and Sarah Lemmen. "Einleitende Überlegungen zu Orientalismen in

Ostmitteleuropa." In *Orientalismen in Ostmitteleuropa*, edited by Robert Born and Sarah Lemmen, 9–28. Bielefeld: Transcript, 2014.

Bozdogan, Sibel. *Modernism and Nation Building: Turkish Architecture and Culture in the Early Republic*. Seattle: University of Washington Press, 2001.

Branczik, Márta. "Exporttervezési munkák." In *Közti 66. Egy tervezőiroda története (1949–1991)*, edited by András Ferkai, vol. 1, 393–453. Budapest: Vince Kiadó, 2015.

Brautigam, Deborah. *The Dragon's Gift: The Real Story of China in Africa*. Oxford: Oxford University Press, 2009.

Bremner, G. Alex. *Imperial Gothic: Religious Architecture and High Anglican Culture in the British Empire, c. 1840–70*. New Haven, CT: Yale University Press, 2013.

———, Johan Lagae, and Mercedes Volait. "Intersecting Interests: Developments in Networks and Flows of Information and Expertise in Architectural History." *Fabrications* 26, no. 2 (2016): 227–45. https://doi.org/10.1080/10331867.2016.1173167.

Brenner, Neil, and Christian Schmid. "Towards a New Epistemology of the Urban?" *City* 19, nos. 2–3 (2015): 151–82.

Browne, Kenneth. "Dubai." *Architectural Review* 161, no. 694 (June 1977): 362–79.

Brzost, Wojciech, and Julia Sułkowska-Kusztelak. "Kształcenie kadr dla krajów rozwijających się w państwach socjalistycznych." *Dydaktyka Szkoły Wyższej* 47, no. 3 (1979): 107–19.

Busch, Annett, and Anselm Franke, eds. *After Year Zero: Geographies of Collaboration*. Warsaw: Muzeum Sztuki Nowoczesnej w Warszawie, 2015.

Butcher, David, Laszlo Huszar, and Tudor G. Ingersoll, eds. *Bui Resettlement Study: A Report for the Ministry of Fuel and Power*. Kumasi: University of Science and Technology, 1966.

Butter, Andreas. "Showcase and Window to the World: East German Architecture Abroad, 1949–1990." *Planning Perspectives* (2017): 249–69. https://www.tandfonline.com/doi/full/10.1080/02665433.2017.1348969.

Carmichael, John. *Together We Build: Fifty Years of Taylor Woodrow in Ghana, 1947–1997*. London: Taylor Woodrow Construction Limited, 1997.

Carr, Jennifer. *Major Companies of Nigeria*. London: Graham and Trotman, 1983.

Casey, Michael S. *The History of Kuwait*. Westport, CT: Greenwood Press, 2007.

Çelik, Zeynep. *Empire, Architecture, and the City: French-Ottoman Encounters, 1830–1914*. Seattle, London: University of Washington Press, 2008.

Chadirji, Rifat. *Concepts and Influences: Towards a Regionalized International Architecture, 1952–1978*. London, New York: KPI, 1986.

Chang, Jiat-Hwee. *A Genealogy of Tropical Architecture: Colonial Networks, Nature and Technoscience*. London, New York: Routledge, 2016.

Chauhan, Akhtar. "Amanat Al Assima Housing." *Indian Institute of Architects Journal* 56, no. 2 (1991): 21–28.

Chen, Jian. "China and the Bandung Conference: Changing Perceptions and Representations." In *Bandung Revisited: The Legacy of the 1955 Asian-African Conference for International Order*, edited by See Seng Tan and Amitav Acharya, 132–59. Singapore: NUS Press, 2008.

Chernev, Mincho, Georgi Malchev, and Mitre Stamenov. *Dela na bulgarskite stroiteli i arkhitekti v chuzhbina/Bulgarian Engineering Achievements in Foreign Countries*. Sofia: Tekhnika, 1963.

Chmielewski, Jan, and Szymon Syrkus. *Warszawa funkcjonalna: przyczynek do urbanizacji regionu warszawskiego*. Warszawa: Wyd. TUP, 1934.

Chukhovich, Boris. "Orientalist Modes of Modernism in Architecture: Colonial/Postcolonial/Soviet." *Études de lettres* 2–3 (2014): 263–94.

Ciborowski, Adolf. *Town Planning in Poland, 1945–1955*. Warsaw: Polonia, 1956.

"Clarity of Plan." *Architects' Journal* 164, no. 35 (September 1, 1976): 390.

Cockburn, Charles. "Educating the Missing Man." *RIBA Journal* 11 (1965): 553–55.

Cody, Jeffrey W. *Exporting American Architecture, 1870–2000*. London: Routledge, 2003.

Collins, Paul D. *Administration for Development in Nigeria: Introduction and Readings*. Lagos: African Education Press, 1980.

"Conservation Projects." *Process: Architecture* 58 (May 1985): 101–11.

Contemporary Architecture of Kuwait. Jack-Art Production, 2013.

Cooper, Frederick, and Randall Packard, eds. *International Development and the Social Science: Essays on the History and Politics of Knowledge*. Berkeley: University of California Press, 1997.

Crawford, Christina E. "Soviet Planning Praxis: From Tractors to Territory." *Centerpiece/Weatherhead Center for International Affairs, Harvard University* 29, no. 2 (2015): 14–20.

Crinson, Mark. *Modern Architecture and the End of Empire*. Aldershot, UK: Ashgate, 2003.

Crowley, David, and Susan E. Reid, eds. *Pleasures in Socialism: Leisure and Luxury in the Eastern Bloc*. Evanston, IL: Northwestern University Press, 2010.

Culot, Maurice, and Thiveaud de Jean-Marie, eds. *Architectures françaises outre-mer*. Liège: Mardaga, 1992.

Cunha Matos, Madalena. "Colonial Architecture and Amnesia: Mapping the Work of Portuguese Architects in Angola and Mozambique." *OASE* 82 (2010): 25–34.

Cutler, Robert M. "East-South Relations at UNCTAD: Global Political Economy and the CMEA." *International Organization* 37, no. 1 (Winter 1983): 121–42.

"Czechoslovak Architects in the World." *Czechoslovak Foreign Trade* 28, no. 11 (1988): 30–31.

Dagne, Haile Gabriel. *Das entwicklungspolitische Engagement der DDR in Äthiopien: eine Studie auf der Basis äthiopischer Quellen*. Münster: Lit, 2004.

Dalton, John H. "Colony and Metropolis: Some Aspects of British Rule in Gold Coast and Their Implications for an Understanding of Ghana Today." *Journal of Economic History* 21, no. 4 (1961): 552–65.

Damluji, Salma Samar. "Brave New Cities." In *The Architecture of the United Arab Emirates*, edited by Salma Samar Damluji, 23–99. Reading, UK: Garnet Publishing, 2006.

———, ed. *The Architecture of the United Arab Emirates*. Reading, UK: Garnet Publishing, 2006.

Danby, Miles. *Grammar of Architectural Design: With Special Reference to the Tropics*. London: Oxford University Press, 1963.

d'Auria, Viviana. "From Tropical Transitions to Ekistic Experimentation: Doxiadis Associates in Tema, Ghana." *Positions* 1 (2010): 40–63.

———. "In the Laboratory and in the Field: Hybrid Housing Design for the African City in Late-Colonial and Decolonising Ghana (1945–57)." *Journal of Architecture* 19, no. 3 (2014): 329–56.

———. "More than Tropical? Modern Housing, Expatriate Practitioners and the Volta River Project in Decolonising Ghana." In *Cultures of Decolonisation: Transnational Productions and Practices, 1945–70*, edited by Ruth Craggs and Claire Wintle, 196–221. Manchester, UK: Manchester University Press, 2014.

———, and Bruno de Meulder. "Unsettling Landscapes: New Settlements for the Volta River Project between Tradition and Transition (1951–1970)." *OASE* 82 (2010): 115–38.

Davaa, Ayuushiyn. "Osnovnoi rychag razvitiia stroitel'nogo proizvodstva MNR." *Ekonomicheskoe Sotrudnichestvo Stran—Chlenov SEV* 2 (1977): 48–52.

Deamer, Peggy. "Architectural Work. Immaterial Labor." In *Industries of Architecture*, edited by Tilo Amhoff, Nick Beech, and Katie Lloyd Thomas, 137–47. London: Routledge, 2016.

———, ed. *The Architect as Worker: Immaterial Labor, the Creative Class, and the Politics of Design*. London: Bloomsbury, 2015.

Deluz, Jean-Jacques. *L'Urbanisme et l'architecture d'Alger*. Liège: P. Mardaga; Algiers: Office des publications universitaires, 1988.

Demchenko, Igor. "Decentralized Past: Heritage Politics in Post-Stalin Central Asia." *Future Anterior: Journal of Historic Preservation, History, Theory, and Criticism* 8, no. 1 (2011): 65–80.

De Raedt, Kim. "Between 'True Believers' and Operational Experts: UNESCO Architects and School Building in Post-colonial Africa." *Journal of Architecture* 19, no. 1 (2014): 19–42.

Dike, K. Onwuka. *The Nigerian Museum Movement*. Lagos: National Commission for Museums and Monuments, 1983.

Ding, Guanghui, and Charlie Q. L. Xue. "China's Architectural Aid: Exporting a Transformational Modernism." *Habitat International* 47 (2015): 136–47.

Dmochowski, Zbigniew. *The Architecture of Poland: A Historical Survey*. London: Polish Research Centre: London, 1956.

———. "Introduction." In *Studies in Polish Architecture*, edited by Jerzy Faczyński, n.p. Liverpool: Liverpool University Press, 1945.

——. *An Introduction to Nigerian Traditional Architecture*. London: Ethnographica; Lagos: National Commission for Museums and Monuments, 1990, 3 vols.

——. "Sprawozdanie z badawczych prac Zakładu Architektury Polskiej i Historji Sztuki Politechniki Warszawskiej w okresie letnim 1933." *Biuletyn historji sztuki i kultury* II, no. 2 (December 1933): 91–92.

——. "Sprawozdanie z pomiaru inwentaryzacyjnego na terenie pow. Stolińskiego, 17.VIII-12. IX.1933." *Biuletyn historji sztuki i kultury* II, no. 2 (December 1933): 93–98.

——. "Sprawozdanie ze studjów nad poleskiem budownictwem drzewnem w r. 1934/5." *Biuletyn historji sztuki i kultury* III, no. 4 (June 1934): 311–34.

Dolinka, Andrej, Katarina Krstić, and Dubravka Sekulić, eds. *Zoran Bojović: Tri tačke oslonca/ Three Points of Support*. Belgrade: Publikum, 2013.

Domosławski, Artur. *Kapuściński Non-Fiction*. Warszawa: Świat Książki, 2010.

"Dossier Lagos." *Cités africaines* 4 (1986): 19–43.

Doxiadis Associates. "The Master Plan of Baghdad." *DA Monthly Bulletin* 9 (1960).

——. "Progress of the Housing Program." *DA Monthly Report* 46 (May 1959).

Doytchinov, Grigor. "Pragmatism, Not Ideology: Bulgarian Architectural Exports to the 'Third World.'" *Journal of Architecture* 17, no. 3 (2012): 453–73.

Drew, Jane. "Recent Work by Fry, Drew, Drake & Partners; and Fry, Drew, Drake & Lasdun in West Africa." *Architectural Design* 25, no. 5 (May 1955): 137–74.

——, Michel Ecochard, and Maxwell Fry. "Deux études d'urbanisme applicables au Sénégal." 1962.

——, and E. Maxwell Fry. *Tropical Architecture in the Humid Zone*. London: Batsford, 1956.

——, E. Maxwell Fry, and Henry L. Ford. *Village Housing in the Tropics*. London: Lund Humphries, 1947.

Dziekan, Marek. "Polsko-irackie związki kulturalne/Polish-Iraqi Cultural Links." In *Słońce nad pustynią. Motywy arabskie w twórczości Romana Artymowskiego (1919–93)/The Sun over the Desert: Arabic Motives in the Work of Roman Artymowski (1919–93)*, edited by Jacek Macyszyn and Józef Grabski, 10–25. Kraków, Warsaw: IRSA, 2004.

"Educational Activity in Physical Planning for Developing Countries Carried Out at the Technical University of Szczecin 1966-84." Themed issue of *Town and Country Planning Research* 8 (1988).

"Einfamilienhäuser am Äquator." *Neue Heimat* 1 (1969): 34–35.

Einheitliche technische Bedingungen für die Projektierung von Betrieben und anderen Objekten, die in der Mongolischen Volksrepublik mit technischer Hilfe der Mitgliedsländer des RGW errichtet werden. Berlin: Bauakademie der DDR, 1976.

Elden, Stuart. "*Mondialisation* before Globalization: Lefebvre and Axelos." In *Space, Difference, Everyday Life: Reading Henri Lefebvre*, edited by Kanishka Goonewardena, Stefan Kipfer, Richard Milgrom, and Christian Schmid, 80–93. Routledge: New York, 2008.

Elsheshtawy, Yasser. "Cities of Sand and Fog: Abu Dhabi's Global Ambitions." In *The Evolving Arab City: Tradition, Modernity and Urban Development*, edited by Yasser Elsheshtawy, 258–304. London: Routledge, 2008.

——. *Dubai: Behind an Urban Spectacle*. New York: Routledge, 2010.

——, ed. *The Evolving Arab City: Tradition, Modernity and Urban Development*. London, New York: Routledge, 2008.

Enderlein, Fritz. *Handbuch der Außenhandelsverträge*. Berlin: Staatsverlag der DDR, 1979–84, 4 vols.

Energoprojekt, 60 Years of Success. Belgrade: Energoprojekt, 2011.

Energoprojekt 1951–1996. Belgrade: Energoprojekt, 1997.

Engerman, David. "The Second World's Third World." *Kritika: Explorations in Russian and Eurasian History* 12, no. 1 (2011): 183–212.

"English Dhabi Winner." *Architects' Journal* 164, no. 30 (July 28, 1976): 159.

Enwezor, Okwui, ed. *The Short Century: Independence and Liberation Movements in Africa 1945–1994*. Munich, London: Prestel, 2001.

"The Execution of Contract on Designing and Construction of Structures in Baghdad—Development Projects of Al Khulafa Street." *Izgradnja* V, no. 11 (2013): 56–65.

Fabbri, Roberto, Sara Saragoça, and Ricardo Camacho. *Modern Architecture Kuwait: 1949–1989*. Zurich: Niggli, 2016.

——, Sara Saragoça, and Ricardo Camacho, eds. *Essays, Arguments and Interviews on Modern Architecture Kuwait: 1949–1989*. Zurich: Niggli, 2018.

Fagg, Bernard. "The Museums of Nigeria." *Museum International* 16, no. 3 (1963): 124–48.

Falola, Toyin, and Matthew M. Heaton. *A History of Nigeria*. Cambridge: Cambridge University Press, 2008.

"Federal Military Government's Views on the Report of the Tribunal of Inquiry into the Finances of the Second World Black and African Festival of Arts and Culture." Lagos: Federal Ministry of Information, 1976.

Feniger, Neta. "Israeli Planning in the Shah's Iran: A Forgotten Episode." *Planning Perspectives* 30 (2014): 231–51.

——, and Rachel Kallus. "Building a 'New Middle East': Israeli Architects in Iran in the 1970s." *Journal of Architecture* 18, no. 3 (2013): 381–401.

Ferguson, Niall, Charles S. Maier, Erez Manela, and Daniel S. Sargent. *The Shock of the Global: The 1970s in Perspective*. Cambridge, MA; London: Belknap, 2010.

Ferkai, András, ed. *Közti 66. Egy tervezőiroda története (1949–1991)*. Budapest: Vince Kiadó, 2015, 2 vols.

Fethi, Ihsan. "Contemporary Architecture in Baghdad: Its Roots and Transition." *Process: Architecture* 58 (May 1985): 112–32.

Filippovich, Irina Nikolaevna. *Osobennosti ob"emno-planirovochnyh reshenii zhilishcha v usloviiakh zharkogo vlazhnogo klimata.*

Moscow: CINIS 1973.

"Fi mutaba'a taḥliliyah min ra'ys al-'itihad al-Kuwaytī li-tijarat wa-sina'at al-'inshā' li-taṣrihāt wazyr al-'isk ān." *Al-Siyāsah*, April 19, 1982, 7.

Firsanov, Vladimir M. *Arkhitektura grazhdanskikh zdanii v ulsoviiakh zharkogo klimata*. Moscow: Vysshaia shkola, 1971.

"First Progress Report on First State Development Plan, 1970/1974." Calabar: Ministry of Economic Development and Reconstruction, 1971.

"First State Development Plan, 1970–74." Calabar: Ministry of Economic Development and Reconstruction, 1971.

Folorunso, Caleb Adebayo. "Ekpo Okpo Eyo (1931–2011)." *Azania: Archaeological Research in Africa* 46, no. 3 (2011): 363–64.

Fox, W. C. "Baghdad: A City in Transition." *East Lakes Geographer* 5 (1969): 5–23.

Frampton, Kenneth. "Towards a Critical Regionalism: Six Points for an Architecture of Resistance." In *The Anti-aesthetic: Essays on Postmodern Culture*, edited by Hal Foster, 16–30. Port Townsend, WA: Bay Press, 1983.

Franch i Gilabert, Eva, Michael Kubo, Ana Miljački, and Ashley Schafer. *OfficeUS Atlas*. Baden: Lars Müller Publishers, 2015.

Fraser, Murray, and Nasser Golzari, eds. *Architecture and Globalisation in the Persian Gulf Region*. Farnham, Surrey, UK: Ashgate, 2013.

Friss, I. "Underdevelopment and Experiences of East-European Socialist Countries." *Acta Oeconomica* 9, nos. 3/4 (1972): 359–64.

Furtak, Zygmunt. "Eksport kompletnych obiektów przemysłowych." *Przegląd budowlany* 10 (1960): 446–49.

Gandhi, Leela. *Postcolonial Theory: A Critical Introduction*. Sydney: Allen and Unwin, 1998.

Gandy, Matthew. "Planning, Anti-planning and the Infrastructure Crisis Facing Metropolitan Lagos." *Urban Studies* 43, no. 2 (2006): 371–96.

Gardiner, Stephen. *Kuwait: The Making of a City*. London: Longman, 1983.

Gawlik, Jan Paweł. "Eksport polskiej architektury." *Życie Literackie* 22 (November 1964): 1.

Gdula, Maciej, in conversation with Michał Sutowski. "Gdula: Co nam zostało z lat 70?" June 4, 2016. http://krytykapolityczna.pl/.

"Ghana." *Edilizia Moderna* 89–90 (1967): 52–64.

"Ghana's Economic Prospects and the Ghana International Trade Fair." *Ghana Review* 7, no. 2 (1967): 9–17.

Giedion, Sigfrid. *Space, Time, and Architecture: The Growth of a New Tradition*. Cambridge, MA: Harvard University Press, 1944.

Gilman, Nils. *Mandarins of the Future: Modernization Theory in Cold War America*. Baltimore, MD: Johns Hopkins University Press, 2007.

Ginelli, Zoltán. "Hungarian Experts in Nkrumah's Ghana." *Mezosfera* (May 2018). http://mezosfera.org.

Ginsburgs, George, and Robert M. Slusser, eds. *A Calendar of Soviet Treaties, 1958–1973*. Alphen aan den Rijn, Netherlands: Sijthoff and Noordhoff, 1981.

Gleń, Włodzimierz. "Models for Urban and Rural

Housing." *Housing Science* 5, no. 4 (1981): 331–43.
Glendinning, Miles. *Modern Architect: The Life and Times of Robert Matthew*. London: RIBA, 2008.
Glissant, Édouard. *Poetics of Relation*. Ann Arbor: University of Michigan Press, 1997 [1990].
Gocking, Roger S. *The History of Ghana*. Westport, CT: Greenwood, 2005.
Godwin, John. "Nigeria: Building in a Boom Economy." *RIBA Journal* 88, no. 7 (1981): 35–40.
———, and Gillian Hopwood. *The Architecture of Demas Nwoko*. Lagos: Farafina, 2007.
———, and Gillian Hopwood. *Sandbank City: Lagos at 150*. Lagos: Kachifo Limited, 2012.
Gosk, Hanna. "Polski dyskurs kresowy w niefikcjonalnych zapisach międzywojennych. Próba lektury w perspektywie postcolonial studies." *Teksty Drugie* 6 (2008): 20–33.
Grabski, Józef, and Jacek Macyszyn, eds. *Słońce nad pustynią. Motywy arabskie w twórczości Romana Artymowskiego (1919–93)/The Sun over the Desert: Arabic Motives in the Work of Roman Artymowski (1919–93)*. Kraków, Warsaw: IRSA, 2004.
Gräfe, Bernhard. "Urbanisierung und städtebauliche Planung im Irak." *Wissenschaftliche Zeitschrift der Technischen Universität Dresden* 23, no. 2 (1974): 479–87.
Grove, David, and Laszlo Huszar. *The Towns of Ghana*. Accra: Ghana Universities Press, 1964.
Grozdanova, Sasha, and Michel Vale. "Trade and Economic Relations between Bulgaria and the Arab Countries." *Soviet and Eastern European Foreign Trade* 21, nos. 1–3 (1985): 120–28.
Grzywnowicz, Stanisław, and Jerzy Kiedrzyński. *Prawa i obowiązki specjalisty*. Warsaw: Wydawnictwa UW, 1972.
Györffy, István. "Az alföldi parasztház." *Tér és Forma* 2, no. 1 (1929): 17–23.
Gyuse, Ruth Shinenge, and Timothy Terver Gyuse. "Kainji Resettlement Housing: 40 Years Later." *Journal of Urbanism* 1, no. 3 (2008): 247–64.
Gzowska, Alicja. "Exporting Working Patterns: Polish Conservation Workshops in the Global South during the Cold War." *ABE Journal* 6 (2014). https://journals.openedition.org/abe/1268.
———, and Lidia Klein, eds. *Postmodernizm polski: architektura i urbanistyka*. Warszawa: 40000 Malarzy, 2013, 2 vols.
Hadik, András. "Nationale und volkstümliche Einflüsse in der ungarischen Baukunst der 1940er und 1950er Jahre/National and Traditional Influences in Hungarian Architecture in the 1940s and 1950s." In *Ungarn: Bauten der Aufbruchszeit 1945–60/Hungary: Architecture in the Era of Awakening*, 124–37. Salzburg: Müry Salzmann, 2014.
Haefele, Michael. "Walt Rostow's Stages of Economic Growth: Ideas and Action." In *Staging Growth: Modernization, Development, and the Global Cold War*, edited by David C. Engerman, Nils Gilma, and Mark H. Haefele, 81–103. Amherst: University of Massachusetts Press, 2003.
"Haifa Street Development." *Process: Architecture* 58 (May 1985): 73–88.
Hakim, Besim Selim. "Co-op Housing, Baghdad: An Evaluation and Recommendations." *Ekistics* 33, no. 196 (1972): 166–72.
Hamilton, Geoffrey. "Conclusion." In *Red Multinationals or Red Herrings?: The Activities of Enterprises from Socialist Countries in the West*, edited by Geoffrey Hamilton, 185–94. London: Frances Pinter, 1986.
Hartmetz, Anne-Kristin, Bence Kocsev, and Jan Zofka. "East-South Relations during the Global Cold War: Economic Activities and Area Studies Interests of East Central European CMEA Countries in Africa." *SFB 1199 Working Paper* 11 (June 2018). www.research.uni-leipzig.de.
Hartung, Ulrich. "Der Industriearchitekt Egon Mahnkopf." *kunstextc.de* 2 (2002). http://www.kunsttexte.de.
Hasty, Jennifer. *The Press and Political Culture in Ghana*. Bloomington: Indiana University Press, 2005.
Healey, Patsy, and Robert Upton, eds. *Crossing Borders: International Exchange and Planning Practices*. London: Routledge, 2010.
Hein, Carola, Jeffry Diefendorf, and Yorifusa Ishida, eds. *Rebuilding Urban Japan after 1945*. London: Palgrave Macmillan, 2003.
Held, Joseph. *Modernization of Agriculture: Rural Transformation in Hungary 1848–1975*. Boulder, CO: East European Monographs, 1980.
Hess, Janet B. "Imagining Architecture [I]: The Structure of Nationalism in Accra, Ghana." *Africa Today* 47, no. 2 (2000): 35–58.
———. "Imagining Architecture II: 'Treasure Storehouses' and Constructions of Asante Regional Hegemony," *Africa Today* 50, no. 1 (2003): 27–48.
Hirsh, Max. "Post-Modern Architectural Exchanges between East Germany and Japan." In *Re-Framing Identities: Architecture's Turn to History, 1970–1990*, edited by Ákos Moravánszky and Torsten Lange, 73–88. Basel: Birkhäuser, 2017.
Hirt, Sonia, Slavomíra Ferenčuhová, and Tauri Tuvikene. "Conceptual Forum: The 'Post-socialist' City." *Eurasian Geography and Economics* 57, nos. 4–5 (2016): 497–520.
Holod, Renata, and Darl Rastorfer, eds. *Architecture and Community: Building in the Islamic World Today: The Aga Khan Award for Architecture*. Millerton, NY: Aperture, 1983.
Hong, Young-Sun. "Through a Glass Darkly: East German Assistance to North Korea and Alternative Narratives of the Cold War." In *Comrades of Color: East Germany in the Cold War World*, edited by Quinn Slobodian, 43–72. New York, Oxford: Berghahn Books, 2015.
"Hôtel de ville d'Abu Dhabi." *Mur vivant* 60 (1981): 27–29.
"How a Yugoslav Company Built an International Market." *New York Times*, March 28, 1983. http://www.nytimes.com/.
Hutchinson, Bruce G., and Galal M. Said. "Spatial Differentiation, Transport Demands, and Transport Model Design in Kuwait." *Transport Reviews* 10, no. 2 (1990): 91–110.
Huwysh, ʿaqīl Nūrī. *al-ʿamārat al-hadithat fi al-ʿiraq: tahlīl moqāran fi handasat al-ʿamārat w al-takhṭīṭ*. Baghdad: Dār al-Shuʾūn al-Thaqāfiyyat al-ʿāmat, 1988.

I. C. "In Memoriam Miro Marasović." *Građevinar* 56 (2004): 323.
Iandolo, Alessandro. "The Rise and Fall of the 'Soviet Model of Development' in West Africa, 1957–64." *Cold War History* 12, no. 4 (2012): 683–704.
Ihekwaba, Stanley. "The Nigerian Institute of Architects, N.I.A." In *Nigeria: The First 25 Years*, edited by Uma Eleazu, 292–96. Lagos: Infodata, 1988.
"Il nuovo Eldorado." Themed issue of *Domus* 595 (1979).
Immerman, Richard H., and Petra Goedde, eds. *The Oxford Handbook of the Cold War*. Oxford: Oxford University Press, 2013.
Immerwahr, Daniel. "The Politics of Architecture and Urbanism in Postcolonial Lagos, 1960–1986." *Journal of African Cultural Studies* 19, no. 2 (2007): 165–86.
Information Book: Hospitals and Dispensaries. Lagos: PWD, 1939.
Isenstadt, Samuel. "'Faith in a Better Future': Josep Lluis Sert's American Embassy in Baghdad." *Journal of Architectural Education* 50, no. 3 (1997): 172–88.
———, and Kishwar Rizvi, eds. *Modernism and the Middle East: Architecture and Politics in the Twentieth Century*. Seattle: University of Washington Press, 2008.
Jackson, Iain. "The Architecture of the British Mandate in Iraq: Nation-Building and State Creation." *Journal of Architecture* 21, no. 3 (2016): 375–417.
———, and Jessica Holland. *The Architecture of Edwin Maxwell Fry and Jane Drew: Twentieth Century Architecture, Pioneer Modernism and the Tropics*. Burlington, VT: Ashgate, 2014.
———, and Nwola Uduku. "Sub-Saharan Africa." In *Architecture and Urbanism in the British Empire*, edited by Alex Bremner, 393–422. Oxford: Oxford University Press, 2016.
Jacobsen, Hanns-Dieter. "Strategy and Focal Points of GDR Foreign Trade." *International Journal of Politics* 12, nos. 1–2 (1982): 125–50.
Jalal, Ferhang. *The Role of Government in the Industrialization of Iraq, 1950–1965*. London: Cass, 1972.
Jałowiecki, Bohdan. *Procesy rozwoju społecznego współczesnej Algierii*. Warszawa: PWN, 1978.
Jamal, Karim. "Destruction of the Middle East?" *Architects' Journal* 164, no. 30 (July 28, 1976): 161–62.
James-Chakraborty, Kathleen. "Beyond Postcolonialism: New Directions for the History of Nonwestern Architecture." *Frontiers of Architectural Research* 3, no. 1 (2014): 1–9.
———. "Reinforced Concrete in Louis Kahn's National Assembly, Dhaka: Modernity and Modernism in Bangladeshi Architecture." *Frontiers of Architectural Research* 3, no. 2 (2014): 81–88.
Jankowski, Stanisław. "Warszawski architekt w biblijnym raju." *Stolica* 51–52 (1962): 10–11.
Jaskot, Paul B. *The Architecture of Oppression: The SS, Forced Labor and the Nazi Monumental Building Economy*. London: Routledge, 2005.
Jędraszko, Andrzej. "Problemy urbanistyczne Bagdadu." *Miasto* 2 (1962): 9–18.
Jones, Peter. *Ove Arup: Masterbuilder of the*

Twentieth Century. New Haven, CT: Yale University Press, 2006.

Jopp, Keith. *Ghana: Ten Great Years, 1951–1960*. Accra: Ghana Information Services, 1960.

Juraszyński, Władysław. "'Budimex'—największy polski eksporter budownictwa." *Przegląd budowlany* 5 (1989): 197–99.

Kaftanov, Andrey. "From International Architecture to Architectural Internationalism." *Project Russia* 16 (2000): 19–24.

Kalinovsky, Artemy. *Laboratory of Socialist Development: Cold War Politics and Decolonization in Soviet Tajikistan*. Ithaca, NY: Cornell University Press, 2018.

Kalinowski, Wojciech. "Prace Jana Zachwatowicza nad spuścizną dziejów architektury w Polsce." *Ochrona Zabytków* 37, no. 2 (1984): 89–91.

Kaliński, Janusz. "Rubel transferowy." *Kwartalnik Kolegium Ekonomiczno-Społecznego. Studia i Prace* 3 (2013): 147–67.

Kalter, Christoph. *The Discovery of the Third World: Decolonization and the Rise of the New Left in France, c. 1950–1976*. Cambridge: Cambridge University Press, 2016.

Kaniewski, Przemysław. *Polska Szkoła Architektury w Wielkiej Brytanii 1942–1954*. Warsaw: Marek Woch, 2013.

Kapuściński, Ryszard. *Gdyby cała Afryka*. Warsaw: Agora, 2011 [1971].

Karagozov, Georgi, et al., eds. *Dictionary of Civil Engineering in Twelve Languages: Bulgarian, Czech, German, Hungarian, Mongolian, Polish, Rumanian, Serbo-Croatian, Spanish, English and French*. Moscow: Russian Language Publishers, 1979.

Karczewski, Anoni. "Uwagi o mierzeniu zabytków." *Ochrona Zabytków Sztuki* 2 (1930–31): 395–402.

Karimi, Zahra Pamela. *Domesticity and Consumer Culture in Iran: Interior Revolutions of the Modern Era*. London, New York: Routledge, 2013.

Katsakioris, Constantin. "Creating a Socialist Intelligentsia: Soviet Educational Aid and Its Impact on Africa (1960–1991)." *Cahiers d'études africaines* 2 (2017): 259–88.

———. "Soviet Lessons for Arab Modernization: Soviet Educational Aid to Arab Countries after 1956." *Journal of Modern European History* 8, no. 1 (2010): 85–106.

Khrushchev, Nikita S. *Memoirs of Nikita Khrushchev*. Providence, RI: Brown University, 2004-7, 3 vols.

Kidd, W. J. "Ahmadu Bello University, Zaria, Nigeria." In *The Architectural Task in Africa Education and the Profession: Final Report and Seminar Papers of a Seminar Held in Nairobi Kenya, 6th and 7th March 1969*, 43–44. Nairobi: United Africa Press, 1968.

Kim, Mina, and Inha Jung. "The Planning of Microdistricts in Post-War North Korea: Space, Power, and Everyday Life." *Planning Perspectives* 32, no. 2 (2017): 199–223.

King, Anthony D. *The Bungalow: The Production of a Global Culture*. London: Routledge and Kegan Paul, 1984.

———, ed. *Urbanism, Colonialism, and the World-Economy: Cultural and Spatial Foundations of the World Urban System*. London: Routledge, 1991.

Kirasirova, Masha. "'Sons of Muslims' in Moscow: Soviet Central Asian Mediators to the Foreign East, 1955–1962." *Ab Imperio* 4 (2011): 106–32.

Kirn, Gal. "Contradictions of Yugoslav Self-management: Class Struggle after the 1965 Market Reform." In *Monuments Should Not Be Trusted*, edited by Linda Džuverović, 100–112. Nottingham, UK: Nottingham Contemporary, 2016.

Kiselevich, L. N., V. A. Kossakovskii, and O. I. Rzhekhina. *Zhilishchnoe stroitel'stvo v usloviiakh zharkogo klimata za rubezhom*. Moscow: Stroiizdat, 1965.

Kłosiewicz, Lech. "Uczące w Bagdadzie." *Polska* 7 (1976): 38, 52–53.

Koenigsberger, Otto, Charles Abrams, Susumu Kobe, Maurice Shapiro, and Michael Wheeler. *Metropolitan Lagos*. New York: United Nations, Commissioner for Technical Assistance, 1964.

Kohlrausch, Martin. "Poland: Planning a European Capital for a New State." In *Atlas of the Functional City: CIAM 4 and Comparative Urban Analysis*, edited by Evelien van Es, Gregor Harbusch, Bruno Maurer, Muriel Pérez, Kees Somer, Daniel Weiss, 320–33. Bussum: Thot, 2014.

Konadu-Agyemang, Kwadwo. "Housing Conditions and Spatial Organization in Accra, 1950s-1990s." *Ghana Studies* 1 (1998): 63–90.

Koós, Károly. "Az erdélyi magyar parasztház." *Tér és Forma* 2, no. 1 (1929): 215–19.

Kornai, János. *The Socialist System: The Political Economy of Communism*. Princeton, NJ: Princeton University Press, 1992.

Kosel, Gerhard. *Unternehmen Wissenschaft: Die Wiederentdeckung einer Idee: Erinnerungen*. Berlin: Henschelverlag Kunst und Gesellschaft, 1989.

Kotkin, Stephen. "The Kiss of Debt: The East Bloc Goes Borrowing." In *The Shock of the Global: The 1970s in Perspective*, edited by Niall Ferguson, Charles S. Maier, Erez Manela, and Daniel S. Sargent, 80–93. Cambridge, MA; London: Belknap, 2010.

Kott, Sandrine. "Cold War Internationalism." In *Internationalisms: A Twentieth-Century History*, edited by Glenda Sluga and Patricia Clavin, 340–62. Cambridge: Cambridge University Press, 2016.

———. *Communism Day-to-Day: State Enterprises in East German Society*. Ann Arbor: University of Michigan Press, 2014.

———. "The Forced Labor Issue between Human and Social Rights, 1947–1957." *Humanity: An International Journal of Human Rights, Humanitarianism, and Development* 3, no. 3 (Winter 2012): 321–35.

Kozłowski, Dariusz. *Dawny dom iracki*. Kraków: Politechnika Krakowska, 1990.

Kraft, Gerhard. *Die Zusammenarbeit der Mitgliedsländer des RWG auf dem Gebiet der Investitionen*. Berlin: Akademie-Verlag, 1977.

Kret, Abigail Judge. "'We Unite with Knowledge.' The Peoples' Friendship University and Soviet Education for the Third World." *Comparative Studies of South Asia, Africa and the Middle East* 33, no. 2 (2013): 239–56.

Krunić, Jovan. "Architectural Traditions and New Architecture in Iraq: The House of Baghdad, Its Old and Modern Concept, an Examination of the Elements and Methods of a Contemporary Synthesis." *Sumer: A Journal of Archaeology and History in Iraq* 18, nos. 1-2 (1962): 33–47.

Krzysztof Wiśniowski, Anna Wiśniowska, Magdalena Wiśniowska, Jan Wiśniowski: 1969–2006. Wrocław: Muzeum Architektury, 2006.

Kula, Marcin. "Między wspomnieniami a badaniem historycznym: Kalecki i Zakład Krajów Słabo Rozwiniętych w Warszawie w latach 1962–1968." *Zdanie* 3-4 (2012): 56–61.

Kulić, Vladimir. "Building the Non-Aligned Babel: Babylon Hotel in Baghdad and Mobile Design in the Global Cold War." *ABE Journal* 6 (2014). https://abe.revues.org.

———. "National, Supranational, International: New Belgrade and the Symbolic Construction of a Socialist Capital." *Nationalities Papers* 41, no. 1 (2013): 35–63.

Kultermann, Udo. *Contemporary Architecture in the Arab States: Renaissance of a Region*. New York, London: McGraw-Hill, 1999.

"Kwame Nkrumah Commercial Area—Accra, Ghana." *Ekistics* 12 (1961): 110–25.

Lagae, Johan, and Denise Laurens. *Claude Laurens: Architecture. Projets et réalisations de 1934 à 1971*. Ghent: Vakgroep Architectuur en Stedenbouw, Universiteit Gent, 2001.

———, and Kim de Raedt. "Global Experts 'Off Radar.'" Themed issue of *ABE Journal* 4 (2013). http://journals.openedition.org/abe/485?lang=en.

———, and Bernard Toulier. "De l'outre-mer au transnational: glissements de perspectives dans l'historiographie de l'architecture coloniale et postcoloniale." *Revue de l'art* 186 (2014): 45–56.

Lampe, John R. *Yugoslavia as History: Twice There Was a Country*. Cambridge: Cambridge University Press, 2000 [1996].

Lange, Torsten. "Form as/and Utopia of Collective Labour: Typification and Collaboration in East German Industrialised Construction." In *Industries of Architecture*, edited by Katie Lloyd-Thomas, Tilo Amhoff, and Nick Beech, 148–59. London: Routledge, 2016.

Lawson, Colin W. "National Independence and Reciprocal Advantages: The Political Economy of Romanian-South Relations." *Soviet Studies* 35, no. 3 (1983): 362–75.

Łazowski, Zygmunt, et al. *Polacy w Nigerii*. Warszawa: Dialog, 1997, 4 vols.

Le Caisne, Rémi. "Les conditions de l'architecture en Afrique tropicale." *Techniques et Architecture* 5-6 (1952): 45–48.

Lee, Rachel. "Negotiating Modernities: Otto Koenigsberger's Works and Network in Exile (1933–1951)." *ABE Journal* 5 (2014). http://dev.abejournal.eu/index.php?id=696.

———, Diane Barbé, Anne-Katrin Fenk, and Philipp Misselwitz, eds. *Things Don't Really Exist Until You Give Them a Name: Unpacking Urban Heritage*. Dar es Salaam: Mkuki na Nyota, 2017.

Lefebvre, Henri. *The Production of Space*. Oxford: Blackwell, 1991 [1974].

———. *The Urban Revolution*. Minneapolis: University of Minnesota Press, 2003 [1970].

Lefebvre, Henri. "The Worldwide Experience." In *State, Space, World: Selected Essays*, edited by Neil Brenner and Stuart Elden, 274–89. Minneapolis: University of Minnesota Press, 2009 [1978].

Legvold, Robert. *Soviet Policy in West Africa*. Cambridge, MA: Harvard University Press, 1970.

Le Normand, Brigitte. *Designing Tito's Capital: Urban Planning, Modernism, and Socialism in Belgrade*. Pittsburgh: University of Pittsburgh Press, 2014.

Le Roux, Hannah. "The Networks of Tropical Architecture." *Journal of Architecture* 8, no. 3 (September 2003): 337–54.

"Lessons from the Fair," *Africa* 78 (1978): 110.

Leszczyński, Adam. *Skok w nowoczesność: polityka wzrostu w krajach peryferyjnych 1943–1980*. Warszawa: PAN, 2013.

Levin, Ayala. "Haile Selassie's Imperial Modernity: Expatriate Architects and the Shaping of Addis Ababa." *JSAH* 75, no. 4 (December 2016): 447–68.

Levine, Neil. *The Urbanism of Frank Lloyd Wright*. Princeton, NJ: Princeton University Press, 2016.

Lewicki, Jakub. "Inwentaryzacja zabytków w okresie dwudziestolecia międzywojennego." *Ochrona Zabytków* 52, no. 4 (1999): 375–90.

Liberska, Barbara. *Polska—Irak: gospodarka, stosunki ekonomiczne*. Warsaw: PWE, 1982.

Livsey, Timothy. "'Suitable Lodgings for Students': Modern Space, Colonial Development and Decolonization in Nigeria." *Urban History* 41, no. 4 (2014): 664–85.

London Survey Committee. *Survey of London*. Vol. 27, *Spitalfields and Mile End New Town*. London: Athlone, 1957.

López, Julio G., and Michaël Assous. *Michal Kalecki*. New York: Palgrave Macmillan, 2010.

Lorenzini, Sara. "Comecon and the South in the Years of Détente: A Study on East–South Economic Relations." *European Review of History* 21, no. 2 (2014): 183–99.

Lu, Duanfang. *Third World Modernism: Architecture, Development and Identity*. New York: Routledge, 2011.

Luuyuugiyn, Lhamsurien. "Pomoshch bratskikh stran v uskorenii razvitiia i povyshenii effektivnosti ekonomiki MNR." *Ekonomicheskoe Sotrudnichestvo Stran—Chlenov SEV* 1 (1977): 25–30.

Lynn, Hyung-Gu. "Globalization and the Cold War." In *The Oxford Handbook of the Cold War*, edited by Richard H. Immerman and Petra Goedde, 584–601. Oxford: Oxford University Press, 2013.

Mabogunje, Akin Ladipo. *Urbanization in Nigeria*. New York: Africana, 1969.

Madden, David J. "City Becoming World: Nancy, Lefebvre, and the Global–Urban Imagination." *Environment and Planning D: Society and Space* 30, no. 5 (2012): 772–87.

Magyar, Peter. *Thought Palaces*. Amsterdam: Architectura and Natura, 1999.

Maier, Jörg, Andreas Huber, and P. O. Adeniyi. *Lagos: Stadtentwicklung einer afrikanischen Metropole zwischen hoher Dynamik und Chaos*. Cologne: Aulis Verlag Deubner, 1989.

Makiya, Kanan. *The Monument: Art, Vulgarity, and Responsibility in Iraq*. Berkeley: University of California Press, 1991.

———. *Post-Islamic Classicism: A Visual Essay on the Architecture of Mohamed Makiya*. London: Saqi Books, 1990.

Makiya, Mohamed. "The Use of Experts in Developing Countries." *Ekistics* 18, no. 107 (1964): 228–29.

Malisz, Bolesław. "Urban Planning Theory: Methods and Results." In *City and Regional Planning in Poland*, edited by Jack C. Fisher, 57–84. Ithaca, NY: Cornell University Press, 1966.

Maner, Hans-Christian. *Galizien. Eine Grenzregion im Kalkül der Donaumonarchie im 18. und 19. Jahrhundert*. Munich: IKGS Verlag, 2007.

Manević, Zoran. *Stojan Maksimović: Stvaralaštvo*. Belgrade: Centar VAM, 2006.

Mark, James, and Quinn Slobodian. "Eastern Europe." In *The Oxford Handbook of the Ends of Empire*, edited by Martin Thomas and Andrew Thompson. Oxford Handbooks Online, 2017. https://doi.org/10.1093/oxfordhb/9780198713197.013.20.

Marr, Phebe. *The Modern History of Iraq*. Boulder, CO; Oxford: Westview, 2004.

Marris, Peter. *Family and Social Change in an African City: A Study of Rehousing in Lagos*. London: Routledge and Paul, 1961.

Marthelot, Pierre. "Bagdad, notes de géographie urbaine." Part 1: *Annales de Géographie* 74, no. 401 (1965): 24–37, and part 2: *Annales de Géographie* 84, no. 464 (1975): 442–53.

Martin, Reinhold. *Utopia's Ghost: Architecture and Postmodernism, Again*. Minneapolis: University of Minnesota Press, 2010.

Masey, Jack, and Conway Morgan. *Cold War Confrontations: US Exhibitions and Their Role in the Cultural Cold War*. Baden: Lars Müller, 2008.

"Master Plan for Metropolitan Lagos. Executive Summary. Prepared by UNDP Sub-Contractor Wilbur Smith and Associates." July 1980.

Matsubara, Kosuke. "Gyoji Banshoya (1930–1998): A Japanese Planner Devoted to Historic Cities in the Middle East and North Africa." *Planning Perspectives* 31, no. 3 (2016): 391–423.

Mazov, Sergey. *A Distant Front in the Cold War: The USSR in West Africa and the Congo, 1956–1964*. Washington, DC: Woodrow Wilson Center Press, 2010.

Mazower, Mark. *Governing the World: The Rise and Fall of an Idea*. London: Allen Lane, 2012.

Mazurek, Małgorzata. "Co się stało z polską szkołą (rozwoju)?" *Krytyka polityczna*, January 22, 2016. http://krytykapolityczna.pl/.

———. "Polish Economists in Nehru's India: Making Science for the Third World in an Era of De-Stalinization and Decolonization." *Slavic Review* 77, no. 3 (2018): 588–610.

McCann, Eugene, Ananya Roy, and Kevin Ward. "Assembling/Worlding Cities." *Urban Geography*, 34, no. 5 (2013): 581–89.

McMillan, Carl H. *Multinationals from the Second World: Growth of Foreign Investment by Soviet and East European Enterprises*. London: Macmillan, 1987.

McNeill, Donald. *The Global Architect: Firms, Fame and Urban Form*. London, New York: Routledge, 2009.

Mëhilli, Elidor. *From Stalin to Mao: Albania and the Socialist World*. Ithaca, NY: Cornell University Press, 2017.

Meuser, Philipp, and Dimitrij Zadorin. *Towards a Typology of Soviet Mass Housing: Prefabrication in the USSR 1955–1991*. Berlin: DOM Publishers, 2015.

Miescher, Stephan F., and Dzodzi Tsikata. "Hydro-Power and the Promise of Modernity and Development in Ghana: Comparing the Akosombo and Bui Dam Projects." *Ghana Studies* 12–13 (2009/2010): 15–53.

Mironov, S. A., and E. N. Malinskii. *Osnovy tekhnologii betona v usloviiakh sukhogo zharkogo klimata*. Moscow: Stroiizdat, 1985.

Mitchell, Timothy. "Economentality: How the Future Entered Government." *Critical Inquiry* 40, no. 4 (2014): 479–507.

Mitrović, Mihajlo. *Na kraju veka: arhitektura Energoprojekta 1951–1995/At the Turn of the Century: The Architecture of Energoprojekt between 1951–1995*. Belgrade: Energoprojekt, 1995.

Moggridge, Hal. "A Dagarti Farmhouse at Mousyiri, Near Lawra, Upper Region, Ghana." *Arena: Architectural Association Journal* 82 (July–August 1966): 42–44.

Möller, Harald. *DDR und Dritte Welt: Die Beziehungen der DDR mit Entwicklungsländern, ein neues theoretisches Konzept, dargestellt anhand der Beispiele China und Äthiopien sowie Irak/Iran*. Berlin: Köster, 2004.

Moravánszky, Ákos. "Peripheral Modernism: Charles Polónyi and the Lessons of the Village." *Journal of Architecture* 17, no. 3 (2012): 333–59.

———, ed. *Das entfernte Dorf: Moderne Kunst und ethnischer Artefakt*. Wien: Böhlau, 2002.

Morris, Milton D. "The Soviet Africa Institute and the Development of African Studies." *Journal of Modern African Studies* 11, no. 2 (1973): 247–65.

Moseley, Malcolm J., and Peter R. Smith. "Hungary: Urban and Rural Planning." *Town and Country Planning* 48 (1979): 85–87.

Moughtin, J. C., ed. *The Work of Z. R. Dmochowski: Nigerian Traditional Architecture*. London: Ethnographica, 1988.

Muehlenbeck, Philip. *Czechoslovakia in Africa, 1945–1968*. New York: Palgrave Macmillan, 2016.

Mühlfriedel, Wolfgang, and Edith Hellmuth. *Carl Zeiss in Jena: 1945–1990*. Köln: Böhlau, 2004.

Mumford, Eric. *The CIAM Discourse on Urbanism, 1928–1960*. Cambridge, MA: MIT Press, 2000.

Murawski, Michał. "Actually-Existing Success: Economics, Aesthetics, and the Specificity of (Still-)Socialist Urbanism." *Comparative Studies in Society and History* 60, no. 4 (2018): 1–31.

Najder, Zdzisław. *Joseph Conrad—A Chronicle*. Cambridge: Cambridge University Press, 1983.

Nancy, Jean-Luc. *The Creation of the World, or, Globalization*. Albany: State University of New York Press, 2007.

Nasr, Joe. "Saba Shiber, 'Mr Arab Planner.'"

Parcours professionnel d'un urbaniste au Moyen-Orient." *Géocarrefour* 80, no. 3 (2005): 197–206.

———, and Mercedes Volait. *Urbanism: Imported or Exported? Native Aspirations and Foreign Plans*. London: Academy Editions, 2003.

The National Action Charter: Proclaimed by President Ahmed Hassan al-Bakr on November 15th 1971. Baghdad: Ministry of Information, 1971.

National Housing Authority (Kuwait). *National Housing Programme*. London: Buchanan, 1976, 5 vols.

"National Physical Development Plan, 1963–1970." Accra: Ghana Town and Country Planning Division, 1965.

Nawrocki, Joachim. "Kombinat für die Genossen." *Die Zeit* 13 (1975). http://www.zeit.de/.

"Neue Heimat International: In vier Kontinenten tätig." *Neue Heimat* 1 (1970): 63–70.

Neveling, Patrick. "The Global Spread of Export Processing Zones and the 1970s as a Decade of Consolidation." In *Changes in Social Regulation—State, Economy, and Social Protagonists since the 1970s*, edited by Knud Andersen and Stefan Müller, 23–40. Oxford: Berghahn Books, 2017.

Newman, Oscar. *CIAM '59 in Otterlo*. Stuttgart: Krämer, 1961.

Nigeria Public Works Department Specifications. Lagos: PWD, 1938.

Nitzan-Shiftan, Alona. "Contested Zionism-Alternative Modernism: Erich Mendelsohn and the Tel Aviv Chug in Mandate Palestine." *Architectural History* 39 (1996): 147–80.

Norberg-Schulz, Christian. *Existence, Space and Architecture*. London: Studio Vista, 1971.

Nowakowska, Joanna. *Osiągnięcia polskich architektów ostatnich dziesięcioleci XX wieku na arenach międzynarodowych (ukierunkowanie na kraje basenu Morza Śródziemnego)—wybrane kraje arabskie—kraje Bliskiego Wschodu. Katalog*. Warsaw: Politechnika Warszawska, 2003-4, 2 vols.

Nowakowska, Zofia. *Metoda określania standardu mieszkaniowego na przykładzie Iraku*. Kraków: Politechnika Krakowska, 1986.

Ntukidem, Anam E. "Calabar Master Plan: An Examination of an Urban Planning Strategy." In *Calabar and Environs: Geographic Studies*, edited by P.E.B. Inyang et al., 63–89. Calabar: University of Calabar, 1980.

Nwaka, Geoffrey I. "Land Administration and Urban Development: A Nigerian Case Study." *Civilisations* 30, nos. 1–2 (1980): 73–82.

Obeidat, Hayssam. *Stosunki Polski z Egiptem i Irakiem w latach 1955–1989*. Toruń: Adam Marszałek, 2001.

Obrist, Hans Ulrich, and Asad Razā, eds. *Mondialité, or the Archipelagos of Édouard Glissant*. Paris: Skira, 2017.

Ogunbadejo, Oye. "Nigeria's Foreign Policy under Military Rule 1966–79." *International Journal* 35, no. 4 (Autumn 1980): 748–65.

Ojo, Olatunde J. B. "Nigerian-Soviet Relations: Retrospect and Prospect." *African Studies Review* 19, no. 3 (1976): 43–63.

Okeke-Agulu, Chika. *Postcolonial Modernism: Art and Decolonization in Twentieth-Century Nigeria*. Durham, NC: Duke University Press, 2015.

Okoye, Ikem Stanley. "Architecture, History, and the Debate on Identity in Ethiopia, Ghana, Nigeria, and South Africa." *JSAH* 61, no. 3 (September 2002): 381–96.

Olgyay, Aladar, and Victor Olgyay. *Solar Control and Shading Devices*. Princeton, NJ: Princeton University Press, 1976.

Olowo-Okere, E. O. "Construction Industry in Nigeria." In *Nigeria: The First 25 Years*, edited by Uma Eleazu, 309–10. Lagos: Infodata, 1988.

Olszewski, Krystyn. "Bagdad—relacja o planie ogólnym." Part 1: *Miasto* 11 (1967): 1–8, and part 2: *Miasto* 12 (1967): 1–11.

Ong, Aihwa. "Worlding Cities, or the Art of Being Global." In *Worlding Cities: Asian Experiments and the Art of Being Global*, edited by Ananya Roy and Aihwa Ong, 1–26. Chichester, UK: Wiley-Blackwell, 2012.

Onimode, Bade. *Imperialism and Underdevelopment in Nigeria: The Dialectics of Mass Poverty*. London: Zed, 1982.

———, John, F. E. Ohiorhenuan, and Tunde Adeniran. *Multinational Corporations in Nigeria*. Ibadan: Les Shyraden Nigeria, 1983.

Oprea, Mirela. "Development Discourse in Romania: From Socialism to EU Membership." *Perspectives on European Politics and Society* 13, no. 1 (2012): 66–82.

Osayimwese, Itohan. *Colonialism and Modern Architecture in Germany*. Pittsburgh, PA: University of Pittsburgh Press, 2017.

Ostrowski, Wacław. *Zespoły zabytkowe a urbanistyka*. Warsaw: Arkady, 1980.

Padányi Gulyás, Jenő. "Heves megyei kisházak." *Tér és Forma* 2, no. 1 (1929): 30–35.

Palutzki, Joachim. *Architektur in der DDR*. Berlin: Reimer, 2000.

"Paradise Gardens and Other Ornaments: Two Mideast Hotels Inspired by the Arts of Islam." *Architectural Record* 168, no. 1 (July 1980): 122–27.

Peil, Margaret. *Lagos: The City Is the People*. Boston: Hall, 1991.

Perišić, Života. *Građevinarstvo Srbije*. Belgrade: Ministarstvo građevina Srbije, 1997.

Pieri, Caecilia. *Bagdad: La construction d'une capitale moderne, 1914–1960*. Beiruth: Ifpo, 2015.

———. "Editing Out the Architectural History of Modern Iraq: Aspects of the Academic Discourse in Iraq (1950s–1980s)." *International Journal of Iraqi Contemporary Studies* 9, no. 1 (2015), 7–20.

Platzer, Monika. "From CIAM to CIAM-Ost, 1928-37. CIAM and Central Europe." In *Shaping the Great City: Modern Architecture in Central Europe, 1890–1937*, edited by Eve Blau and Monika Platzer, 227–31. Munich: Prestel, 1999.

Pletsch, Carl E. "The Three Worlds, or the Division of Social Scientific Labor, circa 1950–1975." *Comparative Studies in Society and History* 23, no. 4 (1981): 565–90.

"Politechnika Gdańska 1945–70. Księga pamiątkowa." Gdańsk: Politechnika Gdańska, 1970.

Polónyi, Charles. "Aménagements touristiques en Hongrie." *L'architecture d'aujourd'hui* 116 (1964): 98–99.

———. *An Architect-Planner on the Peripheries: The Retrospective Diary of Charles K. Polónyi*. Budapest: Műszaki Könyvkiadó, 2000.

———. "The Development of Lake Balaton." *Architectural Design* 5 (1960): 203.

———. "Kumasi 2000." *Arena, the Architectural Association Journal* (July–August 1966): 54–55.

"Pomnik Prezydenta Nkrumaha." *Kontynenty* 5 (June 1964): 8.

Pons, Silvio. *The Global Revolution: A History of International Communism 1917–1991*. Oxford: Oxford University Press, 2014.

Povey, John, Frank Willett, John Picton, and Ekpo Eyo. "Bernard Fagg: 1915–1987." *African Arts* 21, no. 2 (1988): 10, 12.

Prakash, Vikramaditya. *Chandigarh's Le Corbusier: The Struggle for Modernity in Postcolonial India*. Seattle: University of Washington Press, 2002.

Prashad, Vijay. *The Darker Nations: A People's History of the Third World*. New York: New Press, 2007.

"Pride of the City." *Gulf Construction* (August 1985): 20–22.

Projeté, construit, utilisé: Service des projets de modèles et d'expériences/Designed, constructed, utilized/Projektiert, gebaut, genutzt. Berlin: Bauakademie der DDR, 1987.

"Proposals for Restructuring Kuwait." *Architectural Review* 156, no. 931 (1974): 179–90.

Punagin, Vladimir Nikolaevich. *Tekhnologiia betona v usloviiakh sukhogo zharkogo klimata*. Tashkent: Fan, 1977.

Pyla, Panayiota I. "Baghdad's Urban Restructuring, 1958. Aesthetics and Politics of Nation Building." In *Modernism and the Middle East. Architecture and Politics in the Twentieth Century*, edited by Sandy Isenstadt and Kishwar Rizvi, 97–115. Seattle: University of Washington Press, 2008.

Razvojna suradnja kroz nasljeđe Pokreta nesvrstanih/Development Cooperation through the Legacy of the Non-Aligned Movement. Zagreb: Platforma za međunarodnu građansku solidarnost Hrvatske, 2015.

Reisz, Todd. "Plans the Earth Swallows: An Interview with Abdulrahman Makhlouf." *Portal* 9, no. 2 (2013). www.portal9journal.org.

Ren, Xuefei. *Building Globalization: Transnational Architecture Production in Urban China*. Chicago: University of Chicago Press, 2011.

"Report of the United Nations Seminar on Planning Techniques, Moscow, Union of Soviet Socialist Republics, 8–22 July 1964." New York: United Nations, 1966.

Richards, James Maude, ed. *New Buildings in the Commonwealth*. New York: Frederick A. Praeger, 1962.

Richert, Wiktor. *Przestrzenne planowanie regionalne w Ghanie. Zasady i metody, problemy kształcenia, przydatność polskich doświadczeń*. Warszawa: PWN, 1973.

Rimsha, Anatolii Nikolaevich. *Gorod i zharkii klimat*. Moscow: Stroiizdat, 1975.

———. *Gradostroitel'stvo v usloviiakh zharkogo klimata*. Moscow: Stroiizdat, 1972.

———. *Osnovy gradostroitel'stva v usloviiakh zharkogo klimata*. Moscow: Un-t druzhby narodov im. Patrisa Lumumby, 1969.

Rimsha, Anatolii Nikolaevich. *Town Planning in Hot Climates*. Moscow: Mir Publishers, 1976.

"A Road Network Sized for the Products of Detroit." *Construction Today—Middle East* 3 (1979): 30.

Robinson, Jennifer. "Cities in a World of Cities: The Comparative Gesture." *International Journal of Urban and Regional Research* 35, no. 1 (2010): 1–23.

———. "Comparative Urbanism: New Geographies and Cultures of Theorizing the Urban." *International Journal of Urban and Regional Research* 40, no. 1 (2016): 187–99.

———. "Thinking Cities through Elsewhere: Comparative Tactics for a More Global Urban Studies." *Progress in Human Geography* 40, no. 1 (2016): 3–29.

Rogers, Douglas. "Petrobarter: Oil, Inequality, and the Political Imagination in and after the Cold War." *Current Anthropology* 55, no. 2 (2014): 131–53.

Rosen, Seymour Michael. *The Development of Peoples' Friendship University in the U.S.S.R.* Washington, DC: US Dept. of Health, Education, and Welfare, Office of Education, 1973.

Rosenstein-Rodan, Paul. "Problems of Industrialisation of Eastern and South-Eastern Europe." *Economic Journal* 53, nos. 210/211 (1943): 202–11.

Roskam, Cole. "Non-Aligned Architecture: China's Designs on and in Ghana and Guinea, 1955–92." *Architectural History* 58 (2015): 261–91.

Roy, Ananya. "The 21st-Century Metropolis: New Geographies of Theory." *Regional Studies* 43, no. 6 (2009): 819–30.

Rubinstein, Alvin Z. *Yugoslavia and the Nonaligned World*. Princeton, NJ: Princeton University Press, 1970.

Rudner, Martin. "East European Aid to Asian Developing Countries: The Legacy of the Communist Era." *Modern Asian Studies* 30, no. 1 (1996): 1–28.

Sachs, Ignacy. "Revisiting Development in the Twenty-First Century." *International Journal of Political Economy* 38, no. 3 (2009): 5–21.

"Salhia Complex Kuwait." *Arup Journal* 14, no. 2 (July 1979): 2–6.

Sanchez-Sibony, Oscar. *Red Globalization: The Political Economy of the Soviet Cold War from Stalin to Khrushchev*. Cambridge: Cambridge University Press, 2014.

Sanders, Charles L. "Kwame Nkrumah: The Fall of a Messiah." *Ebony* (September 1966): 138–46.

Sayward, Amy L. "International Institutions." In *The Oxford Handbook of the Cold War*, edited by Richard H. Immerman and Petra Goedde, 377–93. Oxford: Oxford University Press, 2013.

Schaefer, Bernd. "Socialist Modernization in Vietnam: The East German Approach, 1976–89." In *Comrades of Color: East Germany in the Cold War World*, edited by Quinn Slobodian, 95–113. New York, Oxford: Berghahn Books, 2015.

Scheffler, Tanja. "Himmelskuppeln aus Jena: Die Architektin Gertrud Schille/Celestial Domes from Jena: The Architect Gertrud Schille." In *Frau Architekt. Seit mehr als 100 Jahren: Frauen im Architektenberuf/Over 100 Years of Women as Professional Architects*, edited by Christina Budde, Mary Pepchinski, Peter Cachola Schmal, and Wolfgang Voigt, 226–33. Tübingen: Wasmuth, 2017.

Schiavone, Giuseppe. *The Institutions of Comecon*. London: Macmillan, 1981.

Schille, Gertrud. "Designing and Building Planetariums for the Carl Zeiss Corporation: An Architect Tells Her Story." In *Women in Industrial Research*, edited by Renate Tobies and Annette B. Vogt, 229–43. Stuttgart: Steiner, 2014.

Schmid, Christian. "Specificity and Urbanization: A Theoretical Outlook." In *The Inevitable Specificity of Cities: Napoli, Nile Valley, Belgrade, Nairobi, Hong Kong, Canary Islands, Beirut, Casablanca*, edited by Roger Diener et al., 287–305. Zurich: Lars Müller, 2015.

———, Ozan Karaman, Naomi C. Hanakata, Pascal Kallenberger, Anne Kockelkorn, Lindsay Sawyer, Monika Streule, and Kit Ping Wong. "Towards a New Vocabulary of Urbanisation Processes: A Comparative Approach." *Urban Studies* 55, no. 1 (2018): 19–52.

Schmitter, Jörg-Peter. *Wohnungsbau in Westafrika: Untersuchungen zur Verbesserung des offiziellen Wohnungsbaus in Kamerun und Ghana*. Darmstadt: Verlag für Wissenschaftliche Publikationen, 1984.

Schreckenbach, Hannah, and Jackson G. K. Abankwa. *Construction Technology for a Tropical Developing Country*. Eschborn: German Agency for Technical Cooperation for the Department of Architecture; Kumasi: University of Science and Technology, 1983.

Schwenkel, Christina. "Affective Solidarities and East German Reconstruction of Postwar Vietnam." In *Comrades of Color: East Germany in the Cold War World*, edited by Quinn Slobodian, 267–92. New York, Oxford: Berghahn Books, 2015.

———. "Traveling Architecture: East German Urban Designs Abroad." *International Journal for History, Culture and Modernity* 2, no. 2 (2014): 155–74.

Scriver, Peter. "Empire-Building and Thinking in the Public Works Department of British India." In *Colonial Modernities: Building, Dwelling and Architecture in British India and Ceylon*, edited by Peter Scriver and Vikramaditya Prakash, 69–92. London: Routledge, 2007.

———. *The Scaffolding of Empire*. Adelaide: Centre for Asian and Middle Eastern Architecture, 2007.

———, and Vikramaditya Prakash, eds. *Colonial Modernities: Building, Dwelling and Architecture in British India and Ceylon*. London: Routledge, 2007.

Seibert, Krystian. *Rozważania i nadzieje*. Kraków: Wydawnictwo Orka Media, 2011.

———. *Urbanizacja Syrii: Przykład specyficznich determinant rozwojowych miast arabskich*. Uniwersytet Warszawski, Instytut Afrykanistyczny: 1978.

Sekulić, Dubravka. "Energoprojekt in Nigeria: Yugoslav Construction Companies in the Developing World." *Southeastern Europe* 41, no. 2 (2017): 200–229.

Šerman, Karin. "Boris Magaš and the Emergence of Postmodernist Themes in the Croatian Modernist Tradition." In *Re-Framing Identities: Architecture's Turn to History, 1970–1990*, edited by Ákos Moravánszky and Torsten Lange, 191–206. Basel: Birkhäuser, 2017.

Sethom, Hafedh. "Les quartiers populaires de Bagdad." In *Politiques urbaines dans le Monde Arabe*, edited by Jean Métral, Françoise Métral, and Georges Mutin, 381–95. Lyon: Maison de l'Orient méditerranéen, 1984.

"Seven-Year Plan for National Reconstruction and Development, 1963/64–1969/70." Accra: Ghana Planning Commission, 1964.

Severino, Renato. *Equipotential Space: Freedom in Architecture*. New York: Praeger, 1970.

Schubert, D. "Bewährte Zusammenarbeit zwischen den Bauschaffenden der RGW-Mitgliedsländer." *Bauplanung—Bautechnik* 11 (1987): 483–85.

Shafi, Shayed S. "Aspects of Iraq's Urbanization: Bibliography and References." Baghdad: United Nations Development Programme, 1972.

———. "Urban Planning in Iraq: Problems and Prospects: Final Report." Baghdad: United Nations Development Programme, 1972.

Shiber, Saba George. *The Kuwait Urbanization: Documentation, Analysis, Critique*. Kuwait: Kuwait Government Printing Press, 1964.

Shin, Gunsoo, and Inha Jung. "Appropriating the Socialist Way of Life: The Emergence of Mass Housing in Post-War North Korea." *Journal of Architecture* 21, no. 2 (2016): 159–80.

Silva, Carlos Nunes, ed. *Urban Planning in Lusophone African Countries*. Burlington, VT: Ashgate, 2015.

Simone, AbdouMaliq. "On the Worlding of African Cities." *African Studies Review* 44, no. 2 (2001): 15–41.

Sit, Victor. "Soviet Influence on Urban Planning in Beijing, 1949–1991." *Town Planning Review* 67, no. 4 (October 1996): 457–84.

Skidmore, Owings, and Merrill. "Computer Capability." 1980.

"Skład osobowy i plan studiów w roku akademickim 1965/66, wg. stanu na dzień 1.VII.65 r." Gdańsk: Politechnika Gdańska, 1965.

Slobodian, Quinn. "The Uses of Disorientation: Socialist Cosmopolitanism in an Unfinished DEFA-China Documentary." In *Comrades of Color: East Germany in the Cold War World*, edited by Quinn Slobodian, 219–42. New York, Oxford: Berghahn Books, 2015.

Słoniewski, Andrzej. "Organizacja i sposoby egzekwowania jakości produkowanych elementów i konstrukcji w warunkach budowy eksportowej w Iraku." *Przegląd budowlany* 1 (1985): 49–52.

Smolansky, Oles M. *The USSR and Iraq: The Soviet Quest for Influence*. Durham, NC; London: Duke University Press, 1991.

Soja, Edward, and Miguel Kanai. "The Urbanization of the World." In *The Endless City: The Urban Age Project by the London School of Economics and Deutsche Bank's Alfred Herrhausen Society*, edited by Richard Burdett and Deyan Sudjic, 54–69. London: Phaidon, 2007.

Souami, Taoufik, and Eric Verdeil, eds. *Concevoir et gérer les villes: milieux d'urbanistes du sud de la Méditerranée*. Paris: Economica/

Anthropos, 2006.

Sovetsko-ganskoe sotrudnichestvo. Accra: Ghana Ministry of Information and Broadcasting, 1961.

Sowa, Kazimierz Z. "Polskie badania socjologiczne w Iraku." *Studia Socjologiczne* 2, no. 65 (1977): 257–61.

Spaulding, Robert Mark. "Trade, Aid, and Economic Warfare." In *The Oxford Handbook of the Cold War*, edited by Richard H. Immerman and Petra Goedde, 394–413. Oxford: Oxford University Press, 2013.

Spivak, Gayatri Chakravorty. "The Rani of Sirmur: An Essay in Reading the Archives." *History and Theory* 24, no. 3 (October 1985): 247–72.

Springer, Philipp. *Verbaute Träume: Herrschaft, Stadtentwicklung und Lebensrealität in der sozialistischen Industriestadt Schwedt.* Berlin: Links, 2006.

Ssorin-Chaikov, Nikolai, ed. *Dary vozhdiam/Gifts to Soviet Leaders.* Moscow: Pinakoteka, 2006.

———. "On Heterochrony: Birthday Gifts to Stalin, 1949." *Journal of the Royal Anthropological Institute* 12, no. 2 (2006): 355–75.

SSSR i strany Afriki: 1946–1962 gg. Dokumenty i materialy. Moscow: Gosudarstennoe izdatel'stvo politicheskoi literatury, 1963, 2 vols.

SSSR i strany Afriki: 1963–1970 gg. Dokumenty i materialy. Moscow: Politizdat, 1982, 2 vols.

Stanek, Łukasz. "Accra, Warsaw, and Socialist Globalization." In *Africa: Big Change, Big Chance*, edited by Benno Albrecht, 162–64. Bologna: Editrice Compositori, 2014.

———. "Architects from Socialist Countries in Ghana (1957–1967): Modern Architecture and Mondialisation." *JSAH* 74, no. 4 (December 2015): 416–42.

———. *Henri Lefebvre on Space: Architecture, Urban Resarch, and the Production of Theory.* Minneapolis: University of Minnesota Press, 2011.

———. "An Image and Its Performance: Techno-Export from Socialist Poland." In *Re-Framing Identities: Architecture's Turn to History, 1970–1990*, edited by Akos Moravánszky and Torsten Lange, 59–71. Berlin: Jovis, 2017.

———. "The Master Plans of Baghdad: Notes on GIS-Based Spatial History," *Jadaliyya,* May 17, 2017. http://www.jadaliyya.com.

———. "Miastoprojekt Goes Abroad: Transfer of Architectural Labor from Socialist Poland to Iraq (1958–1989)." *Journal of Architecture* 17, no. 3 (2012): 361–86.

———. "Mobilities of Architecture in the Global Cold War: From Socialist Poland to Kuwait and Back." *International Journal of Islamic Architecture* 4, no. 2 (2015): 365–98.

———. *Postmodernism Is Almost All Right: Polish Architecture after Socialist Globalization.* Warsaw: Fundacja Bęc-Zmiana, 2012.

———. "PRL™ Export Architecture and Urbanism from Socialist Poland." *Piktogram: Talking Pictures Magazine* 15 (2011): 1–54.

———. "Qahtan Awni, Mustansiriyah University, Baghdad, Iraq." In *SOS Brutalism*, edited by Oliver Elser, Philip Kurz, and Peter Cachola Schmal, 212–13. Zurich: Park Books, 2017.

———. "Second World's Architecture and Planning in the Third World." *Journal of Architecture* 17, no. 3 (2012): 299–307.

———. "Socialist Networks and the Internationalization of Building Culture after 1945." *ABE Journal* 6 (2014). https://journals.openedition.org/abe/1266.

———, ed. "Socialist Networks and the Internationalization of Building Culture after 1945." Themed issue of *ABE Journal* 6 (2014). https://journals.openedition.org/abe/1266.

———, ed. *Team 10 East: Revisionist Architecture in Real Existing Modernism.* Warsaw: Museum of Modern Art; Chicago: University of Chicago Press, 2014.

———, and Tom Avermaete, eds. "Cold War Transfer: Architecture and Planning from Socialist Countries in the 'Third World.'" Themed issue of the *Journal of Architecture* 17, no. 3 (2012).

Steiner, André. "The Globalisation Process and the Eastern Bloc Countries in the 1970s and 1980s." *European Review of History/Revue européenne d'histoire* 21, no. 2 (2014): 165–81.

———, and Kirsten Petrak-Jones. "The Council of Mutual Economic Assistance—An Example of Failed Economic Integration?" *Geschichte und Gesellschaft* 39, no. 2 (2013): 240–58.

Steinhauf, Jerzy. "Bagdad leży nad Wisłą." *Dziennik Polski*, December 10–11, 1967.

Stone, Randall W. *Satellites and Commissars: Strategy and Conflict in the Politics of Soviet-Bloc Trade.* Princeton, NJ: Princeton University Press, 1996.

Stroe, Miruna. *Locuirea între proiect și decizie politică: România 1954–1966.* Bucharest: Simetria, 2015.

Suleiman, Samaila. "Politics of Heritage: Ethnic Minorities and the Politics of Heritage in Northern Nigeria." In *Things Don't Really Exist until You Give Them a Name: Unpacking Urban Heritage*, edited by Rachel Lee, Diane Barbé, Anne-Katrin Fenk, and Philipp Misselwitz, 124–29. Dar es Salaam: Mkuki na Nyota, 2017.

"Survey and Development Plan for Calabar." Calabar: Tesco-Közti Consulting Engineers (NIG), 1969.

Świechowski, Zygmunt, and Jan Zachwatowicz. *Dzieje budownictwa w Polsce według Oskara Sosnowskiego.* Warsaw: PWN, 1964.

Szlajfer, Henryk, ed. *Economic Nationalism in East-Central Europe and South America, 1918–1939/ Le nationalisme économique en Europe du Centre-Est et en Amérique du Sud, 1918–1939.* Geneva: Librairie Droz, 1990.

Szmidt, Bolesław, ed. *The Polish School of Architecture, 1942–1945.* Liverpool: Birchall, 1945.

"Tamale/Kumbungu Survey." Kumasi: Faculty of Architecture, University of Science and Technology, 1970.

Tan, See Seng, and Amitav Acharya, eds. *Bandung Revisited: The Legacy of the 1955 Asian-African Conference for International Order.* Singapore: NUS Press, 2008.

Taylor, Brian Brace. "Kuwait City Waterfront Development." *Mimar* 34 (1990): 13–20.

Tejuoso, Olakunle, et al., eds. *Lagos: A City at Work.* Lagos: Glendora Books, 2007.

Texier, Simon. "Abu Dhabi: l'invention d'une ville." *AMC—Le Moniteur Architecture* 195, no. 3 (2010): 92–96.

———. "Les villes neuves du Golfe, ou les horizons d'Abu Dhabi." *Revue de l'art* 186 (2014): 65–73.

Tipple, A. Graham. *The Development of Housing Policy in Kumasi, Ghana, 1901 to 1981: With an Analysis of the Current Housing Stock.* Newcastle: Centre for Architectural Research and Development Overseas, 1987.

Tłoczek, Ignacy. "W sprawie badań nad architekturą ludową." *Ochrona Zabytków* 11, nos. 1–2 (1958): 19–34.

Todorova, Mariëiia Nikolaeva. *Imagining the Balkans.* New York, Oxford: Oxford University Press, 1997.

Tošković, Dobrivoje. *Kolkata, India: Forty Years of Salt Lake City: From an Idea to a Realization.* Laktaši: Grafomark, 2009.

"The Town of Tema Ghana: Plans for Two Communities." *Ekistics* 13 (1962): 159–71.

"Transportation and Communication in Cross River State." Calabar: Ministry of Communication and Social Development, 1978.

Trentin, Massimiliano. "'Tough Negotiations.' The Two Germanys in Syria and Iraq, 1963–74." *Cold War History* 8, no. 3 (2008): 353–80.

Uduku, Nwola. "Bolgatanga Library, Adaptive Modernism in Ghana 40 Years On." In *The Challenge of Change: Dealing with the Legacy of the Modern Movement—Proceedings of the 10th International DOCOMOMO Conference*, edited by Dirk van der Heuvel, Maarten Mesman, Wido Quist, and Bert Lemmens, 265–72. Amsterdam: IOS Press, 2008.

Uffelmann, Dirk. "Buren und Polen. Metonymischer Manchiäismus und metaphorischer Autoafrikanisierung bei Henryk Sienkiewicz—zur Rhetorik interkultureller Beziehungen." In *Orientalismen in Ostmitteleuropa. Diskurse, Akteure und Disziplinen vom 19. Jahrhundert bis zum Zweiten Weltkrieg*, edited by Robert Born and Sarah Lemmen, 283–312. Bielefeld: Transcript, 2014.

Uji, Zanzan Akaka. "Beyond the Critiques of the Curriculum of Architectural Education in Nigeria." In *Architects and Architecture in Nigeria: A Book of Readings in Honour of Professor Ekundayo Adeyinka Adeyemi*, edited by Uche Obisike Nkwogu, 109–22. Akure: Association of Architectural Educators in Nigeria, 2001.

United Nations, Department of Economic and Social Affairs. "Report of the Study Tour of Building Technologists from Latin America, Africa, Asia and the Middle East to the Union of Soviet Socialist Republics, 3 to 31 July 1963." New York: United Nations, 1964.

United Nations, Mission on Housing, Building and Planning. "Sulphur-Concrete Demonstration." Dubai: Port Said Printing Press, 1977.

"Unterstützung des RGW für Kubas Bauindustrie." *Neues Deutschland*, May 31, 1975, 7.

"Urbaniści 'Miastoprojektu' opracowują plan Bagdadu." *Dziennik Polski,* December 29, 1966, 2.

Urbanistički institut SR Hrvatske. "Conakry. Plan directeur d'urbanisme." Zagreb, 1963.

Uthman, Fuad. "Exporting Architectural Education to the Arab World." *Journal of Architectural*

Education 31, no. 3 (1978): 26–30.
Uyanga, Joseph. "Historical and Administrative Perspective on Nigerian Urban Planning." *Transafrican Journal of History* 18 (1989): 160–72.
Vacher, Hélène. "La planification de la sauvegarde et le détour marocain (1912–1925)." In *Patrimoines en situation. Constructions et usages en différents contextes urbains: Exemples marocains, libanais, égyptien et suisse*, edited by Raffaele Cattedra et al. Beirut: Ifpo, 2010. https://books.openedition.org/ifpo/.
Vago, Pierre. *L'UIA, 1948–1998*. Paris: Épure, 1998.
Vais, Dana. "Exporting Hard Modernity: Construction Projects from Ceaușescu's Romania in the 'Third World.'" *Journal of Architecture* 17, no. 3 (2012): 433–51.
Vaňous, Jan. "Commercial Exchange Rates of East European Countries and Realistic Dollar/Ruble Exchange Rates for Soviet Trade with Eastern Europe." *Soviet and Eastern European Foreign Trade* 22, no. 1 (1986): 83–99.
———. "Soviet and East European Trade and Financial Relations with the Middle East." *Soviet and Eastern European Foreign Trade* 21, nos. 1–3 (1985): 86–119.
Vaz Milheiro, Ana. *Nos trópicos sem Le Corbusier: Arquitectura luso-africana no Estado Novo*. Lisbon: Relógio d'Agua, 2012.
"VEB Industrieprojektierung Dessau: Betriebschronik." n.d., 2 vols.
Vellut, Jean-Luc, ed. *Villes d'Afrique: Explorations en histoire urbaine*. Paris: L'Harmattan, 2007.
Verdeil, Eric. *Beyrouth et ses urbanistes: une ville en plans, 1946–1975*. Beyrouth: Ifpo, 2010.
———. "Expertises nomades au Sud. Eclairages sur la circulation des modèles urbains." Géocarrefour 80, no. 3 (2005). https://journals.openedition.org/geocarrefour/1143.
Verdery, Katherine. "Internal Colonialism in Austria-Hungary." *Ethnic and Racial Studies* 2, no. 3 (1979): 378–99.
Virágh, Pál. *Town Planning in Hungary*. Budapest: Ministry of Building and Urban Development, 1968.
Viski, Károly. "A dunántúli parasztház." *Tér és Forma* 2, no. 1 (1929): 24–29.
Volait, Mercedes. *L'architecture moderne en Égypte et la revue "al-ʿimara," (1939–1959)*. Cairo: CEDEJ, 1988.
"Volta Resettlement Symposium Papers: Papers Read at the Volta Resettlement Symposium, Held at Kumasi, 23–27 March, 1965." Kumasi: Faculty of Architecture, UST, 1965.
Voronina, Veronika Leonidovna. *Arkhitekturnye pamiatniki Srednei Azii*. Leningrad: Avrora, 1969.
———. *Narodnaia arkhitektura severnogo Tadzhikistana*. Moscow: Gosstroiizdat, 1959.
———. *Narodnoe zhilishche arabskikh stran*. Moscow: Stroiizdat, 1972.
———. *Narodnye traditsii arkhitektury Uzbekistana*. Moscow: Gosudarstvennoe izdatel'stvo arkhitektury i gradostroitel'stva, 1951.
———. *Opyt proektirovaniia zdanii v stranakh tropicheskogo klimata*. Moscow: Stroiizdat, 1966.
———. *Sovremennaia arkhitektura stran tropicheskoi Afriki*. Moscow: n.p., 1973.

Wakeman, Rosemary. *Practicing Utopia: An Intellectual History of the New Town Movement*. Chicago: University of Chicago Press, 2016.
Walters, Robert S. *American and Soviet Aid: A Comparative Analysis*. Pittsburgh, PA: University of Pittsburgh Press, 1970.
Ward, Stephen. *Planning the Twentieth-Century City: The Advanced Capitalist World*. Chichester, UK: Wiley, 2002.
———. "Transnational Planners in a Postcolonial World." In *Crossing Borders: International Exchange and Planning Practices*, edited by Patsy Healey and Robert Upton, 47–72. London: Routledge, 2010.
Waterkamp, Rainer. *Das zentralstaatliche Planungssystem der DDR: Steuerungsprozesse im anderen Teil Deutschlands*. Berlin: Duncker and Humblot, 1983.
Waterston, A. *A Practical Program of Planning for Ghana*. Washington DC; Accra: IBRD, 1966.
Wentker, Hermann. "Für Frieden und Völkerfreundschaft? Die DDR als internationaler Akteur." In *Friedensstaat, Leseland, Sportnation? DDR-Legenden auf dem Prüfstand*, edited by Thomas Großbölting, 155–76. Berlin: Links, 2009.
Westad, Odd Arne. *The Global Cold War: Third World Interventions and the Making of Our Times*. Cambridge: Cambridge University Press, 2005.
"West Germans Win on High-Tech." *Middle East Economic Digest* 26, no. 5 (January 29–February 4, 1982): 10.
Wettstein, Domonkos. "The Balaton Region as an Experimental Territory: Positions of Architecture in the Emergence of Regional Planning for Recreation in Hungary." *Építés–Építészettudomány* 44, no. 1–2 (2016): 129–77.
Wiebenson, Dora, and József Sisa, eds. *The Architecture of Historic Hungary*. Cambridge, MA: MIT Press, 1998.
Wigand, Ede. "A magyar parasztház eredete és fejlődése." *Tér és Forma* 2, no. 1 (1929): 4–16.
Wimmelbücker, Ludger. "Architecture and City Planning Projects of the German Democratic Republic in Zanzibar." *Journal of Architecture* 17, no. 3 (2012): 407–32.
Winid, Bogodar. "The Centre of African Studies of Warsaw University." *Studies on Developing Countries* 2 (1972): 151–58.
Wiśniewski, Michał. "Po majątki na Podole…." *Autoportret* 4 (2009): 48–53.
Wolff, Larry. *Inventing Eastern Europe: The Map of Civilization on the Mind of the Enlightenment*. Stanford, CA: Stanford University Press, 1994.
Wright, Gwendolyn. *The Politics of Design in French Colonial Urbanism*. Chicago, London: University of Chicago Press, 1991.
———. "Tradition in the Service of Modernity: Architecture and Urbanism in French Colonial Policy, 1900–1930." *Journal of Modern History* 59, no. 2 (1987), 291–316.
Wyżykowski, Andrzej. "Zagraniczna twórczość architektoniczna Janusza Kraweckiego." *Kwartalnik architektury i urbanistyki* XLI, nos. 3–4 (1996): 339–42.
Yacobi, Haim. *Israel and Africa: A Genealogy of Moral Geography*. London, New York: Routledge, 2016.
Yagodovsky, Leonid Sergeevich. *The World Socialist System—Its Role in the World Today*. Moscow: Novosti Press Agency Publishing House, 1975.
Yamada, Sohiko. "Baghdad: Breaking Tides." *Process: Architecture* 58 (May 1985): 12–25.
Yetunde, Olaiya. "Systemic Shifts: The Case of Abidjan's Urban Planning, 1945–60." *Journal of Architectural Education* 68, no. 2 (2014): 190–98.
Yugoslav Investment Works Abroad. Belgrade: Office for the Federal Chamber of Economy, n.d.
Zachwatowicz, Jan. *Protection of Historical Monuments in Poland*. Warsaw: Polonia, 1965.
Zahariade, Ana-Maria. *Arhitectura în proiectul comunist: România 1944–1989/Architecture in the Communist Project: Romania 1944–1989*. Bucharest: Simetria, 2011.
Zarecor, Kimberly Elman. "What Was So Socialist about the Socialist City? Second World Urbanity in Europe." *Journal of Urban History* 44, no. 1 (2018): 95–117.
Zaremba, Piotr. "Outline of the Polish Physical Planning Methods Adapted to the Needs of Developing Countries." *Town and Country Planning Research* I (1967): 5–39.
Zevin, Leon Zalmanovich. *Economic Cooperation of Socialist and Developing Countries: New Trends*. Moscow: Nauka, 1976.
Ziółek, Maciej. "Problemy budownictwa w warunkach klimatu tropikalnego." *Informacja adresowana* 58 (1968): 3–13.

Index

Note: Page numbers in italic type indicate illustrations.

A

Aalto, Alvar, 176
Abdullah-Bey house, Bukhara (Uzbek Soviet Socialist Republic), *49*
Abercrombie Prize, 110
Abrams, Charles, 110
Abu Dhabi, United Arab Emirates: aerial view, *244*; BCCI building, 252–53, *253*; Bus Station, *258*, 265; Central Bank of the UAE, 245; land use in, 255; Main Bus Terminal, 255, *256*, *257*, 265; master plans for, 243, *245*, 255; Municipality and Town Planning Department, 32–33, *238–39*, 239, 241–43, 254–56, *254–55*, 260, 264, 268, *268–71*, 294
Abusham, Mohamed, 256
Abyssinia, 125
Academy of Architecture (Bauakademie), East Berlin (East Germany), 217, *218*, 219
Academy of Construction and Architecture (Soviet Union), 75
Accra, Ghana, 35–95; architects, planners, and contractors in, 1; Black Star Square, *61*; Cinema-Theater, *51*; Flagstaff House apartment block, 39, 52, 55, *119*; housing in, 65–66, 73–85, *80–83*, *119*, *120*; International Trade Fair (ITF), 31, *34*, 35–36, *36*, 42, *44*, 52, 64, 85–93, *85–90*, 307; Job 600, *53*, 54, 56, 59; Junior Staff Housing, Osu Castle, 63; "Kingsway Street Map of Accra," *38*; Korle Bu Hospital, 39, 42, 56, 60; National Archives Building, *43*; National Museum, *43*; Osu Castle, *51*, 52, 59, *63*; People's Shop, 60, *61*; plans for, 44, 65–66, *65*, 73; population of, 65; post-independence map of, 39, *40*; Presidential Tribune at the Black Star Square, 39, *41*, 59; residential areas in, 73–85, *76–77*, *78*; State House Complex, *53*, 54, *57*; Studio and Practice Hall for the National Orchestra, 44
Accra Airport (Ghana), 42
Accra-Tema-Akosombo metropolitan area plan, 44, *45*, 85
Addis Ababa, Ethiopia, Governmental Center, *12*
Adegbite, Victor (Vic), *34*, 36, *36*, 41, *44*, *45*, *53*, 54, 59, *59*, *62*, 64, 66, 67, 75, *85–90*, 93, *119*
Adeyemi, Adedokun, 142
Adeyemi, Ekundayo Adeyinka, 134, 142–45
Administration Center Hamma, Algiers (Algeria), 25, 264, *264*
Afanas'ev, L., *68*, *70*
Afghanistan, 95, 282
Africa Hall (Women's Hall 6), Kumasi (Ghana), *x*, 59, *59*
"African Architectural Technology" (exhibition), 129
Africanization, 39, 41
Aga Khan Award for Architecture, 280
Aga Khan Foundation, 248
Agency for International Development (United States), 148
Agent, Dan, 230, *233*
agrarian towns (Hungary), 104–5, *105*, 108, 114
Agyeman, O. T., 41
Ahmadu Bello University, Zaria (Nigeria), 122, *123*, 132. *See also* School of Architecture, Ahmadu Bello University, Zaria (Nigeria)
aircraft shelter for Iraq, *217*
Airport Road Housing, Tripoli (Libya), 227, *227*
Akhmedov, Abdullah, 280
Akinloye, A.M.A., 150–51
Akosombo Dam (Ghana), 48
Al Ain, United Arab Emirates, 252, 253–54, 265–66; Municipality Building, 241, 256, 265, *266*, *267*, 268, 270–71
al-Assad, Hafez, 95
Albania, 46
Albenaa (Construction; journal), 248, 251
Alcock, Alfred, and Helga Richards, 84
Alexander Gibb & Partners, 177, 227, 262
Aleppo, Syria, historical center of, *12–13*
Algeria, 95, 235, 331n292
al-Fintas towers, Fintas (Kuwait), *247*
al-Jalili, Naman, 184
al-Muhairy, 256, 258
al-Othman Center, Hawally (Kuwait), 283, 287, *287*, *288*, 290, 297
al-Rahal, Khalid, 209
al-Rayes, Sabah, 274
al-Salem, Abdullah, 245
al-Salman, Falah, 252
al-Sanan, Mohammad, 273, 279
al-Shaab Gate, Kuwait City (Kuwait), *249*
al-Turk, Ismail Fattah, 209
al-Zuhairi, design of rural settlement, *196*
Amartey, A. K., 41
Amin, Samir, 29
Amiri Diwan and Council of Ministers, Kuwait City (Kuwait), 248, *250*, 295
Anastassov, Georgi, 255–56, 265
Andreev, Viktor, *9*
Andreu, Paul, 252
Ankrah, Joseph Arthur, 35, 87
Antipova, E., *21*
Anwar al-Sabah Complex at the Fahad al-Salem Street, Kuwait City (Kuwait), *293*
Apter, Andrew, 130
Arabi Engineers Office, *247*
Arab-Islamic architectural elements, 33, 232, 241, 246, 248, 253–54, 265–71, 280, 282–83, 294, 297
Arab Urban Development Institute, Riyadh (Saudi Arabia), 248
Aradeon, David, 129–30
Araim, Abduljabbar, 189
Archicentre, 248, *250*, 274, *274–75*, 295, 334n163
The Architects Collaborative (TAC), 176, 209, *210*, 274, 280, 297
Architects Co-Partnership, 42, 127
Architects Registration Council of Nigeria, 144
Architectural Associates (Ghana), 41
Architectural Association (London), Department of Tropical Architecture, 5, 91
Architectural Design (journal), 91
Architectural Design Partnership (Ghana), 41
architectural drawings, 135–45
architectural education/training: in Algeria, 331n292; decolonization of, 142–45; in Ghana, 39, 42; Iraq, 179, 205–6, 328n180; Nigeria, 134–35, 142–45; training in planning, 192, 195
Architectural Forum (journal), 6
architectural heritage: in Baghdad, 190–91, 201, 209; in Bulgaria, 259–60, *261*; in Ghana, 63–64; of Gulf states, 248; of Kuwait City, 246, 248, 251–52. *See also* Arab-Islamic architectural elements; vernacular architecture
architectural labor: in Cold War, 92–94; contracts for, 181–82; in Ghana, 85–94; modalities of, 27, 29; in postcolonial Global South, 304–5; socialist (non-free) vs. Western (free), 37, 305; varieties of, 304; in world socialist system, 172–73
Architectural Review (journal), 280
Architecture and Civil Engineering University, Weimar (East Germany), 25
Arcif, 227
Arcom, 22, *24*, 32, 153, 214–15, 221, 222, 224–25, 227, 228, 231–32, *233*, 234, 235, *236*
Arkhitektura SSSR (journal), 64–65
Ariashahr (now Fuladshahr), Iran, 18, *19*
Armabeton, 280
Armah, Ayi Kwei, 63
Aronin, Jeffrey, 91
Arthur Lindsay and Associates, 58
Arup, Ove, 42, 295
Ascobloc, 214–15, 224
Ashanti Empire, 63
Associated Consultants (Ghana), 41
Association of Hungarian Architects, 108
Association of Iraqi Architects, 184
Astra, 150
Atkinson, George A., 91
Audit Bureau Headquarters Building, Kuwait City (Kuwait), *247*, 296, 297
Audu, Ishaya, 143
Austria-Hungary, 126
automobiles, 283
Awni, Kahtan, 15, 201–2, *201–4*, 204
Ázbej, Sándor, *23*
Azikiwe, Nnamdi, 126

B

Baath Party (Iraq), 8, 95, 169–70, 184, 235
backwardness/underdevelopment, 100–106, 122, 125–26, 165, 304–5
Badanov, I., *19*
Baghdad, Iraq, 169–237; al-Khulafa Street Development Project, 210, *210*, *211*; al-Qadisiyah neighborhood in nearby Mahmudiyah, *197–99*, 198; Amanat al-Assima, *168*, 169, 177–78, 180–85, 192, 195, 197, 199, 207, 209, *210*; architects, planners, and contractors in, 2, 15; architectural heritage of, 190–91, 201, 209; "City Centre Rusafa, Civic Centre–Visual Composition," *189*; collaboration and consultation on planning and architecture for, 183–86, 201–35; housing in, 176, 189–90, *191*, 198–200, *199*, 232, *233*; International Airport, 209; land use in, *194*; major architectural commissions in, 176–77; master plans for, 32, *168*, 169, 173–210, *177*, *184*, *185*, *187*, *188*, *193*, *210*, *211*, 327n1; mid-twentieth-century development of, 174–77; Ministry of Oil Building, 210, *212*; Mustansiriyah University, 202, *202–4*; National Electricity Board Building, *204*; office building on Jumhuriyah Street, 201–2, *201*; slaughterhouse, 210–12, *212*, 214–15, *215*, 220–25, *231*, 232, *233*; University of Baghdad, 184, 205–6, *205*, *206–7*; urbanization in, 195–210
Baghdad International Airport, *209*
Bahrain, 293

Bajer, Kazimierz, 183
Bakić, Dragoljub, *276*, 277
Bakić, Ljiljana, 277
Balaton Regional Outline Plan (Hungary), 108–10, *111*, 113
Baloush Bus Terminal, Kuwait City (Kuwait), 290, *290*, *291*
Bamako, Mali, *70*, 71
Baranov, Nikolai, 66
Barnes, Hubbard & Arundel, 42
Barratt, Derek, 63
Barrett, W. H., *65*
barter, 11, 73, 99, 172, 213, 225–27
Basrah, Iraq, 178–79, *180*, 190
Bašta, Vaclav, 205–7, *209*, 248, 280; curriculum booklet, 206, *206–7*; lecture notes on history of architecture, *205*
Baštova, Miroslava, 205
Bauakademie. *See* Academy of Architecture (Bauakademie), East Berlin (East Germany)
Baumiller, Jerzy, *180*, 204–5
Bayan Park Conference Center, Kuwait City (Kuwait), 274, *274–75*, 280, 294, 295
BBPR, 283
BCCI building, Abu Dhabi (UAE), 252–53, *253*
Bechtel Group, 295
Bechtel International Corporation, *26*
Bedouin housing, Kuwait, *276*, 277
Bedri Omar Elias, 266, 268
Beier, Ulli, 141
Beijing Design Institute, 67, *68*
Benin Museum (Nigeria), *133*
Bérczes, István, 108, *109*
Beton, 22, 210, *212*, 300
Besnea, Nicolae, 230, 231, *233*
Biafra, 99, 148
Bida, Nigeria, measured drawing of house in, *137*
Bierbauer, Virgil, 104–5
Bjørn, Malene, 248
Bjørn & Bjørn Design, 248
Bobrowski, Czesław, 106
Bofill, Ricardo, 209, 251
Bogdanov, Dimitar, 25, *238–39*, *254–55*, 255, 264–65, *264*, *268*, *269*, 272, 301
Bohdanowicz, Andrzej, 272–74, *281*, 282, *284*, *285*, 287, *289*, *292*, 294
Bojović, Ljiljana, 161, *162*
Bojović, Zoran, 17, 22, 122, 149, *150–51*, *152*, *154–55*, 155–56, *158*, 159–61, *160–62*, 165, *166*, 210, *211*, 301
Bolgatanga Library (Ghana), 44, *45*
Bond, J. Max, Jr., 44, *45*, 108, 110, 113
Bonnington, John, 295
Botsio, Kojo, 63
Boumédienne, Houari, 95
Bourdieu, Pierre, 69
Brasov system, 228, 232
Brenner, Neil, 33
Bretton Woods, 6, 30
Brezhnev, Leonid, 15, 94, 170, 171, 225
Britain: architectural and construction services of, 5–6; architectural standards and regulations of, 263–64; Ghana and, 37, 41–42; Iraq and, 174–75; Nigeria and, 142–44; as postcolonial reference point, 5–6; West Africa and, 92
British Technical Assistance Programme, 42
Brzezowski, W., *272*
Buchanan & Partners, 246, 282
Budimex, 22, 153

Builders' Brigade (Ghana), 48
building-gifts, 69–73
Building Research Institute (Bulgaria), *96–97*, *98*, *164*, *165*
Building Research Station, Watford (UK), Tropical Building Section, 91
Bui Resettlement Study (Ghana), 112–13
Bulgaria, 15, 16, 21; and Arab countries, 259–60; architectural heritage of, 259–60, *261*; Communist Party in, 265; Ghana and, 46; and international architectural practices, 259–60, 262–64; UAE and, 255–71
Bulgarian Engineering Achievements in Foreign Countries, 259–60, 262
Bulgarproject, *238–39*, 239, 241, *254–58*, 263, 266–69; catalogue of, *18*
Bus Station, Abu Dhabi (UAE), *258*, 265
Butcher, David, 112

C
Calabar, Nigeria, 31, 99–100, 102, 113–22, *116–19*, *121*, *122*
Camus-Setap system, 200
Candilis-Josic-Woods, 283
Cappa & d'Alberto, 155
Carl Zeiss, 21, 219–20, *219*, *220*, 235
cars, 283
Caucasian Soviet Republics, 8, 47
Ceaușescu, Nicolae, 15, 17, 181, 213, 226–27
Čejka, Jan, 205–7, *208*
Center for Studies and Design Abroad. *See* Romproiect
Central Asia, 5, 8, 47–48, 125, 127, 280, 282
Central Bank of the UAE, Abu Dhabi (UAE), 245
Central Research and Design Institute for Housing Construction (TsNIIEP zhilishcha), *82*
Central Scientific Research and Design Institute for Town Planning (TsNIIEP gradostroitel'stva), 18
Centre Scientifique et Technique du Bâtiment, Paris, 91
Chadirji, Rifat, 176, *177*, 199, 201, 202, 207, *208*, 209–10, 248, 251
Chen Deng'ao, 67, *68*
chief's residence, Bolgatanga (Ghana), *64*
China: developing countries and, 11; Ghana and, 11, 37, 46, 50; gift diplomacy of, 73; Soviet Union and, 4, 8; technical assistance and development aid from, 85
Chmielewski, Jan, 104
Chyczewski, L., *285*, 290, *290*, *291*
Chyrosz, Jacek, *34*, 36, *36*, *44*, 50, 52, *64*, 85–90, *90*, *91*, 92
CIAM. *See* International Congresses of Modern Architecture
CIAM-East, 104–5
Ciborowski, Adolf, 182–83, 186; *Town Planning in Poland, 1945–55*, 183
Ciko, Niksa, *x*, 52, *58*, *59*, 321n88
Cinema-Theater, Accra (Ghana), *51*
city planning. *See* planning
civilizing mission, 125, 141
climatic adaptations: in Ghana, 64, 72, 80, 82, 85; in Guinea, 69; in Nigeria, *146–47*; Soviet study of, 47–48; in Soviet Union, 66, 80; tropical architecture and, 88–89. *See also* tropical architecture
Cold War: antagonisms of, 88, 92–93, 95;

architectural discourse in context of, 47, 92–93; architectural labor in, 92–94; crossing of lines during, 55, 94–95; Ghana and, 37; historiography of architecture during, 2, 4, 8, 29, 33; Iraq and, 170; last decades of, 15, 17, 25–26, 33, 298–99; persistence of practices from, 26, 33
collaboration. *See* international exchange and collaboration in architecture
colonialism. *See* postcolonial Global South
Comecon. *See* Council of Mutual Economic Assistance
Comecon building, Moscow (USSR), 172, *172*
Cominform, 148
Committee for the Preservation of the Arab Islamic Architectural Style, 254
Commonwealth Association of Architects, 5–6
computer-aided design (CAD), 295, 297, 298
Conakry, Guinea, *20*, 21, 67
Conference of African and Asian states (Bandung, Indonesia, 1955), 7
Congo crisis (1960), 48
Conrad, Joseph, 125
Consolidated Contractors International Company, 255–56
contracts, 27, 181–82, 196–97, 207
Convention People's Party (CPP, Ghana), 36, 37, 41, 54, 55–56, 60, 63, 93; headquarters building, 56, *57*, 59
Costain, 155
Cottages, Podhale (Poland), *132*
Council of Mutual Economic Assistance (Comecon): barter system of, 148; economic integration of, 221, 225–26; founding of, 8, 171; members of, 8, 16, 171; in 1970s, 16; Permanent Commission for Construction (PCC), 18, 21, 216–17, 221–22, *223*, 236; Permanent Commission for Technical Assistance, 18; technical assistance coordinated by, 8, 11, 21–22, 29, 171–72, 181, 216, 221–22, 224, 236, 303; and world socialist system, 32, 171–73, 216
CPP. *See* Convention People's Party
Cuba, 8, 18, 171, 217, 222
Cubitt, James, 42
cultural emancipation, 127–30
currency, 11, 16–17, 99, 173–74, 181–82, 225
Czechoslovakia, 21, 46, 50, 125

D
Dąbrowski, Hubert, 143, 144
Daczkowska, Zdzisława, 282
Daczkowski, Ryszard, 273, 283, *286*
Dagher, Claude, *22*
Daily Graphic (Ghana, newspaper), 5, 56, 63
Daily Times (Nigeria, newspaper), 127–28, *128*
Dambatta, Nigeria, *123*
Damija, J., *247*
Danby, Miles, 42, 91
Dar al-Handasah, 295
Dar al-Imarah, 195, *197*, *198*
Daszkiewicz, Eligiusz, 55, *62*
decolonization. *See* postcolonial Global South
design-and-build procedure, 210
Design Institute Carpați (Romania), 22, *24*, 213
Design Institute for Housing and Urban Technical and Social Infrastructure (Romania), 99, *124*, *162*

Design Institute for Public Buildings (Hungary). *See* Közti
design institutes, 18, 21–22, 240
development aid, 6, 7
Diwaniyya for H.H. Emir of Kuwait, Kuwait City (Kuwait), *279*
Dmochowski, Zbigniew, 1, 31, 102, 130–45, *131*, *133*, *136–38*, *140*, 165; *Architecture of Poland*, 138; *An Introduction to Nigerian Traditional Architecture*, 130, *130*, 134–35, *136*, *137*, 142, 325n169
D'Olivo, Marcello, 209
Don Arthur, E.G.A., 41
Doxiadis, Constantinos, 2, 37, 44
Doxiadis Associates, *45*, 82, 84–85, 99, 156, *157*, 176, 178, *179*, 189
Doychev, Z., 55
drawings. *See* architectural drawings
Drew, Jane, 2, 42, 60, 88–92, 129; *Tropical Architecture in the Humid Zone*, 42, 89–90, 92
Drewnowski, Jan, 106
Druzhba pipeline, *216*
Drużyński, Jan, *53*, 54
Dubai, United Arab Emirates, 243, 245, 277
Dudok, Willem Marinus, 176
Dumez, 201
Dundakov, Kuno, 17, *18*, 255, *256–58*, 265
Dundakova, Stanka, 17, *18*, 255, *256–58*, 265
Dunikowski, Marek, *28*
Dunkel, William, 176–77
Durbar (Nigeria), 130
Dziennik Polski (Poland, newspaper), 173–74

E
earth scrapers, 118, *119*, 120
Eastern Europe: backwardness of, 103–5, 125; defined, 319n2; diversity within, 4; Global South's relations with, 11; peripheral status of, 31, 100–103, 125–26, 145; plans for postwar reorganization of, 103–6; Soviet Union in relation to, 15, 171–72; West Africa likened to, 31, 100–106, 125, 127, 145, 165, 167; worlding of, 101, 105, 125, 165, 305. *See also individual countries*
Eastern European architects/planners: concepts and tools of, 101; in Ghana, 50, 52, 54–55, 93; in Global South, 1–4, 6, 11, 16–17, 25, 33, 304–5; in historiography of architecture, 2, 4, 8, 33, 55, 303; in Kuwait, 240–41, 271–98; Middle Eastern restrictions on, 258–59; in Nigeria, 31, 99–101, 130–67; non-European training grounds of, 298–99; technological and cultural competence of, 21, 100, 216, 242, 260, 265–72, 274, 292–98; in UAE, 240–41; and West Africa, 31, 33, 93–94, 106–25
East Germany (GDR), 15, 21; Ghana and, 46, 50; Iraq and, 173, 210–25, 237; relations with developing countries, 212–13, 225
Economic Community of West African States (ECOWAS), 6
economics and finances: in Ghana, 48, 50, 66, 85, 88, 106; in Iraq, 170; of less-developed countries, 103–5; liberalization policies and, 6–7; in Nigeria, 99, 153, 155; Soviet model of, 5, 8, 11, 46–48, 50, 64, 85. *See also* socialist development path; world socialist system
education. *See* architectural education/training
Egbor, Augustine, 15, *139*, 143

Egyházi, András, *23*
Eko Hotel, Lagos (Nigeria), 25, *26*, 99
Ekwueme, Alex, 142
Emödy, Attila, 277
Emokpae, Erhabor, 97, *98*
employment. *See* labor
Energoprojekt, 17, 22, *24*, 25, 99, 102, 122, *123*, 145–65, *150–55*, *158*, *160–62*, *166*, 210, *211*, *274*, *276*, 277, 280, 300, 305
Energoprojekt Engineering and Contracting Company, 155
Engmann, E.Y.S., *51*, 72
Erickson, Arthur, 209, 251, 295, *295*
Esie, Nigeria, regional museum, *139*, 140
Esuene, Udoakaha Jacob, *100*
Ethnographica, 134
European Development Fund, 5
Evans, J. E., 128, *128*
Evening News (Ghana, newspaper), 56, *57*, 61
Exhibition Center, Beijing (China), *9*
Eyo, Ekpo, 132

F
Fagg, Bernard, 132, 134
Faisal II, King of Iraq, 169
Falconer, John, 108, 110
Farkas, Tibor, 108–9, *109*
Fathy, Hassan, 248
Fatteh, N., *247*
Federal Secretariat Complex, Ikoyi, Lagos (Nigeria), *153*, 155
Ferens, Robert R., 143
FESTAC (Second World Festival of Black and African Culture), 97, 99, 102, 129–30, 153, 163
Festac Town, Lagos (Nigeria), 99, *124*, 156, *162*, 163
Fidali, Bolesław, *132*
Filipow, Zbigniew, 106
Filippovich, Irina, 64–65
Findeco House, Lusaka (Zambia), *24*
Fintas Center, Fintas (Kuwait), 295, *295*
Fitzroy Robinson Partnership, 252, *253*
5 July 1962 Stadium, Algiers (Algeria), *23*, 113, 265, 300
Flagstaff House apartments, Accra (Ghana), 39, 52, 55, *119*
Fola Alade, Isaac, *153*, 155
Foreign Trade Organization for Complete Industrial Plants (Cekop, Poland), 174; advertisement for, *3*
foreign trade organizations (FTOs), 27, 94, 174, 240, 297–98
France, 42, 67
Friendship Monument, Ulaanbaatar (Mongolia), *10*
Fritz Thier, 214, 221, 222, 225, 231
Fry, Drew, Drake & Lasdun, 42, *43*, 84, 127
Fry, Maxwell, 2, 42, 60, 88–92, 129; *Tropical Architecture in the Humid Zone*, 42, 89–90, 92
FTOs. *See* foreign trade organizations
Functional Warsaw plan, 104, 183

G
Gaddafi, Muammar, 95
Gadomska, Anna, 56
Ganović, Branimir, *24*
Geidenreikh, N. N., *10*
gender, residential considerations pertaining to, 84

General Drafting System (GDS), 295
General Housing Programme for Iraq (GHPI), 32, 195–96, *197–99*, 200–201, *200*
GEO. *See* Gulf Engineering Office
George Paton, 42
Gerlach & Gillies-Reyburn, 42
GDR. *See* East Germany
Germany, 125
Ghana: architects, planners, and contractors in, 4, 30–31; architectural heritage of, 63–64; architectural training for, 39, 42; Britain and, 37, 41–42; China and, 11, 37; Committee for Economic Cooperation with Eastern Countries, 50; Eastern European architects in, 50, 52, 54–55, 93; economy in, 48, 50, 66, 85, 88, 106; housing in, 37, 42, 60, 62, 64–66, 73–85, *80–83*, *112*, *119*, 120; independence of, 5; infrastructure in, 60; international exchange and collaboration in, 36, 39, 50, 52, 55; International Trade Fair (ITF), 37; intersecting politics in, 37; local architects and labor in, 42; Ministry for Fuel and Power, 112; Ministry of Works, 39, 75; modern architecture in, 31, 37–39, 52, 55–64; national control of architecture in, 55–64, 113; National Museum and Monuments Board, 63; National Physical Development Plan, 106–7, *107*; National Planning Commission, 106; persistence of colonial practices in, 39; planning in, 106–8, 110, 112–13; Poland and, 46, 50, 52, 54, 90, 93, 106; Public Works Department (PWD), 39, 41, 50, 52, 55, 56, 63; residential-district plans for, 37, 73–85; social differentiation in, 62; and socialism, 36–37, 44, 46, 64, 73, 87–88, 106–7; socialist path of development in, 48, 50, 64, 85; social unification in, 60; Soviet Union and, 36–37, 44, 46–48, 50, 73–85; Town and Country Planning Division (TCPD), 52, 65, *65*, *84*, 87, 106; United States and, 37, 44
Ghana Farmers' Office, 41
Ghana Housing Corporation, 41, 42
Ghanaian Times (newspaper), 46, *47*, 56
Ghana Institute of Architects, 6, 92
Ghana National Construction Company, 39, *41*, *51*
Ghana National Construction Corporation (GNCC), 30–31, *34*, 36, *36*, 37, 39, 41, 42, 44, *44*, 48, 50, *51*, *53*, 55–64, *59*, 75, 82, *85–90*, 90, 92–94, *119*, 120
GHPI. *See* General Housing Programme for Iraq
Gibb, Alexander. *See* Alexander Gibb & Partners
Gibb, Petermuller & Partners, 245
Gidan Makama, Kano (Nigeria), 132, *137*, 142
Gidroproekt, 112
Giedion, Sigfried, 141
Gierek, Edward, 15, 272
gift diplomacy, 69–73
Gilmour, A., 42
Giprogor (State Institute for the Planning of Cities), 18, *19*, 75–85, *76–83*, 94
Giprostroiindustriia (State Design Institute for the Construction of Industrial Buildings), 75
Giprosviaz (Design Institute of the Ministry of Communication), 179
Giprovuz (State Design Institute for Higher Educational Institutions), 67, *68*, *70*, 71
glass-reinforced concrete (GRC), 294
Glavproekt, 50, *51*
Gleń, Włodzimierz, 200–201, *247*, 273
Glissant, Édouard, 30

INDEX 349

globalization, 30, 241, 259, 303
global socialism, 30
Global South: architects, planners, and contractors in, 1–4, 6, 11, 16–17, 25, 33, 304–5; Global North contrasted with, 7; Soviet Union and, 7–8, 15; urbanization in, 4, 33
GNCC. *See* Ghana National Construction Corporation
Gniadzik, Jan, 144
Godwin, John, 42, 128
Gołąb, Zdzisław, *198*
Gold Coast Society of Architects, 92
Gonchar, L. U., *10*
Gosstroi (State Committee for Construction), 75, 82
Gowon, Yakubu, 99, 163
Greer, J., 128, *128*
Grishin, D., *19*
Gropius, Walter, 176
Gross, Maria, 298
Gruner, 260
Guinea, 11, 36, 46, 50, 67, *68*, 69, 155
Gulf Engineering Office (GEO), 15, 283, *286*
Gulf states: architectural heritage of, 248; housing in, 252; restrictions placed on foreign firms, 258–59; technological and cultural competence in, 265–72, 274, 292–98; urbanization in, 242–54; vernacular architecture in, 252. *See also* Kuwait; United Arab Emirates
Gulf War, first, 4
Gulf Weekly Mirror (Bahrain, newspaper), 243

H

Habitat Associates, 144
Hajdúböszörmény, Hungary, plan of, *105*
Halliday, Anthony, 92
Hallstein Doctrine, 15, 213
Halmágyi, Ildikó, *23*
Hames, J. C., 128
Hammond, R.H.C., 42
Hassan, K., 201
Hausa architecture, 134, 140
Havana, Cuba, 18
Havelka, Jan Amos, *279*, 279, 299
heritage. *See* architectural heritage
Higher Administration School, Bamako (Mali), *70*, 71
Hirst, Philip, 177
historiography of architecture, 2, 4, 8, 33, 55, 303
Hollo, Nick, 144; "Climatic Comfort Design Guide for Nigeria," *146–47*
Hood, Alan G., 65
Hopwood, Gillian, 42, 128
Hotel Camayenne, Conakry (Guinea), 67, *68*, 71
House of Culture and Youth Theater Complex, Darkhan (Mongolia), *21*
house of T. Leśko, Olhomle (Poland), *131*
housing: in Algeria, 235, *236*; in Ghana, 37, 42, 60, 62, 64–66, 73–85, *80–83*, *112*, *119*, *120*; in Gulf states, 252; in Iraq, 169, 176, 189–90, *191*, 195–96, *195*, 198–201, *199*, *200*, 232, *233*, *234*, 235; in Kuwait, *276*, 277, *287*, *294*; in Libya, *231*; in Nigeria, 118, *118–19*, *120*, *124*, 156; prefabrication and mass production in construction of, 66–67, 69, 75, 80, *81*, 85, 200, 228, 232, 235; Soviet, 30, 64–67, 78–80; type designs for, 232, *233*. *See also* mikroraiony
Housing Buildings for Export (Romproiect), 232

Housing estate, Jijel (Algeria), *23*
Howard, Ebenezer, 102
Howard University, Washington, DC (United States), 41
Hryniewiecki, Jerzy, 179, 328n71
Hübner, Tibor, 17, 277
Hungary, 15, 16; City Planning Bureau (VÁTERV), 108–9, *109*; Communist Party in, 93, 102; Ghana and, 46, 50; planning and development of, 104–5; Polónyi's planning work in, 108–10; West Africa and, 93–94
Hussein, Saddam, 95, 209, 214
Huszar, Laszlo, 112
Hydro Power Plant Kpimé (Togo), 150

I

Ideological Institute, Winneba (Ghana), 54, 55
Il'chik, L., 82, *83*
Ilinčev, Orlin, 295, 299
INCO. *See* Kuwait: Industrial and Engineering Consulting Office
indigenous architecture. *See* vernacular architecture
Indonesia, 8, 11
Industrial Development Corporation (Ghana), 39
Industrieprojektierung (Ipro) Dessau, *212*, 214–15, *231*
Ingra, 22, 52, 150
Institute for Town Construction Projects (Gorstroiproekt, Soviet Union), 18
Institute for Town Planning and Housing (Yugoslavia), 122, 151
Institute of Africa, Soviet Academy of Sciences, 46
Institute of Economics of the World Socialist System (Moscow), 170
Institute of Oceanography, Conakry (Guinea), *14*
Institute of Polish Architecture, Warsaw University of Technology (Poland), 131, *131*, 135, 138
Institute of Technological Design for Light Industry (IPIU, Romania), 153, 230–31, *233*
Institute of Tropical Architecture (Poland), 25, 132
Inter-American Housing Center, Bogotá (Colombia), 41
Intercoop, 27
International Bank of Reconstruction and Development. *See* World Bank
International Congresses of Modern Architecture (CIAM), 101, 102, 104–6, 183
international exchange and collaboration in architecture, 3–4, 25–26, 95; benefits of, for Eastern European architects, 299–300; Bulgaria and, 262–64; in Ghana, 36, 39, 50, 52, 55, 85; in Iraq, 201–37; in Kuwait, 239–42, 273–98; in Nigeria, 151–53, 155; and socialist-capitalist relations, 171, 173, 262–64; tropical architecture and, 91–92; in UAE, 239–42, 258–71; in world socialist system, 210–37; Yugoslavia and, 151–53
International Federation of Consulting Engineers (FIDIC), 264
International Monetary Fund, 6, 148
International Organization for Technical-Scientific Cooperation. *See* Tesco
International Postgraduate Course of Urban and Regional Planning for Developing Countries, Szczecin (Poland), 25, 184, 186
International Trade Fair (ITF), Accra (Ghana), 31,

35–36, *36*, 37, 42, *44*, 52, 64, 85–93, *85–90*, 307
International Trade Fair (ITF), Lagos (Nigeria), 22, 31, 52, 99, 102, 149, *150–51*, *154–55*, 155–56, *158*, 159–63, *160–62*, 165, *166*, 307
International Union of Architects (UIA), 3, 110, 260
Inwestprojekt-Wrocław, 272, 273
Ion Mincu University of Architecture (Bucharest), 11, 232, 331n292
IPARTERV, 108
IPIU. *See* Institute of Technological Design for Light Industry
Ipro Dessau. *See* Industrieprojektierung (Ipro) Dessau
Ipro Dresden, 32
Iraq: agricultural consulting and training center, *218*; architects, planners, and contractors in, 4; architectural education/training in, 179, 205–6, 328n180; Britain and, 174–75; Consulting Board for the Affairs of the Master Plan, 184–85, 192; East Germany and, 173, 210–25, 237; economy of, 170; financial terms of technical assistance for, 180–82; housing in, 169, 176, 189–90, *191*, 195–96, *195*, 198–201, *199*, *200*, 232, *233*, *234*, 235; Kuwait invaded by, 298; "Main village," *218*; Ministry of Agriculture and Agrarian Reform, 214; Ministry of Municipalities, 179, *180*; Ministry of Works and Housing, 179, 202, 204; Poland and, 173–210, 237; Qasim's coup in, 4, 95, 169, 176, 213; Revolutionary Command Council, 183, 214; Romania and, 173, 210–15, 221–35; and socialism, 32, 95, 169–71, 179; Soviet Union and, 170, 178–81; State Organization for Housing, 195, 200–201; Yugoslavia and, 210. *See also* Baghdad, Iraq
Islam, 47–48, 134, 150, 241, 243
Islamic architecture. *See* Arab-Islamic architectural elements
Islamic Decree, 253
isometries, 135, 138, 143
Israel, 6, 183, 213
Israel Construction Company–Solel Boneh, 39
Italconsult, 262
Italy, 42, 125
ITF. *See* International Trade Fair (ITF), Accra (Ghana); International Trade Fair (ITF), Lagos (Nigeria)
Ivan Milutinović (PIM), 22, 280, 326n266

J

Jack, William, 127
Jamal, Karim, 251
Jankowski, Stanisław, 179, *180*, 328n71
Japanese Consortium of Consulting Firms, *194*, 327n1
Jarząbek, Wojciech, *247*, *270*, 270, 271, 272–73, 280, *281*, 282–83, *284*, *287*, *288*, 294, *296*, 297, 298, *299*
Job 600, Accra (Ghana), *53*, 54, 56, 59, 63
Joint Factory 718, Beijing (China), 32
joint-intergovernmental committees, 18, 213, 240
joint ventures, 152–53, 155, 161–63, 277
Jonkajtys-Luba, Grażyna, 17, *84*, 93, 324n47
Joseph, Joe, 63
Jos Museum (Nigeria), 132, *133*, 134
Juchnowicz, Stanisław, 122, *123*, 145
Julius Berger, 156

Junior Staff Housing, Osu Castle, Accra (Ghana), 63

K

Kabul, Afghanistan, 18
Kaduna (Nigeria): regional museum, *139*, 140; State House, 128, *128*
Kahn, Louis, 2, 190
Kalecki, Michał, 103
Kalogjera, Berislav, 52
Kamil, Abdullah Ihsan, 176, 184, 205
Kankam, Edwin, 41
Kapuściński, Ryszard, 142
Karaman, Ljubo, 145, 149
Kareem, al-Tayeb Rabel Abdul, 239
Kataev, L., 21
Katamba of Etsu Pategi, Pategi (Nigeria), 138, *138*
Kataria, L. D., 161
Katsarov, Dimitar, 50
KEG. *See* Kuwait Engineering Group
Keita, Modibo, 67, 71
Kennedy, John F., 6
Kessab, Syria, *261*
Kharafi, 277
Khatib & Alami, 169, 327n1
Khishigt, A., *10*
Khrushchev, Nikita, 8, *10*, 15, 30, 36, 46, 66, 69, 80, 85, 99, 171, 221, 225
Kidd, W. J., 143
Kilimani (Zanzibar), *16*
"Kingsway Street Map of Accra," *38*
Kislova, K. D., *9*
Kłosiewicz, Lech, 206
Koenigsberger, Otto, 156
Kola-Bankole, S. I., 142
Kolchev, Stefan, 22, *96–97*, *97*, *98*, *164*, 165
Konovalov, I., *19*
Korle Bu Hospital, Accra (Ghana), 39, 42, 56, 60
Korneeva, G., 82, *83*
Kosel, Gerhard, 216
Kosnikova, I. V., *10*
Kotliński, Jakub, 52
Közti (Design Institute for Public Buildings), 17, 22, *23*, 113, *116–19*, 118, 120, *121*, 122, 125, 160, 265, 300
Krawecki, Janusz, 273, 279
Kumasi Stadium (Ghana), 42
Kuwait: Eastern European architects/planners in, 240–41; housing in, 277, 287, 294; Industrial and Engineering Consulting Office (INCO), 273–74, *281*, 282, *284*, *285*, 290, *290*, *291*, 292; international exchange and collaboration in, 239–42, 273–98; Iraqi invasion of, 298; Kuwait Engineering Office, 15; Ministry of Public Works, *249*, *250*, 274, *279*, 280; National Housing Authority (NHA), 251–52, 280, 282, 294; Poland and, 271, 273–74; relationship to socialism, 95, 240; Soviet Union and, 240; urbanization in, 240, 245–46, 251, 280–91. *See also* Kuwait City, Kuwait
Kuwait City, Kuwait, 15; Al-Shaab Gate, preliminary field study, *249*; Amiri Diwan and Council of Ministers, 248, *250*, 295; Anwar al-Sabah Complex at the Fahad al-Salem Street, *293*; architects, planners, and contractors in, 4; architectural heritage of, 246, 248, 251–52; Audit Bureau Headquarters Building, *247*, *296*, *297*; Baloush Bus Terminal, 290, *290*, *291*; Bayan Park Conference Center, 274, *274–75*, 280, 294; Diwaniyya for H.H. Emir of Kuwait, *279*; Eastern European architects/planners in, 271–98; housing in, *276*; master plans for, 246, *249*, 251; Ministries Complex, 25, 274, *276*; Senior Citizens Housing, *281*, 282; Sief Palace, 248, *250*; Souk Dawliyah, 283, *286*, 290
Kuwait Engineering Group (KEG), *247*, 273, 283, *287*, *288*, 295, *296*, 297
Kuwaiti Architecture: A Lost Identity (film), 251
Kuwait Times (newspaper), 261
Kwiatkowski, B. S., 106
Kyei, Kojo Gyinaye, 41

L

La, Accra, Ghana, 86, 323n239
"Labadi Slum Clearance. Basic Map–Master Plan Proposals," *84*
labor: employment of local residents, 25, 161–62; international division of, 21, 170, 172, 173, 212, 221, 236–37, 305; modalities of, 29; Romanian, 228; study of, 27, 29; treatment of, 161–62, 294. *See also* architectural labor
Lach, Edward, *247*, 270, *270*, *271*, 272–73, 280, *281*, 282–83, *286*, *287*, *288*, 294, *296*, *297*, 298
Lagos, Nigeria, 97–99, 127, 131–67; architects, planners, and contractors in, 1–2, 15; crisis conditions in, 156, 159; Eko Hotel, 25, *26*, 99; Federal Secretariat Complex, Ikoyi, *153*, 155; FESTAC, 97, 99, 102, 129–30, 153, 163; Festac Town, 99, *124*, 156, *162*, *163*; growth in, *157*; housing in, *124*, 156; International Trade Fair (ITF), 22, 31, 52, 99, 102, 149, *150–51*, *154–55*, 155–56, *158*, 159–63, *160–62*, 165, *166*, 307; land use in, *157*; National Arts Theater, 1, 22, *96*, *97*, *98*, 163, *164*, 165
Lake Balaton. *See* Balaton Regional Outline Plan
Lartey, E., *62*
Lasdun, Denys, 274. *See also* Fry, Drew, Drake & Lasdun
Laube, Jan, 52, 56, 63, 90
Lăzărescu, Cezar, 22, *24*, 213, 235
League of Nations, 125
Le Corbusier, 2, 176, 251
Lefebvre, Henri, 29
Legostaev, A., *14*
Leonowicz, Władysław, *191*
Lewis, William Arthur, 47
Libya, 95, 227–28, 230; Airport Road Housing, Tripoli, 227, *227*; housing in, *231*; planetarium, Tripoli, 219–20, *219*, *220*
Limex, 27, 219, 258
Lindström, Sune and Joe, 248
Lloyd, John, 55, 110
Lock, Max, 179
Luba, Jerzy, 17, *84*, 93, 106, 324n47
Ludlam, O. J., *51*
Lumumba University. *See* Patrice Lumumba University
Lumumba, Patrice, 46
Lun'kov, B., *19*
Łyczkowski, Marian, *139*, 140, 144

M

Madfai, Kahtan, 195, 199, 201, 207
Magyar, Peter, 144
Magyar Építőművészet (Hungarian Architecture; journal), 298
Mahmudiyah, Iraq, *197–99*, 198, 199
Main Bus Terminal, Abu Dhabi (UAE), 255, *256*, *257*, 265
Makarycheva, A., *79*
Makhlouf, Abdulrahman, 243
Makiya, Mohamed, 15, 176, 201, 205, 206, 248, 255, 280
Makiya, Munir, Madhloom Associates, 207
Maksimović, Stojan, 274, *274–75*, 294
Mali, 36, 46, 67, *70*, 71
Mańkowski, Tomasz, 190
Mandate system, 125
Manov, Nako, 210, *212*
Mao Zedong, 4, 11
Marasović, Miro, *x*, 52, *58*, *59*
March, Werner, 177
market socialism, 15, 27, 152–53
Markiewicz, Aleksander, *201*, 202
Maroko, S., *75*
Marshall Plan, 6
Marxism, 36, 306
Masallaci Juma'a, Zaria (Nigeria), 135, *136*, 140, 142
Mason, Harold C., 175. *See also* Wilson Mason
Mauss, Marcel, 69
Mayer & Whittlesey, 84
Mazurkiewicz, Małgorzata, *28*
Mbari Club, 129
Medeksza, S., *272*
Meir, Golda, 39
Meissner, Jan Jacek, *28*
Miastoprojekt-Kraków, 17, 32, *168*, 169, 173–74, *178–210*, 184, 185, *187–89*, 193, *195–200*, 243, 245, 273, 277, 306
Middle East Construction (journal), 282
Midhat Pasha, 174
Miecznikowski, Wojciech, *28*
Mieszkowska, Danuta, 198, *198*
Mikhaila, Mallam, 142
mikroraiony (micro-districts), 18, 48, *49*, 67, 78
Milenković, Dušan, *24*, 150
Ministries Complex, Kano (Nigeria), 151, *152*
Ministries Complex, Kuwait City (Kuwait), 25, 274, *276*
Ministry of Defense Building, Kabul (Afghanistan), *26*
Ministry of Oil Building, Baghdad (Iraq), 210
Minoprio, Spencely & Macfarlane, 177–78, *177*, 190, 192, 245
Mlodzianowski, Peter, 252–53, *253*
Mndoiants, A., *172*
modern architecture: as break from past, 127; critiques of, 251–52, 272; in Ghana, 31, 37–39, 52, 55–64; in Gulf states, 251; historiography of, 303; mediation of Arab-Islamic architecture and, 253–54; mobility of, 2–4; in Nigeria, 31, 128–45; space as chief concern of, 141–42; in UAE, 33
modernization: architecture as component of, 29, 90; in Central Asia, 47; dividends of, 29, 110, 118; in Ghana, 36, 60, 63, 90, 305; in Hungary, 105; in Iraq, 214; in Nigeria, 99, 118; socialist, 8, 16, 305
Mohács Island Regional Restoration Plan (Hungary), 108–9, *109*
Molnár, Farkas, 104
Mongolia, 8, 11, 18, 171, 222
Monument of Agostinho Neto, Luanda (Angola), *14*
Monument of Kwame Nkrumah, Winneba (Ghana),

54, *54*
Moravánszky, Ákos, 103
Moscow Architectural Institute (MARKhI), 41, 179
Mosproekt 1, 67, *69*
Mostogradnja, 161
Mostostal-Zabrze, 280
MOTNA. *See* Museum of Traditional Nigerian Architecture
Mubarak al-Kabeer area, Kuwait, *281*, 282–83, *284*, *285*
Mučalov, Živko, 149
Muhammed, Murtala, 99
Municipality and Town Planning Department Building, Abu Dhabi (UAE), 32–33, 238–39, *239*, 241–43, 254–56, *254–55*, 260, 264, 268, *268–71*, 270–71, 294
Municipality Building, Al Ain (UAE), 241, 256, 265, *266*, *267*, 268
Munir, Hisham, 176, 201, 205
Murray, Kenneth, 132, 140, 141
Museum of Traditional Nigerian Architecture (MOTNA), Jos (Nigeria) 130, 132, *133*, 134
Mustansiriyah University, Baghdad (Iraq), 202, *202–3*, 204
Müther, Ulrich, 220
"mutual advantage" principle, 15, 170, 181, 213, 226
Myszkowski, Tadeusz, 199

N
Naidenovich, Ivan, 52
Naiman, Albert, *233*
NAM. *See* Non-Aligned Movement
Namiq, Hazim, 176
Nancy, Jean-Luc, 30
Nasser, Gamal Abdel, 7
National Archives Building, Accra (Ghana), 42, *43*
National Arts Theater, Lagos (Nigeria), 1, 22, *96*, *97*, *98*, 163, *164*, *165*
National Assembly Building, Conakry (Guinea), 67, *68*
National Commission for Museums and Monuments, Lagos (Nigeria), 134
National Construction Company (Pakistan), 294
National Council of Ghana Women, 48
National Electricity Board Building, Baghdad (Iraq), 204
National Housing Corporation (Libya), 227, *227*
National Liberation Movement (Ghana), 63
National Library, Damascus (Syria), *28*, 273
National Museum, Accra (Ghana), 42, *43*
National Stadium, Jakarta (Indonesia), *10*, 11
NECCO. *See* Nigerian Engineering and Construction Company
Nehru, Jawaharlal, 7
neighborhood units, 48, 178, 189, 243, 260
neoliberalism, 6–7
Netherlands, 42
New Culture (journal), 129
New International Economic Order (NIEO), 148, 213
NHA. *See* Kuwait: National Housing Authority
Nianshi, Tai, *9*
Nickson, Borys & Partners, 42, *43*
Niemczyk, E., *272*
Nigeria: architects, planners, and contractors in, 4, 31; architectural education/training in, 134–35, 142–45; Britain and, 142–44; civil war in, 99; decolonization in, 127–45; Department of Antiquities, 131–32, 135; Dmochowski's work in, 130–42; Eastern European architects/planners in, 31, 99–101, 130–67; Eastern Europe compared to, 31, 100–101; economy in, 99; Federal Ministry of Works and Surveys (FMWS), 127; housing in, 118, *118–19*, 120, *124*, 156; indigenization of business and management in, 153, 155; joint venture with Energoprojekt, 102; Ministry of Works, *128*; Ministry of Works and Housing, *139*, 140, 143, 144; modern architecture in, 128–45; Northern Region Public Works Department, 128, *128*; oil production of, 99; planning in, 113–25, 151, 159; Poland and, 131, 145; relationship to socialism, 95, 99–100, 102, 153; traditional politics avoided in, 128; vernacular architecture in, 102, 129–30, 132, 134–35, 142, 143–44; Yugoslavia and, 148, 150–65. *See also* Calabar, Nigeria; Lagos, Nigeria
Nigerian Chronicle (newspaper), 120
Nigerian College of Arts, Science, and Technology, 142
Nigerian Engineering and Construction Company (NECCO), 25, 149, 155–56, 159–63
Nigerian Enterprises Promotion Decree, 153
Nigerian Institute of Architects, 6, 144
Nkrumah, Kwame, 4, 5, 7, 8, 30–31, 35–37, 39, 46–48, 50, 54, 55–56, *57*, 59–60, 66, 73, 87, 92, 102–3, 107, 110, 127, 148, 305, 307
Nok, Nigeria, house, 140, *140*
Non-Aligned Movement (NAM), 240; as alternative to Soviet Union, 37; formation of, 4, 7; Ghana and, 37, 87, 148; Iraq and, 210; Nigeria and, 99; program of, 7; Yugoslavia and, 16, 37, 148–50
Norberg-Schulz, Christian, 141
North Korea, 8
Novozhilova, A., *14*
Nowosadski, Jarosław, 52
Ntukidem, Anam E., 120, 122
Nwoko, Demas, 129, 135, 141

O
Obada, O. E., 155
Obasanjo, Olusegun, 99, 129
Oba's Palace, Benin (Nigeria), *137*
Obtułowicz, Wojciech, *196*
Ochakovo, *82*
office building, Samarra, *180*
Ogaily, Akram, 248, 274
oil: barter for, 171, 173, 213, 226, 230; design and construction exchanged for, 171; embargo on (1973), 16, 170, 171; in Iraq, 192, 213, 226; in Nigeria, 99, 120; reexport of, by Eastern Europe and Soviet Union, 226
Okeke, Uche, 141
Okeke-Agulu, Chika, 141
Olafioye, Tayo, 113
Olęcka, Danuta, *196*
Oleszkiewicz, Ewa, 143
Olgyay brothers, 91
Olumuyiwa, Oluwole, 25, *26*, 128, 129, 142, 144
Onabolu, Aina, 141
Onafowokan, Michael Olutusen, 142, 144
I-464 prefabrication system, 80, 82, 83, 322n220
Ong, Aihwa, 101
Onimode, Bade, 161, 163
OPEC. *See* Organization of the Petroleum Exporting Countries

Organization of African Unity (OAU), 54, 63
Organization of the Petroleum Exporting Countries (OPEC), 7, 170, 240
Orientalism, 125, 141
Ostpolitik, 15
Osu Castle, Accra (Ghana), *51*, 52, 59, 63
Oțoiu, Anca, 277, *278*, 279
Ove Arup & Partners. *See* Arup, Ove
Owusu-Addo, John, x, 58, *59*, 113
Oxford Statistical Institute, 103

P
PACE. *See* Pan Arab Consulting Engineers
Palace of Culture and Sports, Varna (Bulgaria), *97*, *98*
pan-Africanism, 36, 37, 54, 87
Pan Arab Consulting Engineers (PACE), 274, 297
Panfil', A., *78*, *79*, 82, *83*
Pantić, Ivan, 277
Pantó, Gergely, 122
Parliament Building, Khartoum (Sudan), 22, *24*
Patrice Lumumba University (USSR), 25, 46, *47*, 72
PCC. *See* Council of Mutual Economic Assistance (Comecon): Permanent Commission for Construction
Pchel'nikov, K. P., *10*
"peaceful coexistence," 8, 36, 46
Peduase Lodge, near Aburi (Ghana), 59, *59*
People's Art Club of Residential Area, Accra (Ghana), *78*
Peoples' Friendship University. *See* Patrice Lumumba University
People's Shop, Accra (Ghana), 60, *61*
periphery: defined, 145; Eastern Europe as, 31, 100–103, 145; West Africa as, 102, 145, 148, 149; Yugoslavia as, 149
petrobarter, 226, 230
Petrov, Vasil, 256, 265–66, *266*, *267*
Pietilä, Reima, 283
Planetarium, Tripoli (Libya), 219–20, *219*, *220*, 235
planning: in Abu Dhabi, 243, *245*; application of Eastern European ideas to West Africa, 106–22; in Baghdad, 32, *168*, *169*, 173–210; in Eastern Europe, 104–5; in Ghana, 106–8, 110, 112–13; in Hungary, 108–10; joint economic and spatial, 106, 108; in Kuwait, 246, *249*, 251; of less-developed countries, 103–5; in Nigeria, 113–25, 151, 159; in Poland, 106, 183, 186; Polish empirical approach to, 192; regional, 104–10, 114; socialist approach to, 106–8, 110; training in, 192, 195; various city plans, 18, *19*, *20*, 21; in Yugoslavia, 151
Pletsch, Carl, 92
Podolak, Ewa, 143
Point Four Program, 6
Poland, 15, 16, 21, 26; architects, planners, and contractors from, 16; colonialism of, 126; Communist Party in, 93; foreign contracts provided by, 196–97; Ghana and, 46, 50, 52, 54, 90, 93, 106; international participation of, 91; Iraq and, 173–210, 237; Kuwait and, 271, 273–74; Nigeria and, 131, 145; planning in, 106, 183, 186; vernacular architecture in, 131, *132*, *272*; West Africa and, 93–94
Police Headquarters, Accra (Ghana), 39, 56
Polish School of Architecture, Liverpool (UK), 131, 138
Polónyi, Charles (Károly), *12*, 31, 50, 52, 55, 93,

99–103, *100*, 105, 108–26, *109*, *111*, *119*, 145, 148, 165, 167
Polservice, 27, 36, 52, 91, 93–94, 145, 153, 174, 180–82, 192, 196, 204, 227, 265, 271, 273, 297, 306; advertisement for, *28*
Polytechna, 27, 205, 274, 297
Polytechnic Institute, Conakry (Guinea), 67, *68*
Ponti, Gio, 176, *177*
Port Authority, Shuwaikh (Kuwait), 290–91, *292*
Posokhin, M. V., 172, *172*
postcolonial Global South: cultural emancipation in, 127–30; Eastern European architects/planners in, 304–5; Ghana, 62–63; Nigeria, 100, 127–45; persistence of Western and Soviet ties during, 5–6
postmodernism, 209, 251, 254, 280, 299
prefabrication, 66–67, 69, 75, 80, *81*, 200, 217, 219, *228*, 228, 229, 232, *236*
Presidential Tribune at the Black Star Square, Accra (Ghana), 39, *41*, 59
Professional Training Center, housing, Bamako (Mali), *70*
Prommashexport, 179
Ptaszycki, Tadeusz, 183
Public Works Department (PWD, Ghana), 39, 41, 50, 52, 55, 56, 63
Purdom, K.A.R., 127
PWD. *See* Public Works Department

Q

Qabazard, Jasem, 248
Qasim, Abd al-Karim, 4, 95, 169, 176, 179, 181, 183, 189, 210, 213

R

Raczyński, Jerzy, 135
Rad, 22, 210, 274
Radio Moscow, 46
Raitman, S., 75, *76–77*, 78
Raninskii, U. V., *10*
RaPro. *See* Rationalisierung und Projektierung Berlin
Rastan Dam, Syria, 260
Rationalisierung und Projektierung Berlin (RaPro), 214, 220
Ravnikar, Edvard, 209
Reagan, Ronald, 6
regional planning, 104–10, 114
reinforced concrete, 292–94
Repetii, A., *19*
Research and Design Institute for Building Materials Industry (Romania), 232, *235*
Research Center of the Economy of Less-Developed Countries (Warsaw, Poland), 103
RIBA. *See* Royal Institute of British Architects
Richert, Wiktor, 106–7, 145, 148
Rights and Obligations of an Expert, 181–82, 297
Rimsha, Anatolii Nikolaevich, 25; *Town Planning in Hot Climates*, 47–48, *49*
Robaczyński, Lech, 202, *202*, *203*, 204, *204*, 328n175
Robinson, Jennifer, 47
Roller, Henryk, *12–13*
Romania, 15, 16, 17; Algeria and, 331n292; contract and construction arrangements of, 226–28, 232, 235; Ghana and, 46; Iraq and, 173, 181, 210–15, 221–35; relations with developing countries, 212–13
Romconsult, 27, 99, *124*, *162*, 163, 227, 230, 277
Romproiect, 22, 32, 227, *229*, 230, *231*, 232, *233*, 235, *236*, *278*, 279, 300; *Housing Buildings for Export*, 232
Rosenstein-Rodan, Paul, 103
Rostow, Walt Whitman, 6
Royal Institute of British Architects (RIBA), 5, 92; Board of Architectural Education, 142–44; Overseas Relations Committee, 5
Royal Institute of International Affairs (London), 103
Rozanov, E., *14*
rural areas, planning for, 104, 107–8
rural-urban continuum, 113–14, 118
Ryba, Andrzej, 299
Rychlicki, Mieczysław, 282
Rymaszewski, Stanisław, *34*, 36, *36*, *44*, 50, 62, 63, *85–90*, 90, 92, 93
Rynki zagraniczne (Foreign Markets; journal), 29

S

Sabah al-Salem Neighborhood Site C, Mubarak al-Kabeer (Kuwait), *281*, 282–83, *284*, *285*, 290
Sachs, Ignacy, 103
Saida, Algeria, 235, *236*
Salim, Jewad, 177
Salim, Lorna, 206
Salmiya, Kuwait, residential building, 287, *289*
Saudi Arabia, 295
Saukke, A. B., *10*
Sauvy, Alfred, 29
Schille, Gertrud, *219*, 220, *220*
Schlesier, Karlheinz, 29
Schmid, Christian, 33
School of Architecture, Ahmadu Bello University, Zaria (Nigeria), 134, 135, 142–45
School of Architecture, Town Planning and Building, at University of Science and Technology, Kumasi (Ghana), 39, 42, 52, *52*, 102, 112; curriculum of, *114–15*
School of Research and Training in Earthquake Engineering, Roorkee (India), 91
Schreckenbach, Hannah, 54–55
Scott, Kenneth, 42, 92
Scott Brown, Denise, 209, 251
Seibert, Krystian, *22*
self-help programs, 110, 118
Semergiev, R. I., *10*
Senghor, Léopold Sédar, 126
Senior Citizens Housing, Kuwait City (Kuwait), *281*, 282
Senior Staff Club, Kumasi (Ghana), *58*, 59
Sert, Josep Lluís, 177
Service Block for House Groups with 1600–1800 Inhabitants, *79*
Serzhantov, V., *19*
shading devices, *72*
Shafi, Sayed, 183–84, 195
Sham, Mohammad Abul, 255
Shankland Cox Partnership, *249*
Shchusev, A., *14*
Shestopalov, V., *14*
Shiber, Saba George, 245, 283; *Kuwait Urbanization*, 282
Shiber Consult, 270, *270*, *271*, 273, *281*, 282, *284*, *285*, 287, *289*, 334n141
Shifrin, V., *21*
Shiriaevskaia, E. G., *10*
Shorja area competition, 207, *208*
Shumov, E., *14*
Sief Palace, Kuwait City (Kuwait), 248, *250*
Sienkiewicz, Henryk, 125
Sierakowski, Kazimierz, 52
Sim'an, Salam, 199
Simone, AbdouMaliq, 101
Sindermann, Horst, 214
Skanska, 299
Skidmore, Owings & Merrill (SOM), 248, 274, 280, 283, 295
Skokánek, Jan, 52
slaughterhouse, Baghdad (Iraq), 210–12, *212*, 214–15, *215*, 220–25, *231*, 232, *233*
Ślesińska, Alina, 54, *54*
Slijepčević, Aleksandar, 17, 161
Smithson, Alison and Peter, 283
Smuts, Jan, 125
Snam Progetti, 262
socialism: African, 8; Arab, 8; architectural labor in context of, 92–94, 305; architecture grounded in, 216–17; and building-gifts, 69–73; developing countries and, 8, 11, 16–17; diversity within, 4, 167; end of, 298–99; Ghana and, 36–37, 44, 46, 64, 73, 87–88, 106–7; global, 30; hostility toward, 95, 99–100, 102; Iraq and, 95, 169–71, 179; market, 15, 27, 152–53; Nigeria and, 95, 99–100, 102, 153; planning models based on, 106–8, 110; Soviet promotion of, 8; Western discourse on, 92; worldmaking of, 29–33, 305; world system ascribed to, 32; Yugoslavia and, 148, 152–53. *See also* socialist development path; world socialist system
socialist development path, 8, 11, 30–31, 37, 46–48, 64, 66, 85, 94, 100, 125, 170
Society of Engineers (Kuwait), 280
Society of Professional Architects (Nigeria), 144
Sofproekt, 256, 265
Sokolov, E., *14*
Solel Boneh, 39
Solomon, Ana, *124*
Solpol Department Store, Wrocław (Poland), 298, *299*
SOM. *See* Skidmore, Owings & Merrill
Sonetra, 71
Sosnowski, Oskar, 131, 135, 138
Souk Dawliyah, Kuwait City (Kuwait), 283, *286*, 290
souks, 175, 191, 198, *198*, 201, 243, 246, 251, 283, *286*, 290, 297
Soviet Academy of Sciences, 46
Soviet Union: Afghan invasion by, 282; architectural and construction services of, 8, 30; China and, 4, 8; and colonialism, 127; credits (barter) for building assistance supplied by, 73; developing countries' suspicion of, 213; Eastern Europe in relation to, 15, 171–72; Ghana and, 36–37, 44, 46–48, 50, 73–85; gift diplomacy of, 69–73; Global South and, 7–8, 15; Guinea and, 67, 69; Iraq and, 170, 178–81; Kuwait and, 240; Mali and, 71; Ministry of Installation and Special Construction Work, 71; socialist worldmaking undertaken by, 30; technical assistance and development aid from, 8, 11, 15, 17, 29, 180–81; and West Africa, 8, 46, 94; Yugoslavia vs., 4
space, as concern of architecture, 141–42

special economic zones, 26
Spezialbetonbau Binz, 220, 280
Sputnik, 8, 46
Squire, Raglan, 179
SSH, 283
Stalin, Joseph, 7, 148, 171
Stănculescu, Gheorghe Radu, 235, 300
standardization, 222, *223*
Staniszkis, Jerzy, *201*, 202
State Committee on Economic Cooperation (Soviet Union), 46–47
State House, Kaduna (Nigeria), 128, *128*
State House Complex, Accra (Ghana), 53, 54, *57*
State Housing Corporation (Ghana), 66
State Institute for the Restoration of Historic Towns and Monuments (SURPMO, Czechoslovakia), *249*
Ştefan, Dorin, 232
Šterić, Milica, 149, *152*, *276*
Stevenson, Charles C., 127
Stirling, James, 280
Strcula, Ján, 279
Strojexport, 27, 153, *249*, 280
students' housing, University of Ghana, Legon, *62*
Studio A+R, *299*
Studio and Practice Hall for the National Orchestra, Accra (Ghana), 44
Sudanese Union Party, 71
Sukarno, 7, 8, *10*
Sultan, Ghazi, 248
Suwaj, Tadeusz, *191*
Syria, 95, 113, 183, 224, 260, 299
Syrkus, Szymon, 104
Szabados, László, 122

T
Tabqa, Syria, 21, *22*
TAC. *See* The Architects Collaborative
Tashkent, Uzbek Soviet Socialist Republic, 47, 80, 304
Tayeb Engineering, 238–39, *239–40*, *254–55*, 255–56, 258, 262–66, *266*, *267*, *268*, *269*
Taylor Woodrow, 42, 155
TCPD. *See* Ghana: Town and Country Planning Division
Team 10, 55, 110
technical guidelines, for design and construction of buildings, 39, 72, 112, *146–47*, 217
Technical Training College, Accra (Ghana), 42
Technoexportstroy (TES), 1, 17, 22, 25, *26*, *96–97*, *97*, *98*, 99, 153, 161, 163, *164*, *165*, 177, 228, 239–41, 243, 255–72, *261*, 300; catalogues of, 262, *263*
technological adaptation, 228, 230, 232, 235
Tekhnoexport, 71
Tema, Ghana, 44, 73, *74*, 75, 78–80, *80–83*, 82–85, 108
Tema Development Corporation (Ghana), 66
Tér és Forma (Space and Form; journal), 104, *105*
TES. *See* Technoexportstroy
Tesco (International Organization for Technical-Scientific Cooperation), 27, 50, 52, 93, 113, 122, 125, 153, 160, 277, 297
Teshie Nungua, Greater Accra (Ghana), 42
Tetteh, Austin, 106
Thier. *See* Fritz Thier
Tito, Josip Broz, 7, 148, 149
Top, 161

Touré, Ahmed Sékou, 67
town planning. *See* planning
Trades Union Congress Building (Ghana), 48, 56, 59, 69
traditional architecture. *See* architectural heritage; vernacular architecture
Transportmaschinen, 214, 222, 224
Trevallion, B.A.W., *65*
Triad Associates, 144
Tricontinental Conference, 7
Tripoli, Libya, *20*, 21, 219–20, 235
Trocan, Viorel, *278*
tropical architecture: British practice of, 41–42; critiques of, 129; in Ghana, 38, 42, 88–91; in Guinea, 67, 69; international discussions of, 91–92; principles of, 88–91; Soviet practice of, 30, 47, 64, 67, 69, 72; ventilation principles in, 82, 89; vernacular architecture compared to, 129. *See also* climatic adaptations
Truman, Harry, 6
Trzebnica, Poland, residential district in, 272–73, *272*
tubali (cone-shaped, sun-baked bricks), 134
Tulasi, Moses, 41
Tunisia, 21, 183
Turkson, Peter, 52, *84*, 106
type designs/type projects, 216–17, *217*, *218*, 219–20, 222, *223*, 227, *229*, 232, 282

U
UAE. *See* United Arab Emirates
Uji, Zanzan Akaka, 145
Ulaanbaatar, Mongolia: city plan, 18, *19*; Friendship Monument, *10*
UN Conference on Trade and Development (UNCTAD), 7, 99, 148
underdevelopment. *See* backwardness
UNESCO. *See* United Nations Educational, Scientific and Cultural Organization
Union Inženjering, 280
Union of Iraqi Engineers, 184
United Arab Emirates (UAE): architects, planners, and contractors in, 4; architectural heritage of, 253–54; architecture and urban development in, 240; Bulgaria and, 255–71; Currency Board, 245; international exchange and collaboration in, 239–42, 258–71; Khalifah Committee, 243, 253; relationship to socialism, 95, 240; TES in, 255–71; urbanization in, 243, 245. *See also* Abu Dhabi, United Arab Emirates
United Nations: and development, 103, 110; Expanded Programme of Technical Assistance, 7, 37, 66, 156; Higher Course in National Economic Planning for Economists from Less-Developed Countries, 103; Human Settlements Programme, 7; Special Fund, 152
United Nations Educational, Scientific and Cultural Organization (UNESCO), 3, 7, 248
United States: architectural and construction services of, 6; Ghana and, 37, 44; technical assistance and development aid from, 6; Yugoslavia and, 148
Unity Hall (Hall of Residence 5), Kumasi (Ghana), *58*, 59
University College (London), Development Planning Unit, 5
University of Baghdad, Department of Architecture (Iraq), 184, 205–6, *205*, *206–7*
University of Constantine (Algeria), 11
University of Ghana, Legon, *62*
University of Science and Technology (UST), Kumasi (Ghana), *x*, 42, 52, 55, 56, *58*, *59*, 63, 106, 110, 148; Research Department, 112. *See also* School of Architecture, Town Planning and Building, at University of Science and Technology, Kumasi
University of Warsaw, Center for African Studies, 91
urbanization: in Baghdad, 195–210; disenchantment with, 33, 242, 243–52; global, 3; in Global South, 4, 33; in Gulf states, 242–54; in Kuwait, 245–46, 251, 280–91; in Nigeria, 159; in UAE, 243, 245
Urbanowicz, Barbara, 144
urban planning. *See* planning
USSR. *See* Soviet Union
UST. *See* University of Science and Technology (UST), Kumasi
Ustinov, A., *78*
Uthman, Fuad, 205, 207, *208*

V
van Treeck, Martin, 251
Varna, Bulgaria, Regional Planning Office, *96–97*, *97*, *98*, *164*, *165*
VÁTERV (City Planning Bureau), 108–9, *109*
Vaughan-Richards, Alan, 135
VBB, 248
ventilation, 82, 89, 110
Venturi, Robert, 209, 251
vernacular architecture: in Gulf states, 252; in Hungary, 105, 108–10; in Nigeria, 102, 129–30, 132, 134–35, 142, 143–44; in Poland, 131, *132*, *272*; tropical architecture compared to, 129. *See also* Arab-Islamic architectural elements; architectural heritage
Vesnin layout of apartments, 83
Vietnam, 8, 29, 67, 171, 265, 300
villa, Abu Dhabi (UAE), *278*
Virágh, Pál, 108
virgin lands campaign (Soviet Union), 8, 46
Volkov, S., *19*
Volta River Authority, Tema (Ghana), 42
Volta River Project, 37
Volta River Resettlement Project, 110, 112–13
Voronina, Veronika, 48, 64–65

W
Wang Rongshou, 67, *68*
Warner, Burns, Toan & Lunde, *26*
Warsaw Development Consortium (WADECO), *20*, 300
Weiner, Nebojša, 52
West Africa: Britain and, 92; cultural emancipation, 127–30; Eastern European architects/planners and, 31, 33, 93–94, 106–25; Eastern Europe likened to, 31, 100–106, 125, 127, 145, 165, 167; peripheral status of, 102, 145, 148, 149; Soviet Union and, 8, 46, 94; Yugoslavia and, 93–94, 149–65. *See also* Ghana; Guinea; Mali; Nigeria
West African Builder and Architect (journal), 55, 91–93
West Germany, 15, 174, 213, 215

354 INDEX

Wilbur Smith and Associates, 159
William Halcrow & Partners, 243, 255
Willumat, Heinz, *16*
Wilson, James M., 175. *See also* Wilson Mason
Wilson Mason, 299
Wiśniowska, Anna, 282, 290, *290*, *291*
Wiśniowski, Krzysztof, 272–74, *272*, *281*, 282, *284*, *285*, 290, *290*, *291*, *292*
Wnętrzewski, Bogdan, 55
Wojciechowski, Olgierd (Ludlam), 55
Wojczyński, Witold, *51*, *53*, 54, 92
women architects, 54–55
Workers' Brigade (Ghana), 48, 60
World Bank, 6, 7, 37, 103, 107, 148, 152
world-forming, 29
worlding of Eastern Europe, 101, 105, 125, 165, 305
worldmaking: of Eastern European architects, 101; in Ghana, 37; globalization and, 241; international exchange/collaboration and, 95, 241; in Nigeria, 101; socialist, 29–33, 305, 306–7
World Muslim League, 7
worldness, 30
world socialist system, 32, 170–73, 181, 210, 212, 216, 237, 305
Wright, Frank Lloyd, 176
Wrocław University of Technology (Poland), 272–73, 297, 298
Wysocki, Edward, 227, *227*

Y

Yadrov, I. Y., *10*
Yoruba architecture, 140
Young Farmers' League (Ghana), 48
Young Pioneers (Ghana), 48, 60
Yugoslavia, 15–16, 17; Ghana and, 46, 50; international relations of, 148–49; Iraq and, 210; Nigeria and, 148, 150–65; peripheral status of, 149; planning in, 151; socialism in, 148, 152–53; Soviet Union vs., 4; United States and, 148; West Africa and, 93–94, 149–65

Z

Žagar, Zvonimir, 52
Zagreb Urban Planning Institute, *20*
Zakum Construction Company, 256
Zambia, 155
Zambia Engineering & Contracting Company (ZECCO), *24*
Zaremba, Piotr, 26, 106, 186, *187*, 192
Zaria, Nigeria, 122, *123*, *136*
Zaria Art Society, 129, 141
Zaria School of Architecture. *See* School of Architecture, Ahmadu Bello University, Zaria
Zayed bin Sultan al Nahyan, 243, 253, 270
Zevin, Leon Zalmanovich, 170
Zhivkov, Todor, 15, 259
Zhou Enlai, 50
Ziółek, Maciej, 91
Zosimov, G., *19*

Image Credits

25 Years of Jos Museum (Jos: National Museum, 1978) **(3.32)**

First published in Charles Abrams, *Man's Struggle for Shelter* (Cambridge, MA: MIT Press, 1964), 181 **(3.11)**

Académie d'architecture/Cité de l'architecture et du patrimoine/Archives d'architecture du XXe siècle, Paris (France), 390 AA, Box 9 **(5.2)**

Aga Khan Documentation Center, Massachusetts Institute of Technology, Cambridge, MA (US), Mohamed Makiya archive, box 139, "Baghdad—Maps" **(4.12)**

Private archive of Ghada al-Slik, Baghdad (Iraq) **(4.19)**

Archiwum Akt Nowych, Warsaw (Poland) **(1.2)**

Archiwum Międzynarodowych Targów Poznańskich, Poznań (Poland) **(1.25)**

Arhitectura (Romania) 3 (1984): 53 **(4.65)**

Arhitectura (Romania) 6 (1979): 13 **(1.21)**

Arhitectura (Romania) 6 (1980): 56 **(3.24)**

Arhivele Naționale ale României, Bucharest (Romania), f. Romproiect, 7255 **(4.55)**; 7099 **(4.57, 4.61, 4.62)**; 7288 **(4.58)**; 7256 **(4.63, 4.64)**

Arkhitektura (Bulgaria) 7 (1964): 34 **(2.14)**

Arkhitektura SSSR (Soviet Union) 6 (1984): 109 **(1.9)**; 112 **(1.10)**; 103 **(1.14)**

Arkhitektura SSSR (Soviet Union) 9 (1976): 52 **(2.33)**

Private archive of Kazimierz Bajer, Kraków (Poland) **(4.8, 4.9, 4.10, 4.13, 4.15, 4.16, 4.20, 4.22, 4.23, 4.27, 4.28, 5.3)**

Private archive of Tadeusz Barucki, Warsaw (Poland) **(4.29)**

Private archive of Miroslava Baštova, Prague (Czech Republic) **(4.34, 4.35, 4.38, 5.6, 5.7, 5.9)**

Private archive of Jerzy Baumiller, Greenport, NY (US) **(4.6)**

"Beduinsko naselje u Kuvajtu (Housing—Kuwait)," *Architektura Urbanizam* (Yugoslavia) 58 (1969): 25 **(5.34)**

Nicolae Besnea, "Vile în Baghdad," *Arhitectura* (Romania) 6 (1984): 78 **(4.60)**

First published in Thomas Billhardt and Peter Jacobs, *Die Drushba-Trasse* (Berlin: Verlag Neues Leben), 1978 **(4.45)**

Private archive of Borislav Bogdanov, Sofia (Bulgaria) **(5.20, 5.22, 5.23, 5.26, 5.27, 5.28)**

Photo by Zoran Bojović **(3.47)**

Private archive of Zoran Bojović, Belgrade (Serbia) **(3.45, 3.47, 3.50, 3.51, 3.52, 3.53, 3.54, 3.55, 4.39, 4.40, 4.41)**

Max Bond, "A Library for Bolgatanga," *Architectural Forum* (UK) (March 1968): 67 **(2.10)**

Private archive of Zoltán Boór, Budapest (Hungary) **(1.19)**

Bundesarchiv, Berlin (Germany), DG7-748 2 von 2 **(4.44)**; DH2-13970 **(4.46)**; DH2-13884 **(4.47, 4.48, 4.49)**

Private archive of Jan Čejka, Münster (Germany) **(4.36, 4.37)**

First published in Mincho Chernev, Georgi Malchev, and Mitre Stamenov, *Dela na bulgarskite stroiteli i arkhitekti v chuzhbina/Bulgarian Engineering Achievements in Foreign Countries* (Sofia: Tekhnika, 1963), 136 **(5.18)**

Photo by Jacek Chyrosz **(2.2, 2.8, 2.9, 2.58)**

Private archive of Jacek Chyrosz, Warsaw (Poland) **(2.51, 2.54)**

First published in Jacek Chyrosz and Stanisław Rymaszewski, "Międzynarodowe Targi w Akrze, 1.2.1967–19.2.1967," *Architektura* 4 (1969): 146 **(2.55)**

Private archive of Zdenka Ciko, Sydney (Australia) **(2.27, 2.29)**

© Constantinos and Emma Doxiadis Foundation **(3.49)**

Daily Times (Nigeria), May 11, 1960, 24 **(3.26)**

First published in Chen Deng'ao, *Redai Jianzhu* (Beijing: Zhongguo jianzhu gongye chubanshe, 1989) **(2.32)**

Zbigniew Dmochowski, *An Introduction to Nigerian Traditional Architecture* (London: Ethnographica; Lagos: National Commission for Museums and Monuments, 1990), 3 vols., covers **(3.28)**

Zbigniew Dmochowski, "Sprawozdanie ze studjów nad poleskiem budownictwem drzewnem w r. 1934/5," *Biuletyn historji sztuki i kultury* (Poland) III: 4 (June 1934): 317 **(3.29)**

Doxiadis Associates, "Accra–Tema–Akosombo Regional Programme and Plan Interim Report," *Ekistics* (Greece) 11, no. 65 (March 1961): 269 **(2.11)**

Private archive of Stanka Dundakova, Sofia (Bulgaria) **(1.12)**

Private archive of Marek Dunikowski, Kraków (Poland) **(1.26)**

Evening News (Ghana), March 7, 1960, 1 **(2.22)**

Bernard Fagg, "The Museums of Nigeria," *Museum International* (France) 16 (1963): 129 **(3.31)**

"Festac '77," *New Directions* (US) (April 1977): 8 **(3.3)**

First published in Vladimir M. Firsanov, *Arkhitektura grazhdanskikh zdanii v ulsoviiakh zharkogo klimata* (Moscow: 1971), 259 **(2.38)**

Geography and Map Reading Room, Library of Congress, Washington, DC (US), G8854.A2 1958 **(2.3)**; G8854.A2 1965 .G5 **(2.4)**; G8844.L3G4 1974.M3 **(3.48)**; G7614.B3 1973.S6 **(4.18)**

First published in Ghana Town and Country Planning Division, "National Physical Development Plan, 1963–70" (Accra: State Publishing Corporation, 1965) **(3.7)**

Private archive of Alexander Gjurić, Prague (Czech Republic) **(5.8, 5.10)**

John Godwin, "Nigeria: Building in a Boom Economy," *RIBA Journal* (London) 88, no. 7 (1981): 40 **(3.46)**

First published in István Györffy, *Magyar falu, magyar ház* (Budapest: Turul, 1943), 61. Courtesy of Ákos Moravánszky **(3.6)**

Private archive of Ildikó Halmágyi, Budapest (Hungary) **(1.20)**

Private archive of Jan Amos Havelka, Prague (Czech Republic) **(5.36)**

Private archive of Nick Hollo, Sydney (Australia) **(3.43)**

"How Ghana Spent the Great Day," *Evening News* (Ghana), March 7, 1964, 1 **(2.28)**

In Situ (Zambia) (July 1978): 29 **(1.22)**

Photo by Oleg Ivanov, 1966. Sputnik (Russian Federation) **(2.36)**

Private archive of Jovan Ivanovski, Skopje (Macedonia) **(4.42)**

J. Max Bond, Jr., Papers, 1955–2009, Department of Drawings and Archives, Avery Architectural and Fine Arts Library, Columbia University, New York (US) **(3.12)**

Private archive of Stanisław Jankowski, Warsaw (Poland) **(4.7)**

Private archive of Wojciech Jarząbek, Wrocław (Poland) **(5.54, 5.56, 5.57)**

Jenaer Rundschau/Jena Review (German Democratic Republic) 6 (1981): cover **(4.50)**

Private archive of Grażyna Jonkajtys-Luba, Warsaw (Poland) **(2.49)**

Private archive of Stanisław Juchnowicz, Kraków (Poland) **(3.21)**

Kamarata na arkhitektite v Bulgariia, Sofia (Bulgaria), d. "Stefan Kolchev" **(3.2)**

Private archive of Igor Kashmadze. Courtesy of Mikhail Tsyganov **(1.6)**

First published in Gerhard Kraft, *Die Zusammenarbeit der Mitgliedsländer des RWG auf dem Gebiet der Investitionen* (Berlin: Akademie-Verlag, 1977), 54 **(4.52)**; 63 **(4.53)**

Kuwait Times (Kuwait), November 13, 1978, 6 **(5.17)**

Development Office, Kwame Nkrumah University of Science and Technology **(2.26)**

Private archive of Edward Lach, Wrocław (Poland) **(5.29, 5.30, 5.37, 5.43, 5.47)**

Private archive of Władysław Leonowicz, Kraków (Poland) **(4.3, 4.4)**

Private archive of Marian Łyczkowski, Warsaw (Poland) **(3.39, 3.40, 3.41)**

Private archive of Stojan Maksimović, Nahant, MA (US) **(5.32)**

Map and Geospatial Information Center, Peter B. Lewis Library, Princeton University, Princeton, NJ (US) **(4.5)**

Michigan State University Libraries, East Lansing, MI (US) **(4.14)**

Private archive of Peter Mlodzianowski, Bucks (UK) **(5.11)**

Courtesy of Andrzej Mój **(4.17)**

Photo by Ahmad Mousa, 2018 **(4.1)**

Narodowe Archiwum Cyfrowe, Warsaw (Poland) **(3.25)**

Mircea Nicolescu, "8 locuințe pentru Festival Town, Lagos," *Arhitectura* (Romania) 6 (1980): 18 **(3.56)**

Private archive of Anca Oțoiu, Bucharest (Romania) **(5.35)**

Piotr Zaremba Legacy, Loose Files, No. 958, National Archives, Szczecin (Poland) **(4.11)**

Private archive of Wacław Piziorski, Warsaw (Poland) **(1.16)**

Private archive of Anikó Polónyi, Budapest (Hungary) **(1.7, 3.5, 3.8, 3.9, 3.10, 3.13, 3.14, 3.15, 3.16, 3.19)**

Photo by Charles Polónyi, 1964 **(3.17, 3.18)**; 1970s **(3.20)**

First published in Anatolii Nikolaevich Rimsha, *Gorod i zharkii klimat* (Moscow: Stroiizdat, 1975), 193 **(2.13)**

Private archive of Lech Robaczyński, Warsaw (Poland) **(4.30, 4.31, 4.32, 4.33)**

Private archive of Henryk Roller, Warsaw (Poland) **(1.8)**

Courtesy of Cole Roskam **(2.32, 2.34)**

Rossiiskii gosudarstvennyi arkhiv ekonomiki (Moscow, Russian Federation), f. R-850, op. 9–4, d. 38 **(2.39)**; d. 48 **(2.43)**; d. 43 **(2.44, 2.48)**; d. 81 **(2.45)**

Rossiiskii gosudarstvennyi arkhiv ekonomiki (Samara, Russian Federation), f. R-149, op. 1–1, d. 1102, 5 **(2.47)**; d. 1102, 26 **(2.46)**

Rossiiskii gosudarstvennyi arkhiv ekonomiki (Samara, Russian Federation), f. R-150, op. 2–1,

d. 414 (**2.40, 2.41, 2.42**)
Rossiiskii gosudarstvennyi arkhiv ekonomiki (Samara, Russian Federation), f. R-621, op. 5–4, d. 240 (**2.35**); d. 646 (**2.37**)
Private archive of Stanisław Rymaszewski, Warsaw (Poland) (**2.50**)
Private archive of Krystian Seibert, Kraków (Poland) (**1.18**)
Private archive of Mohammed Abul Sham, Abu Dhabi (UAE) (**5.12**)
Photograph from the family archive of Alina Ślesińska (**2.20**)
Ana Solomon, "Proiecte tip destinate programului național de locuințe din Republica Federală a Nigeriei," *Arhitectura* (Romania) 5 (1980): 16 (**3.23**)
Private archive of Gheorghe Radu Stănculescu, Bucharest (Romania) (**4.56**)
Collection Ł. Stanek (**2.15**)
Drawing by Ł. Stanek, postproduction: Kacper Kępiński, software: Gephi (**7.2**); software: Tableau (**7.3**)
Drawing by Ł. Stanek and the students of the Manchester School of Architecture, postproduction: Kacper Kępiński, software: QGIS (**7.4, 7.5, 7.6**); software: Tableau (**7.1**)
Photo by Ł. Stanek, 2012 (**2.1, 2.5, 2.6, 2.7, 2.17, 2.30, 2.52, 2.53, 2.56**); 2014 (**5.5, 5.33, 5.41, 5.42, 5.44, 5.45, 5.46, 5.48, 5.49, 5.50, 5.51, 5.52, 5.53, 5.55**); 2015 (**1.24, 3.1, 3.4, 3.44, 3.57, 3.60, 3.61, 5.1, 5.4, 5.13, 5.14, 5.15, 5.16, 5.21, 5.24, 5.25**); 2017 (**1.3, 1.4, 1.27, 4.2**); 2018 (**1.1, 1.5, 1.13, 1.17, 2.23, 2.25, 2.26**)
"State House Kaduna," *West African Builder and Architect* (Accra) 2, no. 5 (1962): 93 (**3.27**)
Stowarzyszenie Architektów Polskich, Warsaw (Poland) (**1.23, 4.21, 4.24, 4.25, 4.26, 4.54**); d. 498 (**4.21**); d. 375 (**4.24, 4.25**); d. 689 (**4.26**); d. 573 (**4.54**)
First published in Bolesław Szmidt, ed., *The Polish School of Architecture, 1942–45* (Liverpool: Birchall, 1945), 53 (**3.30**)
First published in "Technoexportstroy" (Sofia: Technoexportstroy, n.d.) (**3.58, 5.19**); cover (**3.59**)
First published in B.A.W. Trevallion and Alan G. Hood under the direction of W. H. Barrett, "Accra: A Plan for the Town: The Report for the Minister of Housing" (Accra: Town Country Planning Division, 1958) (**2.31**)
Private archive of Danilo Udovicki, Austin, TX (US) (**3.22**)
Ulrich Müther Archiv, Wismar (Germany), box "Tripoli Zeichnungen" (**4.51**)
First published in "VEB Industrieprojektierung Dessau: Betriebschronik," vol. 2, n.d (**4.43, 4.59**)
First published in Veronika Leonidovna Voronina, *Narodnye traditsii arkhitektury Uzbekistana* (Moscow: Gosudarstvennoe izdatel'stvo arkhitektury i gradostroitel'stva, 1951), 20 (**2.12**)
Photo by Nebojša Weiner, 1967 (**2.57**)
Private archive of Nebojša Weiner, Zagreb (Croatia) (**2.57**)
First published in Ludger Wimmelbücker, "Architecture and City Planning Projects of the German Democratic Republic in Zanzibar," *Journal of Architecture* 17, no. 3 (2012): 417. Courtesy of Ludger Wimmelbücker (**1.11**)

Private archive of Krzysztof Wiśniowski, Wrocław (Poland) (**5.31, 5.38, 5.39, 5.40**)
Private archive of Witold Wojczyński, Warsaw (Poland) (**2.18, 2.19, 2.21**)
Photo by Zvonimir Žagar (**2.16**)
Private archive of Zvonimir Žagar, Zagreb (Croatia) (**2.24**)
First published in Zagreb Urban Planning Institute, "Conakry. Plan Directeur d'Urbanisme," Zagreb, 1963 (**1.15**)
Zbigniew Dmochowski—Archiwum, Gdańsk University of Technology, Gdańsk (Poland) (**3.33, 3.34, 3.35, 3.36, 3.37, 3.38, 3.42**)

Copyright © 2020 by Łukasz Stanek

Published by Princeton University Press, 41 William Street, Princeton, New Jersey 08540

In the United Kingdom: Princeton University Press, 6 Oxford Street, Woodstock, Oxfordshire OX20 1TR
press.princeton.edu

Cover illustrations: (*front*) International Trade Fair, Accra (Ghana), 1962–67, Africa Pavilion and Pavilion A, aerial view. GNCC, Vic Adegbite (chief architect), Jacek Chyrosz, Stanisław Rymaszewski (project architects). Private archive of Jacek Chyrosz, Warsaw (Poland); and (*back*) students at the Department of Architecture, College of Engineering, University of Baghdad (Iraq), 1960s. Private archive of Miroslava Baštová, Prague (Czech Republic).

All Rights Reserved

LCCN 2018966987

ISBN 9780691168708

British Library Cataloging-in-Publication Data is available

Design: Office of Luke Bulman with Carolyn Thomas

This book has been composed in Suisse International and Suisse Neue

Printed on acid-free paper. ∞

Printed in China

10 9 8 7 6 5 4 3 2 1